ANAPHORA

OXFORD STUDIES IN TYPOLOGY AND LINGUISTIC THEORY

SERIES EDITORS: Ronnie Cann, *University of Edinburgh*, William Croft, *University of Manchester*, Anna Siewierska, *University of Lancaster*

This series offers a forum for original and accessible books on language typology and linguistic universals. Works published will be theoretically innovative and informed and will seek to link theory and empirical research in ways that are mutually productive. Each volume will also provide the reader with a wide range of cross-linguistic data. The series is open to typological work in semantics, syntax, phonology, and phonetics or at the interfaces between these fields.

Published:

Indefinite Pronouns
Martin Haspelmath

Intransitive Predication
Leon Stassen

Classifiers: A Typology of Noun Categorization Devices
Alexandra A. Aikhenvald

Anaphora
Yan Huang

In preparation:

The Noun Phrase
Jan Rijkhoff

Double Object Cponstructions
Maria Polinsky

ANAPHORA

A Cross-linguistic Approach

YAN HUANG

OXFORD
UNIVERSITY PRESS

Great Clarendon Street, Oxford OX2 6DP

Oxford University Press is a department of the University of Oxford.
It furthers the University's objective of excellence in research, scholarship,
and education by publishing worldwide in

Oxford New York

Athens Auckland Bangkok Bogotá Buenos Aires Calcutta
Cape Town Chennai Dar es Salaam Delhi Florence Hong Kong Istanbul
Karachi Kuala Lumpur Madrid Melbourne Mexico City Mumbai
Nairobi Paris São Paulo Shanghai Singapore Taipei Tokyo Toronto Warsaw
with associated companies in Berlin Ibadan

Oxford is a registered trade mark of Oxford University Press
in the UK and in certain other countries

Published in the United States
by Oxford University Press Inc., New York

© Yan Huang, 2000

The moral rights of the author have been asserted

Database right Oxford University Press (maker)

All rights reserved. No part of this publication may be reproduced,
stored in a retrieval system, or transmitted, in any form or by any means,
without the prior permission in writing of Oxford University Press,
or as expressly permitted by law, or under terms agreed with the appropriate
reprographics rights organizations. Enquiries concerning reproduction
outside the scope of the above should be sent to the Rights Department,
Oxford University Press, at the address above

You must not circulate this book in any other binding or cover
and you must impose this same condition on any acquirer

British Library Cataloguing in Publication Data

Data available

Library of Congress Cataloging in Publication Data

Data applied for

ISBN 0-19-823529-1 (hbk)
ISBN 0-19-823528-3 (pbk)

10 9 8 7 6 5 4 3 2 1

Typeset in Times
by RefineCatch Limited, Bungay, Suffolk
Printed in Great Britain by
TJ International Ltd., Padstow, Cornwall

For my daughter Elizabeth; my wife Lihua Li; and my parents

Preface

The overall aim of this book is twofold: first, to provide an extensive overview of the major contemporary issues surrounding anaphora and to give a critical survey of the many and diverse contemporary approaches to the study of anaphora; secondly, to offer original observations and analyses and in particular to advance the neo-Gricean pragmatic theory of anaphora as constructed in Huang (1987, 1989, 1991a, 1991b, 1994, 1995, 2000) and Levinson (1987, 1991).

On a topic about which so much has been written, a book such as this inevitably has to be selective in its coverage. Therefore, I have not attempted to present a full survey of all constructions and phenomena that fall under the heading of anaphora; nor have I attempted to provide a full discussion of all approaches to every construction and phenomenon under consideration. Instead, I have concentrated on those areas and approaches I have judged to be the most important and influential in the study of anaphora. For reasons of space, I have omitted two topics altogether. One is concerned with the pyscholinguistics, including the acquisition, of anaphora. The other omission has to do with the sociolinguistics of anaphora. I have, however, included references to important works on both the topics.

The discussion of syntactic approaches to anaphora in Chapter 2 is conducted mainly from the viewpoint of a particular version of generative grammar, namely, Chomsky's (1981, 1982, 1986a, 1986b, 1995, 1998) principles-and-parameters theory and its economy-minimalist descendant. The reason is largely that this is the most widely studied and most dominant of the current syntactic theories under investigation. In addition, I have paid due attention to work on anaphora within the framework of Prince and Smolensky's (1993) Optimality theory, in the belief that this theory, while in its infancy, will yield some exciting results in the next decade. Where relevant and possible, I have also mentioned syntactic analyses made from other generative perspectives such as Generalized Phrase Structure Grammar/Head-Driven Phrase Structure Grammar and Lexical Functional Grammar.

One of the characteristics of this book is that it contains a rich collection of data drawn from around 550 of the world's languages. But such a typological breadth will inevitably result in some loss of depth in the description of anaphoric patterns in individual languages. In order to compensate for this weakness, I have attempted to give the reader some indication of where important works on anaphora in individual languages can be found.

I assume that this book is of interest primarily to scholars and students with some background already in contemporary syntactic, semantic, pragmatic, and discourse theories. For the reader who is unfamiliar with (some of) these theories, I have given additional reference to works that provide an introduction to them.

Since I completed this book, a number of new articles and books on anaphora have appeared. I did not have an opportunity to read them until the final typescript was sent to the publisher. Given that the articles and books in essence affect neither the empirical observations nor the theoretical arguments made in this work, rather than delaying publication further, I have chosen simply to cite them and recommend them to the reader.

The organization of this book is as follows. Chapter 1 outlines the landscape of anaphora and provides typological classifications of anaphora first from the point of view of syntactic category, then from the vantage point of truth-condition, then from the viewpoint of context, and finally from the perspective of reference-tracking in discourse. Chapter 2 is concerned with syntactic approaches to anaphora. The purpose of this chapter is to present a critical overview of the treatment of anaphora within the framework of generative grammar, in particular within the framework of Chomsky's (1981, 1982, 1986a, 1986b) principles-and-parameters theory and its most recent descendant, the minimalist programme (Chomsky 1995, 1998). I also take account of work on anaphora from the viewpoint of Prince and Smolensky's (1993) Optimality theory. Topics that are covered in this chapter include the classical Chomskyan typology of NPs, binding theory and control theory, null subjects and null objects, and long-distance reflexivization. The focus of Chapter 3 is largely on semantic approaches to anaphora. Among the issues that are addressed in this chapter are VP-ellipsis (some syntactic analyses of which are discussed, for ease of exposition), semantically oriented accounts of binding and control, and logophoricity. Chapter 4 is then devoted to pragmatic approaches to anaphora. One of the most interesting developments in the study of anaphora in the last decade has been an increasing awareness of the crucial role played by pragmatics in regulating intrasentential anaphora. The objective of this chapter is to provide a critical survey of the current, ongoing debate about the interaction and division of labour between grammar and pragmatics regarding anaphora and to advance the neo-Gricean pragmatic theory of anaphora I have developed in Huang (1987, 1989, 1991a, 1991b, 1994, 1995, 2000; see also Levinson 1987, 1991). Next, Chapter 5 is concerned with discourse anaphora. One general, distressing feature of the 1980s has been the widening gap between formal syntacticians and discourse analysts. As a corollary, the investigation of discourse anaphora has in general been ignored or positively opposed in formal syntax. Apart from reviewing a number of influential approaches to, and developing a neo-Gricean pragmatic analysis of, discourse anaphora, this chapter also aims to promote cooperation between formal syntax and discourse analysis in this area. The discussion in this chapter covers both reference-tracking systems in a wide variety of exotic languages and discourse anaphora that is found in both written narrative and naturally occurring conversation in a number of more familiar languages. Finally, Chapter 6 summarizes the major findings of the book and accesses the theoretical implications of these findings for linguistic theory.

I am very grateful to many people for support over the years that this research project has proceeded. My greatest debt is to Steve Levinson, John Lyons, Peter Matthews, Anna Morpurgo Davies, and Nigel Vincent, who have taught me how to think about language and linguistics. I owe a special debt of gratitude to Nigel Vincent, who read through a complete draft of this book and made a wide range of enlightening, stimulating, and thoughtful comments in his typical erudite fashion. In the few cases where I have not followed his advice, I may well learn to regret it. Of the many scholars who read through all or part of a draft or material related to the content of this book and provided comments, corrections, and suggestions, or helped me in various other ways, I am particularly grateful to Mira Ariel, Jay Atlas, Walter Bisang, Luigi Burzio, Ronnie Cann, Bernard Comrie, Bruce Connell, David Cram, Bill Croft, Chris Culy, Mary Dalrymple, Denis Delfitto, Mark Durie, Nicholas Evans, Martin Everaert, Ken Hale, Jim Higginbotham, Larry Horn, Eva Koktová, Giulio Lepschy, Steve Levinson, John Lyons, Peter Matthews, Jacob Mey, Anna Morpurgo Davies, Irene Philippaki-Warburton, Manfred Pinkal, Christer Platzack, Ming-Ming Pu, Tanya Reinhart, Luigi Rizzi, Anjum Saleemi, Vieri Samek-Lodovici, Peter Sells, Anna Siewierska, Margaret Speas, Lesley Stirling, David Wilkins, Anne Zribi-Hertz, and Frans Zwarts. I am indebted to the two anonymous referees for Oxford University Press, who supplied me with much needed encouragement at an early stage of this work. Parts of the material contained in this book were presented to various audiences at the Universiteit Antwerpen, the Universitat de Barcelona, the University of Cambridge, Cornell University, the University of Exeter, Fudan University, the Rijks Universiteit Groningen, Harvard University, the University of Lancaster, the Rijks Universiteit Leiden, University College London, Lunds Universitet, the Universität Mainz, MIT, the University of Massachusetts at Amherst, Middlesex University, Nanking University, Nanking Univeristy of Aeronautics and Astronautics, the University of Newcastle upon Tyne, the University of Oxford, the École des Hautes Études en Sciences Sociales Paris, the Université de Paris 6, the Université de Paris 8, the University of Reading, the Universität des Saarlandes, Shanghai International Studies University, the Universiteit Utrecht, the University of Wales at Bangor, and the University of York; I have benefited from the comments received on all these occasions. Needless to say, responsibility for remaining errors is entirely my own. I would like to thank Frances Morphy, John Davey, Nick Green and Jackie Pritchard at Oxford University Press for their professionalism in preparing this work for publication. In particular, I am grateful to Jackie Pritchard for an outstanding job of copy-editing. A special word of thanks is also due to Judith Ayling, former Linguistics Editor of Cambridge University Press, for her interest and encouragement. The research reported on in this book was in part supported by a Research Leave Award from the Humanities Research Board of the British Academy, which provided the time needed to complete a first draft, without the distractions of teaching. In addition, I am indebted to the Research Board of the University of Reading for awarding me a number of grants from its Grant and Travel Fund. On a more personal note, I wish to express my indebtedness to my parents for all they have done for me. I wish also to thank my wife for being a continual source of support and encouragement. Over the six years I spent in preparing this book, she has not only had to carry an extra burden of family responsibilities but has also had to put up with me being even more occupied with anaphora than usual. My little daughter has also contributed in a significant way by preventing me from thinking only about anaphora twenty-four hours a day and giving me good reasons to take time off; it is to them I dedicate this book.

For permission to reprint from my published work, I should like to express my gratitude to Cambridge University Press, John Benjamins BV, Elsevier Science Publishers BV, the Linguistic Society of America, and Walter de Gruyter.

Oxford and Reading Y.H. 黃衍
June 1999

Contents

Abbreviations		xiv
1.	Typologies of Anaphora	1
	1.1. Introduction	1
	1.2. Typologies of anaphora	2
	1.2.1. Anaphora and syntactic categories	2
	1.2.2. Anaphora and truth-conditions	5
	1.2.3. Anaphora and contexts	7
	1.2.4. Anaphora and discourse: reference-tracking systems	8
	1.3. Organization of the book	14
2.	Syntactic Approaches to Anaphora	16
	2.1. Classical Chomskyan theory of anaphora	17
	2.1.1. Typology of NPs	17
	2.1.2. Binding theory	17
	2.1.3. Control theory	38
	2.1.4. Revisions and alternatives	45
	2.1.5. Summary	50
	2.2. Null subjects and null objects	50
	2.2.1. Null subjects	50
	2.2.2. Null objects	78
	2.2.3. Summary	90
	2.3. Long-distance reflexivization	90
	2.3.1. The phenomenon	90
	2.3.2. Properties and theoretical issues	93
	2.3.3. Long-distance reflexivization in generative grammar	101
	2.3.4. Summary	130
	2.4. Conclusion	130
3.	Semantic Approaches to Anaphora	131
	3.1. VP-ellipsis	131
	3.1.1. Definition and properties	131
	3.1.2. Theoretical issues	133
	3.1.3. Two general approaches: syntactically oriented versus semantically oriented	135
	3.1.4. Summary	154

	3.2. Binding and control: some semantic alternatives	156
	3.2.1. Binding	156
	3.2.2. Control	167
	3.2.3. Summary	172
	3.3. Logophoricity	172
	3.3.1. Background	172
	3.3.2. Logophoric pronouns in African languages	176
	3.3.3. Long-distance reflexives in East Asian languages	190
	3.3.4. Discourse representation	199
	3.3.5. Summary	204
	3.4. Conclusion	204
4.	Pragmatic Approaches to Anaphora	205
	4.1. A neo-Gricean pragmatic theory	205
	4.2. A revised neo-Gricean pragmatic theory of anaphora	212
	4.2.1. The general pattern of anaphora	214
	4.2.2. A revised neo-Gricean pragmatic account of anaphora	214
	4.2.3. Application	216
	4.2.4. Summary	246
	4.3. Some other pragmatic/cognitive/functional approaches	247
	4.3.1. Relevance theory	247
	4.3.2. Accessibility theory	253
	4.3.3. Prague School functionalism	257
	4.3.4. Summary	261
	4.4. 'Syntactic' versus 'pragmatic': a new typology of language?	261
	4.4.1. The pragmaticness of anaphora in a pragmatic language	261
	4.4.2. The prominence of Chinese-style topic constructions in a pragmatic language	266
	4.4.3. Explaining the differences: parametric or typological?	276
	4.4.4. Summary	277
	4.5. Conclusion	277
5.	Switch-Reference and Discourse Anaphora	278
	5.1. Switch-reference	278
	5.1.1. The phenomenon	278
	5.1.2. Switch-reference and related phenomena	295
	5.1.3. Two general approaches and beyond: syntactically oriented versus semantically oriented, and perhaps pragmatically oriented	297
	5.1.4. Summary	302

			Contents	xiii
	5.2.	Discourse anaphora		302
		5.2.1.	The problem of anaphoric distribution in discourse	302
		5.2.2.	The topic continuity or distance-interference model	303
		5.2.3.	The hierarchy model	309
		5.2.4.	The cognitive model	314
		5.2.5.	The pragmatic model	318
		5.2.6.	Summary	328
	5.3.	Conclusion		329
6.	Conclusions			330
References				333
Index of Names				371
Index of Languages, Language Families, and Language Areas				380
Index of Subjects				390

Abbreviations

ABL	ablative case	INDIC	indicative
ABS	absolutive case	INF	infinitive
ACC	accusative case	INS	instrumental
ADDR	addressee pronoun	IRR	irrealis
AFF	affirmative	LOC	locative
AGR	agreement	LOG	logophor
ANTIP	antipassive	M	masculine gender
ART	article	MOD	modality
ASP	aspect	NEG	negative
AUX	auxiliary	NOM	nominative/nominalizer
CAUS	causative	OBJ	object
CL	classifier	OBV	obviative
CLI	clitic	PASS	passive
CMP	comparative	PAST	past tense
CNJ	conjunctive	PERF	perfective
COMP	complementizer	PL	plural
CTR	constrastive	POSS	possessive
DAT	dative	PREP	preposition
DECL	declarative	PRES	present tense
DEF	definite	PROG	progressive
DEM	demonstrative	PRON	pronoun
DIR	directional	PROX	proximate
DS	different subject	PRT	particle
DT	different topic	PURP	purposive
DU	dual	Q	question marker
DUR	durative	REAL	realis
EMPH	emphatics	REFL	reflexive
ERG	ergative	REL	relative marker
EVD	evidential	SBJV	subjunctive
F	feminine gender	SBOR	subordinator
FOC	focus	SEQ	sequential
FUT	future	SG	singular
GEN	genitive	SIM	simultaneous
GER	generic	SS	same subject
IMPF	imperfective	ST	same topic
IMPV	imperative	SUBJ	subject
INDEF	indefinite	TNS	tense

TOP	topic	2	second person
1	first person	3	third person

The abbreviations used in the glosses of the original sources are retained, except for those that have been altered for the sake of uniformity. For abbreviations that are too non-conventional and/or language specific, consult the original examples.

1 Typologies of Anaphora

1.1. Introduction

The overall aim of this book is twofold: first to provide an extensive overview of the major contemporary issues surrounding anaphora and to give a critical survey of the many and diverse contemporary approaches to the study of anaphora; secondly to offer original observations and analyses and in particular to advance the neo-Gricean pragmatic theory of anaphora as constructed in Huang (1987, 1989, 1991*a*, 1991*b*, 1994, 1995, 1997) and Levinson (1987, 1991).

The term 'anaphora' is derived from the Greek word αναφορα which may mean 'carrying back'. In contemporary linguistics, it is commonly used to refer to a relation between two linguistic elements, wherein the interpretation of one (called an anaphor) is in some way determined by the interpretation of the other (called an antecedent) (e.g. Lust 1986*b*, Wasow 1986, see also Huang 1994: 1).[1] Linguistic elements that can be employed as an anaphor include gaps (or empty categories), pronouns, reflexives, names, and descriptions.

In recent years, anaphora has not only become a central topic of research in linguistics, it has also attracted a growing amount of attention from philosophers, psychologists, cognitive scientists, and artificial intelligence workers. As pointed out in Huang (1994: 1), it has aroused this interest for a number of reasons. In the first place anaphora represents one of the most complex phenomena of natural language, which, in itself, is the source of fascinating problems. For example, whereas English in general does not allow the dropping of a pronoun from the subject position of a tensed clause, Italian and Spanish do (cf. Chapter 2). In many African languages, the reporting of the perspective of an internal protagonist of a sentence or discourse requires the use of a special, logophoric pronoun (cf. Chapter 3). Both Chinese and Japanese exhibit the blocking effect of long-distance reflexivization, but of a different kind (cf. Chapter 2). Secondly anaphora has for some time been

---

[1] Alternatively, anaphora can be defined as a relation between a linguistic expression and the mental representation/discourse status of the referent denoted by that linguistic expression. This line of definition is particularly popular among studies of anaphora carried out from a cognitive perspective (cf. Chapters 4 and 5).

Also there are at least two other distinct senses of anaphora: (i) anaphors as NPs with the features [+anaphor, −pronominal] versus pronominals as NPs with the features [−anaphor, +pronominal] in the Chomskyan tradition (cf. Chapter 2), and (ii) anaphors as 'backward' versus cataphors as 'forward' in e.g. Halliday and Hasan (1976).

regarded as one of the few 'extremely good probes' in furthering our understanding of the nature of the human mind/brain and thus in facilitating an answer to what Chomsky (1981, 1982, 1986a, 1995) considers to be the fundamental problem of linguistics, namely the logical problem of language acquisition, a special case of Plato's problem. In particular, certain aspects of anaphora have repeatedly been claimed by Chomsky (1981, 1982, 1986a, 1995) to furnish evidence for the argument that human beings are born equipped with some internal, unconscious knowledge of language, known as the language faculty. Thirdly anaphora has been shown to interact with syntactic, semantic, and pragmatic factors. Consequently it has provided a testing ground for a number of competing hypotheses concerning the relationship between syntax, semantics, and pragmatics in linguistic theory.

1.2. Typologies of anaphora

Anaphora can be classified on the basis of (i) syntactic categories, (ii) truth-conditions, (iii) contexts, and (iv) discourse reference-tracking systems.

1.2.1. Anaphora and syntactic categories

Syntactic categories are categories such as NP (or DP), VP, AP, and PP. In terms of syntactic category, anaphora seems to fall into two main categories: NP-, including N-, anaphora and VP-anaphora.

NP-anaphora

In an NP-anaphoric relation, both the anaphor and its antecedent are in general NPs, and both are potentially referring expressions.[2] NP-anaphora corresponds roughly to the semantically defined type of 'identity of reference' anaphora, that is, anaphora in which the anaphor and its antecedent are related in terms of reference. NP-anaphora can be encoded by gaps (or empty categories), pronouns, reflexives, names, and descriptions.

(1.1) (a) Gaps (Chinese)
Xiaoming shuo ø zui xihuan *Tian'ehu*.
Xiaoming say most like swan lake
'Xiaoming says that (he) likes *Swan Lake* most.'

---

[2] An NP-anaphor can sometimes take a CP (i.e. a clause with a complimentizer) or an IP (i.e. a clause) as its antecedent. In that case, the NP-anaphor can best be seen to refer to the action, event, state, or proposition expressed by the CP/IP.

(i) (a) Chopin had a natural gift for the keyboard, and he knew it.
  (b) A: Is this the train for Cambridge?
    B: I hope so.
  (c) John suggested that we join the guided tour around the museum, but I didn't really like the idea.

(b) Pronouns
   John said that he was a music lover.
(c) Reflexives (Tɔrɔ Sɔ, Culy, Kodio, and Togo 1994: 329)
   Mariam₁ Anda₂ wa   unɔ₁/₂ nɛ lagaa be gi.
   Mariam Anda SUBJ REFL OBJ hit   PST said
   'Mariam₁ said that Anda₂ hit her₁/himself₂.'
(d) Names (Thai, Lasnik 1989)
   Cɔɔn₁ khít wâ Cɔɔn₁ chàlāāt.
   John thinks that John is smart
   'John₁ thinks that John₁ is smart.'
(e) Descriptions
   A spokesman for John Major said this morning that the Prime Minister would still be visiting Moscow next week.

N-anaphora

By contrast, in an N-anaphoric relation, both the anaphor and its antecedent are an Ñ rather than an NP, and neither is a potentially referring expression. N-anaphora corresponds roughly to the semantically defined type of 'identity of sense' anaphora, that is, anaphora in which the anaphor and its antecedent are related in terms of sense. Linguistic elements that can be used as an N-anaphor include gaps (or empty categories), pronouns, and nouns.

(1.2) (a) Gaps
   John's favourite composer of the Baroque era is Bach, but Bill's Ø is Handel.
(b) Pronouns
   John bought a new CD, but Bill bought a second-hand one.
(c) Nouns
   John bought a new CD, but Bill bought a second-hand CD.

VP-anaphora

The other main category of anaphora is VP-anaphora. Under this rubric, four types may be isolated.

VP-ellipsis

In VP-ellipsis, also known as VP-deletion, the VP of the second and subsequent clauses is somewhat elided. From a structural point of view, VP-ellipsis can be divided into two types: (i) coordinated VP ellipsis, and (ii) subordinated VP-ellipsis.

(1.3) (a) Coordinated VP-ellipsis
   John adores his cello teacher, and Bill does, too.
(b) Subordinated VP-ellipsis
   The Emperor Napoleon admired himself more passionately than the Duke of Wellington did.

Two issues are of particular interest in the analysis of VP-ellipsis. The first is concerned with the distribution of the strict and sloppy interpretations. The second is concerned with the question of under what conditions VP-ellipsis restricts anaphoric possibilities. We shall return to VP-ellipsis in Chapter 3.

Gapping

Gapping refers to the phenomenon whereby some elements of the second and subsequent conjuncts of a coordinate construction are dropped. What is omitted is typically a repeated, finite verb, but frequently it can also be a sequence of elements containing the verb and some other (usually immediately adjacent) elements. The paradigmatic case of gapping, also known as verb medial gapping, is represented by examples like (1.4).[3]

(1.4) Verb medial gapping
Reading maketh a full man; conference a ready man; and writing an exact man. (Bacon)

(1.4) exemplifies coordination of three clauses. In this conjunction, the first conjunct is complete, but there is a gap in the middle of both the second and third conjuncts. All three conjuncts are parallel in structure, and the antecedent of the missing verb in the second and third conjuncts can be found in the first, complete conjunct.

In addition there are two other, peripheral types of gapping: (i) left node raising and (ii) right node raising. In the first, the leftmost constituent of the second and subsequent conjuncts of a coordinate construction raises to the left-hand side of the first conjunct. Left node raising usually involves coordination of VPs, as in (1.5). In the second, the rightmost element of the first conjunct moves to the rightmost position of the whole conjunction. The coordination in a right node raising construction can be that of clauses, as in (1.6*a*), or that of VPs, as in (1.6*b*).

(1.5) Left node raising
John donated a bassoon to Oxfam and a guitar to Save the Children.
(1.6) Right node raising
(*a*) John adores, but Mary hates, ancient philosophy.
(*b*) Mary found, and started to repair, the antique clock.

Sluicing

Sluicing involves the dropping of an IP (i.e. a clause) within an embedded CP (i.e. a clause with a complementizer as its head), resulting in an elliptical

---

[3] Gapping in its paradigmatic form obtains only language-specifically. Verbs in Chinese and Yoruba (Lawal 1985), for example, do not normally gap.

construction where an IP contains an embedded interrogative CP consisting only of a *wh*-phrase.

(1.7) Sluicing
  (*a*) John donated something to Oxfam, but I don't know what.
  (*b*) John is looking for somebody, but I don't know who.
  (*c*) John has promised to finish the painting in time, but he can't say when.

Stripping

Stripping refers to an elliptical construction in which the ellipsis clause contains only one constituent (and sometimes a clause-initial adverb or negative particle).

(1.8) Stripping
  (*a*) John donated a bassoon to Oxfam, and Bill, too.
  (*b*) John plays the violin, but not Bill.
  (*c*) John plays the violin, but not the piano.
  (*d*) Pavarotti will sing 'Nessun Dorma' again, but not in Hyde Park.

Null complement anaphora

Null complement anaphora refers to an elliptical construction in which a VP or IP complement of a verb is dropped. What is omitted can normally be understood from the preceding clause or context.

(1.9) (*a*) They asked him to pay at least lip-service to the principle, but he refused.
  (*b*) The little boy wanted to pilot a gondola, but his father didn't approve.
  (*c*) John told Mary that the beauty of Cambridge rivals the splendour of Venice, and Peter told Susan.

1.2.2. Anaphora and truth-conditions

Truth-conditions are conditions that the world must meet for a sentence to be true. From a truth-conditional semantic point of view, anaphora can be divided into five types.

Referential anaphora

A referential anaphor is one that refers to some entity in the external world either directly or via its coreference with its antecedent in the same sentence or discourse. In the latter case, a referential anaphor refers to what its antecedent refers to; the anaphor is thus said to be coreferential with its antecedent.

(1.10) Gorbachev knew that he would be remembered as the architect of perestroika.

Bound-variable anaphora

A bound-variable anaphor does not refer to any fixed entity in the external world, as can be shown by sentences like (1.11), but is interpretable by virtue of its dependency on some quantificational expression in the same sentence or discourse, thus seeming to be the natural language counterpart of a bound variable in first-order logic.

(1.11) Nobody thought that he would wish to live with the giants of Brobdingnag.

One interesting characteristic of bound-variable anaphora is that different languages may afford their speakers different types of anaphor to encode such a dependency. For example, to express a bound-variable anaphoric relation between a matrix subject and an embedded subject, while English allows neither gaps nor reflexives,[4] Serbo-Croatian allows gaps, Marathi allows reflexives, and Chinese allows both.

(1.12) (*a*) Gaps (Serbo-Croatian, Lindseth and Franks 1996)
svaki   student misli   da ce   Ø dobiti desetku.
every-M-SG student thinks that will   get   A
'Every student thinks that he will get an A.'
(*b*) Pronouns
Every child wishes that he could visit the land of Lilliput.
(*c*) Reflexives (Marathi, Wali and Subbarao 1991)
sarvããnaa₁ vaaṭṭa ki   aapaṇ₁ libral aahot.
everybody believes that self   liberal is
'Everybody believes that he is liberal.'
(*d*) Gaps and reflexives (Chinese)
Mei ge ren   dou shou Ø/ziji xihuan Zhongguocai.
every CL person all say   self like   Chinese food
'Everybody says that he likes Chinese cuisine.'

Note next that cross-linguistically bound-variable anaphora occasionally can also be encoded by repeating the same lexical NP.

(1.13) Of every ritual bronze that was found in the tomb, it was subsequently discovered that the bronze belonged to the Shang élite.

Finally, as noted in Kempson (1988*a*,1988*b*) and Huang (1994: 292), examples of the following kind can also have a bound-variable interpretation. On such a reading, the supervisor is interpreted as each Ph.D. student's supervisor. Of some particular interest here is that this bound-variable interpretation obtains only by virtue of the addition of the pragmatic inference that every Ph.D. student characteristically has a supervisor.

(1.14) Every Ph.D. student thinks that the supervisor is intelligent.

---

[4] Cf.
(i) Each side proceeds on the assumption that itself loves peace, but the other side consists of warmongers. (Russell)

E-type anaphora

An E-type anaphor is one which, for technical reasons, is neither a pure referential anaphor nor a pure bound-variable anaphor, but which nevertheless appears to constitute a unified semantic type of its own (Evans 1977).

(1.15) Most people who bought a donkey have treated it well.

'Lazy' anaphora

An anaphor of laziness is so called because it is neither a referential anaphor nor a bound-variable anaphor but seems to function as a shorthand for a repetition of its antecedent. In other words, it is a device for a repeated occurrence of the linguistic form, rather than the truth-theoretical content of its antecedent (e.g. Karttunen 1976).

(1.16) The man who gave his paycheque to his wife was wiser than the man who gave it to his mistress.

Bridging cross-reference anaphora

A bridging cross-reference anaphor is one that is used to establish a link of association with some preceding expression in the same sentence or discourse via the addition of background assumption (Clark 1977, Clark and Haviland 1977, Kempson 1988*a*, 1988*b*, Huang 1994: 11, 292, Matsui 1993, 1995). What is tacitly bridged is typically the information that is not structurally retrievable from either the sentence or discourse that triggers the inferential process. Bridging cross-reference anaphora is most commonly encoded in terms of a definite NP.

(1.17) John walked into a concert hall. The chandeliers were magnificent.

We shall have more to say about bridging cross-reference anaphora in Chapter 4.

1.2.3. Anaphora and contexts

One of the classical ways of analysing context is to divide it into three types: (i) encyclopaedic knowledge context, (ii) physical context, and (iii) linguistic context. This three-way 'geographic' division of context, as Ariel (1990: 5) calls it, may then be partially correlated to a three-way 'geographic' division of the paradigmatic use of anaphors (and such related devices as deictics and demonstratives): (i) the paradigmatic use of names and descriptions tends to refer to the encyclopaedic knowledge context, (ii) the paradigmatic use of deictics and demonstratives, to the physical context, and (iii) the paradigmatic use of pronouns and reflexives, to the linguistic context (Clark and Marshall 1981, Ariel 1990: 5–6). Looked at from a slightly different perspective, and in terms of the notion of givenness, names and descriptions may prototypically be regarded as knowledge givenness markers, deictics and demonstratives as physical givenness markers, and pronouns and reflexives as linguistic givenness markers.[5] This partial form–function correlation between anaphor type and context type can be illustrated as follows.

(1.18) (a) As a small boy, Chopin often played in aristocratic homes.
 (b) That man over there is playing a saxophone.
 (c) Chopin once said that he was a Pole not only by birth but by sentiment as well.

1.2.4. Anaphora and discourse: reference-tracking systems

Reference-tracking systems are mechanisms employed in different languages to keep track of the various entities referred to in an ongoing discourse (e.g. Comrie 1989*b*). In general, there are four major types of reference-tracking system operating in discourse, from which a given language may resort to one or more: (i) gender systems, (ii) switch-reference systems, (iii) switch-function systems, and (iv) inference systems. The first is commonly considered to be lexical in nature, the second and third grammatical in nature, and the fourth pragmatic in nature (Foley and Van Valin 1984, Van Valin 1987, Comrie 1989*b*).

Gender systems

In a gender/class system, an NP is morphologically classified for gender/class according to its inherent features, and is tracked through a discourse via its association with the gender/class assigned. The explicit assignment of NPs to gender/class can be accomplished by marking the NPs themselves, by utilizing a verbal affix,[6] and/or by both. Thus, NPs of the same gender/class can be read as coreferential; those of different genders/classes cannot. Note that the term 'gender/class' is used here in a broad sense, and is intended to cover what are traditionally treated as agreement features such as person and number (e.g. Comrie 1989*b*).

---

[5] This, of course, does not entail that we can have a one-to-one correspondence between anaphor type and context type or givenness marker type. It should also be pointed out that Ariel (1990: 5–11) argues against such a correspondence. Also noteworthy are the findings of some recent research that the anaphor/deictic distinction may not be strictly maintained cross-linguistically. Drawing data from English, Ik, Indonesian, Nunggubuyu, and Tagalog, Himmelmann (1996), for example, shows that anaphoric use of deictics and demonstratives is very common in these languages. On the other hand, the investigation by Klein-Andreu (1996) of the evolution and use of the third-person clitics *le/s*, *la/s*, and *lo/s* in five different Spanish dialects indicates that anaphoric systems can engender more deictic functions in the course of development.

[6] In the latter case, NPs whose gender/class are morphologically identified on the verb are typically dropped in discourse once they have been established as topic or given.

Typologies of Anaphora 9

The gender/class system is found to be present in a large variety of languages as genetically different and structurally diverse as Archi, Swahili, and Yimas. A simple version of this system is represented by the English sentence in (1.19).

(1.19) In 1835 when Schumann met Clara again, he wanted to marry her.

Next, consider (1.20) from Nunggubuyu, a non-Pama Nyungan language spoken in the Northern Territory of Australia.

(1.20) (Nunggubuyu, Heath 1980)
Anubani:'lawala, waṛubaj aba   wu=ya-nᵍgi,
after.that   nearby then ANA=go-PAST
ana-baḍirinʸa wu=ya-nᵍgi   waṛubaj,
NC-devil   ANA=go-PAST nearby
ni=yama:-'   ni=nᵍurni-nʸ,
3MSG=do-PAST 3MSG=look.back-PAST
waṛubaj wu=ya-nᵍgi   ana-baḍirinʸa, yinᵍga anawaṛubaj wu=ya-nᵍgi
nearby ANA=go-PAST NC-devil   nearly nearby   ANA=go-PAST
aba   nu:-'ba-gi-yunᵍ   ni=mindhi-nʸ,   na-yaminʸji,
then NC-that-SG-ABS 3MSG=flash-PAST NC-gecko
mari ni=wa-nᵍ,
and 3MSG=kill-PAST
wu=nᵍawi-'-nʸ   nᵍijanᵍ wu-laḷagi-'-nʸ
ANA=die-AUG-PAST more   ANA-get.up-REFL-PAST
ni-ga   aba na-yaminʸji, ... yu:-guni,
3MSG-NOM then NC-gecko   there-ALL
ni=wuwalga-nʸ   Aḷil, ... bagu ni=bura-nᵍa-nʸ,
3MSG=run-PAST [PL-name] there 3MSG=wait-AUG-PAST
ni=ṛanᵍara-nᵍi,   ana-baḍirinʸa ... ni=wa-nᵍ,
3MSG=wait.for-PAST³ NC-devil   3MSG=kill-PAST,
nᵍijanᵍ, ana-baḍirinʸa, ... ni=wa-nᵍ   wu=nᵍawi-'-nʸ,
more, NC-devil   3MSG-kill-PAST ANA=die-AUG-PAST
ni=wuwalga-nʸ   nᵍijanᵍ, ... ana-lha:l,   bani-yunᵍ ...
3MSG=run-PAST more   NC-country there-ABS
niwu=wurdha-nᵍi,   mari.n ...
3MSG→ANA=bury-PAST basket
'After that, the devil came close. He (Gecko) did this, he looked back over his shoulder. It (devil) was going along not far away. It was coming very close. Then that Gecko flashed [lightning] and killed it. It died, then got up again. Then he, Gecko, rushed that way, to that place Aḷil. There he sat and waited for it, the devil. He killed it again, the devil. It died. He ran along again, to that country. He covered up a pandanus basket in the sand.'

Nunggubuyu is well known to be a language with an elaborated system for noun-class marking. For example, there are five categories of noun-class affix for non-human nouns. Human nouns have a distinct class marking mechanism based on number and gender. Noun-class marking is indicated both on independent nouns and to a considerable extent on related verbs (Heath 1983). This is shown in (1.20) above. In the passage, the two protagonists of the narrative *na-yamin^yji* 'gecko' and *ana-baḍirin^ya* 'devil' are given different noun-class prefixes; third-person masculine human *na-* for the former and non-human *ana-* for the latter. In addition, the prefixes on the verb *ni-* and *wu-* cross-reference *na-yamin^yji* and *ana-baḍirin^ya* respectively (see also Van Valin 1987).

Clearly, as a reference-tracking device, the gender/class system is effective only when there is only one NP in each gender/class in the discourse. When the discourse contains more than one such NP, languages may have to utilize additional reference-tracking methods to distinguish between them. One such lexical device is referred to as obviation in the literature.

Obviation

Within obviation,[7] proximate and obviative (also frequently termed misleadingly third- and fourth-person, respectively) are assigned to different third-person NPs on the basis of their relative salience in a discourse. In general, contextually and/or rhetorically more prominent NPs are encoded by means of proximate morphology; contextually and/or rhetorically less central NPs are placed in obviative form.[8] This proximate/obviative opposition is indicated not only on NPs, but, if relevant, on verbs as well. Consequently, only proximates can be interpreted as coreferential with proximates; and obviatives, as coreferential with obviatives. Obviation can thus be seen as representing a natural extension of the gender/class system to the category of person, with proximates marking the unmarked third-person category and obviates, a subsidiary 'fourth-person' category. Obviation is found in some American Indian languages including Algonquian (such as Blackfoot, Cree, and Fox) (e.g. Goddard 1990), Apachean (such as Navajo), Eskimo, Keresan, and Kutenai (e.g. Comrie 1989*b*). Following is a well-quoted example from a Plains Cree text (Bloomfield 1930).

(1.21) Mēkw ē-pimohtē-t ispatināw wāpaht-am,
while CNJ-walk-3PROX hill see-3PROX
ē-āmaciwē-yit ayīsiyiniw-a, nāpēw-a.
CNJ-climb-3OBV person-OBV man-OBV
Ēkwa kitāpam-ē-w kitāpākan
and:then observe-DIR-3PROX spy glass
ē-kanawāpākanēhikē-yit ayīsiyiniw-a
CNJ look:through:spy:glass-3OBV person-OBV
ē-nanātawāpam-ā-yit. Kiskēyim-ē-w ayahciyiniw-a.
CNJ-look:for-DIR-3OBV know-DIR-3PROX Blackfoot-OBV

---

[7] According to Goddard (1990), the term 'obviative' was introduced by Cuoq (1866: 43) as French 'obviatif'. It was first used in English by Trumbull (1877: 150).

[8] As pointed out by Bloomfield (1962: 38): 'The proximate third person represents the topic of discourse, the person nearest the speaker's point of view, or the person earlier spoken of and already known.' Note also that if there is one NP, that NP is usually identified in proximate form.

Ēkwa   o-paskisikan pihtāsō-w;   mōstkīstaw-ē-w   ē-pimisini-yit.
and:then 3PROX-gun load-3PROX attack-DIR-3PROX CNJ-lie–3OBV
'While he (the Cree) was walking he saw a hill on which someone (the Blackfoot), a man, was climbing. And then he (the Cree) observed him (the Blackfoot), as he (the Blackfoot) was looking through a spy glass, as he (the Blackfoot) was looking for people. He (the Cree) knew him (the Blackfoot) for a Blackfoot. And then he (the Cree) loaded his gun and he (the Cree) attacked him (the Blackfoot) as he (the Blackfoot) lay down.'

Switch-reference systems

In a classical switch-reference system, the verb of a dependent clause is morphologically marked to indicate whether or not the subject of that clause is the same as the subject of its linearly adjacent, structurally related independent clause. If both subjects are coreferential, a S[ame]S[ubject] marker is used; otherwise, a D[ifferent]S[ubject] marker is employed. The term 'switch-reference' was introduced by Jacobsen (1967) in his seminal study of three Hokan-Coahuiltecan languages of North America: Kashaya (Southwestern) Pomo, Tonkawa, and Washo, though the relevant phenomenon was noted in the literature on North American Indian languages much earlier (see e.g. Kroeber 1911 on Yuki, Hoijer 1949 on Tonkawa, and Oswalt 1961 on Kashaya; see also Jacobsen 1983 and D. Wilkins 1988 for a historical survey of terminological variants).

Switch-reference is found in many of the native Indian languages spoken in North America (e.g. Jacobsen 1983), of the non-Austronesian languages spoken in Papua New Guinea (e.g. Longacre 1972, 1983, Foley and Van Valin 1984, Stirling 1993), and of the aboriginal languages spoken in Australia, 'in a geographically continuous area, extending from the Indian Ocean across into western Queensland' (e.g. Austin 1981*a*: 329). It has also been found in a number of languages spoken in North Asia (Nichols 1983), and in Africa (e.g. Wiesemann 1982, Comrie 1983).Two examples follow.

(1.22) (Harway, Comrie 1989b)
    (*a*) Ha   döyw nwg^w-ön,   bör dw-a.
        child rat   see-SS   run go:PRES:3SG-DECL
        'The child$_1$ saw the rat and he$_1$ ran away.'
    (*b*) Ha   döyw nwg^w-mön,   bör dw-a.
        child rat   see-DS   run go:PRES:3SG-DECL
        'The child$_1$ saw the rat$_2$ and it$_{2/3}$ ran away.'
(1.23) (Maricopa, Gordon 1983)
    (*a*) nya-ny-yuu-k   'ayuu   '-rav-k.
        when-1/2-see-SS something 1-hurt-ASP
        'When I saw you, I was sick.'
    (*b*) nya-ny-yuu-m   'ayuu   '-rav-k.
        when-3/1-see-DS something 1-hurt-ASP
        'When he saw me, I was sick.'

Switch-function systems

Somewhat related to the switch-reference system is the switch-function system, a term coined by Foley and Van Valin (1984). By switch-function is meant the mechanism that tracks the reference of an NP across clauses in a discourse by means of verbal morphology indicating the semantic function of that NP in each clause. This reference-tracking system is found in a wide range of languages, including a number of Indo-European languages (e.g. English and German), of Mayan languages (e.g. Jacaltec, Datz 1980, Tzotzil, Foley and Van Valin 1984, and Tzutujil, Butler, and Peck 1980), of Australian languages (e.g. Bandjalang, Crowley 1978, Dyirbal and Yidiɲ, Dixon 1972), of Austronesian languages (e.g. Malagasy), and Nootka, a Wakasham language spoken on or near Vancouver Island (e.g. Van Valin 1987).

For a classical illustration, let us take a look at Dyirbal, an aboriginal Australian language spoken in North Queensland. In Dyirbal, the pivot, that is, the grammatically most central NP, of a non-initial clause can be dropped if it is under coreference with that of the initial clause. While the pivot of an intransitive clause is the core-argument of the verb, the pivot of a transitive clause is not its agent but its patient. This is illustrated by (1.24a). But what is of particular interest here is that the suffixation of -*ngurra* to the verb of the second clause in (1.24a) has the effect of switching function, namely, from pivot to pivot in (1.24a) to non-pivot to pivot in (1.24b). In other words, -*ngurra* serves as a switch-function marker.

(1.24) (Dyirbal, Comrie 1989b: 42)
    (a) Bala-n   jugumbil   ba-nggu-l
        CLASS:ABS-F woman:ABS CLASS-ERG-M
        yara-nggu balga-n,   bani-nyu.
        man-ERG hit-REAL come:here-REAL
        'The man hit the woman and she came here.'
    (b) Bala-n   jugumbil   ba-nggu-l
        CLASS:ABS-F woman:ABS CLASS-ERG-M
        yara-nggu balga-n,   bani-ngurra.
        man-ERG hit-REAL come:here
        'The man hit the woman and he came here.'

Switch function can also be achieved by the antipassive voice in Dyirbal. Compare (1.25a) and (1.25b). Given the same function condition, stated above, the non-pivot ergative NP of the second clause cannot be omitted under coreference with the pivot NP of the first clause, hence the ungrammaticality of (1.25a). By contrast, the use of the antipassive voice in (1.25b) renders the agent the pivot of the second clause. Consequently, it can be deleted. Again, the antipassive voice can be viewed as signalling a switch in function.

(1.25) (Foley and Van Valin 1984: 113)
    (a) *Bayi yaṛa   bani-ɲu   balan ḍugumbil bura-n.
        man-ABS(A) come-TNS woman-ABS(U) see-TNS
        'The man came and saw the woman.'
    (b) Bayi yaṛa   bani-ɲu   bagun ḍugumbil-gu buṛal-ɲa-ɲu.
        man-ABS(A) come-TNS woman-DAT(U)   see-ANTIP-TNS
        'The man came and saw the woman.'

But cross-linguistically, the most common way to encode switch-function seems to involve the active/passive voice opposition. The general pattern appears to be that the unmarked, active voice acts as a same function category, while the marked, passive voice indicates a switch in function.

(1.26) (a) John protested in Trafalgar Square and was arrested by the police.
    (b) (Tzotzil, Foley and Van Valin 1984: 154)
        A   li Petal bat-em-Ø   ta xobel max-bil-Ø
        ART   Peter go-PERF-3SG-ABS to town hit-PASS
        yuʔun li   Anton.
        by   ART Anton
        'Peter went to town and got hit by Anton.'

Inference systems

In an inference system, reference-tracking does not depend primarily on the use of any of the three lexical and/or grammatical devices discussed above. Instead, tracking reference in discourse is characterized by (i) the heavy use of zero anaphors, (ii) the appeal to sociolinguistic conventions such as the use of honorifics, and (iii), as the term rightly suggests, the resorting to pragmatic inference. The inference system is particularly common in some East and South-East Asian languages such as Chinese, Japanese, Korean, Javanese, Tamil, and Thai. An illustrative example from Chinese is given below.

(1.27) (Chinese, Huang 1994: 246)
    A: Xianzai zhe zhong xiao bawang
        now   this sort   little despot
        ta   yao   tianshang yao   yueliang
        3SG want sky   want moon
        Ø ye   dei   wa gei ta
        EMPH have to pick for 3SG
        Ø haidi   yao qu lao   yu
            sea bottom want go catch fish
    B:Suoyi   xiaohair bu neng
        therefore child   not should
    A: Ø- ye   dei   lao
        EMPH have to catch
    B: Wo (pause) wo (long pause)
        1SG   1SG
    A: Ø pi   de   budeliao
        naughty CSC exceedingly

B: Wo dao juede xiaohair bu neng tai guan
1SG EMPH think child not should too spoil
A: Nowadays a little brat of this sort
even if he wants the moon in the sky
(you) have to pick (it) for him
Even if (he) wants to catch fish on the sea bottom
B: Therefore children shouldn't
A: (you) have to catch (them)
B: I (pause) I (long pause)
A: (He) is terribly naughty
B: I actually think that children shouldn't be spoilt too much

Reference-tracking systems will be taken up in more detail in Chapter 5.

1.3. Organization of the book

Having outlined the landscape of anaphora, let me point out that this book is not meant to be either a full survey of all constructions and phenomena that fall under the heading of anaphora or a full discussion of all approaches to every construction and phenomenon that is to be considered. Instead, I shall concentrate on those areas I have judged to be the most important and influential in the study of anaphora.

The remainder of this book is organized as follows. Chapter 2 is concerned with syntactic approaches to anaphora. The purpose of this chapter is to present a critical overview of the treatment of anaphora within the framework of generative grammar, in particular within the framework of Chomsky's (1981, 1982, 1986a, 1986b) principles-and-parameters theory and its most recent descendant, namely the minimalist programme (Chomsky 1995). I shall also take account of works on anaphora from the viewpoint of Prince and Smolensky's (1993) Optimality theory. Topics that are covered in this chapter include the classical Chomskyan typology of NPs, binding theory and control theory, null subjects and null objects, and long-distance reflexivization. The focus of Chapter 3 is largely on semantic approaches to anaphora. Among the issues that are addressed in this chapter are VP-ellipsis (some syntactic analyses of which are discussed, for ease of exposition), semantically oriented accounts of binding and control, and logophoricity. Chapter 4 is then devoted to pragmatic approaches to anaphora. One of the most interesting developments in the study of anaphora in the last decade has been an increasing awareness of the crucial role played by pragmatics in regulating intrasentential anaphora. The objective of this chapter is to provide a critical survey of the current, ongoing debate about the interaction and division of labour between grammar and pragmatics regarding anaphora and to advance the neo-Gricean pragmatic theory of anaphora I have developed in Huang

(1987, 1989, 1991*a*, 1991*b*, 1994, 1995, 1997; see also Levinson 1987, 1991). Next, Chapter 5 is concerned with discourse anaphora. One general, distressing feature of the 1980s has been the widening gap between formal syntacticians and discourse analysts. As a corollary, the investigation of discourse anaphora has in general been ignored or positively opposed in formal syntax. Apart from reviewing a number of influential approaches to, and developing a neo-Gricean pragmatic analysis of, discourse anaphora, this chapter also aims to promote cooperation between formal syntax and discourse analysis in this area. The discussion in this chapter covers both reference-tracking systems in a wide variety of exotic languages and discourse anaphora that is found in both written narrative and naturally occurring conversation in a number of more familiar languages. Finally, Chapter 6 summarizes the major findings of this book and assesses the theoretical implications of these findings for linguistic theory.

2 Syntactic Approaches to Anaphora

The ultimate goal of generative grammar is to provide an answer to what Chomsky (1981, 1982, 1986a, 1995) considers to be the fundamental problem of linguistics, namely, the logical problem of language acquisition, a special case of Plato's problem. The answer provided by Chomsky is the innateness hypothesis—the argument that human beings are born equipped with some internal, unconscious knowledge of language, known as the language faculty. The initial state of the language faculty, being a component of the human mind/brain, is subject to a theory of Universal Grammar (UG) which provides a system of universal principles, a finite array of which are parameterized. It is through the interaction of the universal principles with the array of finitely valued parameters that both language universals and language variations which are actually observed can be accounted for (see e.g. Chomsky 1995).

Within the framework of generative grammar, anaphora has for some time been seen as 'the window onto the mind', providing crucial evidence in support of the innateness hypothesis. In this chapter, I shall be concerned with syntactic approaches to anaphora. In particular, I shall be concerned with the treatment of anaphora within the framework of generative grammar, especially within the framework of Chomsky's (1981, 1982, 1986a, 1986b, 1995) principles-and-parameters theory and its minimalist descendant. I shall also take account of work on anaphora from the perspective of Prince and Smolensky's (1993) Optimality theory.[1] I shall discuss the classical Chomskyan typology of NPs, binding theory, control theory, and a number of revisions and alternatives to the standard Chomskyan theory of anaphora in Section 2.1. I shall then proceed to consider both the phenomenology and the many and diverse generative analyses of null subjects and null objects in Section 2.2. Finally, I shall examine long-distance reflexivization in Section 2.3.

---

[1] For the reader who is not well versed in these theories, see e.g. Freidin (1991a) and Haegeman (1994) for an introduction to the principles-and-parameters theory; Cook and Newson (1995), Radford (1997), and Uriagereka (1998) for an introduction to the minimalist programme; and Archangeli and Langendoen (1997) for an introduction to Optimality theory. See also Matthews (1993) for an excellent overview of the background and evolution of some of these theories.

2.1. Classical Chomskyan theory of anaphora

2.1.1. Typology of NPs

Within the principles-and-parameters theory, Chomsky (1981, 1982, 1986a) distinguishes two types of abstract feature for NPs: anaphors and pronominals. An anaphor is a feature representation of an NP which must be referentially dependent and which must be bound within an appropriately defined minimal syntactic domain; a pronominal is a feature representation of an NP which may be referentially dependent but which must be free within such a domain. Interpreting anaphors and pronominals as two independent binary features, Chomsky hypothesizes that one ideally expects to find four types of NP in a language—both overt and non-overt.

(2.1) Chomsky's typology of NPs

		Overt	Empty
(a)	[+anaphor, −pronominal]	lexical anaphor	NP-trace
(b)	[−anaphor, +pronominal]	pronoun	*pro*
(c)	[+anaphor, +pronominal]	—	PRO
(d)	[−anaphor, −pronominal]	name	*wh*-trace/variable

This can be illustrated in (2.2) and (2.3).

(2.2) Overt NPs
    (a) Lexical anaphors
        The composers admire themselves/each other.
    (b) Pronouns
        He is French enough to understand the culture, and yet foreign enough to see its peculiarities.
    (c) Names
        Jonathan Swift wrote an eighteenth-century satire called *Gulliver's Travels*.

(2.3) Empty categories
    (a) NP-traces
        The giant panda seems *t* to live exclusively on bamboo shoots.
    (b) *Pros* (Spanish)
        Carreras sabe   que *pro* es estimado por Domingo.
        Carreras knows that   is esteemed by   Domingo
        'Carreras knows that (he) is respected by Domingo.'
    (c) PROs
        John promised PRO to compose a light orchestral work for his father.
    (d) *Wh*-traces/variables
        Who did Brahms admire *t*.

2.1.2. Binding theory

Of the four types of NP listed in (2.1), anaphors, pronominals, and r[eferential]-expressions, that is, such NPs with the features [−anaphor,

−pronominal] as names and *wh*-traces/variables, are subject to binding conditions A, B and C respectively (see also Chomsky 1995).[2]

(2.4) Chomsky's binding conditions
    A. An anaphor is bound in a local domain.
    B. A pronominal is free in a local domain.
    C. An r-expression is free.

The definition of binding is given in (2.5).

(2.5) α binds β if and only if
    (i) α is in an A-position,
    (ii) α c-commands β, and
    (iii) α and β are coindexed.

Note that given (i) of (2.5), the binding conditions specified in (2.4) apply to A-binding (i.e. binding by a category in argument position) but not to Ā-binding (i.e. binding by a category in non-argument position). C-command is commonly defined as follows:

(2.6) α c-commands β if and only if
    (i) α does not dominate β,
    (ii) β does not dominate α, and
    (iii) the first branching node dominating α also dominates β.

Finally the notion of local domain is standardly defined in terms of governing category (GC) or complete functional complex (CFC),[3] and one common version of GC is given in (2.7).

(2.7) α is a GC for β if and only if α is the minimal category
    (i.e. the smallest NP or IP/S) containing β, a governor of β, and a SUBJECT accessible to β.

With these definitions in place, let us now turn to the four types of NP identified above and see how the binding conditions would predict their distribution. I shall start with lexical NPs and then move on to empty categories.

---

[2] In the minimalist programme, these conditions are recast as interpretative conditions (Chomsky 1995: 211).
  (i) A. If α is an anaphor, interpret it as coreferential with a c-commanding phrase in the relevant local domain D.
      B. If α is a pronominal, interpret it as disjoint from every c-commanding phrase in the relevant local domain D.
      C. If α is an r-expression, interpret it as disjoint from every c-commanding phrase.

One question that arises is at what level of syntactic representation the binding conditions operate. Within the principles-and-parameters framework, there are at least four proposals: (i) at D-structure, (ii) at S-structure, (iii) at LF, and (iv) at both S-structure and LF. In the minimalist programme, given that there are only two syntactic levels, i.e. LF and PF, it is likely that binding theory may obtain exclusively at LF (see also Freidin 1998 and Fox 1999).

[3] CFC may be defined as 'the smallest maximal category containing all the grammatical functions compatible with its head' (Chomsky 1986*b*: 169). Note that this definition is a mixture of both a geometric and a thematic approach to binding domain.

Lexical anaphors

Consider, first, the following paradigmatic examples of reflexives in English.

(2.8) (a) Chopin$_1$ adored himself$_1$.
    (b) Chopin$_1$ thought that Liszt$_2$ adored himself$_{*1/2}$.
    (c) Chopin's$_1$ father$_2$ adored himself$_{*1/2}$.
    (d) Chopin$_1$ believed himself$_1$ to be a poet of the piano.
    (e) *Chopin$_1$ believed that himself$_1$ was a poet of the piano.
    (f) Chopin$_1$ believed Liszt$_2$ to adore himself$_{*1/2}$.

Next, the distribution of reciprocals is essentially identical to that of reflexives in English.

(2.9) (a) They$_1$ adored each other$_1$.
    (b) They$_1$ thought that we$_2$ adored each other$_{*1/2}$.
    (c) Their$_1$ fathers$_2$ adored each other$_{*1/2}$.
    (d) They$_1$ believed each other$_1$ to be poets of the piano.
    (e) *They$_1$ believed that each other$_1$ were poets of the piano.
    (f) They$_1$ believed us$_2$ to adore each other$_{*1/2}$.

As the reader can verify for him- or herself, the distribution of the English reflexives in (2.8) and reciprocals in (2.9) follows straightforwardly from binding condition A.

However, while reflexives can occasionally be bound outside their local domain and/or by a non-c-commanding antecedent in English (see e.g. Kuno 1987, Zribi-Hertz 1989, Pollard and Sag 1992, Reinhart and Reuland 1993), examples of the types (2.10) and (2.11) are systematically allowed in a wide range of other languages.

(2.10) (a) (Chinese)
        Xiaoming$_1$ yiwei Xiaohua$_2$ xihuan ziji$_{1/2}$.
        Xiaoming think Xiaohua like   self
        'Xiaoming$_1$ thinks that Xiaohua$_2$ likes self$_{1/2}$.'
    (b) (Finnish, Korhonen 1995: 73)
        Antti$_1$ kerto-i   Anne-lle$_2$ että Topi
        Antti tell-PAST-3PX Anne-ALL that Topi-NOM
        ihaile-e   hän-tä itseä-än$_{1/*2}$.
        admire-3PX he-PAR REFL-PAR-3PX
        'Antti$_1$ told Anne$_2$ that Topi admires himself$_1$.'
    (c) (Marathi, Wali and Subbarao 1991: 1096)
        Lili$_1$ samajate ki   Suši$_2$ aaplyaa-laa$_{1/*2}$ haste.
        Lili thinks   that Susi self-to   laughs
        'Lili$_1$ thinks that Susi$_2$ laughs at self$_{1/*2}$.'

(2.11) (a) (Japanese, Kato 1994: 39)
        Takasi-ga   zibun-ga tensai da to   omotteiru.
        Takasi-SUBJ self-SUBJ genius is COMP think
        'Takasi thinks that self is a genius.'

(b) (Icelandic, Maling 1984)
Hann sagði að sig vantaði hæfileika.
he said that self lacked-SBJV ability
'He said that self lacked ability.'
(c) (Tuki, Biloa 1991b: 850)
munyinyi mu ta bungana ee mumwamate
birds SUBJ NEG think that themselves
mu nu gwam isi amo.
SUBJ FUT die day some
'Birds don't think that they-selves will die some day.'

(2.10) and (2.11) are examples of so-called long-distance reflexives, and languages that systematically allow long-distance reflexives are called 'long-distance reflexivization' languages. In recent years, a great number of proposals have been put forward in generative grammar to account for long-distance reflexivization, but none of them seems to be adequate. We shall return to long-distance reflexivization in Section 2.3.

A second type of counter-example to binding condition A is presented by the distribution of certain morphologically simplex reflexives in such languages as Dutch and Norwegian. Everaert (1986, 1991) and later Reinhart and Reuland (1991, 1993) note a contrast in the use of this type of reflexive in intrinsic and extrinsic reflexivization contexts: whereas a morphologically simplex reflexive can be locally bound in intrinsic reflexivization contexts, e.g. (2.12a) and (2.13a), as predicted by binding condition A; it cannot be locally bound in extrinsic reflexivization contexts, as in (2.12b) and (2.13b)—a contradiction to binding condition A.

(2.12) (Dutch)
(a) (Everaert 1991: 93)
Jan schaamde zich/*zichzelf.
Jan shamed self/self self
'Jan was ashamed.'
(b) (Reinhart and Reuland 1991: 293)
Jan veracht *zich/zichzelf.
Jan despises self/self self
'Jan despises himself.'
(2.13) (Norwegian)
(a) (Hellan 1991: 33)
Jon skammet seg/*segselv.
Jon shamed self/self self
'Jon was ashamed.'
(b) (Hellan 1988)
Jon foraktet *seg/segselv.
Jon despises self/self self
'Jon despises himself.'

There is thus evidence that cross-linguistically the distribution of reflexives violates binding condition A in both directions: on the one hand, a reflexive can be bound outside its local domain, and on the other, it may not be bound within its local domain.

Pronominals

Next, contrast the distribution of pronominals with that of anaphors in English.

(2.14) (a) Chopin$_1$ adored him$_2$.
    (b) Chopin$_1$ thought that Liszt$_2$ adored him$_{1/*2}$.
    (c) Chopin's$_1$ father$_2$ adored him$_{1/*2}$.
    (d) Chopin$_1$ believed him$_2$ to be a poet of the piano.
    (e) Chopin$_1$ believed that he$_1$ was a poet of the piano.
    (f) Chopin$_1$ believed Liszt$_2$ to adore him$_{1/*2}$.

Clearly, the distribution of pronominals in English abides by binding condition B. But when confronted with languages other than English, binding condition B runs into serious difficulties, for in some of these languages a pronominal can frequently be happily bound in its local domain. First, many languages in the world simply do not have reflexives, and consequently utilize pronominals as one of the means to encode reflexivity. These include some Low West Germanic languages (e.g. Old and Middle Dutch, Old English, Old Frisian, Old Saxon, and perhaps West Flemish and Modern Frisian) (Faltz 1985, 1989, Everaert 1986: 7, 39, 43, Burzio 1996), Bamako Bambara (Zribi-Hertz 1995), Biblical Hebrew (Levinson 1995), Isthmus Zapotec, the majority of Australian languages (e.g. Guugu Yimidhirr) (Levinson 1991), some Austronesian languages (e.g. Kilivila, Senft 1986: 54 and Tahitian, Tryon 1970: 97), and many pidgin and creole languages (e.g. the Spanish-based Palenquero and perhaps Bislama, Chinook Jargon, the French-based Guadeloupe, the Arabic-based KiNubi, Kriyol, Martinique Creole, and Negerhollands) (Carden and Stewart 1988, 1989, Kihm 1996). Some examples follow.

(2.15) (a) (Gumbaynggir, Eades 1979: 312)
       gua:du   bu:rwang   gula:na   magayu.
       3SG-ERG paint-PAST 3SG-ABS red paint-INST
       'He painted himself/him with red paint.'
    (b) (Fijian, Levinson 1991: 135)
       Sa va'a-. dodonu-. ta'ini 'ea   o   Mika.
       ASP correct   3SG-OBJ ART Mika
       'Mike corrected himself/him.'
    (c) (Haitian Creole, Carden and Stewart 1988)
       Emile dwe   ede li.
       Emile should help him
       'Emile should help himself/him.'
    (d) (Old English, Faltz 1985:19)
       Swa hwa swa eadmedath hine.
       whoever   humbles   him-ACC
       'Whoever humbles himself.'

Secondly, there are languages that lack first- and second-person reflexives. In these languages, first- and second-person pronouns are used instead as bound anaphors. Some Germanic and Romance languages, for instance, belong to this type.

(2.16) (*a*) (Danish, Thráinsson 1991: 63)
Jeg barberede mig.
I shaved me
'I shaved myself.'
(*b*) (Italian, Burzio 1991: 83)
Tu pensi solo a te.
you think only to you
'You only think about yourself.'
(*c*) (German, Faltz 1985: 118)
du sahst dich.
2SG-NOM see-PAST 2SG-ACC
'You saw yourself.'

Thirdly, the use of a locally bound third-person pronoun in syntactic structures where its corresponding, third-person reflexive is not available is attested in a range of languages. Following are examples from French, Piedmontese, and Russian. Similar examples can also be found in Catalan, Galician, Portuguese, Romanian, Sardinian; and Spanish (e.g. de Jong 1996).

(2.17) (*a*) (French, Zribi-Hertz 1980)
Victor n'aime que lui.
Victor not-loves but him
'Victor only loves himself.'
(*b*) (Piedmontese, Burzio 1991: 85)
Giuanin a parla sempre d' chiel.
Giuanin CLI-speak always of him
'Giuanin always talks about himself.'
(*c*) (Russian, Timberlake 1979: 115)
Ja emu skazal vse o nem, čto ja dumaju.
I him told all about him that I think
'I told him everything about himself that I was thinking.'

All this clearly indicates that binding condition B is inadequate.

Next, given the standard formulation of binding conditions A and B, it is predicted that anaphors and pronominals be in strict complementary distribution, that is, anaphors can occur only where pronominals cannot, and vice versa. This is because the two binding conditions are precise mirror images of each other.

This distributional complementarity between anaphors and pronominals, however, seems to be a generative syntactician's fantasy world. Even in a 'syntactic' language like English, it is not difficult to find syntactic environments where the complementarity forced by binding conditions A and B breaks down. Well-known cases include (i) 'picture' NPs, (ii) adjunct PPs, including locative and directive PPs, (iii) possessive NPs, and (iv) emphatic NPs (see e.g. Kuno 1987, Keenan 1988, Zribi-Hertz 1989, Safir 1992, Pollard and Sag 1992 and references therein).

(2.18) 'Picture' NPs
Pavarotti₁ saw a picture of himself₁/him₁ in *The Times*.
(2.19) Adjunct PPs
  (a) Locative PPs
  Mary₁ saw a snake near herself₁/her₁.[4]
  (b) Directive PPs
  Pavarotti₁ pulled a box of CDs towards himself₁/him₁.
(2.20) Possessive NPs
  [Pavarotti and Domingo]₁ adore each other's₁/their₁ performances.
(2.21) Emphatic contexts
  (a) As for himself₁/him₁, Pavarotti₁ said that he enjoyed the performance.
  (b) Pavarotti₁ said that tenors like himself₁/him₁ would not sing operas like that.
  (c) Carreras₁ thinks that Pavarotti is more talented than himself₁/him₁.

Worse still, when we take a look at a wider range of languages, we find that the total distributional complementarity entailed by binding conditions A and B stands on more shaky grounds. In the first place, as we have just mentioned, there are long-distance reflexivization languages—languages that systematically allow a reflexive to be bound outside its local domain. These include most East and South-East Asian languages (e.g. Chinese, Korean,

---

[4] Regarding so-called 'snake' sentences like (2.19a), languages can be divided into three groups: (i) those like German, Italian, and (the verbal reflexive construction in) Kinyarwanda, which allow only reflexives, as in (i); (ii) those like Akan, Finnish, and French, which permit only pronouns, as in (ii); and those like Japanese, Spanish, and Turkish, which warrant both reflexives and pronouns, as in (iii).
 (i) (a) (Hindi, Davison 1997)
       raam₁-nee apnee₁/*us₁-kee nazdiik eek sarp deekh-aa.
       Ram-ERG self's/3SG-of near one snake see-PF
       'Ram saw a snake near (him)self.'
    (b) (Serbo-Croatian)
       Ljiljana₁ je videla zmiju pored sebe₁/*nje₁.
       Ljiljana AUX saw   snake next self/her
       'Ljiljana saw a snake next to (her)self.'
 (ii) (a) (Akan, Faltz 1985: 174)
       John₁ hũũ ɔwɔ wɔ *nẽ hõ₁/nẽ₁   nkyɛn.
       John saw snake LOC 3SG-POSS-REFL/3SG-POSS side
       'John saw a snake near himself.'
    (b) (French)
       Pierre₁ a vu un serpent près de *lui-même₁/lui₁.
       Pierre saw a snake near to himself/him
       'Pierre saw a snake near himself.'
 (iii) (a) (Modern Hebrew, Faltz 1985: 111)
       moše₁ raa naxaš al-yad acmo₁/yado₁.
       Moshe saw snake near-3SG-M-REFL/3SG-M
       'Moshe saw a snake near himself/him.'
    (b) (Tagalog, Faltz 1985: 112–13)
       nakakita si   Juan₁ ng   ahas malapit sa
       see-PAST TOP Juan GOAL snake near
       kaniyang sarili₁/kaniya₁.
       3SG-POSS REFL 3SG
       'Juan saw a snake near himself/him.'

and Malay), some Mainland and Insular Scandinavian languages (e.g. Norwegian, Swedish, and Icelandic), some Germanic (other than Scandinavian) and Romance languages (e.g. Dutch, Italian, and Old Provençal), some Slavonic languages (Czech, Polish, and Russian), and languages like Greek, KiNande, and Northern Pomo. In these long-distance reflexivization languages, there is often a systematic syntactic distributional overlap between anaphors and pronominals, as can be exemplified in (2.22).

(2.22) (a) (Malay, Ngoh 1991)
Timah memberitahu Rohani bahawa
Timah tell   Rohani that
Ali memandang rendah akan dirinya/nya.
Ali look   low   to   self-3SG/3SG
'Timah$_1$ told Rohani$_2$ that Ali$_3$ looked down on her$_1$.'
(b) (Norwegian, Hestvik 1992: 578)
John bad   Marit kikke bak   seg/ham.
John asked Mary to-look behind REFL/him
'John asked Mary to look behind him.'
(c) (Northern Pomo, O'Connor 1992a)
tiyi/man   xale yow čima-da   man khebe:n-ye.
NCBR.SG.A/3SF.A tree under sit-ADVCOMP 3SGF.A sing-PERF
'She$_1$ sang while she$_1$ was sitting under the tree.'

Secondly, following in part a suggestion by Burzio (1996), languages can be grouped into three types with respect to bound possessive anaphora: (i) those allowing anaphors but not pronominals (e.g. Danish, Hindi/Urdu, and Mundani), (ii) those permitting pronominals but not anaphors (e.g. English), and (iii) those permitting both anaphors and pronominals (e.g. Japanese, Malayalam, and Tuki). In the first type, the possessive and the antecedent are 'near' enough to allow only a reflexive but not a pronoun.[5] In the second, because either there is no possessive reflexive in the language or the possessive reflexive cannot be used, only a pronominal is permitted. Finally in the third type, the possessive and the antecedent are both 'close' enough to allow a reflexive and at the same time 'distant' enough to permit a pronoun as well.

(2.23) Anaphors only
(a) (Gimira, Breeze 1986:57)
ba/yi   dor gotue.
3REFL/his sheep sold-3M-FIN
'He$_1$ sold self's$_1$/his$_2$ sheep.'
(b) (Norwegian, Hestvik 1992: 578)
John$_1$ fortalte Ola$_2$ om   sin$_1$/*hans$_1$ kone.
John told   Ola about REFL/his wife
'John$_1$ told Ola$_2$ about self's$_1$/his$_2$ wife.'

---

[5] Looked at from a slightly different perspective, (some forms of) possessive pronouns in languages like Danish, Norwegian, and Icelandic seem to be subject-obviative, that is, they must be free from the closest potential subject in a specific syntactic domain (e.g. Vikner 1985, Anderson 1986, Manzini and Wexler 1987, Thráinsson 1991, Hestvik 1992). We shall return to anti-subject orientation of pronouns in Section 2.3.

(c) (Latin, Burzio 1996: 1)
Ioannes₁ sororem suam₁/*eius₁ vidit.
Ioannes sister   self's/his   saw
'Ioannes₁ saw self's₁/his₂ sister.'
(2.24) Pronominals only
(a) Pavarotti₁ adores his₁/₂ performance.
(b) (German, Thráinsson 1991: 63)
Hans₁ sah sein₁/₂ Buch.
Hans saw his   book
'Hans₁ saw his₁/₂ book.'
(c) (Guugu Yimidhirr, Levinson 1987: 390)
John₁-ngun nyulu₁ biiba   nhangu₁/₂   dhaabangadhi.
John-ERG he-NOM father-ABS he-GEN-ABS asked
'John₁ (he₁) asked his₁/₂ father.'
(2.25) Both anaphors and pronominals
(a) (Korean, Kim 1993: 54)
John₁-un caki₁/ku₁/₂-uy emma-lul hyemohanta.
John-TOP self/his-GEN mom-ACC hate
'John₁ hates self's₁/his₁mom.'
(b) (Malayalam, Mohanan 1982)
moohan₁ tante₁/awante₁ bhaaryaye nulli.
Mohan self's/his   wife   pinched
'Mohan₁ pinched self's₁/his₁ wife.'
(c) (Tuki, Biloa 1991b: 848)
Mbara₁ a   mu kusa vakarate vaamate₁/vaa₁.
Mbara SUBJ PL buy books   3SG self/his
'Mbara₁ bought self's₁/his₁ books.'

While binding conditions A and B make correct predications about the distribution of possessive anaphora in 'reflexives only' and perhaps also in 'pronouns only' languages depending on how the binding domain is defined, they certainly make wrong predictions for 'both reflexives and pronominals' languages.

Thirdly, still another type of distributional overlap is found cross-linguistically. This involves certain emphatic contexts. Emphatics can be either morphologically simplex or complex. Morphologically complex emphatics are usually in the form of 'pronoun/reflexive+adjunct/modifier', with the adjunct/modifier having the meaning of 'self', 'same', 'body', 'head', 'eye', 'soul', 'marrow', 'seed', or—in the case of possessives—'own' (Moyne 1971, Zribi-Hertz 1980, 1995, Kuno 1987, Saxon 1990, Burzio 1991, Levinson 1991, McKey 1991, König 1991, König and Siemund 1997, C. Baker 1995, Kemmer 1995; see also Moravcsik 1972 for the origins of emphatics in a number of languages including Arabic, Hausa and Okinawan).[6]

---

[6] Safir (1996) has noted an interesting typological difference between Germanic and Romance languages here. Germanic languages are SELFish ones in that they employ 'self' in complex emphatics whereas Romance languages are SELFless ones in that they use 'same' instead. Other languages that deploy 'same' in (complex) emphatics and are therefore SELFless include Syrian Arabic, Ancient Greek, and Lithuanian (e.g. Moravcsik 1972).

26   *Syntactic Approaches to Anaphora*

These morphologically complex emphatics can alternate with plain pronouns.[7]

(2.26) Pronoun/pronoun+'self'
    (a) Menuhin realized that the boy violinist could be more talented than him/himself.
    (b) (Chinese)
        Li Xiansheng shuo gongyuan li   you ta/ta   ziji sheji de
        Li Mr   say   park   LOC exist 3SG/3SG self design REL
        baota.
        pagoda
        'Mr Li says that in the park there is a pagoda he/he himself designed.'

(2.27) Pronoun/pronoun+'same'
    (a) (French, Zribi-Hertz 1995: 335)
        Pierre pense   que Marie aime Paul plus que lui/lui-même.
        Pierre believes that Marie loves Paul more than him/him-same
        'Pierre believes that Marie loves Paul more than him/himself.'
    (b) (Italian, Burzio 1996)
        Io parlo di   me/me-stesso.
        I talk about me/me-same
        'I talk about myself.'

(2.28) Pronoun/pronoun+'own'
    (a) Chopin adored his/his own performance.
    (b) (Italian, Burzio 1991: 100)
        Gianni legge il   suo/il (suo) proprio libro.
        Gianni reads the his/the his own   book
        Gianni reads his/his own book.'

All this points to the conclusion that the strict distributional complementarity between anaphors and pronominals dictated by binding conditions A and B cannot be maintained.[8]

R-expressions

R-expressions are expressions that (as the term suggests) are inherently referential. Unlike an anaphor or a pronominal which must or can be bound in some domain, an r-expression (being subject to binding condition C) must be free throughout, that is, it must be free in all domains. In other words, there is no configuration in which an r-expression can be bound. This is illustrated by the following paradigmatic examples from English.

(2.29) (a) Chopin$_1$ adored Chopin$_{*1/2}$.
     (b) Chopin$_1$ thought that Chopin$_{*1/2}$ adored Liszt.

---

[7] Notice that except in (2.26b), the emphatics in all the other examples are what Verheijen (1986) has called end reflexives. The emphatic in (2.26b) is a head-bound reflexive.

[8] Cf. the Malagasy example below which also runs contrary to the complementarity predicted by binding conditions A and B for the exceptional case-marking (ECM) construction.

(i) (Malagasy, Randriamasimanana 1986: 279)
    Mihevitra ny tena-ny$_1$/azy$_1$ ho mahay i   Paloly$_1$.
    thinks   the self-his/him as able   ART Paul
    'Paul thinks himself to be able.'

(c) Chopin₁ thought that Liszt adored Chopin*₁/₂.
(d) Chopin's₁ father adored Chopin₁.
(e) *Chopin₁ adored Chopin's₁ father.
(2.30) (a) *He₁ adored Chopin₁.
(b) *He₁ thought that Chopin₁ adored Liszt.
(c) *He₁ thought that Liszt adored Chopin₁.
(d) His₁ father adored Chopin₁.
(e) *He₁ adored Chopin's₁ father.

As is easy to verify by the reader him- or herself, the central distributional pattern of r-expressions in English follows straightforwardly from binding condition C. However, a cursory inspection of a wider range of languages suggests that the binding of r-expressions also varies from language to language. Vietnamese and Thai, for example, are somewhat different from English (Lasnik 1989). Consider the following.

(2.31) (Vietnamese, Lasnik 1989)
(a) *John₁ thúóng John₁.
John likes John
'John likes John.'
(b) John₁ tin John₁ sẽ thắńg.
John thinks John will win
'John thinks that John will win.'
(2.32) (Vietnamese, Lasnik 1989)
(a) *Nó₁ thúóng John₁.
he likes John
'He likes John.'
(b) *Nó₁ tin John₁ sẽ thắńg.
he thinks John will win
'He thinks that John will win.'
(2.33) (Thai, Lasnik 1989)
(a) Cɔɔn₁ chɔ̂ɔp Cɔɔn₁.
John likes John
'John likes John.'
(b) Cɔɔn₁ khít wâa Cɔɔn₁ chàlāāt.
John thinks that John is smart
'John thinks that John is smart.'
(2.34) (Thai, Lasnik 1989)
(a) *Khǎw₁ chɔ̂ɔp Cɔɔn₁.
he likes John
'He likes John.'
(b) *Khǎw₁ khít wâa Cɔɔn₁ chàlāāt.
he thinks that John is smart
'He thinks that John is smart.'

Comparing and contrasting English, Vietnamese, and Thai, two interesting observations emerge. The first is that for binding of an r-expression by a pronoun, binding condition C seems to hold without exception in all three languages. But secondly, in the case of binding of an r-expression by another r-expression, English, Vietnamese, and Thai differ in that binding condition

28   *Syntactic Approaches to Anaphora*

C obtains in all domains in English, but only within a restricted domain (i.e. the GC) in Vietnamese, and in no domain at all in Thai (Lasnik 1989). This has prompted Lasnik to argue, in the spirit of Chomsky (1981: 193, 227), that binding condition C should better be split into two distinct subconditions, to be called binding conditions C_1 and C_2 (see (2.35)), the latter being an instantiation of a hierarchy of referentiality (2.36) (see also Burzio 1991). Furthermore, Lasnik claims that while binding condition C_1 is subject to parametric variation, binding condition C_2 is universal.

(2.35) Lasnik's binding condition C (my phrasing)
   C_1 An r-expression is r-expression-free everywhere
   C_2 An r-expression is pronoun-free everywhere
(2.36) Lasnik's hierarchy of referentiality
   A less referential expression may not bind a more referential one.

But this way of looking at binding condition C patterns does not seem to be seriously entertainable. Let us note first that in fact binding condition C_1 can easily be frustrated in English as well (see e.g. Fodor 1975, Bolinger 1979, Evans 1980, McCray 1980, Carden 1982, Leech 1983, Mittwoch 1983, Reinhart 1983, 1986, Levinson 1987, 1991, Grodzinsky and Reinhart 1993), though perhaps under more restricted circumstances than in Vietnamese and Thai. This difference can further be supported by the fact that the repetition of r-expressions (in various forms) is also extremely common at the discourse level in languages of the latter type (e.g. Huang 1994).

(2.37) (a) (Fodor 1975 :134)
   Only Churchill remembers Churchill giving the speech about blood, sweat, toil and tears.
   (b) (Evans 1980)
   I know what John and Bill have in common. John thinks that Bill is terrific and Bill thinks that Bill is terrific.
   (c) (Levinson 1987)
   Frog went to Frog's house; Toad went to Toad's house.

The question, then, is why binding condition C_1 is less easily violated in English than in, say, Thai. The answer seems to reside in the proposal I made in Huang (1994) that English and Thai belong to different types of language: English is essentially a syntactic language, while Thai is essentially a pragmatic one. I shall return to this issue in Chapter 4.

Next arises the question of whether or not binding condition C_2 can be maintained universally. The answer seems to be negative.

(2.38) (a) (Evans 1980)
   Everyone has finally realized that Oscar is incompetent.
   Even he has finally realized that Oscar is incompetent.
   (b) (Chinese, Huang 1994: 200)
   Zhexia, Yuan Shikai ke   deyi   le, ta   yiwei
   thus   Yuan Shikai EMPH complacent CRS 3SG think

dangjin Zhongguo zhiyou Yuan Shikai cai shi
today China only Yuan Shikai only be
dang huangdi de liao.
act emperor PRT material
'On that occasion, Yuan Shikai₁ was terribly complacent. He₁ thought that in today's China only Yuan Shikai₁ had got the makings of an emperor.'

In (2.38), the r-expression in the second sentence is preceded and c-commanded by a pronoun in the matrix clause of the same sentence, yet it is bound by the pronoun, contra binding condition C_2. One proposal to accommodate counter-examples of this kind has been to reinterpret binding theory as a theory of referential dependency, along the lines of Evans (1980).

(2.39) Evans's theory of referential dependence
A term can be referentially dependent upon an NP if and only if it does not precede and c-command that NP.

On this view, the reference of the pronoun in (2.38) has to be antecedently assigned in the previous sentence, and consequently the pronoun can be accidentally coindexed with the r-expression in question, thus in conformity with binding condition C_2. But such an escape mechanism both over- and under-generates. In the case of (2.40), non-referential dependence between the pronoun and the second instance of *Oscar* should be possible, since there is a possible antecedent in the previous discourse. But this does not seem to be the case (Grodzinsky and Reinhart 1993). On the other hand, in the case of (2.41), the r-expression should not be coindexed with the preceding and c-commanding pronoun without invoking a previous context. But it is.

(2.40) (Grodzinsky and Reinhart 1993)
*Oscar is sad. He thinks that Oscar is incompetent.
(2.41) (Chinese, Huang 1994: 201)
Ta you zai gan zhe xiaozi yiguan gan de shi.
3SG again DUR do this guy always do REL thing
'He is doing what the guy always does.'

This indicates that Evans's proposal may not be valid in explaining away such counter-examples as (2.41) to binding condition C_2. If this is the case, then there is no avoiding the conclusion that binding condition C_2 can also be falsified. All this seems to lead support to Chomsky's (1981, 1982) general discourse principle (2.42) and more generally to Reinhart and Reuland's (1993) position that binding condition C is not a primitive of grammar.

(2.42) Chomsky's general discourse principle
(*a*) Avoid repetition of r-expressions, except when conditions warrant.
(*b*) When conditions warrant, repeat.

As we will see later in Chapter 4, binding condition C, together with (2.42), can be subsumed under or explained by the neo-Gricean pragmatic theory of anaphora I have been developing. When binding condition C and (2.42) work, they follow from that theory; when they do not, they can be explained by that theory.

We move next to binding of ECs. As noted earlier in Section 2.1.1, there are four distinct types of EC in Chomsky's typology of NPs, namely NP-trace, *pro*, PRO, and *wh*-trace. Of these four types, NP-trace and *wh*-trace are ECs which arise, arguably, as a result of some kind of movement. By contrast, *pro* and PRO are considered to be base-generated ECs.

NP-traces

An NP-trace is an EC that is left behind by the movement of an NP. The landing site of an NP-trace is typically an A-position, therefore an NP-trace must be A-bound. In other words, it must be coindexed with the displaced, c-commanding NP with which it forms an A-chain. From a distributional point of view, an NP-trace seems to parallel an anaphor. Therefore, it is taken to be the null analogue of an anaphor, and, as such, is subject to binding condition A. Compare (2.43) with (2.8) above.

(2.43) (*a*) Chopin$_1$ was adored t_1.
     (*b*) *Chopin$_1$ was believed that Liszt adored t_1.
     (*c*) *Chopin's$_1$ father was adored t_1.
     (*d*) Chopin$_1$ was believed t_1 to be a poet of the piano.
     (*e*) *Chopin$_1$ was believed that t_1 was a poet of the piano.
     (*f*) *Chopin$_1$ was believed Liszt to adore t_1.

Wh-traces

By contrast, a *wh*-trace, also called a variable, is an EC which is left behind by the movement of a *wh*-expression. The landing site of a *wh*-trace is typically Spec[ifier] of CP, an Ā-position, therefore a *wh*-trace must be Ā-bound. This amounts to saying that a *wh*-trace must be coindexed with the moved, c-commanding *wh*-element with which it forms an Ā-chain. Notice next that a *wh*-trace is treated like a variable in formal logic, which involves operator binding. In operator binding, an operator such as a quantifier which is outside a proposition binds a variable in the proposition. For example, (2.44) expresses a proposition which informally has the representation (2.45).

(2.44) All Nobel laureates are geniuses.
(2.45) (*a*) Predicate calculus
         $\forall x[\text{NOBEL LAUREATE}(x) . \text{GENIUS}(x)]$
     (*b*) Semantics
         For all x, if x is a Nobel laureate then x is a genius.

Here, the quantifier *all* is represented as an operator ($\forall$), which is peripheral to the proposition and which binds the variable x in the proposition. The variable x denotes a random member of the individuals in the universe of discourse. By exactly the same line of reasoning, if the LF-structure of (2.46) is taken to be something like (2.47), then it seems quite reasonable for us to treat the moved *wh*-expression as a kind of quantifier and its trace as a kind of variable at LF, or at some other levels of syntactic representation, or at some interface levels.

(2.46) [_{CP} who₁ did [_{IP} Chopin adore t_1]]
(2.47) [_{CP} who₁ did [_{IP} Chopin adore x_1]]

This parallelism between binding of variables in formal logic and binding of *wh*-traces in natural language can partially be evidenced by a correspondence of the following well-known paradigmatic examples in English.

(2.48) (a) Who *t* adores her boyfriend?
  (b) ?Whose boyfriend *t* adores her?
  (c) *Who does her boyfriend *t* adore *t*?
  (d) *Whose boyfriend does *t* she adore *t*?
(2.49) (a) Every girl adores her boyfriend.
  (b) ?Every girl's boyfriend adores her.
  (c) *Her boyfriend adores every girl.
  (d) *She adores every girl's boyfriend.

Now, for the purpose of binding theory, just as an NP-trace is treated as a phonetically null anaphor, so is a *wh*-trace classified as a phonetically null r-expression without contradiction. Consequently, like an r-expression, a *wh*-trace is also subject to binding condition C. The following parallel between an r-expression and a *wh*-trace leads support to this line of analysis.

(2.50) (a) *He adored Chopin.
  (b) *Who did he adore *t*.
(2.51) (a) *He thought that Liszt adored Chopin.
  (b) *Who did he think Liszt adored *t*.

It should be mentioned at this point that the (b) sentences of (2.50) and (2.51) are referred to as strong crossover in the literature, a phenomenon that was first discussed by Postal (1971). In strong crossover, the movement of a *wh*-phrase is said to 'cross over' a pronoun which A-binds it. Given binding condition C, the ungrammaticality of strong crossover is entirely expected; the *wh*-trace in question is A-bound, violating that condition. If we reverse the c-command relation, the (b) sentences of (2.50) and (2.51) will become grammatical, as can be shown in (2.52) and (2.53). This is because the *wh*-trace in (2.52) and (2.53) is now A-free, as it is Ā-bound by the moved *wh*-phrase; and the pronoun is also A-free in its respective GC.

(2.52) Who *t* adored him?
(2.53) Who *t* thought Liszt adored him?

Somewhat akin to strong crossover is weak crossover, so-called because the ungrammaticality is less strongly felt.

(2.54) ?Who$_1$ does her$_1$ boyfriend adore t_1?

As in strong crossover, the movement of a *wh*-phrase also 'crosses over' a pronoun in weak crossover. But, unlike in strong crossover, the pronoun in weak crossover does not A-bind the *wh*-trace; though the pronoun is coindexed with it, it does not c-command it. This has the immediate consequence that weak crossover does not fall under binding theory (though various attempts have been made to reduce it to c-command and thus to binding theory, following the footsteps of Reinhart 1983) and has to be accommodated by some other principles of UG. For example, Chomsky (1986*b*) suggests that traces be derived from the ECP. Reinhart and Reuland (1993) are of the view that the local binding of them should be shifted to chain theory. Erteschik-Shir (1997) argues that the interpretation of *wh*-traces is subject to what she labels focus-structure. Furthermore, there are two issues that are of particular interest. The first is concerned with the question whether weak crossover is subject to syntactic configuration only or subject to linear order as well. One view is that linear order plays no role in constraining week crossover and all leftness/directionality effects (i.e. a variable cannot be co-indexed with a pronoun to its left) can be attributed to a linear order-free constraint stated in terms of structural notions such as biuniqueness (Koopman and Sportiche 1983)[9] and parallelism (Safir 1985) (see also Lasnik and Stowell 1991). But Bresnan (1998) has shown convincingly that, contrary to this popular but incorrect view, both syntactic configuration and linear order play an important role in regulating weak crossover, which is a manifestation of a more general prominence condition on binding. Consequently, from a typological point of view, 'weak crossover' languages can be grouped into four types : (i) those like the Bantu languages Chichewa and Kiswahili, which are susceptible only to a syntactic rank condition; (ii) those like Hindi/Urdu and Malayalam, which obey only a linear order constraint, (iii) those like English and Palauan, which have both a syntactic rank constraint and a linear order condition; and (iv) those like German and Korean, which fall under the union of the domain licensed by both syntactic rank and linear order. This typology, Bresnan claims, can largely be predicted by the principles of Optimality theory (see also Pica and Snyder 1995 for a minimalist analysis of weak crossover). Secondly there is the question whether strong and weak crossovers constitute two distinct phenomena or are simply a unified phenomenon. The long-established, traditional view is that they are

---

[9] Cross-linguistically, the argument that *wh*-traces are a result of movement and as such are subject to some kind of island constraints may not be maintained. On the one hand, there are languages such as Dakota, in which *wh*-expressions are found 'in situ' without movement, yet the island constraints obtain. On the other hand, there are languages like Palauan, where *wh*-expressions seem—at least at first sight—to have undergone movement, but no island constraints are observed. I am grateful to Mark Durie for bringing this to my attention (see also Georgopoulos 1991).

distinct. But recent work by Postal (1993) shows that strong crossover falls into two categories, what he has called primary and secondary strong crossover, and that secondary strong crossover should be grouped with weak crossover. Taking Postal's suggestion a step further, Kempson and Gabbay (1998) have attempted to provide a unified analysis of strong and weak crossover in terms of a Labelled Deductive System for natural language processing.

We turn next to the two types of EC that are not derived from movement. We first mention *pro* briefly and then consider PRO in detail.

Pro

A *pro* is considered to be the null analogue of a lexical pronoun, and is hence subject to binding condition B. While it is not assumed to exist in English, it is found in many other languages in the world. These languages have come to be known as 'pro-drop' or 'null subject' languages. We shall discuss null subjects and null objects in detail in Section 2.2.

PRO

As noted above in Section 2.1.1, in the standard Chomskyan typology of NPs, PRO is specified as [+anaphor, +pronominal]. One significant consequence is that from a binding-theoretical perspective, PRO is expected to satisfy the conflicting requirements of both binding conditions A and B. To maintain this, if PRO has a GC, it must be both bound and free in it simultaneously—a contradiction that is irreconcilable. Yet out of this paradox emerges a possible solution: namely PRO cannot have a GC. From this, we derive the PRO theorem (2.55).

(2.55) PRO theorem.
PRO is ungoverned.

Clearly, given (2.55), PRO now trivially satisfies both the requirement that if it has a GC, it is bound in it, and the requirement that if it has a GC, it is free in it, and hence no contradiction arises in connection with binding theory.

Notice that (2.55) is essentially a statement about the distribution of PRO. What it basically says is that PRO can be licensed only in positions where it is ungoverned, for only in these positions will it not have a GC by virtue of lacking a governor. The paradigm in (2.56) and (2.57) shows that this prediction is in general borne out for English.

(2.56) (*a*) *Chopin adored PRO.
    (*b*) *PRO adored Chopin.
    (*c*) *Chopin believed PRO to be a poet of the piano.
(2.57) (*a*) Chopin persuaded Delacrox PRO to paint a portrait of him.

(b) PRO writing a cello sonata is not easy.[10]
(c) In 1831, Chopin settled in Paris PRO contented.

(2.56a) shows that PRO cannot occur as a complement of a lexical head. (2.56b) indicates that it cannot function as the subject of a finite clause. (2.56c) suggests that it cannot appear as the subject of an infinitival clause if it is Case-marked (in this case by an exceptional case-marking (ECM) verb). As the reader can verify for him- or herself, these are all governed positions. Therefore by (2.55) PRO is correctly excluded in these positions. By contrast, (2.57a)–(2.57c) indicate that PRO can act as the subject of a non-Case-marked infinitival clause, a gerundial clause, and a small clause, respectively. Once again, as can easily be verified, this follows straightforwardly from (2.55); these positions are ungoverned.

Another consequence of positing (2.55) is that PRO is predicted to be in complementary distribution with overt NPs. This is because given that an NP characterized as [+anaphor, +pronominal] must be ungoverned, by the binding theory, no overt NP can have such a feature combination. The reason is that within the principles-and-parameters theory, an overt NP requires Case—the central tenet of Case theory. But as the assignment of Case takes place primarily under government, it is impossible for an overt NP to satisfy both the binding theory and the Case Filter, stated in (2.58), simultaneously.

(2.58) Case Filter
*NP if NP has a phonetic metric and has no Case.

It follows therefore that where PRO is sanctioned, overt NPs are not tolerated; where overt NPs are allowed, PRO is not permitted. This prediction in general is also borne out for English, as can easily be verified by the reader.

Finally, both the antecedent of PRO and PRO itself have to be an argument and cannot be an expletive.[11] The latter is captured in Safir's (1985) stipulated Emex Condition.

(2.59) Emex Condition
An expletive EC must be governed.

Cross-linguistic evidence, however, has been given that the distribution of PRO predicted by the PRO theorem may not be correct. There are at least two types of language in which PRO in infinitives can be both governed and Case-

---

[10] Note the following.
(i) PRO to adore Haydn is PRO to adore his music.

In an equative construction like this with multiple PROs, PROs are subject to the condition that they have the same value in reference, for the interpretation of this example is along the lines of 'For x to adore Haydn is for that same x to adore his music.' This contrasts sharply with *pros*. See n. 19 below.

[11] Notice that the statement that PRO has to be an argument does not apply to small clauses, because PRO in small clauses can occur only as adjuncts but not as arguments—a complementarity with PRO in infinitivals. In fact the existence of PRO as subjects in depictive small clause adjuncts is, to say the least, controversial. See e.g. Williams (1992) for arguments against positing PRO in small clauses.

marked. The first is exemplified by Icelandic. PRO in this language, according to Sigurðsson (1991), is both governed and Case-marked but nevertheless remains non-lexical. The evidence provided by Sigurðsson is (i) PRO can occur in 'quirky' constructions—constructions that contain oblique or 'quirky' subjects, as in (2.60a), (ii) PRO can head morphological Case chains, as in (2.60b), and (iii) PRO can trigger or control Case dependent agreements, as in (2.60c). Sigurðsson's own account of non-lexicalization is that PRO in Icelandic is locally assigned Case by Infl/-Agr, which is not a member of the set of proper head governors. Hence PRO is not properly head governed, from which follows the fact that it cannot be lexicalized, whether it is Case-marked or not. The same conclusion that PRO can be (properly) governed and Case-visible has been reached also for both Italian (e.g. Burzio 1991) and Russian (e.g. Franks and Hornstein 1992).

(2.60) (Icelandic, Sigurðsson 1991: 329–36)
  (a) Quirky subject
      Hún vonast til að   PRO vanta ekki vinnu.
      she hopes for to-ACC   lack not job
      'She hopes not to lack a job.'
  (b) Morphological Case chains
      Strákarnir   vonast til að   PRO komast allir   í skóla.
      the boys-NOM hope   for to-NOM   get   all-NOM to school
      'The boys all hope to get to school.'
  (c) Case dependent agreements
      Stelpurnar   vonast til að   PRO verða aðstoðaðar.
      the girls-NOM hope   to-NOM   be   aided-NOM-PL-F
      'The girls hope to be aided.'

The second type of language that falsifies the PRO theorem is represented by Korean and Malayalam. In this type of language, not only can PRO in infinitives be both governed and Case-marked, it can also be lexicalized. Thus, PRO in Korean infinitives can occur in a position that can be filled with a pronoun or an anaphor, which receives nominative Case (Yang 1985, Borer 1989). More or less the same can be said of Malayalam. PRO in this language can occupy a position that can be filled by a lexical NP, which is assigned dative or nominative Case, depending on the embedded verb. The same is also true of Kannada, a sister Dravidian language (Mohanan 1982), and to some extent of Arabic. Another language whose alleged PRO can be lexically filled is Guugu Yimidhirr (Levinson 1987).

(2.61) (a) (Korean, Borer 1989 with errors corrected)
      John$_1$-ka   PRO$_1$/ku$_1$/caki$_1$ ttena-lye-ko   nolyek ha-ess-ta.
      John-NOM   he/self   leave-will-COMP try   do-PAST
      'John tried to leave.'
  (b) (Malayalam, Mohanan 1983)
      Kutti   PRO/awan   wiśakkaan aag̃rahiccu.
      child-NOM   he-DAT hunger-INF desired
      'The child wanted to be hungry.'

36 Syntactic Approaches to Anaphora

Next, the PRO theorem may also be falsified for theory-internal reasons. Note that the validity of the PRO theorem is dependent on the crucial assumption that both anaphors and pronominals have exactly the same GC. But this may not be the case. It has been argued that there is a bifurcation with respect to SUBJECT accessibility in relation to anaphors and pronominals: the accessibility of SUBJECT is relevant to anaphors but irrelevant to pronominals. Consequently the GCs for anaphors and pronominals can be distinct (at least) in languages that allow long-distance reflexivization, the former being larger than the latter (e.g. C.-T. J. Huang 1983, Battistella 1985, Anderson 1986, Chomsky 1986a, Borer 1989, Lasnik 1989: 35, Everaert 1991, Kayne 1991, Steenbergen 1991, Thráinsson 1991). Assuming then that binding condition A applies to a PRO in its anaphoric binding domain, and binding condition B to it in its pronominal domain, the distribution of PRO can be widened to the extent that PRO is licensed in positions in which the two GCs do not coincide. Clearly the embedded subject position of a finite clause in a language such as Chinese is such a position, and therefore the EC in that position can be treated as a PRO.

(2.62) (Chinese)
    (a) Xiaohong shuo ziji hen xihuan la   tiqin.
        Xiaohong say   self very like   play violin
        'Xiaohong says that she likes playing the violin very much.'
    (b) Xiaohong shuo ta   hen xihuan la   tiqin.
        Xiaohong say   3SG very like   play violin
        'Xiaohong says that she likes playing the violin very much.'
    (c) Xiaohong shuo Ø hen xihuan la   tiqin.
        Xiaohong say   very like   play violin
        'Xiaohong says that (I/you/he/she/we/they) like(s) playing the violin very much.'

But this extension of PRO to the subject position of a finite clause may have to be rejected on both theoretical and empirical grounds. From a conceptual point of view, such a radical extension will result in too wide a distribution of PRO. This will give rise to a host of theory-internal problems for the principles-and-parameters theory. One way to tackle this problem has been to speculate that PRO can be excluded from positions in which it must not occur utilizing some other UG principles such as Case theory and θ-theory. But as I pointed out in Huang (1989, 1991a, 1992a, 1992b, 1994), such a move will open a Pandora's box and cannot be seriously entertained. Turning next to the empirical considerations, many problems will arise with such an extension. For one thing, given the assumption that binding condition A is relevant to its anaphoric binding domain and binding condition B is relevant to its pronominal domain, a governed PRO in a finite clause would be expected to be free in its pronominal domain but bound in its anaphoric domain—a contradiction to fact, as can be shown by (2.62c). All this greatly reduces both conceptually and empirically the plausibility of the analysis that PRO can occupy the subject position of a finite clause.

Taking account of the English, Icelandic, Korean, and Chinese facts we have seen above, we can conclude that (i) PRO can occur only in non-finite clauses but maybe in a governed position within such a clause, and (ii) the distribution of PRO is not entailed by binding theory. Consequently the PRO theorem has to be abandoned.

Finally, let us consider the question whether or not PRO (either in the sense of Chomsky or in the sense of the conclusion in (i) above) occurs universally across languages. The answer, I suggest, is negative.

Consider first the case in which we adhere to the classical Chomkyan position that PRO must be ungoverned and un-Case-marked. This will rule out the occurrence of PRO in such languages as Icelandic, Korean, and Malayalam, since, as we have already seen, alleged PRO in these languages clearly is both governed and Case-marked.

Suppose next we abandon the PRO theorem and adopt the definition of PRO as specified in (i) above. By this definition, though PRO can now be both governed and Case-marked, it still occurs only in a non-finite clause. But there are languages which do not have non-finite clauses, and consequently do not contain PRO.

Chinese

One such language is Chinese. As I have demonstrated in detail in Huang (1989, 1991a, 1991b, 1992a, 1992b, 1994), there is no distinction between finite and non-finite clauses in this language, contrary to the claim by C.-T. J. Huang (1984, 1989). Given that this is the case, then there might follow three consequences: (i) there are neither finite nor non-finite clauses in Chinese, (ii) there are only non-finite clauses in Chinese; and (iii) there are only finite clauses in Chinese. Of these positions, (iii) appears to be the most plausible one. If this is the case, then it is not unreasonable to assume that there are only finite clauses in the language. Consequently no PRO as defined by Chomsky or as specified by the definition in (i) above can be allowed in Chinese.

Modern Greek

Another language which clearly does not have PRO in the relevant sense is Modern Greek, as described in Philippaki-Warburton (1987) and Philippaki-Warburton and Catsimali (1999) (see also Joseph 1992). One particular striking characteristic of Modern Greek syntax, argues Philippaki-Warburton (1987), is that there is no infinitive in the language. To see the point, consider (2.63) and (2.64), which are the closest Greek equivalents to an infinitival construction (Philippaki-Warburton 1987: 291–2).

(2.63) o   janis   prospaθise Ø na   fiji.
       the-NOM John-NOM tried-he   SBJV go-he
       'John tried to leave.'
(2.64) δen ine fanero ti   Ø na   kani.
       not is clear what   SBJV do-he
       'It is not clear what he should do.'

In both (2.63) and (2.64), the main verb in the embedded clause is finite in that it contains person agreement features. Furthermore, the finite verb is also accompanied by the subjunctive marker *na*. This shows clearly that the clause in which alleged PRO occurs is a finite one. It follows, therefore, that the EC in such a clause cannot be PRO.[12] Other languages that lack infinitives and hence PRO include KiNande (Authier 1992), Romanian (Kempchinsky 1989), Modern Persian (Hashemipour 1988), and perhaps Salentino (Calabrese 1989).

2.1.3. Control theory

The PRO theorem, it will be recalled from the earlier discussion, is essentially an (incorrect) statement about the distribution of PRO, and has nothing to say about the relation of PRO to its antecedent. Within the principles-and-parameters theory, the module postulated to tackle the problem of assigning an antecedent to PRO is called control theory, to which we now turn.

Definition of control

Control has in general been defined as a relation of referential dependence between an unexpressed subject of a subordinate clause (called a controllee) and an expressed or unexpressed argument of the predicate of the minimal matrix clause (called a controller) (e.g. Bresnan 1982, Mohanan 1983, Andrews 1985, Farkas 1988, but cf. Dziwirek 1998). Defined thus, control appears to have two essential properties, one syntactic and one semantic: the syntactic one being the obligatory omission of the controllee, and the semantic one being the obligatory referential dependence between the controller and the controllee.

But even such a general definition is not without problems. Conceptually, this definition is theory-biased, because the syntactic and semantic status of both the controlled constituent and the controlled element is rather contro-

---

[12] See also Joseph (1992) for a comparison of the control construction in Ancient and Modern Greek, and for an interesting discussion about the control construction in two Albanian dialects, i.e. Arvanítika, the Albanian spoken in Greece, and Shqip, the Tosk dialect of Albanian spoken in Albania. Joseph shows that while the choice of controller in the Shqip gerundic control construction remains intact, that in Arvanítika has narrowed down. This innovative restriction of the semantics of the Arvanítika gerundic control construction, argues Joseph, is the outcome of language contact with Greek through the medium of bilingualism.

versial. As pointed out in Larson et al. (1992) and independently in Huang (1994), four theoretical positions may be isolated. In principles-and-parameters theory, the controlled constituent is assumed to be syntactically clausal and semantically propositional, and the controlled element to be syntactically an EC, i.e. PRO (e.g. Chomsky 1981, 1982, 1986*a*). This can be seen to follow from the fact that the standard Chomskyan theory views control in a narrow, syntactic sense. By contrast, Montague Grammar takes the controlled complement to be neither clausal in its syntax nor propositional in its semantics (e.g. Montague 1974, Dowty 1985). Consequently, there is no reference to an empty syntactic category in this tradition. The third way of looking at the controlled construction is to assume that its syntax is clausal but its semantics is non-propositional, i.e. that of a predicate. This is the position taken by e.g. Williams (1980, 1992) and Chierchia (1989). Finally, in Categorial Grammar (e.g. Bach and Partee 1980), Head-Driven Phrase Structure Grammar (e.g. Sag and Pollard 1991), Lexical-Functional Grammar (e.g. Bresnan 1982), and some semantics-based theories of control (e.g. Culicover and Wilkins 1986), the controlled constituent is viewed syntactically as a VP but semantically as a propositional argument. This position does not posit an empty syntactic category, either.

Next, the definition is also empirically inadequate. On the one hand, crosslinguistically control can take place in a finite clause. Correlating with this is the possibility that the controllee may be lexically expressed. This has been noted for Chamorro (Chung 1989), Chinese (Huang 1989, 1991*b*, 1994), Dogrib (Saxon 1984), Guugu Yimidhirr (Levinson 1987), Japanese (Iida 1996), Korean (Yang 1985, Borer 1989), Modern Greek (Philippaki-Warburton 1987), Modern Hebrew (Borer 1989), Modern Persian (Hashemipour 1988), Serbo-Croatian (Zec 1987), Halkomelem (Sag and Pollard 1991), and several of the Algonquian languages such as Cree and Ojibwa (Joseph 1992).[13]

(2.65) (*a*) (Chinese)
    Xiaoming bi   Xiaohua ziji qu.
    Xiaoming force Xiaohua self go
    'Xiaoming forced Xiaohua to go.'
  (*b*) (Modern Greek, Philippaki-Warburton and Catsimali 1999)
    Anangasan tin Eleni   na   milisi afti i idja.
    They-forced Helen-ACC PRT speaks she herself-NOM
    'They forced Helen herself to speak.'

---

[13] Apart from infinitivals and finite clauses, control can also occur in compound verb-plus-verb units. This is the case of many Algonquian languages (Joseph 1992). Following is an example from Cree. Examples of the same kind can also be drawn from Ojibwa (Rhodes 1985)
(i) (Cree, Ahenakew 1989)
    mitoni kwayask ê-kakwê-pamihât.
    really   properly PV-try-look after-3/3
    'He was really trying to take good care of them.'

(c) (Serbo-Croatian, Zec 1987)
Ana   je   naterala Marija   da (ona) dodje.
Ana-NOM AUX forced   Maria-ACC that (she) come-PRES
'Ana forced Maria to come.'

On the other hand, as we will see shortly, there may be non-strict referential dependence between the controller and controllee.

Types of control

Control can be classified according to whether it is obligatory or optional, whether it is subject or object, and whether it is split or non-split.

Obligatory versus optional control

In obligatory control, the controllee must be controlled and cannot be arbitrary. Furthermore, it must be c-commanded by the controller. These properties seem to point to a parallel between obligatory control and anaphoric binding. By contrast, in optional control, the controllee may be controlled by an argument in the matrix clause, or it may be controlled by an NP which is salient in the discourse, or it may be controlled by an NP which denotes a speech act participant, or it may have an arbitrary interpretation. Furthermore, the controllee need not be c-commanded by the controller. These properties seem to suggest that optional control behaves like pronominal binding. The contrast can be seen by the following.

(2.66) (a) Obligatory control
Chopin tried to take care of himself/*oneself.
(b) Optional control
Chopin finally realized that it was wise to take care of himself/oneself.

Subject versus object control

In subject control, the controller is a subject. Verbs which trigger subject control are called subject control verbs. By contrast, in object control, the controller is an object. Verbs which effect object control are termed object control verbs.

(2.67) (a) Subject control
Pavarotti promised Domingo to sing the part.
(b) Object control
Pavarotti persuaded Domingo to sing the part.

Split versus non-split control

In split control, the controllee has as its controller a non-existent plural NP which is the coordination of two or more NPs occurring separately in the matrix clause. In other words, the controller is split. In non-split control, the controller is not split.

(2.68) Pavarotti told Domingo and Carreras that it would be nice to sing the opera together.

Clearly, in (2.68), the controllee is controlled jointly by both the matrix subject and the conjoined matrix object, as the semantics of the adverb *together* indicates. Note that split control may not be subject to the c-command condition. This leads Williams (1980) to claim that split control is possible only with optional control, but not with obligatory control. However, given examples like (2.69), his generalization is not correct.

(2.69) (*a*) Pavarotti persuaded Domingo to support each other.
    (*b*) (Chinese)
        Zhuren yaoqing keren gong   jin   wucan.
        host   invite   guest together have lunch
        'The host invites the guest to have lunch together.'
    (*c*) (Finnish, Kirsi Hiltunen, personal communication)
        Jussi suostutteli   Tiinan   syömään lounasta yhdessä.
        Jussi persuade-PAST Tiinan-ACC eat-3INF lunch   together
        'Jussi persuaded Tiina to have lunch together.'

Here it may also be mentioned that sometimes control seems to involve referential overlap of some kind.

(2.70) (Chinese)
      Faguo zhongtong shuailing daibiaotuan fangwen Zhongguo.
      French president lead   delegation visit   China
      'The French president leads the delegation to visit China.'

In this example, the matrix subject is most naturally interpreted as included within (rather than strictly coreferential with) the controllee.

Two generalizations

We turn next to a discussion of the two descriptive generalizations, referred to as Bach's Generalization and Visser's Generalization respectively, in the literature. We shall start with Bach's Generalization.

(2.71) Bach's Generalization
      An object controller cannot be omitted.

Now, contrast (2.72) and (2.73).

(2.72) (*a*) Pavarotti promised Domingo to sing the part.
    (*b*) Pavarotti promised to sing the part.
(2.73) (*a*) Pavarotti persuaded Domingo to sing the part.
    (*b*) *Pavarotti persuaded to sing the part.

In (2.72), *promise* is a verb of subject control, and hence the matrix object can be omitted. By contrast, in (2.73), *persuade* is a verb of object control, and hence the matrix object cannot be dropped. In other words, when the object of a control verb is the controller, the verb cannot undergo detransitivization. Bach's Generalization may be seen as a special case of what is occasionally referred to in the literature as Manzini's Generalization — the observation that the controller of a predicate in complement position must be present within the minimal clause containing the complement (Manzini 1983). However, exceptions to Bach's Generalization and hence to Manzini's Generalization are not difficult to find cross-linguistically. Two types can be identified. In the first, the omitted object controller is arbitrary in reference, as in (2.74); in the second, the dropped object controller is definite in reference, as in (2.75).

(2.74) (a) (Italian, Rizzi 1986)
L'ambizione spesso spinge Ø a commettere errori.
the ambition often pushes   make   mistakes.
'Ambition often pushes (one) to make mistakes.'
(b) (French, Authier 1989)
L'ambition amène Ø à commettre des erreurs.
the ambition leads   commit   mistakes
'Ambition leads (one) to make mistakes.'
(c) (Tamil, Authier 1992)
pasí Ø kuTran paNNa vekkardi.
hunger   mistake to do   keep-GER-CAUS
'Hunger forces (one) to make mistakes.'

(2.75) (a) Pavarotti signalled to leave.
(b) (Chinese)
Baba bu rang Ø kan dianshi, mama bu rang Ø ting yinyue.
dad not allow watch TV   mum not allow   listen to music
'Dad did not allow (him) to watch TV and mum did not allow (him) to listen to music.'
(c) (German, Comrie 1984)
Die Mutter bat, das Geschirr abzutragen.
the mother asked the dishes   away to clear
'The mother asked (someone) to clear away the dishes.'
(d) (Guugu Yimidhirr, Levinson 1987: 395)
Muuni nyulu gurray gaari milgamul madhi-nhu.
Muuni he-NOM told NEG ear-PRIV V'IZER-PURP
'Muuni told (them) not to be disobedient.'
(e) (Russian, Comrie 1984)
Predsedatel' poprosil vojti v komnatu.
chairman   asked   enter into room
'The chairman asked (someone) to enter the room.'

We come next to Visser's Generalisation.

(2.76) Visser's Generalisation
Subject control verbs do not passivize.

This descriptive generalization is supported by paradigmatic examples of the following kind.

(2.77) (a) Pavarotti persuaded Domingo to sing the part.
(b) Domingo was persuaded to sing the part (by Pavarotti).

(2.78) (a) Pavarotti promised Domingo to sing the part.
(b) *Domingo was promised to sing the part (by Pavarotti).

(2.77) is an instance of object control and it allows passivization. By contrast, (2.78) is an example of subject control and it prohibits passivization. But as in the case of Bach's Generalization, Visser's Generalization is also faced with counter-examples. One well-known class of counter-example is the so-called double-passive construction, first noted by Hust and Brame (1976), where a switch of control takes place (see also Bresnan 1982).

(2.79) (a) Domingo was promised to be allowed to sing the part.
(b) (Czech, Růžička 1983)
bylo   mu   slíbeno Ø byt zařazen do vybraného mužstva.
(it)was him-DAT promised to be included into the select   team
'He was promised to be included on the select team.'
(c) (German, Růžička 1983)
ihm   war   versprochen worden Ø in   die
him-DAT (it)had been promised   into the
Nationalmannschaft aufgenommen zu werden.
national team   included   to be
'He had been promised to be included on the national team.'
(d) (Russian, Růžička 1983)
emu   bylo   obéščano Ø byt' vključennym v   sbornuju
him-DAT (it)was promised   to be included   into the select
komandu.
team
'He was promised to be included on the select team.'

The assignment of controller

One of the central issues that any adequate theory of control must address concerns the choice of controller. Under the principles-and-parameters approach, the specification of controller has been assumed to be determined essentially in syntactic terms by employing a Rosenbaum-type minimal-distance principle (e.g. Rosenbaum 1967, Chomsky 1981, Larson 1991).

(2.80) The minimal-distance principle
Coindex a controllee with its closest, c-commanding NP.

A well-known problem for this principle is caused by examples like (2.67a) where the subject control verb *promise* is used. In examples of this kind, the matrix subject remains the controller even if the matrix object is a closer, potential controller. In a recent attempt to resurrect the configurational approach to control, Larson (1991) argues that the special behaviour of *promise* can be seen to follow directly from its status as a double-object verb. This verb is structurally subject to the minimal-distance principle, which applies at D-structure. But Larson's analysis, even if it were successful in accounting for examples like (2.67a), would still fail to correctly specify controller choice for a wide range of control cases. These include (i) remote or long-distance control, that is, control from a non-immediate higher clause or from prior discourse, as in (2.81),[14] (ii) exceptions to Bach's Generalization, as in (2.75) above, and (iii) verbs of control that allow either subject or object control or even prefer subject or object control—depending on context and world knowledge, as in (2.82).

(2.81) (a) (Chinese)
Xiaohong de   meimei   shuo mama jueding mingtian
Xiaohong POSS younger sister say   mother decide tomorrow
bu yong qu shang youeryuan.
not need go go to kindergarten
'Xiaohong's$_1$ younger-sister$_2$ says that mum$_3$ has decided that (she$_{1/2/3/4}$ ...) need not go to kindergarten tomorrow.'

(b) (Guugu Yimidhirr, Levinson 1987: 395)
nhangu King Nicholas   gurral-a
he-ACC King Nicholas-ABS tell-IMPV
Ø dhada-nhu dyibarra Laura
  go-PURP south   Laura
nhangu gaari miirriil-a   Ø nhangu nhayun
he-ACC NEG tell-IMPV   he-ACC that-ABS
diiga-nhu   bada.
sent-PURP down
'Tell King Nicholas to go south to Laura. Don't tell him that (they) will take him down south.'

(c) (Modern Greek, Philippaki-Warburton 1987: 292)
sto   telos ton episa   na   fiγune.
at-the end   him persuaded-I SBJV leave-they
'Finally I persuaded him that they should leave.'

(2.82) (a) (Chinese)
Bingren daying   yisheng Ø xiawu   chiyao.
patient promise doctor   afternoon take medicine
'The patient promised the doctor to take medicine in the afternoon.'

(b) Yisheng daying   bingren Ø xiawu   chuyuan.
    doctor promise patient   afternoon leave hospital
'The doctor promised the patient to leave the hospital in the afternoon.'

We can conclude from all this that the structurally oriented minimal-distance principle has to be abandoned, because the selection of controller has to be accomplished on the basis of syntactic, semantic, and pragmatic information (see Martin 1996 and Hornstein 1999 for a minimalist, Section 3.2 for a semantic, and Section 4.2 for a pragmatic approach to control).

---

[14] The existence of examples like (2.81a) would make dubious any attempt to determine control on a purely configurational basis (e.g. Williams 1980, Manzini 1983, Koster 1984a, Larson 1991). The c-command condition, while in general valid for English, has to be weakened for many other languages including those allowing finite control (see also Sag and Pollard 1991).

2.1.4. Revisions and alternatives

In recent years, the standard Chomskyan typology of NPs and subsequently binding and control theories have been subject to a number of attempts at revision. One of the central issues that lies behind these revisions appears to be the discrepancy between the overt and empty categories specified as [+anaphoric, +pronominal] in the standard Chomskyan taxonomy: there is a gap for the overt category with this feature combination in the paradigm. In an effort to tackle this problem, two general lines of approach have presented themselves in the generative literature: (i) to eliminate the hybrid EC PRO, and (ii) to fill the gap by finding some overt category with the features [+anaphoric, +pronominal] or to add new features. Let us call the first the reductionist approach and the second the expansionist approach.

Reductionist

The underlying idea of the reductionist approach is the assumption that no EC should positively be classified as both anaphor and pronominal, and PRO should therefore be reduced to one of the three remaining types of EC (thus mirroring the three types of overt category found in the inventory). This line of revision has been pursued by e.g. Manzini (1983), Bouchard (1984), Koster (1984a), Aoun (1985), Iwakura (1985), Hornstein and Lightfoot (1987), Borer (1989), Chung (1989), C.-T. J. Huang (1989), and Burzio (1991). However, disagreement remains with regard to the crucial issue of which type of EC PRO should be reduced to.

PRO as a pure anaphor and generalized binding

Concentrating on its anaphoric nature, Manzini (1983), for example, suggests that PRO be treated as a pure anaphor, and be subject to a generalized theory of binding (see also Grodzinsky and Reinhart 1993 for a similar view with respect to 'controlled' PRO).

(2.83) Manzini's typology of NPs and generalised binding theory
    (i) Typology of NPs

	Overt	Empty
(a) [+anaphoric, (–pronominal)]	lexical anaphor	NP-trace, PRO
(b) [(–anaphoric), +pronominal]	pronoun	*pro*
(c) [–anaphoric, –pronominal]	r-expression	*wh*-trace

    (ii) Binding conditions A and B
        A. An anaphor is bound in its GC.
        A'. An anaphor without a GC is bound in its domain-GC.[15]
        B. A pronominal is free in its GC.

---

[15] The notion of domain-GC is defined as follows:
    α is a domain-GC for β if and only if (a) α is the minimal category with a subject containing the c-domain of β, and (b) α contains a subject accessible to β.

On this view, PRO is taken to be a pure anaphor that lacks a GC. (The central distributional fact that PRO has to be restricted to ungoverned positions follows independently from Case and θ theories.) As such, it falls under binding condition A'. Clearly, Manzini's approach is a worthwhile attempt to link the control properties and the binding properties of PRO and to unify control and binding theories within the principles-and-parameters framework.

PRO as a pure pronominal and generalized control

In contrast, C.-T. J. Huang (1989), for instance, proposes revising control theory to exploit the pronominal nature of PRO. He suggests that PRO and *pro* be universally collapsed into a single, pronominal EC type, namely *pro*/PRO. The distribution and interpretation of *pro*/PRO is then reduced to a generalized theory of control, determined in terms of a Generalized Control Rule (GCR).

(2.84) C.-T. J. Huang's typology of NPs and generalized control theory
 (i) Typology of NPs

		Overt	Empty
(*a*)	[+anaphoric, −pronominal]	lexical anaphor	NP-trace
(*b*)	[−anaphoric, +pronominal]	pronoun	*pro*/PRO
(*c*)	[−anaphoric, −pronominal]	r-expression	*wh*-trace

 (ii) Generalized Control Rule
 A *pro*/PRO is controlled in its control domain (if it has one).[16]

In this model, then, PRO is considered to be a pure pronominal. Being a pure pronominal, it is naturally linked to *pro* through the proposal that both be subject to the same rule of control.

It should be noted at this point that both approaches share a number of similarities. First, both recognize only three distinct types of EC, namely anaphor, pronominal, and *wh*- trace. Secondly, neither assumes the PRO theorem. Thirdly, Manzini's notion of GC and domain-GC is roughly equivalent to C.-T. J. Huang's notion of control domain. The main conceptual difference, however, is that by reclassifying PRO as a pure anaphor, the Manzini-type analysis attempts to eliminate the need for a separate theory of control by deriving the properties of PRO in terms of a generalized theory of binding, whereas by taking PRO as a pure pronominal, the C.-T. J. Huang-type analysis aims to eliminate the need for a special theory of pro-drop by linking the properties of PRO and those of *pro* via a generalized theory of control (see e.g. C.-T. J. Huang 1989: 205). From a conceptual point of view,

---

[16] The notion of control domain is defined as follows:

α is the control domain for β if and only if it is the minimal category that satisfies both (*a*) and (*b*): (*a*) α is the lowest S or NP that contains (i) β or (ii) the minimal maximal category containing β. (*b*) α contains a SUBJECT accessible to β.

then, other things being equal, the Manzini-type approach is preferred to the C.-T. J. Huang-type approach, for whereas the former needs only a binding theory, the latter still needs both a binding and a control theory (though both still need a pro-drop theory). A second, major difference is that while Manzini bases her theorizing on data drawn mainly from English, C.-T. J. Huang's data come mainly from Chinese. As I have argued in Huang (1994), and as we will see in Chapter 4, while English is a typical 'syntactic' language, Chinese is a typical 'pragmatic' language. As a natural consequence, alleged PRO is expected to behave in a much more syntactic and much less pragmatic way in English than in Chinese. It is therefore not surprising that Manzini and C.-T. J. Huang have come to conclusions that are quite opposite to each other.

Expansionist

In a quite contrary spirit, following work by Saxon (1984) on Dogrib, Enç (1989) on Japanese, Greek, and Turkish, and Wali and Subbarao (1991) on a group of Dravidian languages, Lasnik (1989) argues that 'if a theory with two binary binding features does not provide enough distinctions, the obvious next move is to consider a theory with three features'. More specifically, he suggests that the standard Chomskyan typology of NPs be expanded by incorporating into [±anaphor] and [±pronominal] a third binary binding feature [±referential]. Consequently, there are potentially eight categories in his inventory of NPs.

(2.85) Lasnik's typology of NPs
  (*a*) [+anaphoric, +pronominal, −referential] PRO
  (*b*) [+anaphoric, −pronominal, −referential] anaphor
  (*c*) [−anaphoric, +pronominal, −referential] pronoun
  (*d*) [−anaphoric, −pronominal, +referential] pure r−expression
  (*e*) [−anaphoric, +pronominal, +referential] epithet
  (*f*) [+anaphoric, +pronominal, +referential] ?arbitrary PRO
  (*g*) [+anaphoric, −pronominal, +referential] —
  (*h*) [−anaphoric, −pronominal, −referential] —

What prompts Lasnik's suggestion that we need the binary binding feature [±referential] is the behaviour of a class of NPs that is frequently referred to in the literature as epithets, which was first discussed by Jackendoff (1972: 110). In contrast to names, epithets, argues Lasnik, behave like pure r-expressions on the one hand and pronominals on the other. The argument that epithets have the properties of pronominals can be supported by the following facts: (i) like pronominals but unlike names, epithets can take antecedents from preceding clauses, provided that they are not syntactically bound by them, as in (2.86*a*), (ii) they can participate in left dislocation on a par with pronominals but not with names, as in (2.87*a*), and (iii) while names may bind names, neither epithets nor pronominals can, as in (2.88*a*) (Lasnik 1989).

48   *Syntactic Approaches to Anaphora*

(2.86) (a) John promised to come to Mary's wedding, but he/the idiot missed the train.
   (b) ?John promised to come to Mary's wedding, but John missed the train.
(2.87) (a) John, everyone thinks that he/the idiot should be demoted.
   (b) ?John, everyone thinks that John should be demoted.
(2.88) (Chinese)
   (a) *Ta₁/zhe ge bendan₁ yiwei Xiaoming₁ zui congming.
       3SG/this CL idiot   think Xiaoming most clever
       'He/the idiot thinks that Xiaoming is the cleverest.'
   (b) Xiaoming₁ yiwei Xiaoming₁ zui congming.
       Xiaoming think Xiaoming most clever
       "Xiaoming thinks that Xiaoming is the cleverest.'

In addition, two further pieces of evidence in favour of this analysis are provided by Hornstein and Weinberg (1990): (i) like pronominals, epithets can act as bound variables, as in (2.89), and (ii) like pronominals, epithets license sloppy interpretations under VP-ellipsis, as in (2.90) (cf. Chapter 3).

(2.89) John criticized every mayor in private while praising him/the idiot in public.
(2.90) Every boxer's wife adores him/the idiot, and every wrestler's girlfriend does, too.

Consequently, on the basis of evidence like this, Lasnik argues that two types of r-expressions, namely pure r-expressions like names and pronominal r-expressions like epithets, be distinguished through the introduction of the new binary binding feature [±referential] (but see Dubinsky and Hamilton 1998 for the claim that epithets are antilogophoric pronouns; see also Aoun and Choueiri 1999). Furthermore, the interpretation of pronominal r-expressions is subject to Lasnik's hierarchy of referentiality, repeated here in (2.91).

(2.91) Lasnik's hierarchy of referentiality
   A less referential expression may not bind a more referential one.

Lasnik's typology of NPs is further expanded by Thráinsson (1991). Faced with difficulties posed by the binding behaviour of anaphoric expressions like *ham selv* in Danish, *aapaṇ* in Marathi, and *sig* in Icelandic, Thráinsson claims that NPs should also be distinguished on the basis of whether or not they can be used deictically. If they can, they will be marked by the lexical feature [+deictic] ([+independent reference] in Thráinsson's terminology), otherwise they will be indicated by the lexical feature [−deictic]. Thráinsson's revised classification of NPs looks something like the following.

(2.92) Thráinsson's typology of NPs
   (a) [+deictic, +referential, −anaphoric, +pronominal] epithet
   (b) [+deictic, +referential, −anaphoric, −pronominal] true r-expression
   (c) [+deictic, −referential, −anaphoric, +pronominal] pronoun
   (d) [+deictic, −referential, −anaphoric, −pronominal] possessive pronoun
   (e) [−deictic, −referential, +anaphoric, +pronominal] ?PRO
   (f) [−deictic, −referential, +anaphoric, −pronominal] anaphor

(g) [–deictic, –referential, –anaphoric, +pronominal] ?pronominal long–distance reflexive
(h) [–deictic, –referential, –anaphoric, –pronominal] logophoric long–distance reflexive

Following a proposal by Anderson (1986), Thráinsson suggests the revision of binding theory from the standard Chomskyan one to (2.93), with the compensatory typology of NPs in (2.92) above.

(2.93) Thráinsson's binding theory
   A. A [+anaphoric] NP must be
      (i) bound in its GC, or
      (ii) bound by a superordinate subject in its extended GC.
   B. A [+pronominal] NP must be
      (i) free in its GC, or
      (ii) subject-free (i.e. not bound by a superordinate subject) in its extended GC.
   C. A [+referential] NP must be free.

There are, however, considerable problems with both the reductionist and expansionist approaches. In the case of the reductionist approach, neither the generalized binding, nor the generalized control, model is empirically adequate, for each can at best accommodate half of the central distributional fact attested for PRO. Given the Manzini-type analysis, the pronominal nature of PRO will remain unaccounted for, and equally unfortunately under the C.-T. J. Huang-type account, the anaphoric nature of the EC will be left unexplained. Furthermore, if PRO is taken to pattern with *pro*, as C.-T. J. Huang has argued, then a number of well-known differences between them will need novel explanations. These may include (i) the resumptive pronoun effect, that is, while PRO cannot act as a resumptive pronoun—a pronoun that occupies a position bound by an operator – *pro* can, (ii) the PRO gate effect, that is, while PRO cannot trigger weak crossover effects when paired with *wh*-traces in multiple variable binding contexts, *pro* can, and (iii) the Emex condition effect, that is, while PRO cannot function as an expletive, *pro* can (see Jaeggli and Safir 1989*a*: 15–21 for illustration and further discussion). In addition there is an important problem attendant to C.-T. J. Huang's analysis. As I have argued in detail in Huang (1987, 1989, 1992*a*, 1992*b*, 1994) and as we will see in the next section, the GCR simply does not work.

Turning next to the expansionist enterprise, this line of approach is conceptually undesirable; it runs counter to the metatheoretical desideratum known as 'Occam's razor' ('entities are not to be multiplied beyond necessity'), in particular 'Occam's eraser' (Ziff 1960) or 'modified Occam's razor' (Grice 1978) ('senses or dictionary entries are not to be multiplied beyond necessity'). Conceptually, the proliferation of abstract binding features should a priori be resisted. Next, from an empirical point of view, both

Lasnik's and Thráinsson's analyses are problematic. For example, Lasnik finds it difficult to exemplify the category notated as [+anaphoric, −pronominal, +referential] and the category featured as [−anaphoric, −pronominal, −referential]. A further problem with the expansionist approach bears on the relationship between the expanded typology of NPs and the binding theory. Lasnik does not explicitly draw any connection between them. In Thráinsson's taxonomy, [±deictic], for example, is a lexical rather than a binding feature, and as such it cannot be linked to his binding conditions. Consequently, from a binding perspective, no distinction can be made between pronominals and pronominal long-distance reflexives. Finally, one other, related problem may also be noted. Being [−referential, −anaphoric, −pronominal], both possessive pronouns and logophoric long-distance reflexives are not subject to Thráinsson's binding conditions, either. As a result, new principles would be required to interpret them (see Section 3.2 for semantic, and Section 4.2 for pragmatic, approaches to binding).

2.1.5. Summary

In this section I have examined the classical Chomskyan typology of NPs, binding theory, control theory, and a number of revisions of and alternatives to them. I have demonstrated that these analyses are both conceptually and empirically problematic in accounting for anaphora in a wide range of languages.

2.2. Null subjects and null objects

In the last section, I discussed the classical Chomskyan theory of anaphora. In this section, I shall examine null subjects and null objects.

2.2.1. Null subjects

The phenomenon

Consider the contrast in (2.94) and (2.95).

(2.94) (Italian)
    (*a*) Pavarotti dice che Ø mangia gli spaghetti.
        Pavarotti says that   eat-3SG the spaghetti
        'Pavarotti says that (he) eats spaghetti.'
    (*b*) Ø piove.
        rain-3SG
        '(It) is raining.'

(c) Ø sembra   che Pavarotti mangi   gli spaghetti.
    seem-3SG that Pavarotti eat-SUBJ the spaghetti
    '(It) seems that Pavarotti eats spaghetti
(2.95) (a) *Pavarotti says that Ø eats spaghetti.
    (b) *Ø is raining.
    (c) *Ø seems that Pavarotti eats spaghetti.

As (2.94) indicates, in languages like Italian, the subject of a finite clause can be dropped, whereas as (2.95) shows, in languages like English, the subject of a finite clause cannot be omitted. Within the principles-and-parameters approach, the EC in (2.94) is standardly taken to be a *pro*, the null analogue of an overt pronoun. Languages which allow a subject pronoun in a finite clause to be empty are called null subject or pro-drop languages.[17]

Three types of null subjects

Null subjects can be classified into three types according to a two-way contrast regarding referentiality and argumenthood: (i) referential argumental null subjects, as in (2.94*a*), (ii) non-referential argumental null subjects, as in (2.94*b*), and (iii) non-referential non-argumental null subjects, as in (2.94*c*). Following Chomsky (1982), Rizzi (1986), and Falk (1993), I shall call these three types of null subjects referential, quasi-argumental and expletive null subjects.[18] The notion of argumental (or thematic) null subjects will cover referential and quasi-argumental null subjects, and the notion of non-referential null subjects will subsume quasi-argumental and expletive (i.e.

---

[17] It should be pointed out, however, that a null subject/pro-drop language may allow the occurrence of null subjects only in certain tenses and with certain persons. Modern Hebrew is a well-known example (Borer 1984, 1989), about which more later in this section. Finnish is another (Vainikka and Levy 1999).

[18] Apart from extraposed clauses (2.94*c*), expletive null subjects are commonly found in impersonal passives (i) and existential constructions (ii).

(i) (*a*) (Dutch, Hulk and van Kemenade 1993)
    Op het plein   werdt Ø gedanst.
    in the square was   danced
    'There was dancing in the square.'
   (*b*) (Icelandic, Abraham 1993)
    Var Ø dansað.
    was danced
    'There was dancing.'
(ii) (*a*) (Italian, Platzack 1996)
    Sono cadute alcune pietre.
    fell down some stones
    '(There) fell down some stones.'
   (*b*) (German, Platzack 1996)
    Damals   kamen Ø viele   italienische Immigranten nach USA.
    at-that-time came   many Italian   immigrants   to   USA
    'At that time there came many Italian immigrants to the USA.'

semantically empty, or non-thematic) null subjects. This can be schematically represented in (2.96) (adapted from Saleemi 1992).[19]

(2.96) Three types of null subjects

	R-index	A-position
(a) Referential null subjects	+	+
(b) Quasi-argumental null subjects	−	+
(c) Expletive null subjects	−	−

Generally speaking, the occurrence of referential null subjects entails that of expletive null subjects, that is, if a language allows referential null subjects, it will allow expletive null subjects, but not vice versa. In other words, the properties of expletive null subjects are a subset of the properties of referential null subjects (e.g. Rizzi 1982, 1986, Jaeggli and Safir 1989a, Abraham 1993, Huang 1994: 266, 1995). But there are exceptions. As reported in Platzack (1996), Älvdalsmålet, a Scandinavian language/dialect spoken in a certain region in Dalarna in Sweden, while allowing referential null subjects, does not accept either quasi-argumental or expletive null subjects.

Another point of interest is that whereas the occurrence of referential null subjects is usually optional, the occurrence of non-referential null subjects is frequently obligatory. But there are also null subject and semi-null subject languages (to be elucidated below) which permit overt non-referential subjects. These include Faroese, Modern Hebrew, Irish, Upper Sorbian, Urdu, and Welsh. Some examples follow (see also Saleemi 1992).

---

[19] In addition to the three types of null subject described above, many languages allow non-referential, argumental, arbitrary null subjects (and null objects). Among these languages are Chinese (Huang 1994), Italian (Rizzi 1986), Spanish (Suñer 1983, Jaeggli 1986, Authier 1989), Portuguese, Malayalam, Japanese (Mohanan 1983), Korean (Yang 1985), and Old Icelandic (Sigurðsson 1993).

(i) (a) (Old Icelandic, Sigurðsson 1993)
   Hérna má   Ø dansa.
   here   may   dance
   '(One) can dance here.'
(b) (Korean, Yang 1985)
   iysa-ka   Ø saki-ninkɔs   -in   happi-ta.
   doctor-NOM   deceive-COMP TOP bad-DECL
   'Doctors deceiving (people) are bad.'

This indicates that both the assumption that null subjects and null objects cannot be arbitrary in reference (Chomsky 1982) and the assumption that only third-person plural null subjects can be arbitrary in reference (Jaeggli 1986, Lindseth and Franks 1996) are mistaken.

Notice further that arbitrary *pro*s differ from arbitrary PROs in that unlike the latter, the former do not need to be linked in reference in equative constructions. Following is an example from Spanish (Jaeggli 1986: 59).

(ii) Para que *pro* vengan   a   arreglar la   heladera,
    for that   come-3PL   to   to-fix   the frigerator
    es necesario que *pro* llamen   al   técnico   por
    is necessary that   call-3PL to-the technician by
    lo menos 3 veces.
    the least 3 times
    'In order for (people) to come to fix the refrigerator, it is necessary that (people) call the technician at least three times.'

(2.97) (a) (Faroese, Platzack 1987)
Heani   var (tað) ikke langt til garðarnar.
from-there was there short-way to the farms
'From there it was a short way to the farm sheds.'
(b) (Upper Sorbian, Lindseth and Franks 1996)
(wone) je možno, zo   wón hišce přindźe.
it   is possible that he   still   comes
'It is possible that he still comes.'
(c) (Urdu, Saleemi 1992)
(yi) vaazeh hai ki us   ne jhoot bolaa thaa.
it   obvious is that he-ERG lie spoken   was
'It is obvious that he had lied.'
(d) (Welsh, Awbery 1976)
Mae (hi)'n hwyr.
is   it   late
'It is late.'

A typology of languages with respect to null subjects

Based on a cross-linguistic survey by Gilligan (1987) and following suggestions by Hermon and Yoon (1989), Falk (1993), and Huang (1994: 33–4, 1995), I suggest that languages be grouped into three types with respect to null subjects: (i) full null subject languages, languages which allow all three types of null subjects (e.g. Belorussian, Gothic, and Yukaghir); (ii) non-null subject languages, languages which do not allow any kind of null subjects (e.g. English; but see Börjars and Chapman 1998 on certain dialects of English), French, and Mainland Scandinavian languages, i.e. Danish, Norwegian, and Swedish); (iii) restricted or semi-null subject languages, languages which permit restricted occurrence of null subjects. These languages can further be divided into three subtypes: (i) those which allow only expletive null subjects (e.g. Dutch, German, and perhaps Tagalog), (ii) those which allow both expletive and quasi-argumental null subjects (e.g. Malagasy, Yiddish, and Insular Scandinavian languages, i.e. Icelandic and Faroese), and (iii) those which allow expletive, quasi-argumental, and/or even referential null subjects in certain restricted syntactic environments (e.g. Finnish, Bavarian German, and Ukrainian). As noted by e.g. Rizzi (1994) and Platzack (1996), it is not unreasonable to suggest that the occurrence of null subjects represents the unmarked case, given that (i) most languages in the world seem to allow null subjects of some kind (e.g. Gilligan 1987), and (ii) children acquiring non-null subject languages appear to go through a null subject stage in early syntax (e.g. Hyams 1989, 1992, Radford 1990, Valian 1990, Speas 1994).

The classical version of the null subject/pro-drop parameter

As a step towards providing an account of the cross-linguistic distribution of null subjects/pro-drop, Chomsky (1982) proposes, essentially following Perlmutter (1971), Taraldsen (1978), Jaeggli (1982), Rizzi (1982), among others, setting up what is known as the null subject/pro-drop parameter. The basic idea of this parameter (in its classic version), which has its root in traditional grammar (e.g. Jespersen 1924: 213), is that the distribution of referential null subjects/pro-drop is determined by a process called recoverability (Taraldsen 1978) or identification (Jaeggli 1982); a pronominal may be left out only if its content can be recovered morphosyntactically in one way or another. In particular, the parameter claims that in languages with widespread null subjects (and null objects), there should exist a rich inflectional morphology, especially an elaborated system of verbal agreement. Furthermore, it predicts that only the arguments with which the verb agrees may be encoded in terms of an EC. This position, in its essentials, has recently been reiterated in the minimalist programme (Chomsky 1995). Conceived of in this way, the difference between null subject languages like Italian and Spanish and non-null subject languages like English and French with regard to the possibility of dropping a pronominal subject from a tensed clause boils down to this: the verbal morphology, in particular the nominal features for person, number, and gender, commonly called φ-features, in the former, but not in the latter, is rich enough to determine the content of the missing subject, thus making it redundant and recoverable. Moreover, since no system of verb–object agreement exists either in the Italian-type null subject languages or in the English-type non-null subject languages, no pronominal object may be freely absent from a finite clause in any of these languages (cf. Section 2.2.2 below).

Crucial evidence in support of this agreement-based theory of null subjects/pro-drop can be derived from, apart from the Italian-type languages, languages such as Bani-Hassan Arabic (Kenstowicz 1989), Georgian, Modern Greek (Philippaki-Warburton 1987), Modern Hebrew (Borer 1984, 1989), Irish (McCloskey and Hale 1983), Pashto (C.-T. J. Huang 1984), Slovak, Swahili, and West Flemish (Haegeman 1992). In Georgian, for example, agreement can be marked between the verb and every argument, and consequently every argument can be omitted (C.-T. J. Huang 1984). Irish is a language which contains two parallel types of agreement, one more fully developed than the other. It is also a language that has both expletive and referential null subjects. The interesting point is that Irish has expletive null subjects with its poorer, uninflected, analytic agreement pattern but referential null subjects with its richer, inflected, synthetic anaphoric pattern (McCloskey and Hale 1983). Largely the same can be said of another Celtic language, Breton (Stump 1984, Hendrick 1988: 27–31). Swahili has a mandatory verb–subject, but an optional verb–object, agreement system. Roughly speaking, the verb agrees with the object only when the object is definite or human (e.g. Givón 1976). As correctly predicted by the agreement-based theory, while the subject can be suppressed rather freely, the object can be omitted only if the optional object agreement is present (see also Kim 1993).

(2.98) (Swahili, Kim 1993)
 (a) sisi ha- tu- ki- pendi ki- atu.
  we NEG 1PL (SUBJ AGR)-OBJ AGR-like the shoe
  'We don't like the shoe.'
 (b) Ø ha- tu- ki- pendi Ø.
  NEG 1PL (SUBJ AGR)-OBJ AGR-like
  '(We) don't like (e.g. the shoe).'

Furthermore, one of the most striking pieces of evidence comes from Pashto, a split-ergative language spoken in Afghanistan. Pashto has a rich agreement mechanism, but one that is manifested differently in the present and past tenses. In the present tense configuration, the Agr marks verb–subject agreement in both transitives and intransitives. In the past tense configuration, however, the Pashto agreement system is ergative: the Agr is verb–subject agreement with intransitives, but verb–object agreement with transitives. Now, what is of particular interest is that in Pashto both subjects and objects can be dropped, but only if they agree with the verb. This can be seen by contrasting the (a) and (b) sentences in (2.99) and (2.100), which are cited from C.-T. J. Huang (1984).

(2.99) (a) Ø mana xwr-əm.
  apple eat-1MSG
  '(I) eat the apple.'
 (b) *zə Ø xwr-əm.
  I eat-1MSG
  'I eat (e.g. the apple).'
(2.100) (a) ma Ø wə-xwar-a
  I PRF-eat-3FSG
  'I ate (e.g. the apple).'
 (b) *Ø mana wə-xwar-a.
  apple PRF-eat-3FSG
  '(I) ate the apple.'

In the present tense construction (2.99), the verb agrees with the subject but not the object, hence the subject but not the object can be omitted. By contrast, in the past tense, transitive, construction (2.100), the verb agrees with the object but not the subject, hence the object but not the subject can be lexically null. Swahili and Pashto thus present some compelling evidence for an agreement-based theory of null subjects/pro-drop (see also Bergsland 1997 for the description of Aleut object *pro*s and Baker 1988 for the analysis of Chichewa object *pro*s).

Finally, another source of support for such a theory can be given by some generative work on language acquisition; there is evidence that children seem to set the null subject/pro-drop parameter roughly at the same time as they acquire inflection (e.g. Hilles 1991, Déprez and Pierce 1993 but see Lakshmanan 1991, 1994 for different views).

Two other 'distinctive' properties of null subject languages

Null subjects are further claimed to co-occur with two other distinctive properties: (i) the possibility of having free subject inversion, and (ii) the possibility of extracting a subject long-distance over a lexically filled complementizer. The latter has sometimes been referred to as Perlmutter's Generalization in the literature. In other words, a null subject language exhibits a cluster of three distinctive properties: (i) null subjects, (ii) free subject inversion, and (iii) complement subject extraction. These properties are said to correlate as a function of the positive value of the null subject parameter (e.g. Rizzi 1982). All the languages in (2.101)–(2.106) below are classic null subject languages and all allow both free subject inversion and complement subject extraction as well as null subject, as is expected (see also Bresnan and Mchombo 1987 for an analysis of Chichewa).[20]

(2.101) (Italian, Riemsdijk and Williams 1986)
    (*a*) hanno telefonato le brigate rosse.
        have called the brigades red
        'The red brigades have called.'
    (*b*) Chi credi che Ø verrà?
        who you-believe that will come
        'Who do you believe will come?'

(2.102) (Spanish, Jaeggli 1982)
    (*a*) Vino Juan.
        came Juan
        'Juan came.'
    (*b*) Quién dijiste que Ø llegó ayer?
        Who (you) said that arrived yesterday
        'Who do you say arrived yesterday?'

(2.103) (Modern Greek, Horrocks 1987)
    (*a*) kseçílise to bányo tu arçimídhi.
        overflowed-3SG the bath the-GEN Archimedes-GEN
        'Archimedes' bath overflowed.'
    (*b*) pyos pistévis pos éγrapse aftí tin gritikí?
        who-NOM believe-2SG that wrote-3SG this-ACC the-ACC review-ACC
        'Who do you believe wrote the review?'

---

[20] On the basis of analysis of Modern Greek, Catalan, and Bulgarian, Iatridou and Embick (1997) show that *pro* in an Italian-type, but not in a Chinese-type, pro-drop language cannot take a CP/IP clause as a linguistic antecedent, as can be seen in the Bulgarian example below.
(i) *Ako pristignem kâsno, *pro* šte nakara Ivan da si
    if arrive late FUT make Ivan to REFL
    promeni planovete.
    change plans
    'If we arrive late it will make Ivan change his plans.'

This restriction on the referential property of *pro*, according to Iatridou and Embick, is the outcome of the mismatch in φ-features between *pro* and CP/IP: while *pro* has φ-features, CP/IP is φ-featureless.

(2.104) (Modern Hebrew, Borer 1984)
  (a) kafcu   min   ha-matos Ran ve-Dan.
       jumped from the-plane Ran and-Dan
       'Ran and Dan jumped from the plane.'
  (b) Mi   xasavta   se   Ø 'exer   la-mesiba?
       Who (you) thought that   late-was to-the-party
       'Who do you think was late to the party?'
(2.105) (Bani-Hassan Arabic, Kenstowicz 1989)
  (a) Fariid gaal innu ištarat   al-binit al-libaas.
       Fariid said that bought the girl the dress
       'Fariid said that the girl bought the dress.'
  (b) wayy binit Fariid gaal innu ištarat   Ø al-libaas?
       which girl Fariid said that bought   the dress
       'Which girl did Fariid say bought the dress?'
(2.106) (Slovak, Gabi Bolton, personal communication)
  (a) Prisla   jar.
       arrive-3SG-F-PAST spring-SG-F-NOM
       'Spring arrived.'
  (b) kto myslis   ze   volal?
       who think-2SG-PRES that call-3SG-M-PAST
       'Who do you think has telephoned?'

Problems with the classical version of the null subject parameter

Given the classical version of the null subject/pro-drop parameter, whether null subjects can occur in a language is determined by morphosyntactic recoverability or identification, in particular, by the existence of a rich agreement system in that language. Furthermore, the possibility of having null subjects in a language clusters together with the possibility of having free subject inversion and the possibility of having complement subject extraction in that language.

As I pointed out in Huang (1987, 1989, 1992a, 1992b, 1994, 1995), among others (see e.g. Jaeggli and Safir 1989a), there are, however, considerable difficulties with an agreement-based theory of null subjects/pro-drop like this. First, its prediction, that rich agreement systems constitute both a necessary and a sufficient condition for the licensing of referential null subjects, is empirically falsified in both directions. On the one hand, there are languages such as German, which encodes a slightly greater range of person and number agreement specifications in the verb than Portuguese, yet German does not sanction referential null subjects while Portuguese does. Another case in point involves Icelandic and Älvdalsmålet. Although Icelandic has a richer verbal inflection than Älvdalsmålet, yet Älvdalsmålet but not Icelandic allows referential null subjects (Sigurðsson 1993, see also Platzack 1996, and for a different view concerning referential null subjects in Icelandic, see Rögnvaldsson 1990). Thirdly, a language like Surselvan would also pose problems for such an agreement-based account. Surselvan has a very rich verbal paradigm which distinguishes six persons and the infinitive. However, the occurrence of null subjects in this Swiss dialect of Rhaeto-Romance is restricted to certain persons of the verb and certain syntactic environments (Sprouse and Vance 1999). Still further evidence against the agreement-based theory can be adduced from language change. For example, as reported in Sigurðsson (1993), Old Icelandic is a full null subject (and null object) language, but it lost referential pro-drop of both subjects and objects in the eighteenth and nineteenth centuries, hence Modern Icelandic becomes a semi-null subject language. However, the disappearance of referential pro-drop in the course of development from Old Icelandic to Modern Icelandic is without previous or concomitant weakening of verbal agreement inflection; Icelandic verbal inflection has been retained largely intact from old to modern times. All this seems to be a clear indication that the existence of rich agreement paradigms in a language is not sufficient for that language to permit null subjects.

On the other hand, assuming that the null subject/pro-drop parameter is the relevant one, it fails to account for null subject/object languages such as Chinese, Japanese Korean, Jiwarli, Malayalam, Palauan, and perhaps Tuvaluan either. Since Chinese, for example, has no Agr in I (assuming that the presence or absence of Agr reflects the presence or absence of verb–subject/object agreement system) (e.g. C.-T. J. Huang 1984, Yang 1985, O'Grady 1987), let alone Agr or agreement system that is rich enough to recover the content of a missing argument, an agreement-based theory of pro-drop would incorrectly predict that neither subjects nor objects can be dropped in the language. Another piece of evidence against the agreement-based theory is provided by the Kuki-Chin-Lushai languages–Tibeto-Burman languages spoken in the border areas between Burma and India. As pointed out to me by Chit Hlaing (personal communication), the Kuki-Chin-Lushai languages have both verb–subject and verb–indirect object agreement systems but do not have verb–direct object agreement system. However, contrary to what is predicted by the agreement-based theory of pro-drop, direct objects in these languages can also be dropped.[21] Secondly,

---

[21] A related question arises as to what is the crucial element in the inflectional system of a language that is responsible for pronouns being dropped. It has widely been accepted in the generative literature that the person feature plays the most important role in this respect. This can partially be supported by the fact that languages seem to form a scalar scale here, namely: person/number/gender/case > person/number/gender/ø (as in Tarifit) > person/number/ø (as in Italian) > person/ø/ø (as in Bengali) > ø/ø/ø (as in Maori); see also Cole (1997). Another piece of evidence in support of this assumption comes from the inflectional system of Slavonic languages. Verbs in Slavonic languages potentially manifest both person-number and gender-number agreement markings. However, while person-number inflection is constantly marked in South and West Slavonic languages, it is absent in certain forms in East Slavonic languages. This may explain why subjects are more freely dropped in South and West than in East Slavonic languages (see e.g. Lindseth and Franks 1996 for further discussion about this correlation).

contrary to the standard conception of the null subject/pro-drop parameter, that no referential object pro-drop can be allowed in languages which do not contain object–verb/preposition agreement, non-agreeing or unidentified object pro-drop does exist in a wide range of languages including Chinese, Japanese, Korean, Burmese, Chamorro, Finnish, Thai, Imbabura Quechua, Hungarian, Jiwarli, Palauan, Somali, Malayalam, European Portuguese, and Old Icelandic (to which we shall return in Section 2.2.2). This shows that rich agreement is not necessary for a language to permit pro-drop, either. Thirdly, it is not clear how such an account can automatically carry over to expletive null subjects. There is some evidence that the possibility of dropping expletive subjects is linked to agreement. For example, Icelandic and Faroese have rich verbal agreement and allow expletive null subjects whereas Danish, Norwegian, and Swedish lack rich verbal agreement and disallow expletive null subjects. This difference between Insular and Mainland Scandinavians has been argued to follow from an Agr parameter (e.g. Platzack 1987, Holmberg and Platzack 1995). But such an account cannot be maintained cross-linguistically; Chinese and Korean, for example, have no Agr but nevertheless allow expletive null subjects (see also Abraham 1993 for arguments against both the agreement morphology account and the case morphology account with respect to the development of expletives in the history of German). In fact, according to Gilligan (1987), most languages allow non-referential null subjects whether or not they have verbal agreement systems. This shows that expletive null subjects, like referential null subjects, can be sanctioned irrespective of a rich verbal morphology.

Furthermore, the same can also be said of the cluster of properties which is alleged to be typical of a null subject language. To start with, this diagnostic cannot be applied to agreementless languages such as Chinese, Japanese, and Korean. Next, for those languages to which it is applicable, its predictions are also falsified in both directions. On the one hand, as Safir (1985) notes, languages such as Trentino and Modenese allow free subject inversion and complement subject extraction, yet they do not allow null subjects (but see Brandi and Cordin 1989 for a different view about Trentino and Fiorentino). On the other hand, there are languages such as European Portuguese which exhibit neither free subject inversion nor complement subject extraction, yet they are null subject languages. Other languages that raise serious difficulties for the cluster of properties include Denya, Irish, and many Germanic languages as documented in Law (1993), e.g. Älvdalsmålet, Dutch, German, Icelandic, and West Flemish (see also Gilligan 1987). There is thus clear evidence that such a clustering of properties is neither necessary nor sufficient for a language to be a null subject one. These properties are simply conceptually and empirically independent of each other. All this points to the conclusion that there does not seem to be a universal, direct correlation between the richness of inflection and the occurrence of null subjects on the one hand, and between free subject inversion, complement subject extraction, and null subjects on the other.

Some revisions and alternatives

Licensing versus identification

One of the most significant developments in the generative analyses of null subjects is the separation of the licensing factors from the identification factors. Licensing is a purely formal requirement. It refers to the question of how null subjects are formally sanctioned in a language. Licensing involves verbal features. By contrast, identification is a more substantive or contentful criterion. It is concerned with the question of how the referential content (or at least the φ-features) of null subjects are formally recovered in a language. Identification involves nominal features. While licensing applies to all types of null subjects, identification is a requirement imposed on referential null subjects only.[22] Both licensing and identification are said to be subject to parametric variation.

Rizzi's *pro* module

The analysis

Rizzi's (1986) '*pro* module' consists of two principles: a licensing schema and a recovery convention.

(2.107) Rizzi's '*pro* module'
    (*a*) Licensing schema
        Pro is governed (i.e. Case-marked) by X^o_y.
    (*b*) Recovery convention
        Let X be the licensing head of an occurrence of *pro*: then *pro* has the grammatical specification of the features on X coindexed with it.

Given (2.107*a*), *pro* is now formally licensed under government by a specially designated Case-assigning licensing head X of the type y, where y may range over one or more members of the licensing set. In other words, *pro* can only occur in the structural configuration of its licensing head. Clearly, (2.107*a*) is essentially a syntactic condition on the licensing of the structural domain of *pro*. On the other hand, given (2.107*b*), the content of *pro* is formally recovered via non-standard binding, called head binding, by the φ-features on the licensing head including rich Agr. Put slightly differently, *pro* must have the grammatical features of its licensing head. Evidently, (2.107*b*)

---

[22] This bifurcation seems to be similar to the 'division of labour' between head and antecedent government for traces.

is essentially a morphosyntactic condition on the recoverability of the content of *pro*. Note that in this model, (i) the formal licenser and the content licenser are the same head, and (ii) there seems to be an implicational universal here, namely if a language has the mechanism to identify the content of *pro*, it will have the device to license *pro*, but not vice versa (Hulk and van Kemenade 1993).

To account for the cross-linguistic variation of *pro*, Rizzi suggests that both (2.107*a*) and (2.107*b*) be parameterized. The parameterization of (2.107*a*) has the effect of allowing languages to arbitrarily vary from having an empty set of licensers (namely, no head X is of the type y, that is, no head is a possible licenser) to having a full set of licensers (namely, every head X is of the type y, that is, every head is a possible licenser). Thus, English, French, and Mainland Scandinavian languages do not instantiate the option for a licensing head, while Italian, Spanish, and Portuguese do. Furthermore, the set of licensers can also vary from one pro-drop language to another pro-drop language. In Italian, for example, I functions as the licensing head for null subjects, whereas V and P act as the licensing head for null objects. Old French and Modern Insular Scandinavian languages use C as the licensing head. Modern German differs from Old High German in that in the former C is the choice for licensing head but in the latter I is the choice for licensing head.

Next, how about identification? Recall that identification is a requirement imposed on referential null subjects only. Evidently, one of the main purposes of an identification mechanism is to determine the different ranges of occurrence of null subjects in different languages. Such a mechanism, as Falk (1993) argues, should contain two components. The first is a condition that specifies which φ-features are needed for different types of null subjects. It is commonly assumed that referential null subjects must be identified by features of person and number, that quasi-argumental null subjects must be identified in the form of number marking, and that expletive null subjects need not be identified. This is captured by (2.108).

(2.108) Null subjects and φ-features
    (*a*) Referential null subjects   [+person, +number]
    (*b*) Quasi-argumental null subjects   [Ø, +number]
    (*c*) Expletive null subjects   [Ø, Ø]

The second component is a condition that specifies how the relevant φ-features reach null subjects. This is captured by (2.107*b*) above. Rizzi further stipulates that (2.107*b*) is at work only in languages containing Agr, especially using φ-features. Thus, (2.107*b*) is also subject to parametric variation, allowing some languages to adopt the option fully (e.g. Italian and Spanish), others optionally (e.g. Icelandic and Yiddish), and still others not at all (e.g. English and French). In recent years, Rizzi's work on pro-drop has prompted extensive discussion about null subjects in V2 languages, to which we now turn.

V2, C- versus I-orientation, and null subjects

Verb second, or V2, languages are languages in which a finite verb or Aux is fronted to a second place in a root clause. These languages include German, Dutch, Mainland Scandinavians, Icelandic, Yiddish, Old and Early Middle English, and Old French. V2 languages can further be divided into two types: what Hulk and van Kemenade (1993) call CV2 languages such as German and Swedish, and IV2 languages such as Icelandic (Rögnvaldsson and Thráinsson 1990, but see Sigurðsson 1990*b* for a different view) and Yiddish (Santorini 1989, Diesing 1990). The crucial difference is that in a CV2 language there is a root versus non-root asymmetry with respect to V2, while in an IV2 language there is no such asymmetry, that is, V2 operates in embedded as well as matrix clauses. That is why CV2 languages sometimes are also called asymmetric V2 languages whereas IV2 languages are called symmetric V2 languages.[23]

The above distinction between V2 and non-V2 languages on the one hand, and CV2 and IV2 languages on the other, can be incorporated into a more general typological distinction between CP- or C- versus IP- or I-oriented languages. C-oriented languages are languages in which C is the dominant functional head; I-oriented languages are languages in which I is the dominant functional head. In this typology, then, CV2 languages are C-oriented languages, IV2 and non-V2 languages are I-oriented languages (Hulk and van Kemenade 1993).

Coming back to null subjects, recollect that all types of null subjects must be formally licensed. Now, given Hulk and van Kemenade's C- versus I-language typology, it is suggested that in a C-language, the dominant functional head C can act as a designated Case-assigning licensing head (DCH) which formally sanctions null subjects. It is further argued that in a C-language, a DCH C licenses null subjects in Spec-of-IP. By contrast, in an I-language, the dominant functional head I can function as a DCH, and in such a language a DCH I licenses null subjects in Spec-of-VP. As for the identification of the content of null subjects, which is characteristic of referential null subjects only, Hulk and van Kemenade suggest that it is always

---

[23] More accurately, Icelandic seems to be a mixed V2 language: it is an IV2 language as a whole, but a CV2 language in, say, *wh*-contexts. Note also that Modern English and Modern French are non-V2 languages. But there are syntactic environments in both languages where one can detect typical CV2 properties. These include interrogative and fronted negative constructions in Modern English and subject–clitic and complex inversion constructions in Modern French. In the terminology of Rizzi (1990*b*), they are called 'residual', as opposed to 'full', V2 languages. In other words, Modern English and Modern French are mixed in that they are non-V2 languages as a whole, but CV2 languages under restricted circumstances. See Hulk and van Kemenade (1993) for further discussion.

achieved under I by the mediation of some kind of morphosyntactic agreement system.[24] Thus, the following typological variation of null subjects is predicted.

(2.109) Hulk and van Kemenade's C- versus I-language typology and null subjects

	C	I	
Dutch	DCH	— –phi	expletive null subjects
Mainland Scandinavians	—	— –phi	no null subjects
Italian	—	DCH +phi;	full null subjects
English	—	— –phi	no null subjects
Icelandic	—	DCH –phi	expletive null subjects
Old French	DCH	— +phi	full null subjects in I to C contexts

This typological relation between V2 and null subjects is further strengthened in recent work by Rivero (1993), who argues that V2 and null subjects are also related to the presence or absence of Long Head Movement (LHM) in a language. Following a suggestion by Vanelli, Renzi, and Benincà (1985), Rivero notes that major Old Romance languages can be divided into two distinct typological groups with respect to V2, null subjects, and head movement. The first group include Old Catalan, Old Italian, Old Portuguese, Old Provençal, and Old Spanish, and the second is represented by Old French.[25] They can be contrasted as follows:

(2.110) Rivero's typology of Old Romance
   (*a*) Group 1: Old Catalan, Old Italian, etc.
      (*a*) They have unrestricted null subjects,
      (*b*) They are not V2 languages in the Germanic sense,
      (*c*) They have LHM constructions.
   (*b*) Group 2: Old French
      (*a*) It has restricted null subjects,
      (*b*) It is a V2 language in the prototypical Germanic sense,
      (*c*) It lacks LHM constructions.

Rivero claims that these typological differences are not accidental, but

---

[24] According to Hulk and van Kemenade (1993), the functional features of I also need to be formally licensed by having the properties of being a DCH. Consequently, there are three types of I: (i) I is a DCH, (ii) I is not a DCH but can be related to a DCH C, and (iii) I is not a DCH. Interacting with the option for I to have morphologically overt φ-features, the above typology of I results in a taxonomy of four types of subject–verb agreement relationship: (i) syntactic, as shown in C-oriented languages like Dutch, German, and Mainland Scandinavian languages and I-oriented languages like English and French, (ii) agreement-chain, as shown in Italian, IV2 languages like Icelandic and Yiddish, and C-oriented languages like Dutch and German, (iii) morphological, as shown in Italian and Old French, and (iv) default, as shown in impersonal constructions in Dutch, Old English, Old French, and Icelandic.

[25] Nigel Vincent has pointed out to me that a better term may be 'the earlier stages of the Romance language'. The reason is that there is no historical construct that can be called 'Old Romance', largely because no unified Romance language existed in the period under consideration.

principled. In particular, she argues that LHM and V2 are incompatible with each other as the result of two clashes: (i) non-finite V-raising to C in LHM is in conflict with finite constraints on a root C as licensing head in V2, and (ii) the requirement that Spec-of-CP must be empty in full LHM is in conflict with the usual condition that such a position must be phonologically filled in V2.[26] The requirement of having a phonologically null Spec-of-CP in full LHM, argues Rivero, can be attributed to Chomsky's (1995, 1998) principle of economy of derivation, namely, empty Spec-of-CP functions as a last resort rule to avoid having what is known as the Wackernagel, Tobler, and Mussafia effects in Romance linguistics and philology.

Problems and revisions
Rizzi's analysis, however, is faced with a number of problems, both conceptual and empirical. First of all, to allow languages to vary arbitrarily in terms of a set of licensers fails to explain the crucial question as to why some languages permit null subjects but others do not. Secondly, as noted in Speas (1994), it is not clear conceptually why the phonologically status of *pro* singles it out as requiring a special licensing mechanism. Thirdly, the question arises why quasi-argumental null subjects need to be identified by the φ-feature of number. Such a requirement has also presented technical difficulties for the analysis of V2 languages like Icelandic. In order to maintain Rizzi's position that number must be transmitted to a quasi-argumental null subject from its Case-assigning licensing head (as in Icelandic but not in German), one has to assume that in a V2 language like Icelandic, C always contains number. This has the unwelcome consequence of forcing one to argue that number is invisible in syntactic environments (such as embedded clauses) where C carries no visible number. A rather radical solution to this problem is advocated by Falk (1993), who argues that all types of null subjects must also be identified as a nominal category by the feature of case. Furthermore, she suggests that given their dual status as being both non-referential and argumental, quasi-argumental null subjects can be reduced to either referential or expletive null subjects, depending on which of the two properties is taken to be basic in a particular language. For example, Icelandic takes the non-referential property of quasi-argumental null subjects as basic, therefore quasi-argumental null subjects in the language can be interpreted as basically expletive. Given that Icelandic allows expletive null subjects, quasi-argumental null subjects in the sense of Rizzi are permitted in the language. By contrast, in German, the argumental property is taken as the basic prop-

---

[26] Following Rizzi's (1990*b*) classification of V2 languages, Rivero (1993) claims that LHM languages can be divided into two types: (i) full LHM languages such as certain Old Romance languages (e.g. Old Catalan, Old Italian, and Old Provençal) and Modern Slavonic languages (e.g. Bulgarian, Czech, Serbo-Croatian, Slovak, Slovene), in which LHM operates in all types of root sentence, and (ii) residual LHM languages like Romanian and perhaps Albanian, in which LHM operates only in certain types of root sentence such as interrogatives and exclamatives.

erty. Consequently, German quasi-argumental null subjects can be interpreted as an instance of referential null subjects. Given that German does not allow referential null subjects, quasi-argumental null subjects in the sense of Rizzi are barred in the language. With this bipartite division of null subjects, Falk proposes (2.111) as the identification condition on null subjects.

(2.111) Falk's identification condition on null subjects
    (a) Referential null subjects: [+case, +number, +person]
    (b) Expletive null subjects: [+case, Ø, Ø]

Fourthly, recall that in Rizzi's analysis, the formal licenser and the content licenser must be the same head. But some recent work on null subjects in Old French shows rather convincingly that the formal licenser and the content licenser can be different heads, that is, whereas the formal licensing head is C, the content licensing head can be I, at least in some marked constructions such as *et* V(S) constructions (e.g. Dupuis 1989, Roberts 1993, and Vance 1993). Finally, Chinese-type languages pose a serious challenge to Rizzi's theory. On Rizzi's account, *pro* is locally identified by recovery of φ-features through head binding—the result of the interaction of (2.107b) and (2.108). Since these principles do not apply to Chinese, the question of how *pro* is locally identified in Chinese remains a problem. In fact, Rizzi himself is aware that his '*pro* module' does not apply to Chinese. He points out that if (2.107b) and (2.108) were extended to Chinese, then *pro* would wrongly be restricted to non-argumental use in the language. He also points out that his '*pro* module' does not cover what C.-T. J. Huang (1984, 1989) takes to be *pro* in the embedded subject position of a finite clause in Chinese. This leads C.-T. J. Huang (1984, 1989) to develop an alternative, generalized control analysis of *pro*.

C.-T. J. Huang's generalized control rule

In an attempt to defend the null subject parameter, C.-T. J. Huang (1984, 1989) claims that *pro* can occur in Chinese-type languages despite the absence of Agr in these languages. Specifically C.-T. J. Huang posits a unified analysis of the distribution of *pro* and PRO in terms of a generalized control rule (GCR) (cf. Section 2.1).

(2.112) C.-T. J. Huang's GCR
    A *pro*/PRO is controlled in its control domain (if it has one).

As already mentioned, the notion of control domain is based on the concept of accessible SUBJECT. Thus, in languages with rich Agr (such as Italian), Agr identifies (i.e. controls) *pro* in its control domain. In languages such as English, Agr is too meagre to identify *pro*. Finally, in languages like Chinese, the absence of Agr forces *pro* to be identified by a nominal element from a higher domain. This is an interesting analysis, but it fails to account for the occurrence of null subjects in a wide range of languages.

Chinese

As I have discussed in detail in Huang (1987, 1989, 1992*a*, 1992*b*, 1994), the GCR simply does not work for Chinese. To see the point, consider (2.113), which constitutes a paradigmatic case of null subjects in Chinese.

(2.113) Xiaohong de   meimei   shuo Ø xihuan tan gangpin.
        Xiaohong GEN younger sister say   like   play piano
        'Xiaohong's$_1$ younger sister$_2$ says that (I/you/he/she$_{1/2/3}$/we/you/they ...) love(s) to play the piano.'

Given C.-T. J. Huang's definition of control domain, the matrix sentence is the control domain for the EC, since it is the minimal syntactic domain which contains an accessible SUBJECT. It follows, therefore, that the null subject must be controlled in its control domain. But this is contrary to fact: as the indexes show, the null subject need not be controlled in it (see also (2.145) below and Huang 1992*a*, 1992*b*, 1994: 33–4, 58–69 for detailed arguments).

Modern Hebrew

Modern Hebrew is a full null subject language, but its patterns of dropping subjects are rather complicated. First, there is no restriction on the occurrence of non-referential null subjects. Expletive null subjects, for example, can occur freely in the past, present, and future tenses. Secondly, a third person referential null subject of an embedded clause can occur in the past or the future tense, but not in the present tense. Thirdly, a referential null subject in the matrix sentence is possible only in the first and second persons (Borer 1989, Vainikka and Levy 1999). Now, consider how a third-person referential null subject is identified in terms of C.-T. J. Huang's GCR.

(2.114) (*a*) Talila$_2$ ʔamra le-Itamar$_1$ she Ø$_1$ hicliax.
             Talila said   to-Itamar that   succeeded-M-SG
             'Talia told Itamar that he succeeded.'
        (*b*) Talila$_2$ ʔamra le-Itamar$_1$ she Ø$_2$ hiclixa.
             Talila said   to-Itamar that   succeeded-F-SG
             'Talia told Itamar that she succeeded.'

Given that Modern Hebrew has Agr and Agr qualifies as the identifier or controller, by the GCR the null subject is predicted to be coindexed with Agr, and hence may not be co-indexed with any of the matrix nominal element. But this prediction is not borne out, as can be seen by the fact that the null subject must be coreferential with a c-commanding NP in the matrix clause. Borer's own analysis is that third person Agr in Modern Hebrew is anaphoric, and as such it must be bound by an NP in the matrix clause in order to obtain the φ-features from it. Whether or not Borer's analysis is correct is a different matter; what is relevant here is that the GCR cannot be maintained given the arrays of data from Modern Hebrew. More or less the same can be said of null subjects in controlled complements in Romanian (e.g. Farkas

1985) and in embedded nominalized clauses in Imbabura Quechua (Hermon and Yoon 1989).

(2.115) (a) (Romanian)
Maria₁ l-a   convins   pe Ion₂Ø₂ să   plece.
Maria CLI-has convinced P Ion   SUBJ leave-3SG
'Maria₁ has convinced Ion₂ Ø₂ to leave.'
(b) (Imbabura Quechua)
Juan-ga   Ø llugshi-na-ta   ni-rka.
Juan-TOP   leave-NOM-ACC say-3SG-PAST
'Juan₁ said that (he₁/₂) will leave.'

Old Icelandic
Old Icelandic is a language with widespread argument-drop, a language which is considered to be 'close to freezing point' (Sigurðsson 1993) on C.-T. J. Huang's (1984) 'hot–cool' language temperature scale. First, Old Icelandic has what Sigurðsson calls topic-drop. Second, it has both referential and non-referential pro-drop. Third, it has pro-drop of non-agreeing objects of both verbs and prepositions. Old Icelandic is also very interesting in that it has rich Agr but this rich Agr is incapable of identifying *pro*.

Based on some earlier work, Sigurðsson reports that referential null subjects in Old Icelandic are found mainly in three constructions: (i) root clauses with a lexicalized CP specifier, (ii) subordinate clauses, especially adverbial clauses, and (iii) complement clauses. An example of (i) is given below (Sigurðsson 1993).

(2.116) er   hann kom þar,   er   mest var brunnit þvertréit,
when he   came there where most was burned the beam
þa   brast   Ø niðr   undir honum.
then broke   down   under him
'When he came where the beam was most burned, then (it) broke under him.'

Clearly, this example indicates that (i) the c-command condition is immaterial for a null subject (see also (2.113) from Chinese above), and (ii) a null subject can be coindexed with an NP in the preceding discourse, contrary to C.-T. J. Huang's GCR. Borrowing a discarded idea from Rizzi (1982), Sigurðsson suggests that Agr in Old Icelandic is non-pronominal, that is, it does not have φ-features of its own, and hence it cannot identify *pro*. Instead *pro* in Old Icelandic is identified under free coindexing with an NP in the preceding discourse. But this amounts to saying that the identification of *pro* in Old Icelandic is essentially a pragmatic/discourse strategy.

All this shows clearly that the GCR is a failure as an identification condition for referential null subjects. It will also fail as an licensing condition, because it cannot extend to non-referential null subjects.

Jaeggli and Safir's morphological uniformity hypothesis

On Jaeggli and Safir's (1989a) view, the crucial property in a language to allow null subjects is morphological uniformity. This idea is stated in terms of a morphological uniformity hypothesis.

(2.117) Jaeggli and Safir's morphological uniformity hypothesis
Null subjects are permitted in all and only languages with morphologically uniform inflectional paradigms.

The notion of morphological uniformity is defined as follows:

(2.118) Morphological uniformity
An inflectional paradigm P in a language L is morphologically uniform if and only if P has either only underived inflectional forms or only derived inflectional forms.

Defined thus, morphological uniformity seems to be a paradigmatic notion. But as Hermon and Yoon (1989) have noted, in the licensing of null subjects, it is morphological uniformity of a language as a whole rather than morphological uniformity of a paradigm that counts. If this is correct, then for a language to license null subjects, all paradigms in that language have to be morphologically uniform.

At first sight, this hypothesis seems to make correct predictions for both Italian- and Chinese-type null subject, and English-type non-null subject, languages. Italian is morphologically uniform in that it has derived forms throughout the paradigm; Japanese is morphologically uniform since all forms are inflected for tense/aspect/mood and negation; and Chinese is morphologically uniform in that it has no derived form at all. On the other hand, English is not morphologically uniform, because it has mixed derived and underived forms in the paradigm (see (2.119)). It is thus correctly predicted that while Italian and Chinese are null subject languages, English is not. Other languages that seem to provide supporting evidence for the morphological uniformity hypothesis include Farsi, Russian (e.g. Lindseth and Franks 1996), and Tuki, a Bantu language spoken in Cameroon (Biloa 1991a).[27]

(2.119) (a) (Italian)
　　　　　cammin-o　'walk-1SG'
　　　　　cammin-i　'walk-2SG'
　　　　　cammin-a　'walk-3SG'

---

[27] In a similar vein, C.-T. J. Huang (1984) claims that pro-drop can occur only in languages with rich Agr or no Agr at all. But this generalization is empirically wrong; it fails to cover (i) languages like German and Insular Scandinavian languages which have rich Agr but disallow referential pro-drop (though they allow expletive pro-drop); (ii) languages like Mainland Scandinavian languages which have no Agr but which disallow any type of pro-drop and languages like Duka, Guaymí, and Papiamentu which have no Agr but disallow referential pro-drop; and (iii) languages like Irish which have mixed/weak Agr but have both expletive and referential pro-drop. See Hermon and Yoon (1989) for further discussion.

            cammin-iamo   'walk-1PL'
            cammin-ate   'walk-2PL'
            cammin-ano   'walk-3PL'
(b) (Chinese)
    zou 'walk'
(c) (English)
    walk   1SG, 2SG, 1PL, 2PL, 3PL
    walk-s 3SG

On a closer examination, however, this analysis turns out to be problematic as well. From an empirical point of view, its prediction is falsified in both directions. For example, as Jaeggli and Safir are aware, Mainland Scandinavian languages are morphologically uniform in that they are uniformly affixed with tense, and yet they do not allow null subjects of any kind (Platzack 1987). Essentially the same can be said of Afrikaans, Easter Island Polynesian, Khalkha Mongolian, Mota, and Songhai, as documented in Kameyama (1985: 9–27); and Fon, Haitian, and Vata, as reported in Law (1993), though the details of these languages need to be further studied (see also Cameron 1993). Secondly, as I remarked earlier, Surselvan is a morphologically uniform language in that it distinguishes regularly among six persons of the verb and the infinitive. However, null subjects are sanctioned only in certain persons and certain syntactic contexts. Next, regional variants of a language like Portuguese constitute yet another piece of evidence against this hypothesis. Both European and Brazilian Portuguese are morphologically uniform. Yet while European Portuguese is a null subject language, Brazilian Portuguese, argues Rohrbacher (1994, 1999), is not. Although there is certainly room for dispute about whether Brazilian Portuguese is a full null subject language or not, what is clear, however, is that all this must suffice to show that morphological uniformity may not be sufficient for the licensing of null subjects. This has forced Jaeggli and Safir to weaken their hypothesis to a one-way implication: if null subjects are allowed in a language, the paradigms in that language must be morphologically uniform. But a move of this kind would still leave null subjects in languages like Old French unexplained; Old French is not a morphologically uniform language, but it allows referential null subjects in V2 configurations, where the finite verb raises to C to license under government null subjects in the Spec-of-IP, and it also permits expletive null subjects in both V2 and non-V2 contexts, as has been shown by Adams (1987), Hulk and van Kemenade (1993), Rivero (1993), Roberts (1993), and Vance (1993), on the basis of the original observation made to this effect by Foulet (1930) (see also Hirschbühler 1989). Other languages which are not morphologically uniform but which nevertheless allow referential null subjects include Moroccan Arabic (Cook and Newson 1995) and Dogon (Culy 1994b). Next, most Slavonic languages (except Russian) may be just as much a problem for the morphological uniformity hypothesis. Unless they are forced to be analysed as containing a consonantal ending, as in e.g. Lindseth and Franks (1996), the second- and third-person singular aorist form and the third-person singular present tense form in the conjugation are bare forms, thus rendering the verbal paradigms not morphologically uniform. However, referential null subjects are allowed in these languages. Still another source of counterexample comes from the licensing of expletive null subjects. Here one finds languages like German and Yiddish, where German is morphologically uniform while Yiddish is not. However, not only do both languages allow expletive null subjects, but the range of expletive null subjects permitted in Yiddish is wider than that allowed in German (e.g. Travis 1984, Rohrbacher 1994, Speas 1994). All this indicates that morphological uniformity may not be a necessary licensing condition, either. Furthermore, it is also unclear conceptually why there should be a connection between morphological uniformity and the licensing of null subjects, why morphological uniformity needs to have all derived inflectional forms in some languages and all underived inflectional forms in others, and why some languages are morphologically uniform and others are not (Hermon and Yoon 1989, Huang 1994, 1995).

Now, suppose we accept morphological uniformity as the crucial factor that licenses null subjects in a language (though the right formulation of this hypothesis remains to be spelled out). But this would still leave a null subject language like German undistinguished from a null subject language like Spanish, because both have morphological uniform paradigms. As mentioned earlier, for a referential null subject to occur in a language like Spanish, it must also be morphosyntactically identified. Thus, Jaeggli and Safir's licensing condition would still have to be supplemented by an identification condition, that is, a mechanism which will deal with the characterization of how a referential null subject is identified. But here Jaeggli and Safir simply follow Rizzi's and C.-T. J. Huang's analyses, which we now know are rather problematic themselves.[28]

Two minimalist analyses

Platzack (1996)
More recently, Platzack (1996) proposes a novel approach to null subjects within Chomsky's (1995) minimalist programme. Differentiating between morphologically and syntactically strong/weak AgrS°, he suggests that a null subject in the Spec-of-AgrS° is permitted only if the specifier feature (i.e. the

---

[28] There is evidence from both first and second language acquisition studies that the morphological uniformity hypothesis may not be correct. Weissenborn (1992), for example, finds that French children continue to drop subjects long after they have correctly analysed spoken French as a morphologically non-uniform language. Based on a careful study of the interlanguage (IL) of four children learning English as a second language, Lakshmanan (1994) concludes that there is no convincing evidence that child second language (L2) learners have access to morphological uniformity.

N-feature) of AgrS° is syntactically weak. The reason is that if the specifier feature of AgrS° is strong, it must be checked and eliminated prior to the interface level PF. This has the effect of leaving a DP in Spec-of-AgrS° in overt syntax before Spell-out, hence the blockage of a null subject. By contrast, if the specifier feature of AgrS° is weak, the checking may be carried out in covert syntax. Consequently one may have a DP in Spec-of-AgrS° at the interface level LF, leaving Spec-of-AgrS° empty at PF, to be occupied by a *pro* later. Hence the possibility of having a null subject in Spec-of-AgrS° in overt syntax. Interacting with (2.108), the proposal makes a correct prediction of the cross-linguistic distribution of null subjects in English, German, Icelandic, Italian, and Swedish.

(2.120) Platzack's strong/weak AgrS° and null subjects

Spec-feature of AgrS°	Strong feature	Weak feature
[+ person, + number]	Referential overt subject (English, Swedish, German, Icelandic)	Referential null-subject (Italian)
[Ø, + number]	Quasi-argumental overt subject (English, Swedish, German)	Quasi-argumental null subject (Italian, Icelandic)
[Ø, Ø]	Expletive overt subject (English, Swedish)	Expletive null subject (Italian, German, Icelandic)

This is a very attractive alternative to previous generative analyses within the principles-and-parameters framework, avoiding some of the problems that Rizzi, Jaeggli and Safir, and C.-T. J. Huang have been facing. But conceptually it is not without problems. First, there arises the question of whether Platzack's proposal constitutes the licensing condition for null subjects alone or whether it covers the identification condition as well. This issue is not clearly addressed. Suppose that the analysis forms the licensing condition alone (as seems plausible given Platzack's formulation of his theory), then as far as identification is concerned, the problems pointed out earlier in connection with Jaeggli and Safir's analysis emerge in this theory as well. For example, it is unclear how the identification of the content of null subjects in languages like Chinese, Imbabura Quechua, and Old Icelandic can be made, given this account. Secondly and more worrying is that Platzack's analysis hinges crucially on the concept of syntactically strong/weak specifier features of AgrS°. However, nowhere in his analysis is there any independent evidence provided for this important notion. Unless there is independent evidence to support such a dichotomy, to argue that a syntactically weak specifier feature of AgrS° licenses null subjects and that the occurrence of null subjects in a language presupposes a syntactically weak specifier feature of AgrS° is circular. Furthermore, the empirical scope predicted by the theory, in particular the central claim that null subjects are barred if they are adjacent to a verb without overt agreement morphology in a language with verb raising to AgrS°, needs to be tested against a wider range of languages.

Speas (1994)

Another recent minimalist attempt at predicting the cross-linguistic distribution of null subjects (and null objects) is by Speas (1994). The central descriptive generalization of this account is that null subjects are allowed only in languages with strong Agr (such as Italian) where Agr is base-generated with a morpheme in it or in languages with no Agr at all (such as Chinese), but not in languages with weak Agr (such as English) where Agr is base-generated as part of the verb (see also Rohrbacher 1994). Speas explains this cross-linguistic distribution of null subjects (and null objects) in terms of a sub-principle of Chomsky's (1995, 1998) general principle of economy.

(2.121) Speas's principle of economy
Project XP only if XP has content.

Given (2.121), it is predicted that in a strong Agr language, Agr has content, and AgrP can be projected. Consequently, Spec-of-Agr need not be filled, and hence the possibility of dropping the subject. By contrast, in a weak Agr language, AgrP has to be given content so that it can be projected without contravening (2.121) prior to Spell-out. This has the consequence that weak Agr languages cannot have null subjects, but must have either a pleonastic inserted in, or an NP moved to, Spec-of-Agr. Finally, in a language without Agr, subjects can be omitted because movement does not need to take place since there is no AgrP projection in it.

The main attraction of Speas's account is the theoretical generality it potentially offers. On such an account (if successful), the distribution of null subjects (and null objects) would follow from a very general principle of economy, which conditions the projection of phrases. As a pleasant consequence, a separate stipulated null subject/pro-drop parameter would be eliminated from UG. However, Speas's analysis is not without its share of problems in its present form. In the first place, what has been said of the licensing/identification distinction in relation to Platzack's analysis holds largely for this account. Although Speas has discarded the licensing/identification dichotomy, what her theory attempts to predict is essentially how null subjects (and null objects) are licensed in a language. If this is the case, then the question remains how the content, or at least the φ-features, of null subjects (and null objects) in languages like Chinese, Imbabura Quechua, and Old Icelandic can be identified given this account. A second problem is that, as in the case of Platzack's analysis, there does not seem to be sufficient independent evidence that Agr in Italian is strong, whereas that in English is weak. Finally, problematic also is the issue of how to distinguish between full null subject languages such as Spanish and restricted null subject languages such as German, for both types of language are assumed to have the same type, strong Agr. More or less the same can be said of restricted null object languages such as French, which allows arbitrary and p-licensed null objects, and non-null object languages such as English, which disallow such null objects—a topic to which we shall turn in Section 2.2.2.

Two Optimality-theoretic analyses

We move next to two Optimality-theoretic analyses. Unlike in the principles-and-parameters theory/minimalist programme, in Optimality theory, grammatical regularities are considered to be fundamentally representational and parallel rather than derivational and serial in nature. UG consists of a set of universal but soft (i.e. violable) constraints. The grammatical system contains (i) a lexicon, (ii) a set of constraints, (iii) a ranking of constraints, and (iv) two functions: a generator (GEN), which creates a candidate output for the input, and an evaluator (EVAL), which selects the best (or optimal) candidate for the given input among the candidate output produced by the generator. Thus in Optimality theory, universals are expressed in the universal but violable constraints. Language variation is accounted for in terms of alternative rankings of these universal constraints. Language acquisition is considered to be a process of constraints ranking and re-ranking within the limits set up by UG (e.g. Prince and Smolensky 1993, Archangeli and Langendoen 1997).

Speas (1997)

The first Optimality-theoretical analysis of null subjects (and null objects) to be considered here is the one put forward by Speas (1997). The basic tenet of this analysis is that the cross-linguistic distribution of null subjects (and null objects) can be accounted for in terms of the ranking of three Optimality-theoretical constraints, namely CONTROL, FREE PRONOUN, and MAX (*pro*).

(2.122) Speas's three Optimality-theoretical constraints
(*a*) CONTROL: A null pronoun must be controlled in its control domain.
(*b*) FREE PRONOUN: A pronoun must be free in its governing domain.
(*c*) MAX (*pro*): If *pro* occurs in the input, then its output correspondent is *pro*.

Assuming that there are three types of language with regard to the occurrence of null subjects (and null objects), Speas claims that this typology follows straightforwardly from the different rankings of the three constraints mentioned above. If FREE PRONOUN and MAX (*pro*) outrank CONTROL, *pro* is allowed as both subjects and objects of a finite clause. Thai is one such language. On the other hand, if CONTROL and FREE PRONOUN dominate MAX (*pro*), *pro* cannot occur as either subjects or objects (e.g. English) unless the language has either rich agreement or no agreement at all, in which case *pro* is sanctioned as subjects of a finite clause. Spanish is of the former type and Chinese belongs to the latter type. This can be shown by a consideration of the sentence '(John says) he loves music' in the four

74   *Syntactic Approaches to Anaphora*

languages. Their tableaux are given in (2.123)–(2.126), which are adapted and simplified from Speas (1997).[29]

(2.123) Thai: {FREE PRONOUN, MAX (*pro*)} >> CONTROL

Candidates	FREE PRONOUN	MAX (*pro*)	CONTROL
(*a*) John say he love music		*!	
☞ (*b*) John say *pro* love music			*

(2.124) English: {CONTROL, FREE PRONOUN} >> MAX (*pro*)

Candidates	CONTROL	FREE PRONOUN	MAX (*pro*)
(*a*) *pro* loves music	*!		
☞ (*b*) he loves music			*

(2.125) Spanish: {CONTROL, FREE PRONOUN} >> MAX (*pro*)

Candidates	CONTROL	FREE PRONOUN	MAX (*pro*)
(*a*) he loves music			*!
☞ (*b*) *pro*$_1$ loves$_1$ music			

(2.126) Chinese: {CONTROL, FREE PRONOUN} >> MAX (*pro*)

Candidates	CONTROL	FREE PRONOUN	MAX (*pro*)
(*a*) John say he love music			*!
☞ (*b*) John$_1$ say *pro*$_1$ love music			

In (2.123) candidate (*a*) is not optimal, because its violation of MAX (*pro*) is fatal. By contrast, although candidate (*b*) violates CONTROL, given that the *pro* is not controlled in its control domain in virtue of absence of rich agreement, it satisfies MAX (*pro*). For this input then, there is a conflict between CONTROL on the one hand and MAX (*pro*) on the other. Given the

---

[29] In an Optimality-theoretic tableau, the constraints are ranked across the top, with highest on the left and lowest on the right. Crucial rankings are represented by solid lines and non-crucial ones by dashed lines. Candidates are displayed in the leftmost column, with the optimal candidate indicated by ☞. Violations of constraints are indicated by '*', with fatal violations highlighted by '!' (e.g. Archangeli 1997).

ranking {FREE PRONOUN, MAX (pro)} >> CONTROL, candidate (b) becomes the optimal candidate. Next, as the tableau in (2.124) indicates, candidate (a) falls foul of CONTROL for the same reason given above. This eliminates it as an optimal candidate. On the other hand, candidate (b) violates MAX (pro), but obeys CONTROL. The higher rank of CONTROL relative to MAX (pro) ensures that this conflict is dissolved in favour of CONTROL, thus selecting candidate (b) as the winning candidate. Moving next to (2.125), the ranking established there correctly rules out candidate (a) but chooses candidate (b) as the optimal candidate. This is because for candidate (a), violating MAX (pro) is fatal. In contrast, candidate (b) is violation-free. It abides by CONTROL because the *pro* is controlled by rich agreement in its control domain; it vacuously meets FREE PRONOUN; and it observes MAX (pro) because its input *pro* is matched by its output *pro*. Finally, in (2.126) candidate (a) is excluded because it violates MAX (pro). By contrast candidate (b) emerges as the optimal candidate because it does not incur any violation at all. It satisfies CONTROL because the *pro* is now controlled by the matrix subject in its control domain; in addition, it also adheres to FREE PRONOUN and MAX (pro) for reasons given above.

As promising as Speas's optimality analysis of null subjects (and null objects) is, there are a number of problems attendant to it. In the first place, given that three types of language are assumed, one would expect to find three corresponding rankings of constraint. However, there are only two rankings. Furthermore, it is rather odd, at least intuitively, to see that both pro-drop and non-pro-drop languages (e.g. Spanish and English) and different types of pro-drop languages (e.g. Spanish and Chinese) are put under the same ranking. This indicates clearly that in this analysis, the ranking of Optimality-theoretical constraints alone fails to distinguish between pro-drop and non-pro-drop languages on the one hand and different types of pro-drop languages on the other. To make such distinctions, Speas has to go back to notions like rich agreement, morphological uniformity, and control domain in the principles-and-parameters framework. But as we have already seen, these notions are themselves highly problematic. Secondly, what Speas has put forward here is basically a licensing condition on null subjects (and null objects). If this is the case, then the now familiar question arises how the content of null subjects (and null objects) is determined on this account. Thirdly, it is not clear how the analysis can be extended to expletive null subjects so that full null subject languages such as Italian and semi-null subject languages such as German can be distinguished.

Grimshaw and Samek-Lodovici (1998)
We move next to a second Optimality analysis advanced by Grimshaw and Samek-Lodovici (1998). Once again the underlying idea is that the occurrence of null subjects can be determined in terms of different rankings of a set of

76 Syntactic Approaches to Anaphora

universal Optimality-theoretical constraints governing topic and foci. More specifically Grimshaw and Samek-Lodovici propose three constraints, namely SUBJECT, DROPTOPIC, and PARSE (see also Grimshaw 1997).

(2.127) Grimshaw and Samek-Lodovici's three Optimality-theoretical constraints
  (a) SUBJECT: The highest A-specifier in an extended projection must be filled.
  (b) DROPTOPIC: Leave arguments coreferent with the topic structurally unrealized.
  (c) PARSE: Parse input constituents.

With (2.127), Grimshaw and Samek-Lodovici argue that the occurrence of referential null subjects in a language is the result of the operation of the constraint DROPTOPIC, which requires arguments whose antecedent is a topic to be structurally unrealized or 'unparsed' in the terminology of Prince and Smolensky (1993). The cross-linguistic distribution of referential null subjects can then be explained by the different rankings of the three constraints specified in (2.127). Languages which rank DROPTOPIC higher than SUBJECT and PARSE allow referential null subjects whenever their antecedent has topic status (e.g. Italian, Japanese, and Romani); whereas languages in which SUBJECT and PARSE outrank DROPTOPIC disallow referential null subjects, independent of whether or not the antecedent is a topic (e.g. English, French, and Swedish). To illustrate, let us consider the sentence 'He has come' in Italian and English. Their tableaux are given in (2.128) and (2.129), which are simplified and adapted from Grimshaw and Samek-Lodovici (1998)

(2.128) Italian: DROPTOPIC >> PARSE >> SUBJECT

Candidates	DROPTOPIC	PARSE	SUBJECT
(a) he has come	*!		
(b) has come he	*!		*
☞ (c) *pro* has come		*	*

(2.129) English PARSE >> DROPTOPIC >> SUBJECT

Candidates	PARSE	DROPTOPIC	SUBJECT
(a) *pro* has come	*!		*
(b) has come he		*	*!
☞ (c) he has come		*	

In (2.128) candidate (*a*) satisfies both PARSE and SUBJECT, but violates DROPTOPIC. Next candidate (*b*) obeys PARSE but falls foul of DROPTOPIC and SUBJECT. Finally candidate(*c*) violates PARSE and SUBJECT but abides by DROPTOPIC. Under the ranking established for (2.128), candidate (*c*) which leaves the subject unparsed is the optimal candidate. On the other hand, the ranking for (2.129) predicts that candidate (*c*) is optimal but candidates (*a*) and (*b*) are not. This is because candidate (*c*) violates only the lower-ranked constraint DROPTOPIC. In contrast, the violation of the high-ranked constraint PARSE by candidate (*a*) is fatal, and candidate (*b*) falls foul of one more low-ranked constraint than candidate (*c*). Consequently both candidates (*a*) and (*b*) are rendered suboptimal, hence ungrammatical (see also Samek-Lodovici 1996).

This is a more elegant Optimality-theoretic analysis. From a conceptual point of view, it is not dependent on principles-and-parameters theoretical notions such as rich agreement, morphological uniformity, and control domain, thus avoiding most of the problems the principles-and-parameters analysts have been facing. Empirically, not only does the analysis correctly predict that there are two types of language with regard to null subjects, but it also gives us an opportunity of providing a unified account of Italian-type and Chinese-type null subject languages. For example, on this analysis, a sentence such as '(He) has come' in Chinese can be treated as one which contains a *pro* null subject (on a par with Italian) rather than one which contains a variable, as in virtually all earlier generative analyses. As we shall see shortly in Section 2.2.2, the variable analysis is untenable on both conceptual and empirical grounds.

There are, however, several problems to be pointed out in connection with this proposal and perhaps with Optimality-theoretical analyses in general. First, it seems that Grimshaw and Samek-Lodovici's account forms the licensing condition on referential null subjects only. If this is the case, then the question how referential null subjects are identified remains to be answered. Secondly, there is the problem of circularity. Unless the relevant ranking can be established independently of null subjects, to say that the occurrence of null subjects in a language is determined by, and determines, that ranking is circular. Finally, somewhat related is the issue of what constitutes the set of primitive universal constraints in Optimality theory. The constraints proposed by both Speas and Grimshaw and Samek-Lodovici are in my view too construction-specific, which may lead to a proliferation of Optimality-theoretical constraints—clearly an unwelcome consequence. This is because if one is allowed to invent an Optimality-theoretical constraint for every recalcitrant fact that is actually observed in some language, not only will one have a large number of constraints, but Optimality theory would be too unconstrained to permit the recognition of any counter-examples.

2.2.2. Null objects

Having discussed null subjects, we turn next to null objects.

The phenomenon

Null objects are allowed in many languages despite the absence of an object-identifying clitic or a verb–object agreement feature.[30] The unidentified or non-agreeing object-drop is exemplified in (2.130).

(2.130) (a) (European Portuguese, Raposo 1986)
José sabe   que Maria Ø viu.
José knows that Maria   saw
'José knows that Maria saw (him).'
(b) (Korean, Yang 1985)
John-i   Mary-ka   Ø miwəha-n-ta-kə   malha-əss-ta.
John-NOM Mary-NOM   hate-ASP-DECL-COMP   say-PAST-DECL
'John said that Mary hated (him).'
(c) (KiNande, Authier 1988)
Arlette a-   ka-   lengekanaya ati na-   abiri-anza Ø.
Arlette SUBJ TNS think   that SUBJ TNS love
'Arlette thinks that I have come to love (her).'

Two generative analyses: the variable analysis versus the *pro* analysis

Within the principles-and-parameters framework, null objects have been argued to be of two types: variable and *pro*. On the former account, null objects are treated as a variable Ā-bound by a null operator in Spec-of-CP. In contrast, the central idea of the latter analysis is that null objects are a *pro* because they can be A-bound by a local argument. C.-T. J. Huang (1984, 1989), Hasegawa (1984), Raposo (1986), Campos (1986a, 1986b), and Authier (1988) argue that null objects in Chinese, Japanese, European Portuguese, Spanish, and KiNande, a Bantu language spoken in Zaire, are variables Ā-bound by an empty topic. A similar proposal is also made by Lillo-Martin

---

[30] Null objects, of course, are commonly found in positions where they can be identified by either a clitic, as in (i) or a verb–object agreement marker, as in (ii):
(i) (Modern Greek, Iatridou and Embick 1997)
o   Kostas tin   iδe   *pro*.
the Kostas her-F-SG-ACC saw
'Kostas saw (her).'
(ii) (Chichewa, Baker 1988)
Mikango yanu i-na-zi-thamangits-a   *pro*.
lions   your SUBJ-PAST-OBJ-chase-ASP
'Your lions chased (them).'

These identified or agreeing null objects will not concern us here. Other languages with (only) verb–object agreement include Arosi (Melanesian), Kapampangan (Philippine), Machiguenga (Arawak), Avar (Caucasian), and Mabuiag (Australian) (Keenan 1976), but the data available are not sufficient for us to be certain whether or not they are object-drop languages.

(1986) for null objects in American Sign Language. By contrast, Chung (1984), Yoon (1985), Pingkarawat (1985), Hoonchamlong (1991), Rizzi (1986), Nakamura (1987), Åfarli and Creider (1987), Farrell (1990), Roberge (1991), Sigurðsson (1993), and Landa (1996) claim that null objects in Chamorro, Korean, Thai, Italian, Norwegian, Old Norse, Japanese, Brazilian Portuguese, French, Spanish, Arabic, Old Icelandic, and Basque Spanish are *pro*s. Authier (1992), departing from Authier (1988), suggests that null objects in French, KiNande, and Tamil are Ā-bound *pro*s which are Caseless. In an attempt to reconcile these two accounts, Cole (1987) proposes that languages be grouped into four types with regard to the possibility of unidentified object-drop: (i) those like English that do not allow null objects (but see Massam and Roberge 1989 and Massam 1992 for a different view), (ii) those like Chinese that allow only null variable objects, (iii) those like Imbabura Quechua that allow only (null) *pro* objects, and (iv) those like Thai that allow both null variable and (null) *pro* objects (to which we may add Quiteño, a dialect of Spanish spoken in the city of Quito in Ecuador, as reported in Suñer and Yépez 1988). Furthermore, parameterizing C-T. J. Huang's (1984) GCR to the effect that it applies to both *pro* and PRO in languages that allow only null variable objects but applies only to PRO in languages that allow both null variable and (null) *pro* objects, Cole claims that the full range of possibilities regarding unidentified null objects can be predicted by incorporating an empty topic parameter and a GCR parameter.

The variable analysis

As mentioned above, the central tenet of the variable analysis (or the empty topic hypothesis) is that a variable can be locally Ā-bound by a null operator in Spec-of-CP, which in this case, is an empty topic.[31] Such a variable, i.e. a trace left by a fronted empty topic, can occur in both subject and object positions.

The variable analysis receives some support from so-called 'pronoun zap' in modern Germanic V2 languages (e.g. Ross 1982, C.-T. J. Huang 1984, Sigurðsson 1993), as can be demonstrated by the following examples from colloquial/informal German and Scandinavian languages (Sigurðsson 1993).

(2.131) (*a*) (German)
        Ø kenne   das nicht.
           recognize that not
        '(I) don't recognize that.'

---

[31] There is, however, a good deal of disagreement among the variable analysts regarding whether the empty topic is base-generated in topic position or moved to that position. Raposo (1986), for example, suggests that the empty topic in European Portuguese is base-generated in topic position. By contrast, Authier (1988) argues that the empty topic in KiNande is base-generated in object position and then moved to Spec-of-CP.

(b) (Swedish)
   Ø känner   det inte.
   recognize that not
   '(I) don't recognize that.'
(c) (Icelandic)
   Ø þekki   þa ekki.
   recognize that not
   '(I) don't recognize that.'
(2.132) (a) (German)
   Ø kenne   ich nicht.
   recognize I   not
   '(That) I don't recognize.'
(b) (Swedish)
   Ø känner   jag inte.
   recognize I   not
   '(That) I don't recognize.'
(c) (Icelandic)
   Ø þekki   ég ekki.
   recognize I   not
   '(That) I don't recognize.'

Pronoun zap exhibits a number of rather interesting properties. First, the dropping of an argument is possible only if the argument occupies the sentence-initial, i.e. the topic, position, as shown by (2.131) and (2.132). This is because the argument must first be topicalized before it can be dropped from the topic position, as can best be seen by the V2 requirement in German and Scandinavian languages. Secondly, the lexicalization of Spec-of-CP will render pronoun zap ungrammatical, because the empty topic must be situated in Spec-of-CP, as the following examples show (Sigurðsson 1993).

(2.133) (a) (German)
   *Jetzt kenne   Ø das nicht.
   now recognize   that not
   'Now (I) don't recognize that.'
(b) (Swedish)
   *Nu känner   Ø det inte.
   now recognize   that not
   'Now (I) don't recognize that.'
(c) (Icelandic)
   *Núna þekki   það ekki.
   now   recognize that not
   'Now (I) don't recognize that.'

Thirdly, only one argument can be deleted per sentence, otherwise it will violate the 'one (null) operator per Spec-of-CP' condition (e.g. Ross 1982, C.-T. J. Huang 1984, Sigurðsson 1993). This is because it is generally assumed in generative grammar that a null operator is moved to Spec-of-CP and cannot co-occur with other (overt or null) operators (e.g. Rizzi 1986). The German example in (2.134c) illustrates this property at hand.

(2.134) (C.-T. J. Huang 1984)
  (a) Ich hab' ihn schon gekannt.
      I   have him already known
      'I already knew him.'
  (b) Ø hab' ihn schon gekannt.
        have him already known
      '(I) already knew him.'
  (c) *Ø hab' Ø schon gekannt.
         have   already known
      '(I) already knew (him).'

These properties can readily be accounted for by the variable analysis. Thus, one of the main merits of the variable analysis is that it enables one to maintain the position that neither German nor Swedish nor Icelandic allows a (referential) null subject which is *pro*.

Extending the variable analysis to Chinese and Portuguese, C.-T. J. Huang (1984) speculates that languages may be classified using two parameters: the zero topic parameter distinguishing zero topic from non-zero topic languages and the pro-drop parameter distinguishing pro-drop from non-pro-drop languages. Consequently, there are four types of language: (i) zero topic, pro-drop languages (e.g. Chinese and Portuguese), (ii) non-zero topic, non-pro-drop languages (e.g. English and French), (iii) zero topic, non-pro-drop languages (e.g. German and Swedish) (but notice that German is a semi-pro-drop language), and (iv) non-zero topic, pro-drop languages (e.g. Italian and Spanish).

Coming back to null objects, under the variable analysis, they are treated universally as a variable, i.e. a trace in an argument position that is Ā-bound by an empty topic in Spec-of-CP. Thus, the standard formulation of the pro-drop parameter excludes referential object *pro* (though it allows arbitrary object *pro*, about which see later). From a conceptual point of view, such an analysis seems desirable, because as pointed out by e.g. Sigurðsson (1993), if referential *pro* is allowed in object position, two rather tricky questions will arise: (i) why do prototypical pro-drop languages like Italian and Spanish lack referential object *pro*, and (ii) how can the pro-drop parameter be modified to license and identify referential object pro-drop?[32]

What, then, is the evidence for the variable analysis? One piece of evidence

---

[32] Nigel Vincent points out to me that there seems to be an implicational scale here, namely null objects presupposes null subjects but not vice versa. If this is the case, then there is no reason to expect Italian and Spanish to be null object languages (see also Law 1993). But recently one African language has come to my attention which may constitute a counter-example to such an implicational hierarchy. Marchese (1986) describes Godié, a Kru language spoken in the Sassandra region of Ivory Coast, as one which allows a much freer suppression of objects than subjects.

concerns the so-called subject–object asymmetry in the distribution of null subjects and null objects observed in a number of languages. The asymmetry is that while null subjects can be A-bound, null objects cannot. This can be seen by (2.135) from Portuguese.

(2.135) (Portuguese, C.-T. J. Huang 1984)
(a) João₁ disse que Ø₁ viu o Pedro.
    João said that   saw Pedro
    'João said that (he) saw Pedro.'
(b) *João₁ disse que Pedro viu Ø₁.
    João said that Pedro saw
    'João said that Pedro saw (him).'

Now, if the null subject is a *pro* and the null object, a variable, the asymmetry is explained. Being a *pro*, the null subject falls under binding condition B, which does not prevent it from being A-bound from outside its GC. By contrast, being a variable, the null object obeys binding condition C, hence it cannot be A-bound. Further evidence in favour of the variable analysis comes from the fact that the distribution of null objects is sensitive to subjacency, as the following example from Portuguese shows.

(2.136) (Portuguese, Raposo 1986)
*O rapaz que trouxe Ø mesmo agora da   pastelaria
the boy that brought same now   of the bakery
era o   teu afilhado.
was the your godson
'The boy that brought Ø right now from the bakery was your godson.'

Again, if the null object is a variable, the ungrammaticality of (2.136) is predicted, for variables typically give rise to both crossover effects and island violations.[33]

Moreover, the variable analysis is also motivated by theory-internal considerations. For example, the requirement that a *pro*/PRO is subject to the GCR forces C.-T. J. Huang to analyse null objects universally as variables but not *pro*s. This is because otherwise (null) *pro* objects would entail a contradiction: they must satisfy both the GCR (which requires a *pro* to be controlled in its control domain, i.e. the minimal clause containing the null object) and binding condition B (which prevents a *pro* from being bound in its GC, i.e. again the minimal clause containing the null object).

---

[33] A further piece of evidence supporting the variable analysis is that a null object in Portuguese can license a parasitic gap. Given that parasitic gaps must be licensed by an Ā-bound trace, the null object is taken to be a variable.
(i) (Portuguese, Raposo 1986)
    Vi Ø₁ na TV sem   reconhecer Ø₁.
    saw   on TV without recognizing
    'I saw Ø on TV without recognizing Ø.'

The *pro* analysis

Can the variable analysis of null objects be maintained universally? The answer is clearly no. Rizzi (1986), for example, observes that a limited range of null objects are allowed in Italian. The same seems to be true of French, Arabic, and Tamil (see e.g. Authier 1989, 1992 and Roberge 1991, and also examples in Section 2.2.1 but see Bouchard 1989 for a different view).

(2.137) (a) (Italian, Rizzi 1986)
Il bel tempo invoglia Ø a PRO restare.
the nice weather induces to stay
'The nice weather induces (one) to stay.'
(b) (French, Authier 1992)
Ce gouvernement autorise rarement Ø à PRO vendre des armes.
this government authorizes rarely to sell arms
'This government rarely authorizes (one) to sell arms.'
(c) (Tamil, Authier 1992)
pasí Ø kuTran paNNa vekkardi.
hunger mistake to do keep-GER-(CAUS)
'Hunger forces (one) to make mistakes.'

(2.138) (a) (Italian, Rizzi 1986)
La buona musica riconcilia Ø con se stessi.
the good music reconciles with oneself
'Good music reconciles (one) with oneself.'
(b) (French, Authier 1989)
Une bonne thérapeutique réconcilie Ø avec soi-même.
A good therapy reconciles with oneself
'A good therapy reconciles (one) with oneself.'

(2.139) (a) (Italian, Rizzi 1986)
Questa musica rende Ø allegri.
this music renders happy
'This music renders (one) happy.'
(b) (French, Authier 1989)
Son audace laisse Ø sans voix.
his audacity leaves without voice
'His audacity leaves (one) speechless.'
(c) (Arabic, Roberge 1991)
haaihi al muusiiqaa turziʕu Ø saʕiidan.
this the music renders happy
'This music renders (one) happy.'

The existence of null objects of this kind is supported by the active role they play in syntactic processes such as control, binding, and predication. For example, the null objects in question can act as controllers of a PRO, antecedents of an anaphor, and subjects of predication of small clauses, as shown by (2.137), (2.138), and (2.139) above respectively. Furthermore, Rizzi notes that these null objects have a different interpretation from null subjects; they must always be arbitrary in reference. (Notice that arbitrary null objects in Italian are plural.) On the basis of this wide range of syntactic evidence, Rizzi shows convincingly that these null objects are *pros* rather than variables.[34]

Given that there is no verb–object agreement feature in, say, Italian, these null objects, being *pros*, cannot be identified by means of the φ-features of I. Rizzi's solution is to stipulate that they are licensed by V and identified through coindexation with the appropriate slot in the θ-grid of the V. The slot is given an arbitrary interpretation by the rule in (2.140) below.

(2.140) Rizzi's interpretation rule for pro_{arb}
Assign arb interpretation to the direct θ-role.

The assignment of the arbitrary interpretation is needed, because a slot in a θ-grid of V is intrinsically featureless. Or to put it slightly differently, non-agreeing arbitrary object *pros* have default (i.e. arbitrary) φ-features, therefore, they need not be conventionally identified. Thus, Rizzi's formulation of the pro-drop parameter makes it possible to maintain the position that while the parameter excludes referential object *pro*, it has no bearing on arbitrary object *pro*.

Clearly, the validity of Rizzi's theory depends crucially on the assumption that null objects are always arbitrary in interpretation. But this may not be the case even with Italian. Consider (2.141) below.

(2.141) (Italian, Chierchia 1989)
L'atteggiamento di Giolitti in quell' occasione
the attitude   of Giolitti on that   occasion
lasciò Ø davvero perplessi.
left   really perplexed
'Giolitti's attitude on that occasion left Ø really perplexed.'

According to Chierchia (1989), examples like (2.141) co-occur with non-generic tense and the null object can be interpreted as generic or non-generic depending on context. Another, perhaps clearer counter-example comes from Brazilian Portuguese, where the null object which occurs in similar constructions is clearly ambiguous between an arbitrary and a definite reading.

(2.142) (Brazilian Portuguese, Chao 1992)
Esta decisão faz   Ø feliz.
this decision makes   happy
'This decision makes one/him happy.'

---

[34] Another construction in which arbitrary null pronominal objects can occur involves the causative construction in languages like French, as in (i*a*) and KiNande, as in (i*b*) (Authier 1992).

(i) (*a*) Ce film fait   pleurer Ø
    this film makes cry
    'This film makes (one) to cry.'
(ii) (*b*) efilme eyi yikaliraia   Ø
    film this makes cry-GEN
    'This film makes (one) to cry.'

If this is the case, the question arises how null objects in Brazilian Portuguese can be referential, given that the verb in this language, like its counterpart in Italian and French, also lacks a verb–object agreement feature. But what is most problematic for both the variable analysis and Rizzi's theory of pro-drop is referential null objects of the following type, which are observed in a wide range of languages.

(2.143) (a) (Chamorro, Chung 1984)
Ha-hähassu ha' si Maria na in-bisita Ø
SUBJ(3S)-remember EMP UNM Maria that SUBJ(1P)-visit
gi epitát.
LOC hospital
'Maria₁ remembers that (we) visited (her₁) at the hospital.'
(b) (Imbabura Quechua, Cole 1987)
Juzi nin Marya Ø juyanata.
Jose says Maria will love
'Jose₁ says that Maria will love (him₁).'
(c) (Brazilian Portuguese, Chao 1992)
Pedro disse pra Maria que a plícia veio interrogar Ø.
Pedro told Maria that the police came interrogate
'Pedro₁ told Maria₂ that the police came to interrogate him₁/her₂.'
(d) (Japanese, Nakamura 1987)
John-wa keisatsu-ga Ø mihatteiru koto-o sitteiru.
John-TOP police-NOM are watching fact-ACC know
'John₁ knows that the police are watching him₁.'
(e) (Burmese, Chit Hlaing personal communication)
hkalei amei ahphyit Ø tin-te lou htin-te.
child mother blame put-MOD COMP thinks
'The child₁ thinks that Mum will blame (him₁).'
(f) (Thai, Pingkarawat 1985)
Nit bɔɔk waa Nuan hen Ø.
Nit speak say Nuan see
'Nit₁ said that Nuan saw (her₁).'
(g) (Hungarian, Farkas 1987)
János megmondta Marinak hogy Gabi utálja Ø.
János told Mari-DAT that Gabi hates
'János₁ told Mari₂ that Gabi₃ hates (him₁/her₂/₄/herself₃).'
(h) (Old Icelandic, Sigurðsson 1993)
dvergrinn mælti, at sá baugr skyldi vera
the dwarf said that that ring should be
hverjum hofuðsbani, er atti Ø.
to-anybody a headband that possessed
'The dwarf said that that ring₁ should bring death to anybody who possessed (it₁).'

(i) (Finnish, Kirsi Hiltunen personal communication)
Kalle väittää   että Pekka uhkaili   Ø.
Kalle claim-3SG that Pekka threaten-PAST
'Kalle₁ claims that Pekka₂ threatened (him_{1/3}).'

In these examples, the null (complement) object is most naturally interpreted as being locally A-bound by the matrix subject or object. Thus, it cannot be taken to be a variable, because it violates binding condition C. But it can best be treated as a *pro*, since it obeys binding condition B—a constraint relevant only to a pronominal.

In an attempt to accommodate these counter-examples to Rizzi's identification mechanism, Farrell (1990) suggests that identification be broadened to include intrinsically specified features; in particular he proposes that the following condition be added to (2.107b).

(2.144) Farrell's identification condition
In the absence of identifying φ-features on its licensing head, *pro* is intrinsically specified as [+3 person].

But (2.144) does not have a universal application; for example, it is not extendable to languages like Chinese, since as can be seen in (2.113) above and (2.145) below, both subject and object *pro* in these languages can also be first and second persons.[35]

Finally, both the variable analysis and the *pro* analysis are seriously challenged by null objects in Chinese-style languages. Null objects in Chinese, for example, are simply ambiguous: they could fit in simultaneously with more than one type of EC in the Chomskyan sense, as can be seen by a consideration of (2.145).

(2.145) Xiaoming yiwei laoshi   you   yao zeguai Ø le.
Xiaoming think teacher again will blame   CRS
'Xiaoming₁ thinks that the teacher₂ will blame
(me/you/him_{1/3}/her/himself/herself/us/you/them . . .) again.'

As shown by the indices of this example, the null object could be argued to be a variable, i.e. when it has, say, the index 3. It could also be argued to be a *pro*, i.e. when it is coindexed with the matrix subject. It could even be argued

---

[35] Also worth mentioning here are Xu and Langendoen's arguments against the variable analysis of null objects in Chinese. Xu and Langendoen (1985) and Xu (1986) present three arguments against taking null objects in Chinese as variables. The first argument is that the relation between a null object and a topic is not consistent with the strong crossover condition (cf. Section 2.1. above)—a condition that has long been taken as a standard diagnostic for variable binding in generative grammar. In their second argument, they point out that a topic can simultaneously relate to more than one distinct gap—a violation of Koopman and Sportiche's (1983) bijection principle. Their third argument is that the relation between a null object and a topic is not subject to the island constraint and therefore does not abide by subjacency. For illustration and further discussion, see Huang (1989, 1992a, 1992b, 1994: 49–51).

to be an empty reflexive, i.e. when it is bound by the embedded subject, thus seeming to form a syntactically undifferentiated class. All this indicates that the binding properties of these null objects are not inherently defined, but rather are pragmatically determined. Viewed thus, these null objects, being realized by syntactically undifferentiated gaps rather than specific empty syntactic categories, can only be analysed as empty pragmatic categories, at least as far as their binding properties are concerned (see, e.g. Huang 1989, 1992*a*, 1992*b*, 1994 for further discussion).[36] Clearly none of the existing generative analyses can account for null objects of this kind.

The fact that null objects can be *pro* has non-trivial implications for the pro-drop parameter. First, null subjects and null objects may have different cross-linguistic distributions. French, for example, allows arbitrary null objects but forbids all types of null subjects (cf. Natascha, Crysmann, and Kaiser 1996). Secondly, given the current version of the pro-drop parameter, it is unclear how (null) *pro* objects can be licensed and identified.

Further arguments against the empty topic hypothesis

As already mentioned, the proposal that null objects are variables Ā-bound by a null operator in Spec-of-CP is tied to the hypothesis that the null operator is an empty topic. But as I pointed out in Huang (1987, 1989, 1992*a*, 1992*b*, 1994, 1995), the empty topic hypothesis is incorrect. First, the empty topic is in general a discourse rather than a sentence phenomenon. This can be evidenced by the fact that a topic can be empty only if its chain initial topic is present. Secondly, the proposal that the empty topic can occur in the absence of its chain initial topic has the immediate consequence of forcing one to analyse every sentence as having an empty topic, and, more absurdly, even to analyse every sentence as containing an indefinite number of empty topics. This is because given that an empty topic is an EC which must satisfy the empty category principle (ECP) by being properly head governed (e.g. C.-T. J. Huang 1984), the question arises what it is in Chomsky's typology of ECs. Since it is governed and Case-marked, it cannot be a PRO. Since it has no antecedent, it cannot be an NP-trace. Since it is not locally identified, it cannot be a *pro*. The only alternative left (for those who assume Chomsky's typology) is that it is a variable. The question that comes up next is how it is locally Ā-bound? The answer is likely to be that the empty topic (itself being a variable) is locally Ā-bound by another empty topic, which is in turn locally Ā-bound by

---

[36] Xu (1986) proposes setting up a new class of empty category within the generative framework, namely what he calls a 'free empty category' (FEC) — an all-inclusive EC without specified features. Ironically enough, such a proposal seems to undermine rather than strengthen the generative approach to ECs: it significantly weakens the basic generative assumption that ECs form syntactically differentiated classes.

another empty topic, *ad infinitum*. Thus, one is led to the implausible position that every sentence contains an indefinite number of empty topics. In other words, positing empty topics will result in an infinite regress. Thirdly, the empty topic hypothesis also poses a number of theory-internal problems for the principles-and-parameters theory. One such problem is that, as already mentioned, it runs counter to the generally accepted assumption that a null operator is moved to Spec-of-CP and cannot co-occur with other (overt or null) operators. This 'one operator per Spec-of-CP' constraint has long been used to account for the ungrammaticality of examples of the following type.

(2.146) (European Portuguese, Rizzi 1986)
*Para qual dos filhos é che a Maria comprou?
for which of his children Maria buy
'For which of his children did Maria buy (it)?'

But as we have just seen, given that the empty topic under discussion is a null operator, one is forced to the position that an indefinite number of null operators can occur in Spec-of-CP in a language.

Does *pro* equate to 'pronoun without phonetic matrix'?

Within the principles-and-parameters theory, *pro*, being the null analogue of overt pronoun, is expected to behave in a fashion parallel to its overt counterpart both syntactically and semantically (assuming with e.g. Chomsky 1982, Chung 1989, and Lasnik 1989 that what differentiates ECs from their overt counterparts is nothing but the lack of the phonetic matrix of ECs). This expectation, however, is bound to be disappointed: *pro* often does not share the same range of distribution with its overt counterpart. Thus, in many pro-drop languages only *pro*s but not overt pronouns can admit of a quantifier-variable interpretation. This has been shown to hold for e.g. Chinese (Huang 1989, 1992*a*, 1992*b*, 1994, 1995), Japanese (Saito and Hoji 1983), Korean (Kang 1988), Tarifit (Ouhalla 1988), Catalan (Rigau 1988), Spanish (Montalbetti 1984), Italian, and most West and South Slavonic languages like Czech and Serbo-Croatian (Lindseth and Franks 1996). The contrast can be illustrated by the following examples from Czech, Korean, and Tarifit, a Berber dialect spoken in the Rif area of northern Morocco.

(2.147) (Czech, Lindseth and Franks 1996)
   (*a*) kazdy student$_1$ mysli, ze Ø$_1$ dostane jednicku.
      every-M-SG student thinks that gets A
      'Every student thinks that (he) will get an A.'
   (*b*) *kazdy student$_1$ mysli, ze on$_1$ dostane jednicku.
      every-M-SG student thinks that he gets A
      'Every student thinks that he will get an A.'

(2.148) (Korean, Kim 1993)
- (a) etten salam₁-i Ø₁ Mary-lul poassta-ko malhayssta.
  somebody-NOM Mary-ACC saw-COMP said
  'Somebody said that (he) saw Mary.'
- (b) *etten salam₁-i ku₁-ka Mary-lul poassta-ko malhayssta.
  somebody-NOM he-NOM Mary-ACC saw-COMP said
  'Somebody said that he saw Mary.'

(2.149) (Tarifit, Ouhalla 1988)
- (a) kurižžn₁ y-nna qa Ø₁ ur
  everyone AGR(3M-SG)-said that NEG
  y-ssin ad y-ghnni.
  AGR (3M-SG)-know to AGR (3M-SG)-sing
  'Everyone said that (he) does not know how to sing.'
- (b) *kurižžn₁ y-nna qa ntta₁ ur
  everyone AGR(3M-SG)-said that he NEG
  y-ssin ad y-ghnni.
  AGR (3M-SG)-know to AGR (3M-SG)-sing
  'Everyone said that he does not know how to sing.'

Similarly, in some pro-drop languages, overt pronouns are excluded if the context demands that they function as arbitrary pronouns. In other words, if a pronoun is overtly expressed, then it loses its arbitrary interpretation and becomes referential. Following are examples from Chinese, Malayalam, and Polish, but the same appears to be true of Japanese, Korean (Yang 1985), Serbo-Croatian, and some other West and South Slavonic languages (Lindseth and Franks 1996).

(2.150) (Chinese)
- (a) Laoshi shuo Ø yao chengshi.
  teacher say should honest
  'The teacher says that (one) should be honest.'
- (b) Laoshi shuo ta yao chengshi.
  teacher say 3SG should honest
  'The teacher says that he should be honest.'

(2.151) (Malayalam, Mohanan 1983)
- (a) wakkiilanmaar Ø caṭikkum.
  lawyers-NOM cheat-FUT
  'Lawyers will cheat (one).'
- (b) wakkiilanmaar awane caṭikkum
  lawyers-NOM 3SG cheat-FUT
  'Lawyers will cheat (him).'

(2.152) (Polish, Lindseth and Franks 1996)
- (a) w Holandii Ø hodują tulipany.
  in Holland-PREP grow-3PL tulips
  'In Holland people grow tulips.'

(b) w Holandii   oni hodują   tulipany.
    in Holland-PREP they grow-3PL tulips
    'In Holland they grow tulips.'

There is thus evidence to suggest that *pro*s and overt pronouns may sometimes have complementary distributions.[37]

2.2.3. Summary

In this section, I have offered a critical survey of both the phenomenology and the various extant generative (including principles-and-parameters, minimalist, and Optimality-theoretic) analyses of null subjects and null objects with respect to a wide variety of languages. My conclusions are (i) the conditions that license and identify null subjects and null objects remain to be worked out, and (ii) a single or a few syntactic parameters /features/rankings may never be adequate to account for this complex phenomenon. The reason is that different (groups of) languages may require different licensing and identification strategies, some of which are clearly non-syntactic in nature, as in the case of Chinese, Imbabura Quechua, and Old Icelandic. I shall present a neo-Gricean pragmatic approach to the identification of null subjects and null objects in Chapter 4.

2.3. Long-distance reflexivization

In the preceding section, I discussed null subjects and null objects. In this section, I shall take a look at long-distance reflexivization.

2.3.1. The phenomenon

Long-distance reflexivization[38] refers to the phenomenon whereby a reflexive[39]

---

[37] There is a large body of generative literature on null arguments, especially on null subjects from the perspective of first and/or second language acquisition. Of particular interest are Hilles (1986, 1991), Bloom (1990), Radford (1990), Valian (1990), Hyams (1992), Saleemi (1992), Wang et al. (1992), Weissenborn (1992), Hyams and Wexler (1993), Hamann (1996), Kanno (1996), and Natascha, Crysmann, and Kaiser (1996). See also Solan (1983).

[38] Other terms that are commonly used in the literature include long-distance anaphora/ anaphors (e.g. Koster and Reuland 1991), non-clause-bound reflexivization/reflexives (e.g. Maling 1984, Anderson 1986), and locally free reflexives (C. Baker 1995).

[39] Following Faltz (1985), reflexivization strategies can be divided into two types: verbal and nominal. Disregarding empty reflexives which are found in languages like Chinese (Huang 1989, 1992*a*, 1992*b*, 1994), Chamorro (Chung 1989), Duala (Wiesemann 1986*a*: 441), and Finnish (Steenbergen 1991), overt nominal reflexives may roughly be grouped into two categories: (i) pronominal or morphologically simplex reflexives like *sebja* in Russian, *sich* in German, and *soi* in French; and (ii) compound or morphologically complex reflexives like *zibun zisin* in Japanese, *se stesso* in Italian, and *e féin* in Irish. We shall discuss verbal reflexives in Chapter 3.

can be bound outside its local domain.[40] Central cases of long-distance reflexivation involve binding of a reflexive out of an NP, as in (2.153), out of a small clause, as in (2.154), across an infinitival clause, as in (2.155), across a subjunctive clause, as in (2.156), across an indicative clause, as in (2.157), across sentence boundaries into discourse, as in (2.158), and across speakers/ turns in conversation, as in (2.159).

[40] In many languages, reflexives can also be arbitrary in reference. Three types of construction may be identified. In the first, the reflexive can occur as the possessor of the subject, as in e.g. Chinese, Hindi/Urdu, and Russian (see (i)). The second construction is what Geniušienė (1987) calls the 'reflexive impersonal'. This construction is attested in a variety of languages including Albanian, Kirghiz, Old Cornish, Old Irish, Russian, Slovak, Spanish, Tarahumara, Tatar, Turkish, and Udmurt (see (ii)). In the third, the reflexive occurs in a 'self V self' structure, as in (iii).

(i) (a) (Korean)
   caki-îy   cip-i   hansang gajang alumtapta.
   REFL-GEN house-NOM always   most   beautiful
   'One's own house is always the most beautiful.'
  (b) (Hindi/Urdu, Davison 1997)
   apnaa ghar sab-see acchaa hai.
   self's house all-than good   is
   'One's own house is the best.'
  (c) (Polish, Toman 1991: 166)
   Swój dom   jest zawsze najmilszy.
   self's house is   always dearest
   'One's own house is always the dearest.'
(ii) (a) (German, Everaert 1986: 116)
   Da   wurde sich zurecht geschämt.
   there was   self rightly shamed
   'People are rightly shamed.'
  (b) (Icelandic, Thráinsson 1991: 75)
   það er verið að raka   sig.
   there is being   shaving self
   'One is shaving oneself.'
  (c) (Moldavian, Geniušienė 1987: 287)
   Acolo totdeauna se   lucrează.
   there always   REFL work-PRES
   'There is always working there.'
(iii) (a) (Chinese)
   Ziji kanbuqi   ziji bu hao.
   self look down upon self not good
   'Self looking down upon self is not good.'
  (b) (Korean)
   Caki-ka   caki-lul   soki-nun kes-un   nappu-ta.
   self-NOM self-ACC deceive-COMP-TOP bad-DECL
   'Self deceiving self is bad.'

Regarding (iii), two points are worth noting. First, the two occurrences of the reflexive must both be interpreted as arbitrary in reference—a substantiation of the more general condition that in a construction with multiple occurrences of a reflexive, all the instances of the same reflexive must share the same antecedent. Secondly, (iii) counter-exemplifies the generally accepted generative assumption that the antecedent of an anaphor cannot itself be an unbound anaphor (e.g. Higginbotham 1985, Barss 1986, Battistella 1989). On this assumption, if the reflexive in (iii) is classified as an anaphor, then (iii) would be ruled out for violation of binding condition A. On the other hand, if it is not specified as an anaphor, then the second instance of the reflexive could not be bound by the first. Clearly, neither of the predictions is borne out.

(2.153) (Norwegian, Hellan 1991:30)
Jon₁ likte din artikkel om seg₁.
Jon liked your article about self
'Jon liked your article about self.'

(2.154) (Danish, Pica 1986)
Larsen₁ betragter Jorgen some farlig for sig₁.
Larsen considers Jorgen as dangerous for self
'Larsen considers Jorgen dangerous for self.'

(2.155) (Russian, Progovac 1993:755)
Professor₁ poprosil assistenta₂ PRO₂ čitat' svoj₁/₂ doklad.
Professor asked assistant read self's report
'The professor asked the assistant to read self's report.'

(2.156) (French, Pica 1991)
On₁ souhaite toujours que les gens ne disent pas du mal de soi₁.
one wishes always that the people NEG speak NEG of ill of self
'One always wishes that people do not slander oneself.'

(2.157) (Malay, adapted from Ngoh 1991)
Ali₁ berharap Fatimah₂ akan berkahwin dengan dirinya₁/₂.
Ali hope Fatimah will marry with self-3SG
'Ali hopes that Fatimah will marry himself/herself.'

(2.158) (Icelandic, Maling 1984: 239)
(Hann₁) var að hugsa um, hvað hún yrði hissa,
he was at to-think about what she would-be surprised
þegar hún kæmi á fætur næsta morgun, opnaði dyrnar og
when she would-come to feet next morning would-open doors and
sæi sig₁ á tröppunum; hún sæi sig₁ ef til vill
would-see self on the steps she would-see self if PRT wants
öldungis ekki fyrst, en stigí baraút, ofan á sig₁, . . .
very/right not at first but would-step just out over on self
(Gestur Palsson, *Tilhugalif*)
'(He) was thinking about how surprised she would be when she got up the next morning, opened the door and saw self on the steps; she would see self perhaps not at first, but would just step out, on top of self, . . .'

(2.159) (KiNande, Authier 1988)
A: Nakwa Kambale yo u- li- a- ha
Q Kambale FOC SUBJ TNS TNS give
Arlette₁ yo e-ki ri?
Arlette FOC PV potato
B: Iyehe, iyowenewene₁ yo u- na- li- a- ki-imaya.
no herself FOC SUBJ TNS TNS TNS it-take
A: 'Is it true that Kamble gave Arlette the potato?'
B: 'No, it is herself that took it.'

Languages differ in precisely which types of complement out of which long-distance reflexives can be bound. However, cross-linguistically the variation in the distribution of long-distance reflexives seems to manifest itself in a relatively clear, uniform, and consistent manner. This consistency in variation can be captured in an implicational universal (2.160), extending the idea put forward by Burzio (1996, 1998).

(2.160) An implicational universal for long-distance reflexivization complement types
  (a) At the sentence level
      NPs > small clauses > infinitivals > subjunctives > indicatives
  (b) At the discourse level
      Discourse > different turns in conversation
  (c) Sentence and discourse
      Sentence > discourse

What (2.160) basically says is this: if a language allows long-distance reflexivization into one type of complement, then it will also allow it into every type higher on the hierarchy. Thus, if a language has long-distance reflexivization with indicatives, then it will necessarily have it with (if relevant) subjunctives, infinitives, small clauses, and NPs. This is the case with Old Icelandic (Siguðsson 1990a). Next, Italian is a language in which binding of a long-distance reflexive is normally up to subjunctives whereas Russian is a language which permits long-distance reflexivization at most out of infinitives (Rappaport 1986). Still next, if a language allows 'binding' of a reflexive across different speakers/turns in conversation, then it will also allow the 'binding' of it across sentence boundaries into discourse, as is the case with Chinese. Finally, if a language allows long-distance reflexivization at the discourse level, then it will also allow it at the sentence level. Icelandic, for example, belongs to this type of language.

2.3.2. Properties and theoretical issues

Properties

Long-distance reflexivization exhibits a number of rather interesting properties, or, more accurately, tendencies. These tendencies can roughly be divided into two categories: universal and language-specific.

Universal tendencies

Long-distance reflexivization shows a number of cross-linguistic tendencies, notably:

(2.161) Universal tendencies of long-distance reflexivization
  (a) Antecedents of a long-distance reflexive tend to be subjects (i.e. subject orientation).[41]

---

[41] As noted earlier in Section 2.1, in some languages (e.g. Danish, Norwegian, and Icelandic) the property of subject orientation for anaphors is matched by a property of subject obviation for pronominals. This means that at least in some constructions of this type of language,

(b) Possible antecedents of a long-distance reflexive can in principle be the subject of any matrix clause, but the root clause subject tends to be preferred to any intermediate clause subject (i.e. the maximality effect).

(c) Long-distance reflexives tend to be morphologically simplex (i.e. Pica's Generalization) (Faltz 1985: 153 ff.).

(d) Long-distance reflexives tend to be referentially optional, consequently they are in general not in complementary distribution with pronouns.

These tendencies can be illustrated as follows.

(2.162) Subject orientation (Marathi, Wali 1989: 83)
Minine$_1$ Vinulaa$_2$ Kaḷavle ki aapaṇ$_{1/*2}$ turungaat aahot.
Mini-ERG Vinu-DAT informed that self prison-LOC was
'Mini informed Vinu that self was in prison.'

(2.163) Maximality effects (Chinese)
Xiaoming$_1$ yiwei Xiaohua$_2$ zhidao Xiaolin$_3$ xihuan ziji$_{1>3>2}$.
Xiaoming think Xiaohua know Xiaolin like self
'Xiaoming thinks that Xiaohua knows that Xiaolin likes self.'

(2.164) Morphological simplicity (Icelandic, adapted from Sigurðsson 1990a)
Jón$_1$ segir að María$_2$ elski sig$_1$/sjálfan sig$_{*1/2}$.
John says that Mary loves self/self self
'John says that Mary loves self/self self.'

(2.165) Referential optionality (Inuit, Bittner 1994:147)
Kaali$_1$ uqar-p-u-q Pavia$_2$ immi-nit$_{1/2}$/taa-ssu-managa$_{1/3}$
Kaali say-IND-3SG Pavia self-ABL/DEM-3SG-ABL
angi-nir-u-sinnaa-nngi-tsu-q.
big-CMP-be-can-NEG-PRT-3SG
'Kaali said that Pavia couldn't be taller than self/him.'

However, exceptions to these properties/tendencies have been attested in a wide range of languages. First, subject orientation can easily be violated. Three cases are well known: (i) with psych-verbs, as in (2.166), (ii) with 'hear from'-type verbs, as in (2.167), and (iii) others, as in (2.168).

---

pronominals must be subject-free where anaphors must be subject-bound. Following is an example from Icelandic (Thráinsson 1991).

(i) Pétur$_1$ bað Jens$_2$ Ø$_2$ að raka hann$_{*1/*2}$.
Peter asked Jens to shave him
'Peter asked Jens to shave him.'

A number of proposals have been put forward in the generative literature to account for this kind of subject orientation for anaphors and subject obviation for pronominals. Vikner (1985), Anderson (1986), and Thráinsson (1991), for example, all pursue a parameterization approach. More recently, Hestvik (1992) argues that subject obviation for pronominals should best be analysed in terms of LF-movement, on a par with subject orientation for anaphors. But as we will shortly see, such an analysis will encounter the same difficulties as does an LF-movement analysis of anaphors. Furthermore, Safir (1987) claims that there is a tendency for subject-oriented anaphors and subject-obviative pronominals to correlate in the same language. There is, however, no cross-linguistic evidence to support that claim.

(2.166) (a) (English)
That everyone but herself₁ can play the viola depressed Mary₁.
(b) (Dutch, Anagnostopoulou and Everaert, 1999)
Die beschrijving van hemzelf₁ als communist
that description of himself as communist
ergerde de Gaulle₁.
annoyed de Gaulle
'That description of himself as a communist annoyed de Gaulle.'
(c) (Finnish, Kirsi Hiltunen personal communication)
Se että hän itse₁ ei saa   palkintoa   huolestuttaa Jussia₁.
it that he self no get-3SG prize-PART worry-3SG   Jussi-PART
'That heself does not get a prize worries Jussi.'
(d) (Italian, Giorgi 1984, see also Napoli 1979)
La propria₁ salute preoccupa molto   Osvaldo₁.
the self   health worries very much Osvaldo
'Self's health worries Osvaldo a lot.'
(2.167) (a) (Chinese)
Xiaoming₁ ting Xiaohua₂ shuo ziji₁/₂ zhong le   jiang.
Xiaoming hear Xiaohua say self win   PFV prize
'Xiaoming hears from Xiaohua that self has won a prize.'
(b) (Japanese, Sells 1987)
Taroo wa   Takasi₁ kara Yosiko ga   zibun₁ o
Taroo TOP Takasi from Yosiko SUBJ self   OBJ
nikundeiru koto o   kiita.
be-hating   COMP OBJ heard
'Taroo heard from Takasi that Yosiko hated self.'
(c) (Korean, Kim 1993: 42)
John₁-un   Bill₂-loputhe caki₁/₂-ka tayhak iphaksihem-ey
John-TOP Bill-from   self-NOM college entrance examination-at
hapkyekhayssta-nun iyaki-lul   tulessta.
passed   -that story-ACC heard
'John heard from Bill that self passed the college entrance examination.'
(2.168) (a) (Chinese, adopted from Pan 1995)
Wuqing de   shishi gaosu Lao Liu₁ ziji₁ de   jihua xingbutong.
harsh   POSS fact   tell Lao Liu self POSS plan carry-not-through
'The harsh reality tells Liu that self's plan won't work.'
(b) (Latin, Benedicto 1991)
A Caesare₁   ualde liberaliter inuitor   sibi₁
by Caesar-ABL very generously (I) am invited REFL-DAT
ut   sim   legatus.
COMP be-SBJV legate-NOM
'Caesar most liberally invites me to take a place on self's personal staff.'
(c) (Telugu, Wali and Subbarao 1991)
Vaasu₁ tanu*₁/₂ picci-di ani kamalaa-to₂   ceppeedu.
Vaasu self   crazy-3F that Kamalaa-to-3F told
'Vaasu told Kamala that self is crazy.'

96 Syntactic Approaches to Anaphora

Secondly, in many languages, morphologically complex reflexives either in the form of 'pronoun + self' or in the form of 'self + self' can participate in long-distance reflexivization, as the examples in (2.169) show.

(2.169) (a) (Chinese, see also Pan 1998)
Xiaoming$_1$ shuo leisheng ba ta ziji$_1$ xiao le yi tiao.
Xiaoming say thunder BA 3SG self frighten PERF one CL
'Xiaoming said that the loud clash of thunder had given himself a fright.'
(b) (Malay, Ngoh 1991)
Abdullah$_1$ menolong Aminah mencuci pakaian dirinya$_1$.
Abdullah help Aminah wash clothes self 3SG-POSS
'Abdullah helps Aminah wash himself's clothes.'
(c) (Japanese, Kato 1994)
Takasi$_1$-wa Hirosi-ga zibun-zisin$_1$-ni kasite kureta kuruma-o
Takasi-TOP Hirosi-SUBJ self-self lend give car-OBJ
kowasite simatta.
broken ended up
'Takasi has broken the car which Hirosi lent self-self.'
(d) (German, Katada 1991)
Willi$_1$ dachte, daβ Hans$_2$ mit Fritz$_3$ über sich selbst$_{1/2}$
Willi thought that Hans with Fritz about self self
gesprochen hat.
spoken has
'Willi thought that Hans has spoken with Fritz about self self.'

Furthermore, there are even languages in which the morphologically complex reflexive has to take a long-distance antecedent. These include Finnish;[42] Inuit; and Northern Sámi, a Finno-Ugric language spoken in Norway, Finland, and Sweden (e.g. Vikør 1993).

(2.170) (a) (Inuit, Bittner 1994)
Kaali$_1$ uqar-p-u-q Pavia$_2$ immi-nirmi-nit$_1$
Kaali say-IND-3SG Pavia self-OBV-ABL
angi-nir-u-sinnaa-nngi-tsu-q.
big-CMP-be-can-NEG-PRT-3SG
'Kaali said that Pavia could not be taller than self.'
(b) (Finnish, Steenbergen 1991: 237, errors corrected)
Pekka$_1$ sanoi Jussille$_2$ Matin$_3$ katsovan häntä itseään$_{1/*2/*3}$.
Pekka said Jussi Matin-GEN watch-PTC-GEN he self-POSS
'Pekka said to Jussi that Matin watched himself.'

Thirdly, a long-distance reflexive may be employed in syntactic structures

---

[42] To be more accurate, the Finnish complex reflexive *hän itse* can also be locally bound. What is of particular interest, however, is that when it is locally bound, *hän itse* is object-oriented. This object orientation somewhat parallels the behaviour of the class of anti-subject pronouns in Danish, Icelandic, and Norwegian, as we have just seen. It is this object orientation that distinguishes *hän itse* from the long-distance, simplex reflexive *itse* on the one hand and the long-distance, empty reflexive on the other in the language.

where a pronoun is excluded, hence losing referential optionality and maintaining the reflexive/pronoun complementarity. Examples follow.

(2.171) (a) (Italian, Burzio 1996: 36)
Manuel₁ vide il   toro sopra di sé₁/?*lui₁.
Manuel saw the bull upon of self/him
'Manuel saw the bull upon self/him.'
(b) (Icelandic, Thráinsson 1991: 51, 53)
Pétur₁ bað   Jens₂ um PRO₂ að   raka   sig₁/₂/hann*₁/*₂.
Peter asked Jens   that to shave self/him
'Peter asked Jens to shave self/him.'
(c) (Gimira, Breeze 1986: 58)
yisi₁ ba₁/yi*₁/₂ hamnsue   maki   hayt'ue.
3M-S 3REFL/3M go-FUT-3M-FIN saying-3M told-3M-FIN
'He said that heself/he will go.'

Language-specific properties

In addition, long-distance reflexivization also displays some language-specific properties, notably:

(2.172) Language-specific properties of long-distance reflexivization
(a) Long-distance reflexives can occur only in certain clause types, but not in others (c.f. the implicational universal (2.160)).
(b) Long-distance reflexives may occur in clause types where they are not allowed only when these clauses are embedded under a class of long-distance reflexive-taking, or logocentric predicates (to be elucidated in Chapter 3) (i.e. the skipping effect).[43]
(c) Long-distance binding of a reflexive is possible normally only in case all antecedents agree in person (i.e. the blocking effect).
(d) Binding of a long-distance reflexive may not be subject to the c-command condition.
(e) Antecedents of a (long-distance) reflexive are in general animate (i.e. the animacy condition).

These properties can be illustrated as follows.

(2.173) Clause types (Russian, Progovac 1993: 758)
Vanja₁ znaet čto Volodja₂ ljubit svoju*₁/₂ ženu.
Vanja knows that Volodja loves self's wife
'Vanja knows that Volodja loves self's wife.'
(2.174) Skipping effects (Icelandic, Thráinsson 1976)
Haraldur₁ segir að Jón komi ekki nema María kyssi sig₁.
Harald says that Jon comes not unless Mary kisses self
'Harald says that Jon won't come unless Mary kisses self.'

---

[43] The original term is 'the domino effect', due to Thráinsson (1976). But as the reader can see for him- or herself, it is a misnomer.

(2.175) Blocking effects (Chinese)
Xiaoming₁ yiwei wo₂ bu xihuan ziji*₁/₂.
Xiaoming think 1SG not like   self
'Xiaoming thinks that I do not like self.'
(2.176) Violation of c-command (Malayalam, Mohanan 1982)
Moohante₁ wiswaasam taan₁ dhiiranaan enna aana.
Mohan's   belief   self brave is   that is
'Mohan's belief is that self is brave.'
(2.177) Animacy (Marathi, Wali 1989: 36)
*Itihaas swataaci punaraavrutti karto.
history self's   repetition   makes
'History repeats self.'

As mentioned earlier, Russian is a language which allows long-distance reflexivization at most out of infinitives. Consequently no long-distance reflexives are allowed to occur in a finite indicative, as shown by (2.173). In the Icelandic example (2.174), the embedded adverbial clause cannot take a long-distance reflexive on its own. However, when it is embedded under the logocentric predicate 'say', (2.174) becomes a long-distance reflexivization sentence. The use of the first-person pronoun in the Chinese example (2.175) 'blocks' long-distance reflexivization reading. Next, in the Malayalam sentence (2.176), the antecedent does not c-command the long-distance reflexive, thus violating the c-command condition. The same is true of Malay, Turkish, and many other languages (cf. (2.205)). Finally, (2.177) shows that the antecedent of a (long-distance) reflexive in a language such as Marathi must be animate.

Next, contrary to a generally accepted generative assumption that long-distance reflexives cannot take split antecedents, they vary from language to language. For example, while (some forms of) long-distance reflexives in general cannot have split antecedents in Chinese, Hindi/Urdu (Saxena 1985, Gurtu 1992, Montaut 1994, Srivastav Dayal 1994, and Davison 1997), and Icelandic, they can in Korean, Marathi, and Turkish.[44]

(2.178) (a) (Chinese)
*Xiaoming₁ gaosu Xiaohua₂ Xiaohong bu xihuan ziji₁₊₂.
Xiaoming tell   Xiaohua Xiaohong not like   self
'Xiaoming tells Xiaohua that Xiaohong does not like self.'
(b) (Hindi/Urdu, Davison 1997)
*raam₁-nee syaam₂-see PRO apnii₁₊₂ gaaRii-kii
Ram-ERG   Shyam-with   self's   vehicle-of

---

[44] Note that the Hindi/Urdu possessive reflexive can take split antecedents, as in (i).
(i) (Hindi/Urdu, Davison 1997)
joon₁-nee meerii₂-see kahaa ki apnaa₁₊₂ ghar sab-see acchaa hai.
John-ERG Mary-with say-PF that self's   house all-than good is
'John told Mary that selves' house is the best.'

marammat kar-nee-koo   kah-aa.
repair   do-INF-DAT say-PF
'Ram told Shyam to repair self's vehicle.'
  (c) (Icelandic, Thráinsson 1991)
      *Jon₁ sagði Maríu₂ að þú hefðir svikið   sig₁₊₂.
      John told Mary that you had betrayed self
      'John told Mary that you had betrayed self.'
(2.179) (a) (Korean, Yoon 1989)
        John₁-un Mary₂-eykey caki₁₊₂-tul-i iki-lke-la-ko
        John-TOP Mary-DAT   self-PL-NOM win-FUT-DECL-COMP
        malha-ess-ta.
        tell-PAST-DECL
        'John told Mary that selves will win.'
    (b) (Marathi, Wali and Subbarao 1991)
        Lilini₁   Šaamlaa₂ kaḷavla ki aapaṇ₁₊₂ te kaam karṇa
        Lili-ERG Saam-to informed that self   that job do-INF
        yogya   naahi.
        proper   not
        'Lili informed Saam that self should not do the job.'
    (c) (Telugu, Wali and Subbarao 1991)
        Vaasu₁ taamu₁₊₂ iddaramu picci-waaḷḷamu ani
        Vaasu self-PL both   crazy-AGR-PL   that
        Mohan₂-to ceppeeḍu.
        Mohan-to told
        'Vaasu told Mohan that selves are crazy.'

Finally, the same can be said of long-distance reflexives regarding strict (i.e. pragmatic-coreferential) versus sloppy (i.e. bound-variable) interpretations. While (some forms of) long-distance reflexives in Dutch, Hindi/Urdu, Marathi, and Telugu allow only a sloppy reading, they allow both a strict and a sloppy reading in Finnish, Icelandic, and Norwegian, contrary to e.g. Williams (1977), Bouchard (1984), and Lebeaux (1985).[45]

---

[45] There is also a third possibility. If a language has more than one reflexive form, one of these forms may allow only a strict reading. This seems to be the case with the Dutch reflexive '*mzelf*.
  (i) (Reuland and Koster 1991: 24)
      Ik wantrouw John's beschrijving van 'mzelf en die van Piet ook.
      I distrust   John's description of himself and of Peter too
      'I distrust John's description of John and Peter's description of John too.'
  Somewhat related is the behaviour of reflexives in the comparative deletion construction. If a language has more than one reflexive form or strategy, the general rule is that the morphologically simplex reflexive or the verbal reflexive will allow only a sloppy reading but the morphologically complex reflexive or the nominal reflexive will permit both a strict and a sloppy reading under comparative deletion. Dutch represents the first type (*zich* versus *zichzelf*) (cf. Chinese *ziji* versus *ta ziji*), and Russian (*-sja* versus *sebja*) and Serbo-Croatian (*se* versus *sebe*) belong to the second (see e.g. Sells, Zaenen, and Zec 1987, and Lidz 1996).

(2.180) (*a*) (Dutch, Everaert 1991: 86)
Jan$_1$ zag de sneeuwbal op zich$_1$ afkomen en Piet ook.
Jan saw the snowball to self come and Piet too
'Jan saw the snowball come to self, and Piet too.'
(*b*) (Hindi/Urdu, Davison 1997)
gautam$_1$ apnee (aap$_1$)-koo caalaak samajhtaa   hai,
Gautam self's self-DAT smart   consider-IMPF is
aur vikram bhii Ø.
and Vikram also
'Gautam considers self smart, so does Vikram.'
(*c*) (Marathi, Wali and Subbarao 1991)
Lili-laa$_1$ vaaṭṭa ki   aapali$_1$ bahiṇ libral aahe aaṇi tasac Ravilaa vaaṭṭa.
Lili-to feel   that self's sister liberal is   and same Ravi-to feels
'Lili believes that self's sister is liberal, and Ravi believes the same.'
(2.181) (*a*) (Finnish, Kirsi Hiltunen persernal communication)
Jussi$_1$ käskee   Pekan   pesemään   itsensä$_1,$
Jussi order-3SG Pekan-GEN wash-3INF self-3PX
niin myös Kalle.
so also Kalle
'Jussi orders Pekan to wash self, so does Kalle.'
(*b*) (Icelandic, Thráinsson 1991: 60)
Jón$_1$ sagði að þú hefðir svikið   sig$_1$ og Pétur gerði það líka.
John said that you had betrayed self and Peter did   so too
'John said that you had betrayed self and Peter said so too.'
(*c*) (Norwegian, Hellan 1991:44)
John$_1$ hadde hørt meg snakke nedsettende om seg$_1$
John had   heard me talk   disparagingly about self
og det hadde de   som stod rundt også.
and it had   those who stood around too
'John had heard me talking disparagingly about self, and so had those who were standing around.'

Theoretical issues

There are (at least) five issues that any adequate theory of long-distance reflexivization must address:

(2.182) Theoretical issues
   (*a*) The postulation of a condition which licenses the occurrence of long-distance reflexivization in a language.
   (*b*) The specification of a domain within which an antecedent can be found.
   (*c*) The identification of potential antecedents within the domain specified.
   (*d*) The selection of one out of a number of possible antecedents.
   (*e*) The explanation of the motivation behind the optional use of a long-distance reflexive.

2.3.3. Long-distance reflexivization in generative grammar

Assumptions, problems, and theoretical issues

Within the framework of the principles-and-parameters theory, reflexives, being anaphors, are subject to binding condition A, as stated in (2.4) above. In broad terms, what binding condition A does is to characterize conditions under which an anaphor must be coindexed with an argument in an appropriately defined command relation within an appropriately defined minimal syntactic domain. The standard version of the syntactic prominence condition is c-command, and that of the locality condition is the requirement that an anaphor must be bound in a local domain, canonically coinciding with the local clause.[46]

---

[46] There is another assumption that is generally accepted in the generative literature, namely, long-distance binding of anaphors is restricted to reflexives. Among the strongest empirical evidence in support of this assumption is *siebie* in Polish. *Siebie* is an anaphor which is ambiguous between a reflexive reading and a reciprocal reading. Long-distance binding is allowed only under the reflexive reading but not under the reciprocal reading, as can be shown by the following examples (Reinders-Machowska 1991).

(i) Chłopcy$_1$ rozmawiali ze sobą$_1$.
    boys-NOM talked   with self/each other
    'The boys talked with (them)selves/each other.'

(ii) (*a*) Chłopcy$_1$ czytali dziewcząt$_2$ wspomnienia o   sobie$_{1/2}$.
        boys   read   of-girls   memories   about self
        'The boys read the girls' memories about (them)selves.'
    (*b*) Chłopcy$_1$ czytali dziewcząt$_2$ wspomnienia o   sobie$_{*1/2}$.
        boys   read   of-girls   memories   about each other
        'The boys read the girls' memories about each other.'

Other languages which utilize the same form for reflexives and reciprocals, be it a (grammaticalized/lexicalized) noun, a verbal affix, a particle, or a preposition, include Hebrew (*ni-*) (Wiesemann 1986*a*: 439), Maxakali (*yay*) (Popovich 1986: 355), and Xerénte (*i-si*) (Wiesemann 1986*b*: 375). From a geographic point of view, this polysemous pattern appears to be widespread in African languages. Heine (1997), for example, gives the following list of African languages which use the same form for reflexives and reciprocals: Acholi, Arbore, Balese, Banda, Bango, Dinka, 'Dongo, Gida, Iraqw, Kalenjin, Kara, Kisi, Lele, Luo, Ma, Mangbetu, Margi, Mayogo, Moru, Ndogo, Ngala, Päri, Pokot, Shilluk, Supyire, Urhobo, Xdi, Yoruba, and Zande, to which we can add Gimira (Breeze 1986: 60), Mundani (Parker 1986: 149), Podoko (Burquest 1986: 94), and Zulgo (Wiesemann 1986*a*: 441). The same is also true of most Australian aboriginal languages. For example, according to McGregor (1997), of the ten Nyulnyulan languages (Warrwa, Nyikina, Yawuru, Jukun, Nimanburru, Ngumbarl, Nyulnyul, Jabirrjabirr, Bardi, Jawi), nine (except perhaps Yawuru) employ the same grammatical construction to encode reflexive and reciprocal meaning. Unfortunately, the data available to us are insufficient to confirm or disconfirm the above assumption.

From a historical point of view, it has been hypothesized that reciprocals come from reflexives (e.g. Faltz 1985, Kemmer 1993, Heine 1997, König and Siemund 1997). While languages like Aymara, Karaja, Quechua, Seneca, and Yurok amply witness this evolutional pattern, Mongol and Suislaw are examples of a language in which reciprocals are grammaticalized before reflexives (e.g. Nedjalkov 1980, Wiesemann 1986*a*: 439). There are also languages that have morphological markers to express a reciprocal but not a reflexive relation. These include a group of Oceanic languages (e.g. Mekeo, Tolai, Tigak, Kara, Simbo, Hoava-Kusaghe, Zabana, Nêlêmwâ, To'aba'ita, Fijian, Tongan, Samoan, Futunan) and a number of non-Austronesian languages

102 Syntactic Approaches to Anaphora

One of the major problems caused by long-distance reflexivization for standard binding theory is that the locality restriction imposed by binding condition A is violated: a long-distance reflexive can in principle take antecedents indefinitely far away from it. Other issues that have been figuring prominently in the generative literature on long-distance reflexivization include why a long-distance reflexive is morphologically simplex, why it is subject-oriented, and why it can be blocked under appropriate conditions in some languages but not in others.

Two generative strategies

Within the current framework of generative grammar, there are two general strategies to tackle long-distance reflexivization: (i) to deny the evidence that binding condition A is violated by claiming that a long-distance reflexive is not a true anaphor, and (ii) to modify the standard version of binding theory in such a way as to allow long-distance reflexivization to be accommodated by binding condition A.

Denial of evidence

Let us begin with the first generative strategy. Under this strategy, there are

---

such as Martuthunira (Australian), Tauya (Papuan), Delaware (Algonquian), and Mapun (Chadic) (Lichtenberk 1999, Bril 1999). See also Dench (1987) on reciprocals in a group of Ngayarda languages (Martuthunira, Panyjima, Yinyjiparnti), Nedjalkov and Guentcheva (1999) on reciprocals in Bamana, Djaru, Even, Evenki, Kabardian, Tarian, Yakut, and Warrungu, and Frajzyngier and Curl (forthcoming b) on Amharic, Bilin, and Chinese.

Anyhow, cases of long-distance binding of reciprocals are attested in a number of languages, including Chinese, English (Chomsky 1981: 214, Kuno 1987: 85, Pollard and Sag 1992), and Finnish (Korhonen 1995).

(iii) (a) (Chinese)
    Jiu you   chong feng, bici   dou hen jidong.
    old friend again meet each other all   very excited
    'Having met again, each of the old friends is excited.'
  (b) (English, Pollard and Sag 1992)
    [Bush and Dukakis]$_i$ charged that General Noriega had secretly contributed to each other's$_i$ campaigns.
  (c) (Korean, Yoon 1989)
    Kutul-i   selo-ka   ttokttokha-ta-ko.
    they-NOM each other-NOM be smart-DECL-COMP
    'They think that each other are smart.'
  (d) (Finnish, Korhonen 1995: 57)
    Tytö-t näk-i-vät   toiste-nsa   luke-van.
    girl-PL see-PAST-3PL each other-GEN-PL-3PX read-PTC-GEN
    'The girls saw that each other were reading.'

As Lebeaux (1983) observes, there seem to be some fundamental differences between reflexives and reciprocals in distribution. These differences, on Safir's (1992) view, are disguised by the postulation of a single category of anaphor in Chomsky's typology of NPs. There is some reason to believe that reciprocals may be generated via movement independent of the binding conditions, as argued by Heim, Lasnik, and May (1991).

three ways to pursue such an escape route: (i) to argue that a long-distance reflexive is a (bound) pronominal; (ii) to treat a long-distance reflexive as a pronominal anaphor; and (iii) to claim that a long-distance reflexive is an anaphor of a special kind.

Long-distance reflexive as a (bound) pronominal
Starting with the first generative option, it has long been argued that a long-distance reflexive is not an anaphor but a pronominal in disguise (e.g. Ronat 1982, Bouchard 1984, and, for a different reason, Kameyama 1984, Maling 1984, Sells 1987, Koopman and Sportiche 1989, Pollard and Sag 1992, 1994, and C. Baker 1995). According to Bouchard (1984), for example, although reflexives constitute a coherent morphological class, they do not form a coherent typological class. On the basis of this assumption, Bouchard proposes that anaphors be determined functionally rather than morphologically. Consequently, he makes a distinction between true and false anaphors. What are treated by him as true anaphors are generally those that constitute one of the co-arguments of a predicate (see also Hellan's 1988, 1991 connectedness versus containment anaphor distinction and Reinhart and Reuland's 1991, 1993 reflexivizer versus non-reflexivizer distinction). This has the immediate effect that a long-distance reflexive is ruled out as a true anaphor, and as a result, the fact that it does not conform to the locality requirement imposed by binding condition A does not need an explanation.

However, as I pointed out in Huang (1989, 1994, 1997), what syntactic evidence there is seems to indicate that a long-distance reflexive is an anaphor rather than a pronominal in the Chomskyan sense. Consider (2.183)–(2.185).

(2.183) (Chinese)
Xiaoqiang$_1$, Xiaoming shuo Xiaohua kanbuqi ziji$_{*1}$/ta$_1$.
Xiaoqiang Xiaoming say Xiaohua look down upon self/3SG
'Xiaoqiang, Xiaoming says that Xiaohua looks down upon self/him'.
(2.184) (Marathi, Wali and Subbarao 1991)
Ravi-čaa$_1$ mitraa-laa$_2$ vaatta ki appan$_{*1/2}$/ to$_{1/2}$ husăar aaho.
Ravi's friend thinks that self he smart is
'Ravi's friend thinks that self/he is smart.'
(2.185) (Italian, adapted from Giorgi 1984)
Gianni$_1$ ha convinto Osvaldo$_2$ del fatto che la
Gianni has convinced Osvaldo of the fact that the
propria$_{1/*2}$/sua$_{1/2}$ casa è la più bella del paese.
self/his house is the most beautiful of the village
'Gianni has convinced Osvaldo that self's/his house is the nicest in the village.'

Given the pronominal analysis, the long-distance reflexive in (2.183)–(2.185) is a pronominal. It follows therefore that we would expect that these sentences are grammatical under the indicated interpretation. But this is clearly not the case. Thus, we are owed a reasonable explanation as to why the long-distance reflexive, unlike the real pronominal in (2.183)–(2.185), cannot undergo topicalization, cannot be coindexed with a non-c-commanding NP, and cannot be bound to an object. On the other hand, the ungrammaticality of (2.183)–(2.185) on the assigned reading is entirely expected if the reflexive is an anaphor rather than a pronominal. This is because an anaphor in general has to be bound in the root sentence; the binding of a long-distance anaphor is usually subject-oriented; and an anaphor is sensitive to the c-command condition.

Secondly, on the assumption that a long-distance reflexive is a pronominal, we would expect that it falls under binding condition B. But all binding condition B does is to impose some negative binding restrictions on the choice of antecedents for a pronominal: it specifies only where a pronominal should be free, but not if and where it should be bound. If this is the case, then the question of why and how a long-distance reflexive must normally be bound needs an explanation. One proposal (e.g. Ueda 1986) has been to classify pronominals into two types: one with the feature [+bound], which can be construed as a bound variable; and one with the feature [–bound], which cannot. But such a stipulation would lead to a proliferation of primitives of UG.

Furthermore, given this analysis, the vital question of when a reflexive is predicted to be an anaphor and when it is predicted to be a pronominal remains unanswered. Unless there is independent evidence to suggest otherwise (as seems implausible given the array of syntactic tests above), to argue that a long-distance reflexive is a pronominal simply because it violates binding condition A is circular.[47]

---

[47] A variant of this analysis is to treat a reflexive which can be both long- and short-distance bound uniformly as a bound pronominal (e.g. Fukui 1984, Ueda 1986). But considerable problems arise in connection with this alternative, too. First, the same evidence that has been adduced to argue against treating a long-distance reflexive as a pronominal on the basis of examples like (2.183)–(2.185) can also be used to argue against this analysis. Secondly, as Ueda is aware, on a pronominal hypothesis like this, even examples like (i) would have to be treated as exceptional.

(i) (Japanese)
   Keiko-wa zibun-o aisite-iru.
   Keiko-TOP self-OBJ love
   'Keiko loves self.'

This is a very undesirable situation, as both long- and short-distance uses of a reflexive represent equally well-formed cases of binding in Japanese, and neither should be excluded from the core. Ueda's solution is to claim that the use of locally bound *zibun* is restricted to a certain type of predicate in Japanese (see also Aikawa 1993), but such an analysis cannot be extended to other languages such as Chinese. Therefore, any adequate account of the distribution of reflexives in these languages must treat the reflexive in examples like (i) as unmarked and non-exceptional, at least as far as binding is concerned (see also Sportiche 1986 and Huang 1994 for further arguments against this approach).

Long-distance reflexive as a pronominal anaphor
Alternatively, a long-distance reflexive has been treated as a pronominal anaphor, following suggestions by e.g. Chomsky (1982: 78), Mohanan (1982), Bok-Bennema (1984), Wang and Stillings (1984), Koster (1987), Bickerton (1987), Battistella and Xu (1990), Everaert (1991), and Thráinsson (1991). The central idea underlying this line of analysis is that a long-distance reflexive shares neither the distribution nor the properties of either a pure pronominal or a pure anaphor; rather it combines properties that are normally associated with a pure pronominal only or a pure anaphor only. Consequently it can be characterized as an overt pronominal anaphor with the feature matrix [+anaphoric, +pronominal].

However, if such an analysis is correct, a long-distance reflexive would at first sight be wrongly predicted to be ungoverned. The reason is exactly the same as for its null analogue, i.e. PRO. By virtue of being a pronominal anaphor, it would have to obey both binding conditions A and B simultaneously. It follows therefore that if a long-distance reflexive has a GC, it must be both bound and free in it—a contradiction.[48] Therefore, it cannot have a GC and hence is ungoverned—an absurd conclusion. To circumvent the problem, one could once again argue that thanks to the SUBJECT accessibility bifurcation, the binding domains for anaphors and pronominals can be distinct, the former being larger than the latter (cf. Section 2.1.2.). Assuming then binding condition A applies to a long-distance reflexive in its anaphoric binding domain and binding condition B applies to it in its pronominal binding domain, a long-distance reflexive, being a pronominal anaphor, could then be sanctioned in positions in which the two binding domains do not coincide. Such an analysis seems well suited to account for the use of long-distance reflexives in examples of the following kind, where the embedded subject position is a position with two distinct binding domains (the anaphoric binding domain being the matrix clause and the pronominal binding domain being the embedded clause).

(2.186) (*a*) (Icelandic, Maling 1984)
  Hann$_1$ sagði að sig$_1$ vantaði hæfileika.
  he said that self lacked-SBJV ability
  'He said that self lacked ability.'
 (*b*) (Korean, Kim 1993)
  John$_1$-i caki$_1$-ka aphuta-ko malhayssta.
  John-NOM self-NOM sick-that said
  'John said that self is sick.'

---

[48] As already discussed in Section 2.1.4, there is a gap in the standard Chomskyan typology of NPs, namely the slot of an overt pronominal anaphor with the feature combination [+anaphor, +promominal] is vacant. However, it is partially the sort of contradiction we have just seen that leads to Chomsky's conjecture that this slot cannot be filled by an overt NP.

106   *Syntactic Approaches to Anaphora*

    (c) (Marathi, Wali and Subbarao 1991)
        Lili₁ samajte ki   aapaṇ₁ libral aahot.
        Lili think   that self   liberal is
        'Lili thinks that self is liberal.'
    (d) (Modern Greek, Iatridou 1986)
        O Yanis₁ pistevi oti   o idhios₁ tha kerdhisi.
        John   believes COMP himself   will win
        'John believes that self will win.'
    (e) (Telugu, Wali and Subbarao 1991)
        Kamala₁ tanu₁   libaral ani anukondi.
        Kamula self-NOM liberal that thought
        'Kamula thought that self is liberal.'
    (f) (Tuki, Biloa 1991b: 855)
        visimbi₁ vi   bunganam ee   vimwamate₁ vi   n(u) endam na vita.
        soldiers SUBJ think   that 3PL self   SUBJ FUT go   to war
        'Soliders think that theyselves will go to war.'
    (g) (Norwegian dialect, Moshagen and Trosterud 1990)
        han₁ trudde at   mora   si₁   sto   på taket.
        he   thought that mother REFL-GEN stood on the roof
        'He thought that self's mother stood on the roof.'

There are, however, serious problems attaching to this analysis. First, the analysis makes wrong predictions for examples like (2.187).

(2.187) (a) (Chinese)
        Xiaoming₁ shuo Xiaohua₂ zhidao ziji₁/₂ zui   xihuan gudian   yinyue.
        Xiaoming say   Xiaohua know   self   most like   classical music
        'Xiaoming says that Xiaohua knows that self likes classical music most.'
    (b) (Korean, Kim 1993)
        John₁-un Mary₂-ka   caki₁/₂-ka chencay-la-ko
        John-TOP Mary-NOM self-NOM genius-is-that
        malhankes-ul kiekhanta.
        said-ACC   remembers
        'John remembers that Mary said that self is a genius.'
    (c) (Tuki, Biloa 1991b)
        Mbara₁ a   b- ee   a   t-   idzima ngi omwamate₁ a
        Mbara SUBJ says that SUBJ NEG know   if   3SG self   SUBJ
        mu ongubi
        is thief
        'Mbara says that (he) does not know whether self is a thief.'

On this pronominal anaphor view, the long-distance reflexive in (2.187) would incorrectly be predicted to be bound in the intermediate clause. This is because given that the embedded clause is its pronominal binding domain and the intermediate clause is its anaphoric binding domain, the long-distance reflexive has to be free in the embedded clause but bound in the intermediate clause.

Secondly, on the assumption that a pronominal anaphor can occur only in positions in which the two binding domains are distinct, a long-distance reflexive in examples such as (2.188) cannot be specified as a pronominal anaphor, since the position in which it occurs is one that has the embedded clause as both its anaphoric and pronominal binding domain.[49]

(2.188) (a) (Icelandic, Sigurðsson 1990a)
  Jón$_1$ segir að María elski sig$_1$/hann$_1$.
  John says that Mary love self/him
  'John says that Mary loves self/him.'
 (b) (Norwegian, Hestvik 1992)
  John$_1$ bad Marit kikke bak seg$_1$/ham$_1$.
  John asked Mary to-look behind self/him
  'John asked Mary to look behind self/him.'
 (c) (Malay, Ngoh 1991)
  Timah$_1$ memberitahu Rohani$_2$ bahawa Ali$_3$ memandang rendah
  Timah tell   Rohani   that   Ali   think   low
  akan dirinya$_{1/3}$/kepadanya$_{1/2}$.
  of   self-3SG-POSS/of 3SG
  'Timah told Rohani that Ali looked down on self/her.'

Thirdly, as we have already seen in Section 2.3.1, a long-distance reflexive can even be left unbound within its matrix sentence. Given appropriate conditions, it can be Ā-bound by the topic of a topic-comment construction, as in (2.189), by the head of a relative clause, as in (2.190), and even by the topic of a previous discourse (2.191) or conversation (2.192).

(2.189) (Chinese, Huang 1994)
  Xiaoming$_1$ zuiba$_2$ guan   bu zhu ziji$_{1/*2}$.
  Xiaoming   mouth   control not RV self
  'Xiaoming, mouth cannot control self.'

---

[49] Along somewhat similar lines, Sportiche (1986) suggests that the overall system of overt anaphors and pronominals in Japanese be divided vertically (i.e. column by column) rather than horizontally (i.e. line by line) as in (i):
(i) Sportiche's system of overt anaphors and pronominals in Japanese

	C-command required	C-command not required
Locality condition	1	2
	Reflexives	
Antilocality condition	3	4
	Pronouns as variables	Referential pronouns

Sportiche further speculates that the Japanese reflexive *zibun* covers both slots 1 and 3, whereas the Japanese pronoun *kare* covers only slot 4. This has the consequence that *zibun* would be able to occur in the union of the domains sanctioned by binding conditions A and B, being either an anaphor or a pronominal. But such an analysis has no universal application. For example, it cannot carry over to anaphors and pronominals in Korean (Kang 1988), Chinese (Huang 1994), and some Dravidian languages like Marathi and Telugu (Wali and Subbarao 1991).

108 *Syntactic Approaches to Anaphora*

(2.190) (Tuki, Biloa 1991*b*; 851)
Mbara₁ a   mu   banam okutu   odzu omwamate₁ a   mu   dingam.
Mbara SUBJ FUT marry woman   who   3SG self   SUBJ FUT love
'Mbara will marry the woman that heself will love.'

(2.191) (Faroese, Thráinsson 1991: 58)
hann₁ vildi ikke leypa frá   sínari₁ ábyrgd,
he   would not run   from self's responsibility
tá   ið   hann₁ var komin soleiðis fyri við Sigrid.
now that he   was come   so   for with Sigrid
Hon hevði meiri krav   upp á   seg₁ enn hin.
she had   more demand up on self than the other
'He would not run from self's responsibility now that he had got into this situation with Sigrid. She had more right to self than the other (girl).'

(2.192) (Korean, Kang 1988)
A: ne   John₁ -eykeyse pillyeo-n   chayk-lul po-ass-ni?
    you John from   borrow-REL   book-ACC   see-PAST-INT
    John₁-i   kukes-lul chac-te-la?
    John-NOM   it-ACC   look for-RETRO-DECL
B: nay-ka imi   caki₁-uy   tongsaying-eykey tollyecwu-ass-e.
    I-NOM already   self-POSS   brother-DAT   return-PAST-DECL
A: 'Did you see the book which (I) borrowed from John?
    (I remember that) John was looking for it.
B: I have already returned it to self's brother.'

This turns out to be unexplained under the pronominal anaphor account: if a long-distance reflexive were a pronominal anaphor, it would be expected to be bound in the matrix sentence.

Long-distance reflexive as an anaphor of a special kind
Next, there is the third generative option: appealing to an analysis by Iatridou (1986) of *o idhios* in Modern Greek, a long-distance reflexive has been analysed as an anaphor of a special kind.

Iatridou observes that anaphors and pronominals in Modern Greek do not fit in with the standard binding theory. On the basis of this observation, she proposes that binding theory be readjusted with respect to Modern Greek. Specifically, she suggests that (2.193) be added.

(2.193) Iatridou's setting for binding parameters in Modern Greek

	Narrow domain	Wide domain
Free	Pronouns (condition B)	R-expressions (condition C)
Bound	*ton eafton tou* (condition A)	*o idhios* (condition D)

Logically, Iatridou's proposal seems quite plausible, since the standard binding theory exhibits an asymmetry; it specifies two alternatives for binding within a narrow domain but only one alternative for binding within a wide domain. Furthermore, Iatridou claims that a wide domain anaphor should be regulated by a newly postulated binding condition D or something of the kind (cf. Wali 1979, Koster 1984b, Wang and Stillings 1984, Everaert 1991, Thráinsson 1991, Branco and Marrafa 1999).

(2.194) Iatridou's binding condition D
A wide domain anaphor is bound in its matrix sentence, but free in its GC.

This analysis receives some support especially from the distribution of a class of anti-local, long-distance reflexive (i.e. reflexives which resist binding by a local antecedent) such as *appan* in Marathi, and *taan* in Dravidian languages including Kannada, Malayalam, and Telugu (Wali and Subbarao 1991) (see also Raina 1991 on Kashmiri, Yadava 1998 on Maithili, and Gair and Karunatillake 1998 on Sinhala). Illustrative examples are given below.

(2.195) (a) (Marathi, Wali and Subbarao 1991)
Lili₁ aaplyaa*₁/₂-laa hasli   asa kaḷtaac Ravi₂-ni   ti-čaa-ši
Lili self-to   laughed that know Ravi-ERG her-with
bolna soḍla.
talking stopped
'As soon as Ravi came to know that Lili laughed at self, he stopped talking with her.'
(b) (Kannada, Lidz 1995)
raamu₁ shyaamu₂ tann-annu₁/*₂ priitis-utt-anne   anta
Raamu Shyamu self-ACC   love-PRES-3SG-M that
namb-utt-aane.
believe-PRES-3SG-M
'Raamu believes that Shyamu loves self.'
(c) (Malayalam, Yang 1983)
Moohan₁ tanne*₁/₂/₃ nuḷḷi   ennə amma₂ acchanooṭə
Mohan self   pinched that mother father
parañ̃nu ennə raajaawinə₃ toonni.
said   that king   felt
'The king felt that the mother told the father that Mohan pinched self.'
(d) (Telugu, Wali and Subbarao 1991)
Kamala₁ tana*₁/₂ gurinci ceḍḍagaa maaṭlaaḍindi ani   teliseeka
Kamala self   about   badly   talked   COMP know-after
Ravi₂ aame-to maaṭlaaḍaḍam maaneeseeḍu.
Ravi her with talking   stopped
'As soon as Ravi came to know that Kamala talked badly about self, he stopped talking to her.'

In each of the above sentences the long-distance reflexive in question cannot be bound in its local domain (hence anti-local) but can be bound in its matrix sentence (hence a wide domain anaphor in the sense of Iatridou).

However, when this analysis is applied to a wider range of data, it cannot be maintained. The central distribution predicted by binding condition D is falsified in both directions by such long-distance reflexives as *ziji* in Chinese, *zibun* in Japanese, and *caki* in Korean. On the one hand, these long-distance reflexives allow local binding; in other words, they may be bound in their GC. On the other hand, they may be bound by a topic in the previous discourse; that is to say, they need not necessarily be bound in their matrix sentence. There is thus clear evidence that to treat a long-distance reflexive uniformly as a special kind of anaphor has no universal application.

Modification of binding theory

We move next to the second generative strategy, namely, to treat a long-distance reflexive as an anaphor and to readjust the standard architecture of binding theory so that a long-distance reflexive can be accommodated by binding condition A. Under this strategy, three major types of proposal have presented themselves: (i) to amend the notion of local domain; (ii) to postulate movement at LF; and (iii) to relativize SUBJECTs or antecedents for long-distance reflexives. In addition, there is a fourth generative analysis, which handles long-distance reflexivization in terms of the principles of Optimality theory.[50]

Abandonment, expansion, and parameterization of local domain

Abandonment of local domain. A first line of approach is to redefine the local domain for a long-distance reflexive, with minimal changes in the standard binding theory. One proposal has simply been to argue that there is no GC or CFC for a long-distance reflexive (e.g. Yang 1983, Giorgi 1984). Consequently, the locality condition required by binding condition A is not applicable. Looked at from a generative perspective, this line of analysis, however, is very undesirable: it would amount to admitting that there is no structurally definable domain for the long-distance binding of reflexives.

Expansion of local domain. An alternative is to expand the local domain for a long-distance reflexive. This is the approach taken by e.g. C.-T. J. Huang (1983), Wang and Stillings (1984), Anderson (1986), and Battistella and Xu (1990). As already mentioned above in Section 2.1.2. and this section, the

---

[50] There is, of course, a fifth influential generative approach, namely to recast binding theory in terms of a theory of reflexivity marking (Reinhart and Reuland 1993). Given that marking of reflexivity is essentially a semantically oriented theory, I shall postpone discussion of it until Chapter 3.

A further line of approach involves the *ad hoc* supplementation of language-specific devices. Tang (1989), for example, suggests that binding condition A be supplemented with a feature-copying rule and a reindexing rule to account for long-distance reflexivization in Chinese. Her analysis is essentially one involving cyclic reindexing rather than movement. For further discussion of this approach, see Huang (1994). See also Hukari (1989) for a GPSG analysis of reflexivization in English.

definition of GC can be modified to the effect that the presence of an accessible SUBJECT is relevant to an anaphor but irrelevant to a pronominal. This has the consequence that the GC for anaphors may be larger than the GC for pronominals. The widening of local domain certainly has empirical benefits. By way of illustration, consider (2.186) discussed above. Given the condition of SUBJECT accessibility, the GC for the long-distance reflexive in (2.186) is not the embedded clause but the matrix sentence, hence the possibility of binding of the long-distance reflexive in the matrix sentence.

There are, however, considerable problems at the very core of this analysis. Consider, for example, (2.187) above. Now, by the same analysis, only the intermediate subject would be permitted to be the binder for the long-distance reflexive in these examples. But this is empirically incorrect. As the indexing indicates, it is possible, and in fact preferable, for the long-distance reflexive to be bound to the root subject outside its GC in these sentences. What, then, could a proponent of this line of analysis possibly do to tackle counter-examples of this kind? Of course, he or she could expand the local domain again. Wang and Stillings (1984), for example, argue that the local domain for the Chinese long-distance reflexive *ziji* should consist of the root GC, i.e. the entire root sentence. However, such a move would encounter serious difficulties. One such difficulty is that the notion of root GC would allow equal binding to any subject (in an appropriately defined command relation) in the root sentence (note that in this case, subject orientation needs to be independently stipulated), and consequently it could not accommodate the maximality effect. As a way to account for this effect, Battistella and Xu (1990) stipulate that the local domain for the Chinese *ziji* should be the narrow GC and the root GC but nothing in between. But this move is quite counter-productive: it incorrectly rules out the possibility that the intermediate subjects in principle can also be a binder (though a dispreferred one).

Secondly, as we have already seen, the local domain for a long-distance reflexive may not be limited to the root GC. A long-distance reflexive can be $\bar{A}$-bound by the topic of a topic-comment construction, as in (2.189), by the head of a relative clause, as in (2.190), and by a long-distance antecedent from the previous discourse, as in (2.191) and (2.192). But from a generative point of view, the expansion of local domain perhaps has to stop at the level of root sentence.

Thirdly, the expansion of GC has the unwanted consequence that a principled way for defining GC is lost. The paradox seems to be that in some cases, the most deeply embedded clause remains the GC, whereas in others, the intermediate clause or even the root clause becomes the GC.

Finally, given that GC is enlarged, there will be more than one potential antecedent for a reflexive in it. The problem that arises next will be the question of selecting one out of a number of potential antecedents for it within its GC. This, of course, may not in itself present a problem for binding condition A or any extension of such a syntactic binding principle, since it is not designed to deal with a problem of this kind. Nevertheless, the fact that the selection issue does not fall within the scope of core grammar shows that a syntactic theory *per se* (even if successful) is not in itself adequate to long-distance reflexivization, since it leaves one of the central issues untackled.

Parameterization of local domain. A third move has been to redefine the local domain in a more radical way. Manzini and Wexler (Manzini and Wexler 1987, Wexler and Manzini 1987), for example, suggest parameterizing GC by way of a subset principle, the values of which yield set-theoretically nested languages. More specifically, they define GC in terms of a set of five parametric values, as in (2.196):

(2.196) Manzini and Wexler's governing category parameter (GCP)
γ is a GC for α if and only if γ is the minimal category that contains α and a governor for α and
(*a*) can have a subject or, for α anaphoric, has a subject β, β≠α; or
(*b*) has an Infl; or
(*c*) has a Tense; or
(*d*) has a 'referential' Tense; or
(*e*) has a 'root' Tense;
if, for α anaphoric, the subject β', β≠α, of γ, and of every category dominating α and not γ, is accessible to α

Now, it is claimed that a language can choose among these parametric options for its GC. Thus, the GC for *himself*, *each other*, and *he* in English is determined by value (*a*); that for *sè* in Italian, by value (*b*); that for *hann* in Icelandic, by value (*c*); that for *sig* in Icelandic, by value (*d*); and that for *ziji* in Chinese, *zibun* in Japanese, and *caki* in Korean, by value (*e*). Note that what is crucial here is the claim made by Manzini and Wexler that these parametric values are associated not with particular languages but with particular lexical items in a language. This they call the lexical parameterization hypothesis. Furthermore, both the values (i.e. (*a*), ... , (*e*)) and the languages associated with them (i.e. L(*a*), ... , L(*e*)) are said to be in a strictly nested subset relation. Thus for anaphors, (*a*) is the most restrictive and (*e*), the least restrictive, value; and L(*a*) is properly contained in, say, L(*e*). For pronominals, the reverse holds. This can be represented as follows.

(2.197) (*a*) For anaphors
L(*a*)⊂ L(*b*)⊂L(*c*)⊂L(*d*)⊂L(*e*)

(a) For pronominals
L(e)⊂L(d)⊂ L(c)⊂L(b)⊂L(a)

Manzini and Wexler's parametric variation of GC has a number of conceptual problems. First, given the lexical parameterization hypothesis, the domain property of an anaphoric expression is simply part of the lexical property of that expression. Consequently, the definition of GC has to be parameterized not only for reflexives in different languages, but also for anaphors and pronominals, different types of anaphor (reflexives and reciprocals), and even different forms of reflexive, in a given language. Thus, according to Manzini and Wexler, the GCs for the morphologically complex reflexive *sjálfan sig*, the morphologically simplex reflexive *sig*, the pronoun *hann*, and the reciprocal *hvor annar* in Icelandic are distinct: the GC for *sjálfan sig* is associated with value (*a*); that for *sig*, with value (*d*); that for *hann*, with value (*c*); and that for *hvor annar*, with value (*a*). The same is also true of, say, Japanese and Italian. In Japanese, while the reflexive *zibun* assumes value (*e*), the pronoun *kare* and the reciprocal *otagai* obey value (*a*). Finally, in Italian, while the reflexive *se stesso* (together with the pronoun *lui* and the reciprocal *l'un laltro*) falls under value (*a*), the reflexive *sè* is subject to value (*b*). This would raise a number of conceptual problems for the principles-and-parameters approach. One such problem, noted by Kang (1988) in connection with the Korean reflexive *caki* and reciprocal *sero*, is the question of why reflexives and reciprocals and even different forms of reflexive need different GCs. Clearly, as Kang rightly points out, the original conceptual grounds for separating the GCs for anaphors from the GCs for pronominals do not hold here: unlike pronominals, anaphors by definition are in need of an antecedent. If this is the case, then to stipulate a GC for a particular anaphor or pronominal in a given language would be a significant departure from the standard position taken in generative grammar with respect to parameter setting, namely a principle or a concept that is defined by the general theory of UG can allow only a small range of parametric options, among which individual languages may choose. The kind of parameterization we have seen here would in effect render the definition of GC vacuous as a concept of UG.

A second, somewhat related, problem concerns what Safir (1987) calls the atomization problem. This problem arises from the fact that Manzini and Wexler have to posit different parameters to account for different aspects of long-distance reflexivization, and these parameters cannot be linked. For example, the analysis makes no prediction about the fact that a long-distance reflexive tends to be morphologically simplex. Nor does the GCP say anything about subject orientation. In fact, to capture subject orientation, Manzini and Wexler have to set up a separate parameter, called the proper antecedent parameter.

(2.198) Manzini and Wexler's proper antecedent parameter (PAP)
A proper antecedent for α is
(a) a subset β; or
(b) any element β.

The main problem here, as Hermon (1992) notes, is that there is no way to draw the connection between the GCP and the PAP. Worse still, the values of the two parameters are even in conflict with each other. For example, *ziji* in Chinese, *zibun* in Japanese and *caki* in Korean correspond to value (e) of the GCP, but are subject to value (a) of the PAP. In other words, if the two parameters are made into a single parameter, the new parameter will violate the subset condition; it will yield languages which do not stand in a subset relation to each other. More or less the same can be said of the blocking effect observed in Chinese-type languages, as shown by examples such as (2.175) above. Given the GCP, both subjects are accessible to the reflexive, yet only the local subject can bind it. If the GC is the root sentence, then why can the reflexive not be bound to the root subject? Of course, Manzini and Wexler can posit another independent parameter, say, the blocking effect parameter. But once again the problem is that there is no way to link it and the other two parameters. Put another way, the parameters have to be stipulated as primitives of UG. Such an approach clearly lacks deductive depth and is in direct contradiction to the spirit of the principles-and-parameters framework (see also Cole and Sung 1994).

Finally, it is interesting to note that given the GCP, the GCs for pronominals are predicted to be distinct as well. But this prediction in general is not borne out. As pointed out by Kapur et al. (1993), Reinhart and Reuland (1993), and others, cross-linguistically the GC for pronominals seems to remain relatively constant. In other words, the domains in which a pronominal must be free are much more restricted than those in which an anaphor can be bound. The former does not seem to vary greatly from one language to another, even with long-distance reflexivization languages.

To sum up, given the arrays of data we have considered so far, the domain in which a long-distance reflexive can be anteceded is not restricted to the root sentence. There is thus clear evidence that for part of the environment in which a long-distance reflexive can occur, there is no structurally delimited domain. This would make any attempt to expand and parameterize the syntactically definable binding domain a very dubious enterprise. It would force, and indeed has forced, a generative theorist to posit three different binding domains for a reflexive: a local domain, characterized by the minimal (accessible) subject (i.e. the specified subject condition); a medium-distance domain, characterized by the minimal finite Infl (i.e. the tensed S condition); and a long-distance domain (e.g. Reuland and Koster 1991, Reinhart and Reuland 1991). But a move of this kind is both conceptually and empirically undesirable.

Postulation of movement at LF
The second line of approach under the modification-of-binding-theory strategy can be found in Lebeaux (1983), Pica (1984, 1986), Chomsky (1986*a*), Battistella (1989), Cole, Hermon, and Sung (1990), Huang and Tang (1991), Katada (1991), Reinhart and Reuland (1991), Cole and Sung (1994), and Cole and Wang (1996) (see also Harbert 1995). The basic idea of this approach is to retain somewhat the standard version of binding condition A by proposing LF-movement for reflexives, both long- and short-distance, thus attempting to reduce long-distance reflexivization to 'a sequence of local dependencies' (Cole, Hermon, and Sung 1990). This is, of course, partly reminiscent of various successive-cyclic chain analyses, whether in terms of government-chains (e.g. Everaert 1986, Koster 1987, Benedicto 1991) or Infl-chains (e.g. Steenbergen 1991) or reindexing chains (e.g. Tang 1989). In general, there are two types of LF-movement: (i) a local reflexive is adjoined to a position (such as VP) c-commanded by either a subject or an object, and (ii) a long-distance reflexive is raised to a position (such as Infl) c-commanded only by a subject. In what follows, I shall concentrate on the head movement analysis developed by Cole and his associates (Cole, Hermon, and Sung 1990, Cole and Sung 1994, Cole and Wang 1996), which is representative of this approach.

Following work by Lebeaux (1983), Pica (1984, 1986), Chomsky (1986*a*), and especially Battistella (1989) and drawing largely on selected data from Chinese, Cole, Hermon, and Sung suggest that long-distance reflexivization be analysed in terms of successive-cyclic head-to-head movement from Infl to Infl at LF within Chomsky's (1986*b*) *Barriers* framework. According to this account, a morphologically simplex reflexive (being an $X°$ category) can move into another $X°$ position (such as Infl) by adjunction. In contrast, a morphologically complex reflexive (being an X^{max} category) has to adjoin to another X^{max} position. The movement of both types of reflexive obeys the standard conditions on movement and the binding theory. This can be illustrated by a consideration of (2.199).

(2.199) (Chinese, Huang 1994: 102)
Wang Xiansheng$_1$ yiwei Li Xiansheng$_2$ huaiyi Xu Xiaojie$_3$
Wang Mr   think Li Mr   suspect Xu Miss
kanbuqi   ziji$_{1/2/3}$.
look down upon self
'Mr Wang thinks that Mr Li suspects that Miss Xu looks down upon self.'

The LF structure of (2.199) is given in (2.200).
In (2.200), the reflexive moves from its base-generated object position of IP$_3$ first to V$_3$ and then to I$_3$ (more accurately, adjoined to I$_3$). No barrier is crossed, because VP$_3$ is L-marked by I$_3$ due to the adjunction of the reflexive to I$_3$. This has the consequence that t′ is antecedent-governed by t″. The

116 *Syntactic Approaches to Anaphora*

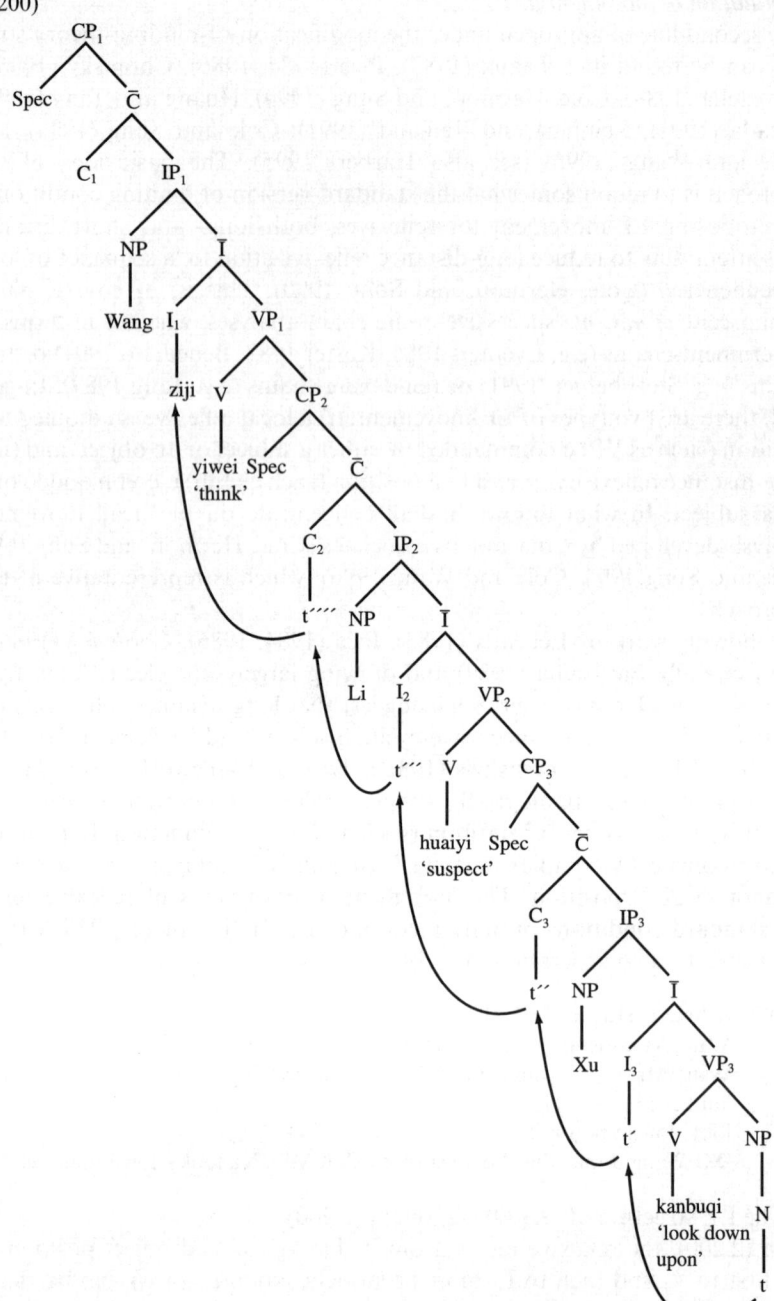

(2.200)

```
                    CP₁
                   /  \
                Spec   C̄
                      /  \
                    C₁    IP₁
                         /  \
                        NP   Ī
                        |   / \
                      Wang I₁  VP₁
                           |   / \
                         ziji V   CP₂
                              |   / \
                           yiwei Spec C̄
                           'think'    / \
                                    C₂  IP₂
                                    |   / \
                                    t''''' NP  Ī
                                           |  / \
                                           Li I₂ VP₂
                                              |  / \
                                             t'''' V  CP₃
                                                   |  / \
                                               huaiyi Spec C̄
                                               'suspect'   / \
                                                         C₃  IP₃
                                                         |   / \
                                                         t''  NP  Ī
                                                             |  / \
                                                             Xu I₃ VP₃
                                                                |  / \
                                                                t'  V   NP
                                                                    |    |
                                                              kanbuqi   N
                                                              'look down |
                                                              upon'      t
```

reflexive moves next from I_3 to C_3. Since IP is by definition not a barrier (though it is a blocking category), the movement does not pose any problem. Next, the reflexive moves from C_3 first to V_2 and then to I_2. Since both CP_3 and VP_2 are L-marked, no barrier will intervene between C_3 and I_2, either. In the same way, movement of the reflexive can continue first from I_2 to C_2, then from C_2 to V_1, and finally from V_1 to I_1.[51]

The principal advantage of this analysis is (claimed to be) that it provides a principled way to draw the connection between the three crucial properties of long-distance reflexivization that have commonly been assumed in generative analyses: (i) long-distance binding, (ii) morphological simplicity, and (iii) subject orientation. Since only $X°$ elements can undergo head-to-head movement, only morphologically simplex reflexives can participate in long-distance reflexivization; since long-distance reflexives are raised to Infl c-commanded only by subjects, given binding condition A they can only be bound by subjects. Furthermore, the analysis, in conjunction with an independently stipulated feature percolation principle (FPP) (to be elucidated below), is said to give a natural explanation for the blocking effect exhibited in languages such as Chinese and Korean.

This is an interesting analysis, but as I pointed out in Huang (1989, 1994, 1996a), it is both empirically inadequate and conceptually problematic. From an empirical point of view, the correlation between locality and $X°$-X^{max} status of reflexives is at best a tendency cross-linguistically. This can be evidenced by the fact that the prediction that morphologically simplex reflexives can be long-distance bound, whereas morphologically complex reflexives cannot, is falsified in both directions. On the one hand, a morphologically simplex reflexive may have to be locally bound, as in (2.201); and on the other, a morphologically complex reflexive can and in some cases even must show long-distance effects, as in (2.169) and (2.170) above.

(2.201) (Togo Kã, Culy, Kodio and Togo 1994: 332)
Omar₁ Anda₂ sã·₁/₂ peju ɛwɛ ĩ wɔ.
Omar Anda self sheep bought know AUX
'Omar knows that Anda bought self's sheep.'

Secondly, there is not a direct correlation between the domain properties

---

[51] The following definitions are given in Chomsky (1986b: 14–15).
(i) Barrier
  γ is a barrier for β if and only if (a) or (b):
  (a) γ immediately dominates δ, δ a blocking category for β;
  (b) γ is a blocking category for β, γ ≠ IP.
(ii) Blocking category
  γ is a blocking category for β if and only if γ is not L-marked and γ dominates β.
(iii) L-marking
  α L-marks β if and only if α is a lexical category that θ-governs β.

and the antecedent properties of reflexives, either. This can be shown by the fact that the prediction that long-distance reflexives are subject-oriented, whereas local ones are not, is also falsified in both directions. On the one hand, a long-distance reflexive can be bound by a non-subject, as in (2.166)–(2.168) above; on the other, a local reflexive may be bound only by a subject, as in (2.202) below.[52]

(2.202) (a) (Inuit, Bittner 1994: 146)
Juuna$_1$-p   Kaali$_2$ immi$_1$-nik uqaluttuup-p-a-a.
Juuna-ERG Kaali self-INS tell-IND-3SG-3SG
'Juuna told Kaali about self.'
(b) (Marathi, Wali and Subbarao 1991)
Lili-ni$_1$ Sŭsi-laa$_2$ swataah-baddal$_{1/*2}$ kaahihi   saangitla naahi.
Lili-ERG Susi-to self-about   anything told   not
'Lili didn't tell Susi anything about self.'
(c) (Lango, Foley and Van Valin 1984: 163)
Lócà$_1$ ò-kwá-ò   dákó$_2$ pìr-έ   kὲnὲ$_{1/*2}$.
man 3SG-A-ask-3SG-U woman about-3SG self
'The man asked the woman about self.'
(d) (Russian, Progovac 1993:762)
Milicioner$_1$ rassprašival arestovannogo$_2$ o   sebe$_{1/*2}$.
policeman questioned suspect   about self
'The policeman questioned the suspect about self.'
(e) (Tɔrɔ Sɔ, Culy, Kodio, and Togo 1994: 329)
Anta$_1$ Omar$_2$ nɛ   sɔ   unɔ$_{1/*2}$ mɔ   sɔaa   be.
Anta Omar OBJ word REFL POSS talked PAST
'Anta talked to Omar about self.'

Note that the examples in (2.166) earlier in this section are so-called psych-sentences. Various solutions have been put forward in the generative literature to explain the 'special' behaviour of these sentences. One such account is to analyse the experiencer in psych-sentences as a covert subject (e.g. Pesetsky 1987, Belletti and Rizzi 1988, but see Cançado 1999, Kuno and Takami 1993 for a critique). But non-subject binding of a long-distance reflexive is not restricted to psych-sentences, and it is difficult to see how the solutions proposed for psych-sentences (even if successful) can be applied

---

[52] Of some interest here is Czech, as described in Toman (1991). Czech has both argumental and possessive/adjective reflexives, and argumental reflexives have both a strong and a weak form. The important point Toman makes is that Czech reflexives are all subject-oriented, even when they are locally bound—a fact that is inconsistent with the generative assumption that the domain properties and the antecedent properties of reflexives are implicationally related. More or less the same can be said of the Malayalam reflexive *swa*. *Swa* can be used both locally and long-distance, depending on its position: and yet it is always subject-oriented (Mohanan 1982). A further class of counter-example to this assumption involves morphologically complex reflexives of the form 'self + self'. As pointed out by e.g. Katada (1991), this type of reflexives is normally local (cf. examples in (2.169d)) but is subject-oriented.

to examples such as (2.167) and (2.168) to analyse them as obeying subject orientation.

Thirdly, the blocking effect does not follow from the head movement analysis. On the head movement analysis, whether or not long-distance reflexives in a language exhibit blocking effects depends on whether or not Infl in that language contains φ-, especially person features. For example, as Chinese has no base-generated φ-features in Infl, by the FPP in (2.203), the features of a reflexive can percolate up to its mother node, i.e. I. This has the consequence that if there is a conflict of features between I and its Spec-of-IP, the blocking effect will arise. By contrast, Italian has fully specified φ-features, so given the FPP the features of a reflexive cannot pass up to I. As a result, the features of a reflexive do not play a role, therefore Italian does not exhibit the blocking effect.

(2.203) The FPP
    (a) The features of the mother node and the features of the daughter nodes will be identical.
    (b) If the features of the daughter nodes conflict, the mother node will havethe features of the head node.

There are, however, serious problems at the very heart of this analysis. Note that the FPP is in part motivated by the relaxation of c-command in configurations known as subcommand, where the subject antecedent is contained in a c-commanding NP which itself is not an antecedent due to inanimacy (e.g. Tang 1989). Tang's subcommand condition is presented in (2.204) and its effect is illustrated in (2.205).

(2.204) The subcommand condition
    β subcommands α if and only if β is contained in an NP that c-commands α or that subcommands α, and any argument containing β is in subject position.

(2.205) (a) (Chinese)
    Xiaoming$_1$ de   taidu   shi ziji$_1$ jue   bu ren   cuo.
    Xiaoming POSS attitude be self EMPH not admit mistake
    'Xiaoming's attitude is that self will never admit any mistake.'
    (b) (Hindu/Urdu, Davison 1997)
    raam$_1$-kee man/dil-meeN apnee$_1$ pitaa-see   ghriNa thii.
    Ram-of   mind/heart-in self's   father-from hatred was
    'Ram's heart was in hatred of self's father.'
    (c) (Icelandic, Maling 1984: 222)
    Skoðun Siggu$_1$ er að   sig$_1$ vanti hæfileika.
    opinion Sigga's is that self lacks talent
    'Sigga's opinion is that self lacks talent.'
    (d) (Korean, Yoon 1989)
    caki$_1$-ka   i   seysang-ese ceyil   yeppu-ke toy-nun-kes-i
    self-NOM this world-in   the most pretty   become-COMP-NOM

Mary₁-uy kkwum-i-tyo-ess-ta.
Mary-GEN dream-NOM-become-PAST-DECL
'It became Mary's dream that self becomes the prettiest in the world.'

But, as I pointed out in Huang (1989, 1991a, 1994, 1996a), the FPP is rather problematic. Consider, for example, (2.206).

(2.206) (Chinese)
Xiaoming₁ de   mao₂ ba ziji₁>₂ xia   le   yi tiao.
Xiaoming POSS cat BA self frighten PFV one CL
'Xiaoming's cat has frightened self.'

In (2.206), the head noun *mao* 'cat' is animate, therefore it is able to antecede the reflexive. Consequently, by the FPP *Xiaoming* cannot be the antecedent. This is because when the features of the daughter nodes are in conflict, the features of the head node *mao* can be percolated up to the mother node, i.e. *Xiaoming de mao* 'Xiaoming's cat'. It follows therefore that only *Xiaoming de mao* but not *Xiaoming* can bind the reflexive. But this is contrary to fact; *Xiaoming* is in fact the preferred antecedent. The key point to note here is that *Xiaoming* is more animate than *mao*. There is thus evidence to suggest that in examples of this kind the choice of antecedent is also affected by a semantically oriented animacy hierarchy.

What is perhaps more interesting is that the FPP has to be further relaxed to allow pragmatic factors as well. For example, while it correctly accounts for (2.207), it makes the wrong prediction for (2.208).

(2.207) (Chinese, Tang 1989)
[[[Zhangsan₁ de]   baba₂ de]   qian]₃ bei   ziji₂ de
   Zhangsan POSS father POSS money PASS self POSS
pengyou tou zou le.
friend   steal RV PFV
'Zhang's father's money was stolen by self's friend.'

(2.208) (Chinese, Huang 1994)
[[[Xiaoming₁ (de)] fuqin₂ de]   turan   qushi]₃ dui
   Xiaoming POSS father POSS sudden death to
ziji daji   hen zhong.
self strike a blow very heavily
'Xiaoming's father's sudden death struck a heavy blow on self.'

In (2.208), the head noun is not a potential antecedent, because it is inanimate. Consequently, no value of the features of this noun is passed up to its mother node NP₃. Instead, according to the FPP the features of *fuqin* 'father' is percolated up the tree, thus rendering NP₂ as the antecedent for the reflexive. However, given world knowledge, NP₂ cannot be the antecedent. It should be clear from the foregoing that while the FPP are syntactic in nature, the conditions under which the c-command condition is relaxed and the FPP is activated is semantic (e.g. animacy) and/or pragmatic (e.g. world knowledge) in nature. Once again, then, evidence for my argument that in imposing configurational restrictions on possible antecedents for a reflexive syntax has to interact with semantics/pragmatics.[53]

Returning to the blocking effect for long-distance reflexives, it is not difficult to see that the FPP again runs into trouble. Consider first (2.209), also from Chinese.

(2.209) Xiaolan$_1$ zhidao tamen$_2$ kanbuqi ziji$_{1/2}$.
Xiaolan know 3PL look down upon self
'Xiaolan knows that they look down upon self.'

One would expect, in accord with the FPP, that the long-distance binding of the reflexive in (2.209) be blocked, for the local and long-distance antecedents do not agree in number. But the long-distance binding of the reflexive is licit here. One solution might simply be to say that number is not an agreement feature in Chinese (e.g. Battistella 1989, Cole, Hermon, and Sung 1990, Cole and Sung 1994). However, this would leave Chinese examples such as (2.210) to be explained, where the mismatch of number between the local and the remote subjects is responsible for the blocking of long-distance reflexivization.

(2.210) Tamen$_1$ zhidao Xiaolan$_2$ kanbuqi ziji$_{*1/2}$.
3PL know Xiaolan look down upon self
'They know that Xiaolan looks down upon self.'

Worse still, occasionally the person feature may also be irrelevant, as in the Chinese sentence (2.211).

(2.211) Xiaozhang$_1$ qing wo$_2$ zuo zai ziji$_{1/*2}$ de shenbian.
principal ask 1SG sit at self GEN side
'The principal asks me to sit beside self.'

Then there is a further, perhaps more troublesome problem: the analysis makes wrong predictions for Japanese. Infl in Japanese, like that in Chinese, does not manifest φ-, especially person features, yet unlike Chinese, Japanese exhibits no blocking effect. This is illustrated in (2.212).[54]

(2.212) (Japanese, Aikawa 1993)
John$_1$-ga watasi$_2$-ga minna-ni Bill$_3$-ga zibun$_{1/2/3}$-o
John-NOM I-NOM everyone-DAT Bill-NOM self-ACC

[53] But the following may be a counter-example to both c-command and sub-command.
(i) (Kobon, Davies 1989)
Kulua$_1$ kain ñi nipe ke$_1$ al-öp.
Kulua dog boy POSS-3SG self shoot-PERF-3SG
'Kulua's son shot self's dog.'

[54] Mainland Scandinavian languages (i.e. Danish, Norwegian, and Swedish) may pose the same problem, given that Infl in these languages may be argued to be devoid of φ-features.

                    hihansita   koto-o   hanasita to   omotte-iru.
                    criticize the fact that-ACC told   that think
                    'John thinks that I told everyone the fact that Bill criticizes self.'

However, Japanese exhibits blocking effects of a different kind—so-called honorific blocking effects (Aikawa 1993). In this language, when the referent of the subject of a sentence is considered socially superior or psychologically distant from the speaker, the predicate can optionally be morphologically marked with a subject honorific suffix. The presence of such a subject, if assigning subject honorification to a predicate (through spec-head agreement), can block the long-distance binding of a reflexive, as in (2.213).

(2.213) (Japanese, Aikawa 1993)
        Masao$_1$-ga   minna-ni   Tanaka-sensee$_2$-ga   zibun$_{*1/2}$-no
        Masao-NOM everyone-DAT Tanaka professor-NOM self-GEN
        kodomo-o o-sikari-ni   natta   koto-o   hanasita.
        child-ACC scolded-[+H] the fact that-ACC told
        'Masao told everyone the fact that Professor Tanaka scolded self's child.'

Two further points regarding the honorific blocking effects in Japanese are worth mentioning here. First, the honorific blocking effect can be induced only if subject honorification is assigned to a reflexive via a predicate, otherwise no such effect will arise. The second point to be noted is that the blockage of long-distance binding of a reflexive is also dependent on whether the first accessible subject triggers subject honorification. If it does, only subject NPs which bear the feature [+honorific] can be a potential antecedent for the reflexive; if it does not, any type of superordinate subject NP can be a potential binder. But what is of direct concern to us here is the fact, pointed out by Aikawa, that honorific blocking effects in Japanese are not solicited by a mismatch in person features between Infl and its Spec-of-IP, but are rather induced by the incompatibility in honorific features between a reflexive and its antecedent. However, it is not clear how this type of blocking effects can be accommodated by the head movement analysis.

Finally, long-distance binding of a reflexive can also be done out of a topic construction, as in (2.189), a relative clause as in (2.190) above, and an adjunct clause as in (2.214).

(2.214) (*a*) (Chechen-Ingush, Nichols 1983: 250)
            Ø$_1$ sie:na$_2$ iza älča iza$_2$ a:rave:lira.
            to:self this said he went out
            'When (someone) said this to self, he went out.'
        (*b*) (Dargi, Nichols 1983: 256)
            abadil$_1$ sinc"e yaj$_{2/3}$ ha'ib-mu:til gal$_2$ aqhic"ij.
            mother to self word said when boy got up
            'When (his) mother spoken to self, the boy got up.'

(c) (Inuit, Bittner 1994: 151)
Juuna₁ immi₂-nut saa-mm-at   Else₂-p   qiviar-p-a-a.
Juuna self-DAT turn-PAST-3SG Else-ERG look at-TNB-3SG-3SG
'When Juuna turned toward self, Else looked at him.'

This would raise considerable difficulties for the head movement analysis, because head-to-head movement is prohibited from crossing island barriers (e.g. Progovac 1993, Huang 1994, 1996a). As an attempt to overcome the problem, Cole and Sung (1994) speculate that head movement of an X° reflexive into Infl renders it lexical, thus L-marking and de-barrierising its CP. But such a move is not seriously entertainable. As pointed out by Progovac (1993), it predicts that adjuncts should be extractable from, say, a relative clause only if it contains a long-distance reflexive—a prediction that is not borne out.

(2.215) (Chinese)
*Xiaoming₁ bu xihuan nage weisheme piping ziji₁/₂ de laoshi₂.
Xiaoming   not like   that why   criticize self REL teacher
*'Xiaoming does not like the teacher who criticizes self why.'

Next, from a theoretical point of view, the head movement analysis leaves a number of important conceptual questions unanswered. Let me start with the question of how long-distance reflexives are licensed in a language. In Cole, Hermon, and Sung (1990), the answer is that long-distance reflexives can occur only in languages in which Infl is lexical. Consequently, VP and CP in these languages are L-marked and do not constitute a barrier for movement. Conceptually the assumption that Infl in languages like Chinese, Japanese, and Korean is lexical is rather odd, given the absence of morphologically overt Agr in these languages (e.g. Aoun et al. 1987, Huang 1989, 1992a, 1992b, 1994, 1996a). Such an account is not empirically sound, either. On the one hand, as Cole, Hermon and Sung are aware, it says nothing about languages like Icelandic; on the other, it wrongly predicts that long-distance reflexivization is never possible in languages like English where Infl is assumed to be functional and hence VP is always a barrier. Though English is not a prototypical long-distance reflexivization language, it does allow long-distance binding of reflexives in restricted contexts (e.g. Kuno 1987, Zribi-Hertz 1989, Pollard and Sag 1992, Safir 1992). In Cole and Sung (1994), however, the assumption that Infl in languages like Chinese is lexical is discarded. Instead, it is claimed that Infl in these languages is functional and can become lexical as the result of the movement of a reflexive into it. There is an obvious weakness in an argument like this—the issue of circularity. What Cole and Sung are saying is that the movement of a reflexive into Infl makes it lexical, thus voiding its barrierhood for the movement of a reflexive. In other words, long-distance reflexivization licenses, and is licensed by, itself. Here Cole and Sung are simply assuming what is to be proven. Furthermore, what is perhaps more worrying is that, under this analysis, it is assumed that X° reflexives not only can, but must, move; and that once an X° reflexive moves, it cannot stop at intermediate positions like V or C, but must end its derivation adjoined to Infl. Clearly, both assumptions, which are crucial to the head movement analysis, need to be explained. The urgency of this need is particularly felt from a minimalist perspective. In the minimalist programme, movement is regarded as a last resort operation. It may take place only when it is triggered, that is, when it is required to escape ungrammaticality—a concept that is sometimes referred to as economy. Evidently, the head movement analysis of long-distance reflexivization is in contradiction to the spirit of economy which requires a movement to be blocked if it does not have to take place.[55]

Relativization of SUBJECTs
Progovac (1992, 1993) considers another syntactic approach to long-distance reflexivization. Rejecting the idea that long-distance reflexives undergo movement at LF, she suggests that SUBJECTs, that is, potential antecedents for reflexives, be relativized.

In accord with the now familiar generative tradition, Progovac also groups reflexives into two types: (i) morphologically simplex X° reflexives and (ii) morphologically complex X^{max} reflexives. In the light of $\bar{X}$ compatibility, she argues that reflexives and their antecedents must have the same $\bar{X}$ status.

---

[55] Also Huang and Tang (1991) and Katada (1991). In the case of Huang and Tang, long-distance reflexivization is analysed as being derived by successive-cyclic IP-adjunction at LF—an instance of A-movement rather than Infl-to-Infl movement. Next, on the basis of analysis of Japanese, Katada introduces a threefold typological classification of reflexives according to a two-way contrast relating to locality and subject orientation: (i) long-distance reflexives with subject orientation, (ii) local reflexives with subject orientation, and (iii) local reflexives with no particular orientation. This can be illustrated cross-linguistically in (i).

(i) Katada's typology of reflexives

	Subject orientation (long-distance)	Subject orientation (local)	No particular orientation (local)
Japanese	zibun	zibun zisin	kare zisin
Korean	caki	caki casin	ku casin
Norwegian	seg	seg selv	ham selv
Dutch	zich	zich zelf	'mzelf
Italian	se	se stesso	lui stesso
Chinese	ziji		ta ziji
English			himself

She argues that this typology can be accounted for in terms of a three-way contrast regarding anaphor raising at LF: (i) long-distance raising, (ii) local raising, and (iii) no raising at all. She calls those anaphors that can raise 'operator anaphors', and those that cannot 'non-operator anaphors', and argues that the former undergo LF raising to an A-position whereas the latter do not. But this analysis is both theoretically and empirically problematic. From an empirical point of view, *ham selv* in Norwegian (Hellan 1988: 105, 130) and *hän itse* in Finnish (Steenbergen 1991: 237), for example, can only be bound by a non-subject in the local domain. For further discussion of both Huang and Tang (1991) and Katada (1991), see Huang (1994).

In particular, she proposes that X° reflexives can be bound only by X° antecedents, and X^{max} reflexives only by X^{max} antecedents. The relativized SUBJECT analysis can be captured in (2.216):

(2.216) Progovac's relativisation of SUBJECTs
    (a) If R is a X° reflexive, then its SUBJECTs are X° categories only, that is, Agr (as the only salient (c-commanding) head).
    (b) If R is a X^{max} reflexive, then its SUBJECTs are X^{max} specifiers, that is, [NP, IP] and [NP, NP].

What (2.216) says in essence is that X^{max} reflexives cannot be bound across specifiers, hence they are local. By contrast, X° reflexives can be bound across specifiers, though they cannot be bound across heads, because they always have to be bound to the first Agr. Therefore, whether or not X° reflexives in a language can be long-distance bound depends on which type of Agr that language has. On Progovac's account, there are two types of Agr, essentially following Borer (1989). The first type is anaphoric Agr which is morphologically null, and the second is referential Agr which is morphologically overt. Only anaphoric but not referential Agr can be linked to a higher Agr for its content, that is, to form an Agr chain. This Agr is then coindexed to its SUBJECT by transitivity. In other words, only when there is an anaphoric Agr chain can X° reflexives participate in long-distance reflexivization. Furthermore, the analysis predicts subject orientation for long-distance reflexivization in terms of $\bar{X}$ compatibility. Since X° reflexives must be bound by Agrs, by coindexation transitivity they must refer to subjects.

Clearly, since Progovac's account does not invoke movement at LF, some of the problems we have seen earlier which are specifically associated with the LF movement analysis can be avoided. This, however, does not mean that the relativized SUBJECT analysis is free from problems in itself. In the first place, contrary to the central claim of this analysis, there is no direct correlation between reflexives and their antecedents with respect to the $\bar{X}$ status. On the one hand, X° reflexives may have to be locally bound by X^{max} antecedents, as in (2.201); on the other, X^{max} reflexives may or even must be long-distance bound by X° antecedents, as in (2.169) and (2.170). Secondly, as in the case of most other generative analyses, Progovac's analysis also fails to allow non-subject binding of long-distance reflexivization, as in (2.166)–(2.168). Thirdly, the distribution of the class of anti-local reflexive in certain South Asian languages, as exemplified in (2.195) above, presents a particularly serious challenge to this analysis. Given that these long-distance reflexives do not allow local binding, hence cannot be bound by the local Agr, the question arises how they can be bound by the remote Agr, since the Agr chain is broken. Fourthly, note that one of the main appeals of this analysis is (claimed to be) that it provides a straightforward explanation for the blocking effect. Given that an anaphoric Agr chain can be formed if and only if all the

Agrs in it must share the same φ-features, it follows therefore that long-distance binding of reflexives cannot be done across Agrs which bear different φ-features, thus the blocking effect. But such an analysis cannot be right, because apart from the Chinese counter-examples such as (2.211), long-distance reflexivization in Japanese and Korean will also pose a serious problem here. This is because Agr in both Japanese and Korean is morphologically empty, hence has to be treated as anaphoric in Progovac's sense. But as (2.212) above shows, a mismatch of φ-features between Agrs in Japanese does not solicit the blocking effect—a contradiction to the prediction of the relativized SUBJECT analysis. Finally, Progovac's analysis is conceptually very unattractive from the point of view of the minimalist programme. Originally, the motivation behind the postulation of the analysis is in part to simplify binding theory by deriving certain aspects of it from $\bar{X}$ theory, perhaps a more primitive component of UG. But if $\bar{X}$ theory itself is taken to be superfluous and is to be eliminated as a fundamental module of UG in the minimalist programme, as advocated by Chomsky (1995), then the conceptual ground on which this analysis is built would collapse.

An Optimality-theoretical analysis
We come finally to an Optimality-theoretical analysis of (long-distance) reflexives. In this analysis, Burzio (1998) put forwards four subhierarchies of soft constraints with a fixed ranking to account for the distribution of (long-distance) reflexives in a number of Germanic, Romance, and Slavonic languages. These subhierarchies are presented in (2.217).

(2.217) Burzio's subhierarchies
    (a) Referential economy
        Reflexives >> pronouns >> r-expressions
    (b) Optimal agreement
        *1/2 >> *3 >> *impersonal
    (c) Optimal antecedent
        Indicatives >> subjunctives >> infinitives >> small clauses >> NPs
    (d) *Morphological complexity
        *Full intensifiers >> *full >> *clitic >> *Ø

What (2.217a) basically says is that in a language or a subsystem within a language, for a bound NP, reflexives are more optimal than pronouns, which in turn are more optimal than r-expressions. This ranking yields an 'avoid pronoun' effect. The idea underlying (2.217b) is that there is an implicational universal for the person of the antecedent of a morphologically simplex reflexive, namely first and second person imply third person, and third person implies zero person (i.e. impersonal). Next, given (2.217c), it is predicted that if a language allows a long-distance reflexive into an subjective (over its subject), it will also allow it into infinitives, small clauses, and NPs (over their subject). In other words, the five types of complement ranked differently in

(2.217c) stand in an implicational relation (cf. (2.160) above). Combined together, (2.217b) and (2.217c) give rise to a counterbalancing effect of 'avoid reflexives'. This is because by (2.217b), when the person of the antecedent of a morphologically simplex reflexive is suboptimal, a pronoun rather than a reflexive will be chosen. The same is also true of (2.217c) when the intended antecedent is not optimal. Finally, the ranked constraints in (2.217d) give an account of the distribution of intensifiers and other anaphoric expressions in terms of their morphological structure. Roughly what it means is that one should try not to use a morphologically complex anaphoric expression if semantically possible, thus engendering an economy of structure effect Burzio calls 'avoid structure'. Note next that the optimization yielded by these subhierarchies can be divided into two types. First, there is what Wilson (1998) calls expressive optimization, which involves selecting the best syntactic structure consistent with a specific semantic interpretation. Expressive optimization is the result of an expressive competition—a competition among sentences that share an intended meaning, but differ with respect to how that meaning is syntactically expressed. The interface here is considered to be the locus of mapping from semantic to syntactic structures. The referential economy constraints (2.217a), for example, belongs to this type. The second type of optimalization is interpretative optimization. This type of optimization involves choosing the best semantic interpretation consistent with a fixed syntactic structure. Interpretative optimization results from an interpretative competition, that is, a competition among sentences that share a common syntactic structure, but differ with respect to the semantic interpretation of that structure. The direction of this interface is the other way round: the locus of mapping is from syntax to semantics. This type of optimization is exemplified by, say, the optimal agreement constraints (2.217b) (see Burzio 1998, Wilson 1998 for more detailed discussion). Furthermore, while the constraints within each subhierarchy have a fixed ranking across languages, the constraints of the four potentially conflicting subhierarchies can be interacted.

This is in my view the best analysis of long-distance reflexivization (and related phenomena) within the framework of generative grammar. It is both conceptually and empirically preferable to all the other generative accounts of long-distance reflexivization we have examined in this section. Conceptually, Burzio's Optimality-theoretic analysis allows a theory of long-distance reflexivization (and anaphora in general) to be built on a ranking of violable constraints whose interaction will yield the best choice from a set of competing candidate derivations. This is not entirely inconsistent with the spirit of the neo-Gricean pragmatic theory of anaphora I have been developing. In fact, some of the insights central to Burzio's analysis such as competition and hierarchy can independently be found in our pragmatic approach, as we will see in Chapter 4. Next, from an empirical perspective, many of the facts that

128   *Syntactic Approaches to Anaphora*

have proven very resistant to the various hard constraint-based generative analyses discussed above can now be brought within the scope of this soft constrain-based account. Consider first examples in (2.171) above. In these examples, there is a reflexive/pronoun complementarity, that is, while the reflexive is long-distance bound, the pronoun is long-distance free. Now, given the account being considered here, this 'avoid pronoun' effect follows straightforwardly from the working of the referential economy constraints (2.217a). The second case in point concerns those examples like (2.16) and (2.17), where pronouns instead of reflexives are used as locally bound anaphors. Once again, this falls neatly under Buzio's analysis, for the ranking of the optimal agreement constraints (2.217b) over the referential economy constraints (2.217a) ensures that a reflexive will be excluded but a pronoun will be allowed in these contexts, since the pronoun is the next optimal candidate. Finally, the contrast shown in the pair of the Italian sentences in (2.218) (Buzio 1998) also receives an elegant explanation from this Optimality theoretical analysis.

(2.218) (a) Gianni$_1$ Ø$_1$/*si$_1$ apre gli occhi.
            Gianni   to-self opens the eyes
            'Gianni opens self's eyes.'
        (b) Gianni$_1$ *Ø/si$_1$ taglia i   capelli.
            Gianni   to-self cuts   the hair
            'Gianni cuts self's hair.'

By the 'avoid structure' constraints (2.217d), it is predicted that the morphological structure employed in (2.218a) be lower on the subhierarchy than that used in (2.218b). This is because the semantics of the former is inherently reflexive but the semantics of the latter is inherently non-reflexive (about which, more in Chapters 3 and 4). Consequently, Ø is optimal in (2.218a) but *si* is optimal in (2.218b)—a prediction that is empirically borne out (see also Lidz 1996: 13–15, 43 on Kannada and Spanish). As we saw earlier, all these facts are beyond the reach of all the other generative analyses we have surveyed in this section.

There are problems with Buzio's analysis, however. Consider first (2.219).

(2.219) (Chinese)
        (a) Xiaoming$_1$ yiwei Xiaohua bu xihua ziji$_1$.
            Xiaoming think Xiaohua not like   self
            'Xiaoming thinks that Xiaohua does not like self.'
        (b) Xiaoming$_1$ yiwei Xiaohua bu xihua ta$_1$.
            Xiaoming think Xiaohua not like   3SG
            'Xiaoming thinks that Xiaohua does not like him.'

In (2.219), there is a systematic referential overlap between a reflexive and a pronoun. Given the referential economy constraints (2.217a), a reflexive is predicted to be preferred to a pronoun. Consequently, (2.219b) should be expected to lose the expressive competition to (2.219*a*). But this expectation is not fulfilled: (2.219*b*) is in fact the preferred structure. This problem does not seem to be solvable by ranking (2.217*b*) and (2.217*c*) higher than (2.217*a*). Equally problematic for the analysis are the examples of the following kind.

(2.220) (Japanese, adapted from Kato 1994: 19)
    (*a*) Pavarotti$_1$-ga   zibun$_1$-ga tensai da to   omotteiru.
        Pavarotti-SUBJ self-SUBJ genius is COMP think
        'Pavarotti thinks that self is a genius.'
    (*b*) Pavarotti$_1$-ga   zibun-zisin$_1$-ga tensai da to   omotteiru.
        Pavarotti-SUBJ self-self-SUBJ genius is COMP think
        'Pavarotti thinks that self self is a genius.'
    (*c*) Pavarotti$_1$-ga   kare-zisin$_1$-ga tensai da to   omotteiru.
        Pavarotti-SUBJ 3SG-self-SUBJ genius is COMP think
        'Pavarotti thinks that heself is a genius.'

In Wilson (1998), (2.217*a*) is recast as a constraint which forbids a coreferential argument to have φ-features. If this is correct, one would expect the Japanese reflexives in (2.220) to be ranked as *zibun* >> *zibun-zisin* >> *kare-zisin*. Now, under this ranking, only (2.220*a*) can be seen as the form that maximises the harmony of the syntactic expression of (2.220). But this will leave unexplained the fact that both (2.220*b*) and (2.220*c*) are equally grammatical.

Next, counter-evidence can also be found with interpretative optimization. As an illustration, take the Chinese example (2.163) above. Given the locality constraint proposed by both Burzio (1998) and Wilson (1998), as is necessary in accounting for relativized minimality exhibited by anaphora in Marathi and other languages (Rizzi 1990*a*), the interpretation that *ziji* is bound to the most local antecedent should be taken to be the optimal one. But this is contrary to fact. As we have seen there, (2.163) displays the maximality effect, that is, the effect that the matrix clause subject is the optimal antecedent. One solution hinted by Wilson is to posit a higher-ranked binding faithfulness constraint which will allow a given reflexive to take multiple antecedents, some of which are more local than others. But such a proposal seems to stipulate precisely what is to be explained, namely, why and how in (2.163), the interpretation that *ziji* is bound to the matrix subject does not lose the interpretative competition to the interpretation that *ziji* is bound to the most embedded subject, since the latter better satisfies the locality condition.

Finally, as in all the other generative analyses we have seen so far, Burzio's analysis also assumes subject orientation and morphological simplicity of long-distance reflexivization. This will have the consequence that non-subject orientation (see e.g. the Telugu example (2.168*c*)) and morphological complexity (see e.g. the Malay example (2.169*b*)) will be just as much a problem for this analysis, given that non-subject antecedents and morphologically complex reflexives are treated as suboptimal under the Optimality-theoretical account.[56]

2.3.4. Summary

In this section, I have discussed various extant generative analyses of long-distance reflexivization, and I have shown that they are inadequate. One of the unifying marks of these analyses is that they assume that cross-linguistically, long-distance reflexivization has three crucial properties: (i) long-distance binding, (ii) morphological simplicity, and (iii) subject orientation. However, these properties can at best be taken as a cross-linguistic tendency. Furthermore, a purely syntactic analysis is not sufficient to specify the domain or the set of potential antecedents for a long-distance reflexive. Nor does it have anything to say about the selection of the actual antecedent of a long-distance reflexive or the motivation behind its use. I shall have more to say about long-distance reflexivization in connection with logophoricity in Chapter 3, and with the neo-Gricean pragmatic theory of anaphora in Chapter 4.

2.4. Conclusion

In this chapter, I have discussed syntactic approaches to anaphora. I have focused on Chomsky's principles-and-parameters theory and its most recent descendant, the minimalist programme. I have also examined work on anaphora from the viewpoint of Optimality theory. In Section 2.1, I have surveyed the classical Chomsky typology of NPs, binding theory, control theory, and a number of revisions of and alternatives to them. In Section 2.2, I have looked at null arguments. Finally, in Section 2.3, I have concentrated on long-distance reflexivization. On the basis of evidence drawn from a wide range of genetically diverse and structurally different languages, I conclude that a purely syntactic approach can never be conceptually and empirically adequate to account for anaphora.

---

[56] For a discussion of long-distance reflexivization from the point of view of first and/or second language acquisition, see e.g. Finer and Broselow (1986), Chien and Wexler (1990), Hirakawa (1990), Finer (1991), Thomas (1991, 1993), Atkinson (1992), Eckman (1994), and Lust, Herman, and Kornfilt (1994). See also Matsuo (1999) for discussion of acquisition of reciprocals.

3 Semantic Approaches to Anaphora

This chapter is largely concerned with semantic approaches to anaphora. One significant development in recent linguistic theorizing is that there has been an increasing involvement of syntactic theory in semantics and of semantic theory in syntax. Consequently, the sorting of data on the one hand, and analyses on the other, into syntactic and semantic has become a more difficult and less theory-neutral task (e.g. Larson et al. 1992). This is particularly true of (studies of) some linguistic phenomena such as VP-ellipsis.

The organization of this chapter is as follows. Section 3.1. discusses a number of analyses of VP-ellipsis including the derived VP rule analysis by Sag (1976) and Williams (1977), the binding theory analysis by Kitagawa (1991), the dependency analysis by Fiengo and May (1994), and the equational analysis by Dalrymple, Shieber, and Pereira (1991). For ease of exposition, the discussion covers both syntactic and semantic approaches. Section 3.2. then reviews a few semantic accounts of binding and control. Finally, Section 3.3. considers the phenomenology of logophoricity, focusing on logophoric pronouns in African languages and logophoric, long-distance reflexives in East Asian languages.

3.1. VP-ellipsis

3.1.1. Definition and properties

As mentioned in Chapter 1, VP-ellipsis may be defined in a relatively theory-neutral way as the phenomenon whereby the VP of the second and subsequent clauses of a structurally parallel construction is lexically suppressed. We have already seen examples from Chinese, Dutch, English, Finnish, Hindi/Urdu, Icelandic, Marathi, and Norwegian in Chapters 1 and 2. Here are a few more examples from languages other than those mentioned above.

(3.1) (*a*) (German)
 Manfred hat sich selbst besser als   sein Anwalt   verteidigt.
 Manfred has self self   better than his lawyer-NOM defended
 'Manfred defended self self better than his lawyer did.'
 (*b*) (Irish, McCloskey 1991)
 Dúirt Ciarán go   labharfadh   sé le-n-a mhac agus
 said Ciarán COMP would-speak he to his son   and

dúirt Eoghnai go   labharfadh   fosta.
said Eoghnai COMP would-speak also
'Ciarán said he would talk to his son, and Eoghnai said he would, too.'

(c) (Japanese, adapted from Hoji 1998: 145)
John-ga   John-o   suisensita,   Bill-mo Ø suisensita.
John-NOM John-ACC recommended Bill-also   recommended
'John recommended John, and Bill did, too.'

(d) (Korean, Otani and Whitman 1991)
Chelswu-ka   caki-uy phyenci-ul peli-ess-ta.
Chelswu-NOM self-of letter-ACC discard-PAST-DECL
Yengmi-to   Ø peli-ess-ta.
Yengmi-also   discard-PAST-DECL
'Chelswu threw out self's letters, and Yengmi did, too.'

(e) (Malay, Md. Salleh 1987)
Ahmad boleh memandu kereta, dan Mary boleh Ø juga.
Ahmad can   act-drive car   and Mary can   too
'Ahmad could drive a car, and Mary could, too.'

(f) (Brazilian Portuguese, Otani and Whitman 1991)
O João encontrou o   seu mestre de elementário,
the João met   the his teacher of elementary
a   Maria também encontrou Ø.
the Maria also   met
'João met his elementary school teacher, and Maria did, too.'

(g) (Serbo-Croatian, Dalrymple, Shieber, and Pereira 1991)
Petar je   sakrio sto hiljada dolara ispod
Petar AUX hid   one hundred dollars underneath
svoje kuće a   to   je   učinio i   Pavle.
self's house and that AUX did   also Pavle
'Petar hid one hundred dollars underneath self's house, and Paul did (that) too.'

(h) (Telugu, Wali and Subbarao 1991)
Kamala tana/aame tammuḍu goppawaaḍu ani anukonṭundi
Kamala self's/her brother   great   that thinks
Sitaa kuuḍaa alaagee anukonṭundi.
Sita also   like that think
'Kamala thinks that self's/her brother is great, and Sita also thinks that way.'

Following Dalrymple, Shieber, and Pereira (1991), let us call the complete antecedent clause the source clause and the elliptical anaphoric clause the target clause. Cross-linguistically, VP-ellipsis seems to exhibit a number of rather interesting properties, notably those specified below (see e.g. Hankamer and Sag 1976, Williams 1977, Chao 1988, Lobeck 1995: 26, Hoji 1998).

(3.2) Properties of VP-ellipsis
  (a) VP-ellipsis can occur in either a coordinate or subordinate clause.
  (b) It engenders a sloppy reading.

(c) It exhibits the locality effect on the sloppy reading.
(d) The sloppy reading is subject to the c-command condition.
(e) It may operate across sentence boundaries.
(f) It may take a pragmatic antecedent.
(g) It may have a split antecedent.

These properties are illustrated by examples from English as follows.

(3.3) (a) Coordinate VP-ellipsis
John defended himself well, and Bill did, too.
(b) Subordinate VP-ellipsis
John defended himself better than Bill did.
(3.4) (a) Mary adores her piano teacher, and Susan does, too.
(b) Mary adores Mary's piano teacher, and Susan adores Susan's piano teacher.
(3.5) (a) Mary adores her piano teacher, and Kate believes that Susan does, too.
(b) Mary$_1$ adores her$_1$ piano teacher, and Kate believes that Susan$_2$ adores her$_2$ piano teacher.
(c) *Mary$_1$ adores her$_1$ piano teacher, and Kate$_2$ believes that Susan adores her$_2$ piano teacher.
(3.6) (Reinhart 1983: 150)
(a) People from LA adore it and so do people from NY.
(b) People from LA adore LA, and people from NY adore LA/*NY.
(3.7) A. John composed a nocturne.
B. Yes, but Bill didn't.
(3.8) (In an appropriate context)
I will, if you will.
(3.9) (Webber 1979)
Wendy is eager to sail around the world and Bruce is eager to climb Kilimanjaro, but neither of them can because money is too tight.

In (3.3a), the source and the target clauses stand in a coordination, but in (3.3b), they involve subordination. The VP-ellipsis in (3.4a) can give rise to the interpretation in (3.4b)—the so-called sloppy reading. (3.5) illustrates the locality effect on the sloppy reading: the antecedent for the sloppily interpreted pronoun must be restricted to the local binder *Susan* but not to the remote binder *Kate*, thus the contrast shown in (3.5b) and (3.5c). In (3.6a), since the antecedent does not c-command the pronoun, (3.6a) allows only a strict but not a sloppy interpretation, as in (3.6b). The source and the target clauses in (3.7) are spread among different speakers in a mini-conversation. The resolution of the VP-ellipsis in (3.8) has to be made contextually. Finally, in (3.9), the antecedent for the VP-ellipsis is a split one.

3.1.2. Theoretical issues

Two issues are of particular interest in the analysis of VP-ellipsis. The first, more traditional one is concerned with the availability and distribution of the strict and sloppy interpretations. This can be illustrated by a consideration of (3.4a), repeated here as (3.10).

(3.10) Mary adores her piano teacher, and Susan does, too.

In (3.10), the second, elided conjunct is ambiguous. It can be understood either in the manner of (3.11a)—the so-called strict reading—or in the manner of (3.11b)—the so-called sloppy reading. Let us call this issue the ambiguity problem.

(3.11) (a) Mary adores Mary's piano teacher, and Susan adores Mary's piano teacher.
(b) Mary adores Mary's piano teacher, and Susan adores Susan's piano teacher.

Secondly, there are what Fiengo and May (1994: 129) have called the eliminative puzzles of VP-ellipsis—the question of why VP-ellipsis reduces the number of possible interpretations of sentences relative to their non-elided counterparts. Of particular concern here are three types of eliminative puzzle: (i) the many-pronouns puzzle (due to Dahl 1974), as shown in (3.12), (ii) the many-clauses puzzle, as exhibited in (3.13), and (iii) the Dahl puzzle (due to Schiebe 1971, Dahl 1973), as shown in (3.14).

(3.12) Mary said that she adored her piano teacher, and Susan did, too.
(3.13) Mary adores her piano teacher, Susan does, too, but Kate doesn't.
(3.14) Mary thinks that she is musical, Susan does, too, but her piano teacher doesn't.

In (3.12), on the assumption that both overt pronouns are anaphorically linked to *Mary*, the elided pronouns are most naturally interpreted across the board: either both are understood strictly or both sloppily. In addition to these two interpretations, (3.12) also has a third, 'mixed' interpretation. On this interpretation, the first pronoun is read as sloppy and the second as strict (see (3.15)). Now, what is of crucial interest to us is that (3.12) does not allow a fourth, mixed interpretation under which the pronouns would be understood in the opposite manner—the first as strict and the second as sloppy. By contrast, when no VP-ellipsis takes place, all the four interpretations are available. Next, in (3.13), the number of ellipses relative to the non-elided pronoun is increased. This has the consequence that (3.13) can be read only in an across-the-board manner, that is, (3.13) has either an across-the-board strict interpretation or an across-the-board sloppy interpretation (see (3.16)). What it does not have are any mixed readings. However, when the elided pronouns are lexically realized, such mixed interpretations are allowed. Finally, in a sentence like (3.14), there is also an across-the-board effect. But what is of direct concern to us here is that in addition to this effect, (3.14) also allows an interpretation in which the medial elided pronoun is understood as sloppy, whereas the final elided pronoun is read as strict relative to the medial elided pronoun, provided that *her* is taken as coreferential with *Susan* (see

(3.17))). Once again, when there is no VP-ellipsis, more than these three interpretations are allowed. The effect of VP-ellipsis, argue Fiengo and May, is thus eliminative.[1]

(3.15) (a) Mary said that Mary adored Mary's piano teacher,
and Susan said that Mary adored Mary's piano teacher.
(b) Mary said that Mary adored Mary's piano teacher,
and Susan said that Susan adored Susan's piano teacher.
(c) Mary said that Mary adored Mary's piano teacher,
and Susan said that Susan adored Mary's piano teacher.
(3.16) (a) Mary adores Mary's piano teacher, Susan adores Mary's piano teacher,
but Kate doesn't adore Mary's piano teacher.
(b) Mary adores Mary's piano teacher, Susan adores Susan's piano teacher,
but Kate doesn't adore Kate's piano teacher.
(3.17) (a) Mary thinks that Mary is musical, Susan thinks that Mary is musical,
but Susan's piano teacher doesn't think that Mary is musical.
(b) Mary thinks that Mary is musical, Susan thinks that Susan is musical,
but Susan's piano teacher doesn't think that Susan's piano teacher is musical.
(c) Mary thinks that Mary is musical, Susan thinks that Susan is musical,
but Susan's piano teacher doesn't think that Susan is musical.

3.1.3. Two general approaches: syntactically oriented versus semantically oriented

As noted by Dalrymple, Shieber, and Pereira (1991) and Lappin (1996, 1999), among others, two general approaches to VP-ellipsis may be identified: (i) syntactically oriented and (ii) semantically oriented. Central to the syntactically oriented analyses is the belief that VP-ellipsis is largely a syntactic phenomenon, and as such references must be made to conditions and constraints that are essentially syntactic in nature. On this view, the interpretation of VP-ellipsis involves the reconstruction of the target clause on the basis of the syntactic structure of the source clause. Semantic representations which are derived syntactically are then assigned to the elided VP in a manner parallel to the antecedent VP. This approach is best represented by Kitagawa (1991) and Fiengo and May (1994) (see also Lobeck 1999 for an minimalist analysis,

---

[1] In addition, there is a third, perhaps less important issue. This involves the different behaviours of (some forms) of reflexives in coordinate and subordinate VP-ellipsis. In coordinate VP-ellipsis, a sloppy construal is strongly preferred (cf. Hoji 1998 on Japanese). By contrast, in subordinate VP-ellipsis, a strict identity is strongly favoured. Following Hestvik (1995), let us call this issue the subordination effect. Hestvik's explanation is roughly that surface reflexives are bound variables at the point of reconstruction, and that these bound variables can be derived from the reflexives themselves under movement at LF. But this analysis is questionable on two grounds. First, from an empirical point of view, Hestvik seems to ignore the fact that there are languages (such as Dutch, Korean, and Norwegian) that contain more than one form of reflexives and that some of these forms can only have a sloppy reading in a subordinate clause. Secondly, the same arguments that have been made against the LF-movement analysis of long-distance reflexivization (cf. Section 2.3.) can also be made against this analysis.

and Kempson, Meyer-Viol and Gabbay 1999 for an account formulated within the framework of Labelled Deductive System; see also Thornton and Wexler 1999 for discussion from an acquisitional point of view). In way of contrast to the syntactically oriented reconstructionist approach, the semantically based approach maintains that VP-ellipsis is essentially a semantic phenomenon. Consequently, it can better be accounted for in semantic terms. Under this approach, the interpretation of VP-ellipsis bears on the identification of a property of the antecedent VP and the assignment of this property to the elided VP. Work by Dalrymple, Shieber, and Pereira (Dalrymple, Shieber, and Pereira 1991, Shieber, Pereira, and Dalrymple 1996) and by Hardt (1992, 1993) belongs to this camp.

Also noteworthy is a second distinction in the study of VP-ellipsis that is independent of the syntactic/semantic approach distinction we have just seen. Based on an earlier observation made by Dahl (1973), Dalrymple, Shieber, and Pereira (1991) note that a distinction can be made between those analyses which trace the strict/sloppy dichotomy to an ambiguity in the representation of the source clause and those which attribute it to the process of recovering a property or relation for the target clause (see also Fiengo and May's 1994: 137 distinction between ambiguity and condition theories of VP-ellipsis). Let us call the first type source ambiguity analyses, and the second type process ambiguity analyses. Next, regarding the source ambiguity accounts, within the syntactic camp, the ambiguity of interpretation can be derived in a partially interpretative way by either deleting the phrase structure of the target clause under the condition of identical semantic interpretation, as in Sag (1976); or by copying the syntactic structure of the source clause to the target clause but requiring identical semantic representation for the two VPs, as in Williams (1977). Within the semantic camp, the multiplicity of interpretation can be obtained in a purely interpretative manner by assuming an unambiguous syntactic analysis of the source clause, as in Gawron and Peters (1990) (see e.g. Dalrymple, Shieber, and Pereira 1991). In what follows, I shall present a critical review of four influential analyses of VP-ellipsis, i.e. the derived VP rule analysis of Sag (1976) and Williams (1977), the binding theory analysis of Kitagawa (1991), the dependency analysis of Fiengo and May (1994), and the equational analysis of Dalrymple, Shieber, and Pereira (1991) (see also Shieber, Pereira, and Dalrymple 1996).

The derived VP rule analysis

Let us start with what is generally known in the literature as the derived VP rule (DVPR) analysis. The basic idea of this predication-based theory is that VP-ellipsis is warranted by a notion of identity of predication. Two most influential versions of the DVPR analysis are what Kitagawa (1991) calls the deletion DVPR approach of Sag (1976) and the interpretative DVPR approach of Williams (1977), both of which are in part inspired by the work of Partee (1973).

On the deletion DVPR account, VP-ellipsis is considered to involve a deletion that takes place in the course of mapping between S-structure and PF. The deleted VP at PF is then recovered at LF on the basis of alphabetic variance that obtains between two λ-expressions. The notion of alphabetic variance is stated as follows:

(3.18) Sag's notion of alphabetic variance
For two λ-expressions, $\lambda x(A)$ and $\lambda y(B)$, to be alphabetic variants,
  (a) Every occurrence of x in A must have a corresponding occurrence of y in B, and verse versa.
  (b) Any quantifier in A that binds variables (in A) must have a corresponding quantifier in B that binds variables in all corresponding positions (in B).
  (c) If there are any variables in A that are bound by some quantifier outside $\lambda x(A)$, then the corresponding variable in $\lambda x(B)$ must be bound by the same operator in order for alphabetic variance to obtain.

In other words, the elided VP is taken to accord with a λ-expression that is an alphabetic variant of the λ-expression that is associated with the antecedent VP.

Next, under the interpretative DVPR approach, the elided VP is claimed to be base-generated as an empty VP. The antecedent VP is derived as a VP with a λ-operator and a variable bound by that λ-operator. The antecedent anaphoric expression is then rewritten as another variable bound by the λ-operator. The rewriting of the anaphoric expression into a λ-bound variable is assumed to be obligatory for reflexives, but optional for pronouns. Finally, a copy of the antecedent VP is made into the elided VP at LF.

In what follows, I shall ignore the technical differences between the two versions of the DVPR analysis and treat both as a conceptually unified class. Now, given the DVPR analysis, the strict/sloppy distinction is to be ascribed to an ambiguity in the representation of the full, source clause of the VP-ellipsis, that is, the antecedent clause with bound pronouns can be taken to express formally distinct predications, depending upon whether as a pronoun or a variable. λ-expressions expressing the elided predicates can differ from their antecedents only in the alphabetic values of their variables. Thus, for (3.10) above, the strict and sloppy construals in (3.11a) and (3.11b) can be formally represented as follows.

(3.19) (a) Strict
Mary$_1$ λx (x adores her$_1$ piano teacher), and Susan$_2$ λy (y adores her$_1$ piano teacher)
(b) Sloppy
Mary$_1$ λx (x adores x's piano teacher), and Susan$_2$ λy (y adores y's piano teacher)

The DVPR analysis represents the first systematic treatment of VP-ellipsis

138 Semantic Approaches to Anaphora

within the context of modern linguistics, and as such it has set the critical background for all subsequent studies of this important topic in theoretical linguistics. However, there are considerable problems at the very core of this analysis. In the first place, the analysis both over- and undergenerates. By way of illustration, let us consider two examples noted by Kitagawa (1991). As pointed out by Kitagawa, the DVPR account wrongly allows the short-distance sloppy reading in examples like (3.20) on the one hand, and incorrectly rules out the long-distance sloppy reading in sentences like (3.21) on the other.[2]

(3.20) Mary wants Susan to support her before Kate does.
(3.21) Mary wants Susan to adore her piano teacher before Kate does.

This is because under the DVPR analysis, the locality effect on the sloppy identity of VP-ellipsis, mentioned above in (3.2c), is captured by the alphabetic variance condition in (3.18), which requires that the antecedent for the sloppily read anaphoric expression be restricted to the binder of the λ expression. Consequently, the application of the rewriting rule will allow the pronoun in the first conjunct of both (3.20) and (3.21) to be rewritten into a variable that is bound by the λ-operator only within the (most deeply) embedded clause, but not in the higher clause, as can be seen by their post-copying LF representations (3.22) and (3.23) respectively.

(3.22) Mary λx (x wants Susan λy (y support $y/\text{*}x$)) before Kate λy
(y support $y/\text{*}x$)
(3.23) Mary λx (x wants Susan λy (y adore y's/*x's piano teacher))
before Kate λy (y adore y's/*x's piano teacher)

But clearly these predictions are empirically wrong (see also Hardt 1992 for further arguments against and counter-examples to the alphabetic variance condition).

Secondly, as observed by Fiengo and May (1994), the DVPR analysis is inadequate in explaining the eliminative puzzles. Recall that on this account, the roots of the strict/sloppy opposition are placed in an ambiguity of the representation of the source clause. Given the alphabetic variance condition, every replication of a predicate must retain whichever reading the antecedent pronoun is given, strict or sloppy. This has the welcome consequence that in the case of the many-clauses puzzle (3.13), the theory predicts that only the across-the-board, but not the mixed, readings be allowed, as in (3.24)—a prediction that is correct.

(3.24) (*a*) Mary$_1$ λx (x adores her$_1$ piano teacher), Susan$_2$ λy (y adores her$_1$ piano teacher), but Kate$_3$ λz (z does not adore her$_1$ piano teacher)

---

[2] These (putative) readings are based on the assumption that the source clause for the ellipsis is the VP complement. Other readings are, of course, available if the source clause is taken to be the matrix clause.

(b) Mary₁ λx (x adores x's piano teacher), Susan₂ λy (y adores y's piano teacher), but Kate₃ λz (z does not adore z's piano teacher)

However, when we turn to the other two puzzles, the DVPR analysis becomes problematic. In the case of the many-pronouns puzzle (3.12), given the same alphabetic variance condition, a four-way ambiguity would be predicted (see 3.25)—a prediction that runs counter to the fact that only three of them (i.e. (3.25a–c)) should be available.

(3.25) (a) Mary₁ λx (x said she₁ adored her₁ piano teacher), and Susan₂ λy (y said she₁ adored her₁ piano teacher)
(b) Mary₁ λx (x said x adored x's piano teacher), and Susan₂ λy (y said y adored y's piano teacher)
(c) Mary₁ λx (x said x adored her₁ piano teacher), and Susan₂ λy (y said y adored her₁ piano teacher)
(d) *Mary₁ λx (x said she₁ adored x's piano teacher), and Susan₂ λy (y said she₁ adored y's piano teacher)

Abstracting away from (3.12), the problem posed by the many-pronouns puzzle for the DVPR analysis, as so nicely stated by Fiengo and May (1994: 133–5), is that while the derivable representations increase exponentially, the number of actual interpretations expand only linearly, that is, for n-many pronouns, only $n+1$ interpretations are available, but 2^n interpretations are generated under the approach being considered here.

Finally, the Dahl puzzle (3.14) can be just as much a problem for the DVPR analysis. This is because if the pronoun is taken to be a pronoun, then all its variants will be read strictly. On the other hand, if the pronoun is treated as a variable, then all its variants will be interpreted sloppily. Once the antecedent pronoun is analysed as a variable, nowhere is there any mechanism in this account to change it back to a pronoun so that a strict reading can be induced for it. As a result, the DVPR analysis fails to engender the pertinent mixed reading that is required for the interpretation of (3.14).

The binding theory analysis

We move next to the binding theory approach of Kitagawa (1991). On this syntactically based reconstructionist account, elided VPs are categorically and lexically treated as an EC (represented as [vp e]) at S-structure (see also Lobeck 1993, 1995). This EC is then reconstructed at LF by a rule of VP copying which copies the antecedent VP into the elided VP. Assuming that binding theory operates at LF, Kitagawa argues that any NP within the copied VP is required to obey the appropriate binding conditions at this level. The concomitant coindexation for binding is allowed to obtain freely, that is, either prior to VP copying or after it, at LF.

Under this analysis, (3.3a) and (3.10) can now be syntactically represented at LF as (3.26) and (3.27) respectively.

140   *Semantic Approaches to Anaphora*

(3.26) John defended himself well, and Bill defended himself well.
(3.27) Mary adores her piano teacher, and Susan adores her piano teacher.

In (3.26), in order to obey binding condition A, the copied reflexive in the reconstructed VP has to be bound to *Bill*, hence we have the sloppy interpretation. On the other hand, in (3.27), binding condition B requires that the copied pronoun in the reconstructed VP be free in its GC, assuming that the GC is the NP *her piano teacher*. Consequently, the copied pronoun is left free to be bound either by the subject of the first conjunct *Mary* or by the subject of the second, reconstructed conjunct *Susan*, giving rise to the strict and sloppy readings respectively.

The main, conceptual, attraction of Kitagawa's analysis is that if it is successful, it can partially reduce the ambiguity problem in the analysis of VP-ellipsis to binding theory, hence rendering a separate theory such as the DVPR analysis superfluous. For example, as Kitagawa points out, the peculiar contrast between (3.3*a*) and (3.10) concerning the strict/sloppy identity (see their respective LF representation (3.26) and (3.27)) can now be derived from the familiar contrast between anaphors and pronominals relevant to binding theory (cf. Chapter 2). Empirically, this analysis is also an improvement over, say, the DVPR analysis. Now, given the LF representations (3.28) and (3.29) and binding conditions A and B, the unavailable short-distance sloppy reading in (3.20) and the available long-distance sloppy reading in (3.21), for instance, will both be correctly predicted.

(3.28) Mary wants Susan to support her before Kate supports her.
(3.29) Mary wants Susan to adore her piano teacher before Kate adores her piano teacher.

Kitagawa's analysis is, however, fraught with problems. In particular, the problems noted for binding theory in the last chapter beset this analysis as well. First, this analysis has clear and fatal counter-examples with regard to binding condition A. These counter-examples fall into two types. The first type is concerned with the behaviour of reflexives in subordinated VP-ellipsis. Consider, for example, (3.3*b*) above. Notice that (3.3*b*) allows both a strict and a sloppy interpretation, with the strict interpretation being the preferred one. Now, given Kitagawa's analysis, (3.3*b*) would be reconstructed at LF along the lines of (3.30).

(3.30) John defended himself better than Bill defended himself.

Clearly, by binding condition A, the copied reflexive has to be bound in its GC. This has the immediate effect that while (3.3*b*) is allowed to have a sloppy reading, it is disallowed to have a strict reading. Furthermore, the problem becomes magnified when we turn to the use of long-distance reflexives in coordinated VP-ellipsis. Recollect that two groups of language can be isolated in this respect. In the first, long-distance reflexives allow only a sloppy identity, whereas in the second, they permit both a strict and a sloppy identity (cf. Section 2.3.). Telugu, for example, belongs to the first group (see (3.1*h*), repeated here as (3.31)), and Finnish is a language of the second group (see (2.181*a*), repeated here as (3.32)).

(3.31) Kamala tana tammuḍu goppawaaḍu ani anukonṭundi
Kamala self's brother great that thinks
Sitaa kuuḍaa alaagee anukonṭundi.
Sita also like that think
'Kamala thinks that self's brother is great, and Sita also thinks that way.'
(3.32) Jussi käskee Pekan pesemään itsensä,
Jussi order-3SG Pekan-GEN wash-3INF self-3PX
niin myös Kalle.
so also Kalle
'Jussi orders Pekan to wash self, so does Kalle.'

Now, given binding condition A, the reconstructed reflexives in both examples are expected to be bound in their respective GCs. This has the consequence that the readings dependent on the long-distance binding of the reflexives are incorrectly ruled out. What, then, could a proponent of the binding theory analysis do to explain away counter-examples of this kind? Of course, he or she could resort to one or more of the generative analyses of long-distance reflexivization described in Section 2.3. These may include the reclassification of a long-distance reflexive as a (bound) pronominal (which is to some extent similar to the idea of 'vehicle change', to which we shall turn in a moment), as a pronominal anaphor, or as an anaphor of a special kind; the parameterization of binding domain, the postulation of movement at LF, and the relativization of antecedents. But as we have already seen, none of these analyses is itself without problems.

Next, what of Kitagawa's analysis relative to binding condition B? The first point to note here is that, as already remarked (cf. Section 2.3.), what binding condition B does is to impose some negative binding restrictions on the choice of antecedent for a pronominal: it specifies only where a pronominal should be free, but not if and where it should be bound. If this is the case, then constraints other than those imposed by binding condition B are needed to tackle the issue of why and how a pronominal must normally be bound in VP-ellipsis. The mechanism employed by Kitagawa to deal with this problem is a rule of coindexation. This rule can apply either before VP copying, to yield strict identity, or after VP copying, to engender sloppy identity. Whereas it correctly rules out the interpretation (3.33) for (3.10) because the index 3 is not copied, it incorrectly allows the interpretation (3.5*c*) for (3.5*a*) because the index 2 is consistent with both binding condition B and the VP-copying rule (see also Fiengo and May 1994: 144).

(3.33) Mary$_1$ adores her$_1$ piano teacher, and Susan$_2$ adores her$_3$ piano teacher.

142   Semantic Approaches to Anaphora

It should perhaps be pointed out at this point that, as in the case of the DVPR analysis, the binding theory analysis too cannot account for the eliminative puzzles (Fiengo and May 1994). Starting with the many-pronouns puzzle, under this analysis, a four-way ambiguity would wrongly be projected, as in (3.34), for all the four interpretations in (3.34) are congruent with binding condition B.

(3.34) (a) Mary$_1$ said that she$_1$ adored her$_1$ piano teacher, and Susan$_2$ said that she$_1$ adored her$_1$ piano teacher.
 (b) Mary$_1$ said that she$_1$ adored her$_1$ piano teacher, and Susan$_2$ said that she$_2$ adored her$_2$ piano teacher.
 (c) Mary$_1$ said that she$_1$ adored her$_1$ piano teacher, and Susan$_2$ said that she$_2$ adored her$_1$ piano teacher.
 (d) *Mary$_1$ said that she$_1$ adored her$_1$ piano teacher, and Susan$_2$ said that she$_1$ adored her$_2$ piano teacher.

Essentially the same point can be made with respect to the many-clauses puzzle. Since binding condition B makes no distinction between the across-the-board and mixed interpretations, all of them would incorrectly be allowed under this analysis.

(3.35) (a) Mary$_1$ adores her$_1$ piano teacher, Susan$_2$ adores her$_1$ piano teacher, but Kate$_3$ does not adore her$_1$ piano teacher.
 (b) Mary$_1$ adores her$_1$ piano teacher, Susan$_2$ adores her$_2$ piano teacher, but Kate$_3$ does not adore her$_3$ piano teacher.
 (c) *Mary$_1$ adores her$_1$ piano teacher, Susan$_2$ adores her$_1$ piano teacher, but Kate$_3$ does not adore her$_3$ piano teacher.
 (d) *Mary$_1$ adores her$_1$ piano teacher, Susan$_2$ adores her$_2$ piano teacher, but Kate$_3$ does not adore her$_1$ piano teacher.

Finally, when we come to the Dahl puzzle, while the analysis is successful in predicting the existing interpretations including the pertinent mixed one, as in (3.17c) it also yields interpretations in (3.36), which should be ruled out.

(3.36) (a) *Mary$_1$ thinks that she$_1$ is musical, Susan$_2$ thinks that she$_2$ is musical, but her$_2$ piano teacher doesn't think that she$_1$ is musical.
 (b) *Mary$_1$ thinks that she$_1$ is musical, Susan$_2$ thinks that she$_2$ is musical, but her$_1$ piano teacher doesn't think that she$_2$ is musical.

Thirdly, Kitagawa's analysis will run into difficulties with r-expressions. Of particular interest here is the behaviour of r-expressions in the Thai/Vietnamese-type languages. As we have already seen in Section 2.1, the binding condition C_1 effect is very weak or even invisible in this type of language. As a case in point, take (3.37) from Chinese (see also Hoji 1998 for examples from Japanese).

(3.37) Xiaoming yiwei Xiaoming zui congming, Xiaohua ye zhiyang yiwei.
 Xiaoming think Xiaoming most intelligent, Xiaohua too so think
 'Xiaoming thinks that Xiaoming is the most intelligent, and Xiaohua thinks the same.'

Given binding condition C in the sense of Kitagawa, it is unclear how the readings of this sentence can be accounted for under the binding theory analysis. Finally, contrary to what (3.2*d*) dictates (e.g. Reinhart 1983), sloppy construals of VP-ellipsis need not be subject to c-command, as the following English example shows (Wescoat 1989, Dalrymple, Shieber, and Pereira 1991; see also Hirschberg and Ward 1991 for experimental evidence).

(3.38) The policeman who arrested John failed to read him his rights, and so did the one who arrested Bill.

Since binding standardly entails c-command, we are owed a reasonable explanation as to how examples of this kind can be handled given Kitagawa's analysis.

The dependency analysis

We turn next to the dependency analysis advocated by Fiengo and May (1994). On this account, VP-ellipsis is dealt with by a syntactic notion of identity. The particular mechanism put forward by Fiengo and May to represent this notion is what they call dependency theory. Central to this theory is the composite notion of index. In Fiengo and May's view, indices consist of two parts: (i) a representation of the semantic value of an index of an expression, called indexical value, and (ii) a representation of the syntactic occurrence of an index of an expression, called indexical type. Within the latter category, two types can further be distinguished: α for a symmetric, independent occurrence of an index, and β for an asymmetric, dependent occurrence of an index, following in part suggestions made by Higginbotham (1983, 1985) in the context of his linking theory. While indexical values are subject to binding theory, indexical types, argue Fiengo and May, should fall in the province of dependency theory.

Indexical dependencies (IDs) are constrained by two syntactic conditions. The first is a well-formedness condition, and this condition is formulated in linear rather than configurational terms. Simply put, the basic idea of the well-formedness condition for IDs is that every β-occurrence is required to occur in a phrase structure factorization that contains a coindexed α-occurrence. The second condition is an identity condition for IDs, where the notion of *i*-copy is invoked. What this identity condition basically states is that IDs are *i*-copies if and only if they differ in no more than their indexical value. In other words, IDs are equivalent just in case they are instances of the same parallel, structural pattern. The particular indexical values they have are of no relevance.

VP-ellipsis is then analysed in terms of the identity condition embedded within a more comprehensive notion of syntactic identity, which Fiengo and May call reconstruction. On this view, VP-ellipsis is possible only if the elided VP and the antecedent VP are reconstructions. Such VPs are reconstructions

144   *Semantic Approaches to Anaphora*

provided that no variation obtains in their indexical type, whether the indexical occurrence is an α- or β-occurrence. This has the consequence that VP-ellipsis is licensed if there is strict identity between the elided material and a non-elided counterpart or if the elided material contains an ID that is an *i*-copy of an ID within a non-elided antecedent. In the former case, we obtain the strict reading, and in the latter, we have the sloppy reading. (3.39) illustrates these two interpretations for (3.10).

(3.39) (*a*) Mary$_1$ adores her$_1^\alpha$ piano teacher, and Susan$_2$ adores her$_1^\alpha$ piano teacher.
(*b*) Mary$_1$ adores her$_1^\beta$ piano teacher, and Susan$_2$ adores her$_2^\beta$ piano teacher.

This is the best syntactic analysis of VP-ellipsis that I am aware of. It provides an elegant analysis of both the ambiguity problem and the eliminative puzzles. To see this, consider how the eliminative puzzles are accounted for under this analysis. First, in the case of the many-pronouns puzzle (3.12), given Fiengo and May's dependency theory, four putative representations are available.[2]

(3.40) (*a*) Mary$_1$ said she$_1^\alpha$ adored her$_1^\alpha$ piano teacher, and
              Susan$_2$ said she$_1^\alpha$ adored her$_1^\alpha$ piano teacher.
(*b*) Mary$_1$ said she$_1^\beta$ adored her$_1^\beta$ piano teacher, and
       Susan$_2$ said she$_2^\beta$ adored her$_2^\beta$ piano teacher.
(*c*) Mary$_1$ said she$_1^\beta$ adored her$_1^\alpha$ piano teacher, and
       Susan$_2$ said she$_2^\beta$ adored her$_2^\alpha$ piano teacher.
(*d*)* Mary$_1$ said she$_1^\alpha$ adored her$_1^\beta$ piano teacher, and
       Susan$_2$ said she$_1^\alpha$ adored her$_2^\beta$ piano teacher.

(3.40*a*) and (3.40*b*) are fairly straightforward: in the former, both elided pronouns bear the α-occurrences, and in the latter, both have the β-occurrences. What is of particular interest to us here, therefore, is how Fiengo and May's analysis distinguishes between (3.40*c*) and (3.40*d*). This is achieved roughly as follows. While the two clauses in (3.40*c*) contain the indexical dependencies which are *i*-copies (see 3.41), those in (3.40*d*) do not (see 3.42), hence the well-formedness of the representation in (3.40*c*) and the ill-formedness of the representation in (3.40*d*).

(3.41) (*a*) <(Mary, she), 1, <NP, V, NP>>
       (*b*) <(Susan, she), 2, <NP, V, NP>>
(3.42) (*a*) <(she, her), 1, <NP, V, NP>>—not an *i*-copy
       (*b*) <(Mary, her), 1, <NP, V, NP, V, NP>>—not realized
       (*c*) <Mary, she, her), 1, <NP, V, NP, V, NP>>—not an indexical dependency

Next, when we turn to the many-clauses puzzle, by the same mechanism, only two well-formed representations are derived. This is when a dependency holds an index in *toto*, that is, either all the three pronouns are α-occurrences or all of them are β-occurrences, as in (3.43).

(3.43) (*a*) Mary$_1$ adores her$_1^\alpha$ piano teacher, Susan$_2$ adores her$_1^\alpha$ piano teacher, but Kate$_3$ does not adore her$_1^\alpha$ piano teacher.

(b) Mary₁ adores her₁$^\beta$ piano teacher, Susan₂ adores her₂$^\beta$ piano teacher, but Kate₃ does not adore her₃$^\beta$ piano teacher.

Finally, in the case of the Dahl puzzle, while the dependency analysis allows the representation in (3.44a), (3.44b), and (3.44c), it disallows, for example, the representations in (3.44d) and (3.44e). This is because in (3.44d) and (3.44e), since the medial clause is read as sloppy, the pronoun in the first clause must bear a β-occurrence. As a consequence, the reconstructed pronoun in the final clause must also bear a β-occurrence. But the final β-occurrence cannot be resolved, hence the ill-formedness of (3.44d) and (3.44e).

(3.44) (a) Mary₁ thinks that she₁$^\alpha$ is musical, Susan₂ thinks that she₁$^\alpha$ is musical, but her₂$^\alpha$ piano teacher doesn't think that she₁$^\alpha$ is musical.
(b) Mary₁ thinks that she₁$^\beta$ is musical, Susan₂ thinks that she₂$^\beta$ is musical, but her₂$^\alpha$ piano teacher₃ doesn't think that she₃$^\beta$ is musical.
(c) Mary₁ thinks that she₁$^\beta$ is musical, Susan₂ thinks that she₂$^\beta$ is musical, but her₂$^\alpha$ piano teacher doesn't think that she₂$^\beta$ is musical.
(d)* Mary₁ thinks that she₁$^\beta$ is musical, Susan₂ thinks that she₂$^\beta$ is musical, but her₂$^\alpha$ piano teacher doesn't think that she₁$^\beta$ is musical.
(e)* Mary₁ thinks that she₁$^\beta$ is musical, Susan₂ thinks that she₂$^\beta$ is musical, but her₁$^\alpha$ piano teacher doesn't think that she₂$^\beta$ is musical.

One of the problems of the dependency analysis, however, is that its central predictions are frustrated in both directions. On the one hand, VP-ellipsis can occur even if syntactic identity is not satisfied. As an illustrating example, take (3.45) (Fiengo and May 1994: 184, see also Rooth 1992).

(3.45) John thought he should run in the race, Bill did, too, but the coach didn't.

(3.45) has a Dahl-reading. But unlike the standard Dahl-sentence in (3.14), it does not have a pronoun in the third conjunct that is coindexed with the subject of the second conjunct. This has the consequence that syntactic identity in its standard form is not observed. In fact, as pointed out by Mary Dalrymple (personal communication), the Dahl-reading is always available in sentences of this kind with proper contextualization, as the following example shows clearly.

(3.46) (Adapted from Mary Dalrymple, personal communication)
Boris Yeltsin thinks that he is a great statesman, Bill Clinton does, too, but Newt Gingrich doesn't.

The fact that this reading is hard to obtain without proper contextualization is largely due to parallelism (about which, more later in this section). The solution put forward by Fiengo and May to tackle the problem caused by (3.45) is to appeal to a notion of discourse sentence (e.g. Roberts 1987, 1989). According to this notion, there is a presuppositional structure that exists between the second and third conjuncts in (3.45). Therefore, the two conjuncts form a discourse sentence, with the final one being subordinate to the medial one. As a result, *the coach* has *Bill* as its antecedent (of some sort), hence making it possible for the second elided pronoun, which bears a β-occurrence, to be resolved. But such an analysis (even if it can be applied to (3.46)) does not follow from syntactic identity itself.

On the other hand, there are cases where syntactic identity is met but where the predicted reading is not available. As a case in point, consider (3.47), also taken from Fiengo and May (1994: 210).

(3.47) John hit himself, and Oscar did, too.

By the dependency theory, two representations would be derived, one giving rise to the strict identity and the other, to the sloppy identity. Faced with the problem of over-generation here, Fiengo and May seek to exclude the unwanted strict reading by appealing to the property of the predicate concerned. Their explanation is in essence that whether or not α-reflexives (i.e. reflexives with strict construals) can be licensed depends on which type of the object the predicate in question takes. While intentional objects allow α-reflexives, extensional ones disallow them. But the need to appeal to the semantics of predicates of VP-ellipsis shows that once again, contrary to Fiengo and May's claim, syntactic identity *per se* is not sufficient to tackle the ambiguity problem.

Secondly, problems arise in connection with Fiengo and May's notion of vehicle change. Within the dependency theory, vehicle change refers to a relation of syntactic identity between expressions that are co-valued and co-typed, irrespective of their particular lexical realizations. By adopting the concept of vehicle change, Fiengo and May allow LF reconstruction to ignore or alter certain features, such as φ-features. This can be seen in (3.48).

(3.48) (*a*) (Person)
Chopin considered himself to be a poet of the piano, and I did, too.
(*b*) (Number)
Chopin considered himself to be a poet of the piano, and John and Bill did, too.
(*c*) (Gender)
Chopin considered himself to be a poet of the piano, and Mary did, too.

But what is of direct interest about vehicle change to us here is that Fiengo and May have extended the notion to account for binding condition violations in VP-ellipsis. It is well known since Sag (1976) that binding theory is sometimes not operative under VP-ellipsis, as can be seen in (3.49).

(3.49) (*a*) (Binding condition A, Sag 1976)
Betsy couldn't imagine herself dating Bernie, but Sandy could.
(*b*) (Binding condition B, Hardt 1992)
Even if George won't, Barbara will vote for him.
(*c*) (Binding condition C, Dalrymple, Shieber, and Pereira 1991)
John got to Sue's apartment before she did.

Now, if we apply vehicle change under reconstruction at LF, we will get (3.50). (3.50) no longer violates binding conditions.

(3.50) (*a*) Betsy couldn't imagine herself dating Bernie, but Sandy could imagine her dating Bernie.
(*b*) Even if George won't vote for himself, Barbara will vote for him.
(*c*) John got to Sue's apartment before she got to her apartment.

As empirically attractive as the notion of vehicle change is,[3] it seems both theoretically and methodologically suspect. One direct consequence of adopting this escape strategy is that any 'objective' test for observation versus violation of binding theory under VP-ellipsis would be lost. Whenever there is a counter-example to binding theory, a proponent of this analysis can dismiss it as a real one simply on the grounds that it can undergo vehicle change to conform to binding theory under reconstruction. This will eventually lead to making it impossible to permit the recognition of any counter-example to binding theory under VP-ellipsis and falsify that theory—a consequence that is at variance with the generally accepted Popperian view that theories of empirically based sciences can only be refuted but not confirmed.

Finally, one empirical challenge for all the syntactically based analyses including that of Fiengo and May is that there is a class of VP-ellipsis that lacks any syntactically matching antecedents (see also properties *e* and *f* of (3.2.)). Examples in (3.51) are of this type.

(3.51) (*a*) (Dalrymple, Shieber, and Pereira 1991)
A lot of this material can be presented in a fairly informal and accessible fashion, and often I do (Chomsky 1982: 41).
(*b*) I will, if you will.
(*c*) (Webber 1979)
Irv and Mary want to dance together but Mary can't since her husband is here.
(*d*) A: Pavrotti fell for his secretary.
B: Yes, but Carreras didn't.

(3.51*a*) is an example of semantically/thematically paralleled VP-ellipsis. The resolution of (3.51*b*) has to be made contextually. Pragmatic inference has to be involved in the interpretation of (3.51*c*); that is, the adjunct *together with Irv* has to be pragmatically implied. Finally, in (3.51*d*), the source and target VPs are in the different turns of a mini-conversation. How these cases of VP-ellipsis can satisfactorily be handled by a syntactically oriented approach is, to say the least, not clear.[4]

---

[3] This, of course, does not mean that there is no technical difficulty in applying the notion of vehicle change to languages other than English. For example, it is not clear how May and Fiengo's analysis of a reflexive in English as [$_{NP}$ [pronoun$^{\alpha/\beta}$] *self*] can be exported into languages which contain bare reflexives.

[4] But see Fiengo and May (1994: 191–203) for a different view. In order to account for examples like (3.51*b*), Fiengo and May have to make appeal to a use component, and in order to handle examples like (3.51*d*), they have to allow syntactic principles to operate across sentence

Note that it is precisely because of the existence of examples of this kind that semantically oriented analyses of VP-ellipsis are motivated. But before we proceed to examine such an analysis, let us briefly consider the question of at what level of syntactic representation reconstruction takes place. Both Kitagawa (1991) and Fiengo and May (1994) argue for reconstruction to obtain at LF. The argument is largely concerned with the characterization of what has become known as the antecedent-contained deletion (ACD) or antecedent-contained ellipsis (ACE) construction, as in (3.52).

(3.52) Mary adored every piano teacher that Susan did.

Assuming that the antecedent in (3.52) is *adored* every piano teacher that Susan did, then the antecedent contains the ellipsis site it is antecedent for. One of the major arguments for stating the reconstruction condition at LF, due to May (1985), is that otherwise an interpretative infinite regress would arise in connection with constructions like (3.52). This is because the copy of the antecedent VP into the elided VP in (3.52) will yield a structure which itself contains an elided VP that must be filled in by another application of the same VP copying rule, and so on *ad infinitum*. This can be illustrated by (3.53). However, as May (1985) observes, if the entire quantified NP object undergoes Quantifier Raising (QR), which adjoins it to the matrix IP at LF, before VP copying takes place, then the regress problem can be avoided, as can be shown in (3.54).

(3.53) Mary adored every piano teacher that Susan did
       adored every piano teacher that Susan did
       ...

(3.54) Every piano teacher that Susan did adore Mary adored.

But the QR analysis of the ACD construction is strongly challenged by Baltin (1987). Based mainly on multiple questions with a *wh*-in-situ in a finite clause such as (3.55), Baltin points out that if May's analysis is correct, then we would expect (3.55) to be ambiguous, with the elided VP being understood either as the reconstructed *thought that Mary read* or as the reconstructed *read*. However, this prediction is empirically not borne out: (3.55) can be interpreted as (3.56a) but not as (3.56b). This shows that there is a boundedness effect on the choice of antecedent VP for an ACD construction. Baltin's own proposal is to require that the relative clause be extraposed at S-structure, resulting in the removal of the elided VP inside the relative clause out of the antecedent that dominates it, hence the evasion of the regress problem. Further, the extraposition of the relative clause is subject to a right

---

boundaries. But if this is the case, then it is unclear that such an analysis can still justifiably be considered to be syntactic in the standard generative sense. See also Lappin (1996) for some relevant discussions.

roof constraint to the effect that the boundedness restriction can be accommodated (but see Larson and May 1990 for counter-arguments against this extraposition approach).

(3.55) Who thought that Mary read how many of the music manuscripts that Susan did.
(3.56) (a) Who thought that Mary read how many of the music manuscripts that Susan read.
(b) *Who thought that Mary read how many of the music manuscripts that Susan thought that she had read.

More recently, Lappin (1996) also argues that reconstruction holds at S-structure rather than at LF. The central idea is that reconstruction is essentially a process by which to identify a correspondence at S-structure between the head and the constituents of a non-elided, antecedent VP and the counterparts of an elided, target VP. On this account, VP-ellipsis is reanalysed as a special case of pseudo-gapping, following a suggestion put forward by Bouton (1970) (see also Jayaseelan 1990 and Lasnik 1999, but see Lobeck 1999 for the view that ellipsis and pseudo-gapping are two distinct grammatical constructions). Thus, in (3.57) below, whereas (a) contains a fully elided VP, (b)–(d) have a partially elided VP.

(3.57) (a) Mary gave a CD to Susan before Kate did.
(b) Mary gave a CD to Susan before Kate did a cassette.
(c) Mary gave a CD to Susan before Kate did to Cathy.
(d) Mary gave a CD to Susan before Kate did a cassette to Cathy.

If we allow VP-ellipsis to be reduced to cases of pseudo-gapping, Lappin argues, then we can avoid the regress problem without recourse to the QR analysis. This can be achieved in the following way. Suppose that the elided VP in (3.52) is not a syntactically unstructured EC at S-structure, but a structured partial EC, which contains a *wh*-trace, as in (3.58). VP-ellipsis would then be resolved via identifying the head verb *adore* of the antecedent VP as the lexical anchor of the partially elided VP. This gives rise to the reconstruction in (3.59). Consequently, the QR analysis becomes unnecessary. In addition to these arguments, Lappin also cites the behaviour of VP-ellipsis in parasitic gaps in ACD constructions and in non-restrictive relative clauses as further evidence in favour of an S-structure approach to reconstruction (see also Lappin 1999 for an analysis made within the framework of Head-Driven Phrase Structure Grammar).

(3.58) Mary [$_{VP}$ adored every piano teacher that$_1$ Susan did [$_{VP}$[$_V$]t_1]]
(3.59) Mary [$_{VP}$ adored every piano teacher that$_1$ Susan [$_{VP}$[$_V$ adored]t_1]]

We need not go into Lappin's arguments in further detail. But one thing seems clear; that is, there are cases of ACD constructions that cannot be accommodated by Lappin's analysis. For example, it is not clear how ACD constructions like (3.60), which can be interpreted only as having a broad scope reading, and which have been shown convincingly by Fiengo and May (1994: 252) to be subject to the QR analysis, can be captured by the S-structure analysis. Furthermore, as Lappin is aware, an S-structure approach like Baltin's and his own is inconsistent with the spirit of the minimalist programme, given that S-structure is to be eliminated as a level of syntactic representation in that framework.

(3.60) Dulles believed everyone that Hoover did to be a spy.

At this point, it is useful to turn briefly to a minimalist approach to ACD constructions put forth by Hornstein (1994, 1995). On this account, ACD constructions are handled in terms of A-movement. Given the standard minimalist assumptions on A-movement, object NPs move out of VP into Spec-AgrO in order to be Case-checked at LF. The consequence relevant to the ACD construction is that the elided VP inside a relative clause is now removed from under the dominating VP that acts as its antecedent, hence avoiding the regress problem. This can be shown in the LF representation (3.61) for (3.52).

(3.61) Mary$_1$ [T [$_{AgrOP}$ [every piano teacher that Sue did Ø]$_2$ [$_{AgrO}$ [$_{VP}$ t_1 [$_{VP_i}$ adore t_1]]]]

Among the evidence in support of this minimalist approach is an array of facts concerning ACD constructions in some East Asian and Romance languages. Japanese, for example, does not allow a sloppy/ACD reading in a normal ACD configuration (3.62). However, if the VP deletion site is moved out of its antecedent, the sloppy/ACD interpretation becomes available, as in (3.63) (Takahashi 1993).

(3.62) John-ga/mo   zibun-no hahaoya-ni Mary-ga Ø   okkutta
John-NOM/also self-GEN mother-to   Mary-NOM sent
dono hon-mo okutta.
every book   sent
'John sent his mother every book that Mary did.'
(3.63) [$_{IP}$ [$_{NP}$ Mary-ga [$_{VP}$*Ø] okutta] dono hon]$_i$-mo [$_{IP}$ John-ga/mo [$_{VP}$ zibun-no hahaoya-ni t_i okutta]]]
'Every book that Mary did, John sent his mother, too.'

As pointed out by Takahashi, these facts pose a serious challenge to the QR analysis of ACD constructions. But what of the minimalist analysis to account for these facts? The explanation for the first is that in Japanese VP-ellipsis, the verb raises above AgrO to a prominent inflectional projection prior to Spell-out (Otani and Whitman 1991). This has the effect that the movement of an object NP to Spec AgrO is not sufficient to sidestep the regress problem. Hence, non-scrambled object NPs do not license sloppy/ACD interpretations in Japanese. This analysis seems to have received additional confirmation from a consideration of the ACD construction in

Spanish and Brazilian Portuguese. As in Japanese, the verb undergoes movement to a prominent inflectional projection above AgrO prior to Spell-out in these two languages. Consequently, the copying cannot proceed without regress. This explains why no sloppy/ACD reading is allowed in both (3.64) and (3.65) below.

(3.64) (Spanish, Hornstein 1995: 91 with errors corrected)
Juan no vio nada que Pedro *(vio).
Juan not saw nothing that Pedro saw
'Juan saw nothing that Pedro did.'
(3.65) (Brazilian Portuguese, Hornstein 1995: 96)
O João disse pra mãe dele tudo que o Pedro disse.
The João said for mother of him everything that the Pedro said
'John said to his mother everything that Pedro said.'

Next, the fact that short-distance scrambling renders the sloppy/ACD reading licit in Japanese can also fall naturally out of the way the minimalist analysis is formulated. This is because within the minimalist framework, short-distance scrambling is standardly taken to be an instance of A-movement whose landing site is a projection higher than AgrO. As a result, the regress problem is overcome, therefore we can have a sloppy/ACD interpretation in a sentence like (3.63).

The equational analysis

We turn finally to a semantically oriented analysis. The central idea of this approach is that the interpretation of VP-ellipsis is essentially a semantic process, involving a semantic rather than a syntactic identity condition between the elliptical, target clause and the non-elliptical, source clause. One such analysis is the equational analysis advocated by Dalrymple, Shieber, and Pereira (Dalrymple, Shieber, and Pereira 1991, Shieber, Pereira, and Dalrymple 1996, see also Crouch 1999) utilizing Huet's (1975) higher-order unificational algorithm (see also Hardt 1992, 1999 for a conceptually different semantic analysis, stated in terms of a dynamic semantic system labelled the incremental interpretation system (Pereira and Pollack 1991)).

The task of ellipsis resolution, according to Dalrymple, Shieber, and Pereira, is no more than to recover a property of the interpretation of the parallel element in the target clause that contains the ellipsis site.[5] This involves two subtasks: (i) a prior determination of the parallel structure

---

[5] But as noted by Fiengo and May (1994: 141–2), among others, VP-ellipsis can also involve semantic types other than property. In (i) below, for example, the elided material expresses a proposition. See Dalrymple, Shieber, and Pereira (1991) for a possible solution to this type of VP-ellipsis within the system they have been advocating.
(i) A: It seems that Debussy was influenced by the cultures of both the Orient and ancient Greece.
B: It certainly does.

between the source and the target clauses (which is beyond the scope of the equational analysis), and (ii) a consequent formation of the implicit relation to be used in the target clause. The latter is in essence a task of recovering admissible solutions for P in the following equation:

(3.66) $P(s_1, s_2, \ldots, s_n) = s$

where s_1 to s_n are the interpretations of the parallel elements of the source, and s is the interpretation of the source itself. Once P is determined, $P(t_1, t_2, \ldots, t_n)$ serves as the interpretations of the target, where t_1 to t_n are the interpretations of the corresponding parallel elements of the target. By using Huet's higher-order unificational algorithm to represent equivalence between two meanings, Dalrymple, Shieber, and Pereira argue that the resolution of VP-ellipsis (and much more beyond) can be satisfactorily achieved. To see how this analysis works, let us return to (3.10). Assuming that the source conjunct has the meaning representation in (3.67a) and the target conjunct has the meaning representation in (3.67b), we derive the equation (3.68) to determine the property P, which serves to generate the interpretation of the target conjunct. Next, the application of the higher-order unificational algorithm yields four solutions (3.69) for the equation (3.68). However, given the primary occurrence constraint, which basically says that no primary occurrences can be included in the solution, (3.69a) and (3.69b) are ruled out. The reason is that both solutions contain a primary occurrence, namely, the first *mary*, which arises directly from the parallel element, the subject *Mary*. This leaves two solutions in (3.70), corresponding to the strict and sloppy interpretations, respectively.

(3.67) (*a*) adores (mary, piano teacher-of (mary))
(*b*) P (susan)
(3.68) P (mary) = adores (mary, piano teacher-of (mary))
(3.69) (*a*) λx.adores (mary, piano teacher-of (mary))
(*b*) λx.adores (mary, piano teacher-of (x))
(*c*) λx.adores (x, piano teacher-of (mary))
(*d*) λx.adores (x, piano teacher-of (x))
(3.70) (*a*) λx.adores (x, piano teacher-of (mary)) (susan) = adores (susan, piano teacher-of (mary))
(*b*) λx.adores (x, piano teacher-of (x)) (susan) = adores (susan, piano teacher-of (susan))

This is an attractive analysis, whose main merits are twofold. Conceptually, it eliminates the need for the stipulation of an ambiguity in the representation of antecedent clauses. Empirically, since it frees the parallelism between the source and target clauses from being defined on purely syntactic terms, its coverage of data has improved (see Shieber, Pereira, and Dalrymple's 1996 analysis of a variety of examples involving the interaction of scope and ellipsis, which pose problems for alternative analyses such as the DVPR analysis, the dependency analysis, and the situation semantic analysis). For instance, cases of VP-ellipsis that are semantically but not syntactically parallel, as noted in (3.51a) above, can in principle be accommodated by the equational account, though the relevant details still remain to be worked out.

One main weakness of the equational analysis, however, is that it too has the problem of over-generation. As an initial illustration, consider how VP-ellipsis with reflexives is handled under this analysis. First, in the case of (3.71), where only a sloppy identity is allowed, in order to rule out the strict interpretation over-generated by the equational mechanism, Dalrymple, Shieber, and Pereira have to resort to an arbitrary, semantic relation-reducing rule, which in effect intransitivizes the verb. Thus for (3.71), we have (3.72).

(3.71) (Dutch, Sells, Zaenen, and Zec 1987)
Zij verdedigde zich beter dan Peter.
She defended self better than Peter
'She defended self better than Peter.'
(3.72) $\lambda x.\lambda y.\text{defend}\,(x, y) \rightarrow \lambda x.\text{defend-self}\,(x)$

There are, however, languages in which sentences equivalent to (3.71) allow both a strict and a sloppy reading (the strict reading frequently being the preferred one) (cf. the subordination effect mentioned in n. 1 above). This is the case of Chinese, German, and Norwegian (see the Chinese example in (3.73)). To give an account of these sentences, a proponent of the equational analysis would have to postulate that the verb is ambiguous between a transitive and an intransitive meaning. But such an analysis should be avoided on (at least) the following two accounts: (i) the ambiguity postulated cannot be derived independently from the lexical meaning of the verb concerned, and (ii) the ambiguity analysis is conceptually undesirable, in that it runs counter to the metatheoretical principle of Occam's razor.

(3.73) Xiaoming bi   Xiaohua gen   xihuan ziji.
Xiaoming than Xiaohua more like   self
'Xiaoming likes self more than Xiaohua.'

Next, the problem of over-generalization again arises in the face of coordinated VP-ellipsis containing possessive reflexives such as (3.1d) and (3.1g) above. By the equational analysis, two solutions will be generated for both (3.1d) and (3.1g). While this works well for those examples which allow both a strict and a sloppy interpretation, as in (3.1d), it over-generates in connection with those which can only be construed in a sloppy fashion, as in (3.1g). Note that in the case of (3.1g), the intransitivization analysis, proposed for (3.71) above, cannot apply, because the reflexive and its antecedent do not constitute the co-arguments of the same predicate. The solution proposed by Dalrymple, Shieber, and Pereira is that the reflexives in (3.1g) would give rise to a primary rather than a secondary occurrence, to be eliminated by the primary occurrence constraint. But this is a stipulation: it does not follow straightforwardly from the equational analysis itself.

154 Semantic Approaches to Anaphora

Finally, the equational analysis also over-generates relevant to the eliminative puzzles. This is particularly true of the Dahl puzzle. As noted by Fiengo and May (1994), among others, given the equational analysis, while the available readings of a Dahl-sentence are predicted, so are the unavailable ones. This is illustrated in (3.74), where the solutions and interpretations of (3.14) generated by the equational mechanism are given. Clearly, (3.74) contains two unavailable interpretations.

(3.74) (a) λx.thinks $(x,$ musical (mary)) (susan) =
thinks (susan, musical (mary)) (piano teacher-of (susan)) =
does not think (piano teacher-of (susan), musical (mary))
(b) λx.thinks $(x,$ musical $(x))$ (susan) =
thinks (susan, musical (susan)) (piano teacher-of (susan)) =
does not think (piano teacher-of (susan), musical (piano teacher-of (susan)))
(c) λx.thinks $(x,$ musical $(x))$ (susan) =
thinks (susan, musical (susan)) (piano teacher-of (susan)) =
does not think (piano teacher-of (susan), musical (susan))
(d) *λx.thinks $(x,$ musical $(x))$ (susan) =
thinks (susan, musical (susan)) (piano teacher-of (susan)) =
does not think (piano teacher-of (susan), musical (mary))
(e) *λx.thinks $(x,$ musical $(x))$ (susan) =
thinks (susan, musical (susan)) (piano teacher-of (mary)) =
does not think (piano teacher-of (mary), musical (susan))

3.1.4. Summary

In this section, I have examined both the phenomenology and the four most influential analyse of VP-ellipsis. By way of summary, three points are worth mentioning. First, the resolution of VP-ellipsis clearly involves syntactic, semantic, and pragmatic factors. If this is the case, then neither a purely syntactic nor a purely semantic approach would be adequate in accounting for VP-ellipsis. Just as a purely syntactic analysis would fail to accommodate semantic cases of VP-ellipsis, so too would a semantic analysis fail to deal with syntactic cases. For example, it is not clear how the equational analysis can adequately handle the 'barrier effects' of the ACD construction, first observed by Haïk (1987). In addition, both syntactic and semantic approaches need to be augmented by a pragmatic component to account for certain pragmatic aspects of VP-ellipsis (cf. Barton 1990). Secondly, all the four analyses being considered here seem to share a common problem, namely, the problem of over-generation. This may be a superficial manifestation of a more deeply rooted problem of parallelism determination. Parallelism is a general constraint which ensures that in VP-ellipsis, the source and target clauses are interpreted in a parallel manner. Fox (1998) notes that two types of parallelism may be needed: (i) referential parallelism, in which NPs in the source and target clauses have the same referential value, and (ii) structural parallelism, in which NPs in the source and target clauses are linked via identical dependencies. But the two types of parallelism do not seem to be sufficient to handle the whole range of data we have seen in this section. In short, solutions to the problem of parallelism determination and beyond are simply not forthcoming at the moment, and a great deal more research remains to be done. Thirdly, one of the major weaknesses in the study of VP-ellipsis is its rather limited cross-linguistic coverage of data. Unlike in the case of analyses of NP-anaphora, there has been a noticeable absence both in breadth and depth of analyses of VP-ellipsis in languages other than English. While VP-ellipsis exhibits a number of universal properties, it also displays a number of language-specific ones. For instance, the English sentence in (3.75) has at least three interpretations, namely, the across-the-board strict reading, the across-the-board sloppy reading, and the mixed strict/sloppy reading (Gawron and Peters 1990). By contrast, its Norwegian analogue, according to Sem et al. (1991), lacks the across-the-board strict reading.

(3.75) John revised his paper before the teacher did, and Bill did, too.

Another case in point involves Chinese-type VP-ellipsis languages. To be noted first is that in this type of language, VP-ellipsis may lack the locality effect on the sloppy reading (with proper contextualization), contrary to (3.2c). The Japanese example in (3.76) illustrates the point at hand (Hoji 1998: 136, see also Doren 1999 on Modern Hebrew).

(3.76) A: John-wa   zibun-no gakusei-o   suisensita.
         John-TOP self-GEN student-ACC recommended
       B: Mary-wa   Bill-ga   Ø suisensita   to   omotteita.
         Mary-TOP Bill-NOM   recommended that thought
       A: 'John recommended self's student.
       B: 'Mary thought that Bill did, too.'

In (3.76), the elliptical clause can mean 'Mary thought that Bill recommended Mary's student'. This may pose problems for any syntactic and semantic theory which has to impose a strict locality condition on the sloppy construal of VP-ellipsis (but see Fox 1998 for a possible solution in terms of Optimality theory). As we shall see in the next chapter, the non-locality effect on the sloppy identity of VP-ellipsis in languages like Japanese may in part be attributed to the fact that these languages are more 'pragmatic' in nature.

A further point of interest is that in the Chinese-type languages, the antecedent and target verbs can be lexically or semantically distinct. The following sentence from Chinese exemplifies this phenomenon (see Otani and Whitman 1991 for examples from Japanese, and Doren 1999 for examples from Modern Hebrew).

(3.77) Li Laoshi piping   le   ziji de   xuesheng,
       Li teacher criticize PFV self GEN student

156 *Semantic Approaches to Anaphora*

        Lin Laoshi que   biaoyang le   Ø.
        Lin teacher CTR praise   PFV
        'Teacher Li has criticized self's student, but Teacher Lin has praised (self's student).'

Clearly, the non-identity of the antecedent and target verbs of this kind is quite unmanageable for any analysis that posits VP copying. From facts like these, there follows one conclusion that a better understanding of VP-ellipsis can be attained only if its cross-linguistic empirical coverage is to be widened and deepened.

3.2. Binding and control: some semantic alternatives

In the last section, I discussed four analyses of VP-ellipsis. In this section, I shall consider a number of semantically oriented accounts of binding and control.

3.2.1. Binding

Thematic prominence

In Chapter 2, I examined a variety of generative analyses of binding. These analyses can be said to be syntactically oriented, because they are formulated predominantly in configurational terms, appealing to purely structural concepts such as c-command, government, and spec-head agreement. In contrast to this 'geometric' approach, the semantically oriented approach attempts to define binding primarily in argument-structure terms, frequently making reference to a thematic hierarchy. This thematic hierarchy is usually defined along the lines of Fillmore (1968) and Jackendoff (1972) (see also e.g. Giorgi 1984, 1991, W. Wilkins 1988, Grimshaw 1990, and Jackendoff 1990).[6]

(3.78) Thematic hierarchy
       Agent > experiencer > goal/source/location/benefactor > theme

Two kinds of empirical fact seem to prompt the semantically based approach to binding. The first is that there are non-configurational effects on binding (both local and long-distance) within individual languages. A well-

---

[6] There is, however, disagreement as to what level of representation thematic prominence obtains. Jackendoff (1990), for example, suggests that thematic prominence is reflected in a lexical-semantic representation called conceptual structure. But this position is not shared by other researchers. On Grimshaw's (1990) account, thematic prominence is considered to be part of a lexical-syntactic representation called predicate argument structure. W. Wilkins (1988) takes still another view that thematic prominence is simply a syntactic primitive.

known example from English, first noted by Postal (1971: 193) and frequently cited in the recent literature (e.g. Kiss 1991, Pollard and Sag 1992, Reinhart and Reuland 1993), is the following.

(3.79) (a) John talked to Mary about herself.
(b) *John talked about Mary to herself.

Given the standard version of binding condition A, both (3.79a) and (3.79b) would be predicted to be either grammatical or ungrammatical, depending on whether the anaphor is analysed as being c-commanded by the antecedent. But either way, the standard version of binding condition A, formulated in configurational terms, fails to bring out the grammaticality/ungrammaticality contrast shown in (3.79). On the other hand, as the reader can verify for him- or herself, this contrast follows directly from the prediction of thematic prominence (see also Hellan and Christensén 1986, Hellan 1988 for a discussion of Norwegian).

Secondly, the extent to which configurational and non-configurational factors interact to determine binding varies from language to language. For example, in contrast to English, Modern Greek is a language in which non-configurational constraints play a more important role than configurational ones. This can be seen by the fact that the binding patterns for nominative anaphors (3.80), in double-object constructions (3.81), and in passive constructions (3.82) in Modern Greek can better be handled in thematic than in configurational terms (e.g. Everaert and Anagnostopoulou 1997).

(3.80) (a) O eaftos tu$_1$ tu   aresi   tu Petru$_1$.
           the self   his-NOM CL-DAT like-3SG the Peter-DAT
           'Himself pleases Peter.'
       (b) *O eaftos tu$_1$ ton   xtipise ton Petro$_1$
           the self   his-NOM CL-ACC hit   the Peter-ACC
           'Himself hit Peter.'
(3.81) (a) Ediksa   s-tin   Maria$_1$ ton eafto   tis$_1$.
           showed-I to-the Mary   the self-ACC her
           'I showed to Mary herself.'
       (b) *Ediksa   tin Maria$_1$ s-ton eafto tis$_1$.
           showed-I the Mary-ACC to-the self her
           'I showed Mary to herself.'
(3.82) (a) ?*To tragoudi   afierothike   s-ton Janni$_1$ apo ton eafto tu$_1$.
           the song-NOM was dedicated to-the John by the self his
           'The song was dedicated to John by himself.'
       (b) To tragoudi   afierothike   apo ton Janni$_1$ s-ton eafto tu$_1$.
           the song-NOM was dedicated by the John to-the self his
           'The song was dedicated by John to himself.'

As pointed out by Everaert and Anagnostopoulou, these examples clearly favour a thematic approach over a syntactic one. The antecedent is thematically more prominent than the anaphor in (3.80a) but not in (3.80b), hence the grammaticality of the former and the ungrammaticality of the latter. Exactly the same can be said of the contrast exhibited in (3.81) and (3.82). Other languages of this type may include Albanian, Malagasy (Randriamasimanana 1986), and Toba Batak (Clark 1992). Following is an example from Malagasy (Randriamasimanana 1986).

(3.83) N-aha-sosotra   an'i   Paoly$_1$ ny tena-ny$_1$.
       PAST-CAUS-angry ACC-ART Paul   the self-his
       'Heself angered Paul.'

Furthermore, of particular interest is the behaviour of binding in so-called flat, polysynthetic/non-configurational languages such as Guugu Yimidhirr (Levinson 1987), Hungarian (Kiss 1991), Kadiwéu (Sandalo 1997), Navajo (Speas 1990), Warlpiri (Hale 1983), and Nepali (see also M. Baker 1995).[7] In such a language, the co-arguments of a predicate mutually c-command each other. Given the standard version of binding condition A, we would expect that in cases like (3.84) in Hungarian both members of the pair be grammatical. But as Kiss (1991) demonstrates, this is not the case. Binding relations between co-arguments in a Hungarian clause are in general not bidirectional but asymmetrical. One of the crucial factors affecting binding possibilities in Hungarian is the relative thematic prominence of the antecedent over the anaphor. This leads Kiss to argue that the configurational, c-command condition be augmented by two other primacy conditions: a linear prominence condition (cf. Kuno 1987) and a thematic prominence condition (along the lines of (3.78) above), with the latter being linked to a lexical argument hierarchy (cf. Kiss 1995).

(3.84) (Hungarian, Kiss 1991)
       (a) A lányok   ismerik egymást.
           the girls-NOM know   each-other-ACC
           'The girls know each other.'
       (b) *A lányokat   ismeri egymás.
           the girls-ACC know   each-other-NOM
           'Each other know the girls.'

While the evidence considered so far suffices to establish the thematic approach as a promising alternative to the syntactic one, counter-evidence has also been forcefully presented in the literature to show that this alternative is not without its sharing of problems. Let me just mention two types of counter-example. To be noted first are English examples of the following kind (Barss and Lasnik 1986, Kiss 1991, Pollard and Sag 1992, 1994).

---

[7] Following the work by Speas (1990: 137–8), non-configurational languages may be summarized as having the following main properties: (i) lack of VP constituents, (ii) lack of pleonastics, (iii) lack of PRO, (iv) presence of nominative reflexives, (v) lack of weak crossover effects, (vi) lack of ECP effects for subjects, and (vii) lack of binding asymmetries. See also Heath (1986) and Austin and Bresnan (1996) for a discussion of non-configurationality with special reference to Australian languages.

(3.85) John explained Mary to herself.

In this type of sentence, an anaphor thematically outranks its antecedent, and yet is bound by the antecedent, thus contradicting one of the critical predictions of the thematic approach (but see W. Wilkins 1988 and Jackendoff 1990 for attempts to rearrange the ordering of thematic roles). The second type involves the contrast shown by the Modern Greek sentences in (3.86) (Everaert and Anagnostopoulou 1997).

(3.86) (a) O Jannis$_1$ edikse tin fotografia   s-ton eafto tu$_1$.
          the Jannis-NOM showed the picture-ACC to-the self his
          'John showed the picture to himself.'
      (b) *O Jannis$_1$ (tu)-edikse   tu eaftu tu$_1$
          the Jannis (CL-DAT)-showed the self   his-DAT
          tin fotografia.
          the picture-ACC
          'John showed himself the picture.'

In (3.86), both the NP- and PP-datives seem to have the same thematic status, and as such are expected to be bindable by the thematically more prominent subject. But this expectation is not borne out; while (3.86a) is grammatical, (3.86b) is not. This indicates that there must be some explanation other than thematic prominence involved here. From facts like these there follows the conclusion that the thematic approach too is inadequate in predicting the full range of binding patterns in a language.[8]

Marking of reflexivity

We move next to a more radical semantically oriented analysis of binding, namely, Reinhart and Reuland's (1993) theory of reflexivity. In this theory, NPs are classified into three groups according to the properties [±SELF] and [±R]: (i) morphologically complex SELF anaphors, (ii) morphologically simplex SE anaphors, and (iii) pronouns. This is schematized in (3.87) (see also Anagnostopoulou and Everaert 1999 for a recent modification).

(3.87) Reinhart and Reuland's typology of NPs
	SELF	SE	Pronouns
Reflexivizing function	+	–	–
R(eferential independence)	–	–	+

Of particular concern to us here is the category of anaphors. While both types of anaphor share the property of referential dependency [–R], they

---

[8] The same conclusion can also be reached about the semantic/thematic approach in relation to long-distance reflexivization. Giorgi (1984), for example, puts forward an account of the distribution of long-distance reflexives which basically says that a long-distance reflexive must be P-bound, that is, bound by the thematically most prominent element in its P-domain (see also Giorgi 1991, and Hellan's 1988, 1991 notion of role command). But cross-linguistically, counterexamples abound (see e.g. Benedicto 1991 for Latin and Pan 1995 for Chinese).

differ in their grammatical functions: whereas SELF anaphors can function as reflexivizers, that is, to render a predicate reflexive, SE anaphors cannot. Consequently, only SE, but not SELF, anaphors are predicted to be subject-oriented and to be able to participate in long-distance binding.

Reviving ideas in traditional grammar (e.g. Jespersen 1924) and drawing in part on work by Riad (1988), Reinhart and Reuland suggest that reflexivity is not a property of NPs, but a property of predicates (see also Keenan 1988). The domain of reflexivity for a predicate is said to be universally licensed in two ways. In the first, called intrinsic reflexivization, a predicate is marked as a reflexive predicate in the lexicon. The verbs in the following examples are all lexically marked as reflexives.

(3.88) (a) (Icelandic, Everaert 1986)
Pétur skammast sín/*sjálfs sín.
Petur shamed self/self self
'Petur was ashamed.'
(b) (Italian, Burzio 1998)
Gianni si vergogna/*se stesso.
Gianni self shames/self same
'Gianni is ashamed.'
(c) (French, Everaert 1986)
On se repentit/*soi-(même).
One self repents/self-same
'One repents itself/oneself.'

Note that in (3.88), only a SE but not a SELF anaphor can occur. This, argues Reinhart and Reuland, is not the direct result of their reflexivity analysis, but follows straightforwardly from a principle of economy: the same property should not be marked twice.

Secondly, the domain of reflexivity can be indicated through the marking of one of the co-arguments of the predicate by means of a SELF anaphor. This is called extrinsic reflexivization, as in (3.89).

(3.89) (a) Pavarotti admires himself.
(b) (Dutch, adapted from Reinhart and Reuland 1991)
Pavarotti bewondert zichzelf.
Pavarotti admires self self
'Pavarotti admires self self.'
(c) (Italian, Giorgi 1984)
Gianni ama solo se stesso.
Gianni loves only self same
'Gianni loves only self self.'

Departing radically from the standard view that binding conditions A and B are designed to account for the mirror-image distribution of anaphors and pronominals respectively, Reinhart and Reuland argue that they are designed to regulate the domain of reflexivity for a predicate. The reflexivity version of binding conditions A and B, with the relevant definitions, are given in (3.90).

(3.90) Reinhart and Reuland's theory of reflexivity
   (*a*) Binding conditions A and B
      A. A reflexive-marked syntactic predicate is reflexive.
      B. A reflexive semantic predicate is reflexive-marked.
   (*b*) Definitions
      (i) The syntactic predicate formed of (a head) P is P, all its syntactic arguments, and an external argument of P (subject).
         The syntactic arguments of P are the projections assigned θ-role or Case by P.
      (ii) The semantic predicate formed of P is P and all its arguments at the relevant semantic level.
      (iii) A predicate (formed of P) is reflexive if and only if two of its arguments are coindexed.
      (iv) A predicate (formed of P) is reflexive-marked if and only if either P is lexically reflexive or one of P's arguments is a SELF anaphor.

In essence, what (3.90) predicts is that if a predicate is lexically reflexive, it may not be reflexive-marked by a SELF anaphor in the overt syntax. And if a predicate is not lexically reflexive, it may become reflexive only via the marking of one of its co-arguments by the use of a SELF anaphor. Stated from a slightly different perspective, what the reflexivity theory basically says is that in the domain of binding, there is a one-to-one mapping between a particular semantic property (i.e. the property of reflexivity) and a particular formal property (i.e. the property of reflexivity-marking), and that there are two ways to realize the formal property.

Reinhart and Reuland's theory of reflexivity constitutes an important step forward in our understanding of binding. By virtue of a shift from viewing binding conditions A and B as principles regulating the distribution of anaphors and pronominals to regarding them as principles governing the well-formedness and interpretation of reflexive predicates, they have made two important contributions. The first is to reinforce the distinction, made by e.g. Farmer and Harnish (1987) and Levinson (1991), of whether or not an anaphor and its antecedent are the co-arguments of the same predicate. And their second contribution is to reapportion the division of labour between syntax and, say, pragmatics by suggesting that the explanation of the marking of non-reflexivity lies outside the purview of binding theory. Consequently, the empirical coverage afforded by the theory improves considerably, avoiding some of the problems that have been embarrassing standard binding theory since its inception. This can best be seen by a consideration of (3.91) and (3.92), which, as we have seen in the last chapter, have long been seriously counter-exemplifying standard binding theory.

(3.91) (Dutch)
   (*a*) Pavarotti bewondert zichzelf.
      Pavarotti admires   self self
      'Pavarotti admires self self.'

(b) *Pavarotti bewondert zich.
   Pavarotti admires   self
   'Pavarotti admires self.'
(3.92) (a) John saw a panda near himself.
  (b) John saw a panda near him.

Given (3.90), the predicate in (3.91a) is both syntactically and semantically reflexive-marked, therefore both binding conditions A and B are satisfied. The ungrammaticality of (3.91b) follows from the violation of binding condition B. Since (3.91b) contains a semantic predicate, it must be reflexive-marked in order to cohere with binding condition B. But the SE anaphor is not a reflexivizer and cannot reflexive-mark the predicate, hence the ungrammaticality of (3.91b). Next, consider (3.92). In the case of (3.92a), although the sentence contains an SELF anaphor, it contains neither a syntactically nor a semantically reflexive-marked predicate. Consequently, both binding conditions A and B are met trivially by not applying. The same also holds for (3.92b). Binding condition A is not relevant, because the pronoun cannot reflexive-mark the predicate; binding condition B is not applicable either, because (3.92b) does not contain a semantic predicate.

There are, however, problems with the reflexivity analysis. In the first place, cross-linguistic evidence has been presented that marking of reflexivity is not limited to the two ways identified by Reinhart and Reuland. In addition to being marked lexically and syntactically, reflexivity can also be indicated morphologically (e.g. Lidz 1996).[9] In the case of morphological marking, a verbal affix (in its broadest sense) is attached to the predicate or predicate

---

[9] Still another way to mark reflexivity is to use a grammaticalized/standardized lexeme usually denoting body and body parts such as 'body', 'head', 'eye', 'heart', 'stomach', 'bone', 'marrow', 'soul', 'skin', 'seed', and 'breath'; and less commonly meaning 'life', 'person', 'owner', 'mask', 'relative', or 'comrade', which might be regarded as a special case of reflexivity being marked syntactically. While this device is attested in a wide variety of languages including Abkhaz, Basque, Biblical Hebrew, Georgian, Lisu, Malagasy, Mojave, and Tamazight (e.g. Faltz 1985: 32–3, 220–2, 245, 282), it seems to be particularly popular among African languages. In Heine (1997), for example, one finds the following African languages which use this device to express reflexivity: Acholi, Anywa, Bagirmi, Bari, Bassa, Didinga, Diola/Dyola, Duala, Ebira, Fulani, Gabu, Gidar, Gisiga, Gola, Hausa, Ibibio, Kanuri, Kenzi, Koromfe, Krongo, Kwami, K'emant, Lamang, Lele, Luo, Maba, Margi, Mina, Moru, Oron, Päri, Pero, Shilluk, So, Swahili, Usak Edet, Vai, Xdi, and Yoruba (see also Heine, Claudi, and Hünnemeyer 1991: 32–4, Hopper and Traugott 1993: 40–1, Frajzyngier 1997, König and Siemund 1997, and Schladt 1997). To this list we can add the Chadic languages Angas, Mandara, and Ngizim (Burquest 1986: 90–4), the Niger-Congo language Fula (Faltz 1985: 32), and the Benue-Congo language Mundani (Parker 1986: 151). Furthermore, Heine (1997) observes that 'body' is the most commonly used expression and has no constraint on areal distribution. By contrast, 'head' seems to be areally confined to West and West-Central Africa, and 'soul' and 'life' appear to be found mainly in North-Central Africa.

From a diachronic point of view, it has been widely believed that lexemes denoting body and body parts are the single most important source for the grammaticalization of reflexives (and other syntactic markers), as the following diagram shows (adapted from e.g. Faltz 1985, Levinson 1991, Kemmer 1993, Heine 1997, König and Siemund 1997).

complex. Such a predicate is then called reflexive verb (RV) (e.g. Geniušienė 1987) or verbal reflexive (VR) (Faltz 1985, Wali et al. forthcoming) in the literature. In some languages, VRs are intransitive, as in (3.93), and in others, they are transitive, as in (3.94).

VRs are discovered in a variety of language families including Algonquian (e.g. South-western Ojibwa), Baltic (Latvian, Lithuanian, and Old Prussian), Dravidian (e.g. Kannada, Tamil, and Telugu), Finno-Ugric (e.g. Estonian, Mansi, and Udmurt), Indo-Aryan (e.g. Gujarati, Punjabi, and Sinhala), Iroquoian (e.g. Tuscarora), Nyulnyulan (e.g. Bardi, Jukun, and Warrwa), Romance (e.g. French, Spanish, and Padovano), Sino-Tibetan (e.g. Chinese, and a Tibeto-Burman language, Mizo), Slavonic (e.g. Russian, Macedonian, and Polish), and Turkic (e.g. Azerbaijani, Turkish, and Uzbek) (e.g. Wali et al. forthcoming, and especially Geniušienė 1987; see also Faltz's 1985 discussion about the origins of VR markers with respect to Abaza, Abkhaz, French, Kinyarwanda, Lakhota, Mojave, and Spanish). They are also considered to be a prominent feature of non-configurational languages (M. Baker 1995). Some examples are given below.

(3.93) (a) (Chinese)
Lao Xie zisha   le.
Lao Xie self-kill CRS
'Lao Xie killed himself.'
(b) (Chuvash, Geniušienė 1987: 309)
Văl   s'ăv-ăn-at'
she-ABS wash-REFL-PRES-3SG
'She washes herself.'

(i) The evolution of reflexives
'Body parts' → (emphatics →) reflexives (→ reciprocals → middles → passives → impersonal passives)

As far as the 'body parts'/reflexives evolution is concerned, there appear to be three stages (e.g. Faltz 1985, Heine 1997). In the first, there is no reflexive in the language and the lexeme concerned is still a noun denoting body etc. A second stage sees that the lexeme begins to acquire the reflexivizing function, but still retains its original lexical meaning. Basque, Krongo, and Malagasy represent this stage. In the third stage, the lexeme loses its original lexical meaning entirely and becomes a fully grammaticalized reflexivizer. Modern Hebrew seems to be on the way to this stage. But what is of particular interest is that during the second, transitional stage, the lexeme has two distinct semantic functions, one with its original lexical meaning and one as a reflexivizing marker. Two examples will serve.

(ii) (a) (Fula, Faltz 1985: 32)
mi   gaañi   hooreqam.
1SG-NOM wound-PERP head-1SG-POSS
'I wounded my head.'
'I wounded myself.'
(b) (Ibibio, Heine 1997)
imé ámà étígha idem (amɔ́)
Ime   shot   body his
'Ime shot his body (as opposed to his head).'
'Ime shot himself.'

(c) (Diyari, Austin 1981b)
ngani muduwa-tadi-yi.
1SG-ABS scratch-REFL-PRES
'I scratch myself.'

(d) (Finnish, Kirsi Hiltunen personal communication)
Pekka pese-yty-i.
Pekka wash-REFL-PAST
'Pekka washed himself.'

(e) (Kinyarwanda, Faltz 1985: 189)
Yohaani yiiguze na Bill.
Yohaani 3SG-PAST-REFL-buy-ASP with Bill
'Yohaani bought himself from Bill.'

(f) (Lithuanian, Geniušienė 1987: 70)
Jon-as ap-si-renge.
Jonas-NOM PERF-RELF-dressed
'Jonas dressed himself.'

Secondly, somewhat related is the problem that VRs of this sort can be doubly marked by a pronoun, as in (3.94a), a SE anaphor, as in (3.94b), and even a SELF anaphor, as in (3.94c).

(3.94) (a) (Padovano, Lidz 1996: 43)
Gianni se varda lu.
Gianni REFL saw him
'Gianni saw himself.'

(b) (Kannada, Lidz 1995)
raamu tann-annu hogal-i-koND-a.
Raamu SE-ACC praise-PP-REFL-PAST-3SG-M
'Raamu praised himself.'

(c) (Spanish)
Ana se vio (a sí misma).
Ana REFL saw to self same
'Ana saw herself.'

In addition, of particular interest to us here is Japanese. According to Aikawa (1993), Japanese has two types of morphologically reflexive-marked predicate: (i) *zi*-V, and (ii) *ziko*-V, a subset of so-called Sino-Japanese predicates. While the former cannot take a direct object, the latter can. And the direct object can be encoded by a pronoun, a SE anaphor or even a SELF anaphor, (3.95) provides a straightforward illustration of this reflexivity-marking pattern of Japanese.

(3.95) (Japanese, Aikawa 1993: 76)
John-ga kare/zibun/zibun-zisin-o ziko hihansita.
John-NOM he/self/self self-ACC self criticized
'John criticized himself.'

Now, given Reinhart and Reuland's analysis, it is not clear how (3.94a), (3.94c), and (3.95) can be accounted for by the principle of economy. The same can also be said of the marking of intrinsic reflexivization. Apart from a SE anaphor, intrinsic reflexivisation can be double marked by a zero anaphor, a pronoun, and even a SELF anaphor. Once again (3.96b) and (3.96c) below would pose a challenge to Reinhart and Reuland's analysis.

(3.96) (a) (Finnish, Kirsi Hiltunen personal communication)
Pekka erehtyi.
Pekka mistake-PAST
'Pekka was mistaken.'
(b) (Frisian, Everaert 1991: 94)
Hy skammet him.
he shames him
'He is ashamed.'
(c) On that occasion, the boys behaved themselves badly.

Next, more worrisome, however, is that the central empirical prediction of the reflexivity analysis, namely, only a reflexive predicate can and must be reflexive-marked, is falsified in both directions. On the one hand, a predicate that is both syntactically and semantically reflexive can be non-reflexive-marked in the sense of Reinhart and Reuland. First, there are many languages which utilize a SE anaphor to reflexive-mark a reflexive predicate, though such an anaphor is considered to be a non-reflexivizer on the reflexivity theory. These languages include Chinese, Hindi/Urdu, Japanese, Juang, Korean, Icelandic, Lithuanian, and Russian. Some illustrative examples are given below.

(3.97) (a) (Chinese)
Xiaoming xihuan ziji/taziji.
Xiaoming like self/3SG-self
'Xiaoming likes self.'
(b) (Korean, Cole, Hermon, and Sung 1990:,18)
Chelswu-nun casin/ku-casin/caki-casin-ul sarangha-n-ta.
Chelswu-TOP self/he-self/self-self-ACC love-PRES-DECL
'Chelswu likes self.'
(c) (Icelandic)
Jón elskar sig/sjálfan sig.
Jon loves self/self self
'Jon loves self.'

Secondly, as remarked earlier in Chapter 2, many languages do not have reflexives, and consequently employ a pronoun as a reflexivizer. Old English, Guugu Yimidhirr and Isthmus Zapotec, for instance, belong to this type of language. Exemplification has been given in (2.15)–(2.17), and I shall not repeat it here. But crucial for our interest is that reflexivity-marking of this type clearly will raise difficulties for Reinhart and Reuland's theory.

On the other hand, a non-reflexive predicate can be reflexive-marked. Let me start, for the purpose of illustration, with an ECM sentence in English.

(3.98) Pavarotti believes himself to be the best tenor.

In (3.98), the SELF anaphor embedded under the ECM verb is the subject of the lower verb, but not an argument of the matrix verb. Consequently, it is predicted not to be able to reflexive-mark the matrix verb. But this is not the case. To circumvent the problem, Reinhart and Reuland argue that a

166 *Semantic Approaches to Anaphora*

distinction should be made between syntactic and semantic predicates (see (3.90) above). As a result, (3.98) contains a syntactic but not a semantic predicate, because although the SELF anaphor is not an argument of the matrix verb, it is part of the syntactic predicate of the matrix verb, for it receives Case from it. This has the effect that binding condition A is met, and therefore (3.98) no longer poses any problem for the reflexivity analysis (see also Lidz 1995). But such an escape hatch cannot be used when we come to examples like (3.99) in a language like Chinese.

(3.99) Xiaoming shuo taziji   hen xihuan *Kamen.*
Xiaoming say 3SG self very like   Carmen
'Xiaoming says that heself likes *Carmen* very much.'

As in (3.98), *taziji* and *Xiaoming* in (3.99) are not the co-arguments of the matrix predicate, therefore (3.99) does not contain a semantic predicate. However, unlike (3.98), there is no way to interpret (3.99) as containing a syntactic predicate, since the matrix verb does not assign Case to *taziji.* Hence the predicate in (3.99) is neither syntactically nor semantically reflexive, yet contrary to what is predicted by Reinhart and Reuland's theory, it is reflexive-marked by a SELF anaphor. A further case in point comes from the reflexive-marking of so-called 'picture' NPs in languages like Kannada and Norwegian.

(3.100) (*a*) (Kannada, Lidz 1995)
raam tann-a   pictur-annu noD-i-koND-a.
Raam SE-GEN picture-ACC see-PP-REFL-PAST-3SG-M
'Raam saw a picture of self.'
(*b*) (Norwegian, Hestvik 1990: 78)
John liker bilder   av seg selv.
John likes pictures of self self
'John likes pictures of self self.'

As noted by Lidz (1995), (3.100*a*) does not contain a syntactic predicate, because *pictur* 'picture' does not have an external argument. It does not contain a semantic predicate, either, because the anaphor is not an argument of the verb. Consequently, it is predicted that no reflexive marking should be possible in a construction like this. But this prediction is not borne out; (3.100*a*) can be morphologically reflexive-marked by the verbal reflexive in Kannada. Exactly the same can be said of (3.100*b*), except that it is syntactically reflexive-marked by the Norwegian complex reflexive *seg selv.* In fact, the Norwegian complex reflexive *seg selv* (at least for some speakers) can also be used as a non-reflexivizer in a small clause—again a contradiction to Reinhart and Reuland's analysis. The same is true for (all speakers of) Chinese.

(3.101) (*a*) (Norwegian, Hestvik 1990: 288)
John satte stolen   foran   seg selv.
John put the chair in front of self self
'John put the chair in front of self self.'

(b) (Chinese)
Xiaoming ba yizi fang zai ta ziji qianmian.
Xiaoming BA chair put in 3SG self front
'Xiaoming put the chair in front of himself.'

Finally, it should be pointed out that on Reinhart and Reuland's theory, neither the configurational nor the thematic effect is attributed to their binding conditions. Instead, both are subject to a condition on chain formation (3.102).

(3.102) Chain formation
A maximal A-chain $(\alpha_1, \ldots, \alpha_n)$ contains exactly one link—α_1—that is both +R and Case-marked.

While (3.102) can account for the configurational effect in (3.103) below and the thematic effect in (3.79) above, it cannot handle the Modern Greek sentences in (3.80), the Malagasy sentence in (3.83), and the Hungarian sentences in (3.84). All this points to the conclusion that chain formation does not apply to these languages (see also Everaert and Anagnostopoulou 1997 for a similar conclusion based on some Modern Greek facts).

(3.103) (Chinese)
(a) Xiaoming$_1$ xihuan ziji$_1$ chui ziji$_1$.
Xiaoming like self boast self
'Xiaoming likes self praising self.'
(b) *Xiaoming$_1$ xihuan ziji$_1$ chui ta$_1$.
Xiaoming like self boast 3SG
'Xiaoming likes self praising him.'

Furthermore, the theory of reflexivity does not in itself provide any account of long-distance reflexivization. Within Reinhart and Reuland's framework, long-distance reflexivization is accommodated in terms of movement at LF. Both SELF and SE anaphors undergo head-to-head movement: SELF anaphors move to V°, whereas SE anaphors raise to Agr, at LF. While this accords with Reinhart and Reuland's position that movement should fall under a chain theory rather than a binding theory, to adopt a head-to-head movement at LF analysis means that most of the problems pointed out earlier in connection with Cole, Hermon, and Sung's analysis will unavoidably emerge in analysis as well.

3.2.2. Control

We turn next to semantically oriented approaches to control. The basic idea underlying these analyses is the belief that control is fundamentally conditioned in semantic terms.

One of the earliest semantic/thematic analyses of control pursued within the framework of generative grammar is Jackendoff (1972). In this work, Jackendoff argues for a specification of the controller in the lexical entry of a complement-taking verb as part of the 'network of reference'. This is also the position taken by Chomsky (1980). In attempting to tackle the problem caused by the *promise*-class verbs for the Rosenbaum-type, 'minimal-distance' analysis (cf. Chapter 2), Chomsky proposes an arbitrary feature [+SC] ('assign subject control') to be included in the lexical entry of these verbs. As for the second major class of control verbs, namely, the *persuade*-class verbs, he suggests that they be marked in the lexicon with the arbitrary feature [+CC] ('assign complement control').

An advance from Jackendoff's thematic analysis is Růžička (1983), who proposes a thematic identity condition (TIC) and a thematic distinctness condition (TDC) for the selection of the controller and the controllee. Roughly speaking, the TIC requires that the controller and the controllee have identical thematic roles, whereas the TDC dictates that they have distinct thematic roles. Consequently, in this model, verbs that are traditionally treated as exhibiting subject control are now assigned [+TI], whereas verbs that are traditionally regarded as taking object control are now given [+TD]. In addition, there are two other features in Růžička's account: [m[arked] TD] and [m[arked] TRC]. The former is meant to encompass verbs such as *propose* in English, *vorschlagen* in German, and *predložit* in Russian, which allow inclusion of the agent as part of the controller. The latter is intended to cover verbs such as *like* in English, *lieben* in German, and *lubić* in Polish, which are (claimed to be) indifferent to thematic relations with regard to the choice of controller.

Another more recent thematically based account of control is presented by Culicover and Wilkins (1986). In this theory, infinitival complements are treated as base VPs. Consequently, there is no use of PRO in the syntax. Instead, the lexical entry for a verb contains a specification of its thematic structure, and thematic roles are assigned algorithmically to a level of representation which Culicover and Wilkins call R-structure. This R-structure is restricted by a completedness constraint and a distributedness constraint. The assignment of controller is then handled by a coindexing rule. What this rule basically says is that if the VP complement does not bear a thematic role, then the controller must be a THEME or a SOURCE; if the VP complement bears the thematic role GOAL, then the controller must be a THEME; and if the VP complement bears the thematic role THEME, then the controller must be a SOURCE (see also Chierchia 1983, 1989 for a controller assignment mechanism in terms of a thematic hierarchy).

Finally, still another semantic analysis, which is conceptually similar to those based on thematic relations, can be found in Sag and Pollard (1991; see also Pollard and Sag 1994). Following a suggestion by Comrie (1984, 1985), Sag and Pollard classify control verbs into three types: (i) the *order/permit-*

type verbs which take object control, (ii) the *promise*-type verbs which take subject control, and (iii) the *want/expect*-type verbs which also take subject control. Notice that each of the three types of control verb identified above shows some semantic regularity. The semantics of the *order/permit*-class verbs involves a state of affairs (SOA) whose relation is of influence type, the semantics of the *promise*-class verbs involves an SOA which contains a relation of commitment, and the semantics of the *want/expect*-class verbs involves an SOA whose relation is of orientation type. Now, for each of the three types of control verb, a role is identified as the controller. This is captured by a controller assignment principle in (3.104).

(3.104) Sag and Pollard's controller assignment principle
Given a non-finite VP or predicative complement C, whose semantic content C' is the SOA-AGR of an SOA S whose relation is R, the unexpressed subject of C is linked to:
(a) the influenced participant of S, if R is of influence type,
(b) the committor participant of S, if R is of commitment type,
(c) the experiencer participant of S, if R is of orientation type.

Let us now subject control to scrutiny using this semantic/thematic framework. From a conceptual point of view, the assignment of arbitrary features to control verbs, as Radford (1981: 381) and Foley and Van Valin (1984: 307) point out, has no predictive or explanatory power. Suppose we ask the question: how do we know that *persuade*, for example, is a verb of 'complement control' or 'thematic distinctness'? It is likely that we will get the non-answer: because it is marked with the feature [+CC] or [+TD] in the lexicon.

Turning next to empirical considerations, one advantage of the semantic/thematic approach over the syntactic/configurational one is that the former has extended the range of data covered. A number of control phenomena that are not captured by a 'minimal-distance' approach can now be accommodated under the semantic/thematic approach. One such case is the so-called controller shift in the double-passive construction, repeated here as (3.105).

(3.105) (a) Domingo was promised to be allowed to sing the part.
(b) (German, Růžička 1983)
ihm   war   versprochen worden Ø in   die
him-DAT (it) had been promised   into the
Nationalmannschaft aufgenommen zu werden.
national team   included   to be
'He had been promised to be included on the national team.'
(c) (Russian, Růžička 1983)
emu   bylo   oběščano Ø byt' vključennym v
him-DAT (it) was promised to be included   into
sbornuju komandu.
the select team
'He was promised to be included on the select team.'

170   *Semantic Approaches to Anaphora*

In (3.105), the controllee of the controlled constitute is a non-agent. Given that 'promise' is a [+TI] verb, by the TIC, it is predicted that the controller will be a non-agent as well—a prediction that is intuitively correct.

On the other hand, however, a number of the problems posed by control for a syntactic approach would remain problematic for the semantic/thematic alternative. But the major problem facing the semantic/thematic approach has to do with verbs that can be used to express different speech acts. The existence of control verbs of this kind has been reported for 'syntactic' languages like English and German (e.g. Comrie 1984, Farkas 1988, Sag and Pollard 1991). In (3.106), we have a nice illustration of this phenomenon from German (Comrie 1984).

(3.106) (*a*) Helga$_1$ versprach Otto$_2$, Ø$_{1/2}$ noch einmal einen Sieg
Helga promised Otto   once again   a   victory
zu erleben.
to experience
'Helga promised Otto to experience victory.'
(*b*) Scipio$_1$ überredete den Senat$_2$, Ø$_{2/1}$ frei handeln zu dürfen.
Scipio persuaded the Senate   free manage to be allowed
'Scipio persuaded the Senate that it/he should be permitted to have a free hand.'

But as I have pointed out in Huang (1991*b*, 1994), this type of 'ambiguous' control verb is more pervasive in a 'pragmatic' language like Chinese and Japanese. Besides (2.82), the following is yet another example from Chinese.

(3.107) (*a*) Xuesheng$_1$ shuofu   laoshi$_2$ Ø$_2$ xiawu   gei ta
pupil   persuade teacher   afternoon for 3SG
buke.
make up lesson
'The pupil$_1$ persuades the teacher$_2$ that (he$_2$) will make up lessons for him$_1$ in the afternoon.'
(*b*) Laoshi$_1$ shuofu   xuesheng$_2$ Ø$_1$ xiawu   gei ta   buke.
teacher persuade pupil   afternoon for 3SG make up lesson
'The teacher$_1$ persuades the pupil$_2$ that (he$_1$) will make up lessons for him$_2$ in the afternoon.'

As (3.107) indicates, *shuofu* 'persuade' can be used to express either a request-for-action or a request-for-permission. In unmarked cases, where the sentence is an iconic reflection of the way the world stereotypically is, *shuofu* expresses a request-for-action. Hence it is a verb of object control, as in (3.107*a*). However, this unmarked interpretation of *shuofu* is merely a strongly favoured one; it can simply be defeated in the face of inconsistency with, say, context and/or world knowledge. This is exactly what happens in

(3.107*b*). Given our knowledge about the world, it is more likely that the speech act expressed is a request-for-permission in (3.107*b*). Consequently, there is a shift of preference for the choice of controller here: the subject control reading becomes the preferred reading in (3.107*b*).

How, then, can this be accounted for by the semantic/thematic approach? Take *shuofu* as an example. Suppose *shuofu* is assigned the feature [+TD] on Růžička's account or treated as a verb whose SOA is of influence type in Sag and Pollard's theory. The TDC or the controller assignment principle will allow (3.107*a*) but rule out (3.107*b*). Suppose then it is given the feature [+TI] or analysed as a verb the SOA of which contains a relation of commitment type. The TIC or the controller assignment principle will permit (3.107*b*) but exclude (3.107*a*). Faced with problems of this kind, what can a proponent of the semantic/thematic approach do? One possibility might simply be to argue that these control verbs have two distinct senses, one marked with the feature [+TI] and the other marked with the feature [+TD]. Or, alternatively, one might even posit that there are two distinct control verbs involved, namely *shuofu*$_1$ and *shuofu*$_2$. But a move like this is not very satisfactory. In the first place, it runs the risk of adducing a proliferation of senses for certain control verbs in a language like Chinese. Secondly, since there is no algorithmic procedure to determine when these verbs are to be assigned the feature [+TD] and when they are to be assigned the feature [+TI], it would leave the feature assignment on a less principled ground. Of course, a proponent of such a proposal might contend that there is a principled way to assign features (at least) to some of these verbs. For example, in the case of the Chinese control verb *qingqiu* 'ask' (though not in the case of *shuofu*), whether it is to be assigned the feature [+TD] or [+TI] depends on the presence or absence of a matrix object. The presence of a matrix object will require the assignment of the feature [+TD]; otherwise the feature [+TI] will obtain, as in (3.108). But examples like (3.109) show that this is not entirely true.

(3.108) (*a*) Xiaoming qingqiu Ø canjia yinyue xiehui.
          Xiaoming ask   join music society
          'Xiaoming asks to join the music society.'
      (*b*) Xiaoming qingqiu ta   canjia yinyue xiehui.
          Xiaoming ask   3SG join music society
          'Xiaoming asks him to join the music society.'
(3.109) (*a*) Bingren qingqiu Ø mingtian gei ta   kaidao.
          patient ask   tomorrow for 3SG operation
          'The patient asks (e.g. the surgeon) to operate on him tomorrow.'
      (*b*) ?Bingren qingqiu yisheng Ø mingtian chuyuan.
          patient ask   doctor   tomorrow leave hospital
          'The patient asks the doctor to leave hospital tomorrow.'

In other words, the correlation between the assignment of [+TD] or [+TI] and the presence or absence of a matrix object is at best a one-way prediction: the presence of a matrix object tends to favour the assignment of [+TD] (unless context or world knowledge tells us otherwise, as in (3.109*b*)), but from the absence of a matrix object, little would be predicted (see also Comrie 1984). If the feature assignment is determined by the speech act the verb expresses, by the contextual environment in which the verb occurs, and/or by our knowledge about the world, then the solution seems to lie in pragmatics rather than semantics. We shall discuss the pragmatic aspects of control in the next chapter.[10]

3.2.3. Summary

In this section, I have examined a number of semantic analyses of binding and control. I have shown that they too are inadequate in accounting for binding and control in a range of languages.

3.3. Logophoricity

In the last section, I considered a number of semantically oriented analyses of binding and control. In this section, I shall examine the concept of logophoricity, focusing on the use of logophoric pronouns in African languages and that of long-distance reflexives in East Asian languages.

3.3.1. Background

Definition

Logophoricity refers to the phenomenon whereby the 'perspective' of an internal protagonist of a sentence or discourse, as opposed to that of the current, external speaker, is being reported by some morphological and/or

---

[10] There are, of course, other semantic approaches to control. In Hintikka and Sandu's (1991) Game-Theoretical Semantics, for example, the specification of controller is effected by the semantic game rules assigned to individual control verbs. These rules contain elements of possible worlds semantics. Put differently, semantic games of this kind are played on sets of possible worlds. By way of illustration, *persuade* is given the game rule in (i) below (adapted from Hintikka and Sandu 1991: 26, 89). This rule will assign a Davidsonic logical form to *persuade* and predict that it will take object control. But see Huang (1993) for a critique of this analysis.

(i) (G. persuade to)
   If the game has reached the sentence a persuades b to X, and the possible world w_1, then Nature chooses a persuade-alternative w_2 to w_1. The game is continued with respect to b X', and the possible world w_2 where X' is exactly like X except that the main verb is in the finite form.

syntactic means.[11] The term 'perspective' is used here in a technical sense and is intended to encompass words, thoughts, knowledge, emotion, perception, and space-location. The concept of logophoricity was introduced in the analysis of African languages like Aghem, Efik, and Tuburi, where there is a separate paradigm of logophoric pronouns which is employed for such a purpose (cf. Culy 1997). As an illustrating example, consider (3.110) taken from Efik, a Niger-Congo language.

(3.110) (Efik, Faltz 1985: 252)
   (a) ámá   étíŋ   étè ké   ikódù   dó.
      3SG-AUX 3SG-say 3SG COMP LOG-MOD-be located there
      'He$_1$ said that he$_1$ was there.'
   (b) ámá   étíŋ   étè ké   ókodù   dó.
      3SG-AUX 3SG-say 3SG COMP 3SG-MOD-be located there
      'He$_1$ said that he$_2$ was there.'

In (3.110a) the use of the logophoric pronoun encodes a coreferential reading between it and the matrix subject. By contrast, in (3.110b) the employment of the regular pronoun indicates a disjoint reference.[12]

Logophoric marking

Cross-linguistically, logophoricity may be morphologically and/or syntactically expressed by one or more of the following mechanisms: (i) logophoric pronouns, which may take free forms (e.g. Donno Sɔ) or be cliticized to the verb (e.g. Ewe),[13] (ii) logophoric addressee pronouns (e.g. Mapun), (iii)

---

[11] There is at least one other, wider definition for logophoricity (e.g. Reinhart and Reuland 1993). Under this definition, any NP, in particular, any anaphor which cannot be bound in its local domain, either in the sense of minimal configuration (e.g. Chomsky 1981) or in the sense of minimal predicate (e.g. Reinhart and Reuland 1993), is taken to be a logophor. An example of logophors of this kind is given below.
(i) John put the music manuscript next to himself.
There is, however, one major problem attendant to this definition of logophoricity, namely the problem of circularity. Unless the notion of logophoricity can be defined independent of binding theory, as in our case, to say that an anaphor is a logophor simply because it violates binding theory is circular.

[12] These regular pronouns may be seen as antilogophoric pronouns of some sort. See e.g. Ruwet (1991) for discussion of antilogophoric clitic pronouns *en* and *y* in French and Hill (1995) for discussion of antilogophoric pronouns in Adioukrou, a Kwa language spoken in Ivory Coast.

[13] If a logophoric language is also a null subject one, then a logophoric pronoun in subject position can be dropped. One such language is Mundani. In this language, a logophoric subject pronoun in a purpose clause is preferred to be omitted (Parker 1986). Another logophoric null subject language is Donno Sɔ, as the following example shows (Culy 1994b).
(i) Oumar minnɛ inyemɛ mɔ̃ gɛndɛzɛm gi.
    Oumar field   LOG   POSS regard:PROG-1SG said
    'Oumar$_1$ said that (he$_1$) will look at his$_1$ field.'
Note also that some languages utilize different sets of logophoric pronouns for different levels of logophoric embedding. For example, Yag Dii uses the 'bi' series for the first level, and 'ii' series for the second-level of embedding. For further discussion, see Bohnhoff (1986).

174 *Semantic Approaches to Anaphora*

logophoric verbal affixes (e.g. Gokana), and (iv) long-distance reflexives (e.g. Kannada). This is illustrated in (3.111a)–(3.114a) and (3.115).

(3.111) Logophoric pronouns: free form
(Donno Sɔ, Culy 1994a)
(a) Oumar Anta inyemɛñ waa be gi.
Oumar Anta LOG-ACC seen AUX said
'Oumar₁ said that Anta₂ had seen him₁.'
(b) Oumar Anta woñ waa be gi.
Oumar Anta 3SG-ACC seen AUX said
'Oumar₁ said that Anta₂ had seen him₃.'
(3.112) Logophoric pronouns: cliticized to the verb
(Ewe, Clements 1975)
(a) Kòfí bé yé-dzó.
Kofi say LOG-leave
'Kofi₁ said that he₁ left.'
(b) Kòfí bé é-dzó.
Kofi say 3SG-leave
'Kofi₁ said that he₂ left.'
(3.113) Logophoric addressee pronouns[14]
(Mapun, Frajzyngier 1985)
(a) n- sat n-wur taji gwar dim n Kaano.
I say BEN-3SG PROHB ADDR go PREP Kano
'I told him₁ that he₁ may not go to Kano.'
(b) n- sat n-wur taji wur dim n Kaano.
I say BEN-3SG PROHB 3SG go PREP Kano
'I told him₁ that he₂ may not go to Kano.'

(ii) Nán ba'ad ø 'ọ̀ moo 'ẹ̀n dà bi tóó bà ka vì bi bà
man work he say for what friend LOG other that SBOR-he ask LOG that
'ii súú wú 'úlá?
LOG repay-him CTR-Q
'The worker₁, he₁ asked why his₁ friend₂, he₂ asked him₁ that he₁ repays him₂?'

[14] The logophoric system in Mapun is represented as follows (Frajzyngier 1985):
(i) Logophoric system in Mapun

	A	B		C
	Subj/Obj	Subj	Obj	Subj
3-M-SG	wur	'di	'dim	gwar
F-SG	war	'de	'de	paa
PL	mo	'du	'dun	nuwa

As can be seen from the table above, addressee pronouns fall under set C. Note that Mapun has genuine logophoric pronouns as well. These are what Frajzyngier calls set B pronouns, as in (ii).
(ii) wur sat ni 'di ta dee n jos.
he say that he stop stay in Jos
'He₁ said that he₁ stoped over in Jos.'
Another language which has both logophiric pronouns and logophoric addressee pronouns is Angas (Frajzyngier 1985).

(3.114) Logophoric verbal affixes[15]
(Gokana, Hyman and Comrie 1981)
(a) à nyímá kɔ aè dɔ-ɛ̀.
he knows that he fell-LOG
'He₁ knows that he₁ fell.'
(b) à nyímá kɔ aè dɔ́.
he knows that he fell
'He₁ knows that he₂ fell.'
(3.115) Long-distance reflexives
(Kannada, Lidz 1995)
raamu shyaamu tann-annu priitis-utt-aane   anta
Raamu Shyamu self-ACC love-PRES-3SG-M that
namb-utt-aane.
believe-PRES-3SG-M
'Raamu₁ believes that Shyamu loves self₁.'

A typology of languages with respect to logophoricity

Following suggestions made by von Roncador (1992) and Culy (1994a), languages can be grouped into three types with respect to logophoricity: (i) full or pure logophoric languages, languages which have special morphological and/or syntactic forms that are employed only in logophoric domains, be the forms a logophoric pronoun, a logophoric addressee pronoun, and/or a logophoric verbal affix (e.g. Babungo, Pero, and Ekpeye); (ii) non-logophoric languages, languages which have no such special morphological and/or syntactic forms (e.g. Arabic, English, and perhaps Abrom, Agni, Bargu, Mambar, and Mooré) (von Roncador 1992); and (iii) semi- or mixed logophoric languages, languages which allow either logophors to be used for non-logophoric purposes (e.g. Igbo, Idoma, and Yoruba) or the extended use of

---

[15] Note that Gokana uses a verbal suffix -ee to encode logophoricity. The general rule is that this logophoric suffix must be marked on the most proximate verb. This sometimes gives rise to multiple ambiguity, as in (i), taken from Hyman and Comrie (1981).
(i) Lébàreè kɔ aè de-è́   a giá.
Lébàreè said he ate-LOG his yams
(a) 'Lébàreè₁ said that he₁ ate his₁ yams.'
(b) 'Lébàreè₁ said that he₁ ate his₂ yams.'
(c) 'Lébàreè₁ said that he₂ ate his₁ yams.'
(d) *'Lébàreè₁ said that he₂ ate his₂ yams.'
The possible range of interpretations indicated in (i) shows that in Gokana, it is both a necessary and a sufficient condition that at least one argument which is made logophoric be coreferential with the matrix subject, and that the argument in question need not be the embedded subject.
A further point of interest is that the Gokana system represents a violation of categorical iconicity, to borrow a term used by Haiman and Munro (1983a) in their description of the switch-reference system. This is because the function of reference tracking is indicated on the verb rather than on the noun itself.
It should also be mentioned here that Ikoro (1995) has recently argued that the logophoric marker in Gokana and Kana is a clitic rather than a verbal suffix.

reflexives in logophoric contexts (e.g. Italian, Malay, and Northern Pomo). Following are some full/pure logophoric languages listed in Culy (1994a).

(3.116) Culy's (1994a) list of full/pure logophoric languages
(i) 26 languages with logophoric pronouns
Aghem, Angas, Babungo, Banda-linda, Bwamu, Donno Sɔ (Dogon), Efik, Ewe, Fon, Gbandili, Gen-Mina, Ibibio, Idoma, Kukuruku (Yekhee), Lele, Mambila, Mapun, Mundang, Mundani, Ngbaka, Ngwo, Noni, Sarangambay, Sura, Tuburi, Yạg Dii (Duru)
(ii) 4 languages with logophoric addressee pronouns
Angas, Mapun, Pero, Tikar
(iii) 6 languages with logophoric verbal inflections
Akɔɔse, Efik, Ekpeye, Gokana, Ibibio, Moru/Logo/Kaliko

In addition, pure logophoric pronouns have been reported for Avatime/Siyasɛ, Banda-Tangbago, Doodwaayaayo/Namshi, Duupa, Feroge, Kresh, Kɔlbila, Mundu, Ndogo, Nkom, Nyang, Nzakara/Pambi/Ngala, Oron, Pape/Dugun, Pere/Kutin, Ténhé, and Yulu; and mixed logophoric marking has been noted for Birri, Bisa, Bongo, Busa, Engenni, Gbaya, Kera, Kposo, Krongo, Mangbetu, Sango, Tiv, Win, and Zande (von Roncador 1992, Culy 1994a, Bohnhoff 1986).

Interestingly enough, as Culy observes, while logophoric languages are found in many places throughout the world, full/pure logophoric languages seem to be found only in Africa.[16] Furthermore, while full/pure logophoric languages are not in a contiguous area, logophoric languages as a whole are in a contiguous area. This geographic distribution of logophoric languages is fascinating as well as surprising, and, for the time being, remains unexplained.

3.3.2. Logophoric pronouns in African languages

With the above background information in place, let us now turn to logophoric pronouns in African languages. I shall start with a description of logophoric pronouns and logocentric triggers.

---

[16] One possible exception might be Maxakali, a Macro-Je language spoken in Brazil, as documented in Popovich (1986). Another might be Lakhota, an American Indian language, and a third might be Wappo—a Yukian language spoken north of San Francisco Bay, California, as described in Faltz (1985: 254, 282). Following is an example from Wappo (cited from Faltz 1985: 282, who credits it to Sandra Thompson).
(i) (a) cephi   me   šawo hak'šeʔ hahšiʔ.
    3SG-NOM LOG bread like   say
    'He₁ says that he₁ likes bread.'
    (a) cephi   te   šawo hak'šeʔ hahšiʔ.
    3SG-NOM 3SG bread like   say
    'He₁ says that he₂ likes bread.'

See also Hale (1999) on the so-called 'logophoric conjunct/disjunct system of verbal inflection' exhibited in the Kathmandu and Bhaktapur dialects of Newari, a Tibeto-Burman language spoken in Nepal.

Logophoric pronouns and logocentric triggers

Person

The general pattern of person distinction for logophoric pronouns can be given as follows. In all languages with logophoric pronouns, logophoric pronouns can be third person; in some, they can also be identified as second person; in a few, they can be distinguished on first person as well.[17] For example, the logophoric pronoun *inyemɛ* in Donno Sɔ, a Dogon language spoken in Mali and Burkina Faso, can be third person only (Culy 1994*b*). The same is true of the logophoric pronoun *ɛpɛ* in Kresh, a Central Sudanic language (Santandrea 1976), the logophoric pronoun *wen* in Noni, a Beboid language (Hyman 1981), the logophoric pronoun *ni* in Sango, a Ubangi language (Zribi-Hertz personal communication), and the logophoric pronoun *ɛnɛ* in Togo Kã, another Dogon language (Culy, Kodio, and Togo 1994). By contrast, in Mundani, a Grassfields Bantu language, the logophoric pronoun *ye* is used for third and second, but not for first person (Parker 1986). Other African languages whose logophoric pronouns can be third and second, but not first person include Akɔɔse, another Bantu language (Hedinger 1984), Moru, a Central Sudanic language (Andersen and Goyvaerts 1986), and Ngbaka, a Ubangi language (Cloarec-Heiss 1986). Finally, in languages like Lele, an East Chadic language (Wiesemann 1986*a*), and Yag Dii, an Eastern Adamawa language (Bohnhoff 1986), logophoric marking can be done in all three persons. All this leads to the setting up of the following implicational universal of person hierarchy for logophoric pronouns (Hyman and Comrie 1981, Wiesemann 1986*a*; see also von Roncador 1992 for a two-way marking system on person based on the argument that some languages, such as Ewe, exhibit syncretism for second and third persons with regard to logophoric pronouns).

(3.117) Person hierarchy for logophoric pronouns
3 > 2 > 1
First-person logophoric pronouns imply second-person logophoric pronouns, and second-person logophoric pronouns imply third-person logophoric pronouns.[18]

A further piece of evidence in favour of (3.117) comes from Gokana, a Cross-River language spoken in Nigeria. In this language, while third-person

---

[17] Logophoric addressee pronouns are in general second person. This raises the issue of whether the logophoric complement should be seen as direct or indirect reported speech—a question whose answer is not forthcoming.

[18] Cf. the similar implicational universal for the person distinction of reflexives (e.g. Comrie 1989*a*: 7)

(i) An implicational universal for the person distinction of reflexives
First-person reflexives imply second-person reflexives, and second-person reflexives imply third-person reflexives.

logophoric marking is obligatory, second-person logophoric marking is optional but preferred, and first-person logophoric marking is optional but dispreferred (Hyman and Comrie 1981).

(3.118) (a) aè kɔ   aè dɔ-ɛ̀.
          he said he fell-LOG
          'He₁ said that he₁ fell.'
       (b) aè kɔ   aè dɔ̀.
          he said he fell
          'He₁ said that he₂ fell.'
(3.119) (a) oò kɔ   oò dɔ-ɛ̀.
          you said you fell-LOG
          'You said that you fell.'
       (b) oò kɔ   oò dɔ̀.
          you said you fell
          'You said that you fell.'
(3.120) (a) mm̀ kɔ   mm̀ dɔ-ɛ̀.
          I   said I   fell
          'I said that I fell.'
       (b) mm̀ kɔ   mm̀ dɔ̀.
          I   said I   fell
          'I said that I fell.'

Clearly, there is a functional/pragmatic explanation for (3.117). For referential disambiguity, the non-deictic third-person distinction is the most, and the deictic first-person distinction the least, useful, with the deictic second-person distinction in between, since third person is closer to non person than either first or second person. It follows, therefore, that the fact that first-person logophoric pronouns are very rare, if not non-existent, in natural languages is hardly surprising, given that logophoric pronouns are one of the (most common) devices the current, external speaker (which is encoded usually in terms of a first-person pronoun) utilizes in reflecting the perspective of anyone else (usually an internal protagonist) but him- or herself.

Number

Next, the general pattern of number specification for logophoric pronouns can be given as follows. While all languages with logophoric pronouns allow singular logophoric pronouns, only some permit plural logophoric pronouns as well. The Eastern Adamawa language Mundang, for example, is a language which has only singular logophoric pronouns (i.e. the weak form ʒì, the strong form áʒì, and the possessive form *min*) (Hagège 1974). Consequently, when reference is made to a set of internal protagonists of a reported event, the plural form of a first-person regular, non-logophoric pronoun is used instead. Other African languages which have only singular logophoric pronouns include Babungo, a Grassfields language (Schaub 1985), Igbo, a

Benue-Congo language (Carrell 1970), and Songhai, a Central Sudanic language (Hutchison 1971). By contrast, Ewe, Gbandili, an Admawa-Ubangi language, and Ngwo, a Grassfields language, are languages whose logophoric pronouns have both singular and plural forms. For Ewe, the singular is *ye*, and the plural is *yèwo* (Clements 1975); for Gbandili, the singular is ʔi/yì, and the plural is *yo* (Cloarec-Heiss 1986); and for Ngwo, the singular is *é*, and the plural is *ô* (Voorhoeve 1980, see also von Roncador 1992 for more examples). This generalization can be captured in another implicational universal for logophoric pronouns (Hyman and Comrie 1981, Wiesemann 1986*a*).

(3.121) Number hierarchy for logophoric pronouns
Singulars > plurals
Plural logophoric pronouns imply singular logophoric pronouns.

Again, from the viewpoint of referential disambiguity, singulars are more important than plurals.

A further point of interest is that a plural logophoric pronoun can be used for a singular antecedent, provided that the antecedent is properly included in the set denoted by the plural logophoric pronoun (and that the singular antecedent and the plural logophoric pronoun accord to the universal for conjunction of different persons, i.e. 1+1, 1+2, 1+3=1plural; 2+2, 2+3=2plural; 3+3=3plural) (e.g. Hyman and Comrie 1981). In contrast, the use of a plural regular pronoun in general does not include the matrix subject. Examples follow.

(3.122) (Ewe, Clements 1975)
    (*a*) Kofi kpɔ be   yèwo-do   go.
        Kofi see COMP LOG-PL-come out
        'Kofi$_1$ saw that they$_{\{1+2\}}$ had come out.'
    (*b*) Kofi kpɔ be   wo-do   go.
        Kofi see COMP 3PL-come out
        'Kofi$_1$ saw that they$_2$ had come out.'

(3.123) (Donno Sɔ, Culy 1994b)
    (*a*) Anta inyemɛmbe yogo   bojen gi.
        Anta LOG-PL tomorrow go-1PL said
        'Anta$_1$ said that they$_{\{1+2\}}$ are going tomorrow.'
    (*b*) Oumar be wa   inyemɛñ kɛɛle obuzɛn   gi.
        Oumar 3PL SUBJ LOG-OBJ money give-PROG-1PL said
        'Oumar$_1$ said that they$_2$ will give him$_1$ money.'

(3.124) (Gokana, Hyman and Comrie 1981)
    (*a*) lébàreè kɔ baè dɔ-ɛ̀.
        Lébàreè said they fell-LOG
        'Lébàreè$_1$ said that they$_{\{1+2\}}$ fell.'
    (*b*) lébàreè kɔ baè dɔ̀.
        Lébàreè said they fell
        'Lébàreè$_1$ said that they$_2$ fell.'

(3.125) (Lele, Wiesemann 1986a: 446)
- (a) Bábá yàá béè kārāndī nāgè   éè cáàní.
  Baba say to children LOG-3PL go field
  'Baba₁ says to (his) children₂ that they₍₁₊₂₎ are going to the field.'
- (b) Bábá yàá béè kārāndī ira-ge   éè cáàní.
  Baba say to children   3PL go field
  'Baba₁ says to (his) children₂ that they₂ are going to the field.'

(3.126) (Mapun, Frajzyngier 1985)
- (a) wur sat ni n nas 'dun.
  he say that I beat LOG
  'He₁ said that I beat them₍₁₊₂₎.'
- (b) wur sat ni n nas mo.
  he say that I beat 3PL
  'He₁ said that I beat them₂.'

Grammatical functions

Languages also vary with respect to the grammatical functions a logophoric pronoun can perform. In Igbo, for example, the logophoric pronoun has only one form, and can occur only as subject. But no such restriction is imposed on logophoric pronouns in the majority of African logophoric languages. As already mentioned, Mundang distinguishes between personal and possessive forms of the logophoric pronoun. In Zande, an Adamawa-Ubangi language, *u* is the logophoric form for third-person singular subject, *rus* the logophoric form for third-person singular object, *ami* the logophoric form for third-person plural subject, and *ra* the logophoric form for third-person plural object (Tucker and Bryan 1966). In a similar way, Mundani also uses different forms for different grammatical functions such as subject, object, possessor, and emphatic (Parker 1986), as the following examples show.

(3.127) Subject
- (a) tá   nē yé ā   lɔ́'ɔ́ ghǎ ėwén.
  3SG-SUBJ that LOG IPFV FUT go market
  'He₁ says that he₁ will go to market.'
- (b) tá   nē tá ā   lɔ́'ɔ́ ghǎ ėwén.
  3SG-SUBJ that 3SG IPFV FTU go market
  'He₁ says that he₂ will go to market.'

(3.128) Object
- (a) Kékɔ̀ŋ nē ... (tá) ŋé'é á vi.
  tortoise that 3SG-SUBJ carry OBJ 3SG-LOG
  'Tortoise₁ said that she₂ should carry him₁.'
- (b) Kékɔ̀ŋ nē ... (tá) ŋé'é á tò.
  tortoise that 3SG-SUBJ carry OBJ 3SG
  'Tortoise₁ said that she₂ should carry him₃.'

(3.129) Possessive
- (a) Kékɔ́ŋ nē ... ví ví ŋé'é á ví.
  tortoise that wife 3SG-LOG-POSS carry OBJ 3SG-LOG
  'Tortoise₁ said that his₁ wife should carry him₁.'
- (b) Kékɔ́ŋ nē ... ví tò ŋé'é á ví.
  tortoise that wife 3SG carry OBJ 3SG-LOG
  'Tortoise₁ said that his₂ wife should carry him₁.'

(3.130) Emphatic
- (a) ńdụ̀ ... Ø-sụ́-á nē ė ká wú zìá.
  giant rat fact-say-IPFV that DS NEG be 3SG-LOG-EMPH
  'Giant Rat₁ was saying that it was not him₁.'
- (b) ńdụ̀ ... Ø-sụ́-á nē ė ká wú tòà.
  giant rat fact-say-IPFV that DS NEG be 3SG-EMPH
  'Giant Rat₁ was saying that it was not him₂.'

Again, there seems to be an implicational universal here, namely:

(3.131) Grammatical function hierarchy for logophoric pronouns
Non-possessives > possessives
Possessive forms/functions imply non-possessive forms/functions.[19]

Logocentric triggers/antecedents

Next, mention should be made of logocentric triggers, namely those NPs that can act as an antecedent for a logophoric pronoun. First, logocentric triggers are generally constrained to be a core-argument of the logocentric predicate of the matrix clause. Secondly, they are typically subjects. In other words, a logophoric pronoun is canonically subject-oriented. Contrariwise, a regular pronoun is not. This contrast is illustrated in (3.132).

(3.132) (Tuburi, Wiesemann 1986a: 448–9)
- (a) Pɔl riŋ Jaŋ gá sὲ lɛ'ɛ.
  Paul said to-John that LOG fell
  'Paul₁ said to John₂ that he₁ fell.'
- (b) Pɔl riŋ Jaŋ gá a lɛ'ɛ.
  Paul said to-John that he fell
  'Paul₁ said to John₂ that he₂/₃ fell.'

But logocentric triggers can also be some other, non-subject argument, provided that this argument represents the 'source' of the proposition or the 'experience' of the mental state that is being reported. Two types of construction are particularly common. The first involves the predicate 'hear from', as in (3.133).

---

[19] Cf. the similar implicational universal for the grammatical function distinction of reflexives (Comrie 1989a: 7):
(i) An implicational universal for the grammatical function distinction of reflexives
  Possessive reflexives imply non-possessive reflexives.

(3.133) (Ewe, Clements 1975)
    (a) Ama se   tso   Kofi gbɔ be   yè-xɔ   nunana.
    Ama hear from Kofi side COMP LOG-receive gift
    'Ama$_1$ heard from Kofi$_2$ that she$_1$/he$_2$ had received a gift.'
    (b) (Donno Sɔ, Culy, Kodio, and Togo 1994)
    mi   inyemɛ yogo   bojo Mariam ibura   ɛgɛm   tube.
    1SG LOG tomorrow go Mariam mouth-LOC heard-1SG said
    'I heard from Mariam$_1$ that she$_1$ is going tomorrow.'
    (c) (Gokana, Hyman and Comrie 1981)
    mǹ dã́   lébàrè gã́   kɔ aè dɔ-ɛ̀.
    1S heard Lébàrè mouth that 3S fell-LOG
    'I heard from Lébàrè$_1$ that he$_1$ fell.'
    (d) (Tuburi, Wiesemann 1986a: 449)
    Pɔl laa   jág Jaŋ gá sɛ   lɛ'ɛ.
    Paul heard from John that LOG fell
    'Paul$_1$ heard from John$_2$ that he$_{1/2}$ fell.'

The second involves 'psychological' predicates expressing emotional states and attitudes, of which the 'experiencer' frequently acts as direct object or object of preposition. This is the case in (3.134) and (3.135).

(3.134) (a) (Gokana, Hyman and Comrie 1981)
    pɔ̀ síí   lébàrè kɔ aè dɔ-ɛ̀.
    fear catches Lébàrè that he fell-LOG
    'Fear catches Lébàrè$_1$ that he$_1$ fell.'
    (b) (Tuburi, Wiesemann 1986a: 449)
    hḗḗné jɔŋ Pɔl gá sɛ̀   lɛ̀' cégè.
    fear has Paul that LOG fall sick
    'Fear grips Paul$_1$ that he$_1$ will fall sick.'
(3.135) (a) (Ewe, Clements 1975)
    e nyo   na Ama be   yè a   dyi vi.
    it be good to Ama COMP LOG SBJV bear child
    'It pleases Ama$_1$ that she$_1$ is with child.'
    (b) (Gokana, Hyman and Comrie 1981)
    à kyɛ́   lébàrè kɔ aè dɔ-ɛ̀.
    it angers Lébàrè that he fell-LOG
    'It angers Lébàrè$_1$ that he$_1$ fell.'
    (c) (Mundani, Parker 1986: 154)
    á bɔ̂   tò ṅdɨ yé ā   kpélé nyá lá.
    it POSS-be fine him how LOG IPFV eat meat SBOR
    'It seemed fine to him$_1$ that he$_1$ could get some meat to eat.'

In fact, there appears to be a cross-linguistic hierarchy for logocentric triggers, in keeping with the familiar grammatical relation hierarchy subject > direct object > oblique first put forward systematically by Keenan and Comrie (1977).

(3.136) Hierarchy for logocentric triggers
Surface structure: subject > object > others
Semantic role: agent > experiencer > benefactor > others (cf. (3.78) above)

What (3.136) basically says is that the higher an NP is on the hierarchy, the more likely it will function as an antecedent for a logophoric pronoun. Given that the subject of the matrix clause is typically the NP that is highest on the hierarchy (and incidentally most animate), it is hardly surprising that it is the typical antecedent for a logophoric pronoun. Hierarchy (3.136) also provides a natural explanation for the examples in (3.134) and (3.135). Because the subjects in these examples are non-referential and non-human, by (3.136), the logophoric pronouns are naturally linked to the next highest NP available on the hierarchy, namely the objects. More or less the same can be said of examples of the following kind, where the antecedent of the logophoric pronoun is a possessor.

(3.137) (Tuburi, Wiesemann 1986a: 449)
ɓil   ɓɛ gɔ   fɛh   wɛr màngá sɛ   ko Jaŋ mɔ̀nɔ̀.
stomach his ACCOM happy because   LOG see John
'He was happy because he saw John.'

Taken together, the above four hierarchies predict that the most basic, unmarked pattern of logophoric marking is one which encodes logophoricity by the use of a third-person, singular, non-possessive, logophoric pronoun which refers to a human subject.

Logophoric domains and logocentric licensers

Logophoric pronouns usually occur in a logophoric domain, that is, a stretch of discourse in which the internal protagonist's perspective is being represented. In general, a logophoric domain starts in a clause which is subordinate to one in which the logocentric trigger is identified, either explicitly or implicitly. Following Culy (1994a), I shall call this part of the logophoric domain the sentential logophoric domain. In contrast, I shall call the logophoric domain which operates across clause boundaries the discourse logophoric domain. Logophoric binding across sentences is found in a number of African languages including Angas (Burquest 1986), Bwamu (Cuenot 1952), Donno Sɔ (Culy 1994b), Ewe (Clements 1975), Fon (Kinyalolo 1993), Gokana (Hyman and Comrie 1981), Tuburi (Hagège 1974), and perhaps Babungo (Schaub 1985) and Mundani (Parker 1986). Following is an example from Donno Sɔ (Culy 1994b).

(3.138) (Donno Sɔ, Culy 1994b)
Endyaana gamma wa: wo le ai   le sɔ   ra
rooster   cat   ADDR 3SG and mouse and word LOC
aa   indyemɛñ kundi ma?
who LOG   put   Q

Indyemɔ̃ togu ra yazɛm ai wa
LOG shelter LOC spend the night mouse SUBJ
bondo ra to kɔ nɛ lɛ taw indyem' mɔ̃ ye to ma?
hole LOC is it in also earth LOG POSS part is Q
'The rooster₁ to the cat₂: who put him₁ in the middle of the difference between him₁ and the mouse? He₁ spends the night in a shelter while the mouse is in a hole. Does it concern him₁?'

The logophoric domain is commonly created by a logocentric licenser, which is of two types: (i) logocentric predicates, and (ii) logocentric complementizers. Logocentric predicates can largely be distinguished on a semantic basis. The most common types of logocentric predicate are predicates of speech and thought. But other types of predicate such as those of mental state, knowledge, and direct perception can also trigger a logophoric domain. Languages differ in precisely which type of predicate they allow to function as a logocentric licenser. For example, while in Ewe and Mundani (Parker 1986), the first four types of predicate mentioned above are allowed to act as a logocentric licenser, in Donno Sɔ, predicates other than those of speech and thought are in general excluded. In Mundang, only predicates of asserting, ordering, and, more rarely, thinking can license a logophoric domain. There are even languages where logocentric predicates are further restricted. Igbo and Mapun are just such languages; the former restricts the logophoric domain to predicates of communication, and the latter just to predicates of speech, and perhaps only to the predicate *sat* 'say' (Frajzyngier 1985). Another African language whose logophoric domain is limited to the predicate *tèlè* 'say' seems to be Sango (Zribi-Hertz personal communication). Furthermore, the types of logocentric predicate may be affected by the grammatical functions the logophoric pronoun performs, as in Togo Kã (Culy, Kodio, and Togo 1994). This is illustrated in (3.139).[20]

(3.139) Logophoric pronouns in subordinate clauses in Togo Kã

	Subject	Object/possessor of object	Possessor of subject
'say'	✓	✓	✓
'think'	✓	✓	×
'hear'	✓	×	×
'know/see'	×	×	×

---

[20] Note that, as pointed out by Culy, Kodio, and Togo (1994), the grammatical positions in which a Togo Kã logophoric pronoun can appear form a hierarchy: the logophoric domain for 'say' is everywhere; that for 'think' does not cover the possessor of subject; that for 'hear' does not include the possessor of subject and object/the possessor of object; and finally no domain exists for 'know/see'. But whether this hierarchy can be applied to other languages is unknown.

But cross-linguistically there does seem to exist an implicational universal for logophoric predicates (Stirling 1993, Culy 1994a, Huang 1994).

(3.140) An implicational universal for logocentric predicates
Speech predicates > epistemic predicates > psychological predicates > knowledge predicates > perceptive predicates[21]

Some of the logocentric predicates in Mundani are given below (adapted from Parker 1986: 153):

(3.141) Some logocentric predicates in Mundani
  (a) Speech predicates
      ēsú 'say', ēbíítē 'ask', ēbɨɨné 'agree'
  (b) Epistemic predicates
      ēmɨɨté 'think', ētàándá 'think (mistakenly)', ēkɨ 'want', ekpá'té 'calculate'
  (c) Psychological predicates
      ēbɔ́ɔ́ 'seem good', ēwú'té ávi 'be happy/proud'
  (d) Perceptive predicates
      ézɔ́ 'hear'

What (3.140) basically says is this: if a language allows (some) predicates of one class to establish a logophoric domain, then it will also allow (some) predicates of every class higher on the hierarchy to do the same. Thus, if a language has logophoric marking with predicates of, say, psychological state, then it will necessarily have it with predicates of thought and communication.

Also worth pointing out is what is called the skipping effect of logophoric marking (cf. Chapter 2). This refers to the phenomenon whereby the embedding under a logocentric predicate of a sentence which originally does not allow logophoric marking can render it logophoric, in that the logophoric pronoun can skip over one or more layers of embedding to reach up the logocentric trigger of the logocentric predicate. For example, in Togo Kã the factual knowledge predicate 'know' does not function as a logocentric

---

[21] By 'perceptive predicates' is meant predicates of direct perception. Following Culy (1994a), I tentatively group non-factive perceptive predicates such as 'hear (that)' and 'see (that)' under the category of 'epistemic predicates'. Some examples follow.
(i) (a) (Babungo, Schaub 1985)
       ŋwɔ́ zɔ́ lāā vɨ́ tíi yi.
       3SG hear that 3PL call LOG
       'He₁ heard that they called him₁.'
   (b) (Mundani, Parker 1986: 154)
       tà zɔ́ nē̄ yé tsè á m̀bi.
       3SG hear that LOG pass LOG first
       'He₁ has heard that he₁ has come first.'
   (c) (Yoruba, Bamgbose 1966, see also Armstrong 1963)
       ó ri pé òún lówó.
       3SG see COMP LOG money
       'He₁ saw that he₁ had money.'
Another difficulty concerns the placement of psychological predicates between epistemic and perceptive predicates. Languages seem to vary here. Much more research is clearly needed.

predicate, hence the ungrammaticality of (3.142a). However, when it is embedded under the logocentric predicate 'say', the sentence becomes grammatical with the interpretation that the logophoric pronoun is coreferential with the matrix subject, as in (3.142b). The same is true of Ewe, as in (3.143).

(3.142) (Togo Kã, Culy, Kodio, and Togo 1994)
    (a) *Omar Anta ɛnɛ ɔɛ Ĩĩ wɔ.
        Omar Anta LOG saw know AUX
        'Omar$_1$ knows that Anta saw him$_1$.'
    (b) Madu Omar wa Ali ɛnɛ laran ɔɛ Ĩĩ wɔ gi.
        Madu Omar SUBJ Ali LOG sister saw know AUX said
        'Madu$_1$ said that Omar$_2$ knows that Ali$_3$ saw his$_{1/*2/*3}$ sister.'
(3.143) (Ewe, Clements 1975)
    (a) *Kofi se Kɔku wò-no yè dzu-m.
        Kofi hear Koku PRON-be LOG insult-PROG
        'Kofi$_1$ heard Koku insulting him$_1$.'
    (b) Kofi gblɔ be yè-se Kɔku wo-nɔ yè dzu-m.
        Kofi say COMP LOG-hear Koku PRON-be LOG insult-PROG
        'Kofi$_1$ said that he$_1$ heard Koku insulting him$_1$.'

Next, note that in some African languages the skipping effect can also arise with respect to clause types. Ewe, for example, is a language which does not allow a logophoric pronoun to be used inside a relative clause, as in (3.144a). But such a restriction is lifted when the relative clause is embedded under the logocentric predicate 'say', as in (3.144b). We shall have more to say about the skipping effect and the relative clause in the next section.

(3.144) (Ewe, Clements 1975)
    (a) *Ama ɖo ŋku nyɔ nuvi hi dze yè gbɔ̰ dyi.
        Ama set eye girl REL stay LOG side on
        'Ama$_1$ remembered the girl who stayed with her$_1$.'
    (b) Ama gblɔ be yè-ɖo ŋku nyɔ nuvi hi dze yè gbɔ dyi.
        Ama say COMP LOG-set eye girl REL stay LOG side on
        'Ama$_1$ said that she$_1$ remembered the girl who stayed with her$_1$.'

The other common type of logocentric licenser is what Stirling (1993: 260) calls 'report-opening' complementizers, such as *be* in Ewe, *kɔ* in Gokana, *se* in Mundang, *ne* in Mundani, and *ga* in Tuburi.[22] These complementizers are

---

[22] Some languages may use different logocentric complementizers for different semantic purposes. For example, Mundani utilizes the complementizer *ne* to introduce purpose clauses whose outcome is uncertain, but the complementizer *mbɨ'i/mbɨ'nè* to introduce purpose clauses whose outcome is certain.

(i) (Mundani, Parker 1986: 156)
    (a) táá fá'á nyáŋ nḕ yé ā bɔ́ ékáb.
        3SG work much that LOG IPFV have money
        'He$_1$ works hard so that he$_1$ may have money (but he may not).'
    (b) táá fá'á nyáŋ mbɨ'nḕ/'mbɨ'i yé á bɔ́ ékáb.
        3SG work much so that LOG IPFV have money
        'He$_1$ works hard so that he$_1$ may have money (and he will).'

often homophonous with the verb 'say' and are often developed historically out of it. Evidence for this evolutionary pattern has been found in a wide range of languages of West Africa (e.g. Ewe), East Asian (e.g. Japanese and Korean), South-East Asian (e.g. Lahu and Thai) and Chinese (e.g Cantonese and Taiwanese), Kriyol, the English-based creole Krio, the Micronesian language Pingilapese, Russian, and Sranan (e.g. Clements 1975, Lord 1976, 1993, Nylander 1985, Ransom 1988, Heine, Claudi, and Hünnemeyer 1991: 180, 216, 246–7, Matisoff 1991, Chui 1994, Kihm 1994, Hwang, Lyovin, and Baika 1998, see also n. 23 below). Some of them still carry the force of speech, as can be seen by the fact that a predicate of speech is frequently omitted before such a complementizer. Besides the Mundani examples in (3.127)–(3.130), below is an example from Tuburi. More or less the same can be said of Lele and many other Chadic languages.[23]

(3.145) (Tuburi, Hagège 1974)
à (ríŋ) wò gā tí sā:rā tʃÍ sā:rā.
they (say) PL COMP head LOG-PL hurt LOG-PL
'They₁ said that they₁ had headaches.'

In many logophoric languages, a complementizer of this kind does seem to play an important role in logophoric marking. Thus, Clements (1975) reports that in Ewe all logophoric constructions contain the complementizer *be*. In a similar way, Hagège (1974) notes that in Tuburi the use of the complementizer *ga* always gives rise to a logophoric domain. Essentially the same can be shown to hold for Gokana where the presence of the complementizer *kɔ* is sufficient for triggering logophoric marking. This connection between complementizers and logophoricity can also be observed in Lele; according to Burquest (1986) and Wiesemann (1986*a*), the whole system of logophoric pronouns in this language has developed from the grammaticalization of the complementizer *na*. Furthermore, Koopman and Sportiche (1989) suggest that there is a correlation between a complementizer and the extended use of independent, regular pronouns in logophoric contexts in Abé—a language which does not have a morphologically distinct class of logophoric pronouns (cf. Zribi-Hertz and Adopo 1992, and von Roncador 1992 on its neighbouring language Attie). Similar observations have also been made of the correlation between complementizers and logophoric marking in other logophoric languages such as Akɔɔse (Hedinger 1986), Banda-linda, and Efik (Welmers 1968, Essien 1975, 1990).

---

[23] See also Frajzyngier (1996), which discusses this link between verbs of saying and complementizers with respect to the following Chadic languages: Hausa, Pero, Tangale, Bole, Angas, Mapun, Ron-Bokkos, Daffo-Butura, Fyer, Ngizim, Pa'a, Zaar, Tera, Ga'anda, Hona, Cibak, Margi, Kapsiki, Mandara, Podoko, Xdi, Lamang, Mafa, Maɗa, Mofu-Gudur, Zulgwo, Gisiga, Mina, Gude, Logone, Munjuk, Mbara, Gidar, Somray, Lele, Kera, Dangla, Bidiya, Masa, and Mesme.

However, as pointed out—correctly, I think—by Culy (1994a), there does not seem to be a universal correlation between complementizers and logophoric marking. On the one hand, logophoric marking can be without complementizers, as in Mundang (Hagège 1974), hence complementizers may not be necessary. On the other hand, complementizers may not result in logophoric marking. Furthermore, of particular interest is that not only are languages different with regard to requiring a complementizer to be present to activate a logophoric domain, so are individual logocentric predicates within a single language. This is the case in Donno Sɔ. In this language, some logocentric predicates require the complementizer gɔ, which is homophonous with a definite determiner rather than the verb 'say', while others do not (Culy 1994a, 1994b).

(3.146) Logophoric marking and complementizers in Donno Sɔ

Predicate	Logophoric marking	Complimentizers
tell	✓	✓
hear from	✓	(✓)
say	✓	✗
know	✗	(✓)

There is thus clear evidence that complementizers do not in and of themselves give rise to a logophoric domain.

The extension of logophoric domains

Logophoric domains can be extended to syntactic constructions which do not seem to be directly related to the reporting of an internal protagonist's perspective. Again, languages vary greatly here and the extension may have to be stipulated on a language-by-language basis. But there do appear to be some common patterns cross-linguistically, two of which are (i) purpose clauses, as in (3.147)[24] and (ii) relative clauses.

(3.147) (a) (Babungo, Wiesemann 1986a: 444)
ŋwə́ nyɨ̀ŋ láā kɨ́ vɔ́ŋ sáŋ yi mé.
3SG ran that NEG 3PL beat LOG not
'He₁ ran away so that they could not beat him₁.'
(b) (Donno Sɔ, Culy 1994b)
Anta ma   sɔ   gɔ inyemɛ le   sɔyyɛ giaa yɛlɛ.
Anta SUBJ:1SG word the LOG with speak said came
'Anta₁ came in order for me to talk with her₁ about the problem.'

---

[24] Hyman and Comrie (1981) claim that, from a semantic point of view, purpose clauses appear to reflect some sort of emotion, intention, or desire of the matrix subject, thus becoming a natural candidate for the extension of logophoric marking. The same can be said of clauses containing 'because' in example (3.159) below.

(c) (Gokana, Hyman and Comrie 1981)
 lébàreè dù kɔ baá mɔn-ɛ̀ɛ̀ ɛ.
 Lébàreè came that they see-LOG him
 'Lébàreè₁ came for them to see him₁.'
(d) (Lele, Wiesemann 1986a: 446)
 Gōjí ày kùlúm kōlō nādū tégè ná kama.
 Goji take jar to LOG get with water
 'Goji₁ takes a jar so that she₁ gets water with it.'
(e) (Yag Dii, Bohnhoff 1986: 114)
 Bà'á Ø nəəy hághá bi hò púggì.
 father bends down LOG sees animal
 'Father bends down to see the animal.'

The case for the relative clause is more complicated. Roughly, three types of language can be identified: (i) languages like Mundang where the relative clause is opaque to logophoricity even if it lies inside a logophoric domain, as in (3.148), (ii) languages like Donno Sɔ and Gokana in which the relative clause becomes transparent to the effects of logophoricity within a logophoric domain (cf. the skipping effect), as in (3.149), and (iii) languages like Mundani and Tuburi where the relative clause is itself the environment for logophoric marking, regardless of the presence or absence of a logocentric predicate, as in (3.150).

(3.148) (Mundang, Hagège 1974: 294)
 à fá mò lɨ dɨb má kàl mè nè?
 he say you know man REL surpass me Q
 'He asked, "Do you know a man who is taller than me?"'
(3.149) (a) (Donno Sɔ, Culy 1994b)
 Anta inyemɛñ i gēnɔ agiya gi.
 Anta LOG-OBJ child robbed:AGT:DF took:3PL said
 'Anta₁ said that they took the child who robbed her₁.'
 (b) (Gokana, Hyman and Comrie 1981)
 lébàreè kɔ aè ziv-èè gíã́ e mm̀ zari.
 Lébàreè said he stole-LOG yams that I bought
 'Lébàreè₁ said that he₁ stole the yams that I bought.'
(3.150) (a) (Mundani, Parker 1986: 155)
 tàá ŋ- kɨ-á álʉ́ yé ā ghɨ̆ lá.
 3SG fact seek-IPFV path LOG IPFV do SBOR
 'He₁ is looking for a way in which he₁ can do it.'
 (b) (Tuburi, Hagège 1974)
 á Dīk ɨ́ māy má:gā sɛ̄ kó n sú: mònò.
 PRON think of young girl REL LOG see yesterday COREL
 'He₁ is thinking of the young girl he₁ saw yesterday.'[25]

---

[25] Little is known about the diachronic evolution of logophoric pronouns. One view is that they are derived from first-person pronouns (e.g. Clements 1975). This can be evidenced by the fact that in some logophoric languages, a logophoric pronoun in subject position requires or may co-occur with first-person agreement/affixation on the verb. This is the case with Donno Sɔ, (see

3.3.3. Long-distance reflexives in East Asian languages

We move next to long-distance reflexives in East Asian languages. In recent years, the notion of logophoricity has also been widely invoked in accounting for long-distance reflexivization though without a detailed, comparative study of these two types of anaphoric linking device (e.g. Bremen 1984, Kameyama 1984, Maling 1984, Kuno 1987, Sells 1987, Huang 1989, 1991*a*, 1994, Yoon 1989, Zribi-Hertz 1989, 1995, Sigurðsson 1990*a*, Levinson 1991, Reinhart and Reuland 1991, 1993, O'Connor 1992*a*, Stirling 1993, C. Baker 1995, Brinton 1995; see also earlier works by Cantrall 1974, Kuno 1972*a*, 1972*b*, Kuroda 1973, Kuno and Kaburaki 1977, Banfield 1982). For example, in her analysis of Icelandic, Maling (1984) observes that antecedents of a long-distance reflexive in this language must be both a logocentric NP and a grammatical subject. Kuno (1987) argues that the difference between the use of a long-distance reflexive and that of a regular pronoun where the choice is not structurally conditioned is essentially one of point of view. Zribi-Hertz (1989) hypothesizes that a long-distance reflexive can be employed if it refers to a minimal subject of consciousness. Sigurðsson (1990*a*) argues that the syntactic notion of 'accessible SUBJECT' be replaced by a semantic notion of 'accessible secondary ego' in long-distance reflexivization in Icelandic. Hellan (1991) is of the opinion that long-distance reflexivization in Norwegian and Icelandic abides by a containment condition, which states that a long-distance reflexive α, bound by an antecedent β, is contained within a constituent γ if γ is, among other things, in the scope or perspective, of β. He calls this relation a perspective command. Along somewhat similar lines, Hintikka and Sandu (1991) propose to derive the contrast between reflexives and pronouns in locative PPs in English from a distinction between perspective and descriptive identification. The basic insight underlying all these analyses is that the use of a long-distance reflexive is closely correlated with a logophoric perspective.

---

the example in n. 13 above) and Nilotic Lotuko. Another piece of evidence comes from the etymology of Sango logophoric pronoun *ni*. *Ni* was a first-person pronoun (Zribi-Hertz personal communication). But this 'first-person origin' hypothesis has been challenged by von Roncador (1992). There is, for instance, evidence that the logophoric marker in both Gokana and Kana is derived from third-person singular pronouns (Ikoro 1995), and the logophoric pronoun in Efik and Ibibio comes from third-person plural pronouns. For the historical origin of pure logophoric systems, see Hyman (1981) on Noni, Hyman and Comrie (1981) on Gokana, and Parker (1986) on Mundani. Parker speculates that the logophoric pronoun in Mundani is derived from reflexives, which are themselves derived from emphatics. What is of interest is that this view dovetails with Levinson's (1991), Heine's (1997), and König and Siemund's (1997) hypothesis that reflexives are diachronically developed from emphatics (cf. n. 9 above). Approaching the issue from an opposite angle, and basing their account on Tɔrɔ Sɔ and Togo Kã, Culy, Kodio, and Togo (1994) speculate that there are two ways in which a logophoric pronoun can lose its logophoricity. The first is by becoming a subject-oriented reflexive, and the second is by being lost without reflex. See also Voorhoeve (1980) for further speculations on the loss of logophoricity.

In this section, I shall survey long-distance reflexives in Chinese, Japanese, and Korean, comparing and contrasting their use with that of logophoric pronouns in African languages.

Long-distance reflexives and logocentric triggers

Person, number, and grammatical functions

The Chinese long-distance reflexive *ziji*, the Japanese long-distance reflexive *zibun*, and the Korean long-distance reflexive *caki* are not specified for person, number, or gender, hence are devoid of φ-features. But what is of relevance to us here is that this pattern of person and number distinctions for long-distance reflexives in Chinese, Japanese, and Korean does not run counter to the person and number hierarchies set up for logophoric pronouns in African languages. As for the grammatical functions it can perform, a long-distance reflexive in East Asian languages can serve as subject, object, indirect object, oblique, and possessor. Examples from Japanese are given in (3.151) (Kato 1994). Again, this is in keeping with the grammatical function hierarchy put forward for logophoric pronouns in African languages.

(3.151) (*a*) Subject
  Takasi-ga   zibun-ga   tensai da to   omotteiru.
  Takasi-SUBJ self-SUBJ genius is COMP think
  'Takasi$_1$ thinks that self$_1$ is a genius.'
 (*b*) Direct object
  Takasi-wa   Hirosi-ga   zibun-o kiratteiru koto-o   sitteiru.
  Takasi-TOP Hirosi-SUBJ self-OBJ hate   COMP-OBJ know
  'Takasi$_1$ knows that Hirosi$_2$ hates self$_1$.'
 (*c*) Indirect object
  Takasi-wa   Hirosi-ga   zibun-ni kasite kureta kuruma-o
  Takasi-TOP Hirosi-SUBJ self-OBJ lend   (give) car-OBJ
  kowasite simatta.
  broken   ended-up
  'Takasi$_1$ has broken the car which Hirosi$_2$ lent self$_1$.'
 (*d*) Possessor
  Takasi-wa   Yukiko-ga   Hirosi-ni   zibun-no syasin-o
  Takasi-TOP Yukiko-SUBJ Hirosi-OBJ self's   photo-OBJ
  miseta to   omotta.
  showed COMP thought
  'Takasi$_1$ thought that Yukiko$_2$ had shown self's$_1$ photo to Hirosi$_3$.'

Next, antecedents for long-distance reflexives in Chinese, Japanese, and Korean also run parallel to those for logophoric pronouns in African languages. First, they are usually limited to be a core-argument of the predicate of the matrix clause. Secondly, they are typically subjects.

(3.152) (a) (Chinese)
Xiaoming gaosu Xiaohua shuo Xiaolan shuo ziji de huaihua.
Xiaoming tell Xiaohua say Xaiolan say self PRT bad words
'Xiaoming$_1$ tells Xiaohua$_2$ that Xiaolan$_3$ talks ill of self$_{1/*2/3}$.'
(b) (Japanese, Aikawa 1993)
John-ga Bill-ni Mary-ga zibun-o hihansita to itta.
John-NOM Bill-DAT Mary-NOM self-ACC criticized that said
'John$_1$ told Bill$_2$ that Mary$_3$ criticized self$_{1/*2/3}$.'
(c) (Korean, Kim 1993)
John-un Bill-eykey caki-ka tayhak iphaksihem-ey
John-TOP Bill-to self-NOM college entrance examination-at
hapkyekhayssta-nun iyaki-lul hayssta.
passed -that story-ACC said
'John$_1$ told Bill$_2$ that self$_{1/*2}$ passed the college entrance examination.'

Again, as in the case of logocentric triggers for logophoric pronouns in African languages, antecedents for long-distance reflexives in Chinese, Japanese, and Korean can also be some non-subject argument, provided that this argument represents the 'source' of the proposition or the 'experience' of the mental states that is being described. Once more, the two most common types of construction are (i) those involving the predicate 'hear from', as in (3.153), and (ii) those involving psychological predicates, as in (3.154).

(3.153) (a) (Chinese)
Ta ting tongshi shuo ziji tishang le jiaoshou.
3SG hear colleague say self promote PFV professor
'He$_1$ hears from the colleague$_2$ that self$_{1/2}$ has been promoted to a professor.'
(b) (Japanese, Sells 1987)
Taroo wa Takasi kara Yosiko ga zibun o nikundeiru
Taroo TOP Takasi from Yosiko SUBJ self OBJ be-hating
to kiita.
COMP heard
'Taroo heard from Takasi$_1$ that Yosiko hated him$_1$.'
(c) (Korean, Kim 1993)
John-un Bill-loputhe caki-ka tayhak iphaksihem-ey
John-TOP Bill-from self-NOM college entrance examination-at
hapkyekhayssta-nun iyaki-lul tulessta.
passed -that story-ACC heard
'John$_1$ heard from Bill$_2$ that self$_{1/2}$ passed the college entrance examination.'
(3.154) (a) (Chinese)
Mama biaoyang le ziji shi Xiaoming hen gaoxing.
Mum praise PFV self make Xiaoming very happy
'That Mum$_1$ praised self$_{1/2}$ makes Xiaoming$_2$ very happy.'

(b) (Japanese, Sells 1987)
　　Yosiko ga　zibun o　nikundeiru koto　ga　Mitiko
　　Yosiko SUBJ self　OBJ be-hating　COMP SUBJ Mitiko
　　o　zetuboo　e　oiyatta.
　　OBJ desperation to drive
　　'That Yosiko₁ hated self₂ drove Mitiko₂ to desperation.'
(c) (Korean, Yoon 1989)
　　John-i　caki-lul　miweha-n-ta-nun　　　　sasil-i
　　John-NOM self-ACC hate-PRES-DECL-COMP fact-NOM
　　Mary-lul　kwelop-hi-ess-ta.
　　Mary-ACC bother-CAUS-PAST-DECL
　　'That John₁ hates self₂ bothered Mary₂.'

Finally, the hierarchy for logocentric triggers may just as well be applied to antecedents for long-distance reflexives in East Asian languages. In other words, NPs that are higher on the hierarchy are more likely to be antecedents of a long-distance reflexive than NPs that are lower on the hierarchy. Note the similarity between (3.137) above and (3.155) below, where both involve a possessor that acts as the antecedent.

(3.155) (Chinese)
　　Xiaoming de　　taidu　　shi ziji jue　　bu ren　　cuo.
　　Xiaoming POSS attitude be self EMPH not admit mistake
　　'Xiaoming's attitude is that self will never admit any mistake.'

Long-distance anaphoric binding domains and logocentric licensers

Turning next to the syntactic and discourse environments in which a long-distance reflexive in East Asian languages is used, one can see that they typically constitute a logophoric domain. The binding domain for long-distance reflexives in East Asian languages is usually triggered by a logocentric predicate. All the five types of predicate listed on hierarchy (3.140) are allowed in these languages to act as a logocentric licenser. This explains why long-distance reflexivization occurs predominantly within the sentential complements of predicates of speech, thought, mental state/attitude, knowledge, and perception in East Asian languages. Following are some of these predicates in Japanese (adapted from Kato 1994).

(3.156) Some logocentric predicates in Japanese
　　(a) Speech predicates
　　　　iu 'say', hanasu 'tell', utiakeru 'confess', tanomu 'ask', tugeru 'inform'
　　(b) Epistemic predicates
　　　　omou 'think', sinziru 'believe', kitai-suru 'expect', utagau 'doubt'
　　(c) Knowledge predicates
　　　　siru 'know'
　　(d) Psychological predicates
　　　　kanasimaseru 'sadden', nayamaseru 'worry', obiesaseru 'frighten', yorokobaseru 'please'

(e) Perceptive predicates
kiku 'hear'

Examples showing that even perceptive predicates can be used as logocentric licensers in Chinese, Japanese, and Korean are furnished in (3.157).[26]

(3.157) (a) (Chinese)
Xiaoming tingjian Xiaohua zai piping ziji.
Xiaoming hear Xiaohua DUR criticize self
'Xiaoming$_1$ hears Xiaohua$_2$ criticizing self$_1$.'
(b) (Japanese, Culy 1994a)
Taro-wa Keiko-ga zibun no imato to hanashi-o
Taro-TOP Keiko-SUBJ self-GEN younger sister-DAT talk-OBJ
siteiru-no-o kiita.
talking-NOM-OBJ heard
'Taro$_1$ heard Keiko talking to self's$_1$ younger sister.'
(c) (Korean)
Kim-nun Inho-ka caki-lul chingchahanun-kes-ul tulessta.
Kim-TOP Inho-NOM self-ACC praise-fact-ACC heard
'Kim$_1$ heard Inho praising self$_1$.'

Now, given the hierarchy for logocentric predicates, one immediate question arises: why is the hierarchy ordered in the way it is? Currently, the most plausible explanation (Culy 1994a) proposes that the hierarchy is associated with a notion of 'reliability'. The link between the hierarchy and reliability is twofold. First, the more reliable the current, external speaker deems the situation to be, the more likely it is that the context will be marked as a logophoric one. Logophoric marking is used in this case to show that the current, external speaker (or the primary ego) is reporting on the logocentric trigger (or the secondary ego) and is not taking responsibility for what he or she is

---

[26] Note that the skipping effect we have seen in Section 3.3.2. above with respect to logophoric pronouns in African languages also shows itself with regard to long-distance reflexives. A simple example of this effect can be found in Icelandic (given that this effect cannot be tested against Chinese, Japanese, and Korean due to the fact that all the five types of predicate listed in hierarchy (3.140) are logocentric predicates in these languages). In Icelandic, factual knowledge predicates such as 'know' normally take indicatives and therefore cannot license the use of a long-distance reflexive, as in (ia). However, when (ia) is embedded under a logocentric predicate such as 'say', its behaviour changes, that is, it can take subjunctives and no longer blocks the use of a long-distance reflexive, as in (ib) (see also Maling 1984, Hellan 1991 on the effect on long-distance reflexivization within a relative clause in Icelandic).
(i) (Icelandic, Sigurðsson 1990a)
(a) *Jón veit að María elskar sig.
John knows-INDIC that Mary loves-INDIC self
'John$_1$ knows that Mary loves self$_1$.'
(b) Anna segir að Jón viti að
Ann says-INDIC that John knows-SBJV that
María elski sig.
Mary loves-SBJV self
'Ann$_1$ says that John knows that Mary loves self$_1$.'

reporting (see also Sigurðsson 1990a and Stirling 1993 for discussion about the notion of 'responsibility'). This notion of s[ituation]-reliability seems to explain why cross-linguistically speech predicates are more likely to generate logophoric marking than all the other predicates on the hierarchy. Unlike the action denoted by the other predicates, the action referred to by speech predicates can be directly perceived. Having direct sensory evidence about the situation is certainly the clearest sign of s-reliability. The second factor affecting the hierarchy is reliability of the report, that is, the less reliable/objective the report is, the more likely it is that the context will be made a logophoric domain. Logophoric marking is used in this case to reflect the subjectivity of the truth, content, or linguistic characterization of the report. This is called r[eport]-reliability. R-reliability appears to be responsible for the fact that cross-linguistically languages are less likely to mark logophoricity with predicates of knowledge and of direct perception than with predicates of speech and of thought. This is because knowledge and direct perception predicates are factive, in that they presuppose the truth of their complements. Furthermore, with predicates of direct perception, the logocentric trigger also has direct, sensory evidence for the report. Consequently, the reports with knowledge and direct perception predicates are more reliable/objective than those with the other predicates, hence logophoric marking is less used with these reports.

In addition, the long-distance binding/logophoric domain in East Asian languages can also be introduced (optionally) by a logocentric complementizer or connective. For example, the logophoric domain in Chinese can be triggered by the semi-complementizer *shuo*. This semi-complementizer is homophonous with the verb *shuo* 'say' and still carries the force of speech. This can be evidenced by the fact that (i) it cannot co-occur with the verb 'say', as in (3.158) and (ii) it can co-occur only with predicates of speech, as in (3.152a) above.

(3.158) (Chinese)
    *Xiaoming shuo shuo Xiaohua bu xihuan ziji.
    Xiaoming say say Xiaohua not like self
    'Xiaoming$_1$ says that Xiaohua$_2$ does not like self$_{1/2}$.'

Another case in point comes from connectives such as *yinwei* in Chinese, *node* in Japanese, and *ttaymuney* in Korean. As noted by e.g. Sells (1987), Yoon (1989), Kim (1993), and Huang (1994), the use of these connectives appears to be sufficient to take long-distance reflexivization into adverbial clauses.

(3.159) (*a*) (Chinese)
    Yinwei laoshi biaoyang le ziji suoyi Xiaoming hen gaoxing.
    because teacher praise PFV self so Xiaoming very happy
    'Xiaoming$_1$ was very happy because the teacher$_2$ had praised self$_{1/2}$.'

(b) (Japanese, Sells 1987)
Takasi-wa Yosiko-ga mizu o zibun no ue ni kobosita
Takasi-TOP Yosiko-SUBJ water OBJ self GEN on LOC spilled
node nurete-simatta.
because wet-got
'Takasi$_1$ got wet because Yosiko$_2$ spilled water on self$_1$.'

(c) (Korean, Yoon 1989)
John-un Mary-ka caki-eykey mwul-ul
John-TOP Mary-NOM self-DAT water-ACC
epsil-ess- ki-ttaymun-e sec-ess-ta.
spill-PAST because got-wet
'John$_1$ got wet because Mary$_2$ spilt water on self$_{1/2}$.'

Furthermore, as with logophoric domains in African languages, long-distance reflexive binding domains in East Asian languages are not restricted to clausal complements of a logocentric predicate, either. First, they can be extended to other types of syntactic construction such as the topic construction, as in (3.160), and the relative construction, as in (3.161).

(3.160) (a) (Chinese)
Xiaoming zuiba guan bu zhu ziji.
Xiaoming mouth control not RV self
'Xiaoming$_1$, mouth$_2$ cannot control self$_1$.'

(b) (Japanese, Kuno 1973)
Sono kodomo-wa zibun-ga kawaigatte-ita inu-ga sinde simatta.
that child-TOP self-SUBJ was fond of dog-SUBJ died ended-up
'That child$_1$, the dog that self$_1$ was fond of died.'

(c) (Korean, Kim 1993)
John-un caki-ka mangchyessta.
John-TOP self-NOM ruined
'John$_1$, self$_1$ ruined.'

(3.161) (a) (Chinese)
Xiaoming xihuan biaoyang ziji de laoshi.
Xiaoming like praise self REL teacher
'Xiaoming$_1$ likes the teacher$_2$ who has praised self$_{1/2}$.'

(b) (Japanese, Kuno 1973)
John-wa zibun-o nikunde-iru onna to kekkon-sita.
John-TOP self-OBJ hate woman with married
'John$_1$ married a woman who hated self$_1$.'

(c) (Korean)
Kim-un caki-lul chingchanha-nun sensayng-ul cohahanta.
Kim-TOP self-ACC praise-to teacher-ACC like
'Kim$_1$ likes the teacher$_2$ who praises self$_{1/2}$.'

Secondly, they can even operate across sentence boundaries, extending over an arbitrarily long stretch of discourse, provided that this portion of discourse falls under the scope, or perspective, of the logocentric NP which antecedes the long-distance reflexive.

(3.162) (a) (Chinese, Huang 1994)
Xiaoming zai sheng mama de qi, yinwei gangcai
Xiaoming DUR take mum PRT offence because just now
baba shuo ziji shi, mama yi sheng ye bu keng.
dad scold self time mum one sound EMPH not utter
'Xiaoming$_1$ is getting angry with Mum, because she did not say a word when Dad scolded self$_1$ a moment ago.'
(b) (Japanese, Sells 1987)
Taroo wa totemo kanasigat-tei-ta. Yosiko ga Takasi
Taroo TOP very sad-PROG-PAST Yosiko SUBJ Takasi
ga zibun o hihansita noni bengosi-nakat-ta kara da.
SUBJ self OBJ criticized though defend-not-PAST because COP
'Taroo$_1$ was very sad. It is because Yosiko did not defend (him) though Takasi criticized self$_1$.'
(c) (Korean, Kim 1993)
Kokayt malu-ey olla-se-ni kuliwun caki cip tungpul-i
hill slope-at rise-stand-as lovely self house lamplight-NOM
poinita.
visible
Sekpong-i-nun ... tanswum-e kokay-lul ttwie naylye kassupnita.
Sekpong-TOP in one breath hill-ACC run down went
'Upon standing on the slope, the lamplight from self's$_1$ lovely home is visible. Sekpong$_1$ ... ran down the hill in one breath.'

Note the use of 'because' in both the Chinese passage (3.162a) and the Japanese passage (3.162b). The use of 'because' here makes clear that the external speaker is making a judgement about the clausal relationship between the two events described in (3.162a) and (3.162b) from the viewpoint of the discourse internal protagonist. Hence the clauses containing the long-distance reflexives are in the scope of the logocentric triggers. In a similar way, in the Korean passage (3.162c), which is written in the so-called *style indirect libre*, the use of the connective ending *-uni* 'as' is also of some significance. (Note that *-uni* becomes *-ni* when preceded by a vowel-ending verb.) According to Kim (1993), *-uni* is usually used by the first-person, current, external speaker. Its use by the narrator of the passage here enables him or her to adopt the point of view of the central character of the story, thus creating a logophoric context.

So far I have been showing that there are strong parallels in the use of logophoric pronouns in African languages and in that of long-distance reflexives in East Asian languages. But there is one pattern of long-distance reflexives in East Asian languages which has not been attested for logophoric pronouns in African languages. This concerns the use of deictically oriented directional predicates such as 'come/go' and 'bring/take'. As can be shown by (3.163)–(3.165), while the use of 'come' in the (a) sentence allows long-distance reflexivization, the use of 'go' in the (b) sentence does not seem to.

Furthermore, note that this contrast is independent of whether or not a logocentric predicate occurs in the matrix clause (see also Kuno 1987: 261 on Turkish).

(3.163) (Chinese)
    (a) Xiaoming shuo mama yihuir hui lai   kan ziji.
        Xiaoming say   mum soon will come see self
        'Xiaoming$_1$ says that Mum$_2$ will come to see self$_1$ soon.'
    (b) ?Xiaoming shuo mama yihuir hui qu kan ziji.
        Xiaoming say   mum soon will go see self
        'Xiaoming$_1$ says that Mum$_2$ will go to see self$_1$ soon.'

(3.164) (Japanese, Kuno 1987)
    (a) Taroo wa   zibun ni ai ni kita hito
        Taroo TOP self   to see to came people
        ni-wa, dare-demo, syokuzi o dasu.
               whoever   meal   offer
        'Taroo$_1$ offers a meal to anybody who has come to see self$_1$.'
    (b) ?Taroo wa   zibun ni ai ni itta hito
        Taroo TOP self   to see to went people
        ni-wa, dare-demo, syokuzi o dasu.
               whoever   meal   offer
        'Taroo$_1$ offers a meal to anybody who has gone to see self$_1$.'

(3.165) (Korean, Kuno 1987)
    (a) John-un, Mary-ka   macimakulo caki-lul   po-la
        John-TOP Mary-NOM last   self-ACC see-to
        w-ass-ul-ttay,   aph-ass-ta.
        come-PAST-when sick-was
        'John$_1$ was sick when Mary$_2$ came to see self$_1$ last.'
    (b) ?John-un, Mary-ka   macimakulo caki-lul   po-la
        John-TOP Mary-NOM last   self-ACC see-to
        ka-ss-ul-ttay,   aph-ass-ta.
        go-PAST-when sick-was
        'John$_1$ was sick when Mary$_2$ went to see self$_1$ last.'

This contrast seems to be attributed to the fact that the use of 'come' in the (a) sentence makes clear what is reported is from the space-location of the matrix subject, therefore the matrix subject is the pivot, or the relativized 'centre of deixis' in the logophoric domain. Hence the possibility of long-distance reflexivization. In other words, 'come' must be interpreted as describing movement towards the matrix subject. On the other hand, the use of 'go' in the (b) sentence is an indication that what is described is not from the 'camera angle' of the matrix subject, rather it indicates movement away from the matrix subject, therefore the matrix subject cannot be the pivot or the logocentric trigger. Hence long-distance reflexivization is rather bad. The deictic nature of the pivot can further be seen by the fact that (3.163b), for example, can be improved if one imagines that Xiaoming is now not in his usual place and his mother will go to see him in the place where he is normally supposed to be. How, then, can these examples be accounted for? One simple solution might be to incorporate deictically oriented directional predicates into hierarchy (3.140) above to derive a new one (3.166):

(3.166) A revised implicational universal for logocentric predicates
Speech predicates > epistemic predicates > psychological predicates > knowledge predicates > perceptive predicates > unmarked directional predicates

Needless to say, much further research is needed to see how these predicates behave in other (semi/mixed) logophoric languages such as Icelandic.

By way of summary, the weight of evidence we have seen strongly indicates that the prototypical use of long-distance reflexives in East Asian languages is indeed logophoric. Given that there are striking parallels between logophoric pronouns in African languages and long-distance reflexives in East Asian languages, the question that comes up next is how to provide a unified, formal account of the two anaphoric linking devices in linguistic theory. The answer seems to reside in an analysis which combines both a Discourse Representation Theory representation (e.g. Kamp 1982, Kamp and Reyle 1993) and a neo-Gricean pragmatic interpretation (e.g. Huang 1989, 1991*a*, 1991*b*, 1994). I shall discuss discourse representation in the next section but postpone the discussion of neo-Gricean interpretation to Chapter 4.

3.3.4. Discourse representation

Without attempting an exact formulation of the semantic ingredients of logophoricity, I shall adopt Sells's (1987) analysis of the concept in terms of three more primitive discourse-semantic notions: (i) the source, namely the 'one who is the intentional agent of the communication', (ii) the self, namely the 'one whose mental state or attitude the content of the proposition describes', and (iii) the pivot, namely the 'one with respect to whose (timespace) location the content of the proposition is evaluated' (cf. Kuno and Kaburaki's 1977 and Kuno's 1987 notion of camera-angle/empathy, see also Stirling 1993 for an alternative, bipartite decomposition of the concept). Clearly, while the self represents the mental aspect of perspective, the pivot represents its physical aspect. Furthermore, Sells claims that these roles are not independent of each other, rather they can be connected in an implicational manner, that is, if the source role is assumed by the internal protagonist, then so is the self role, and if the self role is realized by the internal protagonist, then so is the pivot role. This three-way classification of discourse-semantic roles leads to a four-way classification of discourse environments. The first represents direct speech. In this context, all three discourse-semantic roles coincide on one individual, namely the current, external speaker. Second, there is what Sells calls the context of 'third-person point of view', in which the external speaker has the source and self roles, but the internal protagonist bears the pivot role. Third, then, is the discourse setting for 'psych-verbs'. In this logophoric context, whereas the source role is predicated of the external speaker, the self and pivot roles go to the internal protagonist. The final, fourth type of discourse environment involves what Sells calls 'logophoric verbs', namely verbs of saying and thinking. This constitutes the prototypical logophoric context and all three discourse-semantic roles coincide on the internal protagonist. These four discourse contexts defined by the three roles are listed in (3.167).

(3.167) Sells's (1987) discourse environments

	Direct speech	Third-person point of view	Psych-verb	Logophoric verb
source	external	external	external	internal
self	external	external	internal	internal
pivot	external	internal	internal	internal

Before proceeding to establish the semantic representations for logophoricity, I shall depart from Sells (1987) but follow Stirling (1993) in taking the source, self, and pivot technically, in the sense of the assigned epistemic validating source, self, and pivot. The validating source, self, and pivot are the individual to whom the current, external speaker linguistically assigns responsibility for validation of the truth of a proposition, the actuality of an event, and/or the accuracy of the linguistic expression used in asserting the proposition or describing the event. The advantage of seeing the roles as validating ones emerges quite clearly when we consider examples of the following kind.

(3.168) (a) (Ewe, Clements 1975)
Kofi me-nya be me-kpɔ yè o.
Kofi NEG-know COMP PRON-see LOG NEG
'Kofi$_1$ didn't know that I had seen him$_1$.'
(b) (Chinese)
Xiaoming meiyou shou Xiaohua xihuan ziji.
Xiaoming not say Xiaohua like self
'Xiaoming$_1$ didn't say that Xiaohua$_2$ likes self$_{1/2}$.'

In (3.168), the matrix logocentric predicate is negated, yet the use of a logophoric pronoun/long-distance reflexive remains legitimate. This has long been problematic for Sells's notion of the source, self, and pivot, for what (3.168b), for example, actually says seems explicitly to deny that *Xiaoming* is the source (e.g. Clements 1975, Sells 1987). But to incorporate Stirling's notion of validator allows us to circumvent the problem: even in these cases where the logocentric trigger does not utter the speech, or have the mental or physical experience, it still makes sense to take him or her as responsible for the validation of the content of the speech or experience, even if just to confirm its non-existence (Stirling 1993).

Semantic Approaches to Anaphora 201

Following Sells (1987) and Stirling (1993), we may then represent logophoricity in terms of Discourse Representation Structures (DRSs) developed within the framework of Discourse Representation Theory (Kamp 1982, Kamp and Reyle 1993). In DRT, the meaning of a sentence is determined in the context in which the sentence is embedded. The information of discourse is represented in the form of a DRS, which is built up algorithmically on the basis of syntactic analysis. A DRS has two main components: (i) a set of discourse markers (DMs), called the universe of the DRS, and (ii) a set of conditions on DMs, called DRS-conditions. DMs are typically represented by lower case letters such as $x, y, z, \ldots$ for individuals and $p, q, r, \ldots$ for propositions, and are displayed at the top of the DRS; DRS-conditions are usually displayed at the lower half of the DRS below the universe. What the DRSs in effect do here is to obtain an obligatory equation between the DMs of the logophoric pronoun/long-distance reflexive and those of its logocentric trigger. Using the notations in (3.169), which are adapted from Sells (1987), we can represent the DRS of the three types of logophoric context described above in (3.170)–(3.172) (see also Sells 1987 and Stirling 1993 for two different DRS representations).

(3.169) α represents the validating source
β represents the validating self
γ represents the validating pivot
S represents the current, external speaker

(3.170) The DRS of 'logophoric verbs'
John$_1$ says that Mary$_2$ loves LOG$_1$/self$_1$

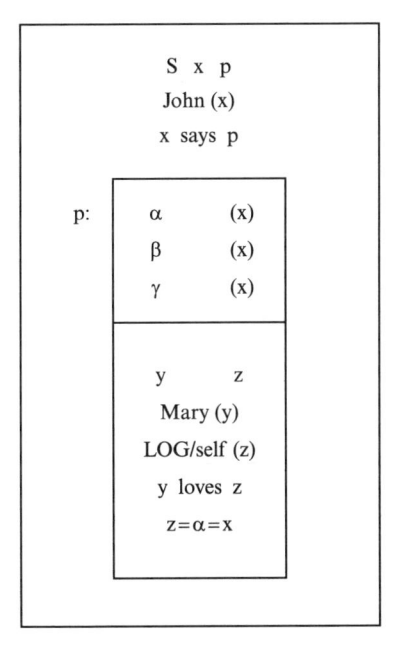

$$
\begin{array}{|l|}
\hline
\quad S \quad x \quad p \\
\quad \text{John}(x) \\
\quad x \text{ says } p \\
\\
p: \begin{array}{|ll|}
\hline
\alpha & (x) \\
\beta & (x) \\
\gamma & (x) \\
\hline
y \quad z \\
\text{Mary}(y) \\
\text{LOG/self}(z) \\
y \text{ loves } z \\
z = \alpha = x \\
\hline
\end{array} \\
\hline
\end{array}
$$

202   *Semantic Approaches to Anaphora*

(3.171) The DRS of 'psych-verbs'
That Mary looks down upon LOG$_1$/self$_1$ saddens John$_1$

```
┌─────────────────────────────────┐
│         S  x  p                 │
│         John (x)                │
│         p saddens x             │
│      ┌──────────────────────┐   │
│      │  α        (S)        │   │
│   p: │  β        (x)        │   │
│      │  γ        (x)        │   │
│      ├──────────────────────┤   │
│      │     y   z            │   │
│      │     Mary (y)         │   │
│      │     LOG/self (z)     │   │
│      │     y looks down     │   │
│      │     upon z           │   │
│      │     z=β=x            │   │
│      └──────────────────────┘   │
└─────────────────────────────────┘
```

(3.172) The DRS of 'third-person points of view'
John$_1$ is happy because Mary comes to see LOG$_1$/self$_1$.[27]

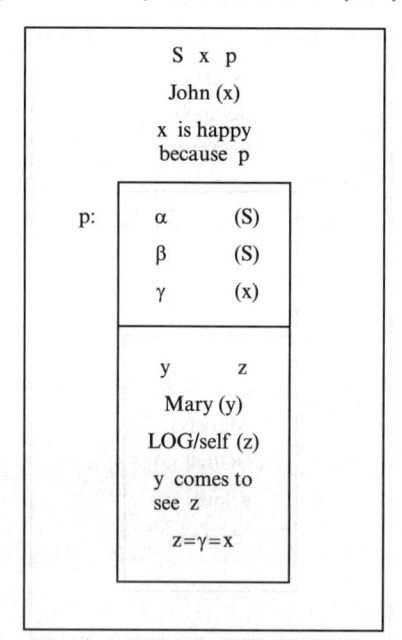

```
┌─────────────────────────────────┐
│         S  x  p                 │
│         John (x)                │
│         x is happy              │
│         because p               │
│      ┌──────────────────────┐   │
│      │  α        (S)        │   │
│   p: │  β        (S)        │   │
│      │  γ        (x)        │   │
│      ├──────────────────────┤   │
│      │     y    z           │   │
│      │     Mary (y)         │   │
│      │     LOG/self (z)     │   │
│      │     y comes to       │   │
│      │     see z            │   │
│      │     z=γ=x            │   │
│      └──────────────────────┘   │
└─────────────────────────────────┘
```

In (3.170), we have the lexical representation of the logocentric verb 'say'. What the DRS indicates here is that 'say' expresses a relation of saying between the individual x and the proposition p. Furthermore, it is a lexical property of 'say' that it dictates that all the three discourse-semantic roles of its complement proposition are realized by its subject. Also shown in the DRS is the anaphoric link established between the role-oriented anaphor and its logocentric trigger: the logophoric pronoun/long-distance reflexive is anteceded by whatever the role predicate it looks for. This is captured by the logophoric pronoun/long-distance reflexive z being linked to the role predicate that is highest on the hierarchy in the DRS, namely the source x. Next, (3.171) presents the lexical representation for the discourse structure of the psych-verb 'sadden'. In this case, the DRS shows that 'sadden' expresses a relation between the proposition p and the individual x: (3.171) is true if and only if one can find a situation in which the proposition p saddens the individual x. Moreover, it indicates that whereas the source role is predicated of the external speaker, the self and the pivot roles are predicated of the internal protagonist. It also shows that the logophoric pronoun/long-distance reflexive takes as its antecedent whatever the highest role predicate, namely the self, is predicated of. Finally, the DRS of the third-person pivot is given in (3.172). In contrast to (3.170) and (3.171), (3.172) is not the discourse representation of a predicate, but is concerned with a construction. Here the only role predicate that is not assumed by the external speaker is the pivot, and consequently the logophoric long-distance reflexive is bound by the pivot.

Clearly, what the DRSs basically do here is (i) to present the lexical representation for the discourse structure of a logocentric predicate or a construction, and (ii) to provide the anaphoric link between the role-oriented anaphor

---

[27] The DRS of, say, (3.168b) may be given as follows.

$$
\begin{array}{|l|l|}
\hline
& \begin{array}{ll} S & x \\ \text{Xiaoming}(x) \end{array} \\
\hline
\sim & \begin{array}{l} p \\ x \text{ shuo } p \end{array} \\
\hline
p: & \begin{array}{|ll|} \hline \alpha & (x) \\ \beta & (x) \\ \gamma & (x) \\ \hline y & z \\ \text{Xiaohua}(y) \\ \text{self}(z) \\ y \text{ xihuan } z \\ z = \alpha = x \\ \hline \end{array} \\
\hline
\end{array}
$$

(i.e. the logophor) and its antecedent (i.e. the logocentric trigger) via the relevant role-predicate. But a DRT analysis of logophoricity is inadequate on at least three accounts. In the first place, it says nothing about which type of predicate can act as a logocentric predicate in a given language. Secondly, nor does it say anything about in what forms a logophor can and must be encoded, for a logophoric pronoun, a long-distance reflexive, and even a regular pronoun are equally allowed to function as a logophor given the DRT account. Thirdly, in the case where a sentence is logophorically ambiguous, as in (3.133a, d) and (3.157) above, a DRT analysis has nothing to say about which logophoric interpretation is the preferred one. While the solution to the first problem can be obtained in the implicational universal for logocentric predicates (3.166) above, the solution to the second and third problems may be sought in the neo-Gricean pragmatic theory of anaphora, to which we shall turn in the next chapter.

3.3.5. Summary

In this section, I have presented an overview of the phenomenology of logophoricity, including ways in which logophoric marking is accomplished cross-linguistically and a typology of languages with respect to logophoricity. I have compared and contrasted the use of logophoric pronouns in African languages and long-distance reflexives in East Asian languages, showing that both anaphoric linking devices are used mainly to encode logophoricity. Finally, I have explored Kamp's (1982) Discourse Representation Theory to provide a semantic analysis of the two logophoric mechanisms.

3.4. Conclusion

I began this chapter by considering VP-ellipsis first from a syntactic, and then from a semantic, point of view. My discussion made it clear that the resolution of VP-ellipsis involves syntactic, semantic, and pragmatic factors. Consequently, neither a purely syntactic nor a purely semantic approach will be adequate in accounting for this elliptical construction. I then turned to an examination of a number of semantic/thematic analyses of binding and control and showed that they too are insufficient. Finally, I discussed logophoricity, concentrating on logophoric pronouns in African languages and long-distance reflexives in East Asian languages, and examined it in terms of Discourse Representation Theory.

4 Pragmatic Approaches to Anaphora

One of the most encouraging developments in the study of anaphora in the last decade has been the increasing awareness of the important role played by pragmatics in regulating anaphora. The main aim of this chapter is twofold. In the first place, I shall reinforce the two important arguments I have made in Huang (1987, 1989, 1991*a*, 1991*b*, 1994, 1995, 1997), namely, (i) syntax, semantics, and pragmatics are interconnected to determine many of the processes of anaphora that are thought to fall within the province of grammar, and (ii) the extent to which syntax, semantics, and pragmatics interact varies typologically. Secondly, I shall advance the neo-Gricean pragmatic theory of anaphora I have constructed in Huang (1987, 1989, 1991*a*, 1991*b*, 1994, 1995, 1997) against a wide variety of genetically unrelated and structurally diverse languages. In addition, I shall survey a number of other pragmatic/cognitive/functional analyses of anaphora.

This chapter is organized as follows. Section 4.1. outlines a neo-Gricean pragmatic theory. The next section is focused on the advancement of the neo-Gricean pragmatic theory I have been developing in Huang (1987, 1989, 1991*a*, 1991*b*, 1994, 1995, 1997). It will be demonstrated that many problems encountered by a syntactic and/or semantic approach to anaphora can readily be tackled in terms of a neo-Gricean pragmatic approach. Next, Section 4.3. examines a number of other pragmatic/cognitive/functional analyses of anaphora, including those formulated within the framework of Relevance theory, Accessibility theory, and Prague School functionalism. Finally, in Section 4.4, using anaphora as a testing ground, I shall consider some typological differences between 'sentence-' and 'discourse-oriented' languages and propose a novel 'syntactic' versus 'pragmatic' language typology.

4.1. A neo-Gricean pragmatic theory

On a general Gricean account of meaning and communication, there are two theories: a theory of meaning$_{\text{-n[on]n[atural]}}$ (Grice 1957, 1989) and a theory of conversational implicature (Grice 1975, 1978, 1989). In the theory of meaning$_{\text{-nn}}$, Grice emphasizes the conceptual relation between natural meaning in the external world and non-natural, linguistic meaning of utterances.

He develops a reductive analysis of meaning$_{nn}$ in terms of the speaker's intentions.

In the theory of conversational implicature, Grice suggests that there is an underlying principle that determines the way in which language is used maximally efficiently and effectively to achieve rational interaction in communication. He calls this governing dictum the cooperative principle and subdivides it into nine maxims classified into four categories. The cooperative principle and its component maxims ensure that in an exchange of conversation the right amount of information is provided, and that the interaction is conducted in a truthful, relevant, and perspicuous manner. They are presented in simplified forms in (4.1).

(4.1) Grice's theory of conversational implicature
    (a) The cooperative principle
        Be cooperative.
    (b) The maxims of conversation
        Quality: Be truthful.
          (i) Don't say what is false.
          (ii) Don't say what lacks evidence.
        Quantity: (i) Don't say less than is required.
        (ii) Don't say more than is required.
        Relevance: Be relevant.
        Manner: Be perspicuous.
          (i) Avoid obscurity.
          (ii) Avoid ambiguity.
          (iii) Be brief.
          (iv) Be orderly.

Assuming that the cooperative principle and its attendant maxims are usually observed by both the speaker and the hearer in a conversational interaction, Grice suggests that conversational implicatures—roughly, a set of non-logical inferences that contains conveyed messages which are meant without being said in the strict sense—can arise from either strictly and directly observing or deliberately and ostentatiously flouting the maxims. Furthermore, he distinguishes between those conversational implicatures which arise without requiring any particular contextual conditions and those which do require such conditions. He calls the first kind generalized conversational implicatures and the second kind particularized conversational implicatures. Grice also points out that conversational implicatures are characterized by a number of distinctive properties, notably (i) cancellability, or defeasibility (conversational implicatures can simply evaporate in certain linguistic or non-linguistic contexts), (ii) non-detachability (any linguistic expression with the same semantic content tends to carry the same conversational implicature (a principled exception is those conversational implicatures that arise via the maxim of Manner)), (iii) calculability (conversational implicatures are calculable via the cooperative principle and its component maxims), (iv) non-conventionality (conversational implicatures, though dependent on what is coded, are non-coded in nature), (v) reinforceability (conversational implicatures can be made explicit without producing too much sense of redundancy), and (vi) universality (conversational implicatures tend to be universal, being motivated rather than arbitrary).

One recent advance on the classic Gricean account is the neo-Gricean pragmatic theory put forward by Levinson (1987, 1991, 1995). Levinson argues that the original Gricean programme (the maxim of Quality apart) should be reduced to three neo-Gricean pragmatic principles or heuristics: what he dubs the Q[uantity]-, I[nformativeness]-, and M[anner]principles.[1]

(4.2) Levinson's Q-, I-, and M-principles
   (*a*) The Q-principle
   Speaker's maxim:
   Do not provide a statement that is informationally weaker than your knowledge of the world allows, unless providing a stronger statement would contravene the I-principle.
   Recipient's corollary:
   Take it that the speaker made the strongest statement consistent with what he knows, and therefore that:
      (i) if the speaker asserted A(W), and <S,W> form a Horn scale (such that A(S) ↦ A(W)), then one can infer K~ (A(S)), i.e. that the speaker knows that the stronger statement would be false;
      (ii) if the speaker asserted A(W) and A(W) fails to entail an embedded sentence Q, which a stronger statement A(S) would entail, and <S, W> form a contrast set, then one can infer ~K(Q), i.e. the speaker does not know whether Q obtains or not.
   (*b*) The I-principle
   Speaker's maxim: the maxim of minimization
   'Say as little as necessary', i.e. produce the minimal linguistic information sufficient to achieve your communicational ends (bearing the Q-principle in mind).
   Recipient's corollary: the rule of enrichment
   Amplify the informational content of the speaker's utterance, by finding the most specific interpretation, up to what you judge to be the speaker's m-intended point. Specifically:
      (i) assume that stereotypical relations obtain between referents or events,

---

[1] Cf. Horn's (1984, 1989) bipartite model. On Horn's view, all of Grice's maxims (except the maxim of Quality) can be replaced with two fundamental and antithetical principles: the Q[uantity]-principle ('Make your contribution sufficient; say as much as you can (given R)') and the R[elation]-principle ('Make your contribution necessary; say no more than you must (given Q)'). Viewing the Q- and R-principles as an instantiation of Zipfian economy (Zipf 1949), Horn explicitly identifies the Q-principle ('a hearer-based economy for the maximization of informational content') with Zipf's Auditor's Economy (the Force of Diversification) and the R-principle ('a speaker-based economy for the minimization of linguistic form') with Zipf's Speaker's Economy (the Force of Unification). He also explicitly identifies the R-principle with Atlas and Levinson's (1981) I-principle. For further discussion, see Huang (1991*a*, 1994).

unless: (1) that is inconsistent with what is taken for granted, (2) the speaker has broken the maxim of minimization by choosing a prolix expression;
  (ii) assume the existence or actuality of what a sentence is 'about' if that is consistent with what is taken for granted;
  (iii) avoid interpretations that multiply entities referred to (assume referential parsimony); specifically, prefer coreferential readings of reduced NPs (pronouns or zeros).
(c) The M-principle
  Speaker's maxim:
  Do not use a prolix, obscure, or marked expression without reason.
  Recipient's corollary:
  If the speaker used a prolix or marked expression M, he or she did not mean the same as he or she would have had he or she used the unmarked expression U—specifically he or she was trying to avoid the stereotypical associations and I-implicatures of U.

In terms of information structure, the metalinguistic Q-principle is a lower-bounding pragmatic principle. The basic idea is that the use of an expression (especially a semantically weaker one) in a set of contrastive semantic alternates Q-implicates the negation of the interpretation associated with the use of another expression (especially a semantically stronger one) in the same set. In other words, the effect of this inference strategy is to give rise to an upper-bounding conversational implicature: a speaker, in saying '... p ...', conversationally implicates that (for all he or she knows) '... at most p ...'. Seen the other way round, from the absence of an informationally stronger expression, one infers that the interpretation associated with the use of that expression does not hold. The Q-principle is particularly pertinent to conversational implicatures that arise from a Horn- or Q-scale (e.g. Horn 1972, Grice 1975, Gazdar 1979, Levinson 1987, 1995). Horn-scales are defined in (4.3) and illustrated in (4.4) and (4.5). (I use the symbol +> to indicate 'conversationally implicate'. The epistemic qualifications are omitted.)

(4.3) Horn-scales
  For <S, W> to form a Horn-scale,
  (i) A(S) must entail A(W) for some arbitrary sentence frame A;
  (ii) S and W must be equally lexicalized;
  (iii) S and W must be 'about' the same semantic relation, or from the same semantic field.
(4.4) $Q_{\text{-scalar}}$: <x, y>
  y +> $Q_{\text{-scalar}}$ ~ x
  <all, some>
  Some of my friends love chamber music.
  +> Not all of my friends love chamber music.
(4.5) $Q_{\text{-clausal}}$: <x, y>
  y +> $Q_{\text{-clausal}}$ ~ x
  <know that p, believe that p>

I believe that John loves chamber music.
+> John may or may not love chamber music
- I don't know which.

Mirroring the effect of the Q-principle, the I-principle is an upper-bounding pragmatic principle. The basic idea is that the use of a semantically general expression I-implicates a semantically specific interpretation. In other words, the working of this inferential mechanism is to induce a lower-bounding conversational implicature: a speaker, in saying '... *p* ...', conversationally implicates that (for all he or she knows) '... more than *p* ...'. More accurately, the conversational implicature engendered by the I-principle is one that accords best with the most stereotypical and explanatory expectation given our knowledge about the world. Schematically:

(4.6) I-scale: [x, y]
    y+>₁ x

Some examples of I-implicature are given below:

(4.7) (Conjunction buttressing)
    p and *q* +> *p* and then *q*
        +> *p* therefore *q*
        +> *p* in order to cause *q*
    John turned the key and the music box opened.
    +> John turned the key and then the music box opened.
    +> John turned the key and thereby caused the music box to open.
    +> John turned the key in order to make the music box open.
(4.8) (Conditional perfection)
    if *p* then *q* +> if ~*p* then ~*q* +> iff *p* then *q*
    If you give me a free Haydn, I'll buy five Mozarts.
    +> If and only if you give me a free Haydn will I buy five Mozarts.
(4.9) (Membership categorization)
    The baby cried. The mummy picked it up.
    +> The mummy was the mother of the crying baby.
(4.10) (Mirror maxim)
    John and Mary bought a piano.
    +> John and Mary bought a piano together, not one each.
(4.11) (Frame-based inference)
    John pushed the cart to the checkout.
    +> John pushed the cart full of groceries to the supermarket
    checkout in order to pay for them, and so on.
(4.12) (Bridging inference)
    John bought a new CD player. The cassette deck doesn't open.
    +> John's new CD player has a cassette deck.
(4.13) (Inference to stereotype)
    Have you met our new nurse?
    +> Have you met our new female nurse?
(4.14) (Indirect speech act)
    Have you got a watch?
    +> If you have got a watch and know the time, please tell me what it is.

(4.15) (Definite reference)
It was a Ming vase and on the base of the vessel were four Chinese characters.
+> It was a Ming vase and on the base of the vase were four Chinese characters.

(4.16) (Lexical narrowing)
John is reading two Modern Languages at Oxford.
+> John is reading two Modern European Languages other than Modern English at Oxford.

The class of I-implicatures is heterogeneous, but the inferences seem to share a number of properties, notably (i) they are more informative than the utterances that generate them, (ii) they are more precise and specific than the corresponding utterances, and (iii) they cannot be cancelled by metalinguistic negation.

Finally, unlike the Q- and I-principles, which operate primarily in terms of semantic informativeness, the metalinguistic M-principle operates primarily in terms of a set of alternatives that contrast in form. The basic idea is that the use of a marked expression M-implicates the negation of the interpretation associated with the use of an alternative, unmarked expression in the same set. In other words, from the use of a marked linguistic expression, one infers that the stereotypical interpretation associated with the use of an alternative, unmarked linguistic expression does not obtain. Schematically:

(4.17) M-scale: {x, y}
$y+>_M \sim x$

Examples illustrating the M-implicature appear in (4.18) and (4.19).

(4.18) (a) The timetable is reliable.
+> to degree n.
(b) The timetable is not unreliable
+> to degree less than n.

(4.19) (a) Mary went from the bathroom to the bedroom.
+> In the normal way.
(b) Mary ceased to be in the bathroom and came to be in the bedroom.
+> In an unusual way, e.g. in a magic show, Mary had by magic been made to disappear from the bathroom and reappear in the bedroom.

Taken together, the I- and M-principles give rise to complementary interpretations: the use of an unmarked linguistic expression tends to convey an unmarked message, whereas the use of a marked linguistic expression tends to convey a marked message.

Given the above tripartite classification of neo-Gricean pragmatic principles, the question that comes up next is how inconsistencies arising from these potentially conflicting inference apparatuses can be resolved. Following a suggestion by Gazdar (1979), Atlas and Levinson (1981), and Horn (1984), Levinson (1987, 1991, 1995) proposes that they can be resolved by an ordered set of precedence.

(4.20) Levinson's resolution schema for the interaction
of the Q-, I-, and M-principles
(a) Level of genus: Q > M > I
(b) Level of species: e.g. $Q_{\text{-clausal}} > Q_{\text{-scalar}}$

This is tantamount to saying that genuine Q-implicatures (where $Q_{\text{-clausal}}$ cancels rival $Q_{\text{-scalar}}$) precede inconsistent I-implicatures, but otherwise I-implicatures take precedence until the use of a marked linguistic expression triggers a complementary M-implicature to the negation of the applicability of the pertinent I-implicature. This can be illustrated by (4.21)–(4.24), with (c) giving the correct implicature of each utterance.

(4.21) Q > I
If Colonel Gadaffi gave you a gun for Christmas, it may have been a real gun.
(a) $Q_{\text{-clausal}}$ <(since p, q), (if p, q)>
+> It may or may not have been a real gun—I didn't know which.
(b) I [gun for Christmas]
+> It was a toy gun.
(c) Q > I
+> Possibly the gun was a real one.

(4.22) Q > M
It is not unlikely that Oxford will win the next boat race, and indeed I think it likely.
(a) $Q_{\text{-clausal}}$ <know p, think p,>
+> It is possible that it is likely that Oxford will win the next boat race.
(b) M {likely, not unlikely}
+> It is less than fully likely that Oxford will win the next boat race.
(a) Q > M
+> It is likely that Oxford will win the next race.

(4.23) M > I
John caused the car to stop.
(a) M
+> not in the normal way, e.g. by use of the emergency brake.
(b) I (John stopped the car.)
+> in the usual manner.
(c) M > I
+> not in the normal way, e.g. by use of the emergency brake.

(4.24) $Q_{\text{-clausal}} > Q_{\text{-scalar}}$
If not all of my friends love chamber music, some of them do.
(a) $Q_{\text{-clausal}}$ <(since p, q), (if p, q)>
+> All of my friends may or may not love chamber music—I don't know which.
(b) $Q_{\text{-scalar}}$ <all, some>
+> Not all of my friends love chamber music.
(c) $Q_{\text{-clausal}} > Q_{\text{-scalar}}$
+> Possibly all of my friends love chamber music.

The resolution schema in (4.20) can in fact be assimilated into a more general implicature cancellation procedure put forward by Gazdar (1979). On Gazdar's view, the informational content of an utterance can be considered to be an ordered set of background assumptions, contextual factors, semantic entailments, conversational implicatures, presuppositions, and so on and so forth. Each incrementation of the informational content of an utterance must be consistent with the informational content that already exists, otherwise it will be cancelled according to the following hierarchy (adapted from Gazdar 1979, Huang 1991a, 1994).

(4.25) The implicature cancellation procedure
    (a) background assumptions
    (b) contextual factors
    (c) semantic entailments
    (d) conversational implicatures
        (i) Q-implicatures
            (1) $Q_{\text{-clausal}}$
            (2) $Q_{\text{-scalar}}$
        (ii) M-implicatures
        (iii) I-implicatures
    (e) presuppositions

4.2. A revised neo-Gricean pragmatic theory of anaphora

We move next to the development of a revised neo-Gricean pragmatic theory of anaphora, based on Huang (1987, 1989, 1991a, 1991b, 1994, 1995, 1997) and Levinson (1987, 1991).[2]

As I have emphasized in Huang (1989, 1991a, 1994, 1995), the pragmatic

---

[2] Earlier attempts to provide a partially Gricean pragmatic account of anaphora within the framework of generative grammar include Dowty (1980) and Reinhart (1983, 1986), though the essential insight may go back at least as far as Lee and Klima (1963). Grodzinsky and Reinhart (1993) is a more recent development of the central ideas in Reinhart (1983, 1986). Some of the modifications proposed in Grodzinsky and Reinhart (1993) are partially motivated by problems relating to what are called expressibility gaps (e.g. Lasnik 1989). Unfortunately, Grodzinsky and Reinhart (1993) are less committed than Reinhart (1983, 1986) to the idea that the interpretation of coreference is part of pragmatics. See Huang (1994) for a discussion of Dowty (1980) and Reinhart (1983, 1986). See also Huang (1991a, 1994) for comments on Levinson's (1987, 1991) 'A-first', 'B-first', and 'A-first plus B-first' analyses, and the development of an alternative analysis within the same theoretical framework.

Chomsky does not put forward any systematic pragmatic theory of anaphora. However, in his work on binding, one does find occasional reference to pragmatic principles. One such principle is the 'avoid pronoun' principle, to be discussed below. Another pragmatic principle is the general discourse principle, as already mentioned in Chapter 1. This principle allows binding condition C_1 to be overridden given the appropriate context under certain circumstances, though the relevant conditions have never been spelled out by Chomsky.

In more recent work on the minimalist programme, Chomsky (1995) has argued that both derivations and representations are subject to a kind of 'least effort' guideline: there are no superfluous steps in derivations and there are no superfluous symbols in representations. The economy of derivations and representations is considered to be the functional driving force behind certain innate grammatical rules such as the last resort constraint on movement and the Full Interpretation Principle. Furthermore, on a more global level, this principle is linked to theory of anaphora I have been advancing does not deny the existence of distinct syntactic, semantic and pragmatic levels and modes of explanation in linguistic theory. On the contrary, it presumes the independence, or at least partial independence, of an irreducible grammatical stratum for pragmatically motivated constraints: calculation of pragmatic inferences of the Gricean sort has to be made over a level of independent syntactic structure and semantic representation (e.g. Gazdar 1979: 56, Levinson 1983: 122, 1991, Horn 1988). What I have been arguing is that syntax interacts with pragmatics to determine many of the anaphoric processes that are thought to be at the very heart of grammar. If this is the case, then a large portion of linguistic explanation concerning anaphora which is currently sought in grammatical terms may need to be shifted to pragmatics, hence the interaction and division of labour between syntax and pragmatics. This interface and division of labour between syntax and pragmatics may be summarized in a Kantian slogan: pragmatics without syntax is empty; syntax without pragmatics is blind (Huang 1994: 259).[3] What pragmatics does here is to provide a set of complementary, explanatory principles that constrains the interpretation or production of an utterance whose linguistic representation has already been antecedently cognized. But these are important and indispensable principles for linguistic explanation, for as Horn (1988: 115) has pointed out, 'an independently motivated pragmatic theory (or several such theories, on the compartmentalized view) should provide simplification and generalization elsewhere in the overall description of language'. Furthermore, the extent to which syntax and pragmatics interact varies typologically. There seems to exist a class of languages (such as Chinese, Japanese, and Korean) where pragmatics appears to play a central role which in familiar European languages (such as English, French, and German) has hitherto been alleged to be played by grammar. In these 'pragmatic' languages, many of the constraints on the alleged grammatical processes are in fact primarily due to principles of language use rather than rules of grammatical structure (see Section 4.4. below). If this is the case, then pragmatics can no longer be treated as an 'epiphenomenon at best' (Chomsky 1986*a*: 25). On the contrary, there is a pressing need for the advancement of the kind of pragmatic theory of anaphora developed in Huang (1987, 1989, 1991*a*, 1991*b*, 1994, 1995, 1997), Levinson (1987, 1991), and the present monograph.

---

some notion of cost in relation to UG principles and language-specific rules. UG principles are less costly than language-particular rules, therefore they obtain wherever possible, with language-specific rules employed only if they are not applicable. Chomsky considers the least effort principle of this kind specific to the human language faculty, but there is reason to believe that it may be an instantiation of some more general pragmatic principles such as our Q-, I- and M-principles.

[3] Cf. Kant's original apophthegm from *Critique of Pure Reason*: 'Concepts without percepts are empty; percepts without concepts are blind.'

214   *Pragmatic Approaches to Anaphora*

The underlying idea of a pragmatic reductionist approach to anaphora like the one being advanced here is that the interpretation of certain patterns of anaphora can be made using pragmatic inference, depending on the language user's knowledge of the range of options available in the grammar, and of the systematic use or avoidance of particular linguistic expressions or structures on particular occasions.

4.2.1. The general pattern of anaphora

Consider the contrast in the (*a*) and (*b*) sentence of (4.26) and (4.27).

(4.26) (*a*) Mozart$_1$ adored his$_{1/2}$ music.
     (*b*) He$_1$ adored Mozart's$_2$ music.
(4.27) (Sanford and Garrod 1981)
     (*a*) The bus$_1$ came trundling round the bend.
         The vehicle$_1$ almost flattened a pedestrian.
     (*b*) The vehicle$_1$ came trundling round the bend.
         The bus$_2$ almost flattened a pedestrian.

There is a clear pattern here: the use of a reduced, semantically general anaphoric expression facilitates a local coreferential interpretation, whereas the use of a full, semantically specific anaphoric expression favours a local non-coreferential interpretation. This can be seen by a consideration of, say, (4.27). In this example, *vehicle* is semantically more general than *bus*, being the superordinate term of *bus*. When it follows *bus*, a local coreferential interpretation is encouraged, as in (4.27*a*); when it is followed by *bus*, a local non-coreferential interpretation is invited, as in (4.27*b*). This pattern applies both intra- and intersententially. Following Levinson (1987, 1991), let us call this the general pattern of anaphora.

(4.28) The general pattern of anaphora
     Reduced, semantically general anaphoric expressions tend to favour locally coreferential interpretations; full, semantically specific anaphoric expressions tend to favour locally non-coreferential interpretations.

4.2.2. A revised neo-Gricean pragmatic account of anaphora

Now, assuming that the general pattern of anaphora (4.28) is largely an instantiation, in the realm of linguistic reference, of the systematic interaction of neo-Gricean pragmatic inferences of some kind, the question that arises next is how it can be given an account in terms of a neo-Gricean pragmatic theory of conversational implicature.

Applying the Q-, I-, and M-principles, sketched in Section 4.1. above, to the domain of anaphoric reference, we can derive a general pragmatic apparatus for the interpretation of zero anaphors, pronouns, reflexives, and lexical NPs. Assuming the semantic content hierarchy in (4.29), this pragmatic apparatus can be presented in (4.30), with a revised version of Farmer and Harnish's (1987) Disjoint Reference Presumption (DRP) given in (4.31).

(4.29) The semantic content hierarchy
Lexical NPs > pronouns > zero anaphors
The inherent semantic content of a lexical NP tends to be semantically more specific than that of a pronoun and the inherent semantic content of a pronoun, than that of a zero anaphor.

(4.30) A revised neo-Gricean pragmatic apparatus for anaphora
(*a*) Interpretation principles
(i) The use of an anaphoric expression *x* I-implicates a local coreferential interpretation, unless (ii) or (iii).
(ii) There is an anaphoric Q-scale $<x, y>$[4], in which case, the use of *y* Q-implicates the complement of the I-implicature associated with the use of *x*, in terms of reference.
(iii) There is an anaphoric M-scale $\{x, y\}$, in which case, the use of *y* M-implicates the complement of the I-implicature associated with the use of *x*, in terms of either reference or expectedness.
(*b*) Consistency constraints
Any interpretation implicated by (*a*) is subject to the requirement of consistency with
(i) The DRP.
(ii) Information saliency, so that
(*a*) implicatures due to matrix constructions may take precedence over implicatures due to subordinate constructions, and
(*b*) implicatures to coreference may be preferred according to the saliency of antecedent in line with the following hierarchy:
topic > subject > object, etc.; and
(iii) General implicature constraints, namely,
(*a*) background assumptions,
(*b*) contextual factors
(*c*) meaning$_{\text{-nn}}$, and
(*d*) semantic entailments.

(4.31) The revised DRP
The co-arguments of a predicate are intended to be disjoint, unless one of them is reflexive-marked.

The basic idea of the DRP is that if the co-arguments of a predicate are not reflexive-marked, they tend to be disjoint in reference. This observation is, of course, far from being wholly original; it is strongly reminiscent of, say, Chomsky's binding condition B. But there is a fundamental difference between the DRP on the one hand and binding condition B on the other. On Farmer and Harnish's view, the DRP is not of a syntactic or semantic but of a pragmatic nature: what it describes is essentially a usage preference (see e.g. Huang 1991*a*, 1994 for evidence from Chinese in support of this line of

---

[4] Or Q-like-scale $<x, y>$, since in this case *x* is semantically stronger than *y*, not because of any relation of entailment, as in classical Q$_{\text{-scalar}}$ implicatures; but because *y* occurs in a position where a semantically stronger *x* could appear, as in, for example, <Professor X, Doctor X> (see Grice 1989). We shall point out why *x* is semantically stronger than *y* here shortly. Anyhow, this technical difference between the two types of Q-implicature will not affect our analysis.

argument). However, it could be equally strongly argued that the DRP is based on world knowledge, given that the fact that one entity tends to act upon another could be due largely to the way the world stereotypically is. The advantage of attributing the DRP to world knowledge is that in that case it will automatically prevent any inconsistent pragmatic implicature from arising or cancel it without violating the hierarchy Q > M > I.

Before applying (4.30) to the interpretation of anaphora, we need to look squarely, though briefly, at two (somewhat related) questions: (i) why is it that a local coreferential interpretation is considered to be semantically more specific, hence informationally richer; and (ii) why is it that the general pattern of anaphora is assumed to be an instantiation of the interaction of neo-Gricean pragmatic principles? According to Atlas and Levinson (1981) and Levinson (1987), answers to both questions can be sought in the analysis of the notion of informativeness made by Bar-Hillel, Carnap, and Popper. In the first place, there is the Bar-Hillelian–Carnapian argument at the level of reference (which might be regarded as one way of operationalizing the Popperian idea of informativeness-relative-to-falsifiability) that the smaller the number of possible state-descriptions which are compatible with a proposition, the more informative the proposition (Bar-Hillel and Carnap 1964: 227 ff.). Since a coreferential interpretation reduces the number of possible entities referred to in the minimal domain of discourse, it is more D[omain]-informative than a corresponding non-coreferential interpretation. It follows, therefore, that the preference for a local coreferential interpretation is the direct result of the I-principle. Secondly, there is the independent Popperian argument at the level of logical form that the fewer existential commitments, the more informative the proposition (Popper 1959: 68 ff.). Given that a coreferential interpretation contains fewer existential quantifiers than its corresponding, non-coreferential one, it is more P[roposition]-informative. Once again, on this view, the preference for a local coreferential interpretation can be seen to follow straightforwardly from the I-principle. Finally, there is the third argument at the level of sense. In a sentence like *Wagner walked into the hall and he kissed Cosima*, regardless of the domain of discourse, the coreferential interpretation is more informative than the corresponding, non-coreferential one (see e.g. Huang 1994 for further discussion).

4.2.3. Application

Having clarified the notion of informativeness, I can now show how (4.30) works. At this point, it is useful to draw the reader's attention to the distinction of whether or not an anaphoric expression and its antecedent are the co-arguments of a predicate. If they are, then the predicate may, in the terminology of Reinhart and Reuland (1993), be reflexive-marked. As we have seen in Chapter 3, a reflexive predicate can in general be reflexive-marked in three distinct ways: (i) lexically by the use of an inherently reflexive verb, as in (3.88), (3.96) above, and (4.32) below,[5] (ii) morphologically by the employment of a reflexive affix attached to the verb, as in (3.93)–(3.95) above and (4.33) below, and (iii) syntactically by the use of a reflexive, as in (3.89) above and (4.34) below, or a grammaticalized lexeme, as in (4.35) below.

(4.32) (a) (Dutch, Reinhart and Reuland 1993)
Max schaamt zich.
Max shames self
'Max is ashamed.'
(b) (German, Everaert 1986)
Johann irrt sich.
Johann mistakes self
'Johann is mistaken.'
(c) (Norwegian, Hellan 1988)
Jon skammer seg.
Jon shames self
'Jon is ashamed.'

[5] Note that intrinsically reflexive predicates can be divided into two types: (i) full intrinsically reflexive predicates such as *schamen* (be ashamed) in Dutch, and (ii) semi-intrinsically reflexive predicates such as *wassen* (wash) in Dutch. The second type is what Jesperson (1924) calls 'verbs with a reflexive pronoun omitted' and what Haiman (1985a) calls 'introverted predicates'. While the former cannot take a referentially distinct object, as in (i), the latter can, as in (ii)–(iv). Thus, the latter are listed twice in the lexicon as both a reflexive and a non-reflexive.
(i) *John behaved him badly.
(ii) (Chinese)
(a) Mama zai xizao.
mum DUR bathe
'Mum is bathing (herself).'
(b) Mama zai gei meimei xizao.
mum DUR for younger sister bathe
'Mum is bathing (my) younger sister.'
(iii) (Godié, Marchese 1986: 229)
(a) ɔ budo.
he wash
'He washed himself.'
(b) ɔ bidɔ yíɔ.
he wash:TRANS child:DEF
'He washed the child.'
(iv) (Udmurt, Geniušienė 1987: 309)
(a) Anaj-Ø diśa-śk-e.
mother-NOM dress-REFL-PRES-3SG
'Mother dresses (herself).'
(b) Anaj-Ø nı̣l-ze diś-a.
mother-NOM daughter-ACC-POSS dress-PRES-3SG
'Mother dresses her daughter.'

In some languages, intrinsic reflexives (both full and semi) are marked morphologically. Modern Hebrew is a good example of a language of this type. In this language, intrinsic reflexives are marked morphologically with a special verb form (*hipael*). While 'shame' occurs only in that form, 'wash' has both that form and a transitive form (Reinhart and Reuland 1993: 666). Another point of interest is that, as observed by Zubizarreta (1987), languages differ in whether they require, permit, or prevent the patient role of their intrinsically reflexive predicates being realized syntactically.

(4.33) (a) (Abaza, Allen 1956)
c-l-ba-x-d.
REFL-3SG-F-see back-PAST
'She saw herself.'
(b) (Abkhaz, Anderson 1976)
l-čə-l-š-wa-yt'.
3SG-F-REFL-3SG-F-kill-ACTIVE-PRES
'She kills herself.'
(c) (Dyirbal, Faltz 1985: 78)
bayi yaṛa buybayirinyu.
the man-ABS hide-REFL-PRES
'The man hides himself.'
(d) (Halkomelem, Gerdts 1988: 54)
ni cən lə́x̌ʷ-əθət.
AUX I blanket-self
'I blanket myself.'
(e) (Kalkatungu, Lidz 1996: 77)
marapai karri-ti-mi thupu-ngku.
woman-NOM wash-REFL-FUT soap-ERG
'The woman will wash herself with soap.'
(f) (Tatar, Geniušienė 1987: 326)
Näfisä ju-vǐn-a.
Nafisa wash-REFL-PRES-3SG
'Nafisa washes herself.'
(g) (Yakut, Geniušienė 1987: 309)
kini sime-n-er.
she-ABS dress up-REFL-PRES-3SG
'She dressed herself up.'
(h) (Yavapai, Kendall 1976)
hmañ-c kwe-wiv-v-i.
child-SUBJ thing-clothe-REFL-TNS
'The child dressed himself.'
(4.34) (a) (Lithuanian, Geniušienė 1987: 239)
Jis gerbia save.
he respects self
'He respects self.'
(b) (Chinese)
Xiaoming piping guo ta ziji.
Xiaoming criticize EXP 3SG self
'Xiaoming has criticized himself.'
(c) (Norwegian, Hellan 1988 with errors corrected)
Jon forakter seg selv.
Jon despises self self
'Jon despises self self.'
(4.35) (a) (Abkhaz, Dumezil 1967)
l-xe y-l-ba-yt'.
3SG-F-head 3SG-M-3SG-F-see-PRES
'She sees herself.'
(b) (Anywa, Heine 1997)
jèy dèet-gi á-jàal-gi.
people bodies-their PFV-blame-they
'The people blamed themselves.'

(c) (Ful, Heine 1997)
'o mbari hoore maako.
he killed head his
'He killed himself.'
(d) (Godié, Marchese 1986: 229)
ɔ ʙɔtɔ ɔ yɔku.
he hit he side
'He hit himself.'
(e) (Ilocano, Schwartz 1976)
kabil-en ti lalaki ti bagi na.
hit-PAT   boy   body his
'The boy hit himself.'

Note futher that the choice of a particular reflexivizing strategy over another is in part determined by the semantics/pragmatics of the reflexive-predicate in question. The meaning of the predicate can roughly be divided into two types here: self-directed and other-directed. By self-directed is meant that the action denoted by the predicate is typically performed by a human agent on him- or herself, whereas in the case of other-directed, the action denoted by the predicate is typically directed against others. Evidently, events such as grooming (e.g. getting dressed, shaving, washing), change of body posture (e.g. lying down, sitting down, standing up), and some emotions (e.g. being ashamed/frightened/proud) are typical examples of self-directed action/attitude. By way of contrast, communication, violent actions, and emotions such as love, hate, and being angry with/jealous of/pleased with fall standardly under the category of other-directed action/attitude (e.g. Kemmer 1993, König and Siemund 1997; see also Moyse-Faurie 1999 on Futunan).

Now, of particular interest is that if we take a careful look at the relationship between the meaning of a reflexive-predicate and the various reflexivizing devices a language has, a cross-linguistic, iconic correlation emerges (adapted from König and Siemund 1997):

(4.36) The predicate meaning/reflexivizing strategy correlation
The more 'marked' a reflexivizing situation (e.g. other-directed), the more 'marked' (i.e. more complex) a reflexivizing strategy will be used to encode it.

What (4.36) basically says is this: if a language has more than one reflexivizing strategy/form, we would expect simplex ones to be employed for inherently reflexive predicates and other self-directed situtations, but complex ones to be utilized for other-directed situations. Different languages, of course, may afford their speakers different means to conform to this correlation. In some languages (e.g. Modern Hebrew, Russian, and Turkish), we find a choice between verbal and nominal strategies; in others (e.g. English, Kannada and Spanish), the opposition is between zero and non-zero anaphors; in yet others, there is an opposition between morphologically simplex and complex reflexives (as in e.g. Dutch, Norwegian, and Swedish); or the choice may be between the use of single versus non-single emphatics (as in

Lezgian, Tsakhur, and Turkish) (see König and Siemund 1997 for further discussion). Some illustrative examples are given below.

(4.37) Verbal versus nominal reflexivizing strategy
(Russian)
(a) Milicioner umyvaet-sja.
policeman washes-REFL
'The policeman is washing (himself).'
(b) Milicioner zastrelil sebja.
policeman shot   self
'The policeman shot himself.'

(4.38) Zero versus non-zero
(Kannada, Lidz 1996: 13)
(a) hari-yu   kannu-gaL-annu tere-d-a.
Hari-NOM eye-PL-ACC   open-PAST-3SG-M
'Hari opened his eyes.'
(b) hari-yu   kannu-gaL-annu tere-du-koND-a.
Hari-NOM eye-PL-ACC   open-PP-REFL-PAST-3SG-M
'Hari opened his eyes (not in a natural way, e.g. with his hands).'

(4.39) Simplex versus complex reflexives
(Dutch)
(a) Rint schaamt zich.
Rint shames   self
'Rint is ashamed.'
(b) Rint veracht zichzelf.
Rint despises selfself
'Rint despises himself.'

(4.40) Single versus non-single emphatics
(Turkish, König and Siemund 1997)
(a) vur-mak
beat
'beat'
(b) (O) kendi kendi-si-ni   vur-du.
3SG self   self-3SG-ACC beat-PAST-3SG
'He beat himself.'

Clearly, all this is explainable in terms of our M-principle: to convey a marked message, use a marked linguistic expresssion.

Next, we have a principle of referential economy for coreferential NPs, along the lines of Huang (1987, 1989, 1991a, 1994), Levinson (1987, 1991), Burzio (1991, 1996), and Richards (1997).

(4.41) A principle of referential economy for coreferential NPs
A referentially dependent anaphoric expression tends to be encoded by a referentially most economic NP.

(4.42) A hierarchy of referential economy for NPs
(a) anaphors
  (i) anaphoric gap
  (ii) self
  (iii) self self
  (iv) pronoun self

(b) pronominals
   (i) pronominal gap/pro
   (ii) pronouns
(c) r-expressions
   (i) epithets
   (ii) definite descriptions
   (iii) names

With all this in place, we can now give a partial pragmatic account of intrasentential anaphora. Let us begin with cases where the anaphoric expression and its antecedent are the co-arguments of the same predicate. Consider first (4.43).

(4.43) (a) Mozart₁ admired himself₁.
       (b) Mozart₁ admired him₂.
       (c) Mozart₁ admired Mozart₂.

Example (4.43) contains, of course, the paradigmatic sentences for binding conditions A, B, and C respectively. How, then, can they be accounted for by our pragmatic apparatus? Take (4.43a) first. Since (4.43a) contains a reflexive predicate and reflexivity is marked in the overt syntax by a reflexive, the DRP is not in operation here. Consequently, the interpretation of the reflexive is subject to the I-principle, which induces a local coreferential interpretation. Next, the binding condition B effect of (4.43b) is the result of the operation of both the Q-principle and the DRP. By the referential economy mechanism (4.41) and (4.42), a reflexive will be chosen if coreference is intended. This has the consequence that if the reflexive is not employed but a pronoun is used instead, a Q-implicature will arise; namely no coreference is intended. In other words, we have a Q-scale <reflexive, pronoun> here, such that the use of the semantically weaker pronoun Q-implicates that the use of the semantically stronger reflexive cannot be truthfully entertained, that is, the coreferential reading which is associated with the use of the reflexive should be avoided. Reflexives are semantically stronger than pronouns in that (i) syntactically, they typically need to be bound in a local domain, and (ii) semantically, they are normally referentially dependent. On the other hand, since the pronoun encodes a co-argument of a potentially reflexive predicate which is not reflexive-marked, it is also subject to the DRP. Thus, the potential, local coreferential interpretation encouraged by the I-principle is ruled out twice, first by the rival Q-principle (Q > M > I) and then by the DRP. Finally in the case of (4.43c), for the same reasoning, the name will again be read first by the Q-principle and then by the DRP as preferably being disjoint in reference with the local subject.

A word of explanation about 'preferred interpretation' is due at this point. By 'preferred interpretation' is meant the interpretation that is the most favoured one out of a number of other, possible interpretations. This interpretation arises without any particular context or specific scenario being necessary. Put slightly differently, in terms of the notion of context, the preferred interpretation arises in a default/unmarked context rather than in a specific/marked one. In other words, it is an instance of Grice's generalized (i.e. default) rather than particularized (i.e. context-induced) conversational implicature.

One advantage of our pragmatic approach over various versions of Chomsky's binding theory can be seen in accommodating those binding patterns where a pronoun is happily bound in its local domain. As we remarked and exemplified in Chapter 2, there are languages in the world which lack first- and/or second-person reflexives. In these languages, first- and second-person pronouns are used instead to encode reflexivity.[6] We saw in (2.16) that Dutch, German, and Italian belong to this type of language. Also of this type are Icelandic, Pima, and Sursurunga. Secondly, in many languages, the use of a locally bound third-person pronoun is required either because the language in question does not have reflexives, or because in the syntactic structure where the pronoun is used, its corresponding, third-person reflexive is not allowed. I showed in (2.15) and (2.17) that this is the case for Fijian, Gumbaynggir, Hatian Creole, Old English, French, Piedmontese, and Russian. The same situation has also been observed for Chamorro, Mundani, Sursurunga, Somoan, and Tsakhur. All this shows that the use of a pronoun as a reflexive in the world's languages is not 'highly marked', as Reinhart and Reuland (1993) have claimed.

(4.44) (a) (Icelandic, Thráinsson 1991)
  Ég rakaði mig.
  I   shaved me
  'I shaved myself.'

---

[6] Recollect the implicational universal for the person distinction of reflexives in n. 18 of Chapter 3, which is repeated here in (i) (see e.g. Faltz 1985: 120, Comrie 1989a: 7, 17, Hawkins 1989, Toman 1991, Kemmer 1993: 47, 223).

(i) An implicational universal for the person distinction of reflexives
First-person reflexives imply second-person reflexives, and second-person reflexives imply third-person reflexives.

Given (i), it is predicted that there will be three types of language with respect to the person distinction of reflexives: (i) those languages with the distinction on all three persons (e.g. Hungarian, Russian, and Wappo), (ii) those languages with the distinction on second and third persons only (e.g. Huichol and Papago), and (iii) those languages with the distinction on just third person (e.g. German, French, and Pre-Old-Norse, in which reflexives are marked on all persons except first-person singular) (e.g. Faltz 1985: 44, Hawkins 1989, but cf. Hubbard 1983, K. Williams 1988 on Albanian, see also van Gelderen 1997 for an account of the development of reflexives from Old to Middle English). In addition, there is a fourth type of language, namely, those languages with no reflexive marking at all (e.g. Anglo-Saxon/Old English, Guugu Yimidhirr, and Palenquero). As Hawkins (1989), among others, has noted, there is a functional explanation here. Evidently, the third-person distinction is the most, and the first-person distinction the least, useful, with the second-person distinction in between. This is in fact motivated and explained by the interaction of the Q-principle ('Say as much as possible in order to be non-ambiguous') and the I-principle ('Say as little as possible in order to be economical').

(b) (Pima, Faltz 1985: 119)
   mañ ñ ñɨit ab TV jɨ̃d.
   I me see DEIC TV from
   'I saw myself on TV.'
(c) (Sursurunga, Hutchisson 1986: 19)
   Iau t'ar iau (sang).
   1SG chop 1SG (EMPH)
   'I cut myself.'

(4.45) (a) (Chamorro, Chung 1989)
   Si Maria$_1$ pära u-lalatdi gui?$_1$.
   UNM Maria will INFL-scold her
   'Maria is going to scold herself.'
(b) (Mundani, Parker 1986: 149)
   bɔ́ɔ́$_1$ ǹ-tíŋ-á á-wɔ́b$_{1/2}$.
   they fact-help-IPFV OBJ-3PL-OBJ
   'They are helping themselves/them.'
(c) (Somoan, Keenan 1976: 314)
   sa sogi joane$_1$ ie ia$_1$ (lava).
   PAST cut John AGT he (EMPH)
   'John cut himself.'
(d) (Sursurunga, Hutchisson 1986: 19)
   A$_1$ t'ar-'ai$_1$ sang.
   he chop-him EMPH
   'He cut himself.'
(e) (Tsakhur, Lyutikova 1997)
   ič-e:$_1$ ʒe-l-e$_{1/2}$ aqlana ha?-a.
   girl-ERG PRON-OBL-SUP-EL laugh do-IPF
   'The girl is laughing at herself/her.'

Now, given the referential economy mechanism in (4.41) and (4.42), the pronoun becomes the most favoured choice for encoding reflexivity in (4.44) and (4.45). Since the DRP is not at work here, given that reflexivity is marked in these cases by a pronoun in the overt syntax, by (4.30) the preference for a local coreferential interpretation induced by the I-principle will go through unblocked. The same can also be said of (2.15)–(2.17). Thus, unlike Reinhart and Reuland's analysis (but like Burzio's Optimality account), our theory allows reflexivity to be marked by a lower-ranked anaphoric expression (such as a pronoun) if its immediately higher-ranked counterpart (such as a reflexive) is not available—an analysis that is empirically more accurate.

But what is of particular interest, from a pragmatic point of view, is the interpretation of cases where an anaphoric expression and its antecedent are not the co-arguments of a predicate. Regarding the reflexive/pronoun distribution, three types can be identified: (i) those permitting reflexives but not pronouns, as in (4.46), (ii) those allowing pronouns but not reflexives, as in (4.47), and (iii) those warranting both, as in (4.48).

(4.46) (Icelandic, Thráinsson 1991)
   Petur$_1$ bad Jens$_2$ um ad raka sig$_{1/2}$/hann$_{*1/*2}$.
   Petur asked Jens shave self/him
   'Petur$_1$ asked Jens$_2$ to shave self$_{1/2}$/him$_{*1/*2}$.'

224   *Pragmatic Approaches to Anaphora*

(4.47)   John₁ said that *heself₁/he₁ is interested in anaphora.
(4.48)   (Korean, adapted from Kim 1993)
   Kim₁-un   caki₁/ku₁-ka   salang-ey ppacyessta-ko malhayssta.
   Kim-TOP self/he-NOM love-in   fell-COMP   said
   'Kim₁ said that self₁/he₁ was in love.'

Note that in all these cases, the DRP is irrelevant; the anaphoric expression and its antecedent being non-co-arguments of the same predicate. Now in the case of (4.46), the interpretation of the reflexive falls under the I-principle, which engenders a local coreferential reading. The interpretation of the pronoun is then due to the working of the Q-principle. The use of a semantically weaker pronoun where a semantically stronger reflexive could occur solicits a classical Q-implicature, to the effect that a local coreferential interpretation is not available. The same analysis can be made of the 'anaphors only' cases of possessive anaphora in (2.23) in Chapter 2 and (4.49) below.[7]

(4.49) (a) (Basque, Rebuschi 1987)
       Peiok₁ bere₁/haren*₁ txakurra ikusi du.
       Peio-k self's/his   dog   seen AUX
       'Peio₁ has seen self's₁/his₂ dog.'
   (b) (Hindi/Urdu, Davison 1997)
       Syaam₁ apniii₁/us₂   praSaNsaa nahiiN kar-taa.
       Shyam self/s'3SG-of praise   not   do-IMPF
       'Shyam₁ does not do self's₁/his₂ praise.'
   (c) (Mundani, Parker 1986: 150)
       tà₁   dzɨ   àkèndè á-zí₁/tò₂.
       3SG PO:eat banana self's/his
       'He₁ has eaten self's₁/his₂ banana.'

We turn next to (4.47). In examples of this kind, because the reflexive is not available as a possible candidate to indicate coreferentiality, there is no Q-scale <reflexive, pronoun> to prevent the pronoun going under the I-principle, which gives rise to a local coreferential interpretation for the pronoun. This is exactly what happens in (4.47). The same is just as true of the 'pronouns only' cases of possessive anaphora in (2.24) in Chapter 2 and (4.50) below.

---

[7] Possessive anaphora in Ingush behaves in a similar way. Note next the use of *ó* versus *ō* in Yaouré (Hopkins 1986: 199).
  (i) (a) Ō   ó   wlùó jɛ̀   ɓiimã̄.
       3PL 3PL head skin comb-ICOMP
       'They₁ combed their₁ hair.'
    (b) Ō   ō   wlùó jɛ̀   ɓiimã̄.
       3PL 3PL head skin comb-ICOMP
       'They₁ combed their₂ hair.'
As the indexing in (ia) shows, *ó* behaves like an anaphor. Therefore, possessive anaphora in Yaouré seems to be another 'anaphors only' case.

(4.50) (a) (Akan, Faltz 1985: 174)
John₁ praa nẽ₁/₂   'fie.
John swept 3SG-POSS house
'John₁ swept his₁/₂ house.'
(b) (Mundani, Parker 1986: 149)
bɔ́₁ lé nɨ́ èghɨ̄ bɔ́b₁/₂.
they 3PL take things their
'They₁ took their₁/₂ things.'
(c) (Spanish)
María₁ quiere a   sus₁/₂ amigos.
Mary   loves ACC 3POSS friends
'Mary₁ loves her₁/₂ friends.'

Finally, of particular interest to us is (4.48), where there is a distributional overlap between the reflexive and the pronoun. Given the referential economy machinery in (4.41) and (4.42), one immediate question arises: why should there be such an overlap? One answer, provided by Burzio (1996), is that this may be the result of a conflict between the 'anaphors first' condition, which favours the use of a reflexive, and the locality condition, which goes against the use of a reflexive and therefore indirectly facilitates the use of a pronoun. Regardless of whether or not this line of explanation is on the right track, within the proposed Gricean pragmatic framework, (4.48) can be interpreted along the following lines. For reference, both the reflexive and the pronoun are subject to the I-principle. However, since the grammar allows the unmarked pronoun to be used to encode coreference, the speaker will use it if such an interpretation is intended. This gives rise to the question as to why the marked reflexive can also be used in (4.48). Put in a slightly different way, a question may be raised as to whether or not there is any systematic semantic/pragmatic contrast between the reflexive on the one hand, and the pronoun on the other. The answer is certainly yes. Intuitively, the use of a reflexive in these locations indicates some sort of unexpectedness (Edmondson and Plank 1978). Examined in a more careful way, this unexpectedness may turn out to be logophoricity, emphaticness/contrastiveness, or something yet to be discovered. But whatever this unexpectedness may turn out to be, we can give it a full account in terms of the systematic interaction of the Q-, I-, and M-principles.

Logophoricity

We begin with logophoricity. Recollect our discussion about the use of logophoric pronouns in African languages and that of long-distance reflexives in East Asian languages in the last chapter. In this subsection, I shall continue to concentrate on the two types of logophor in these two groups of languages. However, the analysis to be offered below will in principle be extendible to the logophoric use of long-distance reflexives in e.g. European, Caucasian, and South Asian languages.

Now, suppose that cross-linguistically logophoric marking is done according to the following hierarchy.

(4.51) Hierarchy of mechanisms for logophoric marking
    (a) Logophoric pronouns [+logophoric, +coreference][8]
    (b) Long-distance reflexives [±logophoric, +coreference][9]

What (4.51) basically says is this: for logophoric marking, a logophoric pronoun will be used if there is one; otherwise, a long-distance reflexive will be used. A second point to be borne in mind is that logophoricity and coreference are two distinct, though intimately related notions; logophoricity entails coreference, but not vice versa.

The use of logophoric pronouns in African languages and that of long-distance reflexives in East Asian languages can then be grouped into two types with regard to coreference: (i) those that are in complementary distribution with regular pronouns, as in (4.52), and (ii) those that are not, as in (4.53) and (4.54).

(4.52) (Igbo, Hyman and Comrie 1981)
    (a) ó sìrì nà yá byàrà.
        he said that LOG came
        'He$_1$ said that he$_1$ came.'
    (b) ó sìrì nà ó byàrà.
        he said that he came
        'He$_1$ said that he$_2$ came.'

(4.53) (Tuburi, Hagège 1974)
    (a) á Dik tí mąy mà:gā sē kó n sú: mònò.
        PRON think of young girl REL LOG see yesterday CORREL
        'He$_1$ is thinking of the young girl he$_1$ saw yesterday.'
    (b) á Dik tí mąy mà:gā à kó n sú: mònò.
        PRON think of young girl REL PRON see yesterday CORREL
        'He$_1$ is thinking of the young girl he$_{1/2}$ saw yesterday.'

(4.54) (Chinese)
    (a) Xiaoming shuo ziji hen xihuan Weierdi de geju.
        Xiaoming say self very like Verdi POSS opera
        'Xiaoming$_1$ said that self$_1$ likes Verdi's operas very much.'

---

[8] Logophoric addressee pronouns and logophoric verbal affixes may also be placed here.
[9] Note that a logophoric pronoun may bind a short-distance reflexive in the same clause.
  (i) (a) (Donno Sɔ, Culy, Kodio, and Togo 1994)
      Omar (inyemɛ) ku inyemɛ mɔ̃ samaa bem gi.
      Omar (LOG) heard LOG POSS congratulated AUX-1S said
      'Omar$_1$ said that (he$_1$) congratulated himself$_1$.'
    (b) (Ewe, Clements 1975)
      Kofi be yè-lɔ̃ yè dokui.
      Kofi said LOG-loves LOG himself
      'Kofi$_1$ said he$_1$ loves himself$_1$.'

Two points are of interest here: (i) the order of the binding relation cannot be reversed, and (ii) if relevant, the complex reflexive is formulated utilizing a logophoric rather than a regular pronoun.

(b) Xiaoming shuo ta   hen xihuan Weierdi de   geju.
    Xiaoming say   3SG very like   Verdi POSS opera
    'Xiaoming₁ said that he₁/₂ likes Verdi's operas very much.'

Take the first type first. By hierarchy (4.51), a logophoric pronoun will be chosen if logophoric marking is intended. Furthermore, given that logophoric pronouns are the only option available in the grammar to encode coreference, any speaker who intends coreference will also have to use a logophoric pronoun. This has the consequence that if the logophoric pronoun is not employed but a regular pronoun is used instead, a Q-implicature will arise; namely, neither logophoricity nor coreference is intended. In other words, we have a Q-scale <logophoric pronoun, regular pronoun> here, such that the use of the semantically weaker regular pronoun Q-implicates that the use of the semantically stronger logophoric pronoun cannot be truthfully entertained, that is to say, both the logophoric interpretation and the coreferential reading which are associated with the use of the logophoric pronoun should be avoided. Logophoric pronouns are semantically stronger than regular pronouns in that (i) syntactically, they usually require to be bound in a local domain, and (ii) semantically, they are canonically referentially dependent. Schematically:

(4.55) <*yá* [+logophoric, +coreference], *ó* [−logophoric, −coreference]>   *ó* +>_Q ~ *yá*

As for the second type, also worth noting is that if relevant, the choice between logophoric pronouns/long-distance reflexives on the one hand, and regular pronouns on the other, is correlated with that between subjunctive and indicative mood: it is common for the use of a logophoric pronoun/long-distance reflexive to go with subjunctive mood, and for the employment of a regular pronoun to go with indicative mood, as the following example shows (see also Coulmas 1986 for the observation that subjunctives are commonly used to mark indirect discourse).

(4.56) (Icelandic, Sigurðsson 1990*a*)
    (*a*) Jón segir   að María elski   sig.
         John says-INDIC that Mary loves-SBJV self
         'John₁ says that Mary loves self₁.'
    (*b*) Jón veit   að María elskar   hann.
         John knows-INDIC that Mary loves-INDIC him
         'John₁ knows that Mary loves him₁.'

Again, the correlation seems to be a reflection of a semantic/pragmatic choice made by the external speaker about the responsibility he or she assumes for the truthfulness of what he or she is reporting. If a regular pronoun and indicative mood are used, it shows that the speaker asserts that the report is true. If on the other hand, a logophoric pronoun/long-distance reflexive and subjunctive mood are deployed, it indicates that the speaker does not take the responsibility for the truth of the report. Thus, the optionality of logophors/non-logophors and of subjunctives/indicatives provides the speaker with a useful means of expressing his or her attitudes toward the truth of what he or she is reporting, or, more broadly, of expressing evidentiality (see e.g. Sigurðsson 1990a, Stirling 1993, and Culy 1994a for further discussion).

Now, come back to the non-complementarity between the logophoric pronoun and the regular pronoun in (4.53), which is usually found in periphrastic logophoric constructions in African languages. Given hierarchy (4.51), a logophoric pronoun will be used for the purpose of encoding logophoricity. However, unlike in (4.52), for coreference, a regular pronoun can be employed. In other words, while the use of a logophoric pronoun encodes both logophoricity and coreference, the use of a regular pronoun may or may not encode coreference, but definitely not logophoricity. This is sufficient enough to form a Q-scale <logophoric pronoun, regular pronoun>, such that the use of the semantically weaker regular pronoun Q-implicates at least a non-logophoric interpretation. Thus, in this context, the Q-induced opposition is one in logophoricity (though it may well be one in reference). Schematically:

(4.57) <sɛ̄[+logophoric, +coreference], à [−logophoric, ±coreference]>   à +>$_Q$ ~ sɛ̄

We move finally to (4.54), where there is a referential overlap between the long-distance reflexive and the pronoun. Essentially the same analysis can be applied to examples of this kind. Given hierarchy (4.51), a long-distance reflexive will be selected if logophoric marking is intended, for there is no logophoric pronoun in the language. Again, we have a Q-scale <long-distance reflexive, regular pronoun> here, to the effect that the unavailability of the semantically stronger long-distance reflexive which may encode both logophoricity and coreference will Q-implicate the speaker's intention to avoid at least one of the features associated with the use of the reflexive, namely, logophoricity (see also O'Connor 1992a, Levinson 1987, 1991). Notice also that the semantics of reflexives requires that they are referentially dependent, which is independent from logophoricity. Schematically:

(4.58) <ziji [±logophoric, +coreference], ta [−logophoric, ±coreference>   ta +>$_Q$ ~ ziji

Alternatively, (4.53) and (4.54) can also be accounted for in terms of the systematic interaction between the I- and M-principles. In the case of (4.53), since the grammar allows the unmarked regular pronoun to be used to encode coreference, the speaker will use it if such an interpretation is intended. On the other hand, if the unmarked regular pronoun is not used, but the marked logophoric pronoun is used instead, then an M-implicature is created, namely, not only coreference but logophoricity as well is intended. Schematically:

(4.59) {à [−logophoric, ±coreference], sɛ̄ [+logophoric, +coreference]}   sɛ̄ +>$_M$ ~ à

Logophoric pronouns can be seen as marked in the following two senses. The first is that they are in general morphologically more prolix than regular pronouns. For example, in Igbo and Yoruba, it is the free/long/independent form that functions as a logophoric pronoun in a logophoric domain (e.g. Green and Igwe 1963, Carrell 1970, Bamgbọse 1966, von Roncador 1992, Culy 1994a). Secondly, logophoric pronouns are functionally marked as well, that is, they are in general forms that are put on a lower rank in a non-logophoric domain but are raised to a higher rank in a logophoric one. Data drawn from around sixty African languages point to the following types of upgrading in a logophoric domain: (i) grammatical function upgrading (a non-subject pronoun may be used as a subject); (ii) emphasis upgrading (an emphatic pronoun may be used as a logophoric pronoun); (iii) gender upgrading (genders or classes for non-humans may be used for humans, e.g. in Zande, pronouns for animal classes are used as logophoric pronouns); and (iv) number upgrading (non-singular markers may be used for singular and plural entities) (von Roncador 1992). Clearly, in each of these cases, a functionally marked form is employed to encode logophoricity.

The same M-based analysis can be shown to hold for (4.54) as well. Again, the use of the marked (morphologically more prolix) reflexive here will convey a message that would not have been conveyed by the use of the unmarked regular pronoun, namely, that of logophoricity. This M-implicature, not being in conflict with the semantics of reflexives (namely, the property of referential dependency) and/or world knowledge, will pass through unchecked. Schematically:

(4.60) {*ta* [–logophoric, ±coreference], *ziji* [±logophoric, +coreference]}   *ziji* +>$_M$ ~ *ta*

Emphaticness/contrastiveness

A second dimension of unexpectedness arising from the use of a long-distance reflexive involves emphaticness/contrastiveness. With regard to differentiation/non-differentiation between emphatics and reflexives, languages can be grouped into two categories: (i) those like the Finno-Ugric, Semitic, and Turkic languages, and Gaelic, Maasai, and Loma, which do not distinguish between emphatics and reflexives, and (ii) those like the Germanic (with English as an exception), Romance, and Slavonic languages, which do (e.g. Moravcsik 1972, König and Siemund 1997, but see n. 6 of Chapter 2 above for differences between Germanic and Romance).

The use of an emphatic is in general subject to the following two semantico-pragmatic conditions proposed by C. Baker (1995) (see also Moyne 1971, Moravcsik 1972, Edmondson and Plank 1978, König 1991, König and Siemund 1997, McKay 1991, Kemmer 1995, and Zribi-Hertz 1995).

(4.61) C. Baker's (1995) theory of use of emphatics
   (a) Contrastiveness condition
       Emphatics are appropriate only in contexts in which emphasis or contrast is desired.
   (b) Relative discourse prominence condition
       Emphatics can only be used to mark a character in a sentence or discourse who is relatively more prominent or central than other characters.

Discourse prominence of a character is determined on the basis of (i) its importance on a real-world hierarchy, (ii) its importance in a given situation, (iii) its importance as the pivot in terms of which some other character is defined, and (iv) its importance as the subject of consciousness (cf. the logocentric trigger) (e.g. C. Baker 1995).

The use of an emphatic typically has the following effects: (i) contrastiveness or being contrary to expectation, (ii) a natural negative gloss, of the sort 'and not anyone else' etc., (iii) inducing a particular anaphoric/referential interpretation, (iv) contrastive stress, and (v) giving rise to a particular scope reading (e.g. Edmondson and Plank 1978, König 1991, and especially Levinson 1991: 131)

With all this in mind, let us now take a look at some examples of long-distance reflexivization. Consider first the Turkish example in (4.62) (Kornfilt 1997).

(4.62) (O) hiss-ed-er-di   ki bu kadin
       he feeling-do-AOR-PAST that this woman
       kendi-sin-i   sev-mi-yor.
       self-3SG-ACC love-NEG-PROG
       'He$_1$ felt that this woman does not love himself$_1$.'

By (4.61), (4.62) describes an emphatic/contrastive situation, though perhaps implicitly. In the first place, the use of the long-distance reflexive here invokes a set of alternatives to the referent of its focus, as an emphatic typically does, for the sentence can be paraphrased as 'He felt that this woman does not love him, but loves someone else'. Secondly, the antecedent for the long-distance reflexive in (4.62) enjoys a prominent or central status, for it is the only logocentric trigger available in the sentence.

This emphatic/contrastive effect can of course be more clearly seen in an overly marked emphatic/constructive context.

(4.63) (Chinese)
   (a) Zhuren zongshi yiwei ta dui, bieren dou bu dui.
       director always think 3SG right other all not right
       'The director$_1$ always thinks that he$_1$ is right, but others are all wrong.'
   (b) Zhuren zongshi yiwei ziji dui, bieren dou bu dui.
       director always think self right other all not right
       'The director$_1$ always thinks that self$_1$ is right, but others are all wrong.'

(c) Zhuren zongshi yiwei ta   ziji dui, bieren dou bu dui.
    director always think 3SG self right other all not right
    'The director always thinks that he self₁ is right, but others are all wrong.'

The use of *bieren* 'others' is a clear indication that (4.63) expresses an emphatic/contrastive event. This seems to explain why intuitively (4.63b) and (4.63c) sound slightly more natural than (4.63a) on the indexed interpretation. Furthermore, (4.63c) is intuitively felt to be more emphatic/contrastive than (4.63b). Within the neo-Gricean pragmatic framework being discussed here, the emphaticness/contrastiveness associated with the use of a long-distance reflexive falls naturally out of the M-principle: it is because the use of a reflexive in these contexts would carry an emphatic/contrastive message that would not be conveyed by the use of either a pronoun or a zero anaphor that it is chosen. Furthermore, the fact that (4.63c) is more emphatic/contrastive than (4.63b) can also be explained by the M-principle. Given this pragmatic principle, it is predicted that the use of a more prolix expression tends to give a more marked message, hence a more emphatic/contrastive reading for (4.63c). Looked at from a slightly different vantage point, what is also partly in operation here is an iconicity principle, namely the more coding material, the more emphatic/contrastive the message. Essentially the same analysis can be made of the use of morphologically complex emphatics, as in (4.64), and that of the 'both anaphors and pronominals' cases of possessive anaphora, as in (4.65).

(4.64) (a) (French, Zribi-Hertz 1995)
        Ce   pauvre type   croit   que Marie aime tout
        that poor   fellow believes that Marie loves all
        le monde excepté lui-même.
        the people except him-same
        'That poor fellow₁ believes that Marie loves everyone except himself₁.'
    (b) (German, C. Baker 1995)
        John möchte, dass seine Mutter ihn selbst
        John wants   that his   mother him self
        vorstellt, bevor sie sich vorstellt.
        introduces before she self introduces
        'John₁ wants her mother to introduce himself₁ before she introduces herself.'
    (c) (Russian, Burzio 1996)
        Ja ... stal rassprasivat' xudoznika o   nem samom.
        I   start question   artist   about him same
        'I ... began to question the artist₁ about himself₁.'
(4.65) (a) (Chinese)
        Xiaoming₁ xihuan ziji₁ /ta₁/₂ de gangqin laoshi.
        Xiaoming like   self /3SG of piano   teacher
        'Xiaoming₁ likes self's₁/his₁/₂ piano teacher.'
    (b) (Malay, Ngoh 1991)
        Aminah₁ mencuci pakaian-dirinya₁/nya₁/₂.
        Aminah wash   clothes-self her/her
        'Aminah₁ washes herself's₁ /her₁/₂ clothes.'

(c) (Tamil, Annamalai 1997)
   kumaar₁ tan₁/avan₁/₂ tambiyeyee   verukraan.
   Kumar self/he   brother-ACC-EMPH hate-PRST-AGR
   'Kumar₁ hates self's₁ /his₁/₂ brother.'

In both types of example, as in the case of (4.62) and (4.63), the (local) coreferential interpretation for both the reflexive/emphatic and the pronoun is due to the working of the I-principle; the emphatic/contrastive reading for the marked reflexive/emphatic is accountable in terms of the M-principle.[10]

Two 'avoid pronoun' effects and beyond

Somewhat related to the emphaticness/contrastiveness generated by the use of an emphatic, discussed above, is that engendered by the employment of an overt pronoun in a pro-drop or zero anaphora language. In such a language, the occurrence of an overt pronoun is in general effected by an emphaticness/contrastiveness constraint, that is, an overt pronoun is typically omitted unless it is required for reasons of emphasis/contrastiveness. This is attested among a variety of zero anaphora languages, as genetically unrelated and structurally different as Arabic, Bengali, Catalan, Chinese, Italian, Korean, Latin, Polish, Spanish, Swahili, and Turkish (see also Sprouse and Vance 1999 on Modern and Medieval Occitan). Some examples follow.

(4.66) (a) (Eastern Bengali, van der Wurff 1989)
       Ami/Ø aslam.
       I-NOM came
       'I came.'
   (b) (Korean, Kim 1993:149)
       John-i   ku-ka/Ø   phikonhata-ko malhayssta.
       John-NOM he-NOM   tired-COMP   said
       'John₁ said that he₁/₂ was tired.'

---

[10] It is also noteworthy that logophoric pronouns and emphatics/reflexives are closely related functionally in some semi/mixed logophoric languages. This functional connection can be seen from two opposite directions. On the one hand, a logophoric pronoun is frequently used as an emphatic/reflexive outside a logophoric domain. This is, for example, the case with the Central Sudanic languages Bango, Birri, Mangbetu, and Songhai, the Kwa language Yoruba, the Adamawa-Ubangi languages Barambu and Ma, the Mande language Busa, and the Ubangi language Gbaya. On the other hand, a possessive reflexive is often used to encode logophoricity in a logophoric domain. This is the case with the Ubangi languages Barambu, Bai, Mayogo, Amadi, the Central Sudanic languages Birri, Bango, Logo, Lendu, Baka, Lugbara, and the Mande languages Bisa and Busa (von Roncador 1992, cf. also n. 9 of Chapter 3).
  Following is an example form Songhai (Hutchison 1981), showing the connection between the marking of logophoricity and possessive reflexivization.
  (i) (a) Ali har ka   ngu go   ta   koy tira.
         Ali say COMP LOG AUX AUX go   school
         'Ali₁ said that he₁ would go to school.'
     (b) Moussa no Ali se ngu   kitaabu di.
         Moussa give Ali to self's book   DET
         'Moussa₁ gave Ali₂ self's₁ book.'

(c) (Spanish, Blackwell 1994)
  Juan cree que él/Ø es listo.
  John believes that he is clever-SG-MASC
  'John$_1$ believes that he$_{1/2}$ is clever.'
(d) (Swahili, Vitale 1981)
  Yeye/Ø a-li-m-piga Juma.
  he 3S-PAST-3S-hit Juma
  'He hit Juma.'
(e) (Turkish, Enç 1986)
  Ben/Ø çarşi-ya gid-iyor-um.
  I market-DAT go-PROG-1SG
  'I am going to the market.'

Again, this contrast follows directly from the interaction of the I- and M-principles. Whereas the reference of both the zero anaphor and the pronoun is subject to the I-principle, the use of the pronoun for emphaticness/contrastiveness is subject to the M-principle: it is because the use of a pronoun in these locations (where there is a referential overlap) would convey a message that would not be conveyed by the use of a zero anaphor that it is chosen. Thus, the I- and M-principles jointly give a complementary interpretation here, but one that contrasts in emphasis rather than reference.

What is of particular interest to us here, however, is the zero anaphor/pronoun opposition of a different kind, which has been observed among many pro-drop or zero anaphora languages. As already mentioned in Chapter 2, in these zero anaphora languages, while a *pro*/zero anaphor can admit of a quantifier-variable interpretation, an overt pronoun cannot. We have already seen examples from Czech, Korean, and Tarifit in (2.147)–(2.149). Following are futher examples from Catalan, Finnish, and Spanish.

(4.67) (Catalan, Picallo 1994)
  (a) Tots els artistes$_1$ creuen que Ø$_1$ són genis.
    all the artists believe that are geniuses
    'All the artists believe that (they) are geniuses.'
  (b) Tots els artistes$_1$ creuen que ells$_{*1/2}$ són genis.
    all the artists believe that they are geniuses
    'All the artists believe that they are geniuses.'
(4.68) (Finnish, Kirsi Hiltunen personal communication)
  (a) Jokainen$_1$ toivoo että Ø$_1$ olisi onnellinen.
    everyone wish-3SG that be-COND happy
    'Everyone wishes that (he) can be happy.'
  (b) Jokainen$_1$ toivoo että hän$_{*1/2}$ olisi onnellinen.
    everyone wish-3SG that he be-COND happy
    'Everyone wishes that (he) can be happy.'
(4.69) (Spanish, Montalbetti 1984)
  (a) Ningún estudiante$_1$ cree que Juan lo vio Ø$_1$.
    no student believe that Juan CLI saw
    'No student believes that Juan saw him.'
  (b) Ningún estudiante$_1$ cree que Juan lo vio à él$_{*1/2}$.
    no student believe that Juan CLI saw him
    'No student believes that Juan saw him.'

234   *Pragmatic Approaches to Anaphora*

In the (*a*) sentence of (4.67)–(4.69), the *pro*/zero anaphor can be construed as a variable bound to the quantificational NP. By contrast, in the (*b*) sentence, the overt pronoun can only be interpreted as a referential pronoun. This contrast is captured by Montalbetti's (1984: 94) Overt Pronoun Constraint.

(4.70) Montalbetti's (1984) Overt Pronoun Constraint
Overt pronouns cannot be linked to formal variables if and only if they occur in a position where the alternative empty/overt is possible.

In the same vein, this empty/overt pronoun opposition holds also for arbitrary interpretation (cf. Chapter 2) in some pro-drop or zero anaphora languages: while a *pro*/zero anaphor can be arbitrary in reference, an overt pronoun cannot. Besides examples from Chinese, Malayalam and Polish in (2.150)–(2.152), we have examples from Serbo-Croatian and Spanish below.

(4.71) (Serbo-Croatian, Lindseth and Franks 1996)
    (*a*) Ø ovdje prodaju kavu.
          sell   coffee   here
       'People sell coffee here.'
    (*b*) oni ovdje prodaju kavu.
          they sell   coffee   here
       'They sell coffee here.'
(4.72) (Spanish, Jaeggli 1986)
    (*a*) Ø llaman   a la   puerta.
          call-3PL at the door
       'People are knocking at the door.'
    (*b*) Ellos llaman a la   puerta.
          they call-3PL at the door
       'They are knocking at the door.'

Along the lines of Montelbetti's Overt Pronoun Constraint, Jaeggli (1986: 66) states this empirical generalization in terms of another bidirectional implication called the Condition on Arbitrary Pronominals.

(4.73) Jaeggli's (1986) Condition on Arbitrary Pronominals
Overt pronouns may not be arbitrary in reference if and only if the overt/empty alternation obtains.

In fact, both (4.70) and (4.73) can be incorporated into Chomsky's (1981, 1982) more general 'avoid pronoun' principle. Given this principle, it is predicted that where there is a zero anaphor/overt pronoun choice left open by the grammar, a zero anaphor is preferred where a local coreferential or bound interpretation is intended. This has the consequence that where a coreferential or bound zero anaphor may occur, the use of an overt pronoun will tend to be taken to solicit disjoint reference. The major difference between (4.70)/(4.73) on the one hand and the 'avoid pronoun' principle on the other, however, is that the former is more firmly grammaticalized than the latter. This can be seen by the fact that the Overt Pronoun Constraint/Condition on

Arbitrary Pronominals effect is in general stronger than the 'avoid pronoun' effect.

Clearly, the Overt Pronoun Constraint/Condition on Arbitrary Pronominals and its overarching 'avoid pronoun' principle have a pragmatic flavour. In fact, they follow directly from the interaction of the I- and M-principles. The I-principle (redundantly) ensures that the *pro*/zero anaphor in the (*a*) sentence of (4.67)–(4.69), for example, takes the quantificational NP as its preferred antecedent. (The I-implicated interpretation is redundant because the quantifier–variable relation is essentially grammatical in nature and therefore can be accounted for by a syntactic rule to that effect.) On the other hand, since the overt pronoun is used where a *pro*/zero anaphor could occur and since the (*a*) sentence is what the speaker should have opted for if he or she intended a quantifier–variable reading, the use of a marked, overt pronoun in the (*b*) sentence will fall under the M-principle, from which a non-quantifier–variable interpretation will be derived. Essentially the same analysis can be made of the *pro*/zero anaphor–overt pronoun contrast with respect to arbitrary interpretation, as shown in (4.71) and (4.72).

There is, however, one pattern of quantifier–variable binding that has received little attention in the literature. This pattern seems to be prominent in languages like Chinese, Japanese, and Korean.

(4.74) (Chinese)
    (*a*) Mei ge ren dou shuo Ø xihuan gudian yinyue.
         every CL person all say   like classical music
         'Everybody$_1$ says that (I/you/he$_{1/2}$/we/they . . .) like(s) classical music.'
    (*b*) Mei ge ren dou shuo ta xihuan gudian yinue.
         every CL person all say 3SG like classical music
         'Everybody$_1$ says that he$_2$ likes classical music.'
    (*c*) Mei ge ren dou shuo ziji xihuan gudian yinyue.
         every CL person all say self like classical music
         'Everybody$_1$ says that self$_1$ likes classical music.'

(4.75) (Japanese, Saito and Hoji 1983)
    (*a*) Daremo-ga   Ø Mary-ni kirawareteiru to
         everyone-NOM Mary-by be-disliked COMP
         omoikondeiru (koto).
         be convinced fact
         'Everyone$_1$ is convinced that (he$_1$) is disliked by Mary.'
    (*b*) Daremo-ga   kare-ga Mary-ni kirawareteiru to
         everyone-NOM he-NOM Mary-by be-disliked   COMP
         omoikondeiru (koto).
         be convinced fact
         'Everyone$_1$ is convinced that he$_2$ is disliked by Mary.'
    (*c*) Daremo-ga   zibun-ga Mary-ni kirawareteiru to
         everyone-NOM self-NOM Mary-by be-disliked   COMP
         omoikondeiru (koto).
         be convinced fact
         'Everyone$_1$ is convinced that self$_1$ is disliked by Mary.'

(4.76) (Korean, Kim 1993: 51, 153)
 (a) amuto   Ø   Mary-lul   cohahanta-ko malhaci anhassta.
   anyone   Mary-ACC like-COMP   say   did not
   'Nobody$_1$ said that (he$_1$) liked Mary.'
 (b) amuto ku-ka   Mary-lul   cohahanta-ko malhaci anhassta.
   anyone he-NOM Mary-ACC like-COMP   say   did not
   'Nobody$_1$ said that he$_2$ liked Mary.'
 (c) amuto caki-ka   Mary-lul   cohahanta-ko malhaci anhassta.
   anyone self-NOM Mary-ACC like-COMP   say   did not
   'Nobody$_1$ said that self$_1$ liked Mary.'

As can be seen by (4.74)–(4.76), in these East Asian languages, a reflexive, in addition to a zero anaphor, can be related to a quantificational NP as a bound variable. Note further that there does seem to be a form/meaning correlation here: the use of a reflexive as a bound variable carries an additional logophoric and/or emphatic/contrastive message. How, then, can this pattern of quantifier-variable binding be accommodated by our pragmatic analysis. Suppose that a bound zero anaphor in Chinese, Japanese, and Korean is grouped together with reflexives as 'zero anaphor/reflexive' on the hierarchy (4.42). This would have the effect that if a speaker in these languages intends to convey a message of quantifier-variable binding, he or she would use either a zero anaphor or a reflexive to that effect. The interpretation of both will (redundantly) fall under the I-principle. Since the zero anaphor is both semantically and formally more minimal/economical than the reflexive, by both the hierarchy (4.42) and the I-principle, it is expected to be employed to express a 'pure' quantifier-variable relation. If, on the other hand, the unmarked zero anaphor is not used, but a marked reflexive is selected instead, then an M-inference is generated, namely, not only quantifier-variable binding but logophoricity and/or emphasis as well is intended. By the same reasoning, the use of an overt pronoun as a non-bound-variable is then the direct outcome of the application of both the Q- and M-principles: the former applied to the Q-contrast set <reflexive, pronoun> and the latter applied to the M-contrast set {Ø, pronoun}. Whenever a reflexive could occur as a bound variable, the use of a semantically weaker pronoun will Q-implicate the non-applicability of the more informative, quantifier-variable interpretation. On the other hand, the use of a more prolix pronoun where a zero anaphor could be used as a bound variable will invite an M-implicature to the effect that the otherwise I-implicated quantifier-variable reading does not obtain.[11]

---

[11] Our analysis informally predicts that if a language does not have the zero anaphor option for encoding quantifier-variable binding, speakers of that language would use reflexives to express such a binding relation. This seems to be the case with Marathi and Telugu, as described in Wali and Subbarao (1991).

Pragmatic Approaches to Anaphora 237

The main advantage of positing a neo-Gricean pragmatic theory of anaphora is that conversational implicatures being cancellable, we can always arrive at an interpretation that is best in keeping with our knowledge about the world. How, then, can conversational implicatures be suspended? According to current pragmatic theory, they tend to disappear in the face of inconsistency with (i) background assumptions (or world knowledge), (ii) contextual information, (iii) meaning$_{nn}$, (iv) semantic entailments, and (v) priority pragmatic inferences (e.g. Levinson 1987, 1991, 1995, Huang 1994). In other words, conversational implicatures are subject to the requirement of consistency with these constraints. As I shall show presently, this holds largely for those conversational implicatures that pertain to anaphoric interpretation.

World knowledge

In the first place, any anaphoric interpretation generated by our pragmatic apparatus must be consistent with real-world knowledge; no interpretation would arise if it is not in keeping with background assumptions. As an initial example, consider (4.77) from Chinese.

(4.77) (a) Bingren shuo yisheng zhidao Ø mingtian gei ta kaidao.
 patient say doctor know tomorrow for 3SG operate
 'The patient$_1$ says that the surgeon$_2$ knows that (I/you/he$_{2/3}$/we/they ...)
 will operate on him$_1$ tomorrow.'
 (b) Yisheng shuo bingren zhidao Ø mingtian gei ta kaidao.
 doctor say patient know tomorrow for 3SG operate
 'The surgeon$_1$ says that the patient$_2$ knows that (I/you/he$_{1/3}$/we/they ...)
 will operate on him$_2$ tomorrow.'

Recall that given our pragmatic apparatus (4.30), the interpretation of an anaphoric expression is subject to the I-principle, unless there is either a Q- or an M-contrast set or both to prevent the applicability of the I-principle. What the I-principle does here is to invite a local coreferential interpretation for the anaphoric expression, provided that such an interpretation does not run contrary to the DRP, information saliency, and the general consistency constraints on conversational implicatures. In fact, there appears to be a rigid I-heuristic here: a local subject is in general preferred to a local object; a non-split antecedent is in general favoured over a split one; and a c-commanding antecedent is in general preferred to a non-c-commanding one. If none of these NPs seems to qualify as a possible antecedent, the next, more remote clause will be examined for possibilities in the same order, and so on until the root clause is reached. Failure to find an intrasentential antecedent will lead to the search for a previous discourse antecedent, preferably a topic, or to settling for an 'arbitrary' interpretation.

Returning to (4.77), given the I-heuristic, the preferred antecedent for the zero anaphor in (4.77a) is correctly predicted to be the subject of the intermediate clause. However, by the same mechanism, the zero anaphor in (4.77b) would first be interpreted as being preferably coreferential with the subject of the intermediate clause. But this interpretation clearly runs counter to our background assumption that it is stereotypically a surgeon who operates on a patient rather than vice versa. This has the immediate consequence that such an interpretation is ruled out as the preferred interpretation. As a result, the zero anaphor under consideration is I-implicated to be preferably coreferential with the matrix subject—a correct consequence.

We next turn to control. Clearly, the choice of controller is very much a function of the lexical semantics of the control verb involved. It has been commonly assumed that verbs of a certain semantic type take subject control, whereas verbs of a different semantic type take object control (cf. Section 2.1.3, see also Radford 1981: 381, Comrie 1984, Foley and Van Valin 1984: 307–11, Farkas 1988, Sag and Pollard 1991). However, on our account, the lexical semantics of control verbs merely plays a role in the selection of controller exactly analogous to the way in which semantic constraints affect pragmatic inferences. In other words, the lexical semantics of control verbs does not determine the actual choice of controller; it merely delimits the set of possible controllers. (If the choice of controller were merely determined by the lexical semantics of control verbs, then control would be an entirely semantic issue.) For example, as already discussed, verbs such as 'promise' and 'persuade' in a language like Chinese can be used to express different speech acts. Given their lexical semantics, it is merely predicted that the possible set of controllers should normally be delimited to the matrix subject (or the AGENT) and the matrix object (or the GOAL). The actual choice between the matrix subject and the matrix object as the preferred controller is then determined by the I-principle in keeping with, say, world knowledge. We have already seen examples of this kind from Chinese in Chapters 1 and 3. Another example of the same type from Japanese is given below (Kumiko Kato personal communication).

(4.78) (a) Kanja$_1$-wa   isya$_2$-ni   asita   Ø$_1$ kusuri-o   nomu
          patient-TOP doctor-to tomorrow   medicine-OBJ take
          koto   o   yakusokusi-ta.
          COMP OBJ promise-PAST
          'The patient$_1$ promised the doctor$_2$ that (he$_1$) will take medicine tomorrow.'
      (b) Isya$_1$-wa   kanja$_2$-ni   asita   Ø$_2$ taiinsuru
          doctor-TOP patient-to tomorrow   leave hospital
          koto   o   yakusokusi-ta
          COMP OBJ promise-PAST
          'The doctor$_1$ promised the patient$_2$ that (he$_2$) will leave hospital tomorrow.'

This analysis is in part reminiscent of the family of analyses by Foley and Van Valin (1984), Farkas (1988), and Sag and Pollard (1991). On Foley and Van Valin's (1984: 309) view, it is the speech acts a control verb may express rather than its lexical meanings that govern controller assignment. Farkas

(1988) uses an abstract notion of responsibility to predict controller choice. The essence of responsibility is that if x can bring a course of action A about, x is potentially responsible for A. Thus on this account, shift of controller is essentially the result of shift of responsibility (see also Larson 1991). Sag and Pollard (1991) are of the opinion that the controller assignment mechanism should be tied to the SOAs described by linguistic expressions rather than linguistic expressions themselves. According to this view, then, controller switch involves a kind of 'accommodation' of interpretation dubbed 'coercion', that is, the semantic content of the controlled complement is 'coerced' into being compatible with the semantics of the control verb involved. It is clear that these analyses are somewhat similar to the one developed here in attempting to account for controller shift on a non-configurational basis. However, they differ from the present one on the issue of whether shift of controller is semantic or pragmatic in nature. While Foley and Van Valin (1984), Farkas (1988), and Sag and Pollard (1991) treat shift of controller as a semantic issue, we take it to be essentially a pragmatic issue. What evidence there is in a language like Chinese favours my position rather than theirs. Note that the object control reading in (4.78b) is only the preferred reading; the other reading, namely the subject control reading, is not impossible. In other words, in examples like (4.78), there are (at least) two possible controllers, one of which is the default but defeasible one. Following Donnellan (1966), Stalnaker (1972), and Horn (1988), we call the systematic ambiguity displayed by control verbs of this kind a pragmatic ambiguity, that is, a built-in duality of use. There is thus clear evidence that it is pragmatics that comes to the fore to make correct predictions for the choice of controller where syntax and/or lexical semantics fail to do so.

Next, let us take a look at (4.79) and (4.80).

(4.79) (Tuburi, Wiesemann 1986a)
Pɔl laa jág Jaŋ gá sɛ̀ ko sɛ̀.
Paul heard from John that LOG see LOG
'Paul$_1$ heard from John$_2$ that he$_{2>1}$ saw him$_{1>2}$.'

(4.80) (Japanese, Kato 1994)
Takasi-ga   Yamada sensei-ni   zibun-ga
Takasi-SUBJ Yamada teacher-OBJ self-SUBJ
siken-ni   goukaku-sita koto-o   kiita.
examination passed   COMP-OBJ heard
'Takasi$_1$ heard from Professor Yamada$_2$ that self$_{1>2}$ passed the examination.'

Note that both (4.79) and (4.80) contain the logocentric predicate 'hear from'. Intuitively, both sentences are two-way ambiguous, the preferred antecedent being *John* in (4.79) and *Takasi* in (4.80). Under the DRT analysis, discussed in Chapter 3, two DRSs are needed for each of (4.79) and (4.80), one linking the logophor with the matrix subject and the other connecting it with the matrix object. Moreover, the DRS analysis tells us nothing about which of the two logophoric interpretations is the preferred one. Now, given the I-heuristic, the two instances of the Tuburi logophoric pronoun *sɛ̀* in (4.79) would first be read as being preferably coreferential with *Pɔl* and *Jaŋ* respectively. But this interpretation clearly does not conform to the background assumption that one does not need to hear that one saw someone else. This has the immediate effect that such an interpretation is ruled out as the preferred interpretation. As a consequence, the two instances of *sɛ̀* are then I-implicated to be preferably coreferential with *Jaŋ* and *Pɔl* respectively—a result that is consistent with our intuition. In contrast to (4.79), in the Japanese example (4.80), the I-principle articulates that the preferred antecedent for *zibun* is the subject of the matrix clause. This I-implicature is further reinforced by the background assumption that it is stereotypically a student rather than a professor who would sit for an examination. Next, essentially the same 'world knowledge' constraint can be shown to hold for the interpretation of a psych-sentence like (4.81).

(4.81) (Chinese)
Tongxuemen laoshi chaonong ziji shi Xiaoming hen kunao.
classmates   always laugh at   self make Xiaoming very worry
'That (his) classmates₁ always laugh at self₂/selves₁ worries Xiaoming₂.'

Given the syntax and semantics of (4.81), the set of possible antecedents for *ziji* would be delimited to *tongxuemen* 'classmates' and *Xiaoming*. Again, two DRS representations are needed here. Now, by the I-heuristic, *tongxuemen* would be implicated to be the preferred antecedent. However, given our knowledge about the world, it is more likely that Xiaoming's worries are caused by his classmates' constant laughing at him rather than at themselves. Consequently, the original I-induced preferred interpretation evaporates, and *ziji* would then be I-implicated to be preferably bound to *Xiaoming*.

Finally, the evaporation of the M-implicated contrast in reference in the following Chinese example shows exactly the same point.

(4.82) (a) Yisheng shuo bingren zhidao Ø mingtian gei ta   kaidao.
           doctor say patient know   tomorrow for 3SG operate
           'The surgeon₁ says that the patient₂ knows that (he₁/₃/I/ you/we/they ...)
           will operate on him₂ tomorrow.'
       (b) Yisheng shuo bingren zhidao ta   mingtian gei ta   kaidao
           doctor say patient know 3SG tomorrow for 3SG operate
           The surgeon₁ says that the patient₂ knows that he₁/₃ will operate on him₂
           tomorrow.'

In (4.82b), *ta* is used where a zero anaphor could occur, as in (4.82a). Given the M-principle, *ta* would be interpreted as preferably disjoint in reference with *yisheng* 'surgeon'. Such an interpretation, however, runs counter to our background assumption that it is stereotypically surgeons who do operations. Therefore, the M-implicature disappears and the use of *ta* is subject to the I-principle, from which follows the coreferential interpretation between *ta* and *yisheng* in (4.82*b*). Perhaps of some further interest is the Spanish equivalent (4.83) (Blackwell 1994), which nicely parallels (4.82) in terms of interpretation. This leads Blackwell (1994: 101–2) to conclude that '[r]egardless of the structural differences between Chinese and Spanish, our background assumption that surgeons usually do the operating is the overriding factor in determining the interpretations of the anaphoric NPs in both languages' (see also Demirci 1997 on how pragmatic knowledge of this kind affects the acquisition of binding of English reflexives by Turkish L2 learners).

(4.83) (*a*) El cirujano dice que el paciente sabe que
the doctor say that the patient know that
Ø va a operarle mañana.
is going to operate-him tomorrow
'The surgeon₁ says that the patient₂ knows that (he_{1/3})will operate on him₂ tomorrow.'
(*b*) El cirujano dice que el paciente sabe que
the doctor say that the patient know that
él va a operarle mañana.
he is going to operate-him tomorrow
'The surgeon₁ says that the patient₂ knows that he_{1/3} will operate on him₂ tomorrow.'

Contextual information

Secondly, any anaphoric interpretation engendered by our pragmatic apparatus is subject to the requirement of consistency with what the linguistic context specifies. One example from Chinese suffices to illustrate this point.

(4.84) (*a*) Chen Xiansheng renwei Liu Xiansheng tai kuangwang,
Chen Mr think Liu Mr too arrogant
Ø zongshi kanbuqi ziji.
always look down upon self
'Mr Chen₁ thinks that Mr Liu₂ is too arrogant, and (he₂) always looks down upon self₁.'
(*b*) Chen Xiansheng renwei Liu Xiansheng tai zibei,
Chen Mr think Liu Mr too self-abased
Ø zongshi kanbuqi ziji.
always look down upon self
'Mr Chen₁ thinks that Mr Liu₂ is too self-abased, and (he₂) always looks down upon self₂.'

Clearly, in the context of (4.84*a*), by the I-principle, *Chen Xiansheng* 'Mr Chen' is the most likely choice for antecedent of *ziji*, whereas in the context of (4.84*b*), *Liu Xiansheng* 'Mr Liu' becomes the most likely candidate for antecedent of *ziji*.

Meaning$_{nn}$

A third constraint on the anaphoric interpretation implicated by our pragmatic apparatus is the requirement that it must accord with what the speaker might clearly intend (i.e. mean$_{-nn}$) given the assumed state of mutual knowledge. To explain by an example, let us return to the Spanish example (4.69). Since there is (4.69a), the use of the pronoun in (4.69b) will M-implicate a non-quantificational interpretation. But now suppose that (i) the hearer knows that the speaker intends to use (4.69b) to mean (4.69a) (for whatever reason), (ii) he or she is expecting the speaker to do so, and (iii) the speaker knows that the hearer knows all that. Then, the speaker uses (4.69b) instead of (4.69a). In that case, what the speaker clearly means$_{-nn}$ is that the pronoun should be interpreted as bound to the quantificational NP. This is enough to cancel the M-implicature that the use of the pronoun in (4.69b) might otherwise generate.

Semantic constraints

Fourthly, any anaphoric interpretation promoted by our pragmatic apparatus must be congruent with semantic constraints. To be noted first is the role played by truth-conditions. Consider (4.85)–(4.87) (adapted from Evans 1980, Reinhart 1983, Levinson 1987).

(4.85) (a) Only John voted for John.
      (b) Only John voted for himself.
(4.86) (a) The poet of the piano was Chopin.
      (b) The poet of the piano was himself.
(4.87) (a) Beethoven and Mozart had one thing in common: Beethoven thought that Mozart was a godsend and Mozart thought that Mozart was a godsend.
      (b) Beethoven and Mozart had one thing in common: Beethoven thought that Mozart was a godsend and Mozart thought that he was a godsend.

Evidently, the (a) sentence of (4.85)–(4.87) contradicts binding condition C. At first sight, it constitutes counter-evidence to our Q- and M-principles as well. In the former case, the use of a semantically weaker lexical NP where a semantically stronger reflexive can occur should Q-implicate a non-coreferential interpretation; and in the latter, the use of a more prolix lexical NP where a more minimal pronoun can occur should M-implicate a non-coreferential interpretation. On a closer examination, however, it turns out that these sentences do not counter-exemplify our pragmatic theory. In the case of (4.85), the (a) and (b) sentences do not share the same truth-condition: for (4.85a) to be true John must have received only one vote, but there is no such truth-condition for (4.85b). Consequently, the use of the lexical NP in (4.85a) triggers no Q-implicature engendered by the possibility of a semantically stronger statement, and therefore the I-principle is applied to invite the preferred coreferential interpretation. In a similar vein, identity

Pragmatic Approaches to Anaphora 243

statements like (4.86a) cannot be paraphrased by the reflexive formulation in (4.86b). In other words, (4.86a) simply does not mean the same thing as (4.86b). Once again, no Q-implicature would arise in (4.86a) to prevent the interpretation of *Chopin* from falling under the I-principle, by which we obtain a coreferential (or coindexed) reading. Finally, in the case of (4.87), the M-implicated disjoint reference fails to arise because the meaning contrast on which it is based does not exist. While (4.87b) can have a bound variable interpretation, (4.87a) cannot. What is topical about (4.87a), according to Reinhart (1983: 168–9), is not having the property of finding oneself a godsend, but rather the property of finding Mozart a godsend. This is enough to cancel the M-implicature, and therefore the I-implicated coreferential interpretation between the two instances of *Mozart* in (4.87a) will then go through unblocked.

We turn next to semantic constraints triggered by the lexical properties of certain predicates, idioms, and anaphoric expressions. Consider first (4.88) from Chinese.

(4.88) (a) Xiaoming shuo Xiaohua xihuan mainong ziji.
Xiaoming say Xiaohua like show off self
'Xiaoming$_1$ says that Xiaohua$_2$ loves to show self$_{*1/2}$ off.'
(b) Xiaoming shuo Xiaohua zai zhui ziji.
Xiaoming say Xiaohua DUR chase self
'Xiaoming$_1$ says that Xiaohua$_2$ is chasing self$_{1/*2}$.'

In (4.88a), *ziji* can only be locally bound. By contrast, in (4.88b) *ziji* can only be long-distance bound. This contrast can be attributed to the contrastive, lexical semantics of the embedded predicates involved: while *mainong* 'show (oneself) off' in (4.88a) is an inherently reflexive predicate, *zui* 'chase' in (4.88b) is an inherently non-reflexive predicate. Consequently, there will be no I-implicated long-distance reflexivization reading for (4.88a) and no I-inferred local reflexivization reading for (4.88b). More or less the same story can be told of the binding patterns in certain inalienable possessives and idiomatic constructions in English (e.g. Helke 1979, Farmer and Harnish 1987).

(4.89) Bound possessive pronouns
   (a) I caught my breath.
   (b) You ate your words.
   (c) She lost her way.
   (d) We crossed our fingers.
(4.90) Non-bound possessive pronouns and reciprocals
   (a) Olivia is the apple of her eye.
   (b) They cramp each other's style.
   (c) They forced each other's hand.

Finally, the application of our pragmatic principles is also constrained by the lexical properties attached to anaphoric expressions themselves. This can be nicely illustrated by the use of reflexive *caki* in the Korean example (4.48) above. In terms of reference, given that the pronoun *ku* can be used here, the use of the more marked *caki* would invite an M-implicated non-coreferential reading. But this interpretation is outlawed by the semantics of referential dependence associated with reflexives. Consequently, the reference of *caki* in (4.48) falls under the I-principle. (Needless to say, the M-implicated logophoric interpretation for *caki* will go through unchecked in (4.48), since it does not run counter to the semantic constraint of referential dependency.)

Antecedent saliency

A further constraint is that any interpretation generated by our pragmatic apparatus may be subject to the requirement of consistency with what is the most salient/relevant. One case in point concerns the interpretation of anaphoric expressions in topic constructions.[12] In Chinese, for example, when there is a topic, the M-implicated referential opposition associated with the use of a pronoun where a zero anaphor could occur seems to evaporate. The use of both the zero anaphor and the pronoun is then subject to the I-implicated coreferentiality with the topic. A good example for illustration is given below.

(4.91) (*a*) Xiaohua, Xiaoming yi   jin   wu.
            Xiaohua Xiaoming as soon as enter room
            Ø jiu   ba men guan shang le.
            EMPH BA door close up   CRS
    'Xiaohua$_1$, as soon as Xiaoming$_2$ enters the house, (he$_1$) closes the door.'
     (*b*) Xiaohua, Xiaoming yi   jin   wu,
            Xiaohua Xiaoming as soon as enter room
            ta   jiu   ba men guan shang le.
            3SG EMPH BA door close up   CRS
    'Xiaohua$_1$, as soon as Xiaoming$_2$ enters the house, he$_1$ closes the door.'

Without the topic *Xiaohua*, there would be a referential contrast between (4.91*a*) and (4.91*b*). But when the sentences undergo topicalization, the original M-contrast in reference vanishes. This seems to be attributable to inconsistency with what is the most salient/relevant. It is clear, at least intuitively, that the topic is the most salient element in a topic construction, around which the comment clause centres. This intuition has been captured by various versions of what is called the 'aboutness' hypothesis concerning the well-formedness of a topic construction in a language. The essence of 'aboutness' is that it is both a necessary and a sufficient condition that the comment clause of a topic construction says something about the topic (e.g.

---

[12] There are at least three distinctive senses of the notion of topic in the literature: (i) topic as sentence/clause topic, which is a part of the grammatical structure of a sentence, (ii) topic as theme in the Prague School tradition—the first element of a sentence, and (iii) topic as discourse topic—what is being talked about in a discourse including the topic participant.

Li and Thompson 1976, Bosch 1983, Xu and Langendoen 1985, Kratochvíl 1986, Huang 1989, 1994). If this is correct, then it is very natural for both the zero anaphor in (4.91a) and the pronoun in (4.91b) to be related to the topic, and hence the disappearance of the original M-implicature. We shall have more to say about 'Chinese-style' topic constructions in Section 4.4.

Clausal linkage

Finally, any interpretation invited by our pragmatic apparatus may be restricted by consistency with what is implicated by the close semantico-conceptual relationship between two clauses. Building on the work of Silverstein (1976), Foley and Van Valin (1984: 269) set up an Interclausal Semantic Relation Hierarchy in (4.92).

(4.92) Foley and Van Valin's interclausal semantic relations hierarchy
Causative > modality > psych-action > jussive > direct perception complements > indirect discourse complements > temporal adverbial clauses > conditionals > simultaneous actions > sequential actions (overlapping) > sequential actions (non-overlapping) > action-action (non-specifed linkage)

They further observe that cross-linguistically there is a correlation between the degree of interclausal semantic connectivity and the choice of anaphoric expressions; the tighter the linkage, the more likely that the coreferential arguments will be encoded by zero anaphors or pronouns (see also Li and Thompson 1979, Chen 1986, and Ariel 1990; and Sections 4.3. and 5.2.5. below). This seems to be the case with the Korean sentence (4.66b) and the Spanish sentence (4.66c): in both sentences there is a relation of indirect discourse complement. Such a tight interclausal semantic linkage, as Levinson (1987) has pointed out, tends to give rise to a 'same agent/patient as the last clause' effect, hence the suspension of the M-implicated contrast in reference and the coreferential interpretation between the zero anaphor/overt pronoun in the embedded clause and the subject of the matrix clause (see e.g. Blackwell 1994, 1998, 2000 for experimental evidence from Spanish in support of some of these constraints).

Now, a question that may come up is this: given that the M-induced contrast in reference in the last two cases is cancelled neither by background assumptions, nor by contextual factors, nor by meaning$_{\text{-nn}}$, nor by semantic entailments, is it defeated by some prevailing pragmatic implicature, and, if so, by which one? The answer appears to be that the M-implicature under discussion is indeed curbed by some priority implicature, namely an I-implicature. How, then, can this be possible, given the hierarchy Q > M > I? The answer to this question, I believe, may be sought in the 'matrix wins' hypothesis concerning the projection of implicatures (Gazdar 1979, Levinson 1983: 142–3, 224). According to this hypothesis, given the cyclic nature of implicature projection, implicatures due to higher constructions may cancel implicatures due to lower constructions. What the 'matrix wins' hypothesis in effect does in both cases is to allow the order of precedence regarding the application of the M- and I-principles, namely M > I, to be overridden when an I-implicature is due to a higher construction and/or an antecedent that is higher in saliency.

The pragmatic theory of anaphora advanced here is not *ad hoc*; rather, it is largely the direct outcome, in the sphere of anaphoric reference, of the systematic interaction of some general neo-Gricean pragmatic principles, constrained by the DRP, information saliency, and general consistency conditions on conversational implicatures. The information saliency constraint is set up primarily in response to the excessive power generated by the M-principle in some cases. The underlying idea here is that given the cyclic nature of implicature projection, the hierarchy of preference regarding the application of the M- and I-principles may be overridden if the I-implicature is due to a higher construction or an antecedent that is higher on the saliency hierarchy. As for the general implicature constraints, they are consistent with Gazdar's (1979) assumption that the informational content of an utterance can be considered to be an ordered set of background assumptions, contextual information, semantic entailments, conversational implicatures, presuppositions, and so on and so forth. Each incrementation of the informational content of an utterance must be consistent with the informational content that already exists, otherwise it will be cancelled according to the hierarchy in (4.25). Furthermore, note that the consistency constraints on conversational implicatures have a twofold function; on the one hand, they force an evaporation of any anaphoric interpretation that runs contrary to them, and on the other, they simultaneously promote another interpretation. This procedure will go on recursively until the anaphoric interpretation that is most compatible with our knowledge about the world is achieved. In other words, the inference generated by our pragmatic apparatus is essentially an inference to the best interpretation.

4.2.4. Summary

In this section, I have developed a revised neo-Gricean pragmatic theory of anaphora. In this theory, anaphora is largely determined by the systematic interaction of three neo-Gricean pragmatic principles, namely the Q-, M-, and I-principles (with that order of priority), constrained by the DRP, information saliency, and general consistency conditons on conversational implicatures. I have demonstrated that by utilizing the three neo-Gricean pragmatic principles and the resolution mechnism organizing their interaction, many patterns of intrasentential anaphora in a wide variety of geographically, typologically, and structurally different languages can be given a more elegant explanation.

4.3. Some other pragmatic/cognitive/functional approaches

In the last section, I developed a revised neo-Gricean pragmatic theory of anaphora. In this section, I shall comment briefly on three other pragmatic/cognitive/functional approaches to anaphora.

4.3.1. Relevance theory

Background

In an attempt to make a 'paradigm change' in pragmatics, Sperber and Wilson (1995), while sharing Grice's view that human communication involves not only an encoding/decoding device, but also an inferential apparatus, nevertheless claim that principles governing this apparatus have their source in the human central cognitive mechanism. Consequently, they propose that the entire Gricean programme be subsumed within a single cognitive principle, namely, the principle of optimal Relevance. On this Relevance theory, which is essentially a modification of the classical Fodorian theory of cognitive modularity (Fodor 1983),[13] it is assumed that the human central cognitive mechanism is a deductive inference-generating device which works in such a way as to maximize Relevance with respect to communication. Thus, the principle of Relevance is claimed to be responsible for the recovery of both the explicit and implicit content of an utterance. In other words, on Sperber and Wilson's view, in interpreting an utterance, one is always maximizing its 'contextual effects' and minimizing its 'processing efforts' to interpret the utterance as optimally relevant, that is, to interpret it in a way which is most consistent with the principle of Relevance.

Kempson (1988a, 1988b)

One of the earliest attempts to analyse anaphora within the Relevance-theoretical framework is Kempson (1988a, 1998b). Kempson observes, among other things, that the pragmatic effect exhibited by bridging cross-reference anaphora (about which, more later) can obtain in bound-variable anaphora— a phenomenon that has commonly been considered to be grammatical in

---

[13] The main thesis of the Fodorian theory of cognitive modularity is that human cognition is modular in the sense of constituting a number of distinct systems, most notably vision, audition, and language. These specialized systems, called modules, are domain-specific, informationally encapsulated, and cognitively impenetrable. One of their major functions is to provide 'input' to the 'central processor' (Fodor 1983: 47–101). The characterization of language as an input system, however, is challenged by Chomsky (e.g. 1986a: 148). On Chomsky's view, the language faculty is a cognitive system of knowledge rather than an input or output system.

nature. Examples (4.93a) and (4.93b) below show this parallelism between bridging cross-reference and bound-variable anaphora.

(4.93) (a) The minister got into a limousine. He chatted to the chauffeur.
(b) Every minister got into a limousine and chatted to the chauffeur.

This leads Kempson to argue for a unitary, pragmatic analysis of pronominal anaphora in terms of Relevance theory. According to this Relevance-theoretical view, the value of an anaphoric expression, say, β, is not directly determined by the grammar. What the grammar provides is merely a set of restrictions that the identified value of the anaphoric expression must satisfy. In the case of the English pronoun *he*, for instance, the set of restrictions imposed by the grammar in its lexicon would be something like: *he*: β [+pronominal, −anaphoric, +male (β), +singular (β)]. Consequently, the identification of the value of an anaphoric expression is left to the working of the principle of Relevance. By this principle, it is assumed that any anaphoric aspect of the propositional content not determined by the logical form output of the grammar is identifiable on the basis of information available to the addressee at minimal processing cost. Put differently, according to this view, the interpretation of different types of anaphora is dependent on different types of information that is immediately available to the addressee. Thus, the establishment of the value of a deictic anaphora is via information that is directly present in the speech environment, that of a referential and bound-variable anaphora, via information that is previously presented in the linguistic context, that of a bridging cross-reference anaphora, via information that is associated with additional premises, and that of a 'lazy' anaphora, via information that is derived from the logical form of the sentence. What these diverse types of anaphora have in common, then, is that they are identified as a set of internal representations which are made accessible to the addressee by the principle of Relevance.

The main merit of Kempson's proposal is that it provides additional evidence that the interpretation of anaphora is basically a semantic/pragmatic, as opposed to a syntactic, process; and consequently, it cannot be adequately dealt with by a syntax-driven model such as Chomsky's principles-and-parameters theory/minimalist programme. But Kempson's analysis is too programmatic and obscure to make clear empirical predictions. For example, it is unclear how the fact that a morphologically simplex reflexive, while being locally bindable in an intrinsic reflexivization context, cannot be locally bound in an extrinsic reflexivization environment, in languages like Dutch and Norwegian (cf. Chapter 2), can be accommodated under this analysis. Also problematic for the account is the issue of how to select the preferred antecedent for a long-distance reflexive in a language like Chinese, Japanese, and Korean.

Matsui (1993, 1995)

Matsui (1993, 1995) presents a Relevance-theoretical analysis of bridging cross-reference anaphora. Before assessing this analysis, let us take a look at the phenomenology of bridging cross-reference anaphora first.

Bridging cross-reference anaphora

Definition and properties
As mentioned in Chapter 1, a bridging cross-reference anaphor is one that is used to establish a link of association with some preceding expression in the same sentence or discourse via the addition of background assumptions. The term 'bridging' was introduced by Clark (1977). Other terms that have been used in the literature include associated anaphora (e.g. Hawkins 1978), indirect anaphora (e.g. Erkü and Gundel 1987), and inferable anaphora (e.g. Prince 1981). A typical example is given in (4.94) below.

(4.94) John walked into a music room. The piano was made in the nineteenth century.

Defined thus, bridging cross-reference anaphora has three characteristic properties: (i) the anaphor, which is usually a definite NP, must occur in the appropriate context of its 'antecedent', which is usually an indefinite NP, (ii) there is some semantic and/or pragmatic relation between the anaphor and its 'antecedent', and (iii) the anaphor and its 'antecedent' do not stand in a strictly coreferential relation. Rather they are linked to each other via the addition of pragmatic inference of some kind.[14]

Issues
There are at least three issues that any adequate theory of bridging cross-reference anaphora must address: (i) what constitutes the well-formedness condition on bridging cross-reference anaphora, (ii) how is bridging cross-reference anaphora interpreted, and (iii) how is the actual, preferred 'antecedent' selected if there is more than one possible antecedent.

---

[14] Note that, on a broader definition, examples of the following kind can also be taken as cases of bridging cross-reference anaphora.
  (i) (Sanford and Garrod 1981: 106)
  Mary dressed the baby. The clothes were made of pink wool.

Notice too that bridging cross-reference anaphora in general cannot be encoded in terms of an informationally poorer anaphoric expression such as a pronoun or a zero anaphor. But as pointed out by Gundel, Hedberg, and Zacharski (1993), among others, there are exceptions. Pronouns are occasionally suited to function as a bridging cross-reference anaphor, provided that the link of association is strong enough to activate a representation of what is referred to by the bridging cross-reference anaphor. This seems to be the case with (ii), an attested example adapted from a novel discussed in Gundel, Hedberg, and Zacharski (1993).

  (ii) There was not a man, woman or child within sight; only a small fishing boat, standing out to sea some distance away. Harriet waved wildly in its direction, but they either didn't see her or supposed that she was merely doing some kind of reducing exercises.

In the past two decades, numerous studies of bridging cross-reference anaphora have been conducted within different disciplines espousing a variety of theoretical perspectives. Thus, within the linguistics tradition, one finds Erkü and Gundel (1987) and Matsui (1993, 1995); within the psycholinguistics tradition, there are Clark (1977), Clark and Haviland (1977), and Sanford and Garrod (1981), and finally within the computational linguistics and artificial intelligence tradition, one finds Sidner (1983). Of these analyses, three models are of particular interest, namely, (i) the topic/focus model, (ii) the scenario model, and (iii) the Relevance-theoretical model.

The topic/focus model
The central idea underlying this approach is that the interpretation of bridging cross-reference anaphora is largely determined by the topic/focus— that which is being talked about—of the previous sentence or discourse.[15] This approach is represented by works such as Sidner (1983) and Erkü and Gundel (1987). In Sidner (1983), for example, there are two types of focus: (i) agent/actor focus and (ii) theme/discourse focus. With discourse focus, the interpretation of bridging cross-reference anaphora is effected by an algorithm which selects the theme/discourse focus roughly on the basis of the following ordered set of preferences: PATIENT > OTHER THEMATIC ROLES > AGENT > VP. Furthermore, the interpretations resulting from the algorithm are subject to the requirement of consistency with world knowledge.

The scenario model
A second influential approach to bridging cross-reference anaphora is what may be called the scenario model. This is the approach that has most enthusiastically been advocated by Sanford and Garrod (e.g. Sanford and Garrod 1981, Garrod and Sanford 1994). The key tenet of this analysis is the idea that in interpreting bridging cross-reference anaphora, one is always referring to an appropriate mental domain of reference. Drawing on notions such as frame (Minsky 1975, see also Fillmore 1982: 111), schema (Rumelhart 1980, see also Chafe 1987: 29), and script (Schank and Abelson 1977), Sanford and Garrod dub this domain of reference a scenario. A scenario, according to Sanford and Garrod, can be foregrounded, that is, can be activated or be in

---

[15] There are at least two distinct senses of the notion of focus in the literature: (i) in the psychological sense of 'centre of attention' (e.g. Linde 1979, Grosz and Sidner 1986), and (ii) in the linguistic sense of 'the position of prominence in the comment part of a sentence' (see also Valldúvi 1992, and Valldúvi and Engdahl 1996 on focus marking in e.g. Catalan, Japanese, and Vute). The psychological notion of 'focusing' may involve differences in importance of a referent, in attention in a referent (cf. the notion of protagonist), or in activation of a referent in memory. As observed by Gundel, Hedbery, and Zacharski (1993), among others, the two senses of focus are related in that, on the one hand, linguistically focused elements are in general a result of focal attention, and on the other the element that is linguistically focused tends to enter the activated memory of both the speaker and the addressee.

focus. This happens when a scenario becomes part of one's working memory. What is focused can then be distinguished on three dimensions: (i) current versus non-current, (ii) explicit versus implicit, and (iii) entity versus role. First, entities that are in the dynamic partitions of memory are considered to be in current focus, whereas entities that are in the static partitions of memory are taken to be in non-current focus. Secondly, explicit foci refer to entities that are directly mentioned in a discourse; by contrast, implicit foci are entities that contain information from situational scenarios that is not explicitly mentioned but is directly relevant to something which is mentioned in a discourse. They consist of 'scenario representations, made up of slots and default specifications, bound together by relational programmatic information' (Sanford and Garrod 1981: 161). This is similar to Chafe's (1987) notion of semi-activeness that is inferentially derived (e.g. Lambrecht 1994: 100). Finally, there is the distinction between entity and role foci. The former represents the individuals who are the main protagonists of a scene, whereas the latter refers to the roles afforded by the scenarios described in the discourse. It is this current, implicit, role focus, Sanford and Garrod further claim, that plays a crucial part in the interpretation of bridging cross-reference anaphora.

The Relevance-theoretical model
The third and final approach to bridging cross-reference anaphora to be discussed here is the Relevance-theoretical model developed by Matsui (1993, 1995). The central idea of this model is that the interpretation of bridging cross-reference anaphora is constrained by the principle of Relevance, as sketched above. Thus, on this account, in interpreting bridging cross-reference anaphora, one is always making a bridging assumption that yields adequate contextual effects but without subjecting the language user to unjustifiable processing efforts to obtain these effects.

Comparison
Let us now compare the three models mentioned above. Consider first (4.95), adapted from Erkü and Gundel (1987).

(4.95) John walked into a restaurant. The waiter was an Italian.

This example can adequately be accounted for by all the three analyses. On the topic/focus account, *restaurant* is the topic/focus of the discourse, hence the antecedent for *waiter*. Next, under the scenario approach, the use of *restaurant* invokes a scenario that contains the implicit focus *waiter*. Finally, within the Relevance-theoretical framework, the bridging assumption that the restaurant John walked into has a waiter arises from the extension of context by encyclopaedic knowledge. This has the consequence that the overall interpretation is consistent with the principle of Relevance. Next, consider (4.96).

(4.96) John stopped for coffee at a cappuccino bar before having dinner at a restaurant. The waiter was an Italian.

This example contains more than one possible antecedent for the bridging cross-reference anaphor *the waiter*, the preferred one being *a cappuccino bar*. This interpretation is correctly predicted by the topic/focus account. Given Sidner's topic/focus algorithm, for example, *a cappuccino bar* will be selected as the topic/focus of the discourse, hence the preferred antecedent for the bridging cross-reference anaphor. In contrast, on the scenario analysis, there would be two currently activated scenarios in (4.96), one for a cappuccino bar and the other for a restaurant, each of which contains a slot for waiters. Since there is no mechanism to choose between the two scenarios, it is not clear how the preferred interpretation could be derived under this approach. Finally, within the Relevance-theoretical framework, (4.96) will be interpreted along the following lines. Assuming *a cappuccino bar* is more accessible than *a restaurant*, it will be tested against, and consequently found consistent with, the principle of Relevance first, hence the preferred antecedent for *the waiter*. However, unless there is an independent mechanism to rank accessibility in Relevance theory, a Relevance-theoretical account of examples like (4.96) would have to be built partially on notions such as topic/focus. Finally, let us turn to (4.97).

(4.97) (*a*) John stopped for coffee at a cappuccino bar before visiting a musical instrument museum. The waiter was an Italian.
(*b*) John stopped for coffee at a cappuccino bar before visiting a musical instrument museum. The curator was an Italian.

Intuitively, (4.97*a*) seems to be slightly more felicitous than (4.97*b*). Why is this the case? As a step towards providing an answer to this question, a number of hypotheses have been put forward in the literature. One set of factors affecting the felicitousness of bridging cross-reference anaphora has been identified by Clark and Haviland (1977) as involving the distance of the bridge (the number of bridging assumptions needed), the plausibility of the bridge (the degree of the truthfulness of bridging assumptions), and the computability of the bridge (the degree of easiness in calculating bridging assumptions). Other factors may include the accessibility of antecedents, the accessibility of contextual assumptions, and the overall coherence of the discourse (see e.g. Matsui 1995 for further discussion). Now, under the topic/focus approach, the factor of accessibility of antecedents seems to play a crucial role in explaining why (4.97*a*) is more felicitous than (4.97*b*): while the antecedent for *the waiter* in (4.97*a*) is the topic/focus of the discourse, the antecedent for *the curator* in (4.97*b*) is not. On the other hand, the scenario model would have to use the notion of accessibility of contextual assumptions to account for the difference between (4.97*a*) and (4.97*b*): the antecedent for *the waiter* in (4.97*a*) is to be found in a context/scenario that is more accessible to the addressee than the antecedent for *the curator* in (4.97*b*), provided, of course, that a mechanism can be worked out to decide on which of the two currently activated scenarios is the more accessible one. Finally, on a Relevance-theoretical analysis, the slight infelicitousness of (4.97*b*) would be attributed to the unjustifiable processing efforts the addressee is subject to in the interpretation of the bridging cross-reference anaphor *the curator* in the discourse. This results from the conflict between the highly accessible topic/focus, namely, *a cappuccino bar*, and the actual intended antecedent, namely, *a musical instrument museum*.

Clearly, the validity of Matsui's analysis of bridging cross-reference anaphora, and indeed of any Relevance-theoretical analysis of anaphora in general, depends crucially on how the principle of Relevance, or, more concretely, 'contextual effects' and its counterbalancing 'processing efforts', can be objectively assessed. Unfortunately nowhere in either Matsui (1993, 1995) or Kempson (1988*a*, 1988*b*) or Sperber and Wilson (1995) is there a satisfactory, independent mechanism to measure this balance of the costs and rewards (see e.g. Levinson 1989). Thus, the principle of Relevance does not seem to be subject to falsifiability, and consequently, both Relevance-theoretical analyses of anaphora we have seen above are empirically difficult to put to the test.[16]

4.3.2. Accessibility theory

Somewhat related to Relevance theory is another cognitive approach known as Accessibility theory (Ariel 1988, 1990, 1994). Following in the spirit of e.g. Prince (1981), Sanford and Garrod (1981), and Givón (1983), Ariel claims

---

[16] There are a number of fundamental differences between neo-Gricean theory and Relevance theory. These differences may include: (i) whether an inferential theory of human communication should be based on the study of usage principles or cognitive principles; (ii) whether such a theory should contain two levels (i.e. a level of sentence-meaning versus a level of speaker-meaning, or, to make use of Lyons's 1977: 13–18 type-token distinction, a level of sentence-type-meaning versus a level of utterance-token-meaning) or three levels (i.e. a level of sentence-meaning versus a level of utterance-meaning versus a level of speaker-meaning, or, again, in terms of Lyons's type-token distinction, a level of sentence-type-meaning versus a level of utterance-type-meaning versus a level of utterance-token-meaning); (iii) whether Gricean inferential principles are a sort of general, functional guidelines agreed between the speaker and the hearer on the basis of the rational nature of human communication or they are merely the automatic reflex of the human metal capacity; (iv) whether the inferential tier of comprehension is governed by a set of specialized principles constituting a pragmatic 'module' or by a non-specialized central inferential process; (v) whether conversational implicature is monotonic or non-monotonic in nature; and (vi) whether there are two types of conversational implicature (i.e. generalized conversational implicature and particularized conversational implicature), or there is only one type of conversational implicature but two types of context (i.e. default context and specific context), or there is neither any distinction in conversational implicature type nor any distinction in context type; all conversational implicatures can be reduced to a kind of context-induced 'nonce'-inference. Since controversies in these areas are deep and far-reaching, it would go well beyond the scope of this book to discuss them in any detail (but see e.g. Levinson 1989 and Sperber and Wilson 1995 for further discussion).

that there is a correlation between the use of anaphoric expressions and the mental entities they represent. All potential anaphoric expressions, according to Ariel, are simply accessibility markers or 'context' retrievers. They each encode the degree of accessibility with which the mental representation is entertained in the addressee's memory as assessed by the speaker, thus enabling the addressee to restrict the set of possible referents.

What, then, are the main factors affecting the degree of accessibility? Careful studies in linguistics, psycholinguistics, and artificial intelligence have pointed to the following ones (ignoring intonation), which may be grouped into two main categories: (i) the salience of the entity/referent/antecedent (cf. Section 4.2. above), and (ii) the connectivity between the referent/antecedent and the anaphoric expression/accessibility marker (cf. (4.92) above) (Ariel 1994). Entity prominence may include factors such as: (i) speech act roles of discourse participants (speaker > addressee > non-participant), (ii) high versus low physical salience, (iii) topic/focus, (iv) surface grammatical functions (e.g. subject > non-subject), (v) humanness/animacy, (vi) surface order of mention (see especially work in Centering theory, Gordon, Grosz, and Gilliom 1993, Grosz, Joshi, and Weinstein 1995, Walker, Joshi, and Prince 1997, and Cornish 1999), (vii) first versus subsequent mention, and (viii) existence versus non-existence of interfering entity/referent/antecedent. Next, connectivity may be affected by (i) the distance between the antecedent and the anaphoric expression, (ii) the connection between the clauses containing the antecedent and the anaphoric expression (cf. the interclausal semantic relations hierarchy in the last section), (iii) the parallel versus non-parallel grammatical function of the antecedent and the anaphoric expression, (iv) the role played by scenarios, and (v) the overall cohesion of the discourse in which the antecedent and the anaphoric expression occur (see also Asher and Wada 1988 for a discussion of the notion of overall salience).

Degrees of mental accessibility, further argues Ariel, are encoded in languages on the basis of three principles: (i) informativity, (ii) rigidity, and (iii) attenuation. Consequently, it is predicted by Accessibility theory that the more accessible an entity/referent/antecedent, the higher an accessibility marker will be selected to code it; and the higher the accessibility marker, the less informative (in terms of the amount of lexical information), the less rigid (i.e. the more general/ambiguous) and the more attenuate (i.e. shorter or less accented) it will be. This leads Ariel to set up a universal accessibility marking scale, along the lines of e.g. Prince's (1981) familiarity scale, Givón's (1983) topic continuity scale, and Gundel, Hedberg, and Zacharski's (1993) givenness hierarchy (cf. Section 5.2, see also Ward, Sproat, and McKoon 1991, Deane 1992, and van Hoek 1995, 1997, who develops similar ideas within the framework of Langacker's 1987, 1991, 1996 Cognitive Grammar).

(4.98) Ariel's accessibility marking scale
Zero > reflexive > agreement marker > cliticized pronoun > unstressed pronoun > stressed pronoun > stressed pronoun + gesture > proximal demonstrative (+NP) > distal demonstrative (+NP) > ... > first name > last name > short definite description > long definite description > full name

Different languages may make different uses of a particular type of anaphoric expression on the scale to encode accessibility, depending on the availability or non-availability of other types of anaphoric expression in those languages. For example, in languages with widespread zero anaphors such as Chinese, Japanese, and Korean, pronouns are frequently utilized to mark lower degrees of accessibility. Languages that lack definiteness markers like the Slavonic ones are expected to resort to demonstratives more freely. Communities with no last names such as the Amish one seem to make more use of definite descriptions instead (Ariel 1990).

Furthermore, the scale in (4.98) is linked to the structure of memory on the one hand and the type of context on the other. Entities that are retrieved from encyclopaedic knowledge are normally stored in long-term memory and therefore are encoded in terms of a low accessibility marker; entities that are present in the physical surroundings the speaker is attending to are usually stored in short-term memory and hence are represented with an intermediate accessibility marker; finally, entities that are mentioned in the immediately preceding linguistic context are frequently stored in the currently activated short-term memory and consequently are indicated by a higher accessibility maker.

There is cross-linguistic evidence in support of Accessibility theory in general and the scale in (4.98) in particular. One such piece of evidence comes from Ariel's (1990, 1994) careful study of the contrastive use of zero anaphors and resumptive pronouns in the relative construction in Modern Hebrew. For example, in (4.99) below, the distance between the antecedent and the anaphoric expression is shorter in the (*a*) than in the (*b*) sentence, therefore the antecedent is more accessible in the former than in the latter. Hence preference for the use of the zero anaphor in (4.99*a*) and of the resumptive pronoun in (4.99*b*), as would be predicted by Accessibility theory. More or less the same can be said of (4.100). (4.100*a*) is a restrictive relative construction, whereas (4.100*b*) is a non-restrictive relative construction. Clearly, there is a tighter clause linkage in (4.100*a*) than in (4.100*b*) (cf. (4.92) above). This explains why the use of a zero anaphor is preferred in (4.100*a*) and that of a resumptive pronoun is allowed in (4.100*b*).

(4.99) (Ariel 1994: 29)
    (*a*) shoshana hi ha isha   she nili   ohevet Ø/ʔota.
        Shoshana is the woman that Nilly loves   her
        'Shoshana is the woman that Nilly loves.'

(b) shoshana hi ha isha   she dani   siper she moshe
    Shoshana is the woman that Danny said that Moses
    rixel   she nili   ohevet ?Ø/ ota.
    gossiped that Nilly loves   her
    'Shoshana is the woman that Danny said that Moses gossiped that Nilly loves.'

(4.100) (Ariel 1994:29)

(a) ha gvarim ha yisreelim she ha cava sholeax Ø/?otam
    the men   the Israelis that the army sends   them
    le hilaxem, hem geza shuvenisti bi   myuxad.
    to fight   are race chauvinist especially
    'The Israeli men that the army sends to fight are an especially chauvinistic lot.'

(b) ha gvarim ha yisreelim she ha cava sholeax Ø/otam
    the men   the Israelis that the army sends   them
    le hilaxem, hem geza shuvenisti bi   myuxad.
    to fight   are race chauvinist especially
    'The Israeli men, whom the army sends to fight, are an especially chauvinistic lot.'

There are, however, problems with Accessibility theory. Let us begin with the binding condition patterns. Under the theory outlined above, binding conditions A, B, and C are treated as a partial grammaticalization of accessibility constraints. Anaphors, being extremely high accessibility markers, are expected to have an extremely highly accessible antecedent, hence being bound by a local antecedent; pronouns, being lower accessibility markers than anaphors, are expected not to have an antecedent that is as highly accessible as that for anaphors; hence being free in the same local domain; finally, r-expressions are the lowest accessibility markers on the scale and therefore they can only have an antecedent that has an extremely low accessibility status, hence they cannot be grammatically bound at all (Ariel 1990, 1994). But such an account cannot be wholly correct because, as we have seen in Chapter 2, in a language like Thai, where there is no binding condition C_1 effect, examples like (4.101) are perfectly grammatical.

(4.101) Cɔɔn₁ chɔ́ɔp Cɔɔn₁.
        John likes John
        'John likes John.'

A second, perhaps more worrisome piece of counter-evidence is provided by the use of morphologically simplex and complex reflexives in a language like Dutch. As discussed in Chapter 2, in such a language, it is the morphologically complex but not the morphologically simplex reflexive that can be locally bound in an extrinsic reflexivization context, as in (4.102)—a contradiction to one of the central predictions of Accessibility theory, given that *zich* is no doubt a higher accessibility marker than *zichzelf*, because the emptier a marker, the higher the accessibility rate.

(4.102) Rint veracht *zich/zichzelf.
Rint despises self/self self
'Rint despises self self.'

Moreover, the cross-linguistic facts concerning long-distance reflexivization are not consistent with the hypothesis of Accessibility theory that the more accessible an antecedent, the higher an accessibility marker will be chosen to represent it. Such a hypothesis would require that if a long-distance reflexivisation language has both morphologically simplex and complex reflexives, morphologically simplex reflexives will be used locally, but morphologically complex reflexives will be used in a long-distance way. This is because a local antecedent is more accessible than a long-distance one. But as we saw in Chapter 2, the cross-linguistic tendency is to the contrary, as can be seen from the contrast shown in the following Icelandic examples.

(4.103) (Icelandic, Hyams and Sigurjónsdóttir 1990)
    (*a*) Jón elskar sjálfan sig.
        John loves self self
        'John loves self self.'
    (*b*) Jón$_1$ segir að María elski sig$_1$.
        John says that Maria loves self
        'John says that Maria loves self.'

Finally, there are cases where the same antecedent can be encoded by more than one accessibility marker, as in (4.104). But it is not clear how this can be accommodated in terms of Accessibility theory.

(4.104) (Chinese)
Xiaoming shuo Ø/ta/ziji/ta ziji/Xiaoming zui xihuan gudian yinyue.
Xiaoming say 3SG self 3SG self Xiaoming most like classical music
'Xiaoming says that Ø/he/self/he self/Xiaoming likes classical music most.'

We shall have more to say about a general cognitive approach with regard to discourse anaphora in Chapter 5.

4.3.3. Prague School functionalism

We finally come to a number of functional accounts of anaphora inspired by the ideas of the Prague School.

Kuno (1972*a*, 1972*b*, 1987)

Kuno (1972*a*, 1972*b*) presents perhaps the first modern functional analysis of anaphora from the standpoint of Functional Sentence Perspective (FSP) (see e.g. Firbas 1992 for an up-to-date account of the theory). Although he assumes the precede and s[entence]-command constraint, which was then generally accepted in the generative literature, he argues that anaphora can better be described incorporating a functional analysis on the basis of flow of information. With this basic assumption, he puts forward three hypotheses attempting to formulate functional-syntactic constraints on backward pronominalization (a configuration in which a pronoun precedes its antecedent in the linear string) (see e.g. McCray 1980, Carden 1982, Mittwoch 1983, Macleod 1984, Reinhart 1986, Ariel 1990, Erteschik-Shir 1997 for further discussion), theme-of-the-sentence pronominalization and exhaustive-listing pronominalization, respectively (but see e.g. Carden 1982 for a critique). In Kuno (1987), anaphora is approached again from a functional perspective, but from one that is much broader in scope. Apart from FSP, Kuno uses two other functional models; what he calls the direct discourse perspective, which 'examines subordinate clauses that represent the utterance, thought or internal feelings of the referent of a main clause element', and the empathy perspective, which 'examines syntactic manifestations of the speaker's camera angles in sentences and in a sequence of sentences' (Kuno 1987: 29) (cf. logophoricity).

Westergaard (1986)

Westergaard's (1986) analysis of anaphora is made also from the viewpoint of FSP. Her main suggestion is that there is an overarching functional principle governing the use of pronouns in a sentence. This principle, which she calls the 'super-principle', states that a pronoun may not be more thematic than the lexical NP from which it acquires its reference (Westergaard 1986: 67). Within this basic guideline, Westergaard formulates a number of sub-principles: a given element tends to be linearly prior to a new element in a sentence; only a given entity can be encoded in terms of a pronoun; and a semantically richer NP is used only if the use of a pronoun causes ambiguity in reference (Westergaard 1986: 64–5). The relative 'rhematicity' of pronouns and their potential antecedents in a sentence is measured by a scalar system which takes into account linear order (i.e. theme versus rheme), information structure (given versus new), stress/focus, and semantic character (pronouns versus NPs).

Koktová (1992)

More recently, Koktová (1992) advances a rather technical analysis of anaphora within the framework of what she calls the Prague Functional Generative Description. Technical details apart, her major claim is that generative-structural concepts such as c-command, binding, and control can entirely be dispensed with by appealing to the Prague School functional notions such as the systematic ordering of dependency and the hierarchy of communicative dynamic in the topic-focus articulation of the sentence.

The main strength of these Prague School functional analyses lies in the insight that non-structural, functionally motivated factors play an extremely important role in regulating anaphora, and as such they can and should be rigorously applied to the study of anaphora. But there are two main weaknesses associated with these accounts. First, many of the basic concepts employed in the Prague School functional analyses such as theme/rheme, topic/comment, and given/new do not seem to be clearly defined. By way of illustration, consider the role played by the notion of given/new information in accounting for anaphora. Within the Prague School tradition, it is generally acknowledged that only given entities can be encoded in terms of a reduced anaphoric expression (e.g. Westergaard 1986: 64). Let us call this hypothesis the 'given-only' hypothesis.

One question that arises naturally if this hypothesis is to be taken seriously is concerned with the issue of what counts as given. However, this question may not be answered satisfactorily. Currently, there are at least three distinct senses of givenness (e.g. Prince 1981). The first, givenness$_{-p}$, is defined in terms of predictability (or recoverability). Thus, in a clause, a particular linguistic item is treated as given if it is recoverable anaphorically or situationally (e.g. Halliday and Hasan 1976: 326). The second sense of givenness, givenness$_{-s}$, is stated in terms of saliency: given information is that knowledge which the speaker assumes to be in the consciousness of the hearer at the time of the occurrence of the utterance (e.g. Chafe 1976, 1987). The third sense of givenness, givenness$_{-k}$, is defined in terms of shared knowledge. Thus, for Clark, Haviland, and Sanford, givenness represents information that the speaker believes that the hearer already knows and can identify uniquely (e.g. Haviland and Clark 1974, Clark and Clark 1977: 92, Clark and Haviland 1977, Sanford and Garrod 1981). Clearly, while givenness$_{-p}$ is linguistics-oriented, givenness$_{-s}$ and givenness$_{-k}$ are psycholinguistics-oriented. The crucial difference seems to be that while the former is restricted to the information status within a clause, the latter is extended to include whatever knowledge the speaker and the hearer may share (Brown and Yule 1983: 183).

It is not difficult to see that the three notions of givenness are not entirely mutually independent: givenness$_{-p}$ might be regarded loosely as a subset of givenness$_{-s}$, which in turn might be seen loosely as a subset of givenness$_{-k}$.

But the fact that there is more than one sense of givenness has the immediate effect that what is taken to be given under one definition may not necessarily be considered to be given under another. If this is the case, then it is inadequate to simply state that only a given entity can be designated by a 'lexically attenuated' anaphoric form. The question of whether or not the 'given-only' hypothesis can be maintained depends on which of the three definitions is to be adopted.

As I pointed out in Huang (1989), however, the 'given-only' hypothesis may not be maintained. This is because on the one hand, examples like

(4.105) show that non-given entities in the sense of givenness$_{-p}$ and givenness$_{-s}$ can in fact be encoded by a reduced anaphoric expression. This is a clear indication that the 'given-only' hypothesis is not a necessary condition for the use of a reduced anaphoric expression. On the other hand, cases of bridging cross-reference anaphora like (4.106) reveals that given entities in the sense of givenness$_{-k}$ cannot be encoded by a reduced anaphoric expression. This shows that the 'given-only' hypothesis is not a sufficient condition for the employment of a reduced anaphoric expression either. Thus, on the one hand, if we take givenness in the narrowest sense, the 'given-only' condition is not necessary; on the other, if we take givenness in the broadest sense, the 'given-only' condition is not sufficient either, for the use of a reduced anaphoric expression.[17]

(4.105) (Chinese)
    C1. A: Zhe qunzi zhen piaoliang!
            this dress really pretty
    C2.   Shei mai de?
            who buy SD
    C3. B: Ta mai de
            3SG buy SD
    E1. A: What a pretty dress!
    E2.   Who bought (it)?
    E3. B: He (e.g. my boyfriend) bought (it)
(4.106) John got some tools out of his bag. The hammer is new.

Secondly, there seems to be a tendency in the Prague School-oriented analyses to completely discard structural factors in anaphora (ironically, in much the same way as functional factors are neglected or positively opposed in orthodox generative analyses). This frequently leads to what might be called wholesale functional reductionism, in which the entire burden of syntactic, semantic, and pragmatic analyses is reduced to extreme functional explanations—a practice that may hinder our efforts to attain a better understanding of anaphora.

---

[17] Another question relating to givenness is whether the given/new distinction is a discrete dichotomy or a matter of degree. Chafe (1976: 32), for example, takes it to be a binary distinction. He argues that givenness has a transitory status: 'One indisputable property of consciousness is that its capacity is very limited. As new ideas come into it, old ones leave. The speaker's treatment of an item as given, therefore, should cease when he judges that item to have left his addressee's consciousness.' By contrast, Westergaard (1986) and Firbas (1992) argue that the given/new distinction is not a matter of yes or no but a matter of more or less. This point of view is consistent with the notion of Communicative Dynamic (CD) within the framework of FSP. The notion of CD presupposes a continuum of givenness, for sentence elements are assumed to carry varying degrees of CD; a higher degree is linked with 'newness' and a low degree with 'givenness'.

4.3.4. Summary

This section discussed three other pragmatic/cognitive/functional approaches to anaphora. Section 4.3.1. surveyed two analyses from the perspective of Relevance theory, focusing on bridging cross-reference anaphora. Section 4.3.2. reviewed Ariel's Accessibility theory. Finally, Section 4.3.3. examined various accounts within the framework of Prague School functionalism.

4.4. 'Syntactic' versus 'pragmatic': a new typology of language?

In this section, I shall consider some typological differences between 'sentence-' and 'discourse-oriented' languages and propose a new 'syntactic' versus 'pragmatic' language typology, using anaphora as a testing ground. The proposal for such a typology is not entirely original; similar ideas can be found in e.g. Givón (1979a), who distinguishes a 'syntactic' versus a 'pragmatic' mode of communication (see the simplified version in (4.107)). But anaphora has never been taken seriously as a diagnostic for such a distinction.

(4.107) Givón's syntactic versus pragmatic modes of communication

Pragmatic mode	Syntactic mode
(i) topic-comment structure	subject-predicate structure
(ii) loose conjunction	tight subordination
(iii) slow rate of delivery	fast rate of delivery
(iv) word-order governed by pragmatic information flow	word-order used to signal semantic case-functions
(v) roughly one-to-one ratio of verbs to nouns in discourse, with verbs being semantically simple	a large ratio of nouns-over-verbs in discourse, with verbs being semantically complex
(vi) no use of grammatical morphology	elaborate use of grammatical morphology

In what follows, I shall discuss some pragmatic properties of anaphora in a pragmatic language in Section 4.4.1. I shall then examine some other pragmatic characteristics of a pragmatic language, focusing on the prominence of 'Chinese-style' topic constructions in Section 4.4.2. Finally, in Section 4.4.3., I shall briefly discuss two possible approaches to these typological differences and argue for the setting up of a new syntactic versus pragmatic language typology as a working hypothesis.

4.4.1. The pragmaticness of anaphora in a pragmatic language

Let me start with the pragmaticness of anaphora in a pragmatic language. If we compare a prototypical pragmatic language (such as Chinese, Japanese, and Korean) with a prototypical syntactic language (such as English, French, and German), we will find that anaphora in the former behaves in a more pragmatic way than that in the latter (see e.g. Huang 1994 for a detailed analysis of Chinese). More specifically, a pragmatic language seems to have the following characteristics as far as anaphora goes.

(4.108) Anaphora in a pragmatic language
- (a) Massive occurrence of zero anaphors
- (b) Existence of pragmatic zero anaphors or empty pragmatic categories
- (c) Pragmatic obligatory control
- (d) Long-distance reflexivization

Massive occurrence of zero anaphors

In the first place, in a pragmatic language, there is massive occurrence of zero anaphors despite the absence of a rich inflectional morphology. This occurrence of zero anaphors is much more widespread than that observed in either an English-style, paradigmatic, non-pro-drop language or an Italian-style, paradigmatic, pro-drop language. This is illustrated by (4.109) and (4.110).

(4.109) At the sentence level.
  (a) (Chinese)
  Baba bu rang Ø Ø kan dianshi,
  dad not allow watch television
  mama bu rang Ø Ø ting yingyue.
  mum not allow listen to music
  'Dad does not allow (me/you/him/her/us/them ...) to watch TV, and mum does not allow (me/you/him/her/us/them ...) to listen to music.'
  (b) (Japanese, Gunji 1987: 102)
  Naomi-wa Ken-ni Ø Ø aisiteiru-to itta.
  Naomi-TOP Ken-to love-COMP say-PAST
  'Naomi told Ken that (she) loved (him).'
  (c) (Korean, Kim 1993: 140)
  John-un Mary-eykey cenhwa-lul hayssta
  John-TOP Mary-to telephone-ACC did
  kulikonun Ø Ø Ø salanghanta-ko malhayssta.
  and then love-COMP said
  'John called Mary and then (he) said that (he) loves (her).'

(4.110) At the discourse level.
  (a) (Chinese)
  A: Ø qu guo Beijing ma?
     go EXP Beijing Q
  B: Ø qu guo Ø.
     go EXP
  A: Have/has (you/he/she/they ...) been to Beijing?
  B: Yes, (I/he/she/they ...) have/has.

(b) (Japanese, Xu 1986)
   A: Kimi-wa kono hon-o   yomi-masi-ta ka?
      you-TOP this book-ACC read-PAST Q
   B: Ø Ø yomi-masi-ta
        read-PAST
   A: Did you read this book?
   B: Yes, (I) read (it).
(c) (Korean, Na and Huck 1993: 188)
   A: Chelswu-ka   Swuni-lul   salanghay-yo?
      Chelswu-NOM Swuni-ACC love-INT
   B: Ney, Ø Ø salanghay-yo
      yes   love-DECL
   A: Does Chelswu love Swuni?
   B: Yes, (he) loves (her).

Existence of pragmatic zero anaphors or empty pragmatic categories

Secondly, in a pragmatic language, there exists a class of pragmatic zero anaphor, or empty pragmatic category. These zero anaphors are simply ambiguous; they could fit in simultaneously with more than one type of empty category in the standard Chomskyan inventory. We have already seen an example from Chinese in Chapter 2 (i.e. (2.145)). The following is yet another example from Chinese illustrating this phenomenon.

(4.111) (a) Laoshi hai zhao bu dao [yi ge [Ø keyi jiao Ø de]   xuesheng].
            teacher still find not   one CL   can teach   REL pupil
            'The teacher still cannot find a pupil whom (he) can teach.'
       (b) Xuesheng hai zhao bu dao [yi ge [Ø keyi jiao Ø de]   laoshi]
            pupil   still find not   one CL   can teach   REL teacher
            'The pupil still cannot find a teacher who can teach (him).'

In the relative clause in both (4.111a) and (4.111b), there are two zero anaphors, one subject and one object. Within the framework of Chomsky's principles-and-parameters theory, the object zero anaphor is treated as a variable Ā-bound by the head of the relative clause (cf. C.-T. J. Huang 1984). But as I pointed out in Huang (1989, 1994), this variable analysis cannot be correct. Given our knowledge about the world, the preferred interpretation for (4.111a) and (4.111b) is exactly the opposite: while the object zero anaphor in (4.111a) is interpreted as being preferably Ā-bound by the head of the relative clause, the object zero anaphor in (4.111b) is interpreted as being preferably A-bound by the matrix subject of the relative construction. The same can be shown to hold for Japanese. Example (4.112), according to Nakamura (1987), is also ambiguous: the object zero anaphor can either be Ā-bound by the head of the relative clause or be A-bound by the subject of the matrix clause (see also Eid 1983 on Egyptian Arabic).

(4.112) John-ga   [[Ø Ø siken-ni   otosita] hito-o] nikunde-iru.
         John-NOM   examination flunk   person hate
(a) 'John hates the person who flunked (him).'
(b) 'John hates the person whom (he) flunked.'

Finally, of further interest is a class of so-called parasitic gap in a pragmatic language. Consider, for example, (4.113) from Chinese (Xu 1990).

(4.113) [women [yinwei Ø changchang chuixu Ø] yanli   piping   guo
         1PL   because   often   boast   severely criticize EXP
         de] na ge ren
         REL that CL person
(a) 'the person whom we severely criticized because (someone) often boasted of (him)'
(b) 'the person whom we severely criticized because (he) often boasted of (someone else)'
(c) 'the person whom we severely criticized because (he) often boasted of (himself)'

Note that the object zero anaphor in the adjunct clause (within the inner brackets) constitutes a parasitic gap in Chinese. Contrary to C.-T. J. Huang, however, the object zero anaphor in question could simultaneously be argued to be a variable, a *pro*, or even an empty reflexive, as in the (a), (b) and (c) readings, respectively. Therefore, it seems to form a syntactically undifferentiated class. Note next that of the three possible readings, the empty anaphor reading seems to be the most preferred interpretation, the *pro* reading the least preferred interpretation, with the variable reading lying somewhere in between, in keeping with world knowledge. All this indicates that the binding properties of empty categories of this kind are not inherently defined, but pragmatically determined. Considered in this way, these zero anaphors, being realized by syntactically undifferentiated gaps rather than specific empty syntactic categories, can only be analysed as empty pragmatic categories, at least as far as their binding properties are concerned.

Pragmatic obligatory control

Thirdly, in a pragmatic language, control enjoys a great freedom in interpretation. For one thing, a pragmatic language allows—rather freely—remote or long-distance control, that is, control by a non-immediate, higher clause or from discourse. An attested example from Chinese is given in (4.114).

(4.114) Ta   xiang dui nainai shuo, ta   kao   shang le
         3SG want to granny say   3SG   pass examination   PFV
         yanjiusheng, renjia duji,   bu rang [Ø qu].
         postgraduate others jealous not allow   go
                                 (Tian Zhonghe, *Wuyue*)

'She wanted to tell Granny that she had passed the entrance examinations for graduate studies, but other people were jealous and (they) did not allow (her) to go.'

For another, a pragmatic language allows obligatory control that is pragmatically determined. Besides the examples given in Chapters 1 and 3 and earlier in this chapter, take (4.115) from Japanese (Kato personal communication).

(4.115) (a) Jokyaku-wa   untensyu-ni imasugu   Ø basu-o   hassya-saseru
            passenger-TOP driver-to   immediately   bus-OBJ start-cause
            yoo ni to   settoku si-ta.
            COMP persuade PAST
            'The passengers persuaded the driver to start the bus immediately.'
       (b) Untensyu-wa jokyaku-ni   imasugu   Ø basu-o   hassya-saseru
            driver-TOP   passenger-to immediately   bus-OBJ start-cause
            yoo ni to   settoku si-ta.
            COMP persuade PAST
            'The driver persuaded the passengers to start the bus immediately.'

As already pointed out, in unmarked cases, 'persuade' is a verb of object control, as in (4.115a). However, this unmarked reading is merely a strongly preferred one; it can be overridden in the face of inconsistency with, say, world knowledge. This is exactly what happens in (4.115b). In (4.115b), there is a shift of preference for the choice of controller: the subject control reading becomes the favoured one. Therefore, a control construction like (4.115) in a pragmatic language is allowed to have (at least) two possible interpretations, in accord with the number of potential antecedents in it. There are thus some grounds for believing that in a pragmatic language like Chinese, Japanese, and Korean, when syntax and world knowledge clash, world knowledge frequently wins. By way of contrast, in a syntactic language like English, French, and German, when there is a conflict between syntax and world knowledge, syntax usually takes the upper hand, as can be seen by the ungrammaticality of the English translations of (4.115b) under the indicated indexing.

Long-distance reflexivization

Fourthly, in a pragmatic language, a reflexive can frequently be long-distance bound. Since I have given a wide array of examples of long-distance reflexivization from Chinese, Japanese, and Korean in Chapter 2, I shall not provide further exemplification here.

By way of summary, using anaphora as a testing ground, we can see that some languages (e.g. Chinese, Japanese, and Korean) are less syntactic and more pragmatic than other languages (e.g. English, French, and German).

This, of course, does not mean that syntax is not relevant to a pragmatic language and pragmatics is not relevant to a syntactic language. On the contrary, syntax is indispensable for a pragmatic language and pragmatics is indispensable for a syntactic language. Therefore, the typological differences between syntactic and pragmatic languages will be one of degree, but of very significant degree.

Now, a question that arises concerns whether or not the pragmaticness of anaphora in a pragmatic language can be 'correlated' to some other pragmatic properties of such a language. In other words, does there exist a clustering of properties of some kind that acts as a function of positive value for a pragmatic language? At the moment, I do not have any definite answer to this question, but the languages we have treated as pragmatic are all topic- as opposed to subject-prominent. Let us now take a look at the prominence of Chinese-style topic construction in a pragmatic language.

4.4.2. The prominence of Chinese-style topic constructions in a pragmatic language

By topic construction is meant a construction containing two parts: a topic, which typically occurs first, and a comment—a clause which follows the topic and says something about it (e.g. Li and Thompson 1976, Gundel 1985, 1988, Xu and Langendoen 1985, Huang 1989, 1994).

Topic constructions in a language can roughly be divided into two types: those whose comment clause is syntactically related to the topic and those whose comment clause is not syntactically but semantically and/or pragmatically related to the topic. Following Chafe (1976) and Xu and Langendoen (1985), we call the former 'English-style' and the latter 'Chinese-style' topic constructions. They are illustrated in (4.116) and (4.117), respectively.

(4.116) (a) (Chinese)
Nei shou gangqin zoumingqu Xiaoming hen xihuan Ø.
that CL piano sonata Xiaoming very like
'That piano sonata, Xiaoming likes very much.'
(b) (Japanese)
Kuruma-wa Taroo-ga Ø kat-ta.
car-TOP Taro-NOM buy-PAST
'That car, Taro bought.'
(c) (Korean, Na and Huck 1993)
Chelswu-nun Swuni-ka Ø salanghay-yo.
Chelswu-TOP Swuni-NOM love-PRES
'Chelswu, Swuni loves.'
(4.117) (a) (Chinese)
Beijing mingshengguji duo.
Beijing historical sites many
'Beijing, historical sites are many.'

(b) (Japanese, McCawley 1976)
   Bukka-wa Nyuu-yooku-ga takakat-ta.
   price-TOP New-York-NOM expensive-PAST
   'Prices, New York was high.'
(c) (Korean, Na and Huck 1993)
   Kkoch-un kwukhwa-ka olaykan-ta.
   flower-TOP chrysanthemum-NOM last long
   'Flowers, chrysanthemums last long.'

In each of the English-style topic constructions in (4.116), the comment clause contains a *wh*-trace which is syntactically bound to the topic. But there is no such syntactic relation between the topic and the comment clause in each of the Chinese-style topic constructions in (4.117); the topic does not correspond to any extraction site within the comment clause. Instead, the topic and the comment clause are related to each other semantically and/or pragmatically (see also Lehmann 1976: 452 on Vedic).

In addition, there is a third type, an 'in-between' type, which provides a natural 'bridge' between clearly English- and clearly Chinese-style topic constructions. By way of illustration, consider (4.118) from Chinese (adapted from Xu and Langendoen 1985).

(4.118) Caiyuanzi   Lao Ma yijing   zhong shang Ø le.
       vegetable garden Lao Ma already plant up   CRS
       'The vegetable garden, Lao Ma has already grown (e.g. vegetables) in (it).'

On Xu and Langenden's (1985) view, (4.118) provides a natural 'bridge' between clearly Chinese-style and clearly English-style topic constructions. The comment clause contains a zero anaphor (as in an English-style topic construction), but the zero anaphor is not syntactically related to the topic (as in a Chinese-style topic construction). The referent of the zero anaphor has to be 'bridge'-inferred from the extended domain of reference. Given our knowledge about the world, the zero anaphor in (4.118) refers most naturally to the vegetables grown in the garden rather than the garden itself.

Chinese-style topic constructions are widespread in Chinese, Japanese, Korean and some South-East Asian languages like Lahu, Lisu, and Zhuang.[18] They are even considered by some scholars to be the basic grammatical relation in the sentential structure of these languages, called topic-prominent languages in the now classic subject- versus topic-prominent language typology put forward by Li and Thompson (1976). In this typology, languages are grouped into four types with regard to subjecthood/topichood: (i) those like English, Malagasy, and Twi, which are subject-prominent; (ii) those like Chinese, Lahu, and Lisu, which are topic-prominent; (iii) those like

---

[18] Two non-East and South-East Asian languages that seem to be topic-prominent are the Kru language Godié, as described in Marchese (1986), and the Indo-European language Hittite, as described in Justus (1976).

Japanese and Korean, which are both subject- and topic-prominent; and (iv) those like the Philippine languages Cebuano, Ilocano, Kalagan, Tagalog, and Waray, which are neither subject- nor topic-prominent.

What, then, are the essential properties of Chinese-style topic constructions? Following Li and Thompson (1976) and Tsao (1977), we can summarize them as follows: (i) the topic must be definite (in its broad sense, according to which proper and generic NPs are understood as definite), (ii) the topic, which is morphologically marked in some languages, is typically in sentence-initial position (cf. Foley and Van Valin 1984: 127–9), (iii) the topic, but not the subject, may be separated from the rest of the construction by a pause particle or something similar, (iv) the subject is in a 'doing' or 'being' semantic relationship with the predicate, but there is no such relationship between the topic and the predicate, and (v) there is often a particular semantic relationship between the topic and the subject; such that the topic is the whole of which the subject is a part. Furthermore, we can set out the well-formedness condition on the topic construction as follows (e.g. Li and Thompson 1976, Dooley 1982 on Guariní, Kitagawa 1982, Huang 1989, 1994, Gundel 1985, Xu and Langendoen 1985, Kratochvíl 1986, Na and Huck 1993, Chafe 1994, Chen 1996, Takami and Kamio 1996).

(4.119) The well-formedness condition on topic constructions
In a topic construction, some constituent of the comment clause or the comment clause as a whole must say something about the topic.

What (4.119) basically says is that in a topic construction, the comment clause must be a statement about the topic. The statement may serve 'to increase the addressee's knowledge about, request information about or otherwise get the addressee to act with respect to' the topic (Gundel 1985: 86) The essence of this 'aboutness' is that it is both a necessary and a sufficient condition that there is a relation between the comment clause and the topic, be it syntactic, semantic, and/or pragmatic. Stated thus, the well-formedness condition applies equally to both English- and Chinese-style topic constructions.

But it should be emphasized that in a Chinese-style topic construction, the relation between the topic and the comment clause is established via semantic and/or pragmatic rather than syntactic means. This can best be seen by a consideration of the following Chinese-style topic constructions, which are drawn from a number of topic-prominent, pragmatic languages.

(4.120) (a) (Japanese, Kuno 1973: 250)
Sakana-wa tai-ga i-i.
fish-TOP red snapper-NOM good-PRES
'Fish, red-snappers are best.'

Pragmatic Approaches to Anaphora 269

(b) (Lahu, Li and Thompson 1976)
hɔ   ɔ̄   na-qhɔ́ yɨ̄   ve   yò.
elephant TOP nose   long PRT DECL
'Elephants, noses are long.'

(c) (Zhuang, Ramsey 1987: 238)
Tapo da:ng reng   la:i.
father body strength much
'(My) father, body strength is great.'

(d) (Chinese, Li and Thompson 1976)
Nei chang huo xingkui   xiaofangdui lai   de   kuai.
that CL   fire fortunately fire brigade come CSC quickly
'That fire, fortunately the fire brigade came quickly.'

(e) (Chinese, Chen 1996)
Zhei ben shu ta   xie   de tai congmang le.
this CL book 3SG write CSC too hurry   CRS
'This book, he wrote in too much of a hurry.'

(f) (Korean, Cole, Hermon, and Sung 1990)
Enehak-un   Chomsky-ka   elyep-ta.
linguistics-TOP Chomsky-NOM difficult-DECL
'Linguistics, Chomsky is hard to read.'

(g) (Chinese)
San ge haizi, liang ge cheng le   zuoqujia.
three CL child two CL become PFV composer
'Of the three children, two became composers.'

(h) (Japanese, Kitagawa 1982)
Taroo-wa   Hanako-ga   iede-si-ta.
Taroo-TOP Hanako-NOM leave-home-do-PAST
'Taro, Hanako ran away from home.'

(i) (Chinese)
Xifang yingyue shi wo shi menwaihan.
western music history 1SG be layman
'History of Western music, I'm a layman.'

In (4.120a)–(4.120e), the comment clauses each contain a lexical item that is somewhat semantically related to the topic. In (4.120a), *tai* 'red snapper' is a hyponym of *sakana* 'fish'. In (4.120b), there is a part–whole relation obtaining between *na-qhɔ́* 'nose' and *hɔ* 'elephant'; *na-qhɔ́* is a part of *hɔ*—a relation that has been referred to in the lexical semantics literature as meronomic (e.g. Cruse 1986).[19] More or less the same can be shown to hold of (4.120c). In (4.120d), *xiaofangdui* 'fire brigade' and *huo* 'fire' are from the same semantic

---

[19] This may be generalized to include the following whole–part relations: (i) set–member, (ii) abstract–instance, (iii) process–step, (iv) object–attribute, and (v) generalization–specific. Some of these semantic relations may go under the rubric of elaboration in Mann and Thompson's (1987) rhetorical structure theory, which we shall discuss in the next chapter.
Another taxonomy is suggested by Na and Huck (1993). In this classification, there are five types of semantic relations: (i) meronomic (*dog–tail*), (ii) qualitative (e.g. *eye–colour*), (iii) conventional (e.g. *man–car*), (iv) conversive (e.g. *parent–child*), and (v) taxonomic (e.g. *fruit–apple*).

field. Furthermore, it is stereotypically a fire brigade whose major job is to put out a fire. Finally, the same can be said of *shu* 'book' and *xie* 'write' in (4.120*e*), On the other hand, in (4.120*f*)–(4.120*i*), the topic and the comment clause are associated with each other pragmatically. In (4.120*f*), *Chomsky* is linked to *enehak* 'linguistics', but the relation is established via the additional premise that Chomsky is a linguist and writes about linguistics. Clearly, this premise is not part of the meaning of the r-expression *Chomsky* but is something which has to be added to the interpretation of the utterance through our background knowledge. In (4.120*g*), the two children mentioned in the comment clause are drawn from among the three children specified in the topic. Next, in (4.120*h*), as Kitagawa (1982) observes, the use of the topic construction indicates that Taro's and Hanako's identities are somehow closely related to each other such as husband and wife, father and daughter, and (we may perhaps add) boss and secretary. Again this sense of identification between the two persons involved can be established only in terms of real-world knowledge. Finally, in (4.120*i*), history of Western music is something about which the speaker is a layman.

A related point of interest is that from an interpretative point of view, Chinese-style topic constructions can be divided into three types: instance, frame, and range topic constructions (e.g. McCawley 1976, Chen 1996).

(4.121) Chen's (1996) three types of pragmatic topics
  (*a*) Instance topic
      An instance topic represents an instance of the object about which a predication is made and assessed. It is typically a definite entity in the cognitive inventory of referential entities in the context.
  (*b*) Frame topic
      A frame topic is one that provides the spatial, temporal, and individual frame within which the proposition expressed by the remaining part of the topic construction, typically a predication made of another expression in the sentence, normally that of the subject, holds true.
  (*c*) Range topic
      A range topic is one that delimits the range of a variable of which the predication is made.

Of the Chinese-style topic constructions (4.120*a*)–(4.120*i*) above, (4.130*e*) is clearly a case of an instance topic construction; the topic provides a specific value for the variable about which a predication is made. Next, in sentences like (4.120*b*), (4.120*c*), (4.20*d*) and (4.120*g*), we have a frame topic. In these cases, as Chafe (1976: 50) notes, the topic appears 'to limit the applicability of the main predication to a certain restricted domain ... [It] sets a spatial, temporal, or individual framework within which the main predication holds.' In other words, the function of the topic of this kind is to establish a frame or domain of reference, or a universe of discourse with respect to which its comment clause or some constituent in it will provide some relevant informa-

Pragmatic Approaches to Anaphora 271

tion (e.g. Dik 1978, Xu and Langendoen 1985). Finally, in examples like (4.120*a*) and (4.120*f*), there is a range topic, which restricts the range of values that a variable in the following predication can take. Thus, in (4.120*a*), for example, the topic specifies the range of the variable x in 'x is best' to a type of fish and states that of the fishes in that range, it is red snappers for which 'x is best' is true. Consequently, this topic construction may informally be interpreted along the following lines: 'Among the x such that x is a type of fish, red snappers are an x such that x is the best' (McCawley 1976, Kitagawa 1982, Na and Huck 1993).

Mention should be made at this point that Chinese-style topic constructions are not restricted to one-topic structures. They can contain multiple topics, provided that the well-formedness condition on the topic construction is met.

(4.122) (*a*) (Chinese)
Zhongguo gudu Beijing mingshengguji duo.
China ancient capital Beijing historical site many
'China, ancient capitals, Beijing, historical sites are many.'
(*b*) (Japanese, Kitagawa 1982: 189)
Bunmeikoku-wa dansei-wa heikin zyumyoo-wa Ø naga-i.
civilized nation-TOP man-TOP average life-span-TOP long-PRES
'Civilized countries, men, the average life-span, (it) is long.'
(*c*) (Korean)
?Hankwuk koto-tulm Sewul yəksa-cək-in kot mantha.
Korea ancient capital-PL Seoul history-of place many
'Korea, ancient capitals, Seoul, historical sites are many.'

Example (4.122*a*), for instance, contains three topic constructions, which are embedded within a domain of predication. In this multiple topic construction, each of the subordinate topics has a twofold function: on the other hand, it acts as the target NP for the preceding topic, and on the other, it functions as the topic for the following comment clause. The structure of (4.122*a*) is given in (4.123).

272   *Pragmatic Approaches to Anaphora*

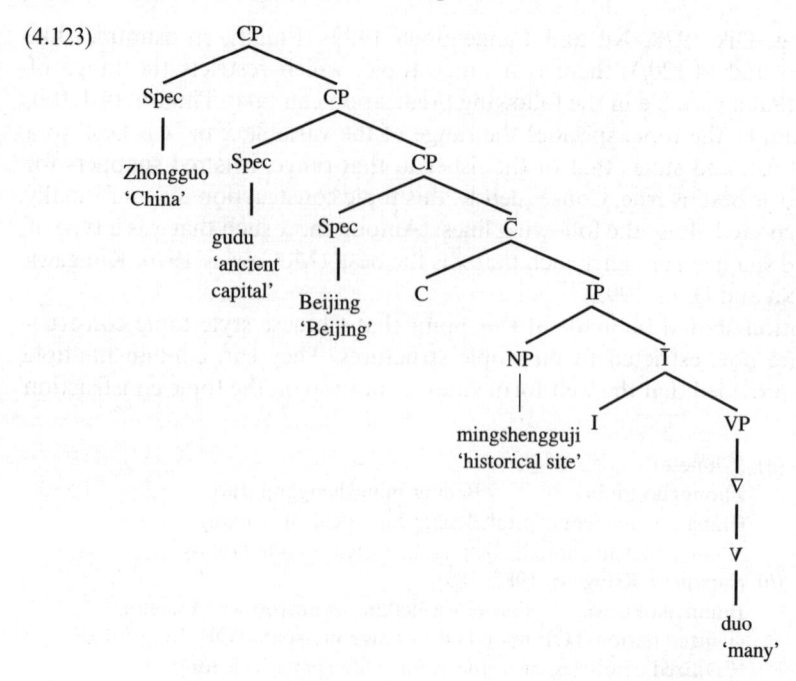

(4.123)

```
                    CP
                   /  \
                Spec   CP
                 |    /  \
             Zhongguo Spec  CP
              'China'  |   /  \
                     gudu Spec  C̄
                   'ancient |   / \
                   capital' Beijing C  IP
                           'Beijing'  / \
                                    NP   I
                                    |   / \
                              mingshengguji I  VP
                              'historical site'  |
                                                 V
                                                 |
                                                 V
                                                 |
                                                duo
                                               'many'
```

Also noteworthy is that Chinese-style topic constructions can sometimes be ambiguous. The ambiguity can be resolved by context and/or world knowledge. Following are two examples from Lisu (Li and Thompson 1976).

(4.124) làthyu nya ánà khṳ̀-a̰.
  people TOP dog bite-DECL
  (a) 'People, dogs bite (them).'
  (b) 'People, (they) bite dogs.'
(4.125) ánà nya làthyu khṳ̀-a̰.
  dog TOP people bite-DECL
  (a) 'Dogs, (they) bite people.'
  (b) 'Dogs, people bite (them).'

As the translations indicate, both (4.124) and (4.125) are ambiguous. This is due to the fact that a simple, transitive, declarative clause in Lisu does not distinguish between agent and patient structurally. The two sentences are, of course, different, but they differ only in terms of topic: *làthyu* is the topic in (4.124), whereas *ánà* is the topic in (4.125). However, given our knowledge about the world, there is no difficulty in determining which interpretation is the preferred one in both (4.124) and (4.125).

Finally, note that the topic of a non-initial Chinese-style topic construction can freely be dropped to the effect that an empty topic chain is formulated. Let us call this 'topic-drop'. In such a construction, the topic established in

Pragmatic Approaches to Anaphora 273

the first topic construction serves as the antecedent of the unrealized topics in the chain of topic constructions following it.

(4.126) (*a*) (Chinese)
Zhongguo fuyuan liaokuo, Ø renkou zhongduo,
China, territory vast population many
Ø lishi youjiu, Ø wenhua canlan.
   history long civilization brilliant
'China, territory is vast; Ø, population is large; Ø, history is long; and Ø civilization is brilliant.'
(*b*) (Japanese)
Zou-wa hana-ga nagaku,
elephant-TOP nose-SUBJ long
Ø o-ga mijikaku,
  tail-SUBJ short
Ø mē-ga chiisai.
  eye-SUBJ small
'Elephants, noses are long; Ø, tails are short; and Ø, eyes are small.'
(*c*) (Korean, Cole, Hermon, and Sung 1990)
Ku cip-un ichung-ita, Ø cipung-i hinsayk-ita.
that house-TOP two storey-is roof-NOM white-is
'That house, two storeys high; and Ø, roof is white.'

Chinese-style relative and passive constructions

The prominence of Chinese-style topic constructions in a pragmatic language has important implications for the syntax of such a language. In this subsection, I shall briefly discuss two constructions that are somewhat correlated to Chinese-style topic constructions: (i) Chinese-style relative constructions, and (ii) Chinese-style passive constructions. Let us take Chinese-style relative constructions first.

Relative constructions in a language can roughly be divided into two categories: English-style and Chinese-style. These two types of relative construction, which correspond to the two types of topic construction we illustrated in e.g. (4.116*a*) and (4.117*a*), are given in (4.127)–(4.128).

(4.127) (Chinese)
[Xiaoming hen xihuan Ø de] nei shou gangqin zoumingqu
Xiaoming very like REL that CL piano sonata
'the piano sonata which Xiaoming likes very much'
(4.128) (Chinese)
[mingshengguji duo de] Beijing
historical sites many REL Beijing
'Beijing (whose) historical sites are many.'

Clearly, in the Chinese-style relative construction (4.128), neither movement nor variable binding is involved. Instead, the head and the target NP in the relative clause are related pragmatically.

Again, there is a third, 'in-between' type of relative constructions, mirroring the 'in-between' type of topic constructions exemplified in (4.118).

(4.129) (Chinese)
[Lao Ma yijing zhong shang Ø le de] caiyuanzi
Lao Ma already plant up CRS REL vegetable garden
'the vegetable garden (in which) Lao Ma has already grown (e.g. vegetables)'

But it should be pointed out at this point that Chinese-style relative constructions are more restricted than Chinese-style topic constructions. Of the three types of Chinese-style topic construction specified above, range topic constructions cannot in general be relativized, as can be seen by the ungrammaticality of the examples in (4.130) below.

(4.130) (a) (Chinese)
*[Zhongwen hen nan xue de] yuyan
Chinese very difficult learn REL language
'language (about which) Chinese is difficult to learn'
(b) (Japanese, Kitagawa 1982)
*[tai-ga i-i] sakana
red snapper-NOM good-PRES fish
'fish, as for which red snapper is the best'
(c) (Korean, Na and Huck 1993)
*[kwukhwa-ka olayka-nun] kkoch
chrysanthemum-NOM last long flower
'flowers such that chrysanthemums last long'

In other words, the aboutness condition stated in (4.119) seems to be a necessary but not a sufficient condition on the well-formedness of Chinese-style relative constructions. Based on McCawley's (1976) observation that restrictive relative constructions may not be formulated by relativizing over a range topic, Na and Huck (1993) claim that what is at stake here is that 'a set denoted by a range topic cannot be mapped by some function directly onto a taxonomically subordinate subset and then partitioned according to whether its members share the property predicated of the subset members'.

Below are three more examples of Chinese-style relative constructions, with the (a) sentences containing their corresponding Chinese-style topic constructions. Notice that all of them are formulated by relativizing over a frame topic.

(4.131) (Chinese)
(a) Nei chang huo xingkui xiaofangdui lai de kuai.
that CL fire fortunately fire brigade come CSC quickly
'That fire, fortunately the fire brigade came quickly.'
(b) [xingkui xiaofangdui lai de kuai de] nei chang huo
fortunately fire brigade come CSC quickly REL that CL fire
'the fire (about which) fortunately the fire brigade came quickly'

(4.132) (Japanese, Kitagawa 1982)
  (a) Taroo-wa   Hanako-ga   iede-si-ta.
      Taroo-TOP Hanako-NOM leave-home-do-PAST
      'Taro, Hanako ran away from home.'
  (b) Hanako-ga   iede-si-ta   Taroo
      Hanako-NOM leave-home-do-PAST Taroo
      'Taro (about whom) Hanako ran away from home.'
(4.133) (Korean, Na and Huck 1993)
  (a) Ku   namca-ka   nwun-i   kalsayk-i-ta.
      DET man-NOM eyes-NOM brown-be-DECL
      'That man, eyes are brown.'
  (b) nwun-i   kalsayk-i-n   namca
      eyes-NOM brown-be-MOD man
      '(the) man (whose) eyes are brown'

Next, more or less the same can be said of Chinese-style passive constructions. As with relative constructions, passive constructions can also be divided into two types: (i) English-style, as in (4.134), and (ii) Chinese-style, as in (4.135).

(4.134) (Chinese)
  Xiaoming bei laoshi   piping   guo Ø.
  Xiaoming by teacher criticize PFV
  'Xiaoming has been criticized by the teacher.'
(4.135) (Chinese)
  Lao Xie bei jichuang zha duan le   shouzhi.
  Lao Xie by lathe   cut off   PFV finger
  'Lao Xie was cut (his) finger by the lathe.'

Evidently, in (4.135), as in the case of the Chinese-style topic and relative constructions we have seen above, there is no syntactic dependency between the subject and the object. Rather, the subject and the object are connected on a semantic basis: the finger is part of Lao Xie.

Once again, there is a third, 'in-between' type of passive constructions, on a par with topic and relative constructions.

(4.136) (Chinese)
  Caiyuanzi   yijing   bei Lao Ma zhong shang Ø le.
  vegetable garden already by Lao Ma plant up   CRS
  'The vegetable garden has already been grown (e.g. vegetables) in (it) by Lao Ma.'

Also worth noting is that Chinese-style passive constructions are in general correlated to frame topics, where the topic stands in a possessor–possessed relation with the target NP in the comment clause. Another example of Chinese-style passive constructions is given below, with the (a) and (b) sentences containing its corresponding Chinese-style topic constructions.

(4.137) (Chinese)
    (a) Shuzhuo Xiaoming ba chouti nonghuai le.
        desk   Xiaoming BA drawer damage PFV
        'The desk, Xiaoming damaged (its) drawer.'
    (b) Shuzhuo chouti bei Xiaoming nonghuai le.
        desk   drawer by Xiaoming damage PFV
        'The desk, the drawer was damaged by Xiaoming.'
    (c) Shuzhuo bei Xiaoming nonghuai le   chouti.
        desk   by Xiaoming damage   PFV drawer
        'The desk was damaged the drawer by Xiaoming.'

4.4.3. Explaining the differences: parametric or typological?

In the preceding sections, I have pointed out some typological differences between syntactic and pragmatic languages. It goes without saying that these are initial observations, and much work remains to be done. However, the differences we have seen appear to suffice to suggest that some languages are more pragmatic than others. In these pragmatic languages, syntactic structure is more closely related to semantic representation and/or pragmatic information.

There might be two general approaches to the typological differences between syntactic and pragmatic languages. One approach is to adopt a null hypothesis from a syntactic perspective, that is, to assume that a single, syntactic model is sufficient to account for both types of language. The typological differences can then be reduced to parameterization. C.-T. J. Huang (1984), for example, posits a sentence-oriented versus discourse-oriented language typology parameter within the framework of Chomsky's principles-and-parameters theory. But as I pointed out in Huang (1989, 1994), such a move would pose considerable problems for the principles-and-parameters theory; it would be a significant departure from the standard position taken in the principles-and-parameters theory with respect to parameter setting: namely, a principle that is allegedly defined by a general theory of UG can allow only a small range of parametric options, among which individual languages may choose. Clearly, a parameter such as the syntactic versus pragmatic language typology one would certainly not be some minor revision of the existing generative machinery. For the notion of parametric variation is not meant to be a way of removing all restrictions on a theory of UG; on the contrary, it is meant to allow only a highly restricted number and limited kinds of typological variants. Thus, to allow a parameter that would in effect classify languages into [+generative] and [–generative] would render the generative theory vacuous as a theory of UG.

Another approach is to assume that languages are typologically different with respect to the extent to which syntax and pragmatics interact, and that some languages are more syntactically oriented and others are more pragmatically oriented. One parameter for distinguishing a syntactic language from a pragmatic one might be the behaviour of intrasentential anaphora in that language. Another might be whether a particular language is topic- or subject-prominent. The step to be taken next is to examine a wide variety of genetically different and structurally diverse languages to see if the two typological parameters can be maintained, if there are other typological parameters (cf. (4.107) above), and if all these parameters can be somewhat related, and eventually be reduced to a set of implicational universals. If the answer to these questions is positive, then we might need two different approaches to the two different types of language: a syntactically centred approach to a syntactic language and a pragmatically centred approach to a pragmatic language.

4.4.4. Summary

In this section, I have considered some typological differences between Chinese- and English-type languages. I have concentrated on two parameters: (i) the syntacticness versus pragmaticness of anaphora, and (ii) the presence versus absence of Chinese-style topic constructions. I have also taken a brief look at both the Chomskyan generative and Greenbergen typological approaches to these differences and argued for the setting up of a novel syntactic versus pragmatic language typology.

4.5. Conclusion

In this chapter, I have concerned myself with pragmatic approaches to anaphora. I have developed a revised neo-Gricean pragmatic theory of anaphora. I have demonstrated that by utilizing this theory many patterns of preferred interpretation regarding intrasentential anaphora in a wide variety of geographically, typologically, and structurally distinct languages can be given a better account. I have also reviewed the Relevance-theoretical, Accessibility-theoretical, and Prague School functional analyses of anaphora. Finally, using anaphora as one of the testing grounds, I have considered some typological differences between sentence-and discourse-oriented languages, and proposed a new syntactic versus pragmatic language typology.

5 Switch-Reference and Discourse Anaphora

In this chapter, I shall be concerned with switch-reference and discourse anaphora. I shall first take a look at switch-reference. As an 'in-between' category, switch-reference seems to provide a natural 'bridge' between pure intrasentential anaphora and pure discourse anaphora. I shall first review the phenomenology of switch-reference in Section 5.1.1. Next, in Section 5.1.2, I shall first make a comparison between switch-reference and other reference-tracking systems and then compare and contrast switch-reference and logophoricity. Finally, in Section 5.1.3, I shall first discuss a syntactic and a semantic, and then sketch a pragmatic approach to switch-reference.

In the second part of this chapter, I shall turn my attention to discourse anaphora. I shall start with the problem of anaphoric distribution in Section 5.2.1. I shall then survey, in Sections 5.2.2–5.2.4, a number of influential approaches to discourse anaphora, focusing on the topic continuity analysis developed by Givón (1983), the hierarchical account represented by Fox (1987), and the cognitive model offered by Chafe (1976), Tomlin and Pu (1991), and Gundel, Hedberg, and Zacharski (1993). Finally, I shall develop a neo-Gricean pragmatic analysis of discourse anaphora in Section 5.2.5.

5.1. Switch-reference

5.1.1. The phenomenon

As mentioned in Chapter 1, one of the mechanisms available in natural languages to keep track of referents in an ongoing discourse is the switch-reference system.[1] In a classical switch-reference system, the verb of a dependent clause is morphologically marked to indicate whether or not the subject of that clause is the same as the subject of its linearly adjacent,

---

[1] In recent years, the notion of switch-reference has been extended by variationists to describe languages such as Egyptian Arabic, Persian, and Spanish, where 'switch-reference' is claimed to be mediated not via verbal morphology but through the optional or variable expression of overt versus null pronominal subjects (see e.g. Parkinson 1987, Haeri 1989, Fleischman 1991, Paredes Silva 1993, Cameron 1994). In this book, however, I shall not adopt such a broad definition for switch-reference.

structurally related independent clause. If both subjects are coreferential, an SS marker is used; otherwise a DS marker is employed, as the following example shows.

(5.1) (Yavapai, Kendal 1976)
   (a) tokatoka-č   savakyuva u-t-k   čikwar-kiñ.
       Tokatoka-SUBJ Savakyuva see-TEMP-SS laugh-COMPL
       'When Tokatoka₁ looked at Savakyuva₂, he₁ laughed.'
   (b) tokatoka-č   savakyuva u-t-m   čikwar-kiñ.
       Tokatoka-SUBJ Savakyuva see-TEMP-DS laugh-COMPL
       'When Tokatoka₁ looked at Savakyuva₂, he₂ laughed.'

Some of the switch-reference languages in the world are listed in (5.2).

(5.2) Switch-reference languages
   (a) American (North)
       Maidu (e.g. Konkow, Nisenan); Muskogean (e.g. Alabama); Northern Cochimi; Uto-Aztecan (e.g Chemehuevi, Hopi); Yokuts (e.g. Chukchansi, Yawelmani, Wikchamni); Zuni
   (b) American (South)
       Cashibo, Guanano, Miskitu, Ancash Quechua, Tunebo, Ulwa
   (c) Australian
       Alyawarra; Djingili; Garawa; Kanyara (Bayungu, Burduna, Dhalandji); Mantharta (e.g. Dhargari, Djiwarli); Martuthunira; Wagaya; Wanyi; Waramungu; West Desert (e.g. Gugada, Pintupi)
   (d) Papuan
       Angaatɨha, Anjam, Bargam, Managalisi, Nobonob, Wojokeso
   (e) Other
       Aghem, Lango, Ngyemboon (African); Nakh (Chechen, Ingush); Didoic (Bezta, Dido); Lezgian (Agul, Udi) (North East Caucasian)

Switch-reference markers

Types

Two main types of switch-reference marker can be identified: (i) verbal affixes, and (ii) independent morphemes. Verbal affixes can further be divided into two subgroups: (i) those that are part of verb concord, and (ii) those that are not. The first subtype is exemplified in many switch-reference languages of Papua New Guinea. In Kanite, for example, switch-reference markers are part of anticipatory subject–verb agreement markers, that is, markers which indicate person/number agreement with the subject of the subsequent clause (Haiman 1983: 112, Stirling 1993: 31). Table (5.3.) below gives the switch-reference markers in Kobon, another language of Papua New Guinea. As can be seen from the table, each of these suffixes encodes not only the SS/DS distinction, but also person and number features.

(5.3) Kobon switch-reference suffixes (Comrie 1983: 20)

		SS	DS
Singular	1	–em	–nö
	2	–(m)ön	–ö
	3	–öm	–ö
Dual	1	–ul	–lo
	2/3	–mil	–lö
Plural	1	–un	–no
	2	–mim	–be/–pe
	3	–öm	–lö

The second subtype of switch-reference markers is found in many American Indian languages. A typical example is Maricopa, a language of the River branch of the Yuman family. In this language, while the subject-verb agreement is shown by a set of prefixes on the verb stem, switch-reference is indicated independently by a pair of suffixes: -*k* for SS and -*m* for DS (Gordon 1983) (cf. Haiman and Munro 1983*a* on languages like Ancash Quechua and Chuave, which are a combination of both the subtypes).

(5.4) (Maricopa, Gordon 1983: 87)
    (*a*) nyaa '-ashvar-k '-iima-k.
        I   1-sing-SS 1-dance-ASP
        'I sang and I danced.'
    (*b*) Bonnie-sh   ashvar-m '-iima-k.
        Bonnie-SUBJ sing-DS 1-dance-ASP
        'Bonnie sang and I danced.'

Alternatively, switch-reference can be marked by independent morphemes, as is found in a number of American Indian languages (Jacobsen 1983) and Australian languages (Austin 1981*a*). In the Lakhota example (5.5), SS is marked by the conjunction *na*, and DS by the conjunction *cha*.

(5.5) (Lakhota, Trask 1993)
    (*a*) Ø-ʔi   na Ø-Ø-kté.
        3SG-arrived and 3SG-3SG-killed
        'He$_1$ arrived and killed him$_2$.'
    (*b*) Øʔi   čha Ø-Ø-kté.
        3SG-arrived and 3SG-3SG-killed
        'He$_1$ arrived and he$_2$ killed him$_1$.'

As (5.5.) indicates, independent morphemes are typically placed in the position for clausal clitics or conjunctions. Next, notice that occasionally they may not need to be adjacent to the verb. This is the case with Pima. In (5.6), the SS/DS markers and the verbs are separated by the deictic particle '*am*.

(5.6) (Pima, Haiman and Munro 1983*a*: p. x)
    (*a*) Hegai 'uuvi 'a-t   'am ṣohñi hegai ceoj c 'am ṣoṣa.
        that woman 3-PERF   hit   that man SS   cry
        'That woman$_1$ hit the man$_2$ and she$_1$ cried.'

(b) Hegai 'uuvi   'a-t   'am ṣohñi hegai ceoj ku-t   'am ṣoṣa.
    that woman 3-PERF   hit   that man DS-PERF   cry
    'That woman₁ hit the man₂ and he₂ cried.'

It is also noteworthy that a language may have multiple switch-reference systems. In some cases, these systems correlate with clause types. For example, Diyari and Dhirari—two Australian languages utilize different sets of markers for implicated clauses, imperfective relative clauses and perfective relative clauses, as the following table shows.

(5.7) Diyari and Dhirari switch-reference suffixes (Austin 1981a: 313)

Clause type		Diyari	Dhirari
Implicated	SS	–lha	–lhali
	DS	–rnanthu	–yani
Imperfective relative	SS	–rna	–rnda
	DS	–rnanhi	–rndanhi
Perfective relative	SS	–rnandu	–rndandu
	DS	–ni(ngurra)	–ni(ngurra)

More or less the same is true of their four neighbouring languages Ngamini, Yarluyandi, Yawarawarga, and Yandruwandha, and another Australian Western Desert language Pitjantjatjara (Austin 1981a: 321). Furthermore, what we have seen here in Australian languages can also be observed in American languages. Choctaw and Chickasaw, for instance, employ one pair of markers for paratactic constructions, and a different pair/array of markers for adverbial, complement, and relative clauses (Jacobsen 1983). Examples (5.8) and (5.9) illustrate this point with respect to Chickasaw. Maxakali—a Macro-Je language—is another language of this type. To indicate coordination, one uses *tu* for SS, and *hu* for DS, but to indicate logical sequence, one utilizes *hu* to encode SS, and *yiy* to encode DS (Wiesemann 1986a: 453).

(5.8) (Chickasaw, Munro 1983: 223)
    (a) hi'lha-cha talowa.
        dance-SS sing
        'He₁ danced and he₁ sang.'
    (b) hi'lha-na talowa.
        dance-DS sing
        'He₁ danced and he₂ sang.'
(5.9) (a) hilha-kat ithaana.
        dance-SS know
        'He₁ knows that he₁ danced.'
    (b) hilha-kã ithaana.
        dance-DS know
        'He₁ knows that he₂ danced.'

In other cases, the distinction concerns additional, secondary meanings. These meanings typically have to do with temporal, logical, and/or epistemic relations between the events described in the clauses. The Uto-Aztecan language Huichol, for example, deploys different sets of switch-reference markers to encode different tenses. We shall have more to say about the secondary functions of switch-reference shortly.

(5.10) Huichol switch-reference systems (Comrie 1983: 19)

	Same-subject	Different-subject
Simultaneous	-ti-	-kaku
Anterior:		
Past	-ka	-ku
Future	-me	-yu

Overt versus covert

With regard to the number of morphologically expressed markers, switch-reference languages can be divided into two types: (i) those that contain both SS and DS markers (e.g. the American Indian languages Kiowa, Choctaw, South-Western and Northern Pomo, Huichol, and Chemehuewi, and the Papua New Guinean language Kobon), and (ii) those that contain only one of the markers. The latter type can further be grouped into two subtypes: (i) those containing SS markers only, as in e.g. some constructions in Cashibo (Wiesemann 1986a: 458) (see (5.11)), and (ii) those containing DS markers only, as in e.g. Washo, Seri, Jamul, and La Huerta dialects of Diegueño, Kâte, Lenakal, Klamath, and Northern Paiute). From a statistical point of view, subtype (i) is much less frequently encountered than subtype (ii). In other words, SS markers are found to be zero indicated much more frequently than DS markers. This distribution of switch-reference markers is consistent with the cross-linguistic fact that SS tends to be unmarked, and DS tends to be marked. For example, in languages like Siroi, SS is marked by dependent verbs, but DS by independent verbs (Foley and Van Valin 1984: 339–40). In Hua, anticipatory subject agreement is indicated not on SS but on DS (Franklin 1983). This asymmetry in terms of markedness can further be evidenced by (i) the different morphological complexities for the two markers (i.e. SS markers are in general morphologically less complex than DS markers), and (ii) the different numbers for the two markers a language has to distinguish (i.e. the number of SS markers is in general smaller than that of DS markers, as in Eastern Pomo, Shoshone, and Tonkawa, but cf. Maidu, Papago, and Tübatulabal) (e.g. Haiman 1983: 106–7, Jacobsen 1983: 164–6, and Stirling 1993: 31–2).[2]

---

[2] With regard to the origins of switch-reference markers, a number of hypotheses have been put forward in the literature. These include (i) SS and DS markers are derived from directional deictics (such as -k 'hither' and -m 'hence' in the Yuman languages) (Jacobsen 1983); (ii) SS and DS markers are developed from case markers (Jacobsen 1983, Dench and Evans 1988); (iii) SS

(5.11) (Cashibo, Wiesemann, 1986a: 458)
 (a) ñu   'aru-tan-cën-xun   cana   pi-a-n.
     things cook-SS-PAST-TR   1S-AFF   eat-PAST-1/2S
     'After I cooked, I ate.'
 (b) 'ën   'aru-cën-xun   ca   pi-a-xin.
     1S-TR cook-PAST-TR   3S-AFF   eat-PAST-3S
     'After I cooked, he ate.'

Switch-reference pivots

Person

The general pattern of person distinction for pivot NPs in a switch-reference system can be expressed by the following implicational hierarchy.

(5.12) Person hierarchy for switch-reference pivot NPs
 3 > 2 > 1
 First-person switch-reference pivot NPs imply second-person switch-reference pivot NPs, and second-person switch-reference pivot NPs imply third-person switch-reference pivot NPs.

In other words, if switch-reference applies to, say, first-person pivot NPs in a language, then it will also apply to second-person pivot NPs in that language. Thus, there should be no language in which only first- and second-person pivot NPs, but not third-person pivot NPs, are SS/DS marked—a prediction that is largely borne out (cf. Kayapo, Wiesemann 1986b: 377).[3] (Incidentally, this implicational hierarchy is also applicable to additional person features attached to switch-reference markers, described above.) Clearly, what is predicted by the hierarchy is not accidental, but is directly related to the primary function of the switch-reference system, namely to avoid referen-

---

and DS markers come from coordinating and subordinating conjunctions (Dench and Evans 1988), (iv) SS and DS markers arise out of a contrast between temporal sequential markers and temporal simultaneous markers (as in Guanano, a Tucanoan language spoken in South America) (Longacre 1983); (v) SS and DS markers originate from a contrast between zero/bound/ unstressed and non-zero/independent/stressed pronouns (as in Lango) (Givón 1983), (vi) SS and DS markers are the result of the evolution from a contrast between first- and non-first-person agreement markers (as in Sherpa, a Tibetan language) (Givón 1983); (vii) SS and DS markers are the result of the development of a contrast between participial/nominalized/non-finite and finite/ other subject-marked clauses (Givón 1983); (viii) SS marked clauses are a reduced version of their corresponding DS marked clauses (Haiman 1983); (ix) DS markers are derived from causative markers, as in Pomo (Oswalt 1977); and (x) DS markers come from subordinating particles or complementizers (as in Augaatiha, Longacre 1983, and Daga, Haiman 1983).

[3] Note that 'third-person only' switch-reference languages are very rare. Cases that have been reported in the literature include Central Yup'ik Eskimo (Woodbury 1983, see also Fortescue 1991 on West Greenlandic), Gokana (Hyman and Comrie 1981, Comrie 1983), and Kaingang (Wiesemann 1982). But the first two, as correctly pointed out by Stirling (1993), do not appear to be canonical switch-reference languages; the Eskimo system represents obviation, and the Gokana system represents logophoricity. Thus, Kaingang remains the only switch-reference language I am aware of that limits SS/DS marking to third-person pivot NPs. However, given that switch-reference in this language is signalled via NPs rather than verbs, Kaingang may not be a prototypical switch-reference language, either.

tial ambiguity in an ongoing discourse. In this respect, as with logophors and reflexives (cf. Chapters 3 and 4), the third-person distinction is the most, the first-person distinction the least useful, with the second-person distinction in between.

Number

Number specifications for pivot NPs are much more complicated than person specifications. To begin with, four situations may be identified: (i) the dominant pivot NP (NP_α) and the dependent pivot NP (NP_β) agree in number (i.e. $NP_\alpha = NP_\beta$), (ii) the dominant NP is properly included in the dependent NP (i.e. $NP_\alpha \subset NP_\beta$), (iii) the dominant NP properly includes the dependent NP (i.e. $NP_\alpha \supset NP_\beta$), and (iv) the dominant and dependent NPs intersect (i.e. $NP_\alpha \cap NP_\beta$). (e.g. Wiesemann 1982, 1986a, Stirling 1993: 35, 212) The first situation is rather straightforward, and I shall not discuss it. With regard to the relation of referential inclusion as displayed in situations (ii) and (iii), there are three cases of interest. The first two show symmetry and the third shows asymmetry. In the first, there is a symmetrical SS marking for both situations (ii) and (iii). Central cases occur in Kashaya (Oswalt 1983), Huichol (Comrie 1983), and Martuthunira (Dench 1988). This is illustrated in (5.13). Secondly, the converse is true, that is, SS marking is symmetrically prohibited for both (ii) and (iii); instead DS marking is employed. This has been reported for Pima by Langdon and Munro (1979) and for Huallaga Quechua by Weber (1980). An example from Huallaga Quechua is given in (5.14). A third occasion involves an asymmetrical marking between (ii) and (iii). In this case, while SS marking is allowed for (ii), it is disallowed for (iii). This can be exemplified by Amele (J. Roberts 1987, Stirling 1993), Diyari (Austin 1981a, Wiesemann 1983) and perhaps Arabana/Wangganguru (Austin 1981a). An Amele example illustrating this point is presented in (5.15). One plausible explanation for this contrast is put forward by D. Wilkins (1988). According to him, the referent of the dominant pivot NP is more prominent in (ii), in that he or she also performs the action described in the dependent clause, but this is not the case in (iii).

(5.13) Symmetrical SS in both (ii) and (iii)
(Huichol, Comrie 1983: 26–7)
(a) taame te-haataʔazia-ka, nee ne-petia.
we 1PL-arrive-SS I 1SG-leave
'When we arrived, I left.'
(b) nee ne-haataʔa-ka, tanaiti te-pekii.
I 1SG-arrive-SS together 1PL-leave
'When I arrived, we left together.'
(5.14) Symmetrical SS disallowed in both (ii) and (iii)
(Huallaga Quechua, Weber 1980: 53)
(a) Chaya*-r/-pti-nchi qoyku-shaq.
arrive*-SS/-DS-1+2 give-1-FUT
'When we (inclusive) arrive, I will give it to him.'

(b) Qam-ta   apari*-r/-pti:-pis   manam chaya-shun-chu.
      you-ACC carry*-SS/-DS-1-even not   arrive-1+2-FUT-NEG
      'Even if I carry you, we (inclusive) will not arrive.'
(5.15) Asymmetrical SS allowed in (ii) but DS allowed in (iii)
      (Amele, Stirling 1993: 213)
      (a) Ege   h-u-me-b   sab j-ig-a.
          1PL come-PRED-SS-1PL food eat-1SG-PAST
          'We came and I ate the food.'
      (b) Ija   ho-co-min   sab jo-qa-a.
          1SG come-PRED-DS-1SG food eat-1PL-PAST
          'I came and we ate the food.'

Other possibilities have also been reported for switch-reference marking of referential inclusion.[4] Most notably, it has been noted that in some languages, either SS or DS marking can be used for both (ii) and (iii). In such cases, the choice seems to be conditioned by a variety of factors, some of which include (i) whether or not the speaker takes the pivots as the same protagonist, as in Maricopa (Gordon 1983); (ii) whether or not the speaker views the pivots as forming a part–whole relation; as in Mparntwe Arrernte (D. Wilkins 1988, see also Maslova 1997 on Tundra or Northern Yukaghir); and (iii) whether or not the speaker regards the pivots as forming a harmonic generation group from an anthropological point of view, again as in Mparntwe Arrernte (D. Wilkins 1988). From all this emerges the following implicational hierarchy.

(5.16) Number hierarchy for switch-reference pivot NPs
      $(NP_\alpha = NP_\beta) > (NP_\alpha \subset NP_\beta) > (NP_\alpha \supset NP_\beta)$
      Dominant NPs including dependent NPs implies dominant NPs being included in dependent NPs, and dominant NPs being included in dependent NPs implies dominant NPs agreeing with dependant NPs.

This implicational scale can be interpreted as follows: in all switch-reference languages, pivot NPs can agree in number; in some, the dominant NP can also be included in the dependent NP; and in a few, the dependent NP can be included in the dominant NP as well. Two exceptional languages that have been documented in the literature are Yankunytijatuara (Dench 1988) and Nasio (Longacre 1972).

A final point to note is that the selection of switch-reference markers may also be affected by the person features of the pivots. In the case of referential

---

[4] Notice that if there is no relation of referential inclusion between the two pivot NPs, then DS markers are likely to be used. Contrast the (a) and (b) sentence below.
(i) (Diyari, Austin 1981a: 316)
    (a) nhulu   nganthi   pardaka-rna warrayi, thanali   thayi-lha.
        he-ERG meat-ABS bring-PART AUX   they-ERG eat-SS
        'He brought the meat for them (him and others) to eat.'
    (b) nhulu   nganthi   pardaka-rna warrayi, thanali   thayi-rnanthu.
        he-ERG meat-ABS bring-PART AUX   they-ERG eat-DS
        'He brought the meat for them (others) to eat.'

inclusion in (ii) and (iii), one common pattern is that if the two pivots agree in person, either SS or DS may be used; otherwise, DS must be employed. This is the case in Kewa and a number of other switch-reference languages in Papua New Guinea (Franklin 1983). Another is that if the two pivots both bear first person, they tend to favour the use of SS marking (see Reesink 1983 and J. Roberts 1988*b* for illustration from Papua New Guinean languages, and Payne 1980 for illustration of a reverse pattern in Chickasaw). Somewhat similar to this is a pattern found for switch-reference marking of referential overlap in situation (iv) in Amele. In this language, either SS or DS markers can be used; but if the dominant pivot is first person, then SS markers must be used. All this is hardly surprising, for difference in person sometimes involves difference in number as well. Since difference in person and difference in number each represents a deviation from sameness, SS marking of pivots which differ in both person and number would be doubly deviate from sameness, and thus not allowed (e.g. Haiman and Munro 1983*a*, Stirling 1993).[5]

Grammatical functions

Switch-reference marking is normally applicable only to subjects. The notion of subject is defined here in its strict syntactic sense and excludes the semantic notion of agent and/or the pragmatic notion of topic. But such a characterization of the grammatical functions switch-reference pivots perform is too narrow and inadequate for the following two reasons: (i) switch-reference marking can be extended to NPs in grammatical functions other than subject, and (ii) switch-reference may involve constructions without subjects or with referentially deficient subjects.

Let us start with the first case first. Two well-documented languages in this respect are Capanahua, a Native American Indian language (Jacobsen 1967) and Warlpiri, an Australian aboriginal language (Simpson and Bresnan 1983, see also Austin 1981*a*). In Capanahua, there are six DS suffixes. Of these suffixes, two link the subject of the dependent clause with the object of its related independent clause, and one identifies the object of the dependent clause with the subject of its independent clause. Warlpiri contains four switch-reference markers. Out of these four markers, two are used to indicate that the subject of the dependent clause is the same as the subject of the independent clause. One SS-marks the subject of the dependent clause with

---

[5] The division of labour between SS and DS may be viewed as a matter of which of the two markers a language takes as the more basic. Languages like Pima take SS to be more basic. In that case, SS marks strict coreference. Consequently, in these languages, what is indicated by DS can then be reduced to what is left by SS marking. For languages like Lak, the reverse is true. In that case, DS signals strict disjoint reference. As a result, SS can, for example, be used to indicate referential inclusion (e.g. Franklin 1983, Comrie 1983, Longacre 1972, Austin 1981*a*, Langdon and Munro 1979, Stirling 1993: 34, 39).

the object of the independent clause, and one links the subject of the dependent clause with the oblique dative argument of the independent clause. This is shown in (5.17). Two other Australian languages, Warlmanpa—another Ngarrka language—and possibly Kaititj—an Arandic language—display a similar pattern.

(5.17) Warlpiri switch-reference markers (Simpson and Bresnan 1983, Sterling 1993)
karra: subject of the marked infinitival clause
       – subject of the independent clause
kurra: subject of the marked clause
       – object of the independent clause
rlajinta: subject of the marked clause
       – subject of the independent clause
rlarni: subject of the marked clause
       – oblique dative argument of the independent clause

Furthermore, in some languages, switch-reference markers may also be needed for marking topics. Barai belongs to this type of language, as the following examples show (Foley and Van Valin 1984: 352).

(5.18) (a) Fu   vua kuae-ga   siare   ije, fu   naebe ume.
           3SG   talk say-DT   betenut DEF   3SG NEG   chew
           'He₁ was talking and, as for betenut, he₁ did not chew it.'
      (b) Fu   vua kuae-ko-ga siare   ije, fu   naebe ume.
           3SG   talk say-DS-DT betenut DEF   3SG NEG   chew
           'He₁ was talking and, as for betenut, he₂ did not chew it.'
(5.19) (a) Ve   ije, fu barone-ko-gana bu   Sakarina ij-ia   va.
           time DEF   3SG die-DS-ST   3PL Sakarina DEF-LOC   go
           'At the time, he was dying and (at the same time) they were going to Sakarina.'
      (b) *Ve ije, fu barone-ko-gana muramura ije,
           time DEF   3SG die-DS-ST   medicine DEF
           bu   Sakarina ij-ia   va.
           3PL Sakarina DEF-LOC   go
           'At the time, he was dying and (at the same time) as for medicine, they were going to Sakarina.'

Examples (5.18) and (5.19) indicate that there are at least two sets of switch-reference marker in Barai: one set (Ø, *ko*) for marking subjects (pragmatic pivots in Foley and Van Valin's terminology), and one set (*gana*, *ga*) for marking topics (see also Olson 1978, 1981).

We move next to switch-reference constructions without subjects or with referentially deficient subjects. The first such construction involves the impersonal construction. While the dependent clause in principle can also be impersonal, as in (5.20), it is typically the independent clause that is impersonal, as in (5.21). Occasionally, both clauses can be impersonal, as in (5.22).

(5.20) (Amele, J. Roberts 1988*a*)
       Ija   co-cob-ig   ija wen-te-ce-b   sab j-ig-a.
       1SG   SIM-walk-1SG-SS   1SG hunger-1SG-DS-3SG   food eat-1SG-PAST
       'As I walked, I became hungry, and I ate.'

(5.21) (Usan, Reesink 1983)
Munon isig eng sarau aib eb-et migeri war-a ...
man old this work big do-SS exhaustion 3SG-U-hit-DS
'The old man₁ is working hard and the exhaustion will hit him₁, and ...'
(5.22) (Barai, Foley and Van Valin 1984: 348)
Na visinam-ie-na do ije ised-ie.
1SG sicken-1SG-SS water DEF displease-1SG
'(Something) sickens me and the water displeases me.'

Secondly, there are constructions with what Stirling (1993) calls referentially deficient subjects. Referentially deficient subjects are of many types, the most common of which includes inanimate subjects (such as inalienably possessed subjects and weather subjects), expletive subjects, and subjects of the passive construction. As with impersonal constructions, referentially deficient subjects usually occur in the independent clause. Some examples follow.

(5.23) Inalienably possessed subjects
(Imbabura Quechua, Stirling 1993: 74)
ñuka chagra-pi trabaja-shpa ñuka-ta uma-ta nana-wa-n-mi.
I field-in work-SS I-ACC head-ACC hurt-1SG-3-EVI
'When I work in the field, my head hurts.'
(5.24) Weather subjects
(Amele, J. Roberts 1987: 300)
Ija co-cob-ig wa hedo-i-a.
1SG SIM-walk-1SG-SS water finish-3SG-PAST
'As I walked along, the rain stopped.'
(5.25) Expletive subjects
(Imbabura Quechua, Cole 1983: 6)
ali-mi kan Juzi-wan parla-ngapaj.
good-EVI you Jusé-with speak-SS-SUBJ
'It is good that you speak with Jusé.'
(5.26) Passive subjects
(Imbabura Quechua, Cole 1983: 8–9)
wawa-ka mama mikuchiy tukushka-mi ama Ø kijari-ngapaj.
child-TOP mother fed became-EVI not complain-SS-SBJV
'The child₁ was fed by the mother₂ in order that (he₁) did not complain.'

Given this array of facts, the traditional view that switch-reference operates only with subjects is clearly inadequate. But this does not mean that cross-linguistically switch-reference applies to grammatical functions in a random fashion. In fact, there seems to be a clear pattern here: if switch-reference applies to, say, objects in a language, then it will apply to subjects as well in that language. This may lead to the setting up of another implicational universal (cf. (3.136) in Chapter 3).

(5.27) Grammatical function hierarchy for switch-reference
Surface structure: subject > object > others
Semantic roles: agent > experiencer > others

Clauses

Types of dependency

Two main types of syntactic dependency can be identified with regard to the two or more clauses to which switch-reference marking applies: (i) subordinate dependency, and (ii) coordinate dependency. In a relation of subordinate dependency, the marked, dependent clause is subordinate to the dominant, independent clause. The dependent clause can be an adverbial clause, as in (5.28), a complement clause, as in (5.29), a relative clause, as in (5.30), and a generalized subordinate clause which Austin (1981a) calls an adjoined clause, following Hale (1976), as in (5.31) (see e.g. Austin 1981a on the documentation of this type of subordinate structure in Diyari, Lardil, Ngiyambaa, Rembarrnga, Yir Yoront, and Warlpiri). Subordinate dependency is most prevalent in the switch-reference languages of North America (Jacobsen 1983) and Australia (Austin 1981).

(5.28) (Guanano, Longacre 1983: 202)
    (a) Tiro waha-ro tjuatasi.
        he when/if/since goes-3SS (he) won't=return
        'When/if/since he$_1$ goes, he$_1$ won't return.'
    (b) to waha-chu tina tjuatasi.
        this when/if/since going-DS they (he) won't=return
        'When/if/since he goes, they won't return.'

(5.29) (Lango, Foley and Van Valin 1983: 162)
    (a) Dákó ò-kób-ò ní ὲ-cám-ò rìŋó.
        woman 3SG-A-say-3SG-U that 3SG-A-(SS)-eat-3SG-U meat
        'The woman$_1$ said that she$_1$ ate meat.'
    (b) Dákó ò-kób-ò ní ò-cám-ò rìŋó.
        woman 3SG-A-say-3SG-U that 3SG-A-(DS)-eat-3SG-U meat
        'The woman$_1$ said that he/she$_2$ ate meat.'

(5.30) (Chickasaw, Munro 1983: 230)
    ihoo yamm-at ofi' pis-tokat illi-tok.
    woman that-SUBJ dog see-SBOR-PAST-SS die-PAST
    'The woman who saw the dog died.'

(5.31) (Diyari, Austin 1981: 313)
    punthapuntha mindi-yi, pangka-nhi widi-lha.
    mouse-ABS run-PRES bed-LOC enter-SS
    (a) 'The mouse runs to get in the bed.'
    (b) 'The mouse runs and gets in the bed.'
    (c) 'The mouse runs before getting in the bed.'

Secondly, in a relation of coordinate dependency, the marked, dependent clause stands in a loose coordination with the unmarked, independent clause. The relation of coordination may be that of clause-chaining, parataxis, or conjunction. Of particular interest here is clause-chaining—a construction that contains a string of clauses without conjunctions. In such a construction, the verb of every dependent clause except that of the last, independent clause is marked for switch-reference. The last verb of the clause chain is termed the final verb; non-final verbs are called medial verbs. To be noted further is that all the medial verbs are inflected with switch-reference morphemes but are not indicated for verbal inflections such as tense/aspect, mood, or agreement, therefore cannot stand on their own. By contrast, the final verb is not marked for switch-reference but is fully inflected for such categories, and this inflection is relevant to the whole clause chain. Switch-reference languages of Papua New Guinea make extensive use of this device. An example is given below.

(5.32) (Koita, Lynch 1983: 210)
    (*a*) daka oro-go-i   era-ga-nu.
        I   come-SG-SS see-SG-PAST
        'I came and saw (him).'
    (*b*) daka oro-go-nuge auki da era-ga-nu.
        I   come-SG-DS he me see-SG-PAST
        'I came and he saw (me).'

In each sentence above, two clauses are linked by clause-chaining without conjunctions. The first appears with a suffix which indicates switch-reference, SS in (5.32*a*) and DS in (5.32*b*).

Constituent order

In subordinate dependency, the dependent clause may precede or follow the independent clause, as in the Chickasaw example (5.33). Occasionally the dependent clause may be centre-embedded in the independent clause, as in the Maricopa example (5.34). But there does seem to exist a geographical diffusion: according to Haiman and Munro (1983*a*), most North American switch-reference languages tend to exhibit the first, cataphoric clausal constituent order; whereas most Australian switch-reference languages tend to have the second, anaphoric order (see also Austin 1981*a*).[6]

(5.33) (Chickasaw, Munro 1983: 232, 236)
    (*a*) aya-l-a'chi-kat ithaana-li.
        go-1SI-IRR-SS know-1SI
        'I know I am going.'
    (*b*) ithaana-li aya-l-a'chi-kat.
        know-1SI go-1SI-IRR-SS
        'I know I am going.'
(5.34) (Maricopa, Gordon 1983: 91)
    Bonnie-sh   nyaa '-ashvar-m iima-k.
    Bonnie-SUBJ I   1-sing-DS dance-ASP
    'Bonnie danced because I sang.'[7]

In coordinate dependency, however, the order of clausal constituency

---

[6] Clause types sometimes may also have a role to play. In Imbabura Quechua, for example, marked adverbial clauses of time precede, and marked adverbial clauses of purpose follow, their independent clauses (e.g. Cole 1983).

[7] Compare (5.34) with the following.

seems to be intimately related to that of affixation. Where the marker is a suffix on the verb, the dependent clause precedes the independent one, as in (5.35). In contrast, where the affix is a prefix, the dependent clause follows the independent clause. This can best be illustrated by a group of Austronesian languages of Southern Vanuatu including Anejom, Lenakel, Sie, and South-West Tanna (Lynch 1983). Examples from Lenakel and South-West Tanna are given in (5.36) and (5.37). This connection may simply reflect a typological correlation at a more basic level—one between the affixation order and the constituent order of a language, namely, suffixation tends to be characteristic of SOV languages, and prefixation tends to go with SVO languages. Given that the majority of switch-reference languages are verb-final languages, it is not surprising that the typical pattern of switch-reference marking is by suffixation on the verb and that the typical constituent order in coordinate dependency is dependent clause preceding independent one (Haiman and Munro 1983*a*).

(5.35) (Choctaw, Heath 1977)
    (*a*) Ø-Ø-pi:sa-ča:, Ø-iya-h.
        3A-3U-see-SS 3A-go-PRES
        'He$_1$ sees him$_2$ and he$_1$ goes.'
    (*b*) Ø-Ø-pi:sa-na:, Ø-iya-h.
        3A-3U-see-DS 3A-go-PRES
        'He$_1$ sees him$_2$ and he$_{2/3}$ goes.'
(5.36) (Lenakel, Lynch 1983: 212)
    (*a*) r-im-va   (kani) m-im-augin.
        3SG-PAST-come (and) SS-PAST-eat
        'He$_1$ came and (he$_1$) ate.'
    (*b*) r-im-va   (kani) r-im-augin.
        3SG-PAST-come (and) 3SG-PAST-eat
        'He$_1$ came and (he$_2$) ate.'
(5.37) (South-West Tanna, Lynch 1983: 217)
    (*a*) natou l-imn-aam   misak m-epi-aiu.
        Natou 3SG-PAST-see Misak SS-SEQ-run
        'Natou saw Misak and ran away.'
    (*b*) natou l-imn-aam   misak l-epi-aiu.
        Natou 3SG-PAST-see Misak 3SG-SEQ-run
        'Natou$_1$ saw Misak$_2$ and he$_2$ ran away.'

(i) (Gordon 1983: 91)
    nyaa '-ashvar-m Bonnie-sh   iima-k.
    I   sing-DS   Bonnie-SUBJ dance-ASP
    (*a*) 'I sang and Bonnie danced.'
    (*b*) 'I sang and then Bonnie danced.'
    (*c*) 'Bonnie danced because I sang.'

  The interesting point is that while (i) has a range of interpretations, (5.34) has only the causal interpretation as indicated. In other words, the centre-embedding of the marked, dependent clause has the semantic effect of forcing a causal interpretation (see Gordon 1983 for further discussion).

Linear adjacency and clause-skipping

In general, the dependent and independent clauses are linearly adjacent to each other. But in many switch-reference languages, this locality condition can readily be violated by clause-skipping—the insertion of one or more intervening clauses between the dependent and independent clauses.

(5.38) (Harway, Comrie 1989*b*)
An ap   mag wr-ön,   yön-aŋ,   nm-n-ŋ-a.
we food   heat-SS cook-CNJ-SG eat-FUT-1PL-DECL
'We will heat the food and, when it is cooked, we will eat it.'

Clause-skipping can roughly be divided into two types, which coincide with the two types of switch-reference marking identified by Oswalt (1983): (i) sequential, and (ii) focal. In sequential marking, an SS/DS maker indicates switch-reference relation with regard to its adjacent clause, whereas in focal marking, an SS/DS marker signals switch-reference relation with respect not to its adjacent clause but to a focal one, usually the final, independent clause. Clause-skipping in the first involves a symmetry of the first and second marked clauses both of which look forward to the same independent clause, as in (5.38) above and (5.39) below; clause-skipping in the second involves subordination to a second dependent clause which is shifted off the grammatical level at which the first and third clauses are joined (Stirling 1993: 23), as in (5.40) (see also Wiesemann 1986*a* on Supyire). From a functional point of view, clause skipping seems to be motivated by facilitating information flow in a discourse, especially in terms of foreground versus background information.

(5.39) (Gahuku, Wiesemann 1986*a*: 454)
nagamiq zeu-ke,   golini zeka-go,   numukuq minuve.
water   after-I-hit-SS rain after-it-hit-DS house-in I-stayed
'After I washed it, after/because it rained, I stayed in a house.'

(5.40) (Kashaya, Oswalt 1983: 280)
mulido mens'in tubic-i·d-em,   hóhwa=tolhqʰaʔ.
QUOT and   get up-DUR-D1   door=toward
mo-qá-·d-em,   ʔul   dace-cí·d-un, pʰala=qan ʔyowal=li
run-out-DUR-D1 then grab-DUR-C1 again=wise former=place
cahcí-hqa-me·d-u.
sit down-CAUS-DUR-ABS
'And, they say, whenever she$_1$ got up and ran out toward the door, he would then grab her$_1$ and make her$_1$ sit back down in the same place.'

Finally, it should be noted that there is no language in the world that has been attested in which switch-reference is exclusively marked between non-adjacent clauses. This gives rise to another implicational universal, namely, if a language has switch-reference between non-adjacent clauses, it will also mark switch-reference between adjacent clauses.

(5.41) Locality hierarchy for switch-reference
Adjacent clauses > non-adjacent clauses

Secondary functions of switch-reference

As mentioned earlier, the primary function of switch-reference is to minimize referential ambiguity in an ongoing discourse. In many languages, however, there are functional extensions of switch-reference. These so-called 'secondary nuances of meaning' (Jacobsen 1967) sometimes may even override the primary function of switch-reference. For example, on the one hand, SS markers can be used even though there is an actual switch of subject. Imbabura Quechua, Kiowa, and Yavapai are examples of a language of this type. In a passive sentence in Imbabura Quechua, for example, when the subject of the matrix clause is a third-person patient and the subject of the subordinate clause is first-person, second-person, or arbitrary in reference, the SS suffix *-ngapaj* rather than the DS suffix *-chun* is actually used (Cole 1983). Next, in the Lenakel example (5.42) below, the obligatory compatibility of number between the subject of the second clause and the object of the preceding clause allows the use of the SS marker even if the two subjects are not coreferential. On the other hand, the use of DS markers to register the same subject has been reported for Choctaw, Northern Pomo, and Yuma. In this usage, the function of switch-reference becomes non-referential. It is used, for example, to signal a discontinuity of some kind in some other aspects of the events described. These may include whether or not the events differ in time, space, or agentivity (J. Roberts 1988*a*). This is the case with Amele. In this language, a change of place and/or time warrants the use of a DS marker even if the subjects in question remain the same. This is illustrated in (5.43).

(5.42) (Lenakel, Lynch 1983: 215)
 magau r-ɨm-ho tom mɨne siak kani m-u-akɨmw.
 Magau 3SG-PAST-hit Tom and Siak and SS-DU-run away
 'Magau hit Tom and Siak and they ran away.'

(5.43) (Amele, Stirling 1993: 216)
 Age ceta gul-do-co-bil l-i bahim na tac-ein.
 3PL yam carry-3SG-DS-3PL go-PRED floor on fill-3PL-PAST
 'They carried the yams on their shoulders and went and filled up the yam store.'

But typically the secondary functions of the switch-reference system are in addition to its primary function and are related to the encoding of some non-referential meanings. Of these non-referential meanings, most commonly involved are the temporal, logical, and epistemic relations between the events described, involving notions of simultaneity, sequence, expectation, causality, condition, and contrast (see e.g. Longacre's 1983 discussion about a group of Papua New Guinean languages including Ek-Nii, Kanite, and Kâte, and

Oswalt's 1983: 272–4 discussion about Kashaya). The Barai examples below illustrate this point.

(5.44) (Barai, Foley and Van Valin 1984: 341–2)
    (a) Bu ire i-kinu vua kuae.
        3PL food eat-SIM/SS talk say
        'They were eating and talking.'
    (b) Bu ire i-ko no vua kuae.
        3PL food eat-SIM/DS 1PL talk say
        'While they were eating, we were talking.'

(5.45) (Barai, Foley and Van Valin 1984: 342)
    (a) Fu juare me-na fae kira.
        3SG garden make-SEQ/SS fence tie
        'He made a garden and then tied a fence.'
    (b) Fu juare me-mo fu fae kira.
        3SG garden make-SEQ/DS 3SG fence tie
        'He$_1$ made a garden and then he$_2$ tied a fence.'

Occasionally, both SS and DS markings can be used for the same construction, but the choice of one over the other frequently effects a change in meaning. In the Amele impersonal construction (5.46), for example, the use of the DS marker in the (b) sentence gives rise to the additional meaning of causality (e.g. J. Roberts 1988a, Stirling 1993: 89–90, 421; see also Stirling's 1993: 87 discussion about the correlation between SS/DS and agentive/non-agentive in Amele). Another case of interest comes from the Barai example (5.47). The use of the SS marker in the (a) sentence indicates that the subject/actor of the marked clause is indefinite. Being indefinite, the subject/actor is outranked by the object/undergoer as the pivot. Consequently, the object/undergoer is elevated to the pivot status and occupies the sentence-initial position. This pivot and the pivot of the second clause are coreferential and hence the use of SS (Foley and Van Valin 1984).[8]

(5.46) (Amele, Stirling 1993: 241)
    (a) Ija co-cob-ig cucui-te-i-a.
        1SG SIM-walk-1SG-SS fear-1SG-3SG-PAST
        'As I walked I was afraid.'

---

[8] Both SS and DS can be used in certain constructions in Maricopa, as is indicated by the following example. However, it is not clear whether there is a semantic difference in the choice of one over the other.
(i) (Maricopa, Gordon 1983: 99)
    (a) nyaa ny-wik-k man-sh 'nym-wik-k nyi-'-wish-k.
        I 1/2-help-SS you-SUBJ 2/1-help-SS nyi-1-do+DU-ASP
        'I helped you and you helped me.'
    (b) nyaa ny-wik-m man-sh 'nym-wik-k nyi-'-wish-k.
        I 1/2-help-DS you-SUBJ 2/1-help-SS nyi-1-do+DU-ASP
        'I helped you and you helped me.'
Another case in point concerns the impersonal passive construction in Tolkapaya Yavapai, as reported in Langdon and Munro (1979) and cited in Stirling (1993: 95–6).

  (b) Ija co-cob-igin   cucui-te-i-a.
    1SG SIM-walk-1SG-DS fear–1SG-3SG-PAST
    'As I walked, something made me afraid.'
(5.47) (Barai, Foley and Van Valin 1984: 350)
  (a) Fu miane sak-i-na barone.
    3SG firestick bite-3SG-SS die
    'A firestick bit him₁ and he₁ died.'
  (b) Miane ije fu sak-i-mo fu barone.
    firestick DEF 3SG bite-3SG-DS 3SG die
    'The firestick bit him₁ and he₂ died.'

5.1.2. Switch-reference and related phenomena

In the last section, I surveyed the phenomenology of switch-reference. In this section, I shall first make a comparison between switch-reference and other reference-tracking systems, and then compare and contrast switch-reference and logophoricity.

Switch-reference and gender/class

Two main differences may be identified between switch-reference and gender/class. First, gender/class is in essence an inherent system, that is, the tracking of reference is dependent on the inherent features of the NPs in question irrespective of the syntactic or semantic functions they perform. By contrast, switch-reference is basically an assigned system, in that it operates on NPs of a particular syntactic (i.e. subject) or semantic (i.e. agent) type; not owing to their inherent lexical features they are assigned syntactically or semantically. The second difference is that between local and global reference-tracking devices and is somewhat related to the first difference. While switch-reference is normally restricted locally to two or more structurally linked clauses, gender/class can operate across structurally unrelated clauses globally through the whole of a discourse. This global characteristic of gender/class is closely tied to the characteristic of lexical inheritance. Since the feature values are not assigned but inherent, on the one hand, they cannot be changed during the course of a discourse, on the other, they are free from the restrictions imposed by syntax and semantics (see e.g. Foley and Van Valin 1984: 333, 363, and Comrie 1989b for further discussion). Thus, switch-reference is more structural in nature than gender/class.

 Also worth noting is the reverse relation between switch-reference and gender/class pointed out by Jacobsen (1967) and Heath (1975), and discussed further by Foley and Van Valin (1983: 361–2), namely, the two reference-tracking systems tend to be mutually exclusive in a language. In other words, languages with rich gender/class tend to lack switch-reference; languages with mature switch-reference are likely to lack gender/class. This is amply evidenced by both North American languages (such as Sierra Miwok and

Tanoan) and Papuan New Guinean languages (such as Kewa and Yimas). In the latter type of language, for example, Yimas is a language that contains a rich gender system and as predicted by the hypothesis, switch-reference is absent in that language. In contrast, Kewa (Franklin 1983) and Fore (Scott 1978) have a developed switch-reference system, and lack gender distinctions for nouns, as would be expected. However, the Bantu languages seem to present a challenge to this hypothesis; they are well known to be languages with elaborated gender/class, yet as reported in Wiesemann (1982), they also sanction switch-reference.

Finally, comparison should also be made between switch-reference and obviation on the one hand, and between gender/class and obviation on the other. Obviation is like gender/class in that it is a global phenomenon, but differs from gender/class in that it is an assigned system. On the other hand, obviation is like switch-reference in that it is an assigned system, but differs from it in that it is a global system. This dual status of obviation has led Foley and Van Valin (1984: 339) to take it as 'an interesting transition point between gender systems and . . . switch-reference system[s]'.

Switch-reference and switch-function

In comparing switch-reference and switch-function, the main similarities are that both are assigned and local. The main difference, however, is that whereas, in switch-reference, what is monitored is a particular syntactic or semantic function and what is signalled is a same or different participant carrying out that function, in switch-function, what is monitored is a participant and what is signalled is a same or different semantic function (see e.g. Comrie 1989*b*). Another difference is that unlike gender/class or switch-reference, the occurrence of switch-function in a language is typically correlated with the existence of voice oppositions in that language.

Note next that in the tracking of referents of NPs in a discourse, most languages resort to more than one system, each compensating for the weaknesses in the other. English, Alamblak, and Yimas are good cases in point. English utilizes both gender/class and switch-function. Alamblak is a language that employs both an unelaborated gender/class system and an undeveloped switch-reference system. The gender/class system used in Yimas is supplemented by an obviation system (see e.g. Foley and Van Valin 1984). A final point of interest is that in most languages, when these lexical and grammatical mechanisms fail to track down the actual referent, pragmatic inference is frequently called in to complete the job.

Switch-reference and logophoricity

Next, let us briefly compare and contrast switch-reference and logophoricity. From a functional point of view, switch-reference is like logophoricity in that it is essentially a device for referential tracking. Structurally, they also share a number of formal properties. In particular, they all imply the same person and grammatical function categories, though they behave slightly differently in terms of number, as we have seen.

There are, however, important differences between switch-reference and logophoricity. In the first place, in switch-reference, the marking is on the verb, but in logophoricity, the marking is on the NP. (A principled exception is, of course, logophoric verbal affixes.) Secondly, in switch-reference, the indication of coreferentiality is unmarked, but in logophoricity, the indication of it is marked. Thirdly and more importantly, switch-reference can in principle apply to predicates of any kind. By contrast, logophoricity is restricted to a set of semantically distinguishable logocentric predicates. In other words, the domain of switch-reference is much wider than that of logophoricity (see Stirling 1993 for further discussion).

Given that switch-reference and logophoricity have different functional applications, it is not surprising to find languages with both systems. Such languages include the Bantu languages Aghem, Bafut, and Noni (Wiesemann 1982), the Caucasian languages Chechen and Ingush (Nichols 1983), and the American language Northern Pomo (O'Connor 1992*a*).

5.1.3. Two general approaches and beyond: syntactically oriented versus semantically oriented, and perhaps pragmatically oriented

There are two main approaches to switch-reference: (i) syntactically oriented, and (ii) semantically oriented. Underlying the syntactic approach is the view that switch-reference is essentially an intrasentential syntactic device to be accounted for by rules of UG such as Chomsky's binding conditions. This approach is best represented by Finer (1985*a*, 1985*b*) (see also Broadwell 1990, 1998 and Hale 1992 within the framework of the principles-and-parameters theory, and Simpson and Bresnan 1983 within the framework of LFG)[9].

Basing his analysis on a subset of switch-reference systems from American Indian languages (especially of the Hokan stock) and Australian languages, Finer (1985*a*, 1985*b*) claims that switch-reference is primarily a syntactic relation subject to binding theory in much the same way as anaphors and pronominals. In particular, he treats switch-reference as an instance of

---

[9] Broadwell's (1990, 1998) analysis is to some extent technically different (for example, he treats DS as a disjoint anaphor in the sense of Saxon's (1984) description of the Athapaskan language Dogrib) but conceptually identical to Finer's analysis. This being the case, what will be said in the next paragraph will undermine the case for Broadwell's analysis as much as it does the case for Finer's analysis.

Ā-binding in the sense of Aoun (1985, 1986). On this generalized binding analysis, the clause marked for SS/DS is assumed to be embedded within its matrix clause. SS/DS is postulated as an abstract operator that is generated in Comp and forms a discontinuous constituent with Infl/Agr. The GC is the matrix clause, the superordinate S̄, and the binding is between Ā-positions, with SS treated as an Ā-anaphor that must be bound by an Ā-binder in its GC, that is, by the Comp of the matrix clause; DS as an Ā-pronominal that must be free of this same Ā-binder in its GC. Next, by a rule of transitivity of indexing relation, SS/DS percolates from Comp through Infl/Arg to the subject NPs of the two hierarchically adjacent clauses and signals obligatory coreference or non-coreference between them.

As promising as Finer's analysis is, there are a number of problems attached to it. First, as pointed out by J. Roberts (1988a), a key assumption of Finer's account is that switch-reference is primarily a property of the syntactic relation between subordination and superordination. While this may be the case for Native American switch-reference languages (e.g. Jacobsen 1983) and perhaps for Australian switch-reference languages (e.g. Austin 1981a) on which Finer has focused, this does not hold for Papuan switch-reference languages. As we noted earlier (cf. Section 5.1.1.), coordinate dependency is most characteristic in Papuan switch-reference languages, and yet this is beyond the scope of Finer's analysis. Secondly, Finer's analysis predicts that SS/DS is determined strictly locally. This follows from the locality condition imposed on binding. Although this prediction is borne out in the majority cases of switch-reference, as can be seen from (5.48), which was cited by Finer (1985b) as crucial supporting evidence for the locality condition, it is falsified in the face of the existence of clause-skipping in many switch-reference languages including Gahuku, Harway, and Kashaya, as we have already seen.

(5.48) (Yavapai, Kendall 1976)
    (a) m-čirav-k   k^{w}e-qalye-m m-tismač-m m-sal-ñu ʔ-k^{w}iθkiñ.
       2-be sick-SS thing-bad-M 2-dream-DS 2-hand   1-hold
       'When you were sick and dreaming of bad things I held your hands.'
    (b) m-čirav-k   k^{w}e-qalye-m m-tismač-k ʔ-sal   n-k^{w}iθkiñ.
       2-be sick-SS thing-bad-M 2-dream-SS 1-hand 2-hold
       'When you were sick and dreaming of bad things you held my hands.'

A third problem for the generalized binding analysis is posed by the fact that in some languages, switch-reference can track reference between NPs other than subjects—a contradiction to Finer's assumption that switch-reference is a syntactic relation that holds between subject NPs only. It will be recalled (cf. 5.1.1.) that three languages are well known in this respect; Capanahua, Warlpiri, and Barai. Another language in point might be Cashinahua, which utilizes different sets of switch-reference markers to indicate SS/DS between subjects themselves and between subjects and objects

(Broadwell 1990) Furthermore, as also mentioned earlier in Section 5.1.1, switch-reference may involve constructions without subjects or with referentially deficient subjects. All these cases of switch-reference will remain unaccounted for under Finer's 'subjects only' analysis. Finally, it is unclear how Finer's analysis will accommodate switch-reference which involves a relation of referential inclusion or overlap. Moreover, the generalized binding account will have nothing to say about so-called secondary functions of switch-reference. But as pointed out by Stirling (1993), these secondary functions are systematic and regular, and should be accounted for by any adequate theory of switch-reference.

In contrast to the generative, syntactic approach, a semantic approach to switch-reference appeals to notions like argumenthood, agency, and eventuality. One such analysis is put forward by Stirling (1993). Stirling's account is formulated within the framework of Unification Categorial Grammar, which associates a syntax based on categorical grammar and a semantics based on Discourse Representation Theory. The underlying idea of Stirling's analysis is that switch-reference is in essence about agreement or non-agreement of indices for eventualities (including both events and states) rather than just about agreement or non-agreement of indices for individuals within those eventualities (see also Tsujimura 1987). Consequently, any adequate theory of switch-reference must provide a unified account of the full range of functions of switch-reference including those secondary functions. To achieve this end, Stirling proposes that each clause be associated with a structured eventuality index, which contains three parameters. The notion of structured eventuality index is formalized as follows:

(5.49) Stirling's notion of structured eventuality index
Let an eventuality index be a triple <Id, Aspect, Parameters>, where:
(i) Id is a uniquely identifying integer 1, 2, 3, . . ., n;
(ii) Aspect is a sorted eventuality variable, chosen from e for an event, s for a state, a for an aspectually unspecified eventuality, and perhaps others, and
(iii) Parameter is a parameter list <Protagonist, Actuality, Location>.
Protagonist is an individual discourse marker chosen from the set $\{x_1, x_2, x_3, \ldots, x_n\}$;
Actuality is a value in the set {actual, non-actual}; and
Location is a sorted discourse marker chosen from the set $\{l_1, l_2, l_3, \ldots, l_n\}$.

The use of SS, then, indicates that the dependent and independent clauses agree in all three eventuality parameters; by contrast, the employment of DS signals non-agreement in at least one parameter, and possibly in others. A second important point made by Stirling is that agency rather than subjecthood should constitute the most important criterion in defining switch-reference pivot NPs.

A Stirling-style analysis has both conceptual and empirical advantages over a Finer-style analysis. Conceptually, the mystery why switch-reference constitutes an instance of categorical iconicity violation, that is, why reference-tracking is marked on the verb rather than on the noun itself, is immediately explained. This is because (i) switch-reference languages tend to be event- rather than object-dominated, or head- rather than dependent-marking, languages (and they also tend to be pro-drop or zero anaphor languages), and (ii) switch-reference marking is essentially a marking of the semantic properties of the clause. It is therefore quite natural that SS/DS will morphologically be indicated on the head of the clause, i.e. the verb. Once this is in place, then it is not difficult to understand why switch-reference markers frequently can have those meanings and functions that are related to the verb (Stirling 1993: 11–13). Next, from an empirical point of view, a Stirling-style analysis is also preferable to a Finer-style analysis. Since it does not depend on configurational notions such as c-command, government, and Ā-binding, it can accommodate both subordinate and coordinate dependencies; it can select switch-reference pivots both locally and non-locally; and it can accommodate switch-reference pivots in grammatical functions other than subject.[10] Furthermore, a Stirling-style analysis can also give an account of the secondary functions of switch-reference. For example, given (5.49), together with an eventuality disagreement mechanism (5.50), which basically says that if DS is used, the default is a switch in Protagonist, but switches in Actuality and/or Location (in that order of priority) are also possible, the full range of the functions of switch-reference including non-referential functions in Eastern Pomo, Lenakel, and Amele, as summarized in (5.51) by Stirling (1993: 152), can now be accommodated.

(5.50) Eventuality disagreement mechanism
    (*a*) Protagonist (a$_1$) $\not\subset$ Protagonist (a$_2$),
    (*b*) $\vee$ Actuality (a$_1$) ≠ Actuality (a$_2$),
    (*c*) $\vee$ Location (a$_1$) ≠ Location (a$_2$).
(5.51) Use of switch-reference markers in Eastern Pomo, Lenakel, and Amele
    (*a*) Eastern Pomo
        If agentivity changes, use DS;
        otherwise, if reference changes, use DS;
        otherwise (i.e. if agentivity and reference stay the same), use SS.
    (*b*) Lenakel
        If tense changes, use DS;
        otherwise, if reference changes, use DS;
        otherwise, if tense and reference stay the same, use SS.
    (*c*) Amele
        If time, place, event sequence, mood changes, use DS;
        otherwise, if reference changes, use DS;
        otherwise, use SS.

---

[10] But it is unclear how Stirling's analysis can handle switch-reference involving object NPs. For a possible solution, see Tsujimura's (1987) account which is largely based on a study of Hopi, Tairora, and Warlpiri.

Before leaving this section, let us consider briefly the question whether or not some aspects of switch-reference can partially be reduced to the neo-Gricean pragmatic theory of anaphora being advanced in this book. The precise answer to this question is yet to be formulated, but my speculation is that a partial neo-Gricean pragmatic analysis is not entirely implausible. Such an account might operate roughly along the following lines, inspired by O'Connor's (1992a, 1993) work on Northern Pomo. Given the grammar of a switch-reference language, any speaker who intends a continuity of eventuality including reference will use SS, otherwise he or she will be in violation of the Gricean principles of cooperative communication. If on the other hand, a SS is not employed but a DS is used instead, then a Q-implicature is generated, namely, the continuity of (some aspects of) eventuality cannot be maintained. In such cases, further inferences based on the I-principle are needed. The default or preferred I-interpretation is that there is a switch in reference. If this is not the case, then the use of DS is likely to reflect a change in some other eventuality parameter such as time, place, and/or world. This seems to be the interpretative strategy which is actually at work in Eastern Pomo, Lenakel, and Amele, as mentioned above.

(5.52) Interpretation of switch-reference markers in Eastern Pomo, Lenakel, and Amele
 (*a*) Eastern Pomo
    If SS is used, then you know reference and agentivity are the same;
    if DS is used, the default is that just reference has changed;
    if DS is used and reference has not changed, agentivity has changed.
 (*b*) Lenakel
    If SS is used, assume tense and reference are the same;
    if DS is used, check whether reference is the same or not;
    if reference is the same, assume just tense has changed.
 (*c*) Amele
    If SS is used, assume same reference, and general continuity of event;
    if DS is used, assume disjoint reference;
    if this doesn't work, assume some other change.

Alternatively, SS/DS can also be accounted for in terms of the systematic interaction between the I- and M-principles. Since the grammar allows the unmarked SS to be used to encode (some aspects of) continuity of eventualities including reference, the speaker will use SS if such an interpretation is intended. On the other hand, if unmarked SS is not employed but marked DS (cf. Section 5.1.1.) is used instead, then an M-implicature is created, namely some discontinuity of eventualities is intended. Furthermore, given our pragmatic theory, it is also predicted that some extra, special techniques tend to be employed by the speaker to pinpoint the exact type of change in the eventuality parameter if it is not a change in default reference. This prediction seems to be largely borne out. For example, in Amele, as pointed out by

J. Roberts (1988a), a change of time indicated by DS is frequently backed up by the use of a temporal expression; a change of place/location marked by DS tends to co-occur with predicates of motion or a locative expression; a change of world indicated by DS is frequently a switch from intended or proposed action to real action or vice versa.

5.1.4. Summary

In this section, I have first discussed the phenomenon of switch-reference. I have then compared and contrasted switch-reference and other reference-tracking systems, and switch-reference and logophoricity. Next, I have provided a critical overview of both a syntactic and a semantic approach. Finally, I have outlined a neo-Gricean pragmatic analysis.

5.2. Discourse anaphora

In the last section, I concentrated on switch-reference, a reference-tracking system that lies in between pure intrasentential anaphora and pure discourse anaphora. In this section, I shall turn my attention to discourse anaphora.

5.2.1. The problem of anaphoric distribution in discourse

One of the central issues in the study of discourse anaphora is concerned with what might be called the problem of anaphoric distribution in discourse, namely, how to account for the choice of a particular referential/anaphoric form at a particular point in discourse. For any entity to which reference is to be made in discourse, there is a (potentially large) set of possible anaphoric expressions each of which, by a correspondence test, is 'correct' and therefore could in principle be used to designate that entity. On any actual occasion of use, however, it is not the case that just any member of that set is 'right'. Therefore, an 'appropriate' anaphoric form from that set has to be selected from time to time during the dynamic course of discourse production. The problem of anaphoric distribution in discourse then boils down to this: on the one hand, from the perspective of anaphoric production, what contributes to the speaker's choice of an appropriate anaphoric form? And on the other, from the vantage point of anaphoric resolution, what enables the addressee to identify the intended referent of that form at a given point in discourse (e.g. Sacks and Schegloff 1979, Fornel 1987, Huang 1989, 1994, 2000, Gundel, Hedberg, and Zacharski 1993)?

Needless to say, anaphoric distribution in discourse is a very complex phenomenon, involving, among other things, structural, cognitive, and pragmatic factors that interact with each other. Nevertheless, currently three main approaches to discourse anaphora can be identified. Simplifying somewhat, anaphoric distribution in discourse is claimed to be determined essentially by the continuity of topic on the first account (to be called the topic continuity model), by the hierarchical structure of discourse on the second (to be termed the hierarchy model), and by cognitive factors such as memory and attention on the third (to be dubbed the cognitive model).

In what follows, I shall first review the three accounts of discourse anaphora noted above (Sections 2.2.2, 2.2.3, and 2.2.4.). In light of the inadequacies of these analyses and given the fact that the pragmatic factor has for some time been a much neglected area here, I shall then develop a neo-Gricean pragmatic approach to discourse anaphora (Section 2.2.5.), which will be complementary to the three extant models. The basic idea underlying the neo-Gricean pragmatic model is that anaphoric distribution in discourse can largely be determined by the systematic interaction of our Q-, M-, and I-principles. I shall demonstrate that by utilizing these principles and the resolution mechanism organizing their interaction, many patterns of discourse anaphora can be given a better explanation. Furthermore, extending the analysis made in Huang (1987, 1989, 1994, 2000) and drawing in part on work by Geluykens (1994), a careful consideration of anaphoric repair systems in conversational discourse shows that the neo-Gricean pragmatic approach developed here is consistent with what interlocutors in conversational discourse are actually oriented to.

5.2.2. The topic continuity or distance-interference model

I shall begin with the topic continuity or distance-interference model, topic being used roughly in the sense of what is being talked about in discourse. This approach is best represented by Givón (1983, 1985, 1990). The main premise of this model is that anaphoric encoding in discourse is essentially determined by topic continuity. The continuity of topic in discourse is measured primarily by factors such as linear distance (the number of clause/sentence between the two mentions of a referent), referential interference (the number of interfering referents), and thematic information (maintenance or change of protagonists). Roughly, what the model predicts is this: the shorter the linear distance, the fewer the competing referents, and the more stable the thematic status of the protagonists, the more continuous a topic; the more continuous a topic, the more likely that it will be encoded in terms of a reduced anaphoric expression. Thus, on this account, different types of anaphoric expression may just be hierarchically reordered as topic-coding devices (e.g. Givón 1983, 1985).

(5.53) Givón's topic-coding devices scale

Most continuous/accessible topic

⬆
zero anaphora

unstressed/bound pronouns or grammatical agreement

stressed/independent pronouns

R-dislocated DEF-NPs

neutral-ordered DEF-NPs

L-dislocated DEF-NPs

Y-moved NPs ('contrastive topicalization')

cleft/focus construction

referential indefinite NPs
⬇

Most discontinuous/inaccessible topic

There is compelling cross-linguistic evidence in support of the topic continuity or distance-interference model. Studies on languages as typologically distinct and structurally diverse as Amharic, Chamorro, spoken and written English, Hausa, Biblical Hebrew, Japanese, spoken Latin-American Spanish, and Ute, originally carried out by Givón and his associates (Givón 1983), show quite convincingly that there is indeed a correlation between topicality and anaphoric encoding in both narrative and conversational discourse. This finding is further corroborated by other independent researches on some East Asian languages. Clancy (1980), for example, has done a comparative study of discourse anaphora in English and Japanese, as represented in *The Pear Stories* (Chafe 1980). She finds that in both languages, when referential distance is short and there is no interfering referent, hence topicality is high, a reduced anaphoric expression is typically used. The same is true of Chinese. Li and Thompson (1979), for instance, point out that the most frequently occurring type of zero anaphora in Chinese discourse is the 'topic chain', where the topic established in the first clause serves as the referent for the unrealized topics in the chain of clauses following it (see also Huang 1989, 1994). Chen (1986) also reports that referents that register high topic continuity in Chinese discourse tend to be encoded by zero anaphors or pronouns. Next, as Tai (1978) observes, when there are two or more referents in a Chinese narrative discourse, it is often the case that a reduced anaphoric form coincides with the topic referent whereas a non- or less-reduced anaphoric form coincides with the non-topic referent. Furthermore, there is also evidence from Chinese narrative discourse to support recency of last mention and existence of interfering referents as the two major factors affecting continuity of topic. Chen (1986) observes that a zero anaphor or pronoun tends to be used to encode a referent with a short distance to its previous mention. Similar results are obtained for the effects of interference. A zero anaphor tends to be selected when there is no interfering referent; a lexical NP tends to be chosen when there is such a referent. Finally, still another piece of evidence for the correlation between topic continuity and anaphoric choice comes from Modern Hebrew. As has been shown by Ariel (1994), in this language, pronouns are predominantly utilized in cases of short distance; demonstratives tend to favour intermediate distance; and lexical NPs are typically employed when the distance is long (see also Du Bois 1987 on Sacapultac, Holisky 1987 on Tsova-Tush, and Durie 1994 on Acehness from a slightly different, Silversteinian point of view).

Also worth noting is that the topic referent is frequently the protagonist, or main character, in a narrative or conversation. The topic protagonist has a number of general characteristics: (i) it is usually agentive or intimately involved in causing the events that constitute the story's actions, (ii) it is higher in animacy than any competing character, (iii) it usually has a primary function in the story in terms of reaching a goal, (iv) it almost always gets named if any characters do, (v) it is referred to more frequently than any other character, and (vi) it occurs in more than one scene and across more than one setting; it is usually introduced in the initial stage of a narrative (McGann and Schwartz 1988). There has been some general consensus in the literature that the protagonist enjoys a special thematic status in a narrative or conversation, thus frequently receiving a minimal anaphoric encoding after initial introduction (e.g. Clancy 1980, Givón 1990: 907–8, Cumming 1995 on Sejarah Melayu, Kibrik 1996; see also Pu 1995 for experimental evidence). Indeed, there are even languages which have a special way to mark the topic character when it is not placed in the canonical, subject position of a sentence. Salishan languages, for example, are of this type. According to Kinkade (1990), at least six or seven out of the twenty-three Salishan languages utilize a special affix to indicate what he calls third-person topic objects. The languages where such an affix has been located are Columbian (Interior Salish), Lushootseed (Central Salish), Cowlitz, Upper Chehalis, Quinault (Tsanosan). Tillamook, and perhaps Lower Chehalis. Following is an example from Upper Chehalis (Kinkade 1990).

(5.54) K^{w}áx^w-mis-n.
arrive-TR-3S-U
λ'áq'-w-n
go out-IMPF-3-U

c   s-ṭánay,
F-IND S-woman
wí   ʔit láx̣ʷ-st-walí.
and PF laugh-CAUS-TOP
'He arrives. A woman goes out, and she laughs at him.'

In (5.54) the subject of the first sentence is the ongoing topic. A new subject is introduced in the second sentence and remains subject of the third sentence. The use of the topic object suffix in the third sentence makes it clear that the referent of the subject in the first sentence is the one that was laughed at. Thus, the primary function of the topic object as opposed to the non-topic (often zero-marked) object in Upper Chehalis is to minimize referential ambiguity in a discourse where there is more than one third-person referent present and the one that assumes topic role has been switched into an object position. In those special circumstances, a special affix is needed to maintain the topicality of the original topic. Other languages with similar devices to mark topic object include Wichita (Rood 1976), Pawnee (Caddoan) (Parks 1976), Tlingit, and some Athapaskan languages such as Navajo and Schaptin (Kinkade 1990).

Next, interestingly enough, in some languages, the centrality, or thematic prominence, of a topic participant may override distance-interference as the main measurement of the continuity of topic in discourse, and subsequently becomes the main determinant of the choice of one type of anaphoric expression over the other. This seems to be the case of To'aba'ita, an Oceanic Austronesian language spoken in the Solomon Islands. To'aba'ita has four basic anaphoric devices: (i) lexical NPs including the proximal deictic *'evi* and the distal deictic *baa*, (ii) independent pronouns, (iii) dependent pronominals including subject/tense markers, object suffixes, and possessive suffixes, and (iv) zero anaphors. Crucial for our current interest, however, is the finding made by Lichtenberk (1996) that in a To'aba'ita narrative, when a newly introduced entity is referred to again in the next clause, both lexical NPs and dependent pronominals can be used to encode it (see also Lichtenberk's (1988) earlier observation that lexical NPs and independent pronouns are the equally common encoding strategies over short distances). But the selection of one type of anaphoric device over the other in this situation is essentially affected by the thematical status of the referents: lexical NPs are accorded to referents that are thematically prominent, and dependent pronominals, to referents that are thematically non-prominent. Another case in point can be found in the North American Indian language Kiowa (Watkins 1990). In Kiowa narratives, while the distribution of anaphoric expressions in 'one-protagonist' stories conforms to the pattern predicted by the topic continuity model, that is, once the prominent character is introduced and named, all future references to it are encoded in terms of zero anaphors, the anaphoric distribution in 'multi-protagonist' stories does not. The key fact is that the alternation between explicitly named referents is largely determined by their alternating 'topic-worthiness'. Participants that are roughly equal in topic-worthiness will receive full NP encoding almost every time they are mentioned again in the narrative. There is thus an iconic motivation for the patterns of anaphoric distribution in Kiowa narratives; the frequency of the use of overt NPs is an iconic reflection of the relative prominence of protagonists (Watkins 1990). Not dissimilar to this is the more familiar phenomenon of obviation (cf. Chapter 1 and Section 5.1.1. above), also particularly common in North American Indian languages.

In fact, as the above discussion about To'aba'ita and Kiowa shows, and as I pointed out in Huang (1989, 1994, 2000), though distance-interference, hence topicality, does bear a close relationship to anaphoric encoding, to explain anaphoric choice merely in terms of distance-interference or topicality would produce incorrect results. Empirically, the predictions of the distance-interference model are violated in both directions. On the one hand, lexical NPs are used in discourse where distance is short and there is no interfering referent, hence there is strong topic continuity. For example, in Chinese conversation, there is a recurring pattern involving the maintenance of reference: a full NP is frequently repeated in the second-pair part of a (question–answer) adjacency pair to encode the referent that is introduced in the first-pair part of that pair (Huang 1989, 1994). An example of this pattern is given in (5.55).

(5.55) C1. A: Na   ta   fuqin gan shenme ne
                uhm 3SG father do   what   Q
→   C2. B: Ta   fuqin zai daxue   li   jiaoshu
                3SG father in university LOC teach
       C3.   Ø jiao   guwen
                teach Classical Chinese
       E1. A: Uhm what is his father doing
       E2. B: His father teaches in a university
       E3.   (He) lectures on Classical Chinese

This is puzzling from the perspective of the distance-interference hypothesis. Since what is repeated is the most recently mentioned referent which has no competing referent, why is a reduced anaphoric expression not used? On the other hand, reduced anaphoric expressions may be used over long distances. For example, in many languages, return of current discussion to a mention other than the linearly most recent one in the preceding discourse can be done by means of a pronoun or zero anaphor—a phenomenon that is generally referred to as 'return pop' in the literature (e.g. Fox 1987, Huang 1989, 1994, Tao 1996). Witness (5.56) from English.

(5.56) (Fox 1987: 30)
1. A. Oh my mother wannduh know how's yer grandmother.
2. B. ˙hhh Uh::, (0.3) I don' know I guess she's aw-she's
3.   awright she went to the uh:: hhospital again tihda:y,
4. A. Mm-hm?
5. B. ˙hh ˙t! ˙hh A:n:: I guess t'day wz d'day she's
6.   supposetuh find out if she goes in ner not.=
7. A. =Oh. Oh::.
8. B. Becuz they're gonna do the operation on the teeuh duct.
9.   -f//fi:rs]t. Before they c'n do t//he cataracts.
10. A. Mm-hm.
11. A. Right.
12. A. Yeah.
13. B. ˙hhh So I don' know I haven:'t yihknow, she wasn' home
14.   by the t-yihknow when I lef'fer school tihday.=
15. A. = Mm hm.
16. B. Tch! ˙hh So uh I don't kno:w,
17.   (0.3)
18. B. En:=
19. A. =°M//hm
20. B. Well my ant went with her anyway this time,
21. A. Mm hm,
    [
22. B. My mother didn't go.
23. A. Mm hm,
→ 24. B. t! ˙hhh But uh? I don' know = She probably haf to go
25.   in soo:n though.

Consider now the use of the pronoun in line 24 (at the arrow). Clearly, the choice of this reduced anaphoric expression would remain unexplained on the distance-interference account. The linearly closest potential antecedent for the pronoun is *My mother*, in line 22. And in fact in line 20, there is another potential antecedent *my a(u)nt*, neither of which can be excluded from candidacy either syntactically or semantically. Yet, contrary to the prediction of the distance-interference model, a pronoun rather than a lexical NP is actually employed to pop back to its referent. This is beyond the explanation offered by the topic continuity model.[11]

One other, perhaps more important point may also be noted. The distance-interference effect language after language largely relies on may be no more than the consistent, secondary correlates of some more deeply rooted cognitive (e.g. Tomlin and Pu 1991) or pragmatic principles (e.g. Huang 1989, 1994)—a possibility of which the proponents of the topic continuity model are aware. For example, Givón (1983) claims that underlying the topic device scale in (5.53) is an iconic coding-quantity principle.

[11] Note that this 'unusual' structural characteristic of return pops can occasionally be exploited to create jokes. For an interesting example from English, see Fox (1987: 36).

(5.57) Givón's topic coding-quantity principle
The less predictable/accessible/continuous a topic is, the more coding material is used to represent it in language.

Looked at from a psychological point of view, the correlation between anaphoric encoding and topicality proposed by Givón can then be taken as a manifestation of the language user's cognitive status (like memory state and attention state). As referential distance and interfering referents increase, so do processing time and mental effort in identifying the intended referent, and hence more coding material (in terms of higher acoustic intensity and more morphological material) is iconically needed (e.g. Givón 1985, Lambrecht 1994: 96–7).

5.2.3. The hierarchy model

We move next to the hierarchy model. Under this approach, it is assumed that the most important factor that influences anaphoric selection is the hierarchical structure of discourse. From this assumption follows the central empirical prediction of the theory, namely, mentions (initial or non-initial) at the beginning or peak of a new discourse structural unit tend to be done by a full NP, whereas subsequent mentions within the same discourse structural unit tend to be achieved by a reduced anaphoric expression. Structural units in discourse can be in the form of e.g. turns, paragraphs, episodes, events, and themes.

This line of approach has been pursued by a number of scholars including Hinds (1978, 1979), Tai (1978), Longacre (1979), and Givón (1983). Hinds (1978, 1979) attempts to account for anaphoric encoding in Japanese narratives in terms of episodic structure of discourse. He argues that the choice of one anaphoric type over another in this language is largely determined by the hierarchical organization of discourse. Tai (1978) has similar findings for the anaphoric pattern in Chinese narratives. Likewise, Longacre (1979) reports that in languages like Gurung of Nepal and Sanio-Hiowe of New Guinea, pronouns cannot be used across paragraph boundaries. Finally, Ariel (1990: 22) too notices the privileged status the beginning of a paragraph enjoys in selecting an anaphoric form in Modern Hebrew. But the most representative of the hierarchy model is Fox's (1987) study of discourse anaphora in both English written texts and conversational discourse.

The key concept underlying Fox's analysis is that anaphoric encoding and discourse organization are closely correlated. She assumes two modes of description: what she calls the 'context-determines-use' mode and the 'use-accomplishes-context' mode. In the first, the hierarchical structure of discourse is claimed to determine the choice of a particular anaphoric form; in the second, the use of a particular anaphoric form is said to establish a particular structural pattern of discourse. In other words, on Fox's view, anaphoric distribution is largely determined by and itself determines the hierarchical structure of discourse.

Anaphora in expository written English texts

Let us take a look at Fox's analysis of anaphora in written English expository prose first. The theoretical framework she has adopted is the rhetorical structure theory developed by Mann, Matthiessen, and Thompson (e.g. Mann and Thompson 1987), drawing in part on work by Grimes (1975). Central to this theory is the belief that texts are made up of hierarchically organized groups of propositions. These proposition groups have internal, r[hetorical]-structures. Most of the r-structures contain a core part (called a nucleus) and an ancillary part (called an adjunct or satellite). Common r-structure relations between nuclei and satellites include (i) issue, (ii) conditional, (iii) circumstance, (iv) list, (v) narrate, (vi) reason, (vii) concession, (viii) opposition, (ix) purpose, (x) response, and (xi) contrast. Looked at from a broader perspective, rhetorical structure theory may be seen as a particular version of a more general coherence model of discourse analysis (see e.g. Halliday and Hasan 1976, Hobbs 1977, 1978, Sanders, Spooren, and Noordman 1992), whose basic assumption is that a discourse (whether written or conversational) is coherent if and only if there is some rhetorical or semantic relation between its constituent parts.

Turning now to Fox's analysis of anaphora in English written texts, her basic claim is that its use is sensitive to the rhetorical structure: pronouns tend to be used to refer to a referent that is mentioned in a rhetorically active or controlling proposition, whereas NPs tend to be employed to demarcate a new rhetorical unit. A proposition is considered to be active if its r-structure partner is being constructed, and to be controlling if its r-structure partner is active. Examples (5.58) and (5.59) illustrate the use of a pronoun whose referent is mentioned in a rhetorically active and controlling proposition, respectively.

(5.58) (a) [1] Purcell's range was wide. [2] He composed everything from bawdy catches to impassioned prayers, intimate chamber music to ceremonial court odes, fresh melodies and dances to elegiac laments. (*The Cambridge Music Guide*)
    (b) R-structure

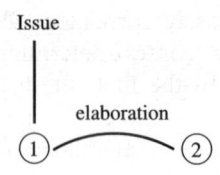

```
        Issue
          |
          |   elaboration
         (1)―――――(2)
```

(5.59) (Fox 1987)
   (a) [1] Leonard saw these as a 'series of psychological curtains which one interposed between oneself and the outside world of "other people."' [2] It was all part of the process of growing up and also a means of self-concealment and self-defence. [3] Particularly valuable in this process was his learning of a peculiar ecstasy which comes from 'feeling the mind work smoothly and imaginatively upon difficult and complicate problems.' (*A House of Lions*)
   (b) R-structure

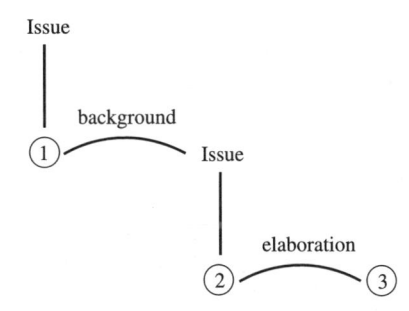

```
Issue
 │
 │ background
 ① ─────── Issue
              │
              │ elaboration
              ② ─────── ③
```

But the most striking piece of evidence in support of Fox's argument comes from the use of pronouns in return pops—return of a physically distant r-structure to a proposition other than the immediately preceding one. Pronouns are commonly used in return pops under two circumstances: (i) when there are mentions of the referent in the popped-over r-structure, and (ii) when the popped-over r-structure is rhetorically non-complex, though it does not contain any mention of the referent. Following is an example illustrating the latter case.

(5.60) (Fox 1987)
   (a) [1] Like most hedonists, he preferred to look neither backward nor forward. [2] The here and now, the picture in front of him, the woman he was with, the bird in flight—this was life: [3] the rest was history. [4] The future could assuredly take care of itself. [5] He found himself at one with Proust in the thought that 'the only certainty in life is change.' (*A House of Lions*)
   (b) R-structure

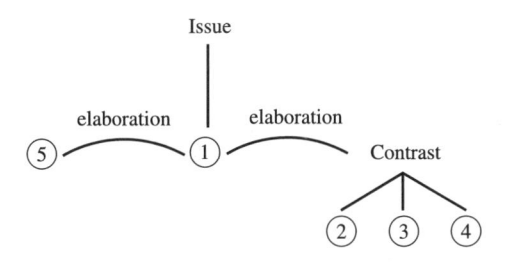

```
           Issue
            │
 elaboration │ elaboration
  ⑤ ─────── ① ─────── Contrast
                       ╱ │ ╲
                      ② ③ ④
```

Note that in this extract, sentence (5) pops over sentences (2), (3), and (4), yet the referent in this sentence is still encoded in terms of a pronoun. Finally, the two repetitions of the name of the central character in the following narrative function to demarcate new rhetorical units, as would be predicted by the hierarchy analysis.

(5.61) Giuseppe Verdi was born in October 1813, near Busseto in north Italy. As a young child he studied music locally; his main schooling was in Busseto, where he had the classical education normal for a middle-class child, and studied music under the church organist. When he was 18 he applied for admission to Milan Conservatory, but was refused: he was past the proper admission age and inadequate as pianist and in counterpoint. He studied in Milan nevertheless, then returned to Busseto in 1835 as town music-master; he was required to teach at the music school and to direct concerts. On the strength of his new appointment he could marry Margherita Barezzi, daughter of his patron. During those years he composed some sacred works, choruses and short orchestral pieces.

In 1839 Verdi felt ready to venture into a wider world; he resigned his post and moved to Milan. Later in the year his first opera, *Oberto*, was staged at La Scala. It was successful enough to interest the leading Italian publisher, Ricordi, and to induce the Scala director to commission further operas from him. His next, a comic work, was a failure. Verdi, whose two infant children and then his wife had just died, went into a depression and resolved to give up composing. He was nursed through it by the Scala director, who found a libretto, on the biblical story of Nebuchadnezzar, to fire him. The result, *Nabucco*, was a triumph when, in 1842, it reached the stage; within a few years it had carried his name to every important musical center in Europe, and then beyond, to America, south as well as north. (*The Cambridge Music Guide*)

All this indicates that anaphoric selection in English written texts is indeed sensitive to the rhetorical structure of text.

Anaphora in English conversation

Next, in her study of anaphora in English conversation, Fox focuses on the relationship between anaphoric distribution and sequential closure/non-closure. Her main argument is that it is the structural notion of sequence, roughly an adjacency pair and any elaboration on that adjacency pair, that establishes the basic distributional pattern of anaphora in English conversation.

(5.62) The basic distributional pattern of anaphora in English conversation
    (i) The first mention of a referent in a sequence is done with a full NP,
    (ii) after the first mention of a referent, a pronoun is used to display an understanding of the sequence as not yet closed,
    (iii) a full NP is used to display an understanding of the preceding sequence containing other mentions of the same referent as closed.

The first clause of (5.62) is rather straightforward. What evidence, then, is there for (5.62ii)? Four types of sequential evidence have been presented. The first is concerned with adjacency pairs. Fox observes that pronouns are regularly employed in the middle, especially in the second-pair part, of an adjacency pair if the referent is mentioned in the first-pair part. This is an indication of the speaker's understanding of the sequence in question as not yet closed.

(5.63) (Levinson 1983: 337)
    C. ... I wondered if you could phone the vicar so that we could ((in-breath)) do the final on Saturday (0.8) morning o:r (.) afternoon or (3.0)
    R. Yeah you see I'll I'll phone him up and see if there's any time free (2.0)

Secondly, there is what Fox calls a 'turn expansion'. In a turn expansion, a turn has arrived at a possible completion place but, owing to the speaker's self-selection, is not closed but continued. Again this continuation of sequence is encoded by means of a pronoun.

(5.64) (Fox 1987: 21)
    M. and then I've got s'mething planned on Sunday with Laura, (0.4)
    M. She she wa- she 'n I 're gonna go out en get drunk at four o'clock in the afternoon

In the third situation, an adjacency pair is linked to another, preceding adjacency pair in the same conversation. Roughly there are two major ways in which adjacency pairs can be so connected: (i) adjacency pairs of the same type can be chained into a series, as in (5.65); and (ii) adjacency pairs can enter a relation of post-elaboration, where a subsequent, 'tying' adjacency pair functions as an elaboration of the content of a preceding, 'tied-to' adjacency pair, as in (5.66). Again, in both cases, the speaker tends to make use of a pronoun to display his or her understanding that the sequence in question is still in progress.

(5.65) A. You know Steve?
        B. Yeah.
        A. Is he still in Cambridge?
        B. No, he's in Nijmegen.
(5.66) (Fox 1987: 23)
        M. A:nd ( ) as far as that goes my father's on his honeymoon.=
           = (y:ah ha ha °ha)
        K. (Oh :::.) Very//nice =
        K. = Where'd he go.

Fourthly, the most striking evidence for Fox's analysis again comes from return pops. In a return pop, an adjacency pair is tied not to its immediately preceding adjacency pair but to a more remote one. Once again, a pronoun is used to indicate that the sequence in question is seen as not being closed but being continued. This has already been illustrated in (5.56) above.

On the other hand, once a sequence is seen as being closed, repetition of NPs occurs, as is predicted by the third clause of (5.62).

(5.67) (Fox 1987: 41)
1. M. W'l (anyway listen) I gotta (go), I gotta(-) do
2. alotta studying
3. (0.3)
4. M. Oh en Hillary said she'd call me if- she was
5. gonna go t'the library with me
6. (0.9)
7. M. But- (0.1) I don't think she will
8. M. So ennyway (0.2) Tch. I'm gonna go have these xeroxed
9. 'n I'll come back inna little bit.
10. (M) ('hhhh/hh)
11. R. (Oka//y. Say]) hi t'Hillary for me.
12. S. Okay.]
13. M. Okay I will.

The main merit of the hierarchy model is its insight that anaphoric distribution in discourse should be accounted for structurally not only in a linear manner, but more importantly from the perspective of the global coherence of discourse as well. Important though the hierarchical organization of discourse may be in selecting one type of anaphoric expression over the other, the hierarchy analysis is not without defects. First, as I pointed out in Huang (1989), at the heart of the analysis lies a fundamental problem, namely, the problem of how to dissect a discourse. Structural units such as paragraphs, segments, and events are vague and difficult to define (see also Pu 1995). Secondly and more importantly, as we shall see in a moment, the hierarchical effects that have been pointed out by the hierarchy theorists may also simply be a superficial, structural manifestation of some more fundamental constraints on the limited capacity of human cognitive resources (see also Tomlin and Pu 1991).

5.2.4. The cognitive model

We come finally to the cognitive model. The basic tenet of this approach is that anaphoric encoding in discourse is largely determined by cognitive processes such as activation and attention. Activation and attention are two intimately related, though distinct cognitive phenomena. Roughly, in the domain of reference, activation of a referent in one's current short-term memory at moment t_n is a result of focusing one's attention on that referent at a previous moment t_{n-1} (e.g. Chafe 1994, Kibrik 1996: 256–7). Furthermore, a distinction should be made between the cognitive status of a particular referent and the means by which that referent achieves a particular cognitive status. Within the former, a further distinction can be made between what Lambrecht (1994) calls the identifiability and the activation of a referent. Identifiability refers to the addressee's knowledge state of a referent, i.e. whether or not a discourse representation of a referent has already been stored in the addressee's mind. By contrast, activation refers to the addressee's consciousness state of the current cognitive representation of an identifiable referent, i.e. whether the degree of the mental representation of an identifiable referent has already been activated, has merely been semi-active, or has simply been inactive, at the time of utterance (e.g. Chafe 1976, 1987, Lambrecht 1994, but see Chafe 1994: 54 for a slightly different view). Next, with regard to the means by which a referent can be identified and activated, there seem to be three major ways: (i) by being introduced into the linguistic context, (ii) through perception of the extralinguistic, spatio-temporal environment shared by the speaker and the addressee, and (iii) by being part of one's general encyclopaedic knowledge and therefore retrievable from one's long-term memory (e.g. Gundel, Hedberg, and Zacharski 1993, Lambrecht 1994: 79–80, Kibrik 1996).

The central empirical claim of the cognitive model is that full NPs are predicted to be used when the targeted referent is currently not addressee-activated, whereas reduced anaphoric expressions such as pronouns and zero anaphors are predicted to be selected when such a referent is estimated to be currently both speaker- and addressee-activated (e.g. Tomlin 1987a, Tomlin and Pu 1991, Gundel, Hedberg, and Zacharski 1993, Kibrik 1996). To capture this correlation between cognitive status and anaphoric form, various hierarchies/scales have been put forward in both the linguistics and psycholinguistics literature. We have already seen one such hierarchy, i.e. Ariel's accessibility marker scale in Chapter 4. Another one is presented in Gundel, Hedberg, and Zacharski (1993).

(5.68) Gundel, Hedberg, and Zacharski's (1993) Givenness Hierarchy[12]
In focus > activated > familiar > uniquely identifiable > referential > type identifiable

These cognitive statuses are then related to anaphoric forms in Chinese, English, Japanese, Russian, and Spanish. While the five languages differ as to which types of anaphoric expression they have, and as to which statuses are needed to constitute a necessary and sufficient condition for the use of a particular type of anaphoric expression, there does seem to be a significant correlation between cognitive status and anaphoric form. For example, the most restrictive cognitive status (i.e. in focus) is realized by the type of anaphoric expression with the least phonological and morphological content, whereas the least restrictive cognitive status (i.e. type identifiable) is reflected in the use of full lexical NPs. Central Pomo provides yet another piece of supporting evidence for this correlation. In this language (apart from logophoric pronouns) there is a three-way distinction between full lexical NPs, utilized for referents that are completely new; zero anaphors, used to encode

---

[12] Gundel, Hedberg, and Zacharski (1993) consider the statuses in the hierarchy as implicationally related, that is, each status entails and is entailed by all lower statuses, but not vice versa. Furthermore, they explicitly link the hierarchy to our Q-principle.

referents that are already within the immediate focal consciousness; and demonstrative pronouns, employed to bring already activated referents back into focal consciousness at significant points of discontinuity in discourse (Mithun 1990; see also Dimitriadis 1997 for supporting evidence from Modern Greek).

This cognitive status/anaphoric form correlation can further be supported by experimental work carried out in psycholinguistics. Within the attention model developed by Tomlin (1987), for example, a series of experiments have been conducted to test the cognitive basis for the selection of an anaphoric form in narrative discourse. By independently manipulating activation of referents during an on-line narrative production task, Tomlin (1987a) and Tomlin and Pu (1991) demonstrate respectively that in both English and Chinese narrative discourse, referents that have been within activated memory regularly take the form of reduced NPs, whereas referents that have only been moved within activated memory are normally signalled by NPs that bear full lexical encodings.

Next, recall that, in Section 5.2.3. above, it was pointed out that one of the most important structural factors governing anaphoric choice is the hierarchical organization of discourse. This correlation between discourse structure and anaphoric choice has also been confirmed by psycholinguistic experiments. Experimental results reported on in Pu (1995), for example, show that speakers of both English and Chinese are sensitive to the episodic structure of narrative discourse. They tend to use full NPs at an episode boundary but to use semantically reduced NPs within the same episode. More or less the same is true of the effects of the internal structure of an episode on anaphoric selection. Full NPs are more likely to occur at the beginning of a subunit within an episode, whereas pronouns and zero anaphors are more likely to appear within such a subunit. This is, of course, largely in line with the findings described in linguistic studies on discourse structure and anaphora, as we have already seen. But under the assumptions of the attention model, discourse units such as episodes or paragraphs are considered to be nothing but structural correlates of cognitive events. As a semantic unit dominated by a macroproposition, an episode is taken merely as the discoursal manifestation of a memory unit that represents sustained attention effort and endures until attention is shifted, that is, until an episode boundary is reached. Consequently, the choice of one type of anaphoric expression over the other is simply a linguistic reflection of attentional states. Pronouns and zero anaphors are used inside an episode or a subunit of an episode, because within such a unit, attention is sustained, the macroproposition is maintained, and the referent remains to be focally activated, thus an attenuated anaphoric expression is sufficient to encode it. On the other hand, NPs are used at episode boundaries, especially at the beginning of an episode or a subunit of an episode, because at such a place, attention is switched, the macroproposition is changed (e.g. with the introduction of new protagonists, times, places, objects, etc. and with a shift between, say, background and foreground information, a change in perspectives, etc.), and the memory status of the referent as activated or not is affected, hence a more explicit anaphoric expression is needed to designate it. In other words, on the attentional view, the alternation between full and reduced NPs inside and outside an episode is merely a function of the limitations imposed on the limited capacity of short-term working memory, which is manifested in the discourse artefact mainly through its episodic structure (for further discussion, see e.g. Pu 1985).

But it should be pointed out here that the correlation between cognitive status and anaphoric form—the critical prediction of the cognitive model—can in fact be frustrated in both directions. On the one hand, there are cases where NPs can and even must be used for activated referents. This is particularly true when potential referential ambiguity may arise from the presence of two or more competing activated referents, as in the attested Russian text (5.69) (cited in Kibrik 1996: 300). On the other hand, pronominal encoding may be used for inactivated referents, as in the attested Chinese conversation (4.105), repeated here in (5.70). Essentially the same usage occurs in both Japanese and Korean.

(5.69) Fedorčuk vskočil.   Davaj   ključ!
 Fedorchuk jumped up give me key/wrench
 kriknul on mexaniku.
 cried   he to mechanic
 Tot   drožaščej   rukoj sunul
 latter with a trembling hand pressed
 emu v ruki   malen'kij gaečnyj ključik.
 him in hands small   nut   key/wrench
 Fedorčuk vyšel   na   krylo.
 Fedorchuk went out onto wing
 'Fedorchuk jumped up. "Give me the wrench!" he cried to the mechanic. The latter, with a trembling hand, pressed a small wrench into his hand. Fedorchuk went out onto the wing.'
(5.70) C1. A: Zhe qunzi zhen piaoliang!
         this dress really pretty
  C2.   Shei mai de?
         who buy SD
  C3. B: Ta   mai de
         3SG buy SD
  E1. A: What a pretty dress!
  E2.   Who bought (it)?
  E3. B: He (e.g. my boyfriend) bought (it)

All this seems to indicate that the cognitive contrast between activation and non-activation of a referent constitutes neither a necessary nor a sufficient condition for the morphological contrast between reduced and full

NPs. This imperfect correlation between cognitive state and anaphoric choice may in part be seen to follow from the differences between a discrete (grammatical) and a non-discrete (cognitive) category. While the anaphoric coding contrast, for example, is in principle a matter of yes or no, activation is in principle a matter of more or less (see also Lambrecht 1994 for further discussion).

5.2.5. The pragmatic model

In the last three sections, I have discussed the topic continuity, hierarchy, and cognitive models of discourse anaphora. In this section, I shall present a neo-Gricean pragmatic approach. The central idea of this model is that anaphoric distribution in discourse can largely be predicted in terms of the systematic interaction of some general pragmatic strategies such as our Q-, I-, and M-principles.[13] In what follows, I shall concentrate on discourse anaphora in its prototypical use: how the establishment, shift, and maintenance of reference to a third-person singular human entity is done in a naturally occurring conversation (e.g. Du Bois 1980, Fox 1987: 2). The data will be drawn mainly from Chinese and English. Although conversation introduces some additional complexities, it also offers the analyst some unique opportunities, for conversation is primarily interactional and processual, and conversational data represent not only a product but also a process. Thus, as pointed out by Levinson (1983: 321),

'Conversation, as opposed to monologue, offers the analyst an invaluable analytic resource: as each turn is responded to by a second, we find displayed in that second turn an analysis of the first by its recipient. Such an analysis is thus provided by participants not only for each other but for the analysts too.'

In other words, the dynamics of conversation may provide a test procedure to confirm or disconfirm a particular analysis.

Let me start by establishing the basic distributional pattern of anaphora in conversation. As already mentioned, anaphoric distribution in discourse (including conversation) is a very complex phenomenon, involving, among other things, structural, cognitive, and pragmatic factors. Nevertheless,

---

[13] Precursors of this analysis may include Sacks and Schegloff (1979), Leech (1983), Huang (1987, 1989, 1994), Takami (1987), and Geluykens (1994). In these analyses except Huang (1987, 1989, 1994), it has been assumed that there are two principles operating in determining discourse anaphora: a principle of economy and a principle of clarity. One such representative can be found in Sacks and Schegloff (1979). They argue that there are two principles at work in the domain of reference to persons in English conversation: a principle of 'minimization' and a principle of 'recognition'. The former amounts to a preference for the use of a 'single' referential form, and the latter amounts to a preference for the use of a 'recognitional'—a referential form that will allow the recognition of its referent to be achieved. Each preference is explicitly bounded in its applicability by the other. But as I pointed out in Huang (1989, 1994, 2000), the principles of clarity and economy are not something *ad hoc*, but a mere instantiation of our more general Q- and I-principles respectively.

allowing for some variations arising from different encoding conventions in different languages, cross-linguistically there does seem to be a basic pattern that underlies the distribution of anaphora in conversation (e.g. Huang 1989, 1994).

(5.71) The basic distributional pattern of anaphora in conversation
- (i) Establishment of reference tends to be achieved through the use of an elaborated form, notably, a lexical NP.
- (ii) Shift of reference tends to be achieved through the use of an elaborated form, notably, a lexical NP.
- (iii) Maintenance of reference tends to be achieved through the use of an attenuated form, notably, a pronoun or a zero anaphor.[14]

This pattern applies regardless of speaker- and/or turn-change in conversation. It is illustrated in (5.72).

(5.72) (Chinese, Huang 1984)
C1. A: Cai Lin zai yinhang gongzuo
    Cai Lin in bank   work
C2. B: Ta airen ne
    3SG spouse Q
C3. A: Ø haoxiang zai xintuo gongsi
      seem   in trust company
C4.   Ao Cai Lin qunian hai qu le   tang Xianggang
       Oh Cai Lin last year also go PFV CL Hongkong
E1. A: Cai Lin works in a bank
E2. B: How about her husband
E3. A: (He) seems to work in a trust company
E4.   Oh Cai Lin even visited Hongkong last year

Clearly, the pattern in (5.71) is in keeping with the interaction of the Q-principle ('Do not say less than is required' or 'Say as much as you need to achieve recognition') and I-principle ('Do not say more than is required' or 'Say as little as you can to achieve minimization'). In the case of establishment of reference, given the hearer-based Q-principle alone, the speaker would have chosen an informationally richer and often morphologically more elaborated referential form such as a long description or a proper name coupled with a description, but this would run counter to minimization (in terms of both meaning and expression). On the other hand, given the speaker-based I-principle alone, the speaker would have selected an informationally poorer and often more minimal form such as a pronoun or a zero anaphor (syntax permitting), but this would go against recognition.[15] Therefore, a compromise is reached between these two potentially conflicting

---

[14] An exception may be Finnish, as described in Hakulinen (1987).

[15] The term 'recognition/identification' is used here in a very loose way. The 'identification' of an intended referent may include: (i) the identification of an individual whom one has actually seen, known, spoken with, etc., as in the sense of Sacks and Schegloff (1979), (ii) the identification of some unique entity in the world (cf. the *de dicto/de re* or attributive/referential distinction

pragmatic principles, resulting in a preference for the use of a 'minimal' but 'recognitional' referential form, which concurrently satisfies both Q- and I-principles.[16] Next, more or less the same can be said of shift of reference. As an illustration, take example (5.72) above. A zero anaphor could have occurred at line C4, but the use of such an anaphoric form could possibly lead the hearer to an incorrect identification of the referent, taking the subject referent at line C3 rather than the subject referent at line C1 as the intended referent. Evidently, this would run counter to recognition. On the other hand, an elaborated description such as *zai yinhang gongzuo de Cai Lin* 'Cai Lin who works in the bank' might have been used as well, but this would run counter to minimisation. Therefore, the use of the proper name at line C4 allows the potential concurrent satisfiability of the Q- and I-based preferences to be realized. Finally, in the case of maintenance of reference, the use of 'lexically attenuated' anaphoric forms is clearly oriented to the concurrent satisfaction of both the Q-based preference for recognition and the I-based preference for minimization.

But the separate involvement of the Q- and I-principles in the management of reference in conversation is most in evidence on occasions when the two principles are not met simultaneously. These occasions arise due to a discrepancy between the speaker's assessment and the hearer's actual state of knowledge. In conversation, both the speaker and the addressee make continuous assessments about each other's state of knowledge (e.g. Clark and Marshall 1981). (Let me assume the mutual knowledge hypothesis without trying to give an account of how it is to be achieved without invoking infinite regress

---

(Donnellan 1978)), and (iii) the identification of a 'discourse referent' via its antecedent. There might be some implicational relations between these different senses of 'identification', but to discuss them here would take me too far afield.

[16] Both proper names and definite descriptions can be used as recognitionals. (The term 'proper names' is intended to cover first names, last names, nicknames, kinship terms, first and last name combinations, titles plus first and/or nickname and/or last name combinations, proper names companied by various sorts of articles, modifiers, and appositives, and proper names embedded in NPs headed by common names. (Downing 1996: 98)) Whether a referent is to be identified through a proper name or a definite description depends on a number of factors. But generally speaking, a definite description will be used when the referent is to be identified via the relevant role, otherwise a proper name will be used (e.g. Fauconnier 1985, Fornel 1987).

However, cross-linguistically there is clear evidence that proper names generally take precedence over definite descriptions, thus becoming the predominant referential form for introducing known human referents into conversation (e.g. Sacks and Schegloff 1979, Huang 1989, 1994, Downing 1996, Schegloff 1996; see also Sanford, Moar, and Garrod 1988 for some psycholinguistic experimental evidence). In fact, Schegloff (1996) has set up a 'name-first' principle: if the recipient knows the referent by name, use a name; indeed, use *that* name. If the recipient knows the referent in some other way, use *that* way as the reference form. Why is this the case? Currently, one view is that the predominant use of proper names is attributable to a preference 'to communicate via the concrete image of a person rather than via the abstract and impersonal image that a description by role creates' (Hofstadter, Clossman, and Meredith 1982). This, of course, does not mean that there is no conversational context in which preference for relevant role is stronger. For discussion of such contexts, see e.g. Fornel (1987).

of the state of knowledge (cf. Clark 1996).) This holds, of course, for referential management in conversation. Given that all referential work in conversation is essentially 'recipient-designed' (Sacks and Schegloff 1979, Schegloff 1996), the speaker, in deciding on a particular referential form, has to ensure that it is one that can serve for the addressee to identify the intended referent. Thus, anaphoric production in conversation depends crucially on the assumptions made by the speaker about how the addressee will recognize the intended referent. However, to assess correctly the addressee's knowledge state is not easy and inevitably mistakes will occasionally occur. These mistakes will sometimes lead to anaphoric repair, an instance of A[ppropriateness]- rather than E[rror]-repair (Levelt 1989), in conversation.

Four types of anaphoric repair are found in conversation: (i) self-initiated self-repair, (ii) self-initiated other-repair, (iii) other-initiated self-repair, and (iv) other-initiated other-repair. Of these, self-initiated self-repair is by far the most common type. This is hardly surprising, given that cross-linguistically conversation is inherently organized in such a way as to favour self- over other-initiation, and self- over other-repair (e.g. Moerman 1977, Schegloff, Jefferson, and Sacks 1977).

The prototypical process of anaphoric repair in conversation is represented by other-initiated self-repair. This type of repair is canonically characterized by a three-stage process (Huang 1989, 1994, Geluykens 1994).

(5.73) Other-initiated self-repair
    (*a*) Speaker A: utterance with a potentially problematic anaphoric expression
    (*b*) Speaker B: initiation of repair (frequently via a class of initiator elements such as *wh*-words)
    (*c*) Speaker A: repair

This type of anaphoric repair can be illustrated by (5.74) from Chinese and (5.75) from English.

(5.74) C1. A: Xiao Zhao hui Zhenjiang le
           Xiao Zhao go back Zhenjiang EXP
→ C2. B: Neige Xiao Zhao
           which Xiao Zhao
   C3. A: Zhao Lisha
           Zhao Lisha
   C4. B: Ao
           oh
   E1. A: Xiao Zhao has returned to Zhenjiang
   E2. B: Which Xiao Zhao
   E3. A: Zhao Lisha
   E4. B: Oh

(5.75) (Survey of English Usage, cited in Geluykens 1994)
       B: ((and)) he said well I'm sorry ((you know)) we don't cater for this you'll just have to change your timetable or work at home ((so)) I said this just means I shall do half as much work# ((and)) he/said 'very well#

→ A: /[k] 'who 'said 'this#
　　B: the/secretary#*.*of the/'school#
→ A: */'m#*/who's 'that#
　　B: /George 'Fornby#

In both (5.74) and (5.75), the speaker anticipates that the addressee will be able to identify the referent, but in fact the addressee cannot. Consequently, an other-initiated recognition search sequence occurs, as in the arrowed lines. This other-initiated recognition search sequence shares all the features of other-initiated self-repair in general (e.g. Schegloff, Jefferson, and Sacks 1977, Moerman 1977). First, it is placed in the turn subsequent to the turn containing the problematic referential form, the position typically occupied by other-initiation. This shows that the addressee systematically withholds the other-initiated recognition search sequence until he or she sees that no self-initiated self-repair of the problematic referential form is likely to occur. Secondly, the sequence is characteristically done by a set of turn-constructional devices distinctive of other-initiation (see e.g. work by Moerman 1977 on Tai conversation), namely, (i) it occupies an entire turn, (ii) it is relatively short, (iii) the turn-constructional devices can be graded according to their relative 'power' to locate the repairable referential form, and (iv) lowest-grade devices are shortest. Thirdly, it is done with a class of initiator techniques typical of other-initiation (e.g. Schegloff, Jefferson, and Sacks 1977), the most common of which are (i) full-turn question words such as 'who', and (ii) partial repetition of the trouble-source turn plus a question word such as *nage Xiao Zhao* 'which Xiao Zhao'.

Now, what is of direct interest to us here is that the other-initiated recognition search sequence will give rise to a step-by-step escalation on the part of the speaker in his or her efforts to secure recognition until recognition is achieved or abandoned. Thus in (5.74) above, upon the other-initiated recognition search sequence by the addressee, a one-step escalation from the use of the referent's surname to the use of her full name is launched on the part of the speaker to secure recognition. Such a step-by-step escalation stops as soon as recognition is achieved, which is signalled by *ao*. There is thus evidence for the application of both Q- and I-principles: the other-initiation of the recognition search sequence is due to the Q-principle, and the gradual relaxation of the use of minimal referential forms is due to the I-principle. On a par with (5.74) from Chinese is (5.75) from English. Here, the two other-initiations are responded to by two self-repairs in terms of more informative forms, but the escalations are made only in a step-by-step manner. Once again, then, evidence for the operation of both Q- and I-principles.

But by far the most common type of anaphoric repair attested in conversation is self-initiated self-repair. Of some interest here is the observation I made in Huang (1989, 1994) that in this type of anaphoric repair, there is frequently an explicitly or implicitly self-initiated check sequence followed by a pause between it and the speaker's repair (see also Geluykens 1994).

(5.76) Self-initiated self-repair
    (a) Speaker A: utterance with a potentially problematic anaphoric expression
    [(b)   recognition check sequence
    (c) Speaker B: (pause)]
    (d) Speaker A: initiation of repair
    (e)   repair

(5.77) (Chinese, Huang 1994)
    C1. A: Pangzi ne ni   xiaode Ø wa
            Fatty PP 2SG know   Q
    C2. B: (pause)
    C3. A: Dapangzi
            Big Fatty
    C4. B: Wo   zhidao Ø
            1SG know
    E1. A: Fatty you know (him)
    E2. B: (pause)
    E3. A: Big Fatty
    E4. B: I know (him)

(5.78) (Sacks and Schegloff 1979: 19)
    A: ... well I was the only one other than than the uhm tch *Fords?*, uh Mrs. Holmes Ford?
    B: (pause)
    A: You know uh//the cellist?
    B: Oh yes. She's she's the cellist.
    A: Yes
    B: Ye//s
    A: Well she and her husband were there.

As can be seen in (5.77) and (5.78), the standard formula for such a sequence is 'You know X?', where X is the problematic referential form. By being introduced typically in a prefatory sequence, this format, as Auer (1984) points out for a similar pattern in German conversation, often serves as a 'pre' for some more 'substantive' talks. Note next that failure to acknowledge recognition in the pause by the addressee is typically interpreted as pragmatically implicating that he or she does not recognize the referent. Again, this will be followed by a step-by-step escalation on the part of the speaker in his or her efforts to secure recognition until recognition is achieved or abandoned. Thus, in (5.77), the speaker is uncertain about whether the referent can be recognized by the addressee, and this uncertainty is expressed explicitly by inserting a self-initiated recognition check sequence following the use of the minimal referential form, i.e. the referent's nickname. The sequence is followed by a pause, which is treated by the speaker as displaying the addressee's failure to recognize the referent. Consequently, the speaker steps up his efforts to achieve recognition by providing more information in the next turn. Thus, the operation of the Q-principle is evidenced by the fact that the kind of self-initiated check sequence we have just seen is essentially oriented to achieving recognition, and that of the I-principle is seen by the fact that more information is provided in a gradual way only after the initial, minimal referential form fails to secure recognition. More or less the same can be said of (5.78) in English. Here the speaker is again uncertain about the recognition of the referent from the addressee. As a consequence, he uses a minimal recognitional form, marked by an upward intonation contour and followed by a brief pause. This, Sacks and Schegloff (1979) and Schegloff (1996) call a 'try-marker', that is, a recognitional form, but one which is marked as a 'try'. It is not difficult for the reader to see that the same step-by-step escalation procedure is employed after the try-marked recognitionals are used.[17]

The third type of anaphoric repair found in conversation is other-initiated other-repair. This is schematized in (5.79) and illustrated in (5.80) from Chinese and (5.81) from English.

(5.79) Other-initiated other-repair
    (a) Speaker A: utterance with a potentially problematic anaphoric expression
    (b) Speaker B: initiation of repair
    (c)   repair
    (d) Speaker A: acknowledgement of repair

(5.80) (Chinese, Huang 1994)
    C1. A: Shang xingqi you lai le ge nüsheng
             last week again come PFV CL girl student
    C2. B: Ø shi bu shi jiao Shang Subo
             be not be call Shang Subo
    C3. A: Shia ni ye renshi Ø
             yes 2SG also know
    C4. B: Dui wo ye renshi Ø
             yes 1SG also know
    E1. A: There came another girl student last week
    E2. B: Is (she) called Shang Subo
    E3. A: Oh yes, you also know (her)
    E4. B: Yes, I also know (her)

(5.81) (Survey of English Usage, cited in Geluykens 1994)
    A: and old Joe who's very [:m] sceptical about these things he's [:m]—you know # *he's he* was /quite / 'very im'pressed with *'this this/' 'Guinness #
    a: *Joe.Joe Lemon m*
    A: /Joe 'Lemon # /ˆyeah # . * (. . .)

In (5.80), the speaker thinks that the referent is unidentifiable to the addressee, and so uses a 'non-recognitional' form; but in fact the referent is

---

[17] This is partly consistent with Geluykens's (1994) analysis of the function of the pause in English conversation. The function of the pause, according to Geluykens, is twofold: (i) it is cognitive, in that it signals a reprocessing on the part of the speaker, and (ii) it is interactional, in that it represents an implicit other-initiation on the part of the recipient. This leads Geluykens to reject—correctly I think—the idea that the initiation of repair is either purely self or purely other, and to call for a more refined inventory of repair types, one which will reflect more fully the collaborative nature of anaphoric repair in conversation. For more discussion, see Huang (1996b).

identifiable to the addressee. The addressee, having been given a 'non-recognitional' form, may find from some other information in the speaker's turn at C1 that he might be able to identify the referent. To confirm his suspicion, the addressee launches an other-initiated other-repair by trying the referent's name at C2, which is confirmed by the speaker at C3. Essentially a similar story can be told about the English conversation in (5.81). Examples of this kind again show that the Q-principle is in force here: one should try to achieve recognition whenever possible. On the other hand, that the I-principle is not irrelevant is also obvious: the addressee tries a minimal referential form first, i.e. the referent's name, even when the success of recognition is uncertain and when some other more elaborated referential forms could be used.[18]

Finally, there is self-initiated other-repair. This is schematized in (5.82).

(5.82) Self-initiated other-repair
    (*a*) Speaker A: utterance with a potentially problematic anaphoric expression
    (*b*)   initiation of repair
    (*c*) Speaker B: repair
    (*d*) Speaker A: acknowledgement of repair

This type of anaphoric repair is rather rare, for the simple reason that if the speaker has started the repair mechanism him- or herself, it is most likely that he or she will do the actual repair. A special case of self-initiated other-repair, which is rather common in conversation, is where the speaker has a 'word-search' problem, and cannot find the name for the referent. He or she may then use a description to help recover the name from his or her own memory (i.e. self-initiated self-repair) or to elicit it from the addressee (self-initiated other-repair).[19] Once the name is provided, the description will be abandoned. Two examples follow.

(5.83) (Chinese)
    C1. A: Nage gen gaogan   erzi jiehun de
             uh   with senior cadre son marry NOM
    C2.   nage nage zhang de   ting haokan de
             uhm uhm grow CSC quite pretty NOM
    C3.   jiao shenme de   le
             call what   NOM PFV
    C4. B: Ao Fan Chunxiao
           Oh Fan Chunxiao
    C5. A: Dui Fan Chunxiao
           yes Fan Chunxiao
    E1. A: There is uhm the person who's married to a senior cadre's son
    E2.   uhm uhm the one who's quite pretty
    E3.   what's (her) name

---

[18] From an interactional point of view, both over- and underestimation are dispreferred acts. The former undermines the addressee's chance to achieve recognition, and the latter threatens his or her 'face' (Brown and Levinson 1987).

[19] The fact that there is a mental process of search on the part of the speaker for the name of the referent can be evidenced by the occurrence of various hesitation markers in these cases.

E4. B: Oh Fan Chunxiao
E5. A: Yes, Fan Chunxiao
(5.84) (Downing 1996:111)
c: <X I saw X> .. the guy with the grave .. what was his name .. Bolz [mann]
A: [\`Bolz]mann
c: ..Bolzmann

Examples of this kind also evidence the operation of the I-principle: despite the fact that the recognition requirement is met, neither the speaker nor the addressee may be satisfied until the minimization requirement is also fulfilled.

One key feature to note regarding both other- and self-initiated other-repair is the role played by the mandatory acknowledgement on the part of the speaker after such a repair is done. Interestingly enough, there are also precise mirror-image parallels in self-initiated self-repair, as we have already seen; success of the recognition of reference must be explicitly acknowledged in the brief pause following the recognition check sequence. The importance of acknowledgements of this kind is that they are a clear indication that anaphoric repair in conversation is essentially an interactional and collaborative process.

Of further interest to us is that in addition, anaphoric repair in conversation also confirms the relative strengths of the Q- and I-principles. The weight of evidence suggested by the kind of occasions we have examined above indicates strongly that the Q-based preference for recognition and the I-based preference for minimization are generally simultaneously satisfied. In cases where the concurrent compatibility of the two preferences is not achieved, the Q-based preference for recognition generally takes precedence over the I-based preference for minimization, and the I-based minimization is generally relaxed step by step in favour of the Q-based preference for recognition. In other words, were minimization preferred to recognition, then, when recognition through minimization was doubtful, more minimal forms would be favoured; and were minimization not relaxed step by step in favour of recognition, then, when recognition was doubtful, non-minimal forms would be preferred, neither of which the repair mechanisms we have seen show to be the case. Therefore, the resolution schema organizing the interaction of the Q- and I-principles in Chapter 4 is once again substantiated.

Having looked at the interaction of the Q- and I-principles from the perspective of anaphoric repair, let us now return to some of the 'unusual' anaphoric patterns described earlier in this chapter and see how they can be accommodated by our pragmatic analysis. We consider return pops first. As we mentioned in both Sections 5.2.2. and 5.2.3., in a return pop, return of current discussion to a mention other than the linearly most recent one in preceding discourse is encoded in terms of a reduced anaphoric expression.

This gives rise to the question; how can the intended antecedent be figured out unambiguously? The answer seems rather straightforward. Given that referential work in conversation is essentially 'recipient-designed', it is reasonable to expect that some special techniques will be employed by the speaker to indicate the intended antecedent if it is not in the 'unmarked', immediately preceding utterance. A number of devices (both cross-linguistic and language-specific) have been observed (see e.g. Huang 1994 for a detailed analysis with respect to Chinese), but the two most commonly used ones cross-linguistically are (i) repetition in the popping utterance of the key lexical items used in the 'popped-back' utterance, (ii) parallel syntactic constructions between the two utterances. This is the case with (5.56). Both devices play an important role in the addressee's inferential strategy (e.g. the use of the I-principle) that leads to the correct identification of the referent.

Next, recall one of the most important findings of both the hierarchy and cognitive models, namely, the distributional pattern that mentions (initial or non-initial) at the beginning or peak of a new discourse structural unit tend to be encoded by a full NP, whereas subsequent mentions within the same discourse structural unit tend to be done by reduced anaphoric expressions. This can be accounted for by the interaction of the I- and M-principles. The crucial point to note here is that while, within the same discourse structural unit, continuity of discourse is strong, at the beginning or peak of a new discourse structural unit the referent has been 'displaced' by some discontinuity in the flow of discourse. This is, in fact, an instance of what Li and Thompson (1979) and Chen (1986) call 'low conjoinability' in discourse. By 'conjoinability' is meant 'the speaker's perception of the degree of "connection" between clauses in discourse' (Li and Thompson 1979). This degree of 'connection', again according to Chen, can be defined in terms of topic continuity and semantic continuity. Conjoinability is affected when the interruption of topic continuity and/or semantic continuity takes place. Topic continuity is interrupted by change of topic and semantic continuity is impaired by factors such as (i) turning from background information to foreground information, or vice versa, (ii) insertion of some digression into the theme development, (iii) insertion of temporal, locative, adversative, or other types of adverbials, and (iv) switch or turn in conversation. Consequently, on these occasions, a less minimal anaphoric expression is likely to be used. Now, under the pragmatic account developed here, the analysis goes roughly thus: given the M-principle, it is predicted that a 'marked' linguistic form will be used to express a 'marked' message. Assuming that low conjoinability is something marked, it is expected that a less minimal anaphoric form will be employed to indicate it. Thus, we obtain a complementary pattern here: other things being equal, the I-principle will favour the use of an 'unmarked' anaphoric form when conjoinability is high, whereas the

M-principle will favour the use of a 'marked' anaphoric form when conjoinability is low.

We move finally to the 'unexpected' use in Chinese and English conversation of NPs that are inverse to each other. Recollect first that, in Section 5.2.2, we pointed out that there is a recurring pattern involving the maintenance of reference in Chinese conversation: a full lexical NP is often repeated in the second-pair part of a (question–answer) adjacency pair to encode the referent that is introduced in the first-pair part of that pair, as in example (5.55) above. As we mentioned there, the repetition of the full NP is left unexplained by the distance-interference theory. Since what is repeated is the most recently mentioned referent which has no competing referent, why is a reduced anaphoric expression not used? However, from an interactional point of view, the repetition of the speaker's topic by the addressee in his or her first turn available explicitly indicates his or her willingness to accept the speaker's topic as the common topic of the subsequent conversation. Once the common topic is established, reduced anaphoric expressions are used to maintain the reference, as would be expected. Two points are noteworthy here: first, in these cases, the interaction of the Q- and I-principles appears to allow the concurrent compatibility of both recognition and minimization to be realized gradually. In other words, by the interaction of the Q- and I-principles, there is an orientation towards the concurrent compatibility of recognition and minimization. Secondly, the I-implicated minimization is also somewhat overridden by the M-implicated message of the establishment of common topic. Finally, the working of the M-principle can also be extended to a recurring pattern of anaphoric distribution in English conversation. As we saw in Section 5.2.3, Fox (1987) reports that English conversational participants frequently use an NP to close a sequence in which previous mentions of that same NP are encoded in terms of a pronoun, as in example (5.67) above. Once again, this can readily be attributed to the M-principle: the use of the NP will convey a message that cannot be conveyed by the use of a pronoun, i.e. to close the sequence in this case. Thus, while the repetition of a full NP at the beginning of a Chinese conversation M-implicates the establishment of common topic, the repetition of a full NP in the middle of an English conversation M-implicates the close of the sequence.

5.2.6. Summary

In this section, I have surveyed three extant theoretical models of discourse anaphora. I have also developed a neo-Gricean pragmatic model. I have demonstrated how the pragmatic factor can best be captured by the pragmatic model. Furthermore, the facts we have examined indicate that of the three interacting factors that are at work in predicting anaphoric distribution in discourse,[20] the structural constraint (both linear and hierarchical) seems largely to be a secondary correlate of the more fundamental cognitive and/or pragmatic constraints. However, the interaction and division of labour between the cognitive and pragmatic constraints are not well understood and need to be further studied.

5.6. Conclusion

In this chapter, I considered first switch-reference and then discourse anaphora. In my discussion of switch-reference, I first examined its phenomenology. I then compared and contrasted it with other reference-tracking systems and logophoricity. Finally, I reviewed a syntactic and a semantic, and sketched a pragmatic approach to switch-reference. In the second part of this chapter, I moved away from considering switch-reference and turned to discourse anaphora. At the outset, I raised the issue of anaphoric distribution in discourse, and then I reviewed three theoretical models. Finally, I proposed a neo-Gricean pragmatic analysis, and demonstrated how this analysis is best suited to account for the pragmatic factor of discourse anaphora.

---

[20] There are, of course, other factors. One such factor concerns the speaker's attitude. In an English conversation, for example, speakers frequently use full NPs to display highly negative attitudes (Fox 1987, Downing 1996). But the reverse is true of Northern Pomo. In this language, speakers tend to avoid names and kinship terms in a negative context (O'Connor 1992*b*). For further discussion about the sociological and cultural dimension, see e.g. Dench (1982), Ariel (1990), Mühlhäusler and Harré (1990), and Payne (1993).

6 Conclusions

In this book, I have provided an extensive overview of the major contemporary issues surrounding anaphora and given a critical survey of the many and diverse contemporary approaches to the study of anaphora. I have also developed a revised neo-Gricean pragmatic theory of anaphora. The survey and analysis are based on a rich collection of data drawn from around 550 of the world's languages, which represent a variety of areal, genetic, and typological characteristics.

The main contributions of this book, I think, are the following: first, the richness and complexity of anaphoric systems in the world's languages are demonstrated; secondly, inadequacies of all current syntactic, semantic, and discourse approaches to the study of anaphora are pointed out; and thirdly, a revised neo-Gricean pragmatic theory of anaphora is constructed.

The findings of this book have important implications for current linguistic theorizing. In the first place, they indicate that any adequate theory of anaphora has to be based on data drawn from a wide range of languages with no geographical, genetic, and typological bias.

Secondly, they force a radical rethink of some of the current claims about the nature of grammatical rules and the way in which they interact with pragmatic principles. As I pointed out in Huang (1989, 1994), to begin with, many grammatical rules underlying anaphoric universals are general, violable tendencies rather than absolute, exceptionless restrictions. Second, certain grammatical rules concerning anaphora are not something *sui generis*, but rather have their origins in language use. In other words, these rules are best seen as, to use Levinson's (1987) metaphor, 'frozen pragmatics'—the outcome of a gradual, diachronic process from utterance-token-meaning via utterance-type-meaning to sentence-type-meaning. This, of course, does not mean that these rules as they are today are not part of the grammar. On the contrary, they are and as such they should be dealt with in the grammar. But the point is that if they are the result of a historical process, they can no longer be held as evidence for biologically pre-programmed human linguistic faculty. Third, syntax and pragmatics are interconnected in regulating anaphora, though they are distinct levels and modes of linguistic explanation. The interface between syntax and pragmatics may in general be summarized in a Kantian apophthegm: pragmatics without syntax is empty; syntax without pragmatics is blind. Furthermore, the extent to which syntax and pragmatics interact varies typologically. There exists a class of language (such as Chinese, Japanese, and Korean) where pragmatics plays a central role which in familiar European languages (such as English, French, and German) has hitherto been alleged to be played by the grammar. In these pragmatic languages, many of the constraints on anaphora are primarily due to principles of language use rather than rules of grammatical structure. From a diachronic viewpoint, languages seem to change from being more pragmatic to more syntactic; from a synchronic perspective, different languages may simply be at different stages of this evolutional circle.

Thirdly, the findings of this book also have important ramifications for current thinkings about universals, innateness, and learnability. On the one hand, anaphora exhibits a number of striking cross-linguistic tendencies; on the other, there are equally striking language-specific exceptions to these tendencies. The Chomskyan generative approach attempts to explain both the universal and the language-specific properties of anaphora in terms of a parameterized UG—the innate language faculty of *homo sapiens*. The logic of the innateness hypothesis is very much grounded in children's learnability, especially in the belief known as 'the problem of poverty or deficiency of stimulus' (e.g. Chomsky 1986*a*). While the findings of this book do not entirely contradict the innateness hypothesis, the fact that so many anaphoric processes in such a wide variety of areally, genetically, and typologically distinct languages are explainable as learnable on the basis of language use does undermine Chomsky's claim to the universality of UG and decrease the plausibility of the innateness hypothesis. This is because anaphora as such can no longer be taken to be instantiations of human mental templates. There are aspects of anaphoric universals which clearly are of a grammatical nature; there are also aspects of anaphoric universals which equally clearly are of a pragmatic nature. Put in a slightly different way, anaphoric universals are the product of both nature and nurture. The challenge before the linguist is, as Hawkins (1988, 1989) has rightly emphasized, to work out what are the grammatical rules and what are the pragmatic principles precisely, what is the relationship between them, and how they interact with each other. The analysis of anaphora made in this book strongly argues for a more interactive approach between the I[nternalized and intensional]- and E[xternalized and extensional]-models of language study. It seems unlikely that we can provide a satisfactory answer to what Chomsky (1986*a*) has referred to as Humboldt's problem and as (a special case of) Plato's problem without even trying to tackle Descartes's problem. In other words, the full understanding of the nature and ontogency of knowledge of language appears to be partially dependent on a better understanding of the (creative) use of that knowledge. If these conclusions are correct, it seems then that a large portion of linguistic explanation of anaphora currently sought in grammatical terms may need to be shifted to pragmatics, and pragmatics may no longer be treated as an 'epiphenomenon at best' (Chomsky 1986*a*: 25). In fact, as we have seen in this book, a refined neo-Gricean pragmatic theory has provided a better alternative to various extant syntactic and semantic analyses of anaphora.

There is an old saying in China which goes 'Qianli zhi xing, shi yu zu xia' (A journey of a thousand miles begins with a single step). While we still have a long way to go to understand anaphora both empirically and theoretically, this book will, I hope, be another step forward in our journey of a thousand miles to attain a better understanding of this fascinating linguistic phenomenon.

References

ABRAHAM, WERNER (1993), 'Null subjects in the history of German: from IP to CP', *Lingua*, 89: 117–42.

ADAMS, MARIANNE (1987), 'From Old French to the theory of pro-drop', *Natural Language and Linguistic Theory*, 5: 1–32.

ÅFARLI, TOR, and CREIDER, CHET (1987), 'Nonsubject pro-drop in Norwegian', *Linguistic Inquiry*, 18: 339–45.

AHENAKEW, FREDA (ed.) (1989), *Kiskinahamawâkan-âcimowinisa* (Saskatoon: Saskatchewan Indian Cultural Centre and Algonquian and Iroquoian Linguistics).

AIKAWA, TAKAKO (1993), 'Reflexivity in Japanese and LF analysis of *zibun* binding', Ph.D. dissertation, The Ohio State University.

ALLEN, W. S. (1956), 'Structure and system in the Abaza verbal complex', *Transactions of the Philological Society*, 127–76.

ANAGNOSTOPOULOU, ELENA, and EVERAERT, MARTIN (1999), 'Toward a more complete typology of anaphoric expressions', *Linguistic Inquiry*, 30: 97–119.

ANDERSEN, TORBEN, and GOYVAERTS, DIDIER L. (1986), 'Reflectivity and logophoricity in Moru-Madi', *Folia Linguistica*, 20: 297–318.

ANDERSON, STEPHEN R. (1976), 'On the notion of subject in ergative languages', in Li (1976: 1–23).

—— (1986), 'The typology of anaphoric dependencies: Icelandic (and other) reflexives', in Hellan and Christensen (1986: 65–88).

ANDREWS, AVERY D. (1985), 'The major functions of the noun phrases', in Shopen (1985:I. 62–154).

ANNAMALAI, E. (1997), 'Lexical anaphors and pronouns in Tamil', to appear in Wali et al. forthcoming.

AOUN, JOSEPH (1985), *A Grammar of Anaphora* (Cambridge, Mass.: The MIT Press).

—— (1986), *Generalized Binding* (Dordrecht: Foris).

—— and CHOUEIRI, LINA (1999), 'Epithets', *Natural Language and Linguistic Theory*, 17.

—— HORNSTEIN, NORBERT, LIGHTFOOT, DAVID, and WEINBERG, AMY (1987), 'Two types of locality', *Linguistic Inquiry*, 18: 539–77.

ARCHANGELI, DIANA (1997), 'Optimality theory: an introduction to linguistics in the 1990's', in Archangeli and Langendoen (1997: 1–32).

—— and LANGENDOEN, D. TERENCE (eds.) (1997), *Optimality Theory: An Overview* (Oxford: Basil Blackwell).

ARIEL, MIRA (1988), 'Referring and accessibility', *Journal of Linguistics*, 24: 65–87.

—— (1990), *Assessing Noun-Phrase Antecedents* (London: Routledge).

—— (1994), 'Interpreting anaphoric expresssions: a cognitive versus a pragmatic approach', *Journal of Linguistics*, 30: 3–42.

ARMSTRONG, ROBERT G. (1963), 'The Kwa working-group at Dakar', *Actes du Second Colloque International de Linguistique Négro-Africaine*, 213–17.

ARNOLD, DOUG, ATKINSON, MARTIN, DURAND, JACQUES, GROVER, CLAIRE, and SADLER, LOUISA (eds.) (1989), *Essays on Grammatical Theory and Universal Grammar* (Oxford: Oxford University Press).

ASHER, N., and WADA, H. (1988), 'A computational account of syntactic, semantic, and discourse principles for anaphora resolution', *Journal of Semantics*, 6: 309–44.

ATKINSON, MARTIN (1992), *Children's Syntax: An Introduction to Principles and Parameters Theory* (Oxford: Basil Blackwell).

ATLAS, JAY DAVID (1989), *Philosophy without Ambiguity: A Logico-linguistic Essay* (Oxford: Oxford University Press).

—— and LEVINSON, STEPHEN C. (1981), '*It*-clefts, informativeness and logical form: radical pragmatics', in Cole (1981: 1–61).

AUER, J. C. PETER (1984), 'Referential problems in conversation', *Journal of Pragmatics*, 8: 627–48.

AUSTIN, PETER (1981a), 'Switch-reference in Australia', *Language*, 57: 309–34.

—— (1981b), *A Grammar of Diyari, South Australia* (Cambridge: Cambridge University Press).

—— (ed.) (1988), *Complex Sentence Constructions in Australian Languages* (Amsterdam: John Benjamins).

—— and BRESNAN, JOAN (1996), 'Non-configurationality in Australian aboriginal languages', *Natural Language and Linguistic Theory*, 14: 215–68.

AUTHIER, J.-MARC P. (1988), 'Null object constructions in KiNande', *Natural Language and Linguistic Theory*, 6: 19–37.

—— (1989), 'Arbitrary null objects and unselective binding', in Jaeggli and Safir (1989b: 45–67).

—— (1992), 'A parametric account of V-governed arbitrary null arguments', *Natural Language and Linguistic Theory*, 10: 345–74.

AWBERY, GWENLLIAN M. (1976), *The Syntax of Welsh* (Cambridge: Cambridge University Press).

BACH, EMMON (1979), 'Control in Montague Grammar', *Linguistics Inquiry*, 10: 525–31.

—— and HARMS, ROBERT T. (eds.) (1968), *Universals in Linguistic Theory* (New York: Holt, Rinehart & Winston).

—— and PARTEE, BARBARA (1980), 'Anaphora and semantic structure', in *Pronouns and Anaphora* (Chicago: Chicago Linguistic Society): 1–28.

BAKER, C. L. (1995), 'Contrast, discourse prominence, and intensification, with special reference to locally free reflexives in British English', *Language*, 71: 63–101.

BAKER, MARK C. (1988), *Incorporation: A Theory of Grammatical Function Changing* (Chicago: The University of Chicago Press).

—— (1995), *The Polysynthesis Parameter* (Oxford: Oxford University Press).

BALTIN, MARK (1987), 'Do antecedent-contained deletions exist?', *Linguistics Inquiry*, 18: 579–95.

BAMGBOSE, AYO (1966), *A Grammar of Yoruba*, West African Language Monographs 5 (Cambridge: Cambridge University Press).

BANFIELD, ANN (1982), *Unspeakable Sentences* (London: Routledge).

BARBOSA, PILAR, FOX, DANNY, HAGSTROM, PAUL, MCGINNIS, MARTHA, and PESETSKY, DAVID (eds.) (1998), *Is the Best Good Enough? Optimality and Competition in Syntax* (Cambridge, Mass.: The MIT Press).

BAR-HILLEL, YEHOSHUA, and CARNAP, RUDOLF (1964), 'An outline of a theory of semantic information', in Y. Bar-Hillel (ed.), *Language and Information* (Reading, Mass.: Addison-Wesley): 221–74.

BARSS, ANDREW (1986), 'Chains and anaphoric dependence', Ph.D. dissertation, MIT.

—— and LASNIK, HOWARD (1986), 'A note on anaphora and double objects', *Linguistic Inquiry*, 17: 347–54.

BARTON, ELLEN L. (1990), *Nonsentential Constituents: A Theory of Grammatical Structure and Pragmatic Interpretation* (Amsterdam: John Benjamins).

BATTISTELLA, EDWIN (1985), 'On the distribution of PRO in Chinese', *Natural Language and Linguistic Theory*, 3: 317–40.

—— (1989), 'Chinese reflexivization: a movement to INFL approach', *Linguistics*, 27: 987–1012.

—— and XU, YONGHUI (1990), 'Remarks on the reflexive in Chinese', *Linguistics*, 28: 205–40.

BELLETTI, ADRIANA, and RIZZI, LUIGI (1988), 'Psych-verbs and θ-theory', *Natural Language and Linguistic Theory*, 6: 291–352.

BENEDICTO, ELENA (1991), 'Latin long-distance anaphora', in Koster and Reuland (1991: 171–84).

BENNIS, HANS, PICA, PIERRE, and ROORYCK, JOHAN (eds.) (1998), *Atomism and Binding* (Dordrecht: Foris).

BERGSLAND, KNUT (1997), *Aleut Grammar* (Fairbanks: Alaska Native Language Center).

BICKERTON, DEREK (1987), '*He himself*: anaphor, pronoun, or . . . ', *Linguistic Inquiry*, 18: 345–8.

BILOA, EDMOND (1991a), 'Null subjects, identification, and proper government', *Linguistics*, 29: 33–51.

—— (1991b), 'Anaphora and binding', *Linguistics*, 29: 845–59.

BITTNER, MARIA (1994), *Case, Scope and Binding* (Dordrecht: Kluwer).

BLACKWELL, SARAH ELIZABETH (1994), 'A neo-Gricean pragmatic approach to Spanish NP anaphora', Ph.D. dissertation, University of Pittsburgh.

—— (1998), 'Constraints on Spanish NP anaphora: the syntactic versus the pragmatic domain', *Hispania*, 81: 606–18.

—— (2000), 'Anaphora interpretations in Spanish utterances and the neo-Gricean pragmatic theory', *Journal of Pragmatics*, 32: 389–424.

BLOOM, PAUL (1990), 'Subjectless sentences in child language', *Linguistic Inquiry*, 21: 491–504.

BLOOMFIELD, LEONARD (1930), *Sacred Stories of the Sweet Grass Cree* (Ottawa: National Museum of Canada).

—— (1962), *The Menomini Language* (New Haven: Yale University Press).

BOHNHOFF, LEE E. (1986), 'Yạg Dii (Duru) pronouns', in Wiesemann (1986b: 103–30).

BOK-BENNEMA, REINEKE (1984), 'On marked pronominal anaphors and Eskimo

pro', in J. Guéron, H.-G. Obenauer, and J.-Y. Pollock, *Grammatical Representation* (Dordrecht: Foris): 1–18.
BOLINGER, DWIGHT (1979), 'Pronouns in discourse', in Givón (1979*b*: 289–309).
BORER, HAGIT (1984), *Parametric Syntax* (Dordrecht: Foris).
—— (1989), 'Anaphoric Agr', in Jaeggli and Safir (1989*b*: 69–109).
BÖRJARS, KERSTI, and CHAPMAN, CAROL (1998), 'Agreement and pro-drop in some dialects of English', *Linguistics*, 36: 71–98.
BOSCH, PETER (1983), *Agreement and Anaphora* (London: Academic Press).
BOUCHARD, DENIS (1984), *On the Content of Empty Categories* (Dordrecht: Foris).
—— (1989), 'Null objects and the theory of empty categories', in Kirschner and DeCesaris (1989: 33–49).
BOUTON, LAWRENCE F. (1970), 'Antecedent-contained pro-forms', *Papers from the Regional Meeting of the Chicago Linguistic Society*. 6: 154–67.
BRANCO, ANTÓNIO, and MARRAFA, PALMIRA (1999), 'Long-distance reflexives and the binding square of oppostion', in G. Webelhuth, J.-P. Koening, and A. Kathol (eds.), *Lexical and Constructional Aspects of Linguistic Explanation* (Stanford, Calif.: CSLI): 163–78.
BRANDI, LUCIANA, and CORDIN, PATRIZIA (1989), 'Two Italian dialects and the null subject parameter', in Jaeggli and Safir (1989*b*: 111–42).
BREEZE, MARY J. (1986), 'Personal pronouns in Gimira', in Wiesemann (1986*b*: 47–69).
BREMEN, K. von (1984), 'Anaphors: reference, binding and domains', *Linguistic Analysis*, 14: 191–229.
BRESNAN, JOAN (1982), 'Control and complementation', in J. Bresnan (ed.), *The Mental Representation of Grammatical Relations* (Cambridge, Mass.: The MIT Press): 282–390.
—— (1998), 'Morphology competes with syntax: explaining typological variation in weak crossover effects', in Barbosa et al. (1998: 59–92).
—— and MCHOMBO, SAM (1987), 'Topic, pronoun and agreement in Chichewa', *Language*, 63: 741–82.
BRIL, ISABELL (1999), 'Values of the reciprocal marker in Nêlêmwâ', in Nedjalkov and Guentcheva (forthcoming).
BRINTON, LAUREL (1995), 'Non-anaphoric reflexives in free indirect style: expressing the subjectivity of the non-speaker', in S. Stein and S. Wright (eds.), *Subjectivity and Subjectivization in Language* (Cambridge: Cambridge University Press): 173–94.
BROADWELL, GEORGE A. (1990), 'Extending the binding theory: a Muskogean case study', Ph.D. dissertation, University of California at Los Angeles.
—— (1998), 'Binding theory and switch-reference', in Bennis, Pica, and Rooryck (1998: 31-49).
BROWN, GILLIAN, and YULE, GEORGE (1983), *Discourse Analysis* (Cambridge: Cambridge University Press).
BROWN, PENELOPE, and LEVINSON, STEPHEN C. (1987), *Politeness: Some Universals in Language Usage* (Cambridge: Cambridge University Press).
BURQUEST, DONALD A. (1986), 'The pronoun system of some Chadic languages', in Wiesemann (1986*b*: 70–102).

BURZIO, LUIGI (1991), 'The morphological basis of anaphora', *Journal of Linguistics*, 27: 81–105.
—— (1996), 'The role of the antecedent in anaphoric relations', in R. Fredin, (ed.), *Current Issues in Comparative Grammar* (Dordrecht: Kluwer): 1–45.
—— (1998), 'Anaphora and soft constraints', in Barbosa et al. (1998: 93–113).
BUTLER, JAMES, and PECK, CHARLES (1980), 'The uses of passive, antipassive, and absolutive verbs in Tzutujil of San Pedro la Laguna', *Journal of Mayan Linguistics*, 2: 40–52.
CALABRESE, A. (1989), 'The lack of infinitival clauses in Salentino', MS.
CAMERON, RICHARD (1993), 'Ambiguous agreement, functional compensation, and non-specific *tú* in the Spanish of San Juan, Puerto Rico, and Madrid, Spain', *Language Variation and Change*, 5: 305–34.
—— (1994), 'Switch reference, verb class, and priming in a variable syntax', in *Variation and Linguistic Theory* (Chicago: Chicago Lingusitic Society): 27–45.
CAMPOS, HÉCTOR (1986*a*), 'Indefinite object drop', *Linguistic Inquiry*, 17: 354–9.
—— (1986*b*), 'Complementos directos indefinidos en romance', *Revista de linguística teórica y aplicada*, 24: 81–90.
CANÇADO, MÁRCIA (1999), 'Exceptional binding with psych verbs?', *Linguistic Inquiry*, 30: 133–41.
CANTRALL, WILLIAM R. (1974), *Viewpoint, Reflexives and the Nature of Noun Phrases* (The Hague: Mouton).
CARDEN, GUY (1982), 'Backwards anaphora in discourse context', *Journal of Linguistics*, 18: 361–87.
—— and STEWART, W. (1988), 'Binding theory, bioprogram and creolization: evidence from Haitian creole', *Journal of Pidgin and Creole Languages*, 3: 1–67.
—— —— (1989), 'Mauritian creole reflexives: a reply to Corne', *Journal of Pidgin and Creole Languages*, 4: 65–101.
CARRELL, PATRICIA L. (1970), *A Transformational Grammar of Igbo*, West African Language Monographs 8 (Cambridge: Cambridge University Press).
CHAFE, WALLACE. L. (1976), 'Givenness, contrastiveness, definiteness, subjects, topics, and point of view', in Li (1976: 25–55).
—— (ed.) (1980), *The Pear Stories: Cognitive, Cultural and Linguistic Aspects of Narrative Production* (Norwood: Ablex).
—— (1987), 'Cognitive constraints on information flow', in Tomlin (1987*b*: 21–51).
—— (1994), *Discourse, Consciousness, and Time: The Flow and Displacement of Conscious Experience in Speaking and Writing* (Chicago: The University of Chicago Press).
CHAO, WYNN (1988), *On Ellipsis* (New York: Garland).
—— (1992), 'Null objects in Portuguese', paper presented at the Oxford Romance Linguistics Seminar.
CHEN, PING (1986), 'Referent introducing and tracking in Chinese narrative', Ph.D. dissertation, University of California at Los Angeles.
—— (1996), 'Pragmatic interpretations of structural topics and relativization in Chinese', *Journal of Pragmatics*, 26: 389–406.
CHIEN, YU-CHIN, and WEXLER, KENNETH (1990), 'Children's knowledge of

locality conditions in binding as evidence for the modularity of syntax and pragmatics', *Language Acquisition*, 1: 225–95.

CHIERCHIA, GENNARO (1983), 'Outline of a semantic theory of (obligatory) control', *Proceedings of the West Coast Conference on Formal Linguistics*, 2: 19–31.

—— (1984), 'Topics in the syntax and semantics of infinitives and gerunds', Ph.D. dissertation, University of Massachusetts.

—— (1989), 'Structural meanings, thematic roles and control', in Chierchia, Partee, and Turner (1989: 131–66).

—— PARTEE, BARBARA, and TURNER, RAYMOND (eds.) (1989), *Properties, Types and Meaning*, 2 vols. (Dordrecht: Kluwer).

CHOMSKY, NOAM (1980), 'On binding', *Linguistic Inquiry*, 11: 1–46.

—— (1981), *Lectures on Government and Binding* (Dordrecht: Foris).

—— (1982), *Some Concepts and Consequences of the Theory of Government and Binding* (Cambridge, Mass.: The MIT Press).

—— (1986a), *Knowledge of Language: Its Nature, Origin and Use* (New York: Praeger).

—— (1986b), *Barriers* (Cambridge, Mass.: The MIT Press).

—— (1995), *The Minimalist Program* (Cambridge, Mass.: The MIT Press).

—— (1998), 'Some observations on economy in generative grammar', in Barbosa et al. (1998: 115–27).

CHUI, KAWAI (1994), 'Grammaticalization on the saying verb *wa* in Cantonese', *Santa Barbara Papers in Linguistics*, 5.

CHUNG, SANDRA (1984), 'Identifiability and null objects in Chamorro', *Proceedings of the Annual Meeting of the Berkeley Linguistic Society*, 10: 116–30.

—— (1989), 'On the notion of "null anaphor" in Chamorro', in Jaeggli and Safir (1989b: 143–84).

CLANCY, PATRICIA M. (1980), 'Referential choice in English and Japanese narrative discourse', in Chafe (1980: 127–202).

CLARK, HERBERT H. (1977), 'Bridging', in P. Wason and P. Johnson-Laird (eds.), *Thinking: Readings in Cognitive Science* (Cambridge: Cambridge University Press): 411–20.

—— (1996), *Using Language* (Cambridge: Cambridge University Press).

—— and CLARK, EVE V. (1977), *Psychology and Language* (New York: Harcourt Brace Jovanovich).

—— and HAVILAND, SUSAN E. (1977), 'Comprehension and the given–new contrast', in R. Freedle (ed.), *Discourse Production and Comprehension* (Hillsdale, NJ: Lawrence Erlbaum): 1–40.

—— and MARSHALL, CATHERINE C. (1981), 'Definite reference and mutual knowledge', in Joshi, Webber, and Sag, (1981: 10–63).

CLARK, ROBIN (1992), 'Towards a modular theory of coreference', in C.-T. J. Huang, and R. May (eds.), *Logical Structure and Linguistic Structure* (Dordrecht: Kluwer): 49–78.

CLEMENTS, GEORGE N. (1975), 'The logophoric pronoun in Ewe: its role in discourse', *Journal of West African Languages*, 10: 141–77.

CLOAREC-HEISS, FRANCE (1986), *Dynamique et équilibre d'une syntaxe: le banda-linda de Centrafrique* (Cambridge: Cambridge University Press).

COLE, MELVYN (1997) 'Pro-drop: a reanalysis of the data', paper presented at the Spring Meeting of the Linguistics Association of Great Britain (Edinburgh: University of Edinburgh).
COLE, PETER (ed.) (1978), *Syntax and Semantics 9: Pragmatics* (London: Academic Press).
—— (ed.) (1981), *Radical Pragmatics* (London: Academic Press).
—— (1983), 'Switch reference in two Quechua languages', in Haiman and Munro (1983*b*: 1–15).
—— (1987), 'Null objects in universal grammar', *Linguistic Inquiry*, 18: 597–612.
—— HERMON, GABRELLA, and SUNG, LI-MAY (1990), 'Principles and parameters of long-distance reflexives', *Linguistic Inquiry*, 21: 1–22.
—— and SUNG, LI-MAY (1994), 'Head movement and long-distance reflexives', *Linguistic Inquiry*, 25: 355–406.
—— and WANG, CHENGCHI (1996), 'Antecedents and blockers of long-distance reflexives: the case of Chinese *ziji*', *Linguistic Inquiry*, 27: 357–90.
COMRIE, BERNARD (1983), 'Switch-reference in Huichol: a typological study', in Haiman and Munro (1983: 17–37).
—— (1984), 'Subject and object control: syntax, semantics, pragmatics', *Proceedings of the Annual Meeting of the Berkeley Linguistics Society*, 10: 450–64.
—— (1985), 'Reflections on subject and object control', *Journal of Semantics*, 4: 47–65.
—— (1989*a*), *Language Universals and Linguistic Typology*, 2nd edn. (Oxford: Basil Blackwell).
—— (1989*b*), 'Some general properties of reference-tracking systems', in Arnold et al. (1989: 37–51).
COOK, VIVIAN J., and NEWSON, MARK (1995), *Chomsky's Universal Grammar*, 2nd edn. (Oxford: Blackwell).
CORBLIN, FRANCIS, GODARD, DANIÈLE, and MARANDIN, JEAN-MARIE (eds.) (1997), *Empirical Issues in Formal Syntax and Semantics* (Bern: Peter Lang).
CORNISH, FRANCIS (1999), *Anaphora, Discourse, and Understanding: Evidence from English and French* (Oxford: Oxford University Press).
COULMAS, FLORIAN (ed.) (1986), *Direct and Indirect Speech* (Berlin: Mouton de Gruyter).
CROUCH, RICHARD (1999), 'Ellipsis and glue languages', in Lappin and Benmamoun (1999: 32–67).
CROWLEY, TERRY (1978), *The Middle Clarence Dialects of Bandjalang* (Canberra: Australian Institute of Aboriginal Studies).
CRUSE, D. A. (1986), *Lexical Semantics* (Cambridge: Cambridge University Press).
CUENOT, JOSEPH (1952), 'Essai de grammaire bobo-oulée', *Bulletin de l'Institut Fondamental d'Afrique Noire série B: sciences humaines*, 14: 996–1045.
CULICOVER, PETER W., and WILKINS, WENDY (1986), 'Control, PRO, and the projection principle', *Language*, 62: 120–53.
CULY, CHRISTOPHER (1994*a*), 'Aspects of logophoric marking', *Linguistics*, 32: 1055–94.
—— (1994*b*), 'A note on logophoricity in Dogon', *Journal of African Languages and Linguistics*, 15: 113–25.

CULY, CHRISTOPHER (1997), 'Logophoric pronouns and point of view', *Linguistics*, 35: 845–59.

—— KODIO, KOUNGARMA, and TOGO, PATRICE (1994), 'Dogon pronominal systems: their nature and evolution', *Studies in African Linguistics*, 23: 315–44.

CUMMING, SUSANNA (1995), 'Agent position in the Sejarah Melayu', in P. Downing and M. Noonan (eds.), *Word Order in Discourse* (Amsterdam: John Benjamins): 51–83.

CUOQ, JEAN-ANDRÉ (1866), *Études philologiques sur quelques langues sauvages de l'Amérique* (Montreal: Dawson Brothers).

DAHL, ÖSTEN (1973), 'On so-called "sloppy identity"', *Synthese*, 26: 81–112.

—— (1974), 'How to open a sentence: abstraction in natural language', in *Logical Grammar Reports* (Göteborg: University of Göteborg).

DALRYMPLE, MARY, SHIEBER, STUART, and PEREIRA, FERNANDO (1991), 'Ellipsis and higher-order unification', *Linguistics and Philosophy*, 14: 399–452.

DATZ, MARGARET (1980), 'Jacaltec syntactic structures and the demands of discourse', Ph.D. dissertation, University of Colorado.

DAVIES, JOHN (1989), *Kobon* (London: Croom Helm).

DAVISON, ALICE (1977), 'Lexical anaphora in Hindi/Urdu', to appear in Wali et al. (1997).

DEANE, PAUL (1992), *Grammar in Mind and Brain: Explorations in Cognitive Science* (Berlin: Mouton de Gruyter).

DE JONG, JELLY JULIA (1996), 'The case of bound pronouns in peripheral Romance', Ph.D. dissertation, University of Groningen.

DEMIRCI, MAHIDE (1997), 'The role of pragmatics in the acquisition of reflexive binding in L2', Ph.D. dissertation, Michigan State University.

DENCH, ALAN (1982), 'Kin terms and pronouns of the Panyjima languages of Northwest Australia', *Anthropological Forum*, 5: 105–20.

—— (1987), 'Kinship and collective activity in the Ngayarda languages of Australian', *Language in Society*, 16: 321–40.

—— (1988), 'Complex sentences in Martuthunira', in P. Austin (ed.), *Complex Sentences in Australian Languages* (Amsterdam: John Benjamins): 97–139.

—— and EVANS, NICHOLAS (1988), 'Multiple case-marking in Australian languages', *Australian Journal of Linguistics*, 8: 1–47.

DÉPREZ, VIVIANE, and PIERCE, AMY (1993), 'Negation and functional projections in early grammar', *Linguistic Inquiry*, 24: 25–68.

DIESING, MOLLY (1990), 'Verb movement and the subject position in Yiddish', *Natural Language and Linguistic Theory*, 8: 41–81.

DIK, SIMON (1978), *Functional Grammar* (Amsterdam: North-Holland).

DIMITRIADIS, ALEXIS (1997), 'When pro-drop languages don't: over pronominal subjects and pragmatic inference', *Papers from the Regional Meeting of the Chicago Linguistic Society*, 32.

DIXON, R. M. W. (1972), *The Dyirbal Language of North Queensland* (Cambridge: Cambridge University Press).

—— (ed.) (1976), *Grammatical Categories in Australian Languages* (Canberra: Australian Institute of Aboriginal Studies).

DONNELLAN, KEITH S. (1966), 'Reference and definite descriptions', *Philosophical Review*, 75: 281–304.

—— (1978), 'Speaker reference, descriptions, and anaphora', in Cole (1978: 47–68).
DOOLEY, ROBERT A. (1982), 'Options in the pragmatic structuring of Guariní sentences', *Language*, 58: 307–31.
DOREN, EDIT (1999), 'V-movement and VP-ellipsis', in Lappin and Benmamoun (1999: 124–40).
DOWNING, PAMELA A. (1996), 'Proper names as a referential option in English conversation', in Fox (1996: 95–143).
DOWTY, DAVID R. (1980), 'Comments on the paper by Bach and Partee', in *Pronouns and Anaphora* (Chicago: Chicago Linguistic Society), 29–40.
—— (1985), 'On recent analyses of the semantics of control', *Linguistics and Philosophy*, 8: 1–41.
DUBINSKY, STANLEY, and HAMILTON, ROBERT (1998), 'Epithets as antilogophoric pronouns', *Linguistic Inquiry*, 29: 685–93.
DU BOIS, JOHN (1980), 'Beyond definiteness: the trace of identify in discourse', in Chafe (1980: 203–74).
—— (1987), 'The discourse basis of ergativity', *Language*, 63: 805–55.
DUMEZIL, GEORGES (1967), *Documents anatoliens sur les langues et les traditions du Daucase*, v: Études abkhas (Paris: Maisonneuve).
DUPUIS, FERNANDE (1989), 'L'Expression du sujet dans les propositions subordonnées en ancien français', Ph.D. dissertation, Université de Montréal.
DURIE, MARK (1994), 'A case study of pragmatic linking', *Text*, 14: 495–529.
DZIWIREK, KATARZYNA (1998), 'Reduced constructions in UG: evidence from Polish object control constructions', *Natural Language and Linguistic Theory*, 16: 53–99.
EADES, D. (1979), 'Gumbaynggir', in R. M. W. Dixon and B. Blake (eds.), *Handbook of Australian Languages*, vol. iii (Canberra: The Australian National University Press): 244–361.
ECKMAN, FRED, R. (1994), 'Local and long-distance anaphora in second language acquisition', in E. E. Tarone, S. M. Gass, and A. D. Cohen (eds.), *Research Methodology in Second Language Acquistion* (Hillsdale, NJ: Erlbaum): 207–26.
EDMONDSON, JEROLD A., and PLANK, FRANS (1978), 'Great expectations: an intensive *self* analysis', *Linguistics and Philosophy*, 2: 373–413.
EID, MUSHIRA (1983), 'On the communicative function of subject pronouns in Arabic', *Journal of Linguistics*, 19: 287–303.
ENÇ MÜRVET (1986), 'Topic switching and pronominal subject in Turish', in D. Slobin and K. Zimmer (eds.), *Studies in Turkish Linguistics* (Amsterdam: John Benjamins): 195–208.
—— (1989), 'Pronouns, licensing, and binding', *Natural Language and Linguistic Theory*, 7: 51–92.
ERKÜ, FERIDE, and GUNDEL, JEANETTE (1987), 'The pragmatics of indirect anaphors', in Verschueren and Bertuccelli-Papi (1987: 533–45).
ERTESCHIK-SHIR, NOMI (1997), *The Dynamics of Focus Structure* (Cambridge: Cambridge University Press).
ESSIEN, OKON (1975), 'Personal pronouns in indirect discourse in Efik', *Work in Progress*, 8: 133–44.
—— (1990), *A Grammar of the Ibibio Language* (Owerri: University Press).

EUBANK, LYNN (ed.) (1991), *Point-Counter-Point: Universal Grammar and Second Language Acquisition* (Amsterdam: John Benjamins).
EVANS, GARETH (1977), 'Pronouns, quantifiers and relative clauses I', *Canadian Journal of Philosophy*, 7: 467–536.
—— (1980), 'Pronouns', *Linguistic Inquiry*, 11: 337–62.
EVERAERT, MARTIN (1986), *The Syntax of Reflexivization* (Dordrecht: Foris).
—— (1991), 'Contextual determination of the anaphor/pronominal distinction', in Koster and Reuland (1991: 77–118).
—— and ANAGNOSTOPOULOU, ELENA (1997), 'Thematic hierarchies and binding theory: evidence from Greek', in Corblin, Godard and Marandin (1997).
FALK, CECILIA (1993), 'Non-referential subjects and agreement in the history of Swedish', *Lingua*, 89: 143–80.
FALTZ, LEONARD M. (1985), *Reflexivization: A Study in Universal Syntax* (New York: Garland).
—— (1989), 'A role for inference in meaning change', *Studies in Language*, 13: 317–31.
FARKAS, DONKA F. (1985), 'Obligatorily controlled subjects in Romanian', *Papers from the Regional Meeting of the Chicago Linguistic Society*, 21: 90–100.
—— (1987), 'Do *pro* in Hungarian', in I. Kenesei (ed.), *Approaches to Hungarian*, vol. ii (Szeged: JATE): 191–213.
—— (1988), 'On obligatory control', *Linguistics and Philosophy*, 11: 27–58.
FARMER, ANN K. (1987), 'They held each other's breath and other puzzles for the binding theory', *Linguistics Inquiry*, 18: 157–63.
—— HALE, KENNETH, and TSUJIMURA, NATSUKO (1986), 'A note on weak crossover in Japanese', *Natural Language and Linguistic Theory*, 4: 33–42.
—— and HARNISH, ROBERT M. (1987), 'Communicative reference with pronouns', in Verschueren and Bertuccelli-Papi (1987: 547–65).
FARRELL, PATRICK (1990), 'Null objects in Brazilian Portuguese', *Natural Language and Linguistic Theory*, 8: 325–46.
FAUCONNIER, GILLES (1985), *Mental Spaces* (Cambridge: Cambridge University Press).
FIENGO, ROBERT, and MAY, ROBERT (1994), *Indices and Identity* (Cambridge, Mass.: The MIT Press).
FILLMORE, CHARLES (1968), 'The case for case', in Bach and Harms (1968: 1–88).
—— (1982), 'Toward a descriptive framework for spatial deixis', in R. Jarvella and W. Klein (eds.), *Speech, Place, and Action* (Chichester: John Wiley & Sons): 31–59.
FINER, DANIEL (1985*a*), *The Formal Grammar of Switch-Reference* (New York: Garland).
—— (1985*b*), 'The syntax of switch-reference', *Linguistic Inquiry*, 16: 35–55.
—— (1991), 'Binding parameters in second language acquisition', in Eubank (1991: 351–74).
—— and BROSELOW, ELLEN (1986), 'Second language acquisition of reflexive binding', *North Eastern Linguistic Society*, 16: 154–68.
FIRBAS, JAN (1992), *Functional Sentence Perspective in Written and Spoken Communication* (Cambridge: Cambridge University Press).
FLEISCHMAN, SUZANNE (1991), 'Discourse pragmatics and the grammar of Old

French: a functional reinterpretation of *si* and the personal pronouns', *Romance Philology*, 44: 251–83.
FODOR, JERRY A. (1975), *The Language of Thought* (Cambridge, Mass.: Harvard University Press).
—— (1983), *The Modularity of Mind* (Cambridge, Mass.: The MIT Press).
FOLEY, WILLIAM A., and VAN VALIN, ROBERT D. (1984), *Functional Syntax and Universal Grammar* (Cambridge: Cambridge University Press).
FORNEL, MICHEL DE (1987), 'Reference to persons in conversation', in Verschueren and Bertuccelli-Papi (1987: 131–40).
FORTESCUE, MICHAEL (1991), 'Switch reference anomalies and "topic" in West Greenlandic: a case of pragmatics over syntax', in Verschueren (1991: 53–77).
FOULET, LUCIEN (1930), *Petite Syntaxe de l'ancien français* (Paris: Honoré Champion). 3rd edition.
FOX, BARBARA A. (1987), *Discourse Structure and Anaphora: Written and Conversational English* (Cambridge: Cambridge University Press).
—— (ed.) (1996), *Studies in Anaphora* (Amsterdam: John Benjamins).
FOX, DANNY (1998), 'Locality in variable binding', in Barbosa et al. (1998: 129–55).
—— (1999), 'Reconstruction, binding theory and the interpretation of chains', *Linguistic Inquiry*, 30: 157–96.
FRAJZYNGIER, ZYGMUNT (1985), 'Logophoric systems in Chadic', *Journal of African Languages and Linguistics*, 7: 23–37.
—— (1996), 'On sources of demonstratives and anaphors', in Fox (1996: 169–203).
—— (1997), 'Affectedness, control and anaphora: the reflexive forms and functions', paper presented at the International Symposium on Reflexives and Reciprocals (Boulder: University of Colorado), to appear in Frajzyngier and Curl (eds.) (forthcoming *a*).
—— and CURL, TRACI (forthcoming *a*), *Reflexives: Forms and Functions* (Amsterdam: John Benjamins).
—— —— (forthcoming *b*), *Reciprocals: Forms and Functions* (Amsterdam: John Benjamins).
FRANKLIN, KARL, J. (1983), 'Some features of interclausal reference in Kewa', in Haiman and Munro (1983*b*: 39–49).
FRANKS, STEVEN, and HORNSTEIN, NORBERT (1992), 'Secondary predication in Russian and proper government of PRO', in Larson et al. (1992: 1–50).
FREIDIN, ROBERT (1991*a*), *Foundations of Generative Grammar* (Cambridge, Mass.: The MIT Press).
—— (ed.) (1991*b*), *Principles and Parameters in Comparative Grammar* (Cambridge, Mass.: The MIT Press).
—— (1998), 'Binding theory on minimalist assumptions', in Bennis, Pica, and Rooryck (1988:141–53).
FUKUI, NAOKI (1984), 'Studies in Japanese anaphora', MS, MIT.
GAIR, JAMES, and KARUNATILLAKE, W. S. (1998), 'Pronouns, reflexives and antianaphora in Sinhala', in J. Gair, *Studies in South Asian Linguistics* (Oxford: Oxford University Press): 126–39.
GARROD, SIMON C., and SANFORD, ANTHONY J. (1994), 'Resolving sentences in a

discourse context', in M. A. Gernsbacher (ed.), *Handbook of Psycholinguistics* (London: Academic Press): 675–98.

GAWRON, MARK, and PETERS, STANLEY (1990), *Anaphora and Quantification in Situation Semantics* (Chicago: The University of Chicago Press).

GAZDAR, GERALD (1979), *Pragmatics: Implicature, Presupposition and Logical Form* (London: Academic Press).

GELUYKENS, RONALD (1994), *The Pragmatics of Discourse Anaphora in English: Evidence from Conversational Repair* (Berlin: Mouton de Gruyter).

GENIUŠIENĖ, EMMA (1987), *The Typology of Reflexives* (Berlin: Mouton de Gruyter).

GEORGOPOULOS, CAROL (1991), *Syntactic Variables: Resumptive Pronouns and Ā-binding in Palauan* (Dordrecht: Kluwer).

GERDTS, DONNA B. (1988), *Object and Absolutive in Halkomelem Salish* (New York: Garland).

GILLIGAN, GARY MARTIN (1987), 'A cross-linguistic approach to the pro-drop parameter', Ph.D. dissertation, University of Southern California.

GIORGI, ALESSANDRA (1984), 'Towards a theory of long distance anaphors: a GB approach', *Linguistic Review*, 3: 307–61.

—— (1991), 'Prepositions, binding and θ-marking', in Koster and Reuland (1991: 185–229).

GIVÓN, TALMY (1976), 'Topic, pronoun and grammatical agreement', in Li (1976: 149–88).

—— (1979a), 'From discourse to syntax: grammar as a processing strategy', in Givón (1979b: 81–112).

—— (ed.) (1979b), *Syntax and Semantics 12: Discourse and Syntax* (London: Academic Press).

—— (ed.) (1983), *Topic Continuity in Discourse: A Quantitative Cross-language Study* (Amsterdam: John Benjamins).

—— (1985), 'Iconicity, isomorphism and non-arbitrary coding in syntax', in Haiman (1985b: 187–219).

—— (1990), *Syntax: A Functional-Typological Introduction*, 2 vols. (Amsterdam: John Benjamins).

GODARD, DANIÈLE (1989), 'Empty categories as subjects of tensed Ss in English or French?', *Linguistics Inquiry*, 20: 497–506.

GODDARD, IVES (1990), 'Aspects of the topic structure of Fox narratives: proximate shifts and the use of overt and inflectional NPs', *International Journal of American Linguistics*, 56: 317–40.

GORDON, LYNN (1983), 'Switch-reference, clause order, and interclausal relationships in Maricopa', in Haiman and Munro (1983b: 83–104).

GORDON, PETER, GROSZ, BARBARA, and GILLIOM, LAURA (1993), 'Pronouns, names, and the centering of attention in discourse', *Cognitive Science*, 17: 311–47.

GREEN, MARGARET M., and IGWE, G. E. (1963), *A Descriptive Grammar of Igbo* (Oxford: Oxford University Press).

GRICE, H. P. (1957), 'Meaning', *Philosophical Review*, 66: 377–88.

—— (1975), 'Logic and conversation', in P. Cole and J. Morgan (eds.), *Syntax and Semantics 3: Speech Acts* (London: Academic Press): 41–58.

—— (1978), 'Further notes on logic and conversation', in Cole (1978: 113–28).

—— (1989), *Studies in the Way of Words* (Cambridge, Mass.: Harvard University Press).
GRIMES, JOSEPH (1975), *The Thread of Discourse* (The Hague: Mouton).
GRIMSHAW, JANE (1990), *Argument Structure* (Cambridge, Mass.: The MIT Press).
—— (1997), 'Projection, heads and optimality', *Linguistic Inquiry*, 28: 373–422.
—— and SAMEK-LODOVICI, VIERI (1998), 'Optimal subjects and subject universals', in Barbosa et al. (1998: 193–219).
GRODZINSKY, YOSEF, and REINHART, TANYA (1993), 'The innateness of binding and coreference', *Linguistic Inquiry*, 24: 69–101.
GROSZ, B. and SIDNER, C. (1986), 'Attention, intensions, and the structure of discourse', *Computational Linguistics*, 12: 175–204.
—— WEINSTEIN, S. and JOSHI, A. (1995), 'Centering: a framework for modeling the local coherence of discourse', *Computational Linguistics*, 21: 203–25.
GUÉRON, J., OBENAUER, H.-G., and POLLOCK, J.-Y. (eds.) (1984), *Grammatical Representation* (Dordrecht: Foris).
GUNDEL, JEANETTE (1985), '"Shared knowledge" and topicality', *Journal of Pragmatics*, 9: 83–107.
—— (1988), 'Universals of topic-comment structure', in M. Hammond, E. Moravcsik, and P. Wirth, (eds.), *Studies in Syntactic Typology* (Amsterdam: John Benjamins): 209–39.
—— HEDBERG, NANCY, and ZACHARSKI, RON (1993), 'Cognitive status and the form of referring expressions in discourse', *Language*, 69: 274–307.
GUNJI, TAKAO (1987), *Japanese Phrase Structure Grammar: A Unification-Based Approach* (Dordrecht: Kluwer).
GURTU, MADHU (1992), *Anaphoric Relations in Hindi and English* (Delhi: Munshiram Manoharlal).
HAEGEMAN, LILIANE (1992), *Theory and Description in Generative Syntax: A Case Study in West Flemish* (Cambridge: Cambridge University Press).
—— (1994), *Introduction to Government and Binding Theory*, 2nd edn. (Oxford: Basil Blackwell).
HAERI, NILOOFAR (1989), 'Overt and nonovert subjects in Persian', *The IPrA Papers in Pragmatics*, 3: 156–67.
HAGÈGE, CLAUDE (1974), 'Les pronoms logophoriques', *Bulletin de la Société de Linguistique de Paris*, 69: 287–310.
HAÏK, ISABELLE (1987), 'Bound VPs that need to be', *Linguistics and Philosophy*, 10: 503–30.
HAIMAN, JOHN (1983), 'On some origins of switch-reference marking', in Haiman and Munro (1983: 105–28).
—— (1985a), *Natural Syntax* (Cambridge: Cambridge University Press).
—— (ed.) (1985b), *Iconicity in Syntax* (Amsterdam: John Benjamins).
—— and MUNRO, PAMELA (1983a), 'Introduction', in Haiman and Munro (1983b: pp. ix–xv).
—— —— (eds.) (1983b), *Switch-Reference and Universal Grammar* (Amsterdam: John Benjamins).
HAKULINEN, AULI (1987), 'Avoiding personal reference in Finnish', in Verschueren and Bertuccelli-Papi (1987: 141–53).
HALE, E. AUSTIN (1999), *Newari/Newar* (Munich: Lincom Europa).

HALE, KENNETH (1976), 'The adjoined relative clause in Australia', in Dixon (1976: 78–105).
—— (1983), 'Warlpiri and the grammar of nonconfigurational languages', *Natural Language and Linguistic Theory*, 1: 5–49.
—— (1992), 'Subject obviation, switch reference, and control', in Larson et al. (1992: 51–77).
HALLIDAY, M. A. K., and HASAN, R. (1976), *Cohesion in English* (London: Longman).
HAMANN, CARNELIA (1996), 'Null arguments in German child language', *Language Acquisition*, 5: 155–208.
HANKAMER, JORGE, and SAG, IVAN A. (1976), 'Deep and surface anaphora', *Linguistic Inquiry*, 7: 391–428.
HARBERT, WAYNE (1995), 'Binding theory, control, and *pro*', in G. Webelhuth (ed.), *Government and Binding Theory and the Minimalist Program* (Oxford: Basil Blackwell): 177–240.
HARDT, DANIEL (1992), 'VP ellipsis and semantic identity', in S. Berman and A. Hestvik (eds.), *Proceedings of the Stuttgart Ellipsis Workshop*, (Stuttgart: University of Stuttgart).
—— (1993), 'Verb phrase ellipsis: form, meaning and processing', Ph.D. dissertation, University of Pennsylvania.
—— (1999), 'Dynamic interpretation of verb phrase ellipsis', *Linguistics and Philosophy*, 22: 185–219.
HASEGAWA, NOBUKO (1984), 'On the so-called "zero pronouns" in Japanese', *Linguistic Review*, 4: 289–341.
HASHEMIPOUR, MEGGY (1988), 'Finite control in Modern Persian', *Proceedings of the West Coast Conference on Formal Linguistics*, 7: 115–28.
HAVILAND, SUSAN E., and CLARK, HERBERT H. (1974), 'What's new? Acquiring new information as a process in comprehension', *Journal of Verbal Learning and Verbal Behaviour*, 13: 512–21.
HAWKINS, JOHN (1978), *Definiteness and Indefiniteness: A Study in Reference and Grammaticality Prediction* (London: Croom Helm).
—— (ed.) (1988), *Explaining Language Universals* (Oxford: Basil Blackwell).
—— (1989), 'Competence and performance in the explanation of language universals', in Arnold et al. (1989: 119–52).
HEATH, JEFFREY (1975), 'Some functional relationships in grammar', *Language*, 51: 89–104.
—— (1977), 'Choctaw case', *Proceedings of the Annual Meeting of the Berkeley Linguistics Society*, 3: 204–13.
—— (1980), *Nunggubuyu Myths and Ethnographic Texts* (Canberra: Australian Institute of Aboriginal Studies).
—— (1983), 'Reference tracking in Nunggubuyu', in Haiman and Munro (1983*b*: 129–49).
—— (1986), 'Syntactic and lexical aspects of nonconfigurationality in Nunggubuyu (Australia)', *Natural Language and Linguistic Theory*, 4: 375–408.
HEDINGER, ROBERT (1984), 'Reported speech in Akɔɔse', *Journal of West African Languages*, 14: 81–102.

HEIM, IRENE, LASNIK, HOWARD, and MAY, ROBERT (1991), 'Reciprocity and plurality', *Linguistic Inquiry*, 22: 63–101.

HEINE, BERND (1997), 'Polysemy involving reflexive and reciprocal markers in African languages', paper presented at the International Symposium on Reflexives and Reciprocals (Boulder: University of Colorado), to appear in Frajzyngier and Curl (eds.) (forthcoming *b*).

—— CLAUDI, ULRIKE, and HÜNNEMEYER, FRIEDERIKE (1991), *Grammaticalization: A Conceptual Framework* (Chicago: The University of Chicago Press).

HELKE, MICHAEL (1979), *The Grammar of English Reflexives* (New York: Garland).

HELLAN, LARS (1988), *Anaphora in Norwegian and the Theory of Grammar* (Dordrecht: Foris).

—— (1991), 'Containment and connectedness anaphors', in Koster and Reuland (1991: 27–48).

—— and CHRISTENSÉN, K. KOCH (eds.) (1986), *Topics in Scandinavian Syntax* (Dordrecht: Reidel).

HENDRICK, RANDALL (1988), *Anaphora in Celtic and Universal Grammar* (Dordrecht: Kluwer).

HERMON, GABRIELLA (1985), *Syntactic Modularity* (Dordrecht: Foris).

—— (1992), 'Binding theory and parameter setting', *Linguistic Review*, 9: 145–81.

—— and YOON, JAMES (1989), 'The licensing and identification of *pro* and the typology of Agr', *Papers from the Regional Meeting of the Chicago Linguistic Society*, 25: 174–92.

HESTVIK, ARILD (1990), 'LF movement of pronouns and the computation of binding domains', Ph.D. dissertation, Brandeis University.

—— (1991), 'Subjectless binding domains', *Natural Language and Linguistic Theory*, 9: 455–96.

—— (1992), 'LF movement of pronouns and antisubject orientation', *Linguistic Inquiry*, 23: 557–94.

—— (1995), 'Reflexives and ellipsis', *Natural Language Semantics*, 3: 211–37.

HIGGINBOTHAM, JAMES (1983), 'Logical form, binding and nominals', *Linguistic Inquiry*, 14: 395–420.

—— (1985), 'On semantics', *Linguistic Inquiry*, 16: 547–93.

HILL, HARRIET (1995), 'Pronouns and reported speech in Adioukrou', *Journal of West African Languages*, 25: 87–106.

HILLES, SHARON (1986), 'Interlanguage and the pro-drop parameter', *Second Language Research*, 2: 33–52.

—— (1991), 'Access to Universal Grammar in second language acquisition', in Eubank (1991: 305–38).

HIMMELMANN, NIKOLAUS P. (1996), 'Demonstratives in narrative discourse: a taxonomy of universal uses', in Fox (1996: 205–54).

HINDS, JOHN (ed.) (1978), *Anaphora in Discourse* (Edmonton: Linguistic Research Inc.).

—— (1979), 'Organizational patterns in discourse', in Givón (1979*b*: 135–57).

HINTIKKA, JAAKKO, and SANDU, GABRIEL (1991), *On the Methodology of Linguistics* (Oxford: Basil Blackwell).

HIRAKAWA, MAKIKO (1990), 'A study of the L2 acquisition of English reflexives', *Second Language Research*, 6: 60–85.
HIRSCHBERG, JULIA, and WARD, GREGORY (1991), 'Accent and bound anaphora', *Cognitive Linguistics*, 2: 101–21.
HIRSCHBÜHLER, PAUL (1989), 'On the existence of null subjects in embedded clauses in Old and Middle French', in Kirschner and DeCesaris (1989: 155–75).
HOBBS, JERRY R. (1978), 'Resolving pronoun references', *Lingua*, 44: 311–38.
—— (1979), 'Coherence and coreference', *Cognitive Science*, 3: 67–90.
HOEKSTRA, TEUN, and SCHWARTZ, BONNIE D. (1994), *Language Acquisition Studies in Generative Grammar* (Amsterdam: John Benjamins).
HOFSTADTER, D., CLOSSMAN, G., and MEREDITH, M. (1982), *Shakespeare's Plays Weren't Written by Him but by Someone Else of the Same Name: An Essay on Intentionality and Frame-Based Knowledge Representation Systems* (Bloomington: Indiana University Linguistics Club).
HOIJER, H. (1949), 'Tonkawa syntactic suffixes and anaphoric particles', *South-Western Journal of Anthropology*, 5: 37–55.
HOJI, HAJIME (1998), 'Null object and sloppy identity in Japanese', *Linguistic Inquiry*, 29: 127–52.
HOLISKY, D. A. (1987), 'The case of the intransitive subject in Tsova-Tush (Batsbi)', *Lingua*, 71: 103–32.
HOLMBERG, ANDERS, and PLATZACK, CHRISTER (1995), *The Role of Inflection in Scandinavian Syntax* (Oxford: Oxford University Press).
HOONCHAMLONG, YUPHAPHANN (1991), 'Some issues in Thai anaphora: a Government and Binding approach', Ph.D. dissertation, University of Wisconsin at Madison.
HOPKINS, ELIZABETH B. (1986), 'Pronouns and pronoun fusion in Yaoure', in Wiesemann (1986*b*): 191–204).
HOPPER, PAUL, and TRAUGOTT, ELIZABETH (1993), *Grammaticalization* (Cambridge: Cambridge University Press).
HORN, LAURENCE R. (1972), 'On the semantic properties of logical operators in English', Ph.D. dissertation, University of California at Los Angeles.
—— (1984), 'Toward a new taxonomy for pragmatic inference: Q-based and R-based implicature', in Schiffrin (1984: 11–42).
—— (1988), 'Pragmatic theory', in Newmeyer (1988: i. 113–45).
—— (1989), *A Natural History of Negation* (Chicago: The University of Chicago Press).
HORNSTEIN, NORBERT (1994), 'An argument for minimalism: the case of antecedent contained deletion', *Linguistic Inquiry*, 25: 455–80.
—— (1995), *Logical Form: From GB to Minimalism* (Oxford: Basil Blackwell).
—— (1999), 'Movement and control', *Linguistic Inquiry*, 30: 69–96.
—— and LIGHTFOOT, DAVID (1987), 'Predication and PRO', *Language*, 63: 23–52.
—— and WEINBERG, AMY (1990), 'The necessity of LF', *Linguistic Review*, 7: 129–67.
HORROCKS, GEFFREY (1987), *Generative Grammar* (London: Longman).
HUANG, C.-T. JAMES. (1983), 'A note on the binding theory', *Linguistic Inquiry*, 14: 554–61.

—— (1984), 'On the distribution and reference of empty pronouns', *Linguistic Inquiry*, 15: 531–74.
—— (1989), 'Pro-drop in Chinese: a generalized control theory', in Jaeggli and Safir (1989b: 185–214).
—— (1991), 'Remarks on the status of the null object', in R. Freidin (ed.), *Principles and Parameters in Comparative Grammar* (Cambridge, Mass.: The MIT Press): 56–76.
—— and TANG, C.-C. JANE (1991), 'The local nature of the long-distance reflexive in Chinese', in Koster and Reuland (1991: 263–82).
HUANG, YAN (1987), 'Zero anaphora in Chinese: toward a pragmatic analysis', Cambridge College Research Fellowship Competition dissertation, University of Cambridge.
—— (1989), 'Anaphora in Chinese: toward a pragmatic analysis', Ph.D. dissertation, University of Cambridge.
—— (1991a), 'A neo-Gricean pragmatic theory of anaphora', *Journal of Linguistics*, 27: 301–35.
—— (1991b), 'A pragmatic analysis of control in Chinese', in Verschueren (1991: 113–45).
—— (1992a), 'Against Chomsky's typology of empty categories', *Journal of Pragmatics*, 17: 1–29.
—— (1992b), 'Hanyu de kongfanchou (Empty categories in Chinese)', *Zhongguo Yuwen*, 5: 383–93.
—— (1993), 'Review of Hintikka, J. and Sandu, G., *On the Methodology of Linguistics*', *Journal of Pragmatics*, 19: 487–501.
—— (1994), *The Syntax and Pragmatics of Anaphora: A Study with Special Reference to Chinese* (Cambridge: Cambridge University Press).
—— (1995), 'On null subjects and null objects in generative grammar', *Linguistics*, 33: 1081–123.
—— (1996a), 'A note on the head-movement analysis of long-distance reflexives', *Linguistics*, 34: 833–40.
—— (1996b), 'Review of Geluykens, R., *The Pragmatics of Discourse Anaphora in English*', *Language*, 72: 164–7.
—— (1997). 'Interpreting long-distance reflexives: a neo-Gricean pragmatic approach', paper presented at the LSA Workshop on Long-Distance Reflexives (Cornell University).
—— (2000), 'Discourse anaphora: four theoretical models', *Journal of Pragmatics*, 32: 151–176.
HUBBARD, P. L. (1983), 'Albanian reflexives: violations of proposed universals', *Kansas Working Papers in Linguistics*, 8: 63–71.
HUET, GÉRARD (1975), 'A unification algorithm for typed $\bar{\lambda}$-calculus', *Theoretical Computer Science*, 1: 27–57.
HUKARI, THOMAS E. (1989), 'The domain of reflexivization in English', *Linguistics*, 27: 207–44.
HULK, AAFKE, and VAN KEMENADE, ANS (1993), 'Subjects, nominative case, agreement and functional heads', *Lingua*, 89: 181–215.
HUST, JOEL, and BRAME, MICHAEL (1976), 'Jackendoff on interpretive semantics', *Linguistic Analysis*, 2: 243–77.

HUTCHISON, JOHN P. (1981), 'Coreferent pronominalization in Diré Songhai', *Studies in African Linguistics*, 2: 83–103.

HUTCHISSON, DON (1986), 'Sursurunga pronouns and the specific uses of quadral number', in Wiesemann (1986*b*: 1–20).

HWANG, JYA-LIN, LYOVIN, ANATOLE, and BAIKA, TADASHI (1998), 'On the grammaticalization of saying verbs: evidence from Taiwanese, Russian and Japanese', paper presented at the 27th Annual Meeting of the Linguistic Association of the Southwest.

HYAMS, NINA M. (1986), *Language Acquisition and the Theory of Parameters* (Dordrecht: D. Reidel).

—— (1989), 'The null subject parameter in language acquisition', in Jaeggli and Safir (1989*b*: 215–38).

—— (1992), 'A reanalysis of null subject in child language', in Weissenborn, Goodluck, and Roeper (1992: 249–69).

—— and SIGURJÓNSDÓTTIR, SIGRIDUR (1990), 'The development of "long-distance anaphora"': a cross-linguistic study with special reference to Icelandic', *Language Acquisition*, 1: 57–93.

—— and WEXLER, KENNETH (1993), 'On the grammatical basis of null subjects in child language', *Linguistics Inquiry*, 24: 421–60.

HYMAN, LARRY (1979), 'Phonology and noun structure', in L. Hyman (ed.), *Aghem Grammatical Structure* (Los Angeles: Department of Linguistics, University of Southern California): 1–72.

—— (1981), *Noni Grammatical Structure* (Los Angeles: Department of Linguistics, University of Southern California).

—— and COMRIE, BERNARD (1981), 'Logophoric reference in Gokana', *Journal of African Languages and Linguistics*, 3: 19–37.

IATRIDOU, SABINE (1986), 'An anaphor not bound in its governing category', *Linguistic Inquiry*, 17: 766–72.

—— (1988), 'Clitics, anaphors, and a problem of coindexation', *Linguistic Inquiry*, 19: 698–703.

—— and EMBICK, DAVID (1997), 'Apropos *pro*', *Language*, 73: 58–78.

IIDA, MASAYO (1996), *Context and Binding in Japanese* (Stanford, Calif.: CSLI).

—— WECHSLER, STEPHEN, and ZEC, DRAGA (eds.) (1987), *Working Papers in Grammatical Theory and Discourse Structure: Interactions of Morphology, Syntax and Discourse*, (Stanford, Calif.: CSLI).

IKORO, S. (1995), *The Kana Language* (Leiden: CNWS).

IWAKURA, KUNIHIRO (1985), 'The binding theory and PRO', *Linguistic Analysis*, 15: 29–55.

JACKENDOFF, RAY (1972), *Semantic Interpretation in Generative Grammar* (Cambridge, Mass.: The MIT Press).

—— (1987), 'The status of thematic relations in linguistic theory', *Linguistic Inquiry*, 18: 369–411.

—— (1990), *Semantic Structures* (Cambridge, Mass.: The MIT Press).

JACOBSEN, WILLIAM H. (1967), 'Switch-reference in Hokan-Coahuiltecan', in D. Hymes and W. Bittle (eds.), *Studies in Southwestern Ethnolinguistics* (The Hague: Mouton): 238–63.

—— (1983), 'Typological and genetic notes on switch-reference systems in North American Indian languages', in Haiman and Munro (1983*b*: 151–83).
JAEGGLI, OSVALDO A. (1982), *Topics in Romance Syntax* (Dordrecht: Foris).
—— (1986), 'Arbitrary plural pronominals', *Natural Language and Linguistic Theory*, 4: 43–76.
—— and SAFIR, KENNETH J. (1989*a*), 'The null subject parameter and parametric theory', in Jaeggli and Safir (1989*b*: 1–44).
—— —— (eds.) (1989*b*), *The Null Subject Parameter* (Dordrecht: Kluwer).
—— and SILVA-CORVALÁN, CARMEN (eds.) (1986), *Studies in Romance Linguistics* (Dordrecht: Foris).
JAYASEELAN, K. A. (1990), 'Incomplete VP deletion and gapping', *Linguistic Analysis*, 20: 64–81.
JESPERSEN, OTTO (1924), *The Philosophy of Grammar* (London: Allen & Unwin).
JOSEPH, BRIAN (1992), 'Diachronic perspectives on control', in Larson et al. (1992: 195–234).
JOSHI, ARAVIND K., WEBBER, BONNIE C., and SAG, IVAN A. (eds.) (1981), *Elements of Discourse Understanding* (Cambridge: Cambridge University Press).
JUSTUS, CAROL (1976), 'Relativization and topicalization in Hittite', in Li (1976: 213–45).
KAMEYAMA, MEGUMI (1984), 'Subjective/logophoric bound anaphor *zibun*', *Papers from the Regional Meeting of the Chicago Linguistic Society*, 20: 228–38.
—— (1985), 'Zero anaphora: the case of Japanese', Ph.D. dissertation, Stanford University.
KAMP, HANS (1982), 'A theory of truth and semantic representation', in J. Groenendijk, T. Janssen, and M. Stokhof (eds.), *Formal Methods in the Study of Language* (Amsterdam: Matematisch Centrum): 277–321.
—— and REYLE, UWE (1993), *From Discourse to Logic: Introduction to Modeltheoretic Semantics of Natural Languages, Formal Logic and Discourse Representation Theory* (Dordrecht: Kluwer).
KANG, BEOM-MO (1988), 'Unbounded reflexives', *Linguistics and Philosophy*, 11: 415–56.
KANNO, KAZUE (1996), 'Access to universal grammar in second-language acquisition: data from the interpretation of null arguments in Japanese', *Linguistics*, 34: 397–412.
KAPUR, S., LUST, B., HARBERT, W., and MARTOHARDJONO, G. (1993), 'Universal grammar and learnability theory', in E. Reuland and W. Abraham (eds.), *Knowledge and Language: Issues in Representation and Acquisition* (Dordrecht: Kluwer).
KARTTUNEN, LAURI (1976), 'Discourse referents', in J. McCawley (ed.), *Syntax and Semantics 7: Notes from the Linguistic Underground* (London: Academic Press): 363–85.
KATADA, FUSA (1991), 'The LF representation of anaphors', *Linguistic Inquiry*, 22: 287–313.
KATO, KUMIKO (1994), 'On reflexives in Japanese: some syntactic and pragmatic approaches', MA dissertation, University of Reading.
KAYNE, RICHARD S. (1991), 'Romance clitics, verb movement, and PRO', *Linguistic Inquiry*, 22: 647–86.

KEENAN, EDWARD L. (1976), 'Towards a universal definition of "subject"', in Li (1976: 303–33).
—— (1988), 'On semantics and the binding theory', in Hawkins (1988: 105–44).
—— and COMRIE, BERNARD (1977), 'Noun phrase accessibility and universal grammar', *Linguistic Inquiry*, 8: 63–99.
KEMMER, SUZANNE (1993), *The Middle Voice* (Amsterdam: John Benjamins).
—— (1995), 'Emphatic reflexive *-self*', in S. Stein and S. Wright (eds.), *Subjectivity and Subjectivization in Language* (Cambridge: Cambridge University Press): 55–82.
KEMPCHINSKY, P. (1989), 'Directionality of government and nominative Case assignment in Romanian', in Kirschner and DeCesaris (1989: 208–24).
KEMPSON, RUTH (1988*a*), 'Grammar and conversational principle', in Newmeyer (1988: ii. 139–63).
—— (1988*b*), 'Logical form: the grammar cognition interface', *Journal of Linguistics*, 24: 393–431.
—— and GABBAY, DOV (1998), 'Crossover: a unified view', *Journal of Linguistics*, 34: 73–124.
—— MEYER-VIOL, WILFRIED and GABBAY, DOV (1999), 'VP-ellipsis: toward a dynamic, structural account', in Lappin and Benmamoun (1999: 227–89).
KENDALL, MARTHA (1976), *Special Problems in Yavapai Syntax: The Verde Valley Dialect* (New York: Garland).
KENSTOWICZ, MICHAEL (1989), 'The null subject parameter in Modern Arabic dialects', in Jaeggli and Safir (1989*b*: 263–76).
KIBRIK, ANDREJ A. (1996), 'Anaphora in Russian narrative prose: a cognitive calculative account', in Fox (1996: 255–303).
KIHM, ALAIN (1994), *Kriyol Syntax* (Amsterdam: John Benjamins).
—— (1996), 'Reflexivity in Kriyol: a case of half-hearted grammaticalization', in P. Baker and A. Syea (eds.), *Changing Meanings, Changing Functions* (London: Westminster University Press).
KIM, SUN-HEE (1993), 'Division of labor between grammar and pragmatics: the distribution and interpretation of anaphora', Ph.D. dissertation, Yale University.
KINKADE, M. DALE (1990), 'Sorting out third persons in Salishan discourse', *International Journal of American Linguistics*, 56: 341–60.
KINYALOLO, KASANGATI K. (1993), 'The logophoric pronoun *émi* as a LF operator/anaphor', *North East Linguistic Society*, 23: 223–37.
KIRSCHNER, CARL, and DECESARIS, J. (eds.) (1989), *Studies in Romance Linguistics* (Amsterdam: John Benjamins).
KISS, KATALIN É. (1991), 'The primacy condition of anaphora and pronominal variable binding', in Koster and Reuland (1991: 245–62).
—— (1995), 'NP movement, operator movement, and scrambling in Hungarian', in K. É. Kiss (ed.), *Discourse Configurational Languages* (Oxford: Oxford University Press): 207–43.
KITAGAWA, CHISATO (1982), 'Topic constructions in Japanese', *Lingua*, 57: 175–214.
KITAGAWA, YOSHIHISA (1991), 'Copying identity', *Natural Language and Linguistic Theory*, 9: 497–536.
KLEIN-ANDREU, FLORA (1996), 'Anaphora, deixis, and the evolution of Latin Ille', in Fox (1996: 305–31).

KOKTOVÁ, EVA (1992), 'On new constraints on anaphora and control', *Theoretical Linguistics*, 18: 101–78.
KÖNIG, EKKEHARD (1991), *The Meaning of Focus Particles: A Comprehensive Perspective* (London: Routledge).
—— and SIEMUND, PETER (1997), 'Intensifiers and reflexives: a typological perspective', paper presented at the International Symposium on Reflexives and Reciprocals (Boulder: University of Colorado), to appear in Frajzyngier and Curl (eds.) (forthcoming *a*).
KOOPMAN, HILDA, and SPORTICHE, DOMINIQUE (1983), 'Variables and the bijection principle', *Linguistic Review*, 2: 139–63.
—— —— (1989), 'Pronouns, logical variables and logophoricity in Abe', *Linguistic Inquiry*, 20: 555–89.
KORHONEN, Anna-LEENA (1995), 'A comparative study of binding theory in English and Finnish', MA dissertation, University of Reading.
KORNFILT, JAKLIN (1997), 'Long-distance (and other) reflexives in Turkish', paper presented at the LSA Workshop on Long-Distance Reflexives (Cornell University).
KOSTER, JAN (1984*a*), 'On binding and control', *Linguistic Inquiry*, 15: 417–59.
—— (1984*b*), 'Reflexives in Dutch', in J. Guéron, H.-G. Obenauer, and J.-Y. Pollock (eds.), *Grammatical Representation* (Dordrecht: Foris): 141–67.
—— (1987), *Domains and Dynasties: The Radical Autonomy of Syntax* (Dordrecht: Foris).
—— and REULAND, ERIC (eds.) (1991), *Long-Distance Anaphora* (Cambridge: Cambridge University Press).
KRATOCHVÍL, PAUL (1986), 'Subject or topic? Extreme-orient extreme-occident', *Cahiers de recherches comparatives*, 8: 269–320.
KROEBER, A. (1911), 'The languages of the coast of California north of San Francisco', *University of California Publications in American Archaeology and Ethnology*, 9: 273–435.
KUNO, SUSUMU (1972a), 'Pronominalization, reflexivization, and direct discourse', *Linguistic Inquiry*, 3: 161–95.
—— (1972*b*), 'Functional sentence perspective: a case study from Japanese and English', *Linguistic Inquiry*, 3: 269–320.
—— (1973), *The Structure of the Japanese Language* (Cambridge, Mass.: The MIT Press).
—— (1987), *Functional Syntax: Anaphora, Discourse and Empathy* (Chicago: The University of Chicago Press).
—— and KABURAKI, ETSUKO (1977), 'Empathy and syntax', *Linguistic Inquiry*, 8: 627–72.
—— and TAKAMI, KEN-ICHI (1993), *Grammar and Discourse Principles* (Chicago: The University of Chicago Press).
KURODA, S.-Y. (1973), 'On Kuno's direct discourse analysis of the Japanese reflexive *zibun*', *Papers in Japanese Linguistics*, 2. 136–47.
LAKSHMANAN, USHA (1991), 'Morphological uniformity and null-subjects in child second language acquisition', in Eubank (1991: 389–411).
—— (1994), *Universal Grammar in Child Second Language Acquisition: Null Subjects and Morphological Uniformity* (Amsterdam: John Benjamins).

LAMBRECHT, KNUD (1994), *Information Structure and Sentence Form: A Theory of Topic, Focus and the Mental Representations of Discourse Referents* (Cambridge: Cambridge University Press).

LANDA, ALAZNE (1996), 'Conditions on null objects in Basque Spanish and their relation to "leismo" and clitic-doubling', Ph.D. dissertation, University of Southern California.

LANGACKER, RONALD W. (1987), *Foundations of Cognitive Grammar*, i: *Theoretical Prerequisites* (Stanford, Calif.: Stanford University Press).

—— (1991), *Foundations of Cognitive Grammar*, ii: *Descriptive Application* (Stanford, Calif.: Stanford University Press).

—— (1996), 'Conceptual grouping and pronominal anaphora', in Fox (1996: 333–78).

LANGDON, MARGARET, and MUNRO, PAMELA (1979), 'Subject and (switch)-reference in Yuman', *Folia Linguistica*, 13: 321–44.

LAPPIN, SHALOM (1996), 'The interpretation of ellipsis', in S. Lappin (ed.), *Handbook of Contemporary Semantics* (Oxford: Basil Blackwell): 145–75.

—— (1999), 'An HPSG account of antecedent-contained ellipsis', in Lappin and Benmamoun (1999: 68–97).

—— and BENMAMOUN, ELABBAS (eds.) (1999), *Fragments: Studies in Ellipsis and Gapping* (Oxford: Oxford University Press).

LARSON, RICHARD K. (1991), '*Promise* and the theory of control', *Linguistic Inquiry*, 22: 103–39.

—— and MAY, ROBERT (1990), 'Antecedent-containment or vacuous movement: reply to Baltin', *Linguistics Inquiry*, 21: 103–22.

—— IATRIDOU, SABINE, LAHIRI, UTPAL, and HIGGINBOTHAM, JAMES (eds.) (1992), *Control and Grammar* (Dordrecht: Kluwer).

LASNIK, HOWARD (1989), *Essays on Anaphora* (Dordrecht: Kluwer).

—— (1999), 'Pseudogapping puzzles', in Lappin and Benmamoun (1999: 141–74).

—— and STOWELL, TIM (1991), 'Weakest crossover', *Linguidstic Inquiry*, 22: 687–720.

LAW, PAUL (1993), 'On null subjects and null arguments', *Canadian Journal of Linguistics*, 38: 1–41.

LAWAL, NIKE S. (1985), 'Why verbs do not gap in Yoruba', *Journal of African Languages and Linguistics*, 7: 155–61.

LEBEAUX, DAVID (1983), 'A distributional difference between reciprocals and reflexives', *Linguistic Inquiry*, 14: 723–30.

—— (1985), 'Locality and anaphoric binding', *Linguistic Review*, 4: 343–63.

LEECH, GEOFFREY N. (1983), *Principles of Pragmatics* (London: Longman).

LEES, R., and KLIMA, E. (1963), 'Rules for English pronominalization', *Language*, 39: 17–28.

LEHMANN, W. P. (1976), 'From topic to subject in Indo-European', in Li (1976: 445–56).

LEVELT, WILLEM J. M. (1989), *Speaking: From Intention to Articulation* (Cambridge, Mass.: The MIT Press).

LEVINSON, STEPHEN C. (1983), *Pragmatics* (Cambridge: Cambridge University Press).

—— (1987), 'Pragmatics and the grammar of anaphora: a partial pragmatic reduction of Binding and Control phenomena', *Journal of Linguistics*, 23: 379–434.

—— (1989), 'A review of Relevance', *Journal of Linguistics*, 25: 455–72.
—— (1991), 'Pragmatic reduction of the Binding Conditions revisited', *Journal of Linguistics*, 27: 107–61.
—— (1995), 'Three levels of meaning', in F. Palmer (ed.), *Grammar and Meaning: Essays in Honour of Sir John Lyons* (Cambridge: Cambridge University Press): 90–115.
LI, CHARLES N. (ed.) (1976), *Subject and Topic* (London: Academic Press).
—— and THOMPSON, SANDRA A. (1976), 'Subject and topic: a new typology of language', in Li (1976: 457–98).
—— —— (1979), 'Third-person pronoun and zero anaphora in Chinese discourse', in Givón, (1979*b*: 311–35).
LICHTENBERK, FRANTISEK (1985), 'Multiple uses of reciprocal constructions', *Australian Journal of Linguistics*, 5: 19–41.
—— (1988), 'The pragmatic nature of nominal anaphora in To'aba'ita', *Studies in Language*, 12: 299–344.
—— (1996), 'Patterns of anaphora in To'aba'ita narrative discourse', in Fox (1996: 379–411).
—— (1997), 'Reciprocals without reflexives', paper presented at the International Symposium on Reflexives and Reciprocals (Boulder: University of Colorado), to appear in Frajzyngier and Curl (eds.) (forthcoming *b*).
—— (1999), 'Reciprocals and related meanings in To'aba'ita', in Nedjalkov and Guentcheva (1999).
LIDZ, JEFFREY (1995), 'Morphological reflexive marking: evidence from Kannada', *Linguistic Inquiry*, 26: 705–10.
—— (1996), 'Dimensions of reflexivity', Ph.D. dissertation, University of Delaware.
LILLO-MARTIN, DIANE (1986), 'Two kinds of null arguments in American Sign Language', *Natural Language and Linguistic Theory*, 4: 415–44.
LINDE, CHARLOTTE (1979), 'Focus of attention and the choice of pronouns in discourse', in Givón (1979*b*: 337–54).
LINDSETH, MARTINA, and FRANKS, STEVEN (1996), 'Licensing and identification of null subjects in Slavic', in J. Toman (ed.), *Formal Approaches to Slavic Linguistics* (Ann Arbor: Michigan Slavic Publications): 197–244.
LOBECK, ANNE (1993), 'Strong agreement and identification: evidence from ellipsis in English', *Linguistics*, 31: 777–811.
—— (1995), *Ellipsis* (Oxford: Oxford University Press).
—— (1999), 'VP-ellipsis and the minimalist program: some speculations and proposals', in Lappin and Benmamoun (1999: 98–123).
LONGACRE, ROBERT E. (1972), *Hierarchy and Universality of Discourse Constituents in New Guinea Languages*, vol. ii (Washington: Georgetown University Press).
—— (1979), 'The paragraph as a grammatical unit', in Givón (1979*b*: 115–34).
—— (1983), 'Switch reference systems from two distinct linguistic areas: Wojokeso (Papua New Guinea) and Guanano (Northern South America)', in Haiman and Munro (1983*b*: 185–207).
LORD, CAROL (1976), 'Evidence for syntactic reanalysis: from verb to complementizer in Kwa', in *Diachronic Syntax* (Chicago: Chicago Linguistic Society): 179–91.

—— (1993), *Historical Change in Serial Verb Constructions* (Amsterdam: John Benjamins).

LUST, BARBARA (1986a), 'Introduction', in Lust (1986b: i. 3–106).

—— (ed.) (1986b), *Studies in the Acquisition of Anaphora*, 2 vols. (Dordrecht: D. Reidel).

—— HERMAN, GABRIELLA, and KORNFILT, JAKLIN (eds.) (1994), *Syntactic Theory and First Language Acquisition: Cross-linguistic Perspectives*, vol. ii (Hillsdale, NJ: Lawrence Erlbaum).

LYNCH, JOHN (1983), 'Switch-reference in Lenakel', in Haiman and Munro (1983: 209–21).

LYONS, JOHN (1977), *Semantics*, 2 vols. (Cambridge: Cambridge University Press).

LYUTIKOVA, EKATERINA A. (1997), 'Reflexives and emphasis in Tsakhur (Nakh-Dagestanian)', paper presented at the International Symposium on Reflexives and Reciprocals (Boulder: University of Colorado), to appear in Frajzyngier and Curl (eds.) (forthcoming a).

MCCAWLEY, JAMES D. (1976), 'Relativization', in M. Shibatini, (ed.), *Syntax and Semantics 5: Japanese Generative Grammar* (London: Academic Press): 209–306.

MCCLOSKEY, JAMES (1991), 'Clause structure, ellipsis and proper government', *Lingua*, 85: 259–302.

—— and HALE, KENNETH (1983), 'On the syntax of person-number inflection in Modern Irish', *Natural Language and Linguistic Theory*, 1: 487–534.

MCCRAY, ALEXA (1980), 'The semantics of backward anaphora', *Proceedings of the North Eastern Linguistics Society*, 10: 329–44.

MCGANN, WILLIAM, and SCHWARTZ, ARTHUR (1988), 'Main character in children's narrative', *Linguistics*, 26: 215–33.

MCGREGOR, WILLIAM (1997), 'Reflexive and reciprocal constructions in the Nyulnyulan languages (Dampier Land and Kimberley, Western Australia)', paper presented at the International Symposium on Reflexives and Reciprocals (Boulder: University of Colorado), to appear in Frajzyngier and Curl (eds.) (forthcoming b).

MCKAY, THOMAS J. (1991), 'He himself: undiscovering an anaphor', *Linguistic Inquiry*, 22: 368–73.

MCKEE, C., NICHOL, J., and MCDANIEL, D. (1993), 'Children's application of binding during sentence-processing', *Language and Cognitive Processes*, 8: 265–90.

MACLEOD, N. (1984), 'More on backward anaphora and discourse structure', *Journal of Pragmatics*, 8: 321–7.

MALING, JOAN (1984), 'Non-clause-bounded reflexives in Modern Icelandic', *Linguistic and Philosophy*, 7: 211–41.

—— and ZAENEN, ANNIE (eds.) (1990), *Syntax and Semantics 24: Modern Icelandic Syntax* (London: Academic Press).

MANN, W. C., and THOMPSON, SANDRA A. (1987), 'Rhetorical Structure Theory: a theory of text organization', in Polanyi (1987).

MANZINI, M. RITA (1983), 'On control and control theory', *Linguistic Inquiry*, 14: 421–46.

—— and WEXLER, KENNETH (1987), 'Parameters, binding theory, and learnability', *Linguistic Inquiry*, 18: 413–44.

MARCHESE, LYNELL (1986), 'The pronominal system of Godie', in Wiesemann (1986*b*: 217–55).
MARTIN, R. (1996), ' A minimalist theory of PRO and control', Ph.D. dissertation, University of Connecticut.
MASCARÓ, JOAN, and NESPOR, MARINA (eds.) (1990), *Grammar in Progress: GLOW Essays for Henk van Riemsdijk* (Dordrecht: Foris).
MASLOVA, ELENA (1997), 'Reciprocals in Yukaghir languages', paper presented at the International Symposium on Reflexives and Reciprocals (Boulder: University of Colorado), to appear in Frajzyngier and Curl (eds.) (forthcoming *b*).
MASSAM, DIANE (1992), 'Null objects and non-thematic subjects', *Journal of Linguistics*, 28: 115–37.
—— and ROBERGE, YVES (1989), 'Recipe context null objects in English', *Linguistic Inquiry*, 20: 134–9.
MATISOFF, JAMES A. (1991), 'Ariel and universal dimensions of grammaticalization in Lahu', in Traugott and Heine (1991: 383–453).
MATSUI, TOMOKO (1993), 'Bridging reference and the notions of "topic" and focus', *Lingua*, 90: 49–68.
—— (1995), 'Bridging and relevance', Ph.D. dissertation, University College London.
MATSUO, AYUMI (1999), 'Reciprocity and binding in early child grammar', *Linguistic Inquiry*, 30: 310–17.
MATTHEWS, P. H. (1993), *Grammatical Theory in the United States from Bloomfield to Chomsky* (Cambridge: Cambridge University Press).
MAY, ROBERT (1985), *Logical Form, its Structure and Derivation* (Cambridge, Mass.: The MIT Press).
MD. SALLEH, R. (1987), 'Fronted constituents in Malay: base structures and move α in a configurational non-Indo European language', Ph.D. dissertation, University of Washington.
MINSKY, M. (1975), 'A framework for representing knowledge', in P. Wason (ed.), *The Psychology of Computer Vision* (New York: McGraw-Hill).
MITHUN, MARIANNE (1990), 'Third-person reference and the function of pronouns in Central Pomo natural speech', *International Journal of American Linguistics*, 56: 361–76.
MITTWOCH, ANITA (1983), 'Backward anaphora and discourse structure', *Journal of Pragmatics*, 7: 129–39.
MOERMAN, MICHAEL (1977), 'The preference for self-correction in Tai conversational corpus', *Language*, 53: 872–82.
MOHANAN, KARUVANNUR P. (1982), 'Grammatical relations and anaphora in Malayalam', *MIT Working Papers in Linguistics*, 4: 163–90.
—— (1983), 'Functional and anaphoric control', *Linguistic Inquiry*, 14: 641–74.
MONTAGUE, RICHARD (1974), *Formal Philosophy* (New Haven: Yale University Press).
MONTALBETTI, MARIO (1984), 'After binding: on the interpretation of pronouns', Ph.D. dissertation, MIT.
MONTAUT, ANNIE (1994), 'Réflexivisation et focalisation en hindi/ourdou', *Bulletin de la Société Linguistique de Paris*, 89: 83–120.

MORAVCSIK, EDITH A. (1972), 'Some cross-linguistic generalizations about intensifier constructions', *Papers from the Regional Meeting of the Chicago Linguistic Society*, 8: 271–7.

MOSHAGEN, SJUR N., and TROSTERUD, TROND (1990), 'Non-clause-bounded reflexives in Mainland Scandinavian', *Working Papers in Scandinavian Syntax*, 46: 47–52.

MOYNE, J. A. (1971), 'Reflexive and emphatic', *Language*, 47: 141–63.

MOYSE-FAURIE, CLAIRE (1999), 'Reciprocal constructions in Futunan', in Nedjalkov and Guentcheva (1999).

MÜHLHÄUSLER, PETER, and HARRÉ, ROM (1990), *Pronouns and People* (Oxford: Basil Blackwell).

MUNRO, PAMELA (ed.) (1980), *Studies of Switch-Reference* (Los Angeles: University of California at Los Angeles).

—— (1983), 'When "same" is not "not different"', in Haiman and Munro (1983): 223–43).

NA, YOUNG HEE, and HUCK, GEOFFREY J. (1993), 'On the status of certain island violations in Korean', *Linguistics and Philosophy*, 16: 181–229.

NAKAMURA, MASARU (1987), 'Japanese as a *pro* language', *Linguistic Review*, 6: 281–96.

NAPOLI, DONNA J. (1979), 'Reflexivization across clause boundaries in Italian', *Journal of Linguistics*, 15: 1–28.

NATASCHA, MÜLLER, CRYSMANN, BERTHOLD, and KAISER, GEORG A. (1996), 'Interaction between the acquisition of French object drop and the development of the C-system', *Language Acquisition*, 5: 35–63.

NEDJALKOV, V. P. (1980), 'Reflexive constructions: a functional typology', in G. Brettschneider and C. Lehmann (eds.), *Wege zur Universalienforschung* (Tübingen: Narr): 222–8.

—— and GUENTCHEVA, Z. (eds.) (1999), *Typology of Reciprocal Constructions* (Munich: Lincom Europa).

NEWMEYER, FREDERICK J. (ed.) (1988), *Linguistics: The Cambridge Survey*, 4 vols. (Cambridge: Cambridge University Press).

NGOH, GEOK LUN (1991), 'A pragmatic analysis of long-distance reflexivization in Malay', MS, University of Cambridge.

NICHOLS, JOHANNA (1983), 'Switch-reference in the Northeast Caucasus', in Haiman and Munro (1983b: 245–65).

NYLANDER, DUDLEY K. (1985), 'Serial verbs and the empty category principle in Krio', *Canadian Journal of Linguistics*, 30: 15–32.

O'CONNOR, MARY C. (1992a), *Topics in Northern Pomo Grammar* (New York: Garland).

—— (1992b), 'Third-person reference in Nothern Pomo conversation: the indexing of discourse genre and social relations', *International Journal of American Linguistics*, 56: 377–409.

—— (1993), 'Disjoint reference and pragmatic inference: anaphora and switch reference in Northern Pomo', in W. A. Foley (ed.), *The Role of Theory in Language Description* (Berlin: Mouton de Gruyter): 215–42.

O'GRADY, WILLIAM (1987), 'The interpretation of Korean anaphora', *Language*, 63: 251–77.

OLSON, MICHAEL (1978), 'Switch-reference in Barai', *Proceedings of the Annual Meeting of the Berkeley Linguistics Society*, 4: 140–57.
—— (1981), 'Barai clause junctures: toward a functional theory of interclausal relations', Ph.D. dissertation, Australian National University.
OSWALT, ROBERT L. (1961), 'A Kashaya grammar (South-western Pomo)', Ph.D. dissertation, University of California at Berkeley.
—— (1976), 'Switch-reference in Maiduan: an areal and typological contribution', *International Journal of American Linguistics*, 42: 297–304.
—— (1977), 'The causative as a reference switching mechanism in Western Pomo', *Proceedings of the Annual Meeting of the Berkeley Linguistics Society*, 3: 46–54.
—— (1983), 'Interclausal reference in Kashaya', in Haiman and Munro (1983*b*: 267–90).
OTANI, KAZUYO, and WHITMAN, JOHN (1991), 'V-raising and VP-ellipsis', *Linguistic Inquiry*, 22: 345–58.
OUHALLA, JAMAL (1988), 'A note on bound pronouns', *Linguistic Inquiry*, 19: 485–94.
PAN, HAIHUA (1995), 'Locality, self-ascription, discourse prominence, and Mandarin reflexives', Ph.D. dissertation, University of Texas at Austin.
—— (1998), 'Closeness, prominence, and binding theory', *Natural Language and Linguistic Theory*, 16: 771–815.
PAREDES SILVA, VERA L. (1993), 'Subject omission and functional compensation: evidence from written Brazilian Portuguese', *Language Variation and Change*, 5: 35–49.
PARKER, ELIZABETH (1986), 'Mundani pronouns', in Wiesemann (1986*b*: 131–66).
PARKINSON, DILWORTH (1987), 'Constraints on the presence/absence of "optional" subject pronouns in Egyptian Arabic', in K. Denning, S. Inkelas, F. McNair-Knox, and J. Rickford (eds.) *Variation in Language* (Stanford, Calif.: Stanford University Press): 348–60.
PARKS, DOUGLAS R. (1976), *A Grammar of Pawnee* (New York: Garland).
PARTEE, BARBARA (1973), 'Some transformational extensions of Montague Grammar', *Journal of Philosophical Logic*, 2: 509–34.
PAYNE, DORIS (1980), 'Switch-reference in Chickasaw', in Munro (1980: 89–118).
PAYNE, THOMAS E. (1993), *The Twins Stories: Participant Coding in Yagua Narrative* (Berkeley and Los Angeles: University of California Press).
PEREIRA, FERNANDO C., and POLLACK, MARTHA (1991), 'Incremental interpretation', *Artificial Intelligence*, 50: 37–82.
PERLMUTTER, DAVID (1971), *Deep and Surface Constraints in Syntax* (New York: Holt, Rinehart & Winston).
PESETSKY, DAVID (1987), 'Binding problems with experiencer verbs', *Linguistic Inquiry*, 18: 126–40.
PHILIPPAKI-WARBURTON, IRENE (1987), 'The theory of empty categories and the pro-drop parameter in Modern Greek', *Journal of Linguistics*, 23: 289–318.
—— and CATSIMALI, GEORGIA (1999), 'On control in Greek', in A. Alexiadou, G. Horrocks, and M. Stavrou (eds.), *Studies in Greek Syntax* (Dordrecht: Kluwer): 153–68.

PICA, PIERRE (1984), 'Subject, tense and truth: towards a modular approach to binding', in J. Guéron, H.-G. Obenauer and J.-Y. Pollock, (eds.), *Grammatical Representation* (Dordrecht: Foris): 259–91.
—— (1986), 'Liage et contiguité', in J.-C. Milner, (ed.), *Recherches sur l'anaphore* (Paris: Université de Paris-7): 119–64.
—— (1991), 'On the interaction between antecedent-government and binding: the case of long-distance reflexivization', in Koster and Reuland (1991: 119–35).
—— and SNYDER, WILLIAM (1995). 'Weak crossover, scope and agreement in a Minimalist framework', *Proceedings of the 13th West Coast Conference on Formal Linguistics*, 334–49.
PICALLO, M. CARME (1994), 'Catalan possessive pronouns: the Avoid Pronoun Principle revisited', *Natural Language and Linguistic Theory*, 12: 259–99.
PINGKARAWAT, NAMPTIP (1985), 'Distribution and reference of empty pronouns in Thai', MS, University of Illinois.
PLATZACK, CHRISTER (1987), 'The Scandinavian languages and the null-subject parameter', *Natural Language and Linguistic Theory*, 5: 377–401.
—— (1996), 'Null subjects, weak Agr and syntactic differences in Scandinavian', in H. Thráinsson, S. D. Epstein, and S. Peter (eds.), *Studies in Comparative Germanic Syntax*, vol. ii (Dordrecht: Kluwer): 180–96.
POLANYI, LIVIA (ed.) (1987), *The Structure of Discourse* (Norwood, NJ: Ablex).
POLLARD, CARL, and SAG, IVAN A. (1992), 'Anaphors in English and the scope of binding theory', *Linguistic Inquiry*, 23: 261–303.
—— —— (1994), *Head-Driven Phrase Structure Grammar* (Chicago: The University of Chicago Press).
POPOVICH, HAROLD (1986), 'The nominal reference system of Maxakali', in Wiesemann (1986*b*: 351–8).
POPPER, KARL (1959), *The Logic of Scientific Discovery* (London: Hutchinson).
—— (1973), *Objective Knowledge* (Oxford: Oxford University Press).
POSTAL, PAUL M. (1971), *Cross-Over Phenomenon* (New York: Holt, Rinehart & Winston).
—— (1993), 'Remarks on weak crossover effects', *Linguistic Inquiry*, 24: 539–56.
PRINCE, ALAN, and SMOLENSKY, PAUL (1993), *Optimality Theory: Constraint Interaction in Generative Grammar* (To be published by Cambridge, Mass.: The MIT Press).
PRINCE, ELLEN F. (1981), 'Toward a taxonomy of given-new information', in Cole (1981: 223–55).
PROGOVAC, LJILJANA (1992), 'Relativized SUBJECT: long-distance reflexives without movement', *Linguistic Inquiry*, 23: 671–80.
—— (1993), 'Long-distance reflexives: movement-to-Infl versus relativized SUBJECT', *Linguistic Inquiry*, 24: 755–72.
PSATHAS, GEORGE (ed.) (1979), *Everyday Language: Studies in Ethnomethodology* (New York: Irvington).
PU, MING-MING (1995), 'Anaphoric patterning in English and Mandarin narrative production', *Discourse Processes*, 19: 279–300.
RADFORD, ANDREW (1981), *Transformational Syntax* (Cambridge: Cambridge University Press).

—— (1990), *Syntactic Theory and the Acquisition of English Syntax* (Oxford: Basil Blackwell).
—— (1997), *Syntax: A Minimalist Introduction* (Cambridge: Cambridge University Press).
RAINA, ACHLA MISRI (1991), 'An s-selectional approach to grammar: some issues in Kashmiri syntax', Ph.D. dissertation, Indian Institute of Technology, Kanpur.
RAMSEY, S. ROBERT (1987), *The Languages of China* (Princeton: Princeton University Press).
RANDRIAMASIMANANA, CHARLES (1986), *The Causatives of Malagasy* (Honolulu: The University of Hawaii Press).
RANSOM, E. N. (1988), 'The grammaticalization of complementizers', *Proceedings of the Annual Meeting of the Berkeley Linguistics Society*, 14: 364–74.
RAPOSO, EDUARDO (1986), 'On the null object in European Portuguese', in Jaeggli and Silva-Corvalán (1986: 373–90).
RAPPAPORT, GILBERT C. (1986), 'On anaphor binding in Russian', *Natural Language and Linguistic Theory*, 4: 97–120.
REBUSCHI, GEORGE (1987), 'Defining the three binding domains of Basque', *Proceedings of the Conference on the Basque Languages*.
REESINK, P. (1983), 'Switch-reference and topicality hierarchies', *Studies in Language*, 7: 215–46.
REINDERS-MACHOWSKA, EWA (1991), 'Binding in Polish', in Koster and Reuland (1991: 137–50).
REINHART, TANYA (1983), *Anaphora and Semantic Interpretation* (London: Croom Helm).
—— (1986), 'Center and periphery in the grammar of anaphora', in Lust (1986*b*: 123–50).
—— and REULAND, ERIC (1991), 'Anaphors and logophors: an argument perspective', in Koster and Reuland (1991: 283–321).
—— —— (1993), 'Reflexivity', *Linguistic Inquiry*, 24: 657–720.
REULAND, ERIC, and KOSTER, JAN (1991), 'Long distance anaphora: an overview', in Koster and Reuland (1991: 1–25).
RHODES, RICHARD (1985), *Eastern Ojibwa–Chippewa–Ottawa Dictionary* (Berlin: Mouton).
RIAD, TOMAS (1988), 'Reflexivity and predication', *Working Papers in Scandinavian Syntax*, 36.
RICHARDS, NORVIN (1997), 'Competition and disjoint reference', *Linguistic Inquiry*, 28: 178–87.
RIEMSDIJK, HENK VAN, WILLIAMS, EDWIN (1986), *Introduction to the Theory of Grammar* (Cambridge, Mass.: The MIT Press).
RIGAU, GEMMA (1988), 'Strong pronouns', *Linguistic Inquiry*, 19: 503–11.
RIVERO, MARÍA-LUISA (1993), 'Long head movement vs. V2, and null subjects in Old Romance', *Lingua*, 89: 217–45.
RIZZI, LUIGI (1982), *Issues in Italian Syntax* (Dordrecht: Foris).
—— (1986), 'Null objects in Italian and the theory of *pro*', *Linguistic Inquiry*, 17: 501–57.
—— (1990*a*), *Relativized Minimality* (Cambridge, Mass.: The MIT Press).

RIZZI, LUIGI (1990b), 'Some speculations on residual V2 phenomena', in Mascaró and Nespor (1990: 375–87).
—— (1994), 'Early null subjects and root null subjects', in Hoekstra and Schwartz (1994: 151–76).
ROBERGE, YVES (1991), 'On the recoverability of null objects', in D. Wanner and D. A. Kibbee (eds.), *New Analyses in Romance Linguistics* (Amsterdam: John Benjamins): 299–312.
ROBERTS, CRAIGE (1987), 'Modal subordination, anaphora, and distributivity', Ph.D. dissertation, University of Massachusetts.
—— (1989), 'Modal subordination and pronominal anaphora in discourse', *Linguistics and Philosophy*, 12: 683–721.
ROBERTS, IAN (1993), *Verbs and Diachronic Syntax* (Dordrecht: Kluwer).
ROBERTS, JOHN (1987), *Amele* (London: Croom Helm).
—— (1988a), 'Amele switch-reference and the theory of grammar', *Linguistic Inquiry*, 19: 45–63.
—— (1988b), 'Switch-reference in Papuan languages: a syntactic or extrasyntactic device?', *Australian Journal of Linguistics*, 8: 75–117.
ROEPER, THOMAS, and WILLIAMS, EDWIN (1987), *Parameter Setting* (Dordrecht: D. Reidel).
RÖGNVALDSSON, EIRÍKUR (1990), 'Null objects in Icelandic', in Maling and Zaenen (1990: 367–79).
—— and THRÁINSSON, HÖSKULDUR (1990), 'On Icelandic word order once more', in Maling and Zaenen (1990: 3–40).
ROHRBACHER, BERNHARD W. (1994), 'The Germanic VO languages and the full paradigm: a theory of V to I raising', Ph.D. dissertation, University of Massachusetts.
—— (1999), *Morphology-Driven Syntax: A Theory of V to I Raising and Pro-drop* (Amsterdam: John Benjamins).
RONAT, M. (1982), 'Une solution pour un apparent contre-exemple à la théorie du liage', *Lingvisticae Investigationes*, 6: 189–98.
ROOD, DAVID S. (1976), *Wichita Grammar* (New York: Garland).
ROOTH, MATS (1992), 'Ellipsis redundancy and reduction redundancy', in S. Berman and A. Hestvik (eds.), *Proceedings of the Stuttgart Ellipsis Workshop* (Stuttgart: University of Stuttgart).
ROSENBAUM, PETER S. (1967), *The Grammar of English Predicate Complement Constructions* (Cambridge, Mass.: The MIT Press).
ROSS, JOHN R. (1982), 'Pronouns deleting processes in German', paper presented at the Annual Meeting of the Linguistic Society of America.
RUMELHART, DAVID (1980), 'Schemata: the basic building blocks of cognition', in R. Spiro, B. Bruce, and W. Brewer (eds.), *Theoretical Issues in Reading Comprehension* (Hillsdale, NJ: Erlbaum).
RUWET, NICHOLAS (1991), '*En* et *y*: deux clitiques pronominaux antilogophoriques', *Langages*, 97: 51–81.
RŮŽIČKA, RUDOLF (1983), 'Remarks on control', *Linguistic Inquiry*, 14: 309–24.
SACKS, HARVEY, and SCHEGLOFF, EMANUEL A. (1979), 'Two preferences in the organization of reference to persons in conversation and their interaction', in Psathas (1979: 15–21).

—— —— and JEFFERSON, GAIL (1974), 'A simplest systematics for the organization of turn-taking in conversation', *Language*, 50: 696–735.

SAFIR, KENNETH J. (1985), *Syntactic Chains* (Cambridge: Cambridge University Press).

—— (1987), 'Comments on Wexler and Manzini', in Roeper and Williams (1987: 77–89).

—— (1992), 'Implied noncoreference and the pattern of anaphora', *Linguistics and Philosophy*, 15: 1–52.

—— (1996), 'Semantic atoms of anaphora', *Natural Language and Linguistic Theory*, 14: 545–89.

SAG, IVAN A. (1976), 'Deletion and logical form', Ph.D. dissertation, MIT.

—— and POLLARD, CARL (1991), 'An integrated theory of complement control', *Language*, 67: 63–113.

SAITO, MAMORU, and HOJI, HAJIME (1983), 'Weak crossover and move-α in Japanese', *Natural Language and Linguistic Theory*, 1: 245–60.

SALEEMI, ANJUM P. (1992), *Universal Grammar and Language Learnability* (Cambridge: Cambridge University Press).

SAMEK-LODOVICI, VIERI (1996), 'Constraints on subjects: an Optimality theoretic analysis', Ph.D. dissertation, Rutgers University.

SANDALO, FILOMENA (1997), 'Case, binding and polysynthesis in Kadiwéu', paper presented at the International Symposium on Reflexives and Reciprocals (Boulder: University of Colorado).

SANDERS, T., SPOOREN, W., and NOORDMAN, L. (1992), 'Toward a taxonomy of coherence relations', *Discourse Processes*, 15: 1–35.

SANFORD, ANTHONY J. and GARROD, SIMON C. (1981), *Understanding Written Language* (Chichester: John Wiley & Sons).

—— MOAR, K., and GARROD, SIMON C. (1988), 'Proper names as controllers of discourse focus', *Language and Speech*, 31: 43–56.

SANTANDREA, STEFANO (1976), *The Kresh Group, Aja and Daka Languages (Sudan): A Linguistic Contribution* (Naples: Instituto Universitario Orientale).

SANTORINI, BEATRICE (1989), 'The generalization of the verb second constraint in the history of Yiddish', Ph.D. dissertation, University of Pennsylvania.

SAXENA, ANJU (1985), 'Reflexivization in Hindi: a reconsideration', *International Journal of Dravidian Linguistics*, 14: 225–37.

SAXON, LESLIE (1984), 'Control and agreement in Dogrib', *Proceedings of the First Eastern States Conference on Linguistics*, 128–39.

—— (1986), 'The syntax of pronouns in Dogrib (Athapaskan): some theoretical consequences', Ph.D. dissertation, University of California at San Diego.

—— (1990), 'On one's own: the semantics and pragmatics of reflexives', in C. Georgopoulos and R. Ishihara (eds.), *Interdisciplinary Approaches to Language* (Dordrecht: Kluwer).

SCHANK, ROGER C., and ABELSON, ROBERT (1977), *Scripts, Plans, Goals, and Understanding: An Inquiry into Human Knowledge Structures* (Hillsdale, NJ: Lawrence Erlbaum).

SCHAUB, WILLI (1985), *Babungo* (London: Croom Helm).

SCHEGLOFF, EMANUEL A. (1996), 'Some practices for referring to persons in talk-in-interaction: a partial sketch of a systematics', in Fox (1996: 437–85).
—— JEFFERSON, GAIL, and SACKS, HARVEY (1977), 'The preference for self-correction in the organization of repair in conversation', *Language*, 53: 361–82.
SCHIEBE, T. (1971), 'Zum Problem der grammatisch relevanten Identität', in F. Kiefer and N. Ruwet (eds.), *Generative Grammar in Europe* (Dordrecht: Kluwer).
SCHIFFRIN, DEBORAH (ed.) (1984), *Meaning, Form, and Use in Context: Linguistic Applications* (Washington: Georgetown University Press).
SCHLADT, MATHIAS (1997), 'The typology and grammaticalization of reflexives with special reference to body parts', paper presented at the International Symposium on Reflexives and Reciprocals (Boulder: University of Colorado), to appear in Frajzyngier and Curl (eds.) (forthcoming *a*).
SCHWARTZ, ARTHUR (1976), 'On the universality of subjects: the Ilocano case', in Li (1976: 519–43).
SCOTT, GRAHAM (1978), *The Fore Language of Papua New Guinea* (Canberra: Linguistic Circle of Canberra).
SELLS, PETER (1987), 'Aspects of logophoricity', *Linguistic Inquiry*, 18: 445–79.
—— ZAENEN, ANNIE, and ZEC, DRAGA (1987), 'Reflexivization variation: relations between syntax, semantics and lexical structure', in P. Sells et al. (eds.), *Working Papers in Grammatical Theory and Discourse Structure* (Stanford, Calif.: CSLI): 169–238.
SEM, HELLE, SÆBØ, KJELL, VERNE, GURI, and VESTRE, ESPEN (1991), 'Parameters: dependence and absorption', in J. Barwise et al. (eds.), *Situation Theory and its Applications*, vol. ii (Stanford, Calif.: CSLI): 499–516.
SENFT, GUNTER (1986), *Kilivila, the Language of the Trobriand Islands* (Berlin: Mouton de Gruyter).
SHIEBER, STUART, PEREIRA, FERNANDO, and DALRYMPLE, MARY (1996), 'Interactions of scope and ellipsis', *Linguistics and Philosophy*, 19: 527–52.
SHOPEN, TIM (ed.) (1985), *Language Typology and Syntactic Description*, 3 vols. (Cambridge: Cambridge University Press).
SIDNER, CANDECE (1983), 'Focusing and discourse', *Discourse Processes*, 6: 107–30.
SIGURÐSSON, HALLDÓR A. (1990*a*), 'Long-distance reflexives and moods in Icelandic', in Maling and Zaenen (1990: 309–46).
—— (1990*b*), 'V1 declaratives and verb raising in Icelandic', in Maling and Zaenen (1990: 41–96).
—— (1991), 'Icelandic case-marked *pro* and the licensing of lexical arguements', *Natural Language and Linguistic Theory*, 9: 327–63.
—— (1993), 'Argument-drop in Old Icelandic', *Lingua*, 89: 247–80.
SILVERSTEIN, MICHAEL (1976), 'Hierarchy of features and ergativity', in Dixon (1976: 112–71).
SIMPSON, JANE, and BRESNAN, JOAN (1983), 'Control and obviation in Warlpiri', *Natural Language and Linguistic Theory*, 1: 49–65.
SOLAN, LAWRENCE (1983), *Pronominal Reference: Children Language and the Theory of Grammar* (Dordrecht: Reidel).
SPEAS, MARGARET (1990), *Phrase Structure in Natural Language* (Dordrecht: Kluwer).

—— (1994), 'Null arguments in a theory of economy of projection', *University of Massachusetts Occasional Papers in Linguistics*, 17: 179–208.

—— (1997), 'Optimality theory and syntax: null pronouns and control', in Archangeli and Langendoen (1997: 177–99).

SPERBER, DAN, and WILSON, DEIRDRE (1995), *Relevance: Communication and Cognition*, 2nd edn. (Oxford: Basil Blackwell).

SPORTICHE, DOMINIQUE (1986), '*Zibun*', *Linguistic Inquiry*, 17: 369–74.

SPROUSE, REX A., and VANCE, BARBARA (1997), 'An explanation for the decline of null pronouns in certain Germanic and Romance languages', in M. DeGraff (ed.), *Language Creation and Language Change: Creolization, Diachrony, and Development* (Cambridge Mass.: The MIT Press): 257–84.

SRIVASTAV DAYAL, VENEETA (1994), 'Binding facts in Hindi and the scrambling phenomenon', in M. Butt, T. H. King, and G. Ramchand (eds.), *Theoretical Perspectives on Word Order in South Asian Languages* (Stanford, Calif.: CSLI): 237–62.

STALNAKER, ROBERT (1972), 'Pragmatics', in D. Davidson and G. Harman (eds.), *Semantics of Natural Language* (Cambridge: Cambridge University Press): 380–97.

STEENBERGEN, MARLIES VAN (1991), 'Long-distance binding in Finnish', in Koster and Reuland (1991: 231–44).

STIRLING, LESLEY (1993), *Switch-Reference and Discourse Representation* (Cambridge: Cambridge University Press).

STUMP, GREGORY T. (1984), 'Agreement vs. incorporation in Breton', *Natural Language and Linguistic Theory*, 2: 289–348.

SUÑER, MARGARITA (1983), '*Pro_{arb}*', *Linguistic Inquiry*, 14: 188–91.

—— and YÉPEZ, MARIA (1988), 'Null definite objects in Quiteño', *Linguistic Inquiry*, 19: 511–19.

TAI, JAMES H. Y. (1978), 'Anaphoric constraints in Mandarin Chinese narrative discourse', in Hinds (1978: 279–338).

TAKAHASHI, D. (1993), 'On antecedent contained deletion', MS, University of Connecticut.

TAKAMI, KEN-ICHI (1987), 'Anaphora in Japanese: some semantic and pragmatic considerations', *Journal of Pragmatics*, 11: 169–91.

—— and KAMIO, AKIO (1996), 'Topicalization and subjectivization in Japanese: characterizational and identificational information', *Lingua*, 99: 207–35.

TANG, C.-C. JANE (1989), 'Chinese reflexives', *Natural Language and Linguistic Theory*, 7: 93–121.

TAO, LIANG (1996), 'Topic discontinuity and zero anaphora in Chinese discourse: cognitive strategies in discourse processing', in Fox (1996: 487–513).

TARALDSEN, TARALD (1978), *On the NIC, Vacuous Application, and the That-Trace Filter* (Bloomington: Indiana University Linguistic Club).

THOMAS, MARGARET (1991), 'Universal grammar and the interpretation of reflexives in a second language', *Language*, 67: 211–39.

—— (1993), *Knowledge of Reflexives in a Second Language* (Amsterdam: John Benjamins).

THORNTON, ROSALIND, and WEXLER, KENNETH (1999), *Principle B, VP Ellipsis, and Interpretation in Child Grammar* (Cambridge, Mass.: The MIT Press).

THRÁINSSON, HÖSKULDUR (1976), 'Reflexives and subjunctives in Icelandic', *Proceedings of the North-Eastern Linguistics Society*, 6: 225–39.

—— (1991), 'Long-distance reflexives and the typology of NPs', in Koster and Reuland (1991: 49–75).

TIMBERLAKE, ALAN (1979), 'Reflexivization and the cycle in Russian', *Linguistics Inquiry*, 10: 109–41.

TOMAN, JINDŘICH (1991), 'Anaphors in binary trees: an analysis of Czech reflexives', in Koster and Reuland (1991: 151–70).

TOMLIN, RUSSELL (1987a), 'Linguistic reflections of cognitive events', in Tomlin (1987b: 455–80).

—— (1987b), *Coherence and Grounding in Discourse* (Amsterdam: John Benjamins).

—— and PU, MING MING (1991), 'The management of reference in Mandarin discourse', *Cognitive Linguistics*, 2: 65–95.

TRASK, ROBERT, L. (1993), *A Dictionary of Grammatical Terms in Linguistics* (London: Routledge).

TRAUGOTT, ELIZABETH, C. and HEINE, BERND (1991), *Approaches to Grammaticalization*, 2 vols. (Amsterdam: John Benjamins).

TRAVIS, LISA (1984), 'Parameters and effects of word order variation', Ph.D. dissertation, MIT.

TRUMBULL, J. HAMMOND (1877), 'The Algonkian verb', *Transactions of the American Philological Association*, 146–71.

TRYON, DARRELL T. (1970), *Conversational Tahitian* (Canberra: The Australian National University Press).

TSAO, FENG-FU (1977), 'A functional study of topic in Chinese: the first step toward discourse analysis', Ph.D. dissertation, University of Southern California.

TSUJIMURA, N. (1987), 'A comprehensive theory of switch-reference', Ph.D. dissertation, University of Arizona.

TUCKER, ARCHIBALD N., and BRYAN, MARGARET A. (1966), *Linguistics Analyses: The Non-Bantu Languages of North-Eastern Africa* (Oxford: Oxford University Press).

UEDA, MASANOBU (1986), 'On a Japanese reflexive *zibun*: a non-parameterization approach', MS, University of Massachusetts.

URIAGEREKA, JUAN (1998), *Rhyme and Reason: An Introduction to Minimalist Syntax* (Cambridge, Mass.: The MIT Press).

VAINIKKA, ANNE, and LEVY, YONATA (1999), 'Empty subjects in Finnish and Hebrew', *Natural Language and Linguistic Theory*, 17: 613–71.

VALIAN, VIRGINIA (1990), 'Null subjects: a problem for parameter-setting models of language acquisition', *Cognition*, 35: 105–22.

VALLDUVÍ, ENRIC (1992), *The Information Component* (New York: Garland).

—— and ENGDAHL, ELIZABETH (1996), 'The linguistic realization of information packaging', *Linguistics*, 34: 459–519.

VANCE, BARBARA (1993), 'Verb-first declaratives introduced by *et* and the position of *pro* in Old and Middle French', *Lingua*, 89: 281–314.

VAN DER WURFF, W. (1989), 'The syntax of participial elements in Eastern Bagali', *Journal of Linguistics*, 25: 373–416.

VANELLI, LAURA, RENZI, LORENZO, and BENINCÀ, PAOLA (1985), 'Typologie des pronoms sujets dans les langues romanes', *Actes du XVIIe Congrès International de Linguistique et Philologie Romanes*, iii. 163–76.

VAN GELDEREN, ELLY (1997), 'Historical binding domains', paper presented at the International Symposium on Reflexives and Reciprocals (Boulder: University of Colorado), to appear in Frajzyngier and Curl (eds.) (forthcoming *a*).

VAN HOEK, KAREN (1995), 'Conceptual reference points: a Cognitive Grammar account of pronominal anaphora constraints', *Language*, 71: 310–40.

——(1997), *Anaphora and Conceptual Structure* (Chicago: The University of Chicago Press).

VAN VALIN, R. D. (1987), 'Aspects of the interaction of syntax and pragmatics: discourse coreference mechanisms and the typology of grammatical systems', in Verschueren and Bertuccelli-Papi (1987: 513–31).

VERHEIJEN, RON (1986), 'A phrase structure for emphatic *self*-forms', *Linguistics*, 24: 681–95.

VERSCHUEREN, JEF (ed.) (1991), *Levels of Linguistic Adaptation* (Amsterdam: John Benjamins).

—— and BERTUCCELLI-PAPI, MARCELLA (eds.) (1987), *The Pragmatic Perspective* (Amsterdam: John Benjamins).

VIKNER, STEN (1985), 'Parameters of binder and binding category in Danish', *Working Papers in Scandinavian Syntax*, 23.

VIKØR, LARS S. (1993), *The Nordic Languages: Their Structure and Interrelations* (Oslo: Novus Press).

VITALE, ANTHONY J. (1981), *Swahili Syntax* (Dordrecht: Foris).

VON RONCADOR, MANFRED (1992), 'Types of logophoric marking in African languages', *Journal of African Languages and Linguistics*, 13: 163–82.

VOORHOEVE, JAN (1980), 'Le Pronom logophorique et son importance pour la reconstruction du proto bantou', *Sprache und Geschichte in Afrika*, 2: 173–87.

WALI, KASHI (1979), 'Two Marathi reflexives and the causative structure', *Studies in Language*, 3: 405–38.

—— (1989), *Marathi Syntax: A Study of Reflexives* (Patiala: Institute of Language Studies).

—— and SUBBARAO, K. V. (1991), 'On pronominal classification: evidence from Marathi and Telugu', *Linguistics*, 29: 1093–110.

—— LUST, BARBARA, GAIR, JAMES, and SUBBARAO, K. V. (eds.) (forthcoming), *Lexical Anaphors and Pronouns in Selected South Asian Languages: A Principled Typology* (Berlin: Mouton de Gruyter).

WALKER, MARILYN, JOSHI, ARAVIND K., and PRINCE, ELLEN (eds.) (1997), *Centering Theory in Discourse* (Oxford: Oxford University Press).

WANG, J. L. and STILLINGS, J. T. (1984), 'Chinese reflexives', in *Proceedings of the First Harbin Conference on Generative Grammar* (Harbin: Heilongjiang University Press): 100–9.

WANG, Q., LILLO-MARTIN, D., BEST, C., and LEVITT, A. (1992), 'Null subjects and objects in the acquisition of Chinese', *Language Acquisition*, 2: 221–54.

WANNER, D., and KIBBEE, D. A. (eds.) (1991), *New Analyses in Romance Linguistics* (Amsterdam: John Benjamins).

WARD, GREGORY, SPROAT, RICHARD, and MCKOON, GAIL (1991), 'A pragmatic analysis of so-called anaphoric islands', *Language*, 67: 439–73.

WASOW, TOM (1986), 'Reflections on anaphora', in Lust (1986*b*: i. 107–22).

WATKINS, LAUREL J. (1990), 'Noun phrase versus zero in Kiowa discourse', *International Journal of American Linguistics*, 56: 410–26.

WEBBER, BONNIE L. (1979), *A Formal Approach to Discourse Anaphora* (New York: Garland).

WEBER, DAVID (1980), 'Switch-reference: Quechua', in Munro (1980: 48–64).

WEISSENBORN, J. (1992), 'Null subjects in early grammars: implications for parameter setting theories', in Weissenborn, Goodluck, and Roeper (1992: 269–301).

—— GOODLUCK, H., and ROEPER, T. (eds.) (1992), *Theoretical Issues in Language Acquisition* (Hillsdale, NJ: Lawrence Erlbaum).

WELMERS, W. (1968), *Efik* (Ibadan: University of Ibadan).

WESCOAT, MICHAEL (1989), 'Sloppy readings with embedded antecedents'. MS, Stanford University.

WESTERGAARD, MARIT R. (1986), *Definite NP Anaphora: A Pragmatic Approach* (Oslo: Norwegian University Press).

WEXLER, KENNETH, and MANZINI, M. RITA (1987), 'Parameters and learnability in Binding Theory', in Roeper and Williams (1987: 41–76).

WIESEMANN, URSULA (1982), 'Switch-reference in Bantu languages', *Journal of West African Languages*, 12: 42–57.

—— (1986*a*), 'Grammaticalized coreference', in Wiesemann (1986*b*: 437–64).

—— (ed.) (1986*b*), *Pronominal Systems* (Tübingen: Narr).

WILKINS, DAVID (1988), 'Switch-reference in Mparntwe Arrernte (Aranda): form, function and problems of identity', in Austin (1988: 147–76).

WILKINS, WENDY (1988), 'Themantic structure and reflexivisation', in W. Wilkins (ed.), *Syntax and Semantics 21: Thematic Relations* (London: Academic Press): 191–213.

WILLIAMS, EDWIN S. (1977), 'Discourse and logical form', *Linguistic Inquiry*, 8: 101–39.

—— (1980), 'Predication', *Linguistic Inquiry*, 11: 203–38.

—— (1992), 'Adjunct control', in Larson et al. (1992: 297–322).

WILLIAMS, KEMP (1988), 'Exceptional behaviour of anaphors in Albanian', *Linguistic Inquiry*, 19: 161–8.

WILSON, COLIN (1998), 'Bidirectional optimization and the theory of anaphora', MS, The Johns Hopkins University.

WILT, KOOS VAN DER (1985), 'Long distance anaphora in Dutch and Icelandic: a remark on learnability', *Linguistic Analysis*, 15: 177–86.

WOODBURY, ANTHONY C. (1983), 'Switch reference, syntactic organization, and rhetorical structure in central Yup'ik Eskimo', in Haiman and Munro (1983*b*: 291–315).

XU, LIEJONG (1986), 'Free empty categories', *Linguistic Inquiry*, 17: 75–93.

—— (1990), 'Are they parasitic gaps?', in Mascaró and Nespor (1990: 455–61).

—— and LANGENDOEN, D. TERENCE (1985), 'Topic structures in Chinese', *Language*, 61: 1–27.

YADAVA, YOGENDRA (1998), *Issues in Maithili Syntax: A Government-Binding Approach* (Munich: Lincom Europa).

YANG, DONG-WHEE (1983), 'The extended binding theory of anaphors', *Language Research*, 19: 169–92.

—— (1985), 'On the integrity of control theory', *Proceedings of the North-Eastern Linguistics Society*, 15: 389–408.

YOON, JAMES (1985), 'On the treatment of empty categories in topic prominent languages', MS, University of Illinois.

YOON, JEONG ME (1989), 'Long-distance anaphors in Korean and their cross-linguistic implications', *Papers from the Regional Meeting of the Chicago Linguistic Society*, 25: 479–95.

ZEC, DRAGA (1987), 'On obligatory control in clausal complements', in Iida, Wechsler, and Zec (1987: 139–68).

ZIFF, P. (1960), *Semantic Analysis* (Ithaca, NY: Cornell University Press).

ZIPF, G. K. (1949), *Human Behavior and the Principle of Least Effort* (Cambridge, Mass.: Addison-Wesley).

ZRIBI-HERTZ, ANNE (1980), 'Coréférences et pronoms réfléchis: notes sur le contraste *lui/lui-même* en français', *Linguisticae Investigationes*, 4:131–79.

—— (1989), 'Anaphor binding and narrative point of view: English reflexive pronouns in sentence and discourse', *Language*, 65: 695–727.

—— (1995), 'Emphatic or reflexive? On the endophoric character of French *lui-même* and similar complex pronouns', *Journal of Linguistics*, 31: 333–74.

—— and ADOPO, CHARLEMAGNE (1992), 'The syntax of Attie pronominals', *Linguistic Review*, 9: 69–108.

ZUBIZARRETA, MARIA (1987), *Levels of Representation in the Lexicon and in the Syntax* (Dordrecht: Foris).

Index of names

Abelson, R. 250
Abraham, W. 51, 52, 59
Adams, M. 69
Adopo, C. 187
Åfarli, T. 79
Ahenakew, F. 39
Aikawa, T. 104, 121, 122, 164, 192
Allen, W. S. 218
Anagnostopoulou, E. 157, 159, 167
Andersen, T. 177
Anderson, S. 24, 36, 49, 90, 94, 95, 110, 218
Andrews, A. 38
Annamalai, E. 231
Aoun, J. 45, 48, 123, 298
Archangeli, D. 16, 73, 74
Ariel, M. 7, 8, 245, 253, 254, 255, 256, 258, 261, 305, 309, 315, 329
Armstrong, R. 185
Asher, N. 254
Atkinson, M. 130
Atlas, J. 207, 210, 216
Auer, J. 232
Austin, P. 11, 158, 164, 280, 281, 284, 285, 286, 289, 290, 298
Authier, J.-M. 38, 42, 52, 78, 79, 83, 84, 92,
Awbery, G. 53

Bach, E. 39
Baika, T. 187
Baker, C. L. 25, 90, 103, 190, 229, 230, 231
Baker, M. 55, 78, 158, 163
Baltin, M. 148, 150
Bamgbose, A. 185, 229
Banfield, A. 190
Bar-Hillel, Y. 216
Barss, A. 91, 158
Barton, E. 154

Battistella, E. 36, 91, 105, 110, 111, 115, 121
Belletti, A. 118
Benedicto, E. 95, 115, 159
Benincà, P. 63
Bergsland, K. 55
Best, C. 90
Bickerton, D. 105
Biloa, E. 20, 25, 68, 106, 108
Bittner, M. 94, 96, 118, 123
Blackwell, S. 233, 241, 245
Bloom, P. 90
Bloomfield, L. 10
Bohnhoff, L. 173, 176, 177, 189
Bok-Bennema, R. 105
Bolinger, D. 28
Borer, H. 35, 36, 39, 45, 51, 54, 57, 66, 125
Börjars, K. 53
Bosch, P. 245
Bouchard, D. 45, 83, 99, 103
Bouton, L. 149
Brame, M. 43
Branco, A. 108
Brandi, L. 59
Breeze, M. 24, 97, 101
Bresnan, J. 32, 38, 39, 43, 56, 158, 286, 287, 297
Bril, I. 102
Brinton, L. 190
Broadwell, G. 297, 298, 299
Broselow, E. 130
Brown, G. 259
Brown, P. 325
Bryan, M. 180
Burquest, D. 101, 163, 183, 187
Burzio, L. 21, 22, 24, 25, 26, 28, 35, 45, 93, 126, 127, 128, 129, 160, 220, 223, 225, 231
Butler, J. 12

Index of names

Calabrese, A. 38
Cameron, R. 69, 278
Campos, H. 78
Cançado, M. 118
Cantrall, W. 190
Carden, G. 21, 28, 258
Carnap, R. 216
Carrell, P. 179, 229
Catsimali, G. 37, 39
Chafe, W. 250, 251, 259, 260, 266, 268, 270, 278, 304, 314, 315
Chao, W. 84, 85, 132
Chapman, C. 53
Chen, P. 245, 268, 269, 270, 304, 305, 327
Chien, Y.-C. 130
Chierchia, G. 39, 84, 168
Chomsky, N. 1, 2, 14, 16, 17, 18, 28, 29, 32, 36, 39, 43, 51, 53, 54, 64, 70, 72, 88, 102, 103, 105, 115, 117, 126, 130, 168, 173, 212, 213, 215, 222, 234, 247, 248, 263, 276, 277, 297, 331
Choueiri, L. 48
Christensén, K. 157
Chui, K. 187
Chung, S. 39, 45, 79, 85, 88, 90, 223
Clancy, P. 304, 305
Clark, E. 259
Clark, H. 7, 249, 250, 252, 259, 320, 321
Clark, R. 158
Claudi, U. 162, 187
Clements, G. 173, 179, 182, 183, 186, 187, 189, 200, 226
Cloarec-Heiss, F. 177, 179
Clossman, G. 320
Cole, M. 58
Cole, P. 79, 85, 114, 115, 121, 123, 165, 166, 269, 273, 288, 290, 293
Comrie, B. 8, 10, 11, 12, 42, 168, 170, 172, 175, 177, 178, 179, 181, 182, 183, 188, 189, 190, 222, 226, 238, 280, 282, 283, 284, 286, 292, 295, 296
Cook, V. 16, 19
Cordin, P. 59
Cornish, F. 254
Coulmas, F. 227
Creider, C. 79

Crouch, R. 151
Crowley, T. 12
Cruse, D. 269
Crysmann, B. 87, 90
Cuenot, J. 183
Culicover, P. 39, 168
Culy, C. 3, 69, 117, 118, 173, 174, 175, 176, 177, 179, 182, 183, 184, 185, 186, 188, 189, 190, 194, 226, 228, 229
Cumming, S. 305
Cuoq, J.-A. 10
Curl, T. 102

Dahl, Ö. 134, 136, 139, 142, 145, 154
Dalrymple, M. 131, 132, 135, 136, 143, 145, 146, 147, 151, 152, 153
Datz, M. 12
Davies, J. 121
Davison, A. 23, 98, 100, 119, 224
Deane, P. 254
de Fornel, M. 302, 320
de Jong, J. 22
Demirci, M. 241
Dench, A. 102, 282, 283, 284, 285, 329
Déprez, V. 55
Descartes, R. 331
Diesing, M. 62
Dik, S. 271
Dimitriadis, A. 316
Dixon, R. M. W. 12
Donnellan, K. 239
Dooley, R. 268
Doren, E. 155
Downing, P. 320, 326, 329
Dowty, D. 39, 212
Dubinsky, S. 48
Du Bois, J. 305, 318
Dumezil, G. 218
Dupuis, F. 65
Durie, M. 32, 305
Dziwirek, K. 38

Eades, D. 21
Eckman, F. 130
Edmondson, J. 225, 229, 230
Eid, M. 263

Embick, D. 56, 78
Enç, M. 47, 233
Engdahl, E. 250
Erkü, K. 249, 250
Erteschik-Shir, N. 32, 258
Essien, O. 187
Evans, G. 7, 28, 29, 242
Evans, N. 282, 284
Everaert, M. 20, 21, 36, 95, 100, 105, 109, 115, 157, 159, 160, 165, 167, 217

Falk, C. 51, 53, 61, 64, 65
Faltz, L. 21, 22, 23, 90, 94, 101, 162, 163, 164, 173, 177, 218, 222, 223, 225
Farkas, D. 38, 66, 85, 170, 238, 239
Farmer, A. 161, 215, 243
Farrell, P. 79, 86
Fauconnier, G. 320
Fiengo, R. 131, 134, 135, 136, 138, 139, 141, 142, 143, 144, 145, 146, 147, 148, 150, 151, 154
Fillmore, C. 156, 250
Finer, D. 130, 297, 299, 300
Firbas, J. 257, 260
Fleischman, S. 278
Fodor, J. 28, 247
Foley, W. 8, 11, 12, 13, 118, 169, 238, 239, 245, 268, 282, 287, 288, 289, 294, 295, 296
Fortescue, M. 283
Foulet, L. 69
Fox, B. 287, 307, 308, 309, 310, 311, 312, 313, 314, 318, 328, 329
Fox, D. 18, 154, 155
Frajzyngier, Z. 102, 162, 174, 180, 184, 187
Franklin, K. 282, 286, 296
Franks, S. 6, 35, 52, 53, 58, 68, 70, 88, 89, 234
Freidin, R. 16, 18
Fukui, N. 104

Gabbay, D. 33, 136
Gair, J. 109
Garrod, S. 214, 249, 250, 251, 253, 259, 320
Gawron, M. 136, 155

Gazdar, G. 207, 210, 211, 212, 213, 245, 246
Geluykens, R. 303, 318, 321, 323, 324
Geniušienė, E. 91, 163, 164, 217, 218
Georgopoulos, C. 32
Gerdts, D. 218
Gilligan, G. 53, 59
Gilliom, L. 254
Giorgi, A. 95, 103, 110, 156, 159, 160
Givón, T. 54, 253, 261, 278, 283, 303, 304, 305, 308, 309
Goddard, I. 10
Gordon, L. 11, 280, 285, 290, 291, 294
Gordon, P. 254
Goyvaerts, D. 177
Green, M. 229
Grice, H. P. 49, 205, 206, 207, 208, 215, 222, 247, 310
Grimes, J. 310
Grimshaw, J. 75, 76, 77, 156
Grodzinsky, Y. 29, 45, 212
Grosz, B. 250, 254
Guentcheva, Z. 102
Gundel, J. 249, 250, 266, 268, 278, 302, 315
Gunji, T. 262
Gurtu, M. 98

Haegeman, L 16, 54
Haeri, N. 278
Hagège, C. 178, 183, 187, 188, 189, 226
Haïk, I. 154
Haiman, J. 175, 217, 278, 280, 282, 283, 286, 290, 291
Hakulinen, A. 319
Hale, E. 177
Hale, K. 54, 158, 289, 297
Halliday, M. A.. K. 1, 259, 310
Hamann, C. 90
Hamilton, R. 48
Hankamer, J. 132
Harbert, W. 115
Hardt, D. 136, 138, 146, 151
Harnish, R. 161, 215, 243
Harré, R. 329
Hasan, R. 1, 259, 310
Hasegawa, N. 78

Index of names

Hashemipour, M. 38, 39
Haviland, S. 7, 249, 252, 259
Hawkins, J. 222, 249, 331
Heath, J. 9, 158, 291, 295
Hedberg, N. 249, 250, 278, 302, 315
Hedinger, R. 177, 187
Heim, I. 102
Heine, B. 101, 162, 163, 187, 190, 218, 219
Helke, M. 243
Hellan, L. 20, 92, 100, 103, 124, 157, 159, 190, 194, 217, 218
Hendrick, R. 54
Hermon, G. 53, 67, 68, 70, 114, 115, 121, 123, 130, 165, 166, 269, 273
Hestvik, A. 24, 94, 107, 135, 166
Higginbotham, J. 91, 143
Hill, H. 173
Hilles, S. 55, 90
Hiltunen, K. 41, 86, 95, 100, 164, 165, 233
Himmelmann, N. 8
Hinds, J. 309
Hintikka, J. 172, 190
Hirakawa, M. 130
Hirschberg, J. 143
Hirschbühler, P. 69
Hlaing, C. 58, 85
Hobbs, J. 310
Hofstadter, D. 320
Hoijer, H. 11, 88
Hoji, H. 132, 135, 142, 155, 235
Holisky, D. 305
Holmberg, A. 59
Hoonchamlong, Y. 79
Hopkins, E. 224
Hopper, P.162
Horn, L. 207, 208, 210, 213, 239
Hornstein, N. 35, 44, 45, 48, 150, 151
Horrocks, G. 56
Huang, C.-T. 36, 37, 45, 46, 47, 49, 54, 55, 58, 65, 66, 67, 68, 70, 71, 78, 79, 80, 81, 82, 110, 115, 124, 263, 264, 276
Huang, Y. 1, 6, 7, 13, 14, 15, 28, 29, 36, 37, 39, 47, 49, 52, 53, 57, 66, 70, 86, 87, 88, 90, 103, 104, 107, 110, 117, 120, 123, 124, 170, 172, 185, 190, 195, 197, 199, 205, 206, 212, 213, 215, 216, 220, 237, 245, 259, 262, 263, 266, 268, 276, 302, 303, 304, 307, 308, 314, 318, 319, 320, 321, 322, 323, 324, 327, 330
Hubbard, P. 222
Huck, G. 263, 266, 269, 271, 274
Huet, G. 151, 152
Hukari, T. 110
Hulk, A. 51, 61, 62, 63, 69
Hünnemeyer, F. 162, 187
Hust, J. 43
Hutchison, J. 232
Hutchisson, D. 223
Hwang, J.-L.187
Hyams, N. 53, 90, 257
Hyman, L. 175, 177, 178, 179, 182, 183, 186, 188, 189, 190, 226, 283

Iatridou, S. 56, 78, 106, 108, 109
Igwe, G. 229
Iida, M. 39
Ikoro, S. 175, 190
Iwakura, K. 45

Jackendoff, R. 47, 156, 159, 168
Jacobsen, W. 11, 280, 281, 282, 289, 293, 295, 298
Jaeggli, O. 49, 52, 53, 54, 56, 57, 68, 69, 70, 71, 234
Jayaseelan, K. 149
Jefferson, G. 160, 217, 321, 322,
Jespersen, O. 54
Joseph, B. 37, 38, 39
Joshi, A. 254
Justus, C. 267

Kaburaki, E. 190, 199
Kaiser, G. 87, 90
Kameyama, M. 69, 103, 190
Kamio, A. 268
Kamp, H. 199, 201, 204
Kang, B.-M. 88, 107, 108, 113
Kanno, K. 90
Kant, I. 213, 330
Kapur, S. 114

Karttunen, L. 7
Karunatillake, W. 109
Katada, F. 96, 115, 118, 124
Kato, K. 19, 96, 129, 191, 193, 238, 239, 265
Kayne, R. 36
Keenan, E. 22, 78, 160, 182, 223
Kemmer, S. 25, 101, 162, 219, 222, 229
Kempchinsky, P. 38
Kempson, R. 6, 7, 33, 136, 247, 248, 253
Kendall, M. 218, 279
Kenstowicz, M. 54, 57
Kibrik, A. 305, 314, 317
Kihm, A. 21, 287
Kim, S.-H. 25, 54, 55, 89, 95, 105, 106, 192, 195, 196, 197, 224, 232, 236, 262
Kinkade, M. 305, 306
Kinyalolo, K. 183
Kiss, K. 157, 158
Kitagawa, C. 268, 269, 270, 271, 274, 275
Kitagawa, Y. 135, 136, 138, 139, 140, 141, 143, 148
Klein-Andreu, F. 8
Klima, E. 212
Kodio, K. 3, 117, 118, 177, 182, 184, 190, 226
Koktová, E. 258
König, E. 25, 101, 162, 190, 219, 220, 229
Koopman, H. 32, 86, 103, 187
Korhonen, A.-L. 19, 102
Kornfilt, J. 130, 230
Koster, J. 44, 45, 90, 99, 105, 109, 114, 115
Kratochvíl, P. 245, 268
Kroeber, A. 11
Kuno, S. 19, 22, 25, 102, 118, 123, 158, 190, 196, 198, 199, 257, 268
Kuroda, S.-Y. 190

Lahiri, U. 131
Lakshmanan, U. 55, 70
Lambrecht, K. 309, 314, 315, 317, 318
Landa, A. 79
Langacker, R. 254
Langdon, M. 284, 286, 294

Langendoen, D. 16, 73, 86, 245, 266, 267, 268, 271
Lappin, S. 135, 148
Larson, R. 39, 43, 44, 131, 148, 149, 239
Lasnik, H. 3, 27, 28, 32, 36, 47, 48, 50, 88, 102, 149, 158, 212
Law, P. 59, 69, 81
Lawal, N. 4
Lebeaux, D. 99, 102, 115
Leech, G. 28, 318
Lees, R. 212
Lehmann, W. 267
Levelt, W. 321
Levinson, S. 1, 15, 21, 25, 28, 35, 39, 42, 44, 158, 161, 162, 190, 207, 208, 210, 212, 213, 214, 216, 220, 228, 230, 237, 242, 245, 253, 313, 318, 325, 330
Levitt, A. 90
Levy, Y. 51, 66
Li, C. 245, 266, 267, 268, 269, 272, 304, 327
Lichtenberk, F. 102, 306
Lidz, J. 99, 109, 128, 162, 164, 166, 175, 220
Lightfoot, D. 45
Lillo-Martin, D. 78
Linde, C. 250
Lindseth, M. 6, 52, 53, 68, 70, 88, 89, 234
Lobeck, A. 132, 135, 137, 149
Longacre, R. 11, 283, 285, 289, 309
Lord, C. 187
Lust, B. 1, 130
Lynch, J. 290, 291, 293
Lyons, J. 253
Lyovin, A. 187
Lyutikova, E. 223

McCawley, J. 267, 270, 271, 274
McCloskey, J. 54
McCray, A. 28, 258
McGann, W. 305
McGregor, W. 101
McKay, T. 25, 229
McKoon, G. 254
Macleod, N. 258
Maling, J. 20, 90, 92, 105, 119, 190, 194

Index of names

Mann, W. 269, 310
Manzini, M. 24, 42, 44, 45, 46, 47, 49, 112, 113, 114
Marchese, L. 217, 219, 267
Marrafa, P. 109
Marshall, C. 7, 320
Martin, R. 44
Martohardjono, G. 114
Maslova, E. 285
Massam, D. 79
Matisoff, J. 187
Matsui, T. 7, 249, 250, 251, 253
Matsuo, A. 130
Matthews, P. 16
May, R. 102, 131, 134, 135, 136, 138, 139, 141, 142, 143, 144, 145, 146, 147, 148, 149, 150, 151, 154
Mchombo, S. 56
Md.Salleh, R. 132
Meredith, M. 320
Meyer-Viol, W. 136
Minsky, M. 250
Mithun, M. 316
Mittwoch, A. 28, 258
Moar, K. 320
Moerman, M. 321, 322
Mohanan, K. P. 25, 35, 38, 52, 89, 98, 105, 118
Montague, R. 39
Montalbetti, M. 88, 233, 234
Montaut, A. 98
Moravcsik, E. 25, 229
Moshagen, S. 106
Moyne, J. 25, 229
Moyse-Faurie, C. 219
Mühlhäusler, P. 329
Munro, P. 175, 280, 284, 286, 289, 291, 294

Na, Y. H. 263, 266, 267, 268, 269, 271, 274, 275
Nakamura, M. 79, 85, 263
Napoli, D. 95
Natascha, M. 87, 90
Nedjalkov, V. 101, 102
Newson, M. 69
Ngoh, G. L. 24, 92, 96, 107, 231

Nichols, J. 11, 122, 297
Noordman, L. 310
Nylander, D. 187

O'Conner, C. 24, 190, 228, 297, 301, 329
O'Grady, W. 58
Olson, M. 287
Oswalt, R. 11, 283, 284, 292, 294
Otani, K. 132, 150, 155
Ouhalla, J. 88, 89

Pan, H. 95, 96, 159
Paredes Silva, V. 278
Parker, E. 101, 162, 182, 183, 184, 185, 186, 189, 190, 223, 224, 225
Parkinson, D. 278
Parks, D. 173, 306
Partee, B. 39, 137
Payne, D. 286
Payne, T. 329
Peck, C. 12
Pereira, F. 131, 132, 135, 136, 143, 146, 147, 151, 152, 153
Perlmutter, D. 53, 56
Pesetsky, D. 118
Peters, S. 136, 155
Philippaki-Warburton, I. 37, 39, 44, 54
Pica, P. 32, 92, 94, 115
Picallo, M. 233
Pierce, A. 55
Pingkarawat, N. 79, 85
Plank, F. 225, 229, 230
Plato 2, 16
Platzack, C. 51, 52, 53, 57, 59, 69, 70, 71, 72
Pollack, M 151
Pollard, C. 19, 39, 44, 102, 103, 123, 157, 158, 168, 170, 171, 238, 239
Popovich, H. 101
Popper, K. 216
Postal, P. 31, 33, 157
Prince, A. 14, 16, 73, 76
Prince, E. 249, 253, 254, 259
Progovac, L. 92, 97, 118, 123, 124, 125
Pu, M.-M. 278, 305, 308, 314, 315, 316

Radford, A. 16, 53, 90, 169, 238
Raina, A. 108

Index of names

Ramsey, S. 269
Randriamasimanana, C. 26, 158
Ransom, E. 187
Raposo, E. 78, 79, 182
Rappaport, G. 93
Rebuschi, G. 224
Reesink, P. 286, 288
Reinders-Machowska, E. 101
Reinhart, T. 19, 20, 29, 32, 45, 103, 114, 115, 133, 143, 157, 159, 160, 161, 164, 165, 166, 167, 173, 190, 212, 216, 217, 222, 223, 242, 243, 258
Renzi, L. 63
Reuland, E. 19, 20, 29, 32, 90, 99, 103, 114, 115, 157, 159, 160, 161, 164, 165, 166, 167, 173, 190, 216, 217, 222, 223
Reyle, U. 199, 201
Rhodes, R. 39
Riad, T. 160
Richards, N. 220
Rigau, G. 88
Rivero, M.-L. 63, 64, 69
Rizzi, L. 42, 51, 52, 56, 60, 61, 62, 64, 65, 67, 71, 79, 81, 83, 84, 85, 86, 118, 129
Roberge, Y. 79, 83
Roberts, C. 145
Roberts, I. 65, 69
Roberts, J. 284, 286, 287, 288, 293, 294, 298, 302
Rögnvaldsson, E. 57, 62
Rohrbacher, B. 69, 70, 72
Ronat, M. 103
Rood, D. 306
Rooth, M. 145
Rosenbaum, P. 43, 168
Ross, J. 79, 80
Rumelhart, D. 250
Ruwet, N. 173
Růžička, R. 43, 168, 169, 171

Sacks, H. 302, 318, 319, 320, 321, 322, 323, 324
Sæbø, K. 155
Safir, K. 22, 25, 32, 34, 49, 52, 57, 59, 68, 70, 71, 94, 102, 113, 123

Sag, I. 19, 22, 39, 44, 102, 103, 123, 131, 132, 136, 137, 146, 157, 158, 168, 170, 171, 238, 239
Saito, M. 88, 235
Saleemi, A. 52, 53, 90
Samek-Lodovici, V. 75, 76, 77
Sandalo, F. 158
Sanders, T. 310
Sandu, G. 172, 190
Sanford, A. 214, 249, 250, 251, 253, 259, 320
Santandrea, S. 177
Santorini, B. 62
Saxena, A. 98
Saxon, L. 25, 39, 47, 297
Schank, R. 250
Schaub, W. 178, 183, 185
Schegloff, E. 302, 318, 319, 320, 321, 322, 323, 324
Schiebe, T. 134
Schladt, M. 162
Schwartz, A. 219, 305
Scott, G. 296
Sells, P. 95, 99, 103, 153, 190, 192, 193, 195, 196, 197, 199, 200, 201
Sem, H. 155
Senft, G. 21
Shieber, S. 131, 132, 135, 136, 143, 146, 147, 151, 152, 153
Sidner, C. 249, 250
Siemund, P. 25, 101, 162, 190, 219, 229
Sigurðsson, H. 35, 52, 57, 58, 62, 67, 79, 80, 81, 85, 93, 107, 190, 194, 195, 227, 228
Sigurjónsdóttir, S. 257
Silverstein, M. 245
Simpson, J. 287, 297
Smolensky, P. 14, 16, 73, 76
Snyder, W. 32
Solan, L. 90
Speas, M. 53, 64, 70, 72, 73, 74, 75, 158
Sperber, D. 247, 253
Spooren, W. 310
Sportiche, D. 32, 86, 103, 104, 107, 187
Sproat, R. 254
Sprouse, R. 58
Srivastav Dayal, V. 98

378   Index of names

Stalnaker, R. 239
Stewart, W. 21
Stillings, J. 105, 108, 110, 111
Stirling, L. 11, 185, 190, 195, 199, 200, 201, 228, 279, 282, 283, 284, 285, 286, 287, 288, 292, 293, 294, 295, 297, 299, 300
Stowell, T. 32
Stump, G. 54
Subbarao, K. V. 6, 19, 47, 95, 99, 103, 106, 107, 109, 132, 235
Suñer, M. 52, 79
Sung, L.-M. 114, 115, 118, 121, 123, 165, 166, 269, 273

Tai, J. 304, 309
Takahashi, D. 150
Takami, K. I. 118, 268, 318
Tang, C.-C. 110, 115, 119, 120, 124
Taraldsen, T. 53, 54
Thomas, M. 130
Thompson, S. 117, 245, 266, 267, 268, 269, 272, 304, 310, 327
Thornton, R. 136
Thráinsson, H. 22, 24, 25, 36, 48, 49, 50, 62, 94, 97, 105, 108, 222, 223
Timberlake, A. 22
Togo, P. 3, 117, 118, 177, 182, 184, 186, 190, 226
Toman, J. 118, 222
Tomlin, R. 278, 308, 314, 315, 316
Trask, R. 280
Traugott, E. 162
Travis, L. 70
Trosterud, T. 106
Trumbull, J. 10
Tryon, D. 21
Tsujimura, N. 299, 300
Tucker, A. 180

Ueda, M. 104
Uriagereka, J. 16

Vainikka, A. 51, 66
Valian, V. 53, 90
Vallduví, E. 250
Vance, B. 58, 65, 69

van der Wurff, W. 232
Vanelli, L. 63
van Gelderen, E. 222
van Hoek, K. 254
van Kemenade, A. 51, 61, 62, 63, 69
van Riemsdijk, H. 56
van Steenbergen, M. 36, 90, 96, 115, 124
Van Valin, R. 8, 10, 11, 12, 13, 118, 169, 238, 239, 245 268, 282, 287, 288, 289, 294, 295, 296
Verheijen, R. 26
Verne, G. 155
Vestre, E. 155
Vikner, S. 24, 94
Vikør, L. 96
Vincent, N. 63, 81, 87
Visser, F. 41, 42, 43
Vitale, A. 233
von Bremen, K. 190
von Humboldt, W. 331
von Roncador, M. 175, 176, 177, 179, 187, 190, 229
Voorhoeve, J. 190

Wada, H. 254
Wali, K. 6, 19, 47, 94, 95, 98, 99, 100, 103, 106, 107, 108, 109, 118, 132, 163, 235
Walker, M. 254
Wang, C. 111, 115
Wang, J. 105, 108, 110
Wang, Q. 90
Ward, G. 143, 254
Wasow, T. 1
Watkins, L. 306, 307
Webber, B. 133, 147
Weber, D. 284
Weinberg, A. 48
Weinstein, S. 254
Weissenborn, J. 70, 90, 101
Welmers, W. 187
Wescoat, M. 143
Westergaad, M. 258, 259, 260
Wexler, K. 24, 90, 112, 113, 114, 130, 136
Whitman, J. 132, 150, 155

Wiesemann, U. 11, 90, 177, 179, 180, 181, 182, 183, 187, 188, 189, 239, 281, 282, 283, 284, 292, 296
Wilkins, D. 11, 284, 285
Wilkins, W. 39, 156, 159, 168
Williams, E. 34, 39, 41, 44, 56, 99, 131, 132, 136, 137
Williams, K. 222
Wilson, C. 127, 129
Wilson, D. 247, 253
Woodbury, A. 283

Xu, L. J. 86, 245, 263, 264, 266, 267, 268, 271
Xu, Y. 105, 110, 111

Yadava, Y. 109

Yang, D.-W. 35, 39, 52, 58, 78, 89, 109, 110
Yépez, M. 79
Yoon, J. 53, 67, 68, 70, 79, 99, 102, 119, 195, 196
Yoon, J. M. 190, 193
Yule, G. 259

Zacharski, R. 249, 250, 278, 302, 315
Zaenen, A. 99, 153
Zec, D. 39, 40, 99, 153
Ziff, P. 49
Zipf, G. 207
Zribi-Hertz, A. 19, 21, 22, 25, 26, 123, 177, 184, 187, 190, 229, 231
Zubizarreta, M. 217

Index of languages, language families, and language areas

This index includes all the individual languages, larger genetic groupings of languages, and larger non-genetic, geographic groupings of languages referred to in the book.

Abaza 163, 218
Abé 187
Abkhaz 162, 163, 218
Abrom 175
Acehness 305
Acholi 101, 162
Adamawa 177, 179, 180, 232
Adamawa, Eastern 178
Adamawa-Ubangi 177, 180, 232
Adioukrou 173
African languages 1, 81, 101, 131, 162, 172, 173, 176, 177, 178, 179, 180, 181, 182, 183, 184, 185, 186, 187, 188, 189, 191, 194, 197, 199, 204, 225, 226, 229, 279
Afrikaans 69
Aghem 173, 176, 279, 297
Agni 175
Agul 279
Akan 23, 225
Akɔɔse 176, 177, 187
Alabama 279
Alamblak 296
Albanian 38, 64, 91, 158, 222
Aleut 55
Algonquian 10, 39, 102, 163
Älvdalsmålet 52, 57, 59
Alyawarra 279
Amadi 232
Amele 284, 285, 286, 287, 288, 293, 294, 295, 300, 303
American Indian languages 10, 11, 176, 280, 281, 282, 286, 297, 298
American Indian languages, North 11, 279, 289, 290, 295, 306, 307
American Indian languages, South 279

American Sign Language 79
Amharic 102, 304
Anejom 291
Angaatiha 279, 283
Angas 162, 174, 176, 183, 187
Anglo-Saxon 222
Anjam 279
Anywa 162, 218
Apachean 10
Arabana 284
Arabic 35, 83, 175, 232
Arabic, Bani-Hassan 54, 57
Arabic, Egyptian 263, 278
Arabic, Moroccan 69
Arabic, Syrian 25
Arandic 287
Arawak 78
Arbore 101
Archi 9
Arosi 78
Arrernte, Mparntwe 285
Arvanítika 38
Asian languages, East 13, 23, 131, 150, 187, 190, 191, 192, 193, 194, 195, 196, 197, 198, 199, 200, 201, 202, 203, 204, 225, 226, 232, 304
Asian languages, South 225
Asian languages, South-east 13, 23, 187, 267
Athapaskan 297, 306
Attié 187
Australian languages 12, 21, 78, 101, 102, 158, 279, 280, 281, 286, 287, 289, 290, 297, 298, 306
Austronesian 12, 21, 291
Avar 78
Avatime/Siyasɛ 176

Index of languages, language families, and language areas 381

Aymara 101
Azerbaijani 163

Babungo 175, 176, 178, 183, 185, 188
Bafut 297
Bagirmi 162
Bai 232
Baka 232
Balese 101
Baltic 163
Bamana 102
Bambara, Bamako 21
Banda 101
Banda-linda 176, 187
Banda-Tangbago 176
Bandjalang 12
Bango 101, 232
Bantu 32, 68, 78, 177, 296, 297
Bantu, Grassfields 177, 178, 179
Barai 287, 288
Barambu 232
Bardi 101, 103
Bargam 279
Bargu 175
Bari 162, 294, 295, 298
Basque 162, 163, 224
Bassa 162
Bayungu 279
Beboid 177
Belorussian 53
Bengali 58, 232
Bengali, Eastern 232
Benue-Congo 162, 179
Berber 88
Bezta 279
Bidiya 187
Bilin 102
Birri 176, 232
Bisa 176, 232
Bislama 21
Blackfoot 10
Bole 187
Bongo 176
Breton 54
Bulgarian 56, 64
Burduna 279
Burmese 59, 85

Busa 176, 232
Bwamu 176, 183

Caddoan 306
Cantonese 187
Capanahua 286, 298
Cashibo 219, 282, 283
Cashinahua 298
Catalan 22, 56, 232, 233, 250
Catalan, Old 63, 64, 88
Caucasian languages 78, 225, 297
Caucasian languages, North-east 279
Cebuano/Sebuano 268
Celtic 54
Chadic 102, 162, 187
Chadic, East 177
Chamorro 39, 59, 79, 85, 90, 222, 223, 304
Chechen 122, 279, 297
Chehalis, Lower 305
Chehalis, Upper 305, 306
Chemehuewi 279, 282
Chichewa 32, 55, 56, 78
Chickasaw 281, 286, 289, 290
Chinese 1, 2, 4, 6, 13, 14, 19, 23, 26, 28, 29, 36, 37, 39, 41, 42, 44, 47, 48, 52, 56, 58, 59, 65, 66, 68, 69, 71, 72, 73, 74, 75, 76, 77, 78, 79, 81, 86, 88, 89, 90, 91, 92, 93, 94, 95, 96, 98, 99, 102, 103, 104, 106, 107, 110, 111, 112, 114, 115, 117, 119, 120, 121, 123, 124, 126, 128, 129, 131, 142, 147, 153, 155, 156, 159, 163, 165, 166, 167, 170, 171, 187, 191, 192, 194, 195, 196, 197, 198, 200, 213, 215, 217, 218, 226, 227, 230, 231, 232, 234, 235, 236, 237, 238, 239, 240, 241, 243, 244, 248, 255, 257, 260, 261, 262, 263, 264, 265, 266, 267, 269, 270, 271, 272, 273, 274, 275, 276, 277, 304, 305, 307, 309, 315, 316, 317, 318, 319, 321, 322, 323, 324, 325, 326, 327, 328, 330
Chinook Jargon 21
Choctaw 281, 282, 291, 293
Chuave 163, 280

382 Index of languages, language families, and language areas

Chukchansi 279
Chuvash 163
Cibak 187
Cochimi, Northern 279
Columbian 305
Cornish, Old 91
Cowlitz 305
Cree 10, 39
Creole, Haitian 21, 222
Creole, Martinique 21
Creole languages 21
Cross-River 177
Czech 24, 43, 64, 88, 118, 233

Daffo-Butura 187
Daga 283
Dakota 32
Dangla 187
Danish 22, 24, 48, 53, 59, 92, 93, 96, 121
Dargi 122
Delaware 102
Denya 59
Dhalandji 279
Dhargari 279
Dhirari 281
Didinga 162
Dido 279
Didoic 279
Diegueño, Jamul, and La Huerta dialects 282
Dinka 101
Diola/Dyola 162
Diyari 164, 281, 284, 285, 289
Djaru 102
Djingili 279
Djiwarli 279
Dogon 69, 176, 177
Dogrib 39, 47, 297
Dongo 101
Donno Sɔ 173, 174, 176, 177, 179, 182, 183, 184, 188, 189, 226
Doodwaayaayo/Namshi 176
Dravidian 35, 47, 107, 109, 163
Duala 90, 162
Duka 68
Dutch 20, 24, 51, 53, 59, 62, 63, 95, 99, 100, 124, 131, 135, 153, 160, 161, 162, 217, 219, 220, 222, 248, 256, 257
Dutch, Middle 21
Dutch, Old 21
Duupa 176
Dyirbal 12, 218

Ebira 162
Efik 173, 176, 187, 190
Ek-Nii 293
Ekpeye 175
Engenni 176
English 1, 8, 9, 12, 19, 21, 22, 24, 26, 27, 28, 31, 32, 33, 34, 37, 44, 47, 51, 53, 54, 61, 62, 63, 65, 68, 69, 70, 71, 72, 73, 74, 75, 76, 79, 81, 95, 102, 114, 123, 124, 131, 133, 143, 147, 155, 157, 158, 168, 170, 175, 187, 213, 219, 229, 248, 262, 265, 266, 267, 268, 277, 296, 304, 307, 308, 309, 310, 311, 312, 313, 314, 315, 316, 318, 321, 322, 323, 324, 325, 326, 328, 329, 331
English, Early Middle 62, 222
English, Old 21, 62, 164
Eskimo 10
Eskimo, Central Yup'ik 283
Estonian 163
Even 102
Evenki 102
Ewe 173, 174, 176, 179, 182, 183, 184, 186, 187, 200, 226

Faroese 52, 53, 59, 108
Farsi 68
Feroge 176
Fijian 21, 101, 22
Finnish 19, 23, 41, 51, 53, 59, 85, 90, 95, 96, 97, 100, 102, 124, 131, 141, 164, 165, 233, 319
Finno-Ugric 96, 163, 229
Fiorentino 59
Flemish, West 21, 54, 59
Fon 69, 176, 183
Fore 296
Fox 10

Index of languages, language families, and language areas

French 22, 23, 26, 42, 53, 54, 61, 62, 63, 70, 72, 73, 76, 79, 81, 83, 84, 85, 87, 90, 92, 160, 163, 173, 213, 222, 231, 262, 265, 331
French, Old 61, 62, 63, 65, 69, 222
Frisian 21, 165
Frisian, Old 21
Ful 219
Fula 162, 163
Fulani 162
Futunan 101, 219
Fyer 187

Ga'anda 187
Gabu 162
Gaelic 229
Gahuku 292, 298
Galician 22
Garawa 279
Gbandili 176, 179
Gbaya 176, 232
Gen-Mina 176
Georgian 54, 162
German 12, 22, 24, 25, 32, 51, 53, 57, 59, 61, 62, 63, 64, 65, 68, 70, 71, 72, 75, 79, 80, 81, 90, 91, 96, 131, 153, 168, 169, 170, 213, 217, 222, 231, 262, 265, 331
German, Bavarian 53
German, Old High 61
Germanic 21, 22, 23, 25, 42, 43, 59, 79, 126, 229
Gida 101, 187
Gidar 162
Gimira 24, 97, 101
Gisiga/Giziga 162, 187
Godié 81, 217, 219, 267
Gokana 174, 177, 178, 179, 182, 183, 186, 187, 189, 190, 283
Gola 162
Gothic 53
Greek 24, 37, 38, 39, 44, 47, 54, 56, 78, 106, 108, 157, 159, 167, 316
Greek, Ancient 25, 38
Greenlandic, West 283
Guadeloupe 21
Guanano 279, 283, 289

Guariní 268
Guaymí 68
Gude 187
Gugada 279
Gujarati 163
Gumbaynggir 21, 222
Gurung 309
Guugu Yimidhirr 21, 25, 35, 39, 42, 44, 158, 165, 222

Haitian 69
Halkomelem 39, 218
Harway 11, 292, 298
Hausa 25, 162, 187, 304
Hebrew 23, 39, 51, 52, 54, 57, 66, 101, 155, 163, 217, 219, 255, 256, 309
Hebrew, Biblical 21, 162, 304, 305
Hindi 23, 24, 32, 91, 98, 99, 100, 119, 131, 165, 224
Hittite 267
Hoava-Kusaghe 101
Hokan-Coahuiltecan 11, 297
Hona 187
Hopi 279, 300
Hua 282
Huichol 222, 282, 284
Hungarian 59, 85, 158, 167, 222

Ibibio 162, 163, 176, 190
Icelandic 20, 24, 35, 37, 48, 51, 53, 57, 58, 59, 61, 62, 63, 64, 71, 72, 80, 81, 96, 97, 98, 99, 100, 105, 107, 112, 113, 119, 131, 160, 165, 190, 194, 222, 223, 227, 257
Icelandic, Old 52, 58, 59, 67, 71, 85, 90, 91, 92, 93, 94
Idoma 175, 176
Igbo 175, 178, 180, 184, 226, 229
Ik 8
Ilocano 219, 268
Indo-Aryan 163
Indo-European 12, 267
Indonesian 8
Ingush 122, 224, 279, 297
Inuit 94, 96, 118, 123
Iraqw 101
Irish 52, 54, 59, 68, 90, 131

Index of languages, language families, and language areas

Irish, Old 91
Iroquoian 163
Italian 1, 22, 23, 24, 26, 35, 42, 50, 51, 52,
 54, 56, 58, 61, 63, 65, 68, 69, 71, 72,
 75, 76, 77, 79, 81, 83, 84, 85, 88, 90,
 93, 95, 97, 103, 112, 113, 119, 124,
 128, 160, 176, 222, 232
Italian, Old 63, 64

Jabirrjabirr 101
Jacaltec 12
Japanese 1, 13, 19, 23, 24, 39, 47, 52, 58,
 59, 68, 76, 78, 79, 85, 88, 89, 90, 95,
 96, 104, 107, 110, 112, 113, 114, 121,
 122, 123, 124, 126, 129, 132, 150,
 151, 155, 164, 165, 187, 191, 192,
 193, 194, 195, 196, 197, 198, 213,
 235, 236, 238, 239, 240, 245, 248,
 250, 255, 261, 262, 263, 264, 265,
 266, 267, 268, 269, 271, 273, 274,
 275, 304, 309, 315, 317, 330
Javanese 13
Jawi 101
Jiwarli 58, 59
Juang 165
Jukun 101, 163

Kabardian 102
Kadiwéu 158
Kaingang 283
Kaititj 287
Kalagan 268
Kalenjin 101
Kaliko 176
Kalkatungu 218
Kana 175, 190
Kanite 279, 293
Kannada 35, 109, 128, 163, 164, 166, 174,
 175, 219, 220
Kanuri 162
Kanyara 279
Kapampangan 78
Kapsiki 187
Kara (African) 101
Kara (Oceanic) 101
Karaja 101
Kashaya 11, 284, 292, 294, 298

Kashmiri 109
Kâte 282, 293
Kayapo 283
K'emant 162
Kenzi 162
Kera 176, 187
Keresan 10
Kewa 286, 296
Kilivila 21
KiNande 24, 38, 78, 79, 84, 92
KiNubi 21
Kinyarwanda 23, 163, 164
Kirghiz 91
Kisi 101
Kiswahili 32
Kiowa 282, 293, 306, 307
Klamath 282
Kobon 121, 279, 280, 282
Koita 290
Kɔlbila 176
Konkow 279
Korean 13, 23, 25, 32, 35, 37, 39, 52, 58,
 59, 78, 79, 88, 89, 91, 95, 98, 99, 102,
 105, 106, 107, 108, 110, 112, 113,
 114, 117, 119, 120, 123, 124, 126,
 132, 135, 165, 187, 191, 192, 193,
 194, 195, 196, 197, 198, 213, 224,
 232, 233, 235, 236, 244, 248, 255,
 262, 263, 265, 266, 267, 268, 269,
 271, 273, 274, 275, 317, 330
Koromfe 162
Kposo 176
Kresh 176, 177
Krio 187
Kriyol 21, 187
Krongo 162, 163, 176
Kru 81, 267
Kuki-Chin-Lushai 58
Kukuruku (Yɛkhee) 176
Kutenai 10
Kwa 173, 232
Kwami 162

Lahu 187, 267, 269
Lak 285
Lakhota 163, 176, 280
Lamang 162, 187

Index of languages, language families, and language areas

Lango 118, 279, 283, 289
Lardil 289
Latin 25, 95, 159, 232
Latvian 163
Lele 101, 162, 176, 177, 180, 187, 189
Lenakel 282, 291, 293, 300
Lendu 232
Lezgian 220, 279
Lisu 162, 267, 272
Lithuanian 25, 163, 164, 165, 218
Logo 176, 232
Logone 187
Loma 229
Lotuko, Nilotic 190
Lugbara 232
Luo 101, 162
Lushootreed 305

Ma 101, 232
Maasai 229
Maba 162
Mabuiag 78
Macedonian 163
Machiguenga 78
Macro-Je/Macro-Gê 176, 281
Mada 187
Mafa 187
Maidu 279, 282
Maithili 109
Malagasy 12, 26, 53, 158, 162, 163, 166, 267
Malay 24, 92, 96, 98, 109, 129, 132, 176, 231
Malayalam 24, 25, 32, 35, 37, 52, 58, 59, 89, 98, 109, 118, 234
Mambar 175
Mambila 176
Managalisi 279
Mandara 162, 187
Mande 232
Mangbetu 101, 176, 232
Mansi 163
Mantharta 279
Maori 58
Mapun/Mupun 102, 173, 174, 176, 184, 187

Marathi 6, 19, 48, 94, 98, 99, 100, 103, 106, 107, 109, 118, 129, 131, 235
Margi 101, 162, 187
Maricopa 11, 280, 285, 290, 294
Martuthunira 102, 279, 284
Masa 187
Maxakali/Maxacali 101, 176, 281
Mayan 12
Mayogo 101, 232
Mbara 187
Mekeo 101
Melanesian 78
Melayu, Sejarah 305
Mesme 187
Micronesian 187
Mina 162, 187
Miskitu 279
Miwok, Sierra 295
Mizo 163
Modenese 59
Mofu-Gudur 187
Mojave 162, 163
Moldavian 91
Mongal 101
Mongolian, Khalkha 69
Mooré 175
Moru 101, 162, 176, 177
Moru-Madi 177
Mota 69
Mundang 176, 178, 180, 184, 186, 188, 189
Mundani 24, 101, 162, 173, 176, 177, 180, 182, 183, 184, 185, 186, 187, 189, 190, 222, 223, 224, 225
Mundu 176
Munjuk 187
Muskogean 279

Nakh 279
Nasio 285
Navajo 10, 158, 306
Ndogo 101, 176
Negerhollands 21
Nêlêmwâ 101
Nepali 158
Newari, Bhaktapur 176
Newari, Kathmandu 176

Index of languages, language families, and language areas

Ngala 101
Ngamini 281
Ngarrka 287
Ngayarda 102
Ngbaka 176, 177
Ngiyambaa 289
Ngizim 162, 187
Ngumbarl 101
Ngwo 176, 179
Ngyemboon 279
Niger-Congo 162, 173
Nimanburru 101
Nisenan 279
Nkom 176
Nobonob 279
Noni 176, 177, 190, 297
Nootka 12
Norse, Old 79
Norse, Pre-old 222
Norwegian 20, 24, 53, 59, 79, 92, 93, 96, 99, 100, 106, 107, 121, 124, 131, 135, 153, 157, 166, 190, 217, 218, 219
Nunggubuyu 8
Nyang 176
Nyikina 101
Nyulnyul 101
Nyulnyulan 101, 163
Nyungan 9
Nzakara/Pambi/Ngala 176

Occitan, Medieval 232
Occitan, Modern 232
Oceanic 101, 306
Ojibwa 39
Ojibwa, South-western 163
Okinawan 25
Oron 162, 176

Pa'a 187
Padovano 163, 164
Paiute, Northern 282
Palauan 32, 58, 59
Palenquero 21, 222
Panyjima 102
Papago 222, 282
Pape/Dugun 176
Papiamentu 68

Papuan languages 102, 279, 282, 286, 290, 293, 296, 298
Päri 101, 162
Pashto 54, 55
Pawnee 306
Pere/Kutin 176
Pero 162, 175, 176, 187
Persian 38, 39, 278
Philippine languages 78, 268
pidgin languages 21
Piedmontese 22, 222
Pima 222, 223, 280, 281, 284, 286
Pingilapese 187
Pintupi 279
Pitjantjatjara 281
Podoko 101, 187
Pokot 101
Polish 24, 89, 91, 101, 163, 168, 232, 234
Polynesian, Easter Island 69
Pomo 11, 283
Pomo, Central 315
Pomo, Eastern 283, 300, 301
Pomo, Northern 24, 176, 282, 293, 297, 301, 329
Pomo, South-western 11, 282
Portuguese 22, 52, 57, 61, 81, 82
Portuguese, Brazilian 69, 79, 84, 85, 132, 151
Portuguese, European 59, 69, 78, 79
Portuguese, Old 63
Provençal, Old 24, 63, 64
Prussian, Old 163
Punjabi 163

Quechua, 101
Quechua, Ancash 279, 280
Quechua, Huallaga 284, 285
Quechua, Imbabura 59, 67, 72, 79, 85, 90, 288, 290, 293
Quinanlt 305
Quiteño 79

Rembarrnga 289
Rhaeto-Romance 58
Romance 22, 24, 25, 63, 64, 126, 150, 163, 229
Romance, Old 63, 64

Romani 76
Romanian 22, 38, 66
Ron-Bakkos 187
Russian 22, 24, 35, 42, 43, 68, 69, 90, 91, 92, 93, 97, 98, 99, 118, 163, 165, 168, 169, 187, 219, 220, 222, 231, 315, 317

Sacapultec 305
Salentino 38
Salishan 305
Salishan, Central 305
Salishan, Interior 305
Sámi, Northern 96
Samoan 101
Sango 176, 177, 184, 190
Sanio-Hiowe/Saniyo-Hiyowe 309
Sarangambay 176
Sardinian 22
Saxon, Old 21
Scandinavian languages 52, 62, 63, 79
Scandinavian languages, Insular 24, 53, 59, 68
Scandinavian languages, Mainland 24, 53, 59, 61, 68, 69, 121
Schaptin 306
Semitic 229
Seneca 101
Serbo-Croatian 6, 23, 39, 40, 64, 88, 89, 99, 132, 234
Seri 282
Sherpa 283
Shilluk 101, 162
Shoshone 282
Shqip 38
Sie 291
Simbo 101
Sinhala 109, 163
Sino-Tibetan 163
Siroi 282
Slavonic 24, 58, 64, 69, 126, 163, 229, 255
Slavonic, East 58
Slavonic, South 58, 88, 89
Slavonic, West 58, 89
Slovak 54, 57, 64, 91
Slovene 64
So 162
Somali 59

Somoan 222, 223
Somray 187
Songhai 69, 179, 232
Sorbian, Upper 52, 53
Spanish 1, 17, 22, 23, 52, 54, 56, 61, 70, 71, 73, 74, 75, 78, 81, 91, 128, 151, 163, 164, 219, 225, 232, 233, 234, 241, 242, 245, 278, 315
Spanish, Basque 79
Spanish, dialects 8
Spanish, Latin American 304
Spanish, Old 63
Sranan 187
Sudanic languages 117
Sudanic languages, Central 177, 179, 232
Suislaw 101
Supyire 101, 292
Sura 176
Surselvan 57, 58, 69
Sursurunga 222, 223
Swahili 9, 54, 55, 162, 232, 233
Swedish 24, 53, 59, 62, 71, 76, 80, 81, 121, 219

Tagalog 8, 23, 53, 268
Tahitian 21
Tai 322
Tairora 300
Taiwanese 187
Tamazight 162
Tamil 13, 42, 79, 83, 163, 231
Tangale 187
Tanna, South-west 291
Tanoan 296
Tarahumara 91
Tarian 102
Tarifit 58, 88, 89, 233
Tatar 91, 218
Tauya 102
Telugu 95, 99, 106, 107, 109, 129, 132, 141, 163, 235
Ténhé 176
Tera 187
Thai 3, 13, 27, 28, 59, 74, 79, 85, 142, 187, 256
Tibetan 283
Tibeto-Burman 58, 163, 176

Tigak 101
Tikar 176
Tillanook 305
Tiv 176
Tlingit 306
To'aba'ita 101, 306, 307
Toba Batak 158
Togo Kã 117, 177, 184, 186, 190
Tolai 101
Tongan 101
Tonkawa 11, 282
Tɔrɔ Sɔ 3, 118, 190
Trentino 59
Tsakhur 220, 222, 223
Tsanosan 305
Tsova-Tush 305
Tübatulabal 282
Tuburi/Tupuri 173, 176, 181, 182, 183, 186, 187, 189, 226, 239, 240
Tucanoan 283
Tuki 20, 24, 25, 68, 106, 108
Turkic 163, 229
Tunebo 279
Turkish 23, 47, 91, 98, 163, 219, 220, 230, 232, 233, 241
Tuscarora 163
Tuvaluan 58
Twi 267
Tzotzil 12
Tzutujil 12

Ubangi 177, 180, 232
Udi 279
Udmurt 91, 163, 217
Ukrainian 53
Ulwa 279
Urdu 24, 52, 53, 91, 98, 99, 100, 119, 131, 165, 224
Urhobo 101
Usak Edet 162
Usan 288
Ute 304
Uto-Aztecan 282, 279
Uzbek 163

Vai 162
Vata 69

Vedic 267
Vietnamese 27, 28, 142
Vute 250

Wagaya 279
Wakasham 12
Wangganguru 284
Wanyi 279
Wappo 176, 222
Waramungu 279
Waray 268
Warlmanpa 287
Warlpiri/Walbiri 158, 286, 287, 289, 298, 300
Warrungu 102
Warrwa 101, 163
Washo 11, 282
Welsh 52, 53
Western Desert 279, 281
Wichita 306
Wikchamni 279
Win 176
Wojokeso 279

Xdi 101, 162, 187
Xerénte 101

Yag Dii/Duru 173, 174, 176, 177, 189
Yakut 102, 218
Yandruwandha 281
Yankunytijatuara 285
Yaouré 224
Yarluyandi 281
Yavapai 218, 279, 293, 298
Yavapai, Tolkapaya 294
Yawarawarga 281
Yawelmani 279
Yawuru 101
Yekhee 176
Yiddish 53, 61, 63, 70
Yidiɲ 12
Yimas 9, 296
Yinyjiparnti 102
Yir Yoront 289
Yokuts 279
Yoruba 4, 101, 162, 175, 185, 229, 232
Yukaghir 53

Yukaghir, Northern/Tundra 285
Yuki 11
Yukian 176
Yulu 176
Yuma 293
Yuman 280, 282
Yurok 101

Zaar 187
Zabana 101
Zande 101, 176, 180, 229
Zapotec, Isthmus 21, 165
Zhuang 267, 269
Zulgwo 101, 187
Zuni 279

Index of subjects

accessibility 253–257
accessibility marking scale 255
Accessibility theory 253–257
alphabetic variance condition 137–138
anaphor 108–110, 124
   connectedness vs. containment 103
   narrow vs. wide domain 108–110
   operator vs. non-operator 124
anaphora 1–332
   associated 249
   bound-variable 88–89, 233–234, 235–236
   and contexts 7–8
   definition of 1
   discourse 301–329
   and discourse 8–13, 302–329
   distributional pattern of 312, 319
   E-type 7
   general pattern of 214
   indirect 249
   inferrable 249
   'lazy' 7
   N- 3
   NP- 2–3
   null complement 5
   possessive 24–25, 224–225, 231–232
   referential 5
   revised neo-Gricean pragmatic apparatus for 215
   revised neo-Gricean pragmatic theory of 212–277, 301–302, 318–329
   semantic content hierarchy of 215
   and syntactic categories 2–5
   and truth conditions 5–7
   typologies of 2–14
   VP- 3–5
   zero 17, 30–38, 50–90, 262–265
animacy condition 97–98
antecedent-contained deletion/ellipsis (ACD)/(ACE) 148–151

antecedent saliency 244–245
antilocality condition 109
antilogophoric pronoun 48, 173
arbitrary interpretation 89–91, 234–235
Arbitrary Pronominals, Condition on (CAP) 234–235
'avoid pronoun' effect 232–236
'Avoid Pronoun' Principle 234–235

Bach's Generalization 41, 42, 44
background assumption 237–241, 263–265
binding 17–33, 45–46, 88–89, 148, 156–167, 222, 233–236, 297–299
   A- vs. Ā- 18, 30, 297–299
   bound/quantifier-variable 88–89, 233–236
   definition of 18
   domain 18
   logophoric 172–204, 225–229
binding condition A 18–26, 30, 139–143, 146, 157–162
binding condition A' 45
binding condition B 18, 22–26, 139–143, 146, 160–162
binding condition C 18, 26–30, 142–143, 146
binding condition D 109–110
binding theory 17–33, 45–46, 148, 156–167, 222, 297–299
   generalized 45–46, 297–299
blocking effect 1, 97–98, 114, 117, 119, 121
bound-variable anaphora/binding/interpretation 88–89, 233–234, 235–236
bridging cross-reference 7, 249–253
   definition of 7, 249
   properties of 249

Relevance-theoretical model of 251–253
scenario model of 250–253
topic/focus model of 250–253

causative construction 84
c-command 18, 44, 98, 119–121, 143
  binding and 119–121
  control and 44
  definition of 18
  relaxation of 98, 119–121
  VP-ellipsis and 133, 143
Centring theory 254
clause chaining 289–290
clause linkage 245–246
Cognitive Grammar 254
cognitive modularity, Fodorian theory of 247
command 18, 44, 98, 119–121, 143, 190
  c- 18, 44, 98, 119–121, 143
  perspective 190
  sub- 119–120
configurational vs. non-configurational language 156–159, 163
conjoinability principle 327
connectivity 245–246, 327
context 7–8, 212, 241, 253
  and anaphora 7–8, 241
  default/unmarked vs. specific/marked 253
  and implicature cancellation/generation 212
control 38–44, 46–47, 167–172, 238–239
  definition of 38–39
  domain 46
  finite 39–40
  long-distance/remote 44, 246
  obligatory vs. optional 40
  properties of 38
  split vs. non-split 40–41
  subject vs. object 40, 238, 264–265
controller assignment principle 169
control theory 38–44, 46–47, 167–172, 238–239
  generalized 46
conversation, maxims of 206–207
  Manner 206

Quality 206–207
Quantity 206
Relation 206
conversational implicature 206–212
  and anaphora 212–277, 301–302, 318–329
  definition of 206
  generalized vs. particularized 206, 222
  projection of 210–212
  properties of 206–207
  typologies of 207–210
co-operative principle 206
CP/C-oriented language 62–64

Descartes's problem 331
discourse anaphora 302–329
  cognitive model of 314–318
  distributional pattern of 312, 319
  hierarchy model of 309–314
  neo-Gricean pragmatic model of 318–328
  topic contiuity/distance-interference model of 303–309
discourse-oriented language 261
Discourse Representation Theory (DRT) 199–204
Disjoint Reference Presumption (DRP) 215–216

economy, principle of 64
E-language 331
eliminative puzzle 134–135, 138–139, 142, 144–145, 154
  Dhal-puzzle 134–135, 138–139, 142, 145, 154
  many-clauses puzzle 134–135, 138–139, 142, 144
  many-pronouns puzzle 134–135, 138–139, 142, 144
Emex condition 34
empathy 258
emphaticness/contrastiveness 229–232
  semantico-pragmatic conditon on 230
emphatics 25–26, 127
empty category (EC) 17, 30–38, 86–87, 263–264
  free (FEC) 87

392   Index of subjects

typologies of 17, 30–38
empty topic 78–82, 87–88
empty topic hypothesis/parameter 79, 87–88
epithet 47–48
Exceptional Case Marking (ECM) construction 34
existential construction 51
expletive 51–52, 71

focus 250–251
Functional Sentence Perspective (FSP) 257–258

Game-Theoretical Semantics (GTS) 172
gapping 4
  pseudo- 149
gender system 8–10, 295–296
general discourse principle 29
Generalized Control Rule (GCR) 46, 65–67, 79, 82
Generalized Control Rule (GCR) parameter 79
'given-only' hypothesis 259–260
given vs. new information 259–260
governing category (GC) 18, 110–113
  for anaphors 110–113
  definition of 18
  for pronominals 110–113
governing category (GC) parameter 112–113

Head-Driven Phrase Structure Grammar (HPSG) 39, 149
Humboldt's problem 331

iconicity 219, 231, 308
I-implicature 207, 209–210
I-language 331
impersonal passive construction 51
implicature cancellation procedure 212
inference system 13–14
information saliency 215, 244–245
informativeness 216
Interclausal Semantic Relation Hierarchy 245

IP/I-oriented language 62–64
I-principle 207, 209–210

Lexical-Functional Grammar (LFG) 39
local domain 110–115
  abandonment of 110
  expansion of 110–112
  parameterization of 112–115
logocentric complementizer 184, 186–188, 195–196
logocentric licenser 183, 193–196
logocentric NP 177, 181–183, 191–193
logocentric predicate 184–186, 193–195
  implicational universal for 185, 193, 198
logocentric trigger 177, 181–183, 191–193
  hierarchy for 182–183, 193
logophoric addressee pronoun 173–177
logophoric context/domain 176, 183–189, 193–197
logophoricity 172–204, 225–229
  definition of 172–173
  discourse representation of 199–204
  skipping effect of 185–186, 189, 194
logophoric long-distance reflexive 174–175, 190–204
logophoric marking mechanism hierarchy 226
logophoric vs. non-logophoric language 175–176
  full/pure 175–176
  geographical distribution of 176
  semi/mixed 175–176
logophoric pronoun 1, 173–189, 225–232
logophoric verbal affix 174–175
long-distance reflexive 103–110
  as anaphor of a special kind 108–110
  as (bound) pronominal 103–105
  as pronominal anaphor 105–108
long-distance reflexivization 1, 19–20, 90–130, 159, 167, 174–175, 190–204, 225–232, 256
  blocking effect of 97–98, 114, 117, 119, 121
  definition of 90–91

domino effect of 97
and emphaticness/contrastiveness 229–232
head movement analysis of 115–124
honorific blocking effect of 122
implicational universal for complement type 92–93, 127
licensing of 123
and logophoricity 172–204, 225–229
maximality effect of 94, 129
Optimality-theoretical analysis of 126–130
properties of 93–100
relativization of SUBJECT analysis of 124–126
skipping effect of 97
and split antecedents 98–99
and strict vs. sloppy interpretation 99–100
and sub-command condition 119–120
and subjunctive 126, 227–228

Manzini's Generalization 42
'matrix wins' hypothesis 246
meaning$_{nn}$ 205–206, 242
M-implicature 208, 210
'minimal distance' principle 43
minimalist programme 32, 70–73, 135, 150–151
minimization, principle of 318
morphological uniformity hypothesis 68–70
movement 63–64, 115–116
   head-to-head 115–116
   Infl-to-Comp-to-Infl 115–116
   Infl-to-Infl 115–116
   long head (LHM) 63–64
   short head (SHM) 63–64
M-principle 208, 210
mutual knowledge hypothesis 320

neo-Gricean pragmatic theory 205–212, 253
neo-Gricean pragmatic theory of anaphora 212–277, 301–302, 318–329

NP 2–3
   classifications/typologies of 17, 30, 45–50, 159
NP-trace 30
null object 54, 59, 78–87
   variable vs. *pro* analysis of 78–87
null object parameter 78–90
null operator 78–82, 87–88
null subject 50–77
   and Agr[eement] 53–55, 57–60, 65–68, 72–73
   C vs. I-language typology and 62–65
   expletive 51–52, 71
   licensing vs. identification of 60, 65, 71–72
   minimalist analyses of 70–73
   Optimality-theoretic analyses of 73–77
   and φ-features 61, 63, 65–67, 72
   quasi-argumental 51–52, 71
   referential 51–52, 71
   strong/weak AgrS^0 and 70–72
   typology of languages with repect to 53
null subject language 53–77
   properties of 53–57
null subject parameter 50–70

object-drop 78
obviation 10–11, 283, 296, 307
Occam's razor/eraser 49, 153
   modified 49
Optimality theory 32, 73–77, 126–130
Overt Pronoun Constraint (OPC) 234–235

parallelism 154–155
   referential 154
   structural 154
parasitic gap 264
passive construction 275–276, 293
   Chinese-style 275–276
   English-style 275
   in between 275
Perlmutter's Generalization 56
φ-features 56, 61, 63, 65–67, 72, 84, 86, 119–121, 126, 129, 191
Pica's Generalization 94
pivot 199–204

394 Index of subjects

Plato's problem 2, 16, 331
pragmatic language 261–277
   'clustering' properties of 262
Prague school functionalism 257–260
predicate meaning/reflexivizing strategy correlation 219–220
principles-and-parameters theory 14, 16, 17, 297
PRO 33–38
   distribution of 33–34
   governed vs. ungoverned 34–38
   properties of 33
pro 33, 50–87, 88–90
   cross-linguistic distribution of 54
   expletive 51–52, 71
   and language typology 53
   licensing of 54
   local determination of 54
   recovery of 54
   referential 51–52, 71
pro-drop language 50–90
pro-drop parameter 53–70
pronominal 21–23
pronoun zap 79–81
proper antecedent parameter 114
proper name 320
protagonist 305
PRO theorem 33, 35–38
psych-sentence 94, 118–119

Q-, I-, and M-principles, interaction of 211, 326
Q-implicature 207–209
   $Q_{\text{-clausal}}$ implicature 207–209
   $Q_{\text{-scalar}}$ implicature 206–209
Q-principle 207–209
quantifier-variable binding/construction/intrepretation 88–89, 233–234, 235–236

recipient design, principle of 321
reciprocal 19, 101–102
recognition, principle of 318
reference-tracking system 8–14, 278–302
   gender/class 8–10, 295–296
   inference 13–14
   obviation 10–11, 283, 296, 307

switch-function 12–13, 296
switch-reference 11, 278–302
referential dependency, theory of 29
referential hierarchy 28, 48, 126
reflexive/reflexivization 19–20, 90, 94–96, 101–102, 117, 160, 177, 217–220, 222, 243
   extrinsic 20, 160, 218–220
   implicational universal for the person distinction of 177, 222
   intrinsic 20, 160, 217, 243
   morphologically simplex vs. complex 20, 94–96, 117
   typologies of 90
reflexivity marking 110, 159–167, 216–217
referential economy for NPs, hierarchy of 220–221
referential economy for NPs, principle of 220–221
relative construction 188–189, 196, 255–256, 263–264, 273–274
   Chinese-style 273–274
   English-style 273–274
   in between 273–274
Relevance, principle of 247
Relevance theory 247–253
repair, anaphoric 321–329
   self- vs. other-initiated 321–326
   self- vs. other-repair 321–326
return pop 307–308, 311, 313, 326–327
revised DRP 215
revised neo-Gricean pragmatic apparatus for anphora 215
revised neo-Gricean pragmatic theory of anaphora 212–277, 301–302, 318–329
r-expression 26–30
r[hetorical]-structure 269, 310–312
rhetorical structure theory 269, 310–312

self 199–204
SELFish language 25
SELFless language 25
self- vs. other-directed action/situation 219–220
sentence-oriented language 261

Index of subjects

sloppy interpretation 4, 99–100, 133–134, 137–141, 144, 152–153
sluicing 4–5
source 199–204
split antecedent 40–41, 98–99, 133
strict interpretation 4, 99–100, 133–134, 137–141, 144, 152–153
stripping 5
strong crossover 31–33
sub-command 119–120
  binding and 119–120
  definition of 119
subject-object asymmetry 82
subject obviation 24, 93–94
subject of consciousness 190
subject orientation 93–95, 117–118, 181–183, 191–193
subject- vs. topic-prominent language typology 266–268
subset principle 112–113
switch-function 12–13, 296
switch-reference 11, 278–302
  coordinate vs. subordinate dependency in 289–290
  definition of 11, 278
  and gender/class 295–296
  and logophoricity 296–297
  marker 279–283
  neo-Gricean pragmatic analysis of 301–302
  pivot 283–288
  S[ame]S[ubject] vs. D[ifferent]S[ubject] 11, 279, 281–283, 286, 289–294, 298–299, 301
  secondary functions of 293–295
  semantic analysis of 298–300
  and switch-function 296
  syntactic analysis of 297–298
syntactic language 47, 170, 261–277
syntactic vs. pragmatic language typology 261–277
syntax-pragmatics interface 212–277, 330–331

Thematic Distinctness Condition (TDC) 168–172
thematic hierarchy 156

Thematic Identity Condition (TIC) 168–172
topic 78–82, 87–88, 196, 244–245, 266–276, 287, 303–309
  empty/null 78–82, 87–88
  frame 270–271
  instance 270–271
  range 270–271
topic chain 304
topic coding device scale 304, 309
topic construction 78–82, 87–88, 196, 244–245, 266–276, 287, 303–309
  'aboutness' hypothesis of 244, 268
  Chinese-style 266–276
  definition of 266
  English-style 266–268
  in between 267
  typology of 266–268
  well-formedness condition on 268
topic-drop 272–273
topic-prominent language 266–273

unexpectedness 225–232
universal grammar (UG) 16, 126, 213, 276, 297, 331

V2 62–63
  CV2 62–63
  IV2 62–63
vehicle change 146–147
verbal reflexive (VR) 163–164
verb/predicate 20, 40–43, 160, 163–164, 167–172, 197–199, 217–220, 238–239, 243
  control 40–43, 167–172, 238–239
  deictically oriented directive 197, 198, 199
  epistemic 185, 193, 199
  knowledge 185, 193, 199
  perceptive 185, 194, 199
  psychological 185, 193, 199
  reflexive 20, 160, 163–164, 217–220, 243
  speech 185, 193, 199
Visser's Generalization 42–43

Index of subjects

VP-ellpsis/deletion 3–4, 131–156
  binding theory analysis of 139–143
  coordinated vs. subordinated 3, 133, 135
  definition of 3, 131
  dependency analysis of 143–147
  derived VP rule (DVPR) analysis of 136–139
  eliminative puzzles of 134–135, 138–139, 142, 144–145
  equational analysis of 151–154
  properties of 132–133
  strict vs. sloppy interpretation 4, 133–134, 137–141, 144, 152–153
  subordinate effect 135, 148

weak crossover 31–33
wh-trace 30–33
world knowledge 237–241, 263–265

zero anaphor/anaphora 17, 30–38, 50–90, 262–265
zero anaphor/overt pronoun contrast 88–90, 232–237